Modern Finance and Risk Management

Festschrift in Honour of
Hermann Locarek-Junge

Transformations in Banking, Finance and Regulation

Print ISSN: 2752-5821
Online ISSN: 2752-583X

Series Editors: Sabri Boubaker
(*EM Normandie Business School, France & Swansea University, UK*)
Duc Khuong Nguyen
(*IPAG Business School, France*)

Presently, the banking and finance sectors evolve within a globalized and highly uncertain environment. Each business and financial decision requires careful consideration of country-specific and international factors due to high levels of shock transmission and volatility spillovers. Furthermore, it would be remiss to omit the COVID-19 health crisis, which caused harmful effects to all areas of the real economy and made profound changes in the way our firms, economies, and markets used to function.

Many other already well-known aspects, including the repercussions of quantitative easing policies, disruptive technologies in finance (e.g., FinTech, Big Data, Data Analytics, Artificial Intelligence, and Blockchains), as well as innovative financing instruments for startups (e.g., ICOs and crowdfunding) are currently revolutionizing banking and finance and posing numerous challenges to regulatory bodies and policymakers. Climate change emergencies also put pressure on governments and firms worldwide to improve policy on governance, corporate social responsibility, and sustainability practices.

This book series "Transformations in Banking, Finance, and Regulation" attempts to address these issues by focusing on transformative perspectives in banking and finance. Accordingly, it provides evidence-based guidance, recommendations, and pathways to assist businesses and policy decision-makers through an interdisciplinary and in-depth understanding of ongoing changes in the behavior of economic agents.

Published

Vol. 4 *Modern Finance and Risk Management: Festschrift in Honour of Hermann Locarek-Junge*
edited by Tony Klein, Sven Loßagk, Mario Straßberger and Thomas Walther

Vol. 3 *Finance with a Purpose: FinTech, Development and Financial Inclusion in the Global Economy*
by Frederic de Mariz

Vol. 2 *Institutional Change and China Capitalism: Frontier of Cliometrics and its Application to China*
edited by Antoine Le Riche, Antoine Parent and Lei Zhang

For the complete list of volumes in this series, please visit
www.worldscientific.com/series/tbfr

Transformations in Banking, Finance and Regulation

Volume 4

Modern Finance and Risk Management

Festschrift in Honour of Hermann Locarek-Junge

Editors

Tony Klein
Queen's University Belfast, UK

Sven Loßagk
Berufsakademie Sachsen, University of Cooperative Education Dresden, Germany

Mario Straßberger
Zittau/Görlitz University of Applied Sciences, Germany

Thomas Walther
Utrecht University, The Netherlands

World Scientific

NEW JERSEY • LONDON • SINGAPORE • BEIJING • SHANGHAI • HONG KONG • TAIPEI • CHENNAI • TOKYO

Published by

World Scientific Publishing Europe Ltd.

57 Shelton Street, Covent Garden, London WC2H 9HE

Head office: 5 Toh Tuck Link, Singapore 596224

USA office: 27 Warren Street, Suite 401-402, Hackensack, NJ 07601

Library of Congress Cataloging-in-Publication Data

Names: Locarek, Hermann, honoree. | Klein, Tony, editor. |
Loßagk, Sven, editor. | Straßberger, Mario, editor.
Title: Modern finance and risk management : Festschrift in honour of Hermann Locarek-Junge /
editors, Tony Klein, Queen's University Belfast, UK,
Sven Loßagk, Berufsakademie Sachsen, University of Cooperative Education Dresden, Germany,
Mario Straßberger, Zittau/Görlitz University of Applied Sciences, Germany,
Thomas Walther, Utrecht University, The Netherlands.
Description: Hackensack, NJ : World Scientific, 2022. | Series: Transformations in banking,
finance and regulation, 2752-5821 ; Vol. 4 | Includes bibliographical references and index.
Identifiers: LCCN 2021059102 | ISBN 9781800611900 (hardcover) |
ISBN 9781800611917 (ebook) | ISBN 9781800611924 (ebook other)
Subjects: LCSH: Investments. | Risk management. | Banks and banking.
Classification: LCC HG4521 .M63 2022 | DDC 332.6--dc23/eng/20220126
LC record available at https://lccn.loc.gov/2021059102

British Library Cataloguing-in-Publication Data

A catalogue record for this book is available from the British Library.

For any available supplementary material, please visit
https://www.worldscientific.com/worldscibooks/10.1142/Q0351#t=suppl

Desk Editors: Soundararajan Raghuraman/Michael Beale/Shi Ying Koe

Typeset by Stallion Press
Email: enquiries@stallionpress.com

https://doi.org/10.1142/9781800611917_fmatter

Grußwort

Prof. Dr. Hermann Locarek-Junge feiert im Mai 2022 seinen 65. Geburtstag. Aus diesem Anlass haben sich ehemalige Assistenten und Doktoranden entschlossen, ihn mit der vorliegenden Festschrift zu überraschen und zu ehren. Diese Festschrift soll die vielfältigen Themen der modernen Finanzwirtschaft, vor allem aber auch die zentralen Forschungsschwerpunkte von Hermann Locarek-Junge, behandeln, u.a. Risikomanagement, Vermögensmanagement, Krisen und Anomalien am Kapitalmarkt.

Aus seiner Vita ist bekannt, dass Hermann Locarek-Junge zunächst ein Doppelstudium absolvierte. Nach seinem Abitur studierte er parallel Betriebswirtschaftslehre an der Universität Augsburg und Informatik an der Fernuniversität Hagen. Während seiner sich anschließenden Assistentenzeit am Institut für Statistik und Mathematische Wirtschaftstheorie der Universität Augsburg interessierte er sich zunächst für die Konstruktion DV-basierter Systeme zur Integration von Expertenwissen in statistische Auswertungsprogramme. Gleichzeitig näherte er sich interessanten offenen Problemen des modernen Finance und folgte nach einer vierjährigen Professur an der Universität Essen für Betriebliche Informationssysteme einem Ruf an die TU Dresden auf einen Lehrstuhl für Finanzwirtschaft und Finanzdienstleistungen.

Neben seiner Haupttätigkeit als Lehrstuhlinhaber lehrte er viele Jahre im Masterprogramm an der Dresden International University und war als Studienleiter und Dozent der Sächsischen Verwaltungs- und Wirtschaftsakademie tätig. International war Hermann Locarek-Junge zu allen Zeiten ein gefragter Fachmann. So war er Jahre lang

Dozent in den MBA-Programmen der Pfeiffer University in Charlotte/North Carolina sowie des Instituts für Industrie und Finanzmanagement (IPFM) Prag. Bis heute ist er Gastprofessor an der Wirtschaftsuniversität in Wroclaw (Breslau). Im Rahmen zahlreicher Mitgliedschaften bei wissenschaftlichen Gesellschaften und in Aufsichtsräten organisierte er nationale und internationale Tagungen sowie Zusammenkünfte von Arbeitsgruppen, und er war auch Herausgeber entsprechender Ergebnisbände.

Die Autoren dieses Grußwortes haben ihren ehemaligen Mitarbeiter Hermann Locarek-Junge in sehr positiv-lebhafter Erinnerung. Unmittelbar nach Amtsantritt als wissenschaftlicher Assistent engagierte er sich nachhaltig für die Entwicklung der Datenverarbeitung am Institut und war zu jeder Zeit ansprechbar und in der Lage, zielgerecht zu helfen, wenn sich Probleme ergaben. Parallel dazu betrieb er mit Akribie und Zielstrebigkeit seine Forschungsinteressen in den Bereichen Datenverarbeitung, statistische Methoden, später zunehmend im Bereich Finanzwirtschaft und erzielte stets innovative und interessante Ergebnisse. Wegen seiner hilfsbereiten und offenen Art war Hermann Locarek-Junge ein hoch geschätzter Mitarbeiter, der sehr wesentlich zur Forschungsstruktur und Lebensart des Instituts für Statistik und Mathematische Wirtschaftstheorie beitrug. Nach seiner Ernennung zum ordentlichen Professor an der TU Dresden besuchte er viele Jahre im Advent sein früheres Institut in Augsburg, um einen Dresdner Stollen zu überreichen, dessen Qualität er stets wortstark herausstellte.

Mit Hermann Locarek-Junge hat die TU Dresden einen Kollegen, der seit knapp 30 Jahren das Erscheinungsbild der Wirtschaftswissenschaftlichen Fakultät entscheidend mitprägt.

Auf Grund seiner fachlich-wissenschaftlichen Qualitäten und seiner verständnisvollen und umgänglichen Art war es für seine ehemaligen Assistenten und Doktoranden ein Herzensanliegen, Hermann Locarek-Junge durch die vorliegende Festschrift zu ehren.

Für die Zukunft wünschen wir Hermann Locarek-Junge alles Gute!

Günter Bamberg
Otto Opitz

https://doi.org/10.1142/9781800611917_fmatter

Foreword

In May 2022, Professor Dr. Hermann Locarek-Junge will celebrate his 65th birthday. To mark this occasion, former associates and doctoral students have decided to surprise and honour him with this Festschrift. This Festschrift aims to cover the wide range of topics in modern Finance that align with Hermann Locarek-Junge's central research areas, including risk management, asset management, crises, and anomalies in capital markets.

It is known from his vita that Hermann Locarek-Junge completed a double degree. After graduating from high school, he studied Business Administration at the University of Augsburg and Computer Science at the FernUniversität Hagen. In subsequent times as a research assistant at the Institute for Statistics and Mathematical Theory of Economics at the University of Augsburg, he first became interested in the design of computer-based systems for the integration of expert knowledge into statistical evaluation programs. During this time, he narrowed his interest on promising, open problems in modern Finance and, after holding a four-year professorship in Business Information Systems at the University of Essen, he followed a call of the TU Dresden as chair in Finance and Financial Services.

In addition to his main activity as Finance chair, he taught in the master's program at the Dresden International University and served as director of studies and professor at the Saxon Academy of Administration and Economics for many years. Hermann Locarek-Junge is an internationally sought-after expert. For example, he was an adjunct professor in the MBA programs of Pfeiffer University in Charlotte/North Carolina as well as the Institute for Industrial and

Financial Management (IPFM) Prague. Currently, he still is a visiting professor at the University of Economics in Wroclaw. He has held numerous memberships in scientific societies and supervisory boards, has organised national and international conferences and meetings of working groups, and has also edited the corresponding proceedings.

The authors of these greeting remarks have very positive and vivid memories of their former colleague Hermann Locarek-Junge. Immediately after taking up his post as a research assistant, he made a sustained commitment to the development of data processing at the institute and was always approachable and available to provide targeted help when problems arose. In parallel, he pursued with high meticulousness and determination his research interests in the areas of data processing, statistical methods, and later with increasing focus in the area of financial economics. He always obtained innovative and interesting results. Because of his helpful and open nature, Hermann Locarek-Junge was a highly valued colleague who contributed very significantly to the research structure and way of life of the Institute of Statistics and Mathematical Economic Theory. After his appointment as full professor at the TU Dresden, he regularly visited his former institute in Augsburg for many years during Christmas time to bring a Dresden Stollen, the quality of which he always eloquently emphasised.

In Hermann Locarek-Junge, the TU Dresden has a colleague who has decisively shaped the image of the Faculty of Economics for almost 30 years. Given his professional-scientific qualities and his understanding and amiable manner, it was without hesitation that his former assistants and doctoral students have decided to honour Hermann Locarek-Junge through this commemorative publication, the present Festschrift.

We wish Hermann Locarek-Junge all the best for the future!

Günter Bamberg
Otto Opitz

https://doi.org/10.1142/9781800611917_fmatter

About the Editors

Tony Klein is Associate Professor in Finance at Queen's Management School, Queen's University Belfast, UK. He holds Ph.D. in Finance (2017) and Master's degree in Financial Mathematics (2013) from Technische Universität Dresden. His research interests include econometric modeling and machine learning within the fields of finance, energy finance, and energy economics; the financialisation of commodity markets and connectedness to stock and fixed-income markets; and volatility forecasting with application in financial risk management and portfolio optimisation. He is Senior Editor for *Finance Research Letters* and regularly serves as reviewer for several journals.

Sven Loßagk is Professor of Finance with the Berufsakademie Sachsen, University of Cooperative Education Dresden. Before that, he was Head of Finance at VSB Neue Energien Deutschland GmbH. He received his Diploma in Business Administration (2007) and his Doctoral degree in Business & Economics (2013) from Technische Universität Dresden. His current research interests are project financing and the financing of renewable energies.

Mario Straßberger is Professor of Finance and Financial Services with Zittau/Görlitz University of Applied Sciences. Prior to this, he was Financial Risk Manager at KfW Banking Group in Frankfurt, Assistant Professor at Friedrich-Schiller-Universität Jena, and Research Associate at Technische Universität Dresden. He received B.A. (1996) from University of Wolverhampton, UK, Diploma degree (1997) and Doctoral degree (Ph.D., 2002) from Technische Universität Dresden. He is also an alumnus of the German Academic Scholarship Foundation. His current research interests are asset and risk management, statistical and econometric applications in finance, and financial decision making.

Thomas Walther is Assistant Professor of Finance (Tenure Track) with the Utrecht School of Economics, Utrecht University. Formerly, he was Assistant Professor for Energy Finance (Non-Tenure Track) at the University of St. Gallen. He is also Research Fellow for Finance at the Technische Universität Dresden from which he received a B.Sc. (2010) and M.Sc. (2013) in Industrial Engineering and Management and a Ph.D. (2017) in Business & Economics. His research focuses on commodity/energy/climate finance and financial econometrics with applications to risk management. He is Associate Editor of the journal *Finance Research Letters*.

https://doi.org/10.1142/9781800611917_fmatter

About the Contributors

Günter Bamberg is Professor Emeritus at the University of Augsburg. He studied Mathematics at the Universities of Saarbrücken and Bonn. After a doctorate (dr. rer. nat.) in 1968 at the University of Saarbrücken and the Habilitation (venia legendi in Statistics and Econometrics) in 1970 at the Technical University of Karlsruhe, he was appointed Full Professor of Statistics at the Faculty of Business and Economics of the University of Augsburg. He held the Chair from 1970 to 2009 despite calls to the Universities of Osnabrück and Heidelberg. He has authored several books on Statistics, Decision Theory, Incentives, and Agency Theory and numerous papers in journals like *OR Spectrum*, *Review of Managerial Science*, *German Economic Review*. In 2006, he was given an honorary doctorate by the University of Tübingen.

Kerstin Bergk received her postdoctoral qualification in Business Administration from Friedrich Schiller University Jena and holds B.Sc. and M.Sc. degrees in Business Administration from Friedrich Schiller University Jena, respectively. Her research focuses on risk measurement and portfolio selection with application to bank regulation.

Mario Brandtner is Professor of Finance at Jena University of Applied Sciences. Prior to that, he was Associate Professor at Friedrich Schiller University Jena. He received his Diploma degree (2006) and Doctoral grade (2010) from Friedrich Schiller University Jena. He is a Research Affiliate with Halle Institute for

Economic Research. His research focuses on financial risk management, portfolio optimisation and asset management, financial decision making, and banking regulation.

Thomas Burkhardt is Full Professor of Finance at Koblenz-Landau University, Germany. He graduated in Physics (Diplom 1990) and Economics (Diplom 1992), Doctoral degree 1994, all from Göttingen University. He received his Habilitation (2000) from the Technical University of Freiberg. Since 2001, he holds the Chair of Finance at Koblenz-Landau University, Campus Koblenz. Further call to Chair in Banking at Innsbruck University, Austria, but declined by him. Primary research interests are financial decision making, asset management, derivatives, and long term investment decisions, including forest investments. Preferred methods include mathematical modeling and optimisation as well as economic experiments.

Karl Dietrich is an SAP Consultant specialised in logistics for a leading consulting firm and an alumnus from Technische Universität Dresden. He graduated in 2020, receiving a Diploma in Industrial Engineering. During his studies, his focus was on supply chain management and production.

Alexander Fox is Lecturer (Assistant Professor) in the Group for Research in Finance at Technische Universität Ilmenau. He received his Diploma in Media Economics (2003) and a Doctoral grade (Ph.D., 2010) from Technische Universität Ilmenau. His current research interests are valuation of renewable energy projects, crowdfunding, mezzanine financing instruments and fan bonds. Prior to his time in academia, he was Controller at Allianz insurance in Leipzig.

Benjamin Hammer is Lecturer (Assistant Professor) in Accounting & Finance at Lancaster University Management School (LUMS). He joined LUMS in 2020 from HHL Leipzig Graduate School of Management where he served as Assistant Professor of Finance and Executive Director of the Center for Corporate Transactions & Private Equity (CCTPE). Dr Hammer's research focuses on private equity and venture capital and has been published in highly-ranked journals such as the *Journal of Corporate Finance* or the *British Journal of Management*. Dr. Hammer studied at HHL Leipzig Graduate School of Management (Leipzig, Germany) and Tulane University

(New Orleans, USA) as a scholarship holder of the German Academic Scholarship Foundation. He completed his Ph.D. in Finance with distinction in 2017. Prior to his time in academia, Dr. Hammer worked in consulting and investment banking.

Nils Härtel is Group Director Growth at Serviceware SE. In his role, he leads the HR department and is responsible for the M&A activities of the company. Before that, he was a Consultant at the strategy consulting company Boston Consulting Group (BCG). He received B.Sc. in International Business Administration (2012) from the University of Tübingen, M.Sc. in Finance (2014) from Stockholm School of Economics and his Doctoral degree in Economics and Business Administration (2019) from HHL Leipzig Graduate School of Management, with a research focus on performance, secondary buyouts, and specialisation in the private equity industry.

Sebastian Heiden is postdoctoral Researcher at the University of Augsburg. He holds Diploma in Business Economics (2008), Master's degree in Management et Gestion des Entreprises (2009) and Ph.D. in Business Economics (2013) from the Universities of Augsburg and Rennes, France. His research interests include behavioural finance, financial econometrics, portfolio optimisation and risk management.

Lars Hengmith is Data Privacy Manager at 50Hertz Transmission GmbH. From 2009 to 2020, he was the riskmanager of this company. From 2003 to 2009, he was Assistant at the Chair of Finance and Financial Services at TU Dresden where he received his Doctoral degree in Economics and Business Administration. Before that, he worked at KPMG in Stuttgart in the information risk department. In 2000, he received his Diploma in Business Administration from Technische Universität Chemnitz.

Nikolas Höhnke is a startup-Consultant at the HTW-Berlin. He obtained his Ph.D. from the University of Rostock for his research on the growth of social banks in the aftermath of the global financial crisis. His research interests include social banking, impact investing, and entrepreneurship.

Susanne Homölle is Professor of Banking and Finance at the University of Rostock. She obtained her Ph.D. in Business Administration from the University of Münster in 1998 and finished her

Habilitation in 2004. Her research interests include bank regulation, risk management of banks, sustainability in banking business as well as bank customers' behaviour.

Andreas Horsch is Full Professor of Investment and Finance at Technische Universtität Bergakademie Freiberg, Germany, and since 2019, also Dean of Freiberg's Faculty of Business Administration. He studied Economics at Ruhr-Universität Bochum, Germany, graduating with a Diploma in 1992. Having joined Bochum's Chair of Banking & Finance (Prof. Dr. Dr. h.c. Joachim Süchting), he received his Ph.D. in 1998 based on a dissertation on insurance guarantee funds. After a three-year stint with the second largest German bank of that time, he returned to academia in 2001, finishing his Habilitation on Rating and Regulation at Bochum University in 2007. Following two years as an Interim Professor at Freiberg University, he became Full Professor in 2008. His primary research interests are financial (dis)intermediation, financial regulation, securitisation, and project finance.

Steffi Höse is Professor of Statistics and Operations Research at Zittau/Görlitz University of Applied Sciences. Prior to this, she was temporary Professor at the Brandenburg University of Technology Cottbus-Senftenberg and at the Karlsruhe Institute of Technology. From 2004 to 2010, she was a trainer in the SRP/IRB qualification programme for supervisors of the Deutsche Bundesbank and the German Federal Financial Supervisory Authority. She received a Diploma degree, a Doctoral degree and a Habilitation in Quantitative Methods from the Technische Universität Dresden. Her research focuses on quantitative risk management, in particular the modelling of dependence structures using risk factor and mixture models, the simultaneous estimation of dependence and default parameters, and the quantification of the involved model risk.

Ulf Hübenbecker is a Ph.D. student and Research Assistant at the Chair of Banking and Finance at the University of Rostock. His research interests are the philosophy of science and the future of banks from a theory-driven approach.

Steffen Hundt is Interim Professor at TU Bergakademie Freiberg. He is also the founder and CEO of the renewable energy advisory firm Think RE GmbH. He holds a Doctoral degree in Economics and Business Administration (2015) from TU Bergakademie Freiberg, where he also graduated with a Diploma (2010). Before returning to Freiberg as Interim Professor of Resource Management in 2021, he was Interim Holder of the Chair Banking & Finance at the University of Paderborn after he had senior manager positions at Nordex SA, PNE AG, and PricewaterhouseCoopers. He also had several senior lecturer positions at Frankfurt School of Finance and New Design University St. Pölten. His research interests cover sustainability finance, renewable energy management, risk management, and econometrics.

Stefan Huschens held the Chair of Quantitative Methods, especially Statistics at the Technische Universität Dresden from 1994 until his emeritus status in 2017. He received a Diploma degree, a Doctoral degree and a Habilitation in Statistics and Economics from the Ruprecht-Karls Universität Heidelberg. His research focuses on decision theory, non-parametric statistical estimation methods, factor models and statistical methods for risk quantification. Together with the honoree of this volume, he organised from 1998 to 2018 a series of symposia (Dresdner Risikotutorium) on current topics in risk quantification.

Krzysztof Jajuga is Full Professor of Finance at Wrocław University of Economics and Business, Poland. He is the Chairman of the Department of Financial Investments and Risk Management. He holds Master, Doctoral and Habilitation degrees from Wrocław University of Economics and Business, titular professor given by President of Poland, honorary doctorate from Cracow University of Economics and honorary professorship from Warsaw University of Technology. He carries out research and published numerous papers and monographs in the area of financial markets, risk management, household finance, multivariate statistics and quantitative methods in economic sciences. He is Editor-in-Chief of *Argumenta Oeconomica* (JCR journal). Among others, he is the Founder and President of CFA Society Poland and holds the position of Chairman of the Committee of Statistics and Econometrics of the Polish Academy of Sciences.

Harald Kinateder is Associate Professor of Finance at the University of Passau, Germany. Since 2012, he is Visiting Lecturer at the Corvinus University of Budapest. He received his Ph.D. in Finance and Habilitation from the University of Passau. He regularly serves as a referee for well-known research journals and he is a Subject Editor of *Journal of International Financial Markets, Institutions and Money* and Associate Editor of *Studies in Economics and Finance.* His research focuses on asset pricing, climate finance, corporate finance, cryptocurrencies, energy economics and risk management.

Siegfried Köstlmeier is a Research Associate and Ph.D. student at the University of Regensburg. He received his M.B.A. from the University of Regensburg. His research interests include empirical asset pricing and macro-finance.

Wolfgang Kürsten is Full Professor and Chair of Finance, Banking and Risk Management at Friedrich Schiller University Jena. Prior to this, he was Full Professor of Finance and Financial Markets at Otto-von-Guericke-University of Magdeburg. He studied Mathematics at the University of Erlangen-Nürnberg, received his postdoctoral qualification in Business Administration, and his Doctoral degree in Economics from University of Passau, respectively. He received various appointments at other universities as, e.g., the Ordinary of Banking at University of Zurich, Switzerland. He is Editor-in-Chief of *Review of Managerial Science*, together with Ralf Ewert and Sascha Kraus, and is a member of the Advisory Board of the Eurasian Business and Economics Society (EBES). His current research interests include theory and applications of monetary risk measures, financial contracts and asymmetric information, corporate risk management and optimal derivatives hedging, and business valuation under uncertainty.

Katarzyna Kuziak is Associate Professor of Finance at Wroclaw University of Economics and Business, Poland. She works for the Department of Financial Investments and Risk Management. She holds Master's, Doctoral and Habilitation degrees from Wroclaw University of Economics and Business. In her research, she focuses on the area of financial markets, risk management and quantitative methods in finance. She published a few textbooks for students and many papers in the area of quantitative methods in finance. She belongs to the editorial team of *Argumenta Oeconomica* (JCR journal).

Rainer Lasch holds the Chair of Business Management, esp. Logistics, at the Faculty of Business and Economics at Technische Universität Dresden, has been Visiting Professor at the Università degli Studi di Trento since 2002 and the Academic Head of the Department of Economics, Law and Management at Dresden International University since 2006. He is the author of numerous textbooks and internationally recognised publications as well as a reviewer for several international journals. In addition, Rainer Lasch is a distinguished research partner of the Federal Ministry of Education and Research (BMBF) and industry, particularly in the areas of benchmarking in logistics, market-oriented process design, supply chain management, risk management, spare parts logistics, governance, blockchain and quantitative planning methods in logistics. He is a member of numerous scientific societies and associations and also a member of the Scientific Advisory Board of the Association Supply Chain Management, Procurement and Logistics (BME).

Sophia Licht is a working student in the area of project controlling at 50Hertz Transmission GmbH. She received her Bachelor's degree in Industrial Engineering/Mechanical Engineering in 2020 from the Beuth University of Applied Sciences in Berlin. There she is currently completing her Master's degree on the same topic.

Dominik Möhring received B.Mus. (2016) from HfM Dresden, B.Sc. in Computer Science and also B.Ed. in Mathematics and Computer Science from Koblenz-Landau University in 2021. He works at Debeka insurance company in the areas of risk management and capital investments.

Jörg Müller trained as a banker and then worked in practice for more than 10 years, including about 7 years as a corporate client advisor. He then completed Bachelor's degree in Economics, followed by Master's degree in Finance at the Chemnitz University of Technology. Since graduating with an M.Sc., he has been working as Research Assistant and doctoral candidate at the Chair of Finance and Banking at the Chemnitz University of Technology.

Suleiman Naiem is Senior Associate at McKinsey&Company. He received an M.Sc. in Finance and Accounting from WU Wien and a Doctoral degree in Economics and Business Administration (2019) from HHL Leipzig Graduate School of Management. His research focused on secondary and SME-buyouts.

Krzysztof Piontek is Associate Professor of Finance at Wroclaw University of Economics and Business, Poland. He is a member of the Department of Financial Investments and Risk Management. He holds Master's degree from Wroclaw University of Science and Technology, Bachelor, Doctoral and Habilitation degrees ('Construction and Verification of Quantile-Based Market Risk Measurement Models') from Wrocław University of Economics and Business. He specialises in the use of mathematical methods in finance, with a particular focus on time series analysis. He is also a member of the Classification and Data Analysis Section (SKAD) of the Polish Statistical Association (PTS).

Klaus Röder is Professor of Finance with the University of Regensburg. Before that, he was Professor of Finance with the University of Münster. He holds a Dr. rer. pol. (1994) and a Dipl.-Kfm. degree (1991) from the University of Augsburg. His research interests include empirical capital markets and futures markets. Currently, he is Dean of Fakultät Wirtschaftswissenschaften at University of Regensburg.

Bernhard Schwetzler is Professor at HHL Leipzig Graduate School of Management, where he holds the Chair for Financial Management and Banking. He received his Doctoral and Habilitation degrees at the University of Regensburg and held several positions as Guest Professor and Research Fellow at international universities. His research focuses on private equity, takeover regulation and corporate valuation.

Gerhard Stahl is a member of the Executive Board of HDI Service AG. He holds the position of the Chief Risk Officer of the HDI Group and heads the department 'Group Risk Management'. He has studied Mathematics at TU Karlsruhe. From 1995 to 2007, he was with the Federal Financial Supervisory Authority (BaFin). Until 2007, he headed the Risk Modelling Group (QRM), which is in charge of on-site inspections of risk management models. He was assigned to represent the BaFin in several working groups in Basel and in the

Committee of European Banking Supervisors. Prior to joining the BaFin, he had been a Research Fellow at the Economic Faculty of Heidelberg. He was a member of the Advisory Board of the CASE Institute at Humboldt and a Fellow of the Centre for Financial Studies, Frankfurt. He holds an honorary doctor (Dr. rer. pol. h. c.) from the University of Bamberg for his scientific contributions to financial risk management. Since 2008, he has been an Adjunct Professor at the University of Ulm and since 2010 at the University of Hanover.

Ulrike Stopka is the holder of the Chair of Information and Communication Business Management & Economics at the 'Friedrich List' Faculty of Transportation and Traffic Sciences, Technische Universität Dresden. Before this, she completed a teaching and research stay at the University of Bayreuth, Faculty of Law, Economics & Management. She received the Diploma degree in 1976, the Ph.D. in 1981, and was habilitated in 1986 at the University of Transport and Traffic Sciences, Dresden. In 1992, she was appointed Professor of Business Administration & Management at the University of Applied Sciences, Dresden, and one year later, she received the appointment to the Technische Universität Dresden. Her research activities are telecommunications, internet and network economics, business models, investment appraisal and financing.

Friedrich Thießen is Full Professor of Banking and Finance at the Chemnitz University of Technology. He received his Doctorate in Economics from the University of Cologne. His postdoctoral lecture qualification was obtained at the University of Frankfurt. He is Managing Director of the Rhine-Main Institute, Darmstadt, and the Center for Municipal Finance Management (ZKFM). He is a member of the board of the Federal Association against Aircraft Noise. His research focuses on investment banking, digitalisation in banking and finance, sustainability and regional economics. He is the author of 20 books and more than 250 articles.

Ralf Trost is Full Professor of Finance and Head of the Group for Research in Finance at the Technical University of Ilmenau. He received his Diploma in mathematics at the Technical University of Darmstadt (formerly Technische Hochschule Darmstadt). After a Doctorate and the Habilitation (venia legendi in Statistics and Quantitative Methods of Business Economics) at the University of

Augsburg, he substituted professorships of Controlling (University of Ulm) and Quantitative Methods of Business Economics (University of Bielefeld). His main research interests, besides current developments in finance like crowdfunding, focus on financial and decision theory.

Niklas Wagner is Professor of Finance at the University of Passau, Germany, where he holds the Chair in Finance and Financial Control. After receiving his Ph.D. from Augsburg University under the supervision of Professor Günter Bamberg, he held postdoctoral appointments at U.C. Berkeley, Stanford GSB and TU Dresden and completed his habilitation thesis at TU Munich. Dr. Wagner has co-authored contributions in the areas of asset pricing, asset management, corporate finance, applied financial econometrics and risk management. In recent years, he has been an academic guest to universities in Asia, Australia, Europe and the U.S. Besides at Passau, he taught finance courses at TU Dresden, TU Munich, Handelshochschule Leipzig, Zeppelin University Friedrichshafen, Leibniz University Hannover, Corvinus University of Budapest and at EDHEC Business School in London, Nice and Singapore. He currently serves as Editor-in-Chief of *Studies in Economics and Finance* and as an Associate Editor of finance and economics journals (*Economic Modelling, Finance Research Letters, International Review of Financial Analysis, Journal of International Financial Markets, Institutions and Money*). In 2009, Handelsblatt Betriebswirte-Ranking listed him as a top 100 researcher at age below 40 in the German-speaking business administration research community.

Philipp Winskowski is a Ph.D. student and Research Assistant at the Chair of Banking and Finance at the University of Rostock. He received his Master's in Economics at the Technical University of Dresden in 2016. His current research interests are the punishment for fan misbehaviour in football and stakeholder management.

https://doi.org/10.1142/9781800611917_fmatter

Contents

https://doi.org/10.1142/9781800611917_0001

Chapter 1

Introduction

Tony Klein[*,¶], **Sven Loßagk**[†,‖], **Mario Straßberger**[‡,**], **and Thomas Walther**[§,††]

[*]*Queen's University Belfast, Queen's Management School, United Kingdom*
[†]*Berufsakademie Sachsen, University of Cooperative Education Dresden, Germany*
[‡]*Zittau/Görlitz University of Applied Sciences, Faculty of Business Administration and Economics, Germany*
[§]*Utrecht University, Utrecht School of Economics, The Netherlands*
Technische Universität Dresden, Faculty of Business and Economics, Germany
[¶]*t.klein@qub.ac.uk*
[‖]*sven.lossagk@ba-sachsen.de*
[**]*m.strassberger@hszg.de*
[††]*t.walther@uu.nl*

The field of modern finance and risk management is characterised by fundamental changes and further developments in recent years. Theoretical and empirical analysis of asset prices, implementation of behavioural finance approaches, and time series analysis with time-varying volatility are topics that were honoured by the Nobel Prize committee.

Some of these developments are picked up in the present volume which is dedicated to our academic mentor Hermann Locarek-Junge. He contributed to the field of portfolio management and risk management of his own during the last four decades as Ph.D. student and post-doc at the University of Augsburg, Professor at the University of Essen/Duisburg, Professor at the Technische Universität Dresden, Chairman of the German Finance Association (Deutsche Gesellschaft für Finanzwirtschaft E.V.) and host of various conferences. This volume comprises twenty chapters from scholars in finance who learned and worked with Hermann Locarek-Junge in various ways. Their contributions cover some of the latest and most relevant topics in finance research dealing with questions of modern finance, modern risk management, and modern commodity finance.

In the first section of this Festschrift, authors address current topics of *modern finance* including asset management, entrepreneurship, and behavioural finance.

Günter Bamberg and *Sebastian Heiden* take a closer look at the notion of returns. They show that confounding the return notions leads to incorrect results in portfolio optimisation and performance measurement.

Ralf Trost and *Alexander Fox* discuss the role of emotionally involved investors in finance and decision theory and use an example of a German football fan bond. They conclude that currently emotional aspects seem to be too complex to be incorporated into mathematically driven models.

Friedrich Thießen and *Jörg Müller* investigate the performance of various risk-reduced investment strategies during the COVID-19 pandemic. They document limited risks throughout the sample of funds. Further, they find heterogeneous returns within strategies but homogeneous returns across strategies which is due to the low degree of commitment to an investment strategy by fund managements.

Susanne Homölle, Nikolas Höhnke, Ulf Hübenbecker, and *Philipp Winskowski* focus on the growth of social banks, which typically have higher deposits-to-assets ratios than conventional banks due to excess liquidity. The empirical results of 23 European social banks show a tremendous growth in deposits since the financial crisis leading to excess liquidity risks with strict self-restrictions.

Ulrike Stopka compares approaches in practice for determining the eligible cost of capital for different regulated infrastructure network companies (telecommunication, electricity, and railway) in Germany. Although the regulation is applied by the Bundesnetzagentur for all three industries, the methodological framework is different in detail.

Benjamin Hammer, Nils Härtel, Suleiman Naiem, and *Bernhard Schwetzler* examine the enterprise value growth of private equity backed buyouts. They show that the rate of growth of enterprise value for small and medium-sized enterprises (SME) is higher than that for non-SMEs. Furthermore, they investigate the effects of different portfolio firm- and deal-characteristics, e.g., financial market development, private equity fund size, or management buyouts, on the growth of enterprise value.

The second section of this Festschrift covers different contributions to *risk management* including aspects of risk measurement, risk controlling, and regulation.

From a statistical point of view, *Steffi Höse* and *Stefan Huschens* give answers on estimating probabilities of risky events if no occurrence of such events has been observed before. They present a variety of point estimates and interval estimates for the Bernoulli parameter based on different approaches to statistical inference.

Kerstin Bergk, Mario Brandtner, and *Wolfgang Kürsten* compare Conditional Value-at-Risk and Tail Nonlinearly Transformed Risk Measure as a basis of regulatory capital constraints for banks. Imposing both risk measures on the classical portfolio selection problem, the authors show that the first constraint might be less effective than the second one in inducing lower risk takings. But, the effectiveness depends on the bank's grade of risk aversion.

Lars Hengmith and *Sophia Licht* attempt to objectify subjective risk assessments using systematic opinion combining techniques. The applicability of the proposed methodology is tested by expert interviews in the electricity industry.

Stefan Huschens and *Gerhard Stahl* develop an approach for capturing model risk by a multiplicative risk factor instead of additively aggregating it to other risks. They consider and compare the standard additive (location) model, a multiplicative (scale) model, and a location-scale model.

Krzysztof Jajuga considers model risk in option pricing focussing on the uncertainty with respect to the estimates of underlying price volatility. He proposes to measure model risk by sensitivity measures. One of the sources of model risk is identified with the volatility index VIX which is not an appropriate estimator for expected volatility.

Rainer Lasch and Karl Dietrich develop a framework for success factors of resilient supply chains and analyse reactions of supply chains to disruptions by a case study in the mobile phone sector.

Katarzyna Kuziak and *Krzysztof Piontek* examine systemic risk in the German banking sector. They report differences in systemic risk assessment depending on selected financial ratios, normalisation and ordering methods, and group of banks.

In the third section of this Festschrift, authors deal with topics of *commodities and energy finance* considering oil, gold, and cryptocurrencies as well as power purchase agreements and renewable energy sources.

The impact of oil-market variables on short-term stock market returns is examined by *Harald Kinateder* and *Niklas Wagner*. They report significant positive effects of oil prices on stock returns across different markets but a negative influence of oil price volatility.

Sven Loßagk undertakes an assessment of the German Renewable Energy Sources Acts over time regarding the risk situation of lenders and shareholders by using Monte-Carlo simulation and by applying different risk metrics of project finance. He demonstrates a decrease in financial risk for equity and debt.

The use of Power Purchase Agreements (PPA) for purposes of corporate risk reduction is outlined by *Andreas Horsch* and *Steffen Hundt*. They analyse gain and risk structures of major PPA types and recommend that buyers should carefully match their risk appetite and price expectation with the PPA's price mechanism.

Thomas Burkhardt and *Dominik Möhring* review a model for predicting gold price movements proposed in popular literature. Next to a sceptical analysis, they apply appropriate out-of-sample tests for model evaluation and identify the model to be inadequate.

Siegfried Köstlmeier and *Klaus Röder* consider gold as an additional component to German stock portfolios. While hedging perspectives suggest increasing the share of gold in stock portfolios, they find that investors should rather decrease its share in Germany when maximising the Sharpe ratio.

Tony Klein and *Thomas Walther* deal with dynamic correlation of precious metal and equities. Their findings suggest that Gold and Silver serve as short-term safe-haven with decreasing correlation towards zero during equity market recessions, while Platinum and Palladium show features of a diversifier.

Finally, *Mario Straßberger* includes Bitcoin in German equities portfolios and examines diversification benefits and hedging abilities. He reports improved performances and significant diversification effects for stock market investors but almost no hedging abilities of Bitcoin.

We are deeply grateful to all contributors for participating in the realisation of this Festschrift by submitting their original papers. Furthermore, we are highly indebted to many colleagues helping us with friendly reviews of the various chapters: *Dirk Baur, Lanouar Charfeddine, Simon Cornée, Robert Czudaj, Jeroen Derwall, Gregor Dorfleitner, Tom Dudda, Matthias Fengler, Rüdiger Kiesel, Ladislav Kristoufek, Eran Manes, Paul Schure, Daniel Tillich, Christian Walkshäusl*, and *Florian Ziel*. We are also grateful to *Duc Khuong Nguyen* and World Scientific for their kind support throughout the process.

Finally, we would like to thank Hermann Locarek-Junge for his manifold support on our way into the academic world. During our time as research assistants, we benefited greatly from his experience and guidance through the challenging process of research, in particular by allowing for an unbounded development of research topics within the realms of modern finance. Unforgotten are the annual trips to Saxon Switzerland, where we discussed recent research topics during daytime and other interesting issues afterwards. And of course, every recent staff member will remember the regular all-staff meetings which usually included either ice cream or — depending on the time of the year — Dresdner Stollen. For all this, we are deeply grateful and wish him all the best for his future.

PART I

Aspects of Modern Finance

https://doi.org/10.1142/9781800611917_0002

Chapter 2

Confounding the Return Notions Could Be Dangerous

Günter Bamberg* and Sebastian Heiden†

Department of Statistics, Faculty of Business and Economics, University of Augsburg, Germany

**guenter.bamberg@wiwi.uni-augsburg.de*

†*sebastian.heiden@wiwi.uni-augsburg.de*

In numerous finance publications, the term 'return' appears at first only as a necessary element for further research. Seemingly, it is so basic that it does not require a precise definition. However, the inappropriate use of 'return' has serious consequences. This chapter shows that confounding the return notions and inappropriate approximations lead to wrong results in portfolio optimisation. Using log-returns instead of ordinary (or simple) returns in a traditional Markowitz framework can feign arbitrage opportunities which are nonexistent in reality. Furthermore, this chapter highlights the huge numerical differences between key figures of log-return and ordinary returns. For instance, calculating the Sharpe ratio with log-returns can signalize a bad investment, whereas it is a really highly profitable investment.

1. Introduction

It is well known that the notion 'return' can be defined in two different ways: as (simple or ordinary) return and as (continuously compounded rate of) return. Instead of the clumsy terms 'continuously compounded rate of return' or equivalently 'natural logarithm of gross return' the shorter notion 'log-return' will be used. The former is used in the Markowitz and the CAPM world, whereas 'log-return' is predominant in time series analysis and in empirical finance. For instance, the entire literature on realised volatility (see, e.g., Andersen and Teräsvirta, 2009) is based on log-returns. Advantages of log-returns are as follows:

- additivity along the time axis;
- simple annualising formulas;
- the whole real line as support.

Disadvantages in the context of portfolio selection are as follows:

- portfolio log-return is nonlinear in the weights and the individual log-returns;
- short sales must be excluded.

To circumvent the nasty nonlinearity of portfolio log-return, a linear approximation has been widely used in the literature. With respect to this linear approximation, we show that

- it leads to a wrong capital market line and a wrong minimum variance portfolio;
- it is unable to exploit the true diversification potential.

Furthermore, we point out the striking difference between the numerical values of moments and other key figures of the returns. For instance, the Sharpe ratio can turn from positive values to negative ones if we switch from ordinary return to the corresponding log-return. Moreover, the covariance matrix of log-returns may be singular, whereas the corresponding covariance matrix of ordinary returns is regular. Finally, we point out that the estimation of moments from one category of returns to the other category is hardly possible.

Of course, some pros and cons of the two return notions and the consequences of confounding them have been addressed in several papers (Dorfleitner, 2002, 2003; Meucci, 2010). Our intention is to add some additional aspects to this stream of literature.

The chapter is organised as follows: In Section 2, we provide and discuss lower and upper bounds to the portfolio log-return. Section 3 analyses properties of the portfolio log-return and drawbacks of the linear approximation. Section 4 deals with the numerical differences of key figures if we switch from one return notion to the other.

In Section 5, we sketch the problem to infer empirical evidence from one return notion to the other. Section 6 concludes.

2. Upper and Lower Bounds of Portfolio Log-Return

We use the following notation:

- P_t is the price at time t of a certain security (adjusted for dividends, stock splits, etc.) or the value of a performance index like the German DAX,
- $R_t = \frac{P_t - P_{t-1}}{P_{t-1}}$ is the ordinary return with respect to period $[t-1; t]$,
- $r_t = \ln\left(\frac{P_t}{P_{t-1}}\right)$ is the log-return with respect to period $[t-1; t]$,

where r_t is the natural logarithm of gross return $1 + R_t$. Hence $P_t = P_{t-1} \cdot e^{rt} = P_{t-1}(1+R_t)$. To utilise the small letter r_t for the log-return makes sense, since the inequality $r_t \leq R_t$ always holds. Dropping the time index t and denoting by r^i the log-return of share number i, the relative weight by w_i and by r^P the portfolio log-return we get the (nonlinear) formula

$$r^P = \ln\left(\sum_{i=1}^{n} w_i e^{r^i}\right) \quad \text{subject to} \sum w_i = 1, w_i \geq 0 \tag{1}$$

which can be inferred from

$$e^{r^P} = \sum_{i=1}^{n} w_i e^{r^i}.$$

In (1) the restriction $w_i \geq 0$ for the portfolio weights is essential. Otherwise, the argument of ln could be negative (at least with a certain probability) and r^P would not be a properly defined random variable. An upper bound with respect to r^P follows from

$$\begin{aligned} r^P &= \ln\left[1 + \sum_{1}^{n} w_i(e^{r^i} - 1)\right] \\ &= \ln\left[1 + \sum_{1}^{n} w_i R^i\right] \leq \sum_{1}^{n} w_i R^i. \end{aligned} \tag{2}$$

The first equality stems from $\sum w_i = 1$, the second one stems from $e^{r^i} - 1 = R^i$ and the inequality results from $\ln(1 + x) \leq x$ for all $x > -1$. A lower bound for r^P can be derived as well:

$$r^P = \ln \left[\sum_1^n w_i e^{r^i} \right] \geq \sum_1^n w_i \ln(e^{r^i}) = \sum w_i r^i = \hat{r}. \tag{3}$$

The inequality sign holds because of the concavity of ln and Jensens inequality. Obviously, both bounds are linear in the weights and the returns. The upper bound is the (stochastic) goal function of the Markowitz world. The lower bound $\hat{r}$ defined in (3) is referred to in the literature as 'linear approximation'. One can also read $\hat{r}$ as the Markowitz goal function in which the ordinary returns are erroneously replaced by log-returns, a common practise in many empirical papers. Upper and lower bounds constitute a (stochastic) interval

$$\left[\sum_1^n w_i r^i ; \sum_1^n w_i R^i \right]$$

whose length is a random variable. Example 1 shows that the expected length could be infinite.

Example 1. Log-returns r^i are assumed to be student distributed ($r^i \sim t_\nu$) with arbitrary degrees of freedom (ν). Then $E(r^i) = 0$ and $E\left[\sum_1^n w_i r^i\right] = 0$ and expected lower bound $= 0$. However, the expected upper bound is no longer finite since $E(e^{r^i})$ is larger than every positive number ($=\infty$ for short). Therefore,

$$E\left[\sum_1^n w_i R^i\right] = \sum_1^n w_i E(R^i) = \sum_1^n w_i E(e^{r^i}) - 1 = \infty.$$

It is well known that r^i has Pareto tails and thus no finite exponential moment $E(e^{r^i})$. (Compare, for instance, Bamberg and Dorfleitner, 2002). By the way, the tail index coincides with the degrees of freedom ν.

3. Properties of Portfolio Log-Return and Drawbacks of Its Linear Approximation

Ordinary portfolio return $R^P = \sum_1^n w_i R^i$ allows the separation of moments: $E(R^P)$ depends only on the first moments $E(R^i)$, $\mathrm{Var}(R^P)$ depends only on the second moments of the R^i. Portfolio log-return $r^P = \ln\left(\sum w_i e^{r^i}\right)$ does not have this separation property. Therefore, things like efficient frontier, capital market line, etc. have no meaning in the log-return world. The considerations about portfolio selection in the Markowitz world are mainly based on the (σ_R, μ_R)-plane. There is no counterpart in the (σ_r, μ_r)-plane. The optimisation problem

$$\max_{\sum w_i = 1, w_i \geq 0} E(R^P)$$

is trivial. It selects the asset with the highest $E(R_i)$ and leads to non-diversification. In contrast to this,

$$\max_{\sum w_i = 1, w_i \geq 0} E(r^P) \tag{4}$$

is a well-defined optimisation problem which will be discussed in Section 3.1.

3.1. *Expected log-return and decision theory*

From the decision theoretic point of view, the problem (4) is very specific. The solution w^* of (4) is the optimal portfolio of a loginvestor, who aims at maximising the expected utility of end-of-period wealth. Indeed, $\sum w_i e^{r^i}$ is the end-of-period wealth stemming from one unit of money invested. Expected utility of the loginvestor is

$$E\left[\ln\left(\sum w_i e^{r^i}\right)\right]$$

and thus identical to $E(r^P)$. Since ln belongs to the class of utility functions with constant relative risk aversion, w^* is the optimal portfolio not only for one unit invested, but for an arbitrary initial investment. A second property of w^* is noteworthy and will be discussed in Section 3.2.

3.2. *Expected log-return and long-term investment*

If one aims at maximising the long-term growth rate of final wealth, then w^*, interpreted as constant mix strategy, should be adopted. To implement the strategy w^*, one has to reshuffle the portfolio in every period such that the weights w_i^* are maintained. In the relevant literature, this procedure is referred to as the Kelly criterion or as the maximum expected log (MEL) criterion. For details and assumptions, compare, for instance, Kelly (1956), Latané (1959), Markowitz (1976) or Bamberg and Neuhierl (2012).

3.3. *An informative example*

Example 2 is tailor-made for revealing drawbacks of the linear approximation. As already mentioned, by linear approximation is meant the approximation of the exact r^P through its lower bound (3):

$$r^P = \hat{r} = \sum_{i=1}^{n} w_i r^i. \tag{5}$$

Example 2. There are three investment opportunities:

(1) a riskless investment with a log-return $r_f = 0.05$.
(2) two stochastic log-returns r^1, r^2 with common distribution according to Figure 1.

Thus, the marginal distribution of r^i and the first two moments are

$$r^i = \begin{cases} -1 & \text{with probability } 1/3 \\ 0 & \text{with probability } 1/3 \\ 1 & \text{with probability } 1/3, \end{cases}$$

$$E(r^i) = 0, \quad \mathrm{Var}(r^i) = \frac{2}{3}, \quad \mathrm{Corr}(r^1, r^2) = -1,$$

$$\mathrm{Cov}(r^1, r^2) = \begin{pmatrix} 2/3 & -2/3 \\ -2/3 & 2/3 \end{pmatrix}.$$

The covariance matrix is singular. Since we intend to compare the optimal portfolios resulting from r^P and $\hat{r}$ with those obtained in the Markowitz framework, we have to display the situation by means of ordinary returns R^1, R^2. Here, R^i is still a three-point distribution:

$$R^i = \begin{cases} e^1 - 1 & \text{with probability } 1/3 \\ 0 & \text{with probability } 1/3 \\ e^{-1} - 1 & \text{with probability } 1/3. \end{cases}$$

The first three moments are

$$E(R^i) = 0.36, \quad \mathrm{Var}(R^i) = 0.986, \quad \mathrm{Corr}(R^1, R^2) = -0.866.$$

Now there is no perfect negative correlation. The covariance matrix

$$\mathrm{Cov}(R^1, R^2) = \begin{pmatrix} 0.986 & -0.850 \\ -0.850 & 0.986 \end{pmatrix}$$

is no longer singular. Instead of Figure 1 we get Figure 2.

3.4. *The linear approximation does not detect the existing diversification potential*

We refer to Example 2 and compare the optimal portfolio with respect to log-return r^P and with respect to the linear approximation

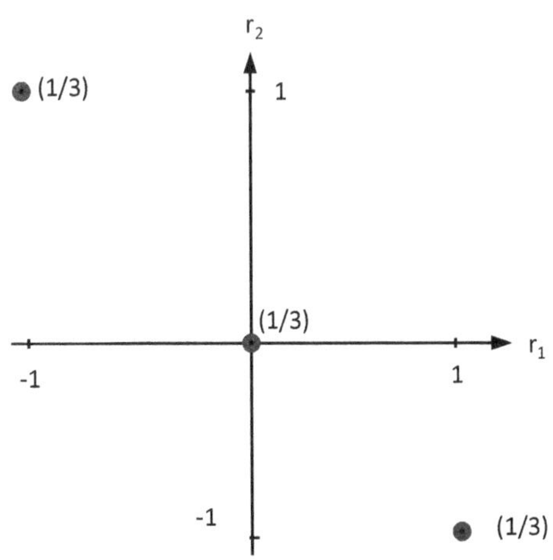

Fig. 1. Common probability function of log-returns r^1, r^2. The three bold-typed points have the probability $\frac{1}{3}$ (each).

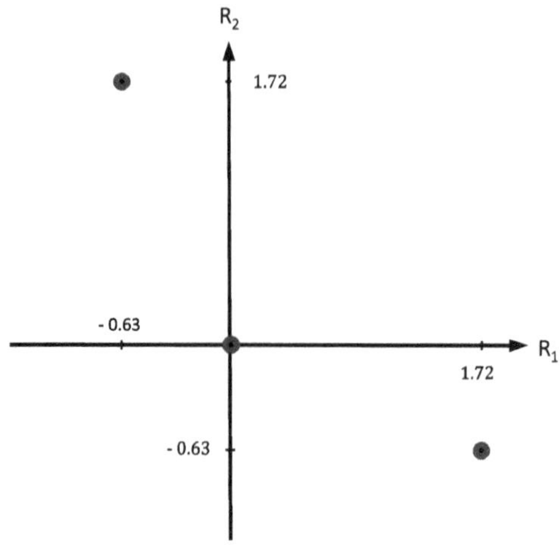

Fig. 2. Common probability function of ordinary returns R^1, R^2. Again each of the three bold-typed points has probability $\frac{1}{3}$. Now the three points are no longer on a straight line.

$\hat{r}$ (given by (3)). In order to have r^P properly defined, the weights must be nonnegative:

$$w_1 \geq 0, \quad w_2 \geq 0, \quad 1 - w_1 - w_2 \geq 0. \tag{6}$$

Appendix A shows that maximising

$$E(r^P) = E\{\ln[w_1 e^{r^1} + w_2 e^{r^2} + (1 - w_1 - w_2)e^{0.05}]\}$$

under the restriction (6) results in the portfolio

$$w^* = (0.5;\ 0.5;\ 0)$$

with expected log-return 0.29 (and standard deviation 0.20). On the other hand, $\hat{r}$, due to its linearity, allows to construct the efficient frontier. Since

$$Var(\hat{r}) = (w_2 - w_1)^2 \cdot 2/3 \tag{7}$$

vanishes for $w_1 = w_2$ and

$$E(\hat{r}) = (1 - w_1 - w_2) \cdot 0.05 \tag{8}$$

moves from zero (for $w_1 + w_2 = 1$) to 0.05 (for $w_1 + w_2 = 0$), we get the (degenerated) efficient frontier illustrated in Figure 3.

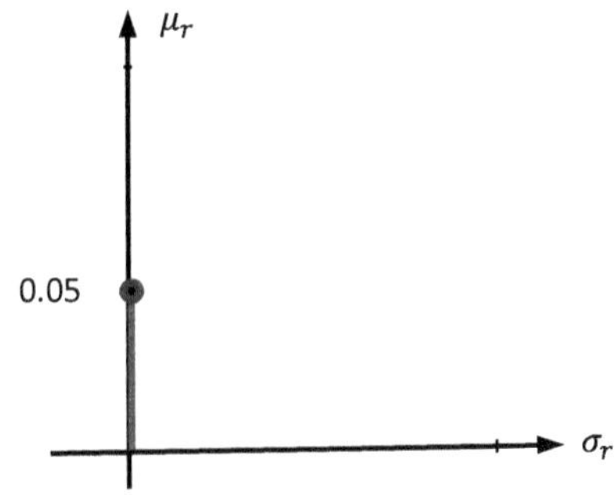

Fig. 3. The efficient frontier resulting from the linear approximation and the data of Example 2. Clearly, the optimal portfolio is $(0; 0; 1)$ since it has risk zero and the maximum expectation.

Note that the $\hat{r}$-optimal portfolio $(0; 0; 1)$ eliminates risks by eliminating the risky assets instead of exploiting the diversification opportunities. An obvious third approach is made up by totally avoiding log-returns, describing Example 2 by ordinary returns and applying the Markowitz machinery. As pointed out in Appendix B, the efficient frontier degenerates to a single point corresponding to the strategy $(0.5; 0.5; 0)$. This strategy constitutes the minimal variance portfolio (of the risky assets) as well. The resulting expected (ordinary) return is 0.36.

3.5. *The linear approximation possibly feigns arbitrage opportunities*

Again, we consider the data of Example 2, but this time without the restriction (6) on the weights w_1 and w_2. The consideration of r^P does not make sense. However, the linear approximation $\hat{r}$ can be considered for arbitrary weights w_1 and w_2 as well. By (7), portfolios with $w_1 = w_2$ have vanishing risk. According to (8), the corresponding expected return is $E(\hat{r}) = (1 - 2w_1) \cdot 0.05$. For instance, the strategy $(-1000;\ -1000;\ 1+2000)$ stands for shortselling the risky assets and investing the proceeds risk free. It leads to the (seemingly) riskless return of $(2001) \cdot 0.05 = 100.05$. Obviously, it is possible to generate unlimited arbitrage opportunities, which do not exist in reality.

3.6. *Different opinions concerning the linear approximation: Some quotes from the literature*

Many papers do not bother about the return notion. They use the notion 'return' without making it more precise. Of course, this blurs the distinction between the exact portfolio logreturn and the linear approximation. Maybe, this attitude exists due to influential authors like Fama, who states: 'For daily and monthly data, distributions of simple and continuously compounded returns have the same general properties' (Fama, 1976, p. 27). Famas statement is no longer tenable if extreme events or heavy tails (compare Example 1) are taken into account. Example 2 shows that the statement is unsuitable and misleading even under less extreme price movements. Some papers use the linear approximation to avoid nasty nonlinearities. The way of proceeding is often accompanied by escape clauses like 'The approximation is extremely good for all practical purposes' (cf. Sornette *et al.*, 2000, p. 531) or 'We adopt the usual linear approximation' (cf. Valle *et al.*, 2015, p. 850). Finally, there are papers like Blattberg *et al.* (1974), which do not distinguish r^P and $\hat{r}$. They take the equality $r^P = \hat{r}$ at face value and use the linear approximation as taken for granted. Also, Bollerslev *et al.* (2018, p. 81) use the linear approximation without any notes on its approximative nature. Finally, the prestigious Deutsche Börse AG published beta factors calculated by means of log-returns instead of rightly calculating the factors by ordinary return. At least this practice is documented in Deutsche Börse AG (March 2005).

4. Without Precise Definition of the Term 'Return', Reporting Key Return Figures Makes No Sense At All

In the following examples, we consider the same situation, once described by log-return r and once again by ordinary return R. We limit ourselves to popular scalar return measures (such as moments, etc.) and illustrate the striking difference of the corresponding figures. That multidimensional measures can also differ considerably has been shown in Example 2, where a singular covariance with respect to r turns into a regular one with respect to R.

4.1. *Example with light tails*

A prominent member of the class of light-tailed distributions is the normal distribution. Since ordinary return R has support $[-1;\infty)$ and log-return r has support $(-\infty:\infty)$, it seems more plausible to model r (than R) as normally distributed.

Example 3. Assume that log-return r is normally distributed with $\mu_r = 0$ and $\sigma_r = 0.3$, i.e., $r \sim N(0; 0.09)$. Then $R = e^r - 1$ is a shifted lognormal distribution and we get the following key figures:

	Return	
Key figure	Log-return r	Ordinary return R
Expectation	0	0.046
Variance	0.09	0.103
Skewness	0	0.95
Kurtosis	3	4.645
Sharpe ratio (with $r_f = 1\%$)	−0.033	0.11

Note that the symmetric and mesokurtic r turns into a positively skewed and leptokurtic R. The Sharpe ratio changes its sign. This ratio is designed for the Markowitz world and has a well-defined meaning in the CAPM framework (namely, slope of the capital market line). Plugging in the moments of log-return r is clearly a misuse of this ratio. Nevertheless, one can find it in many papers. In our case, the negative ratio with respect to r (erroneously) signalises a bad investment, whereas R reveals that it is indeed a profitable investment.

4.2. *Example with heavy tails*

The normal distribution used in the previous example has light tails. Many papers (for instance, Cont, 2001 and the literature therein) give an overview of the 'stylised facts' governing return data. One stylised fact, taken for serious in numerous papers, is the heavy tailedness. If we take this 'fact' at face value, the discrepancy between the key figures gets even chaotic.

Example 4. Instead of $r \sim N(0; 0.09)$ we assume $r \sim t_5$, the Student distribution with 5 degrees of freedom. Then the figures in the

r-column remain finite. However, the figures in the R-column are ∞ or indeterminate, due to the upper Pareto tail of t_5.

Key figure	Return	
	Log-return r	Ordinary return R
Expectation	0	∞
Variance	1.67	∞
Skewness	0	$\frac{\text{not defined}}{\text{not defined}}$
Kurtosis	9	$\frac{\text{not defined}}{\text{not defined}}$
Sharpe ratio (with $r_f = 1\%$)	-0.008	$\frac{\text{not defined}}{\text{not defined}}$

Note that the problems delineated in Example 4 do not only emerge with Pareto tails but also with some kinds of exponentially decaying tails (for instance of the Laplace distribution). A consequence of heavy-tailed log-returns is the strange effect that investing of money today entails an infinite expected wealth tomorrow. Therefore, we consider heavy-tailed log-returns as rather questionable.

5. Inference From Log-Return r to Return R

Up to now, we postulated given distributions for r and R. This assumption enabled us to generate clear cut effects and paradoxes. Obviously, no empirical researcher has such a state of knowledge. If we leave the theoretical framework, the situation is quite different. Instead of knowing the truth, we have to rely only on empirical return data. Very often, empirical studies are gathering log-return data. Such data arise from the ever growing literature of realised volatility, realised covariances, etc. If only properties of time series matter, there is no further problem. But if also portfolio issues matter, one has to switch from r-data to R-data. Here, we will restrict, by way of example, to the seemingly simplest case. Namely, the estimation of $\mu_R = E(R)$ from log-return data. As can be seen from

$$\mu_R = E(R) = E(e^r - 1) \tag{9}$$

there is no simple correspondence between μ_R and $\mu_r = E(r)$. In fact, μ_R depends on the exponential moment and hence on all power moments of r. Of course, inference from r-data to μ_R makes only sense if r has light tails; otherwise μ_R does not exist. Because of $r \leq R$, we have

$$\mu_r \leq \mu_R.$$

If $\hat{\mu}_r$ is an unbiased estimator with respect to μ_r we get

$$E(\hat{\mu}_r) = \mu_r \leq \mu_R \tag{10}$$

which means that $\hat{\mu}_r$ underestimates μ_R systematically. In order to reduce the degree of underestimation, Hudson and Gregoriou (2015) proposed to estimate μ_R by means of an estimator

$$\hat{\mu_r} + \frac{1}{2}\hat{\sigma}_r^2 \tag{11}$$

where $\hat{\sigma}_r^2$ is an unbiased estimator for σ_r^2. They justified (11) through Taylor expansions. In order to see whether (11) eliminates the underestimation, we investigate the special, but nevertheless important, normal case. Let $r \sim N(\mu_r, \sigma_r^2)$. Then the expectation of (11) can be evaluated as follows.

$$E\left(\hat{\mu_r} + \frac{1}{2}\hat{\sigma}_r^2\right) = \mu_r + \frac{1}{2}\sigma_r^2 \leq \exp\left(\mu_r + \frac{1}{2}\sigma_r^2\right) - 1 = \mu_R. \tag{12}$$

The first equality sign in (11) stems from the unbiasedness, the inequality sign stems from $x \leq \exp(x) - 1$ and the last equality sign from the expectation of a lognormal distribution. Hence, (11) brings forth an underestimation as well. On the other hand, the estimator

$$\exp\left\{\hat{\mu_r} + \frac{1}{2}\hat{\sigma}_r^2\right\} - 1 \tag{13}$$

overestimates μ_R systematically which can be seen from Jensens inequality:

$$E\left[\exp\left\{\hat{\mu_r} + \frac{1}{2}\hat{\sigma}_r^2\right\} - 1\right] \geq \exp\left\{E\left[\hat{\mu_r} + \frac{1}{2}\hat{\sigma}_r^2\right] - 1\right\}$$
$$= \exp\left\{\mu_r + \frac{1}{2}\sigma_r^2\right\} - 1 = \mu_R.$$

By calculating both (11) and (13), we get an interval

$$\left[\hat{\mu_r} + \frac{1}{2}\hat{\sigma}_r^2; \quad \exp\left\{\hat{\mu_r} + \frac{1}{2}\hat{\sigma}_r^2\right\} - 1\right]$$

which could serve as a rather reliable interval forecast of μ_R. The situation is less transparent if we address higher moments or the multivariate case. Maybe it could be more favourable to transform the original r-dataset into the corresponding R-dataset and to apply traditional sampling estimators on the R-dataset.

6. Conclusions

The problem we addressed here has been investigated by other scholars. For instance Dorfleitner (2003), nearly two decades ago, argued that more awareness of the suited return term is necessary. He showed that wrong beta factors, wrong efficient frontiers, etc. emerge from replacing the (correct) ordinary returns by log-returns. Despite these findings, quite a number of contemporary papers use the term 'return' without giving a precise definition. This is the gateway for misunderstandings and errors. Another gateway is the unspecific use of genuine symbols like r (for return), μ and σ. Simply put, one can say that log-return is suited for time series analysis such as GARCH models, etc. Log-return is also the correct return term in the Black–Scholes world. On the other hand, ordinary return is the correct return notion in the Markowitz world.

Appendix A: Maximising the Expected Log-Return of Portfolio

We have to maximise

$$E(r^P) = E\left\{\ln\left[w_1 e^{r^1} + w_2 e^{r^2} + (1 - w_1 - w_2)e^{0.05}\right]\right\} \tag{14}$$

subject to (6). Due to the symmetric role of the variables r^1 and r^2, optimising (14) is tantamount of optimising

$$E\left\{\ln\left[we^{r^1} + we^{r^2} + (1 - 2w)e^{0.05}\right]\right\}$$
$$\text{subject to } w \geq 0, w \leq 0.5 \tag{15}$$

(15) is a concave function of w. The maximum (without the restriction on w) is far beyond 0.5 (namely, 8.25). Thus, (15) is increasing on the interval $[0; 0.5]$ and has the maximiser $w_* = 0.5$ on the boundary.

Appendix B: Efficient Frontier and Capital Market Line

Again, we refer to Example 2. The common distribution of ordinary returns R_1, R_2 is depicted in Figure 2. The moments are

$$E(R^1) = E(R^2) = 0.36, \quad \mathrm{Var}(R^i) = 0.986, \quad \sigma_R^i = 0.993,$$

$$\mathrm{Cov}(R^1, R^2) = \begin{pmatrix} 0.986 & -0.850 \\ -0.850 & 0.986 \end{pmatrix}.$$

The minimisation

$$\min_w \begin{pmatrix} w & 1-w \end{pmatrix} \begin{pmatrix} 0.986 & -0.850 \\ -0.850 & 0.986 \end{pmatrix} \begin{pmatrix} w \\ 1-w \end{pmatrix}$$

yields the minimum variance portfolio which is identical to $(0.5; 0.5)$. Here, the efficient frontier is no longer the familiar hyperbola in the $(\sigma_R; \mu_R)$-plane. Rather, it collapses to a single point, since both expected returns $E(\hat{R}) = 0.36$ are identical. This particular case has been overlooked by Merton (1972). This single point also corresponds to the minimum variance portfolio. The coordinates in the $(\sigma_R; \mu_R)$-plane are $(0.26; 0.36)$. If one is restricted to portfolios made up by risky assets, 50/50 is clearly optimal. If the riskfree asset is taken into account the whole capital market line is the new efficient frontier. Figure B.1 illustrates this situation.

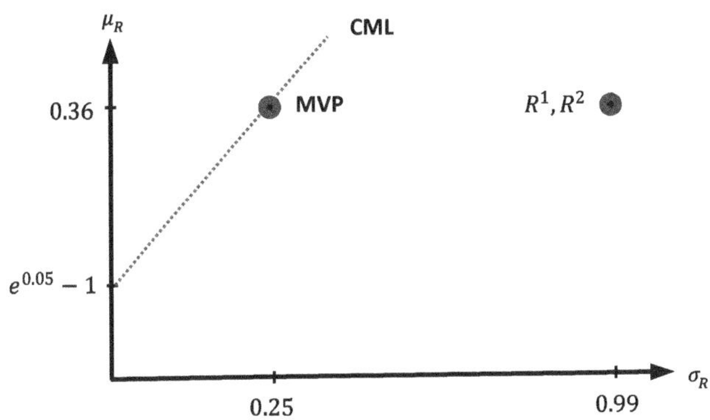

Fig. B.1. Since both expected returns $E(R^i) = 0.36$ are identical, the efficient frontier degenerates to the single point $(0.26; 0.36)$ which also corresponds to the minimum variance portfolio MVP. The capital market line CML goes through this point and the point linked to the riskfree asset.

Acknowledgements

The authors thank Christian Conrad for valuable advice on relevant literature.

References

Andersen, T.G. and Teräsvirta, T. (2009). *Realized Volatility.* Berlin, Heidelberg: Springer Berlin Heidelberg, pp. 555–575.

Bamberg, G. and Dorfleitner, G. (2002). Is traditional capital market theory consistent with fat-tailed log returns? *Zeitschrift für Betriebswirtschaft* **72**(8), 865–873.

Bamberg, G. and Neuhierl, A. (2012). Growth optimal investment strategy: the impact of reallocation frequency and heavy tails, *German Economic Review* **13**(2), 228–240.

Blattberg, R.C., Gonedes, N.J. *et al.* (1974). A comparison of the stable and student distributions as statistical models for stock prices, *The Journal of Business* **47**(2), 244–280.

Bollerslev, T., Patton, A.J., and Quaedvlieg, R. (2018). Modeling and forecasting (un) reliable realized covariances for more reliable financial decisions, *Journal of Econometrics* **207**(1), 71–91.

Cont, R. (2001). Empirical properties of asset returns: stylized facts and statistical issues. *Quantitative Finance* **1**, 223–236.

Deutsche Börse A.G. (March 2005). Leitfaden zu den Indexkennzahlen der Deutschen Börse, Version 1.5.

Dorfleitner, G. (2002). Stetige versus diskrete Renditen: Überlegungen zur richtigen Verwendung beider Begriffe in Theorie und Praxis. *Kredit und Kapital* **35**, 216–241.

Dorfleitner, G. (2003). Why the return notion matters, *International Journal of Theoretical and Applied Finance* **6**, 73–86.

Fama, E. (1976). Foundations of finance, *Basic Books, New York. Futures Markets* **2**, 1–17.

Hudson, R.S. and Gregoriou, A. (2015). Calculating and comparing security returns is harder than you think: A comparison between logarithmic and simple returns, *International Review of Financial Analysis* **38**, 151–162.

Kelly, J. (1956). A new interpretation of information rate, *Bell Systems Technical Journal* **35**, 917–926.

Latané, H.A. (1959). Criteria for choice among risky ventures, *Journal of Political Economy* **67**(2), 144–155.

Markowitz, H.M. (1976). Investment for the long run: New evidence for an old rule, *The Journal of Finance* **31**(5), 1273–1286.

Merton, R.C. (1972). An analytic derivation of the efficient portfolio frontier, *Journal of Financial and Quantitative Analysis*, **7**(4), 1851–1872.

Meucci, A. (2010). Quant Nugget 2: Linear vs. Compounded Returns-Common Pitfalls in Portfolio Management. GARP Risk Professional.

Sornette, D., Andersen, J., Simonetti, P. *et al.* (2000). Portfolio theory for "fat tails", *International Journal of Theoretical and Applied Finance (IJTAF)* **3**(03), 523–535.

Valle, C.A., Meade, N., and Beasley, J.E. (2015). Factor neutral portfolios, *OR Spectrum* **37**(4), 843–867.

https://doi.org/10.1142/9781800611917_0003

Chapter 3

Emotionally Involved Investors — Is There Any Finance Theory Fitting to Ethical, Crowdfunding and Fan Bond Investors?

Ralf Trost* and Alexander Fox

TU Ilmenau, Department of Economic Sciences and Media, Germany

**ralf.trost@tu-ilmenau.de*

It is quite obvious that emotions influence human decision-making. Conventional finance theory as well as conventional decision theory assume strictly rational behaviour. Behavioural finance, on the contrary, assumes bounded rationality causing humans to make mistakes. In this chapter we argue that both perspectives do not adequately cover decisions influenced by emotions and depict three very different kinds of emotional involvement in making investment decisions, one of them illustrated by empirical data. At the end, it shows it is fruitless to try to incorporate such phenomena in formal theories as well as declaim this impossibility once more and complain about normative theories not being descriptive.

1. Introduction

According to conventional understanding, the behaviour of investors is based on the balance between the expected return to be achieved and the risk involved. However, it is well known that investors do not always act rationally and make investments where the expected return does not correspond to the risk taken. There are a variety of reasons for this. In some cases in particular, emotional motives seem to play a role. In crowdfunding, for instance, social or intrinsic determinants influence the funding decision. Another matter we deal with in this chapter are bonds emitted by football clubs. It is more than a guess, as we will show in Section 4, that emotions also play a crucial role in the success of bond emissions. The rising number of so-called ethical investments, also known as environmental, social, and governance (ESG) investments, may be considered a third example.

In all these cases and presumably many other situations, investors' emotions may have a decisive influence on their investment decisions. These investors are addressed throughout this chapter by the wording *emotionally involved investors* (EII). However, dealing with this observation is a challenge in terms of both theory and practice in finance. Some fundamental questions arise in the process. Obviously, the first one is whether finance theories are, in principle, *able* to factor in this kind of behaviour. To find an answer to this, we have to distinguish between descriptive and normative theories. Next, are we dealing with *formal* or *non-formal* models? And, ultimately: *Should* models replicate this emotional behaviour at all?

The remainder of this chapter is structured as follows: Section 2 provides a short survey of the main theories in finance regarding investors' behaviour from the angle of emotional involvement. In Section 3, we discuss our concept of emotionally involved investors and give three examples, all of them assumed to be well-known. In Section 4, an empiric data set illuminates — admittedly in an extreme case — investments that are almost completely driven by emotions, which in our opinion cannot however be dismissed *per se* as irrational or bounded rational. Section 5 presents the conclusions.

2. Financial Theories and Emotionally Involved Investors

Since the 1950s (Modern portfolio theory, MPT by Markowitz, 1952) and 1960s (Capital asset pricing model, CAPM by Sharpe (1964), Lintner (1965), and Mossin (1965)), the classical understanding of individuals investing money in financial projects is based on the paradigm of the so-called *homo economicus* (e.g., Persky, 1995). Despite the assumption of perfect information, the homo economicus is characterised by strictly rational behaviour (Savage, 1954). Since the (μ, σ)-preferences in both the models are compatible with a certain combination of assumptions, sometimes called hybrid model (see Lintner, 1969, 1970; Bamberg, 1986), within the decision-theoretic model of the expected utility theory (EUT), rational behaviour, in our case, at least aims at maximising the expected utility of personal wealth (von Neumann and Morgenstern, 1944).

It is no news at all that these theories are inadequate in describing people's observable behaviour, but they still may be a valuable part of normative decision theory or capital market theory. However, regardless of whether we take a descriptive point of view or whether we are looking for a convincing normative theory, it is desirable that investment decision models do not conflict systematically with real behaviour. In the first case, gaining insights into the characteristics of human decision-making is the analysis' aim *per se*. In the latter case, we have to anticipate that even if we want to behave as rationally as possible, other people's decisions affect the markets and should therefore be considered. So, since the CAPM was proposed, the question was whether the aim of modelling real human behaviour in decision-making within formal decision models is a reachable aim at all. Simple modifications of the CAPM or arbitrage pricing theory (APT) (Ross, 1976) do not deal with this topic. More recent considerations of asymmetrical distribution of information are subject to the principal–agent model (see Jensen/Meckling, 1976; for the wording 'agency': Ross, 1973). The decision maker, however, is still assumed to be the homo economicus.

Let us now look at the decision-theoretical aspects. Classical EUT is based on one-dimensional utility functions defined on the decision maker's final wealth. In particular, the usual assumption of risk-adverse behaviour, associated with concave utility functions, cannot explain the engagement of EII. In the case of football fan bonds, for example, risk-averse investors should prefer any alternative with non-negative and riskless return, since fan bonds empirically show high risks and low interests (Weimar and Fox, 2021). Moreover, high default risks may result in negative expected returns. A (partially) risk-prone attitude could be seen an explanation because some protagonists in financial markets or participants in lotteries see investments of lower amounts as a kind of play money. A partially convex and partially concave utility function could cover this behaviour (like the value function in the prospect theory by Kahneman and Tversky (1979)) but the doubtable assumption that only the financial dimension drives the investors' decisions would remain.

Conversely, the cases of the poorly placed fan bonds of Hansa Rostock and TSV 1860 München (Weimar and Fox, 2012) show that altruistic motives on their own cannot explain the observed behaviour (cf. Section 3.3). The study by Trost *et al.* (2017) argues the same, i.e., a demand for worthy rewards as a sort of payment-in-kind for reward-based crowdfunding. At the same time, negative returns can be seen in crowdfunding as well (cf. Section 3.2). One-dimensional constructs cannot fit these observations. It is plausible that investors simultaneously pursue several goals and the achieved utility results from the aggregation of the different degrees of fulfilment. In neoclassical terms, this is reflected by multi-dimensional utility functions (multi-attributive expected utility theory (MAUT); see, e.g., Keeney und Raiffa (1976)), where wealth is only one criterion and emotion-based goals play an additional role. In this context, two questions must be considered. First, what kind of interdependencies exist between the multiple criteria? This depends on individual preferences. The interaction may be additive, multiplicative, or multilinear (Keeney and Raiffa, 1976). A simple additive utility function, for example, would reflect a trade-off between the different criteria. A lower return could be compensated by the good feeling in supporting a good goal. Simple multiplicative utility functions cannot explain the acceptance of negative returns as mentioned previously. What kind of interaction is appropriate could be tested empirically if the second, far more difficult question would be answered: How to operationalise the non-monetary dimension(s) of the utility function? This is subject to the situation under consideration. In our empirical example regarding football fan bonds in Section 4, we won't operate on the basis of utility functions but of empiric observable behaviour. This enables us to establish a measure for the emotional involvement of the investors in football fan bonds.

Incidentally, from a descriptive point of view, the expected utility theory doesn't capture human decision-making satisfactorily, regardless of whether it is one- or multi-dimensional. Consequently, behavioural finance became a popular field of financial research in the recent past (see, e.g., Daxhammer and Fascar, 2018). Behavioural finance tries to explain empirical findings about human behaviour in financial decision-making using psychological und behavioural science-based aspects (Camerer and Loewenstein, 2004; De Bondt *et al.*, 2008). Therefore, at first glance, behavioural finance seems to be an adequate framework for analysing EIIs. It is based on the findings of Simon (1957) and assumes the so-called bounded rationality, situated between strictly rational and irrational behaviour. Individuals try to act rationally but they are restricted in recognising and evaluating the available decision alternatives. The restriction results from limited information (market imperfections, information costs, etc.), restricted cognitive abilities (leading to simplifications and heuristics) and psychological stress because of, e.g., time pressure or fear of loss (Simon, 1957). It shows that the decision-making process of investors is affected by various factors. They may influence the cognition of information, the processing and evaluation of information and the decision-making itself (Daxhammer and Fascar, 2018). Numerous effects have been researched in recent years to explain the various behaviours of financial market players (for a summarising overview, see, e.g., De Bondt *et al.* (2008)).

However, the lack of selectivity between the effects to date is an enormous disadvantage. In many cases, it is difficult to associate certain effects with a certain behaviour. Moreover, as stated, for instance, by Klug *et al.* (2009), not every observation discussed in behavioural finance is necessarily irrational or bounded-rational. With regard to EII, it can be assumed that there are situations in which they behave rationally in a traditional sense and other situations in which they don't. For a football fan, it could, e.g., be quite rational to invest capital, even at high risk and lacking monetary return, to help ensure the continued existence of something important (namely the football club in this case). It would be inadequate and arrogant to call this kind of behaviour irrational or bounded-rational. Therefore, considerations based on this understanding of behavioural finance are not appropriate for adequately describing the aspect of emotional involvement itself.

Concurrently, as for any other investor, behavioural finance can be used to describe certain additional effects that have an impact on the behaviour of the emotionally involved investors and subsequently the success of the financing (see Huth *et al.*, 2014; Fox and Heim, 2015). The following is an example of potential bounded rationality, which in our opinion can be traced back to a pattern of well-known effects in behavioural finance: To a remarkable degree, fan bond investors are willing to waive interest and/or redemption payments (see the study in Section 4). We suppose that this is due to the so-called endowment effect. It was first mentioned by Thaler (1980) and states that individuals assign different utility to one and the same asset depending on whether they already possess it or are considering acquiring it. A variation of this effect is the status quo effect, which suggests that people have a bias towards leaving things as they are (Samuelson and Zeckhauser, 1988), while in the framing effect (Thaler, 1980; Kahneman and Tversky, 1986), decisions vary with the reference point relative to which a situation is evaluated. Because of loss aversion (Kahneman and Tversky, 1979), losses outweigh gains of the same amount. Prospect theory captures this property in the shape of the so-called value function, replacing the utility function of the expected utility theory (Kahneman and Tversky, 1979). In the case of emotionally involved fan bond investors, we assume a similar effect as described in a sequential setting: At the time of the bond issue, the investment replaces an (hypothetical) alternative, i.e., the direct donating of the money to the club instead of buying the bond. However, the bond investment avoids the impression of losing money. Subsequently, the status quo changes. The recovery of the money would be a gain that has less weight than the corresponding loss in the beginning. Depending on the dimension of this effect, it may tempt some investors to waive re-payments. Surely, at least from an ex-post point of view, it would have been rational to give planning security to the club by donating the money from the beginning on. As is often the case in behavioural finance, this explanation (or should we call it a story?) is possible but not compelling at all. Further, it doesn't explain the aspect of emotions, because they don't play any role in this argumentation.

In some publications by Taffler and Tuckett, we can find the term *emotional finance* (see, e.g., Taffler and Tuckett, 2010; Taffler, 2018). They address the role of the unconscious in financial decision-making, especially in securities' management, and focus on phenomena like the dotcom bubble in 2000 and the financial crisis in 2008 et seqq. by utilising concepts of psychoanalysis. While some authors recognise a great potential in this approach (Aren and Hamamci, 2020), it has received severe critiques too: "Nearly a decade on, their ideas have largely failed to achieve traction in the academic literature, and continue to struggle to find empirical validation ... Although it is fruitful to analyse the role of emotions in financial markets, more precise, rigorous and realistic approaches to these problems are needed" (Coffman, 2020, p. 1). Taffler and Tuckett located their approach in behavioural finance, but, later on, this kind of research moved further on towards a specific research area called neurofinance (Peterson, 2010; Konovalov and Krajbich, 2019; Miendlarzewska *et al.*, 2019), a sub-branch of neuroeconomics (Camerer *et al.*, 2004; Bechara and Damasio, 2005; Peterson, 2010). Neurofinance entails 'combining insights from psychology and neuroscience with theories of finance' and 'studies how the brain processes financial information' (Miendlarzewska *et al.*, 2019, p. 196). 'By combining these experiments with computational models, neurofinance aims to provide an alternative explanation for the apparent failure of classic finance theories' (Miendlarzewska *et al.*, 2019, p. 196). Obviously, despite a supposed relationship because of the same term 'emotion' this research has nothing in common with the subject of our chapter. To make the differences clearer, the following section starts with some remarks on the term 'emotion'.

3. Emotional Involvement in Making Investment Decisions

3.1. *Emotionally involved investors: Concept and examples*

The term 'emotion' is defined or interpreted in different ways, especially across different scientific communities. In the context of economic decisions, it is used in various ways, sometimes by economists but mainly by psychologists, sociologists und neuroscientists. The view of the latter group is descriptive, and they focus on unconscious emotions. For Loewenstein (2000, p. 26), emotions like anger or fear are 'visceral factors'. Other visceral factors include the so-called drive states such as hunger or feeling states like pain. According to the aforementioned paradigm of emotional finance, proposed by Taffler and Tuckett, decision makers are not conscious about the influence of their emotions on their decisions: 'Although visceral factors also play an essential (probably the dominant) role in human behaviour, people's introspections about the causes of their own behaviour lead them to underappreciate the influence of visceral factors and to exaggerate the importance of higher-level cognitive processes' (Loewenstein, 2000, p. 427). The distinction by Kahneman between 'thinking fast and slow' (Kahneman, 2011) fits for these considerations. Consequently, most discussions about the impact of emotions in economic decisions focus on the unconscious effects of emotions (e.g., Virlics, 2013) and can therefore be subsumed under the area of neurofinance. Furthermore, the effect of this emotional behaviour is often judged as biased (e.g., Virlics, 2013). This argumentation links neurofinance to behavioural finance.

Rick and Loewenstein (2008, p. 138) systemise emotions as follows: The expected emotions are considered by decision makers as possible ex post feelings like regret. In fact, there is a formal decision-theoretic model called regret theory (Loomes and Sugden, 1982). Due to its nevertheless descriptive character (Trost, 1991, p. 94–97), this model, just like Kahneman/Tversky's prospect theory, is to be seen as an early element of behavioural economics. On the contrary, according to Rick and Loewenstein (2008, p. 138), immediate emotions 'are experienced at the moment of choice'. There are two variants of immediate emotions. Incidental emotions arise from 'sources objectively unrelated to the task at hand, e.g., the TV program playing in the background' (Rick and Loewenstein, 2008, p. 138); see also the literature cited by Andrade and Ariely (2009). The other kind of immediate emotion is called integral emotion. Like the expected emotions, they relate to the decision's consequences, but unlike expected emotions, they are felt in the moment of decision-making. To make things even more complicated, we have to distinguish between emotions and the feelings evoked by emotions (Lucey and Dowling, 2005, p. 214).

When considering the examples given in this chapter, especially the investors in football bonds, we have to confess that there is no concrete indication whether one of the definitions of emotion is applicable. On the other hand, we are quite sure that emotions in a quite general sense do play a decisive role. So, and because of the variety of definitions, we feel free to define the term in our own way. For the purposes of this chapter, it is sufficient to take the non-scientific definition by the Merriam-Webster dictionary as a basis: Emotion is "a conscious mental reaction (such as anger or fear) subjectively experienced as strong feeling usually directed toward a specific object and typically accompanied by physiological and behavioural changes in the body" (Merriam-Webster, 2021).

It is evident that emotions have an impact on decision-making, and doubtlessly there is a wide range of human emotions. So, more precisely, we are not interested in the mistakes people make due to of emotions. We call it a mistake if investors would want to reconsider their decision when becoming aware of it. Many of the effects in behavioural finance are of this kind. However, there have been a lot of cases wherein the investors wouldn't revise their decision at all. Not all the remaining effects are caused by emotions. The emotional involvement we deal with is a characteristic of a certain person making a certain investment decision. In that case, we discuss an emotionally involved investor (EII). Another person in the same decision-making situation or the same person in another decision-making situation but with the same monetary outcome, i.e., facing the same monetary random variable, may show no emotional involvement at all. On the other hand, as every investor, the EII is interested in money. The investment decision rests on, at least, two dimensions. On a large scale, we know this from successful business people who nevertheless spend enormous amounts of money on their beloved football club, showing both profit orientation and emotion-driven funding in the same person. In contrast, most other people would not give a penny to support these clubs.

We argued in Section 2 that it would be wrong to declare investment decisions that are wholly or partially driven by emotional involvement as irrational or bounded-rational. Considering a firm offering products and services that are unique and not even partially substitutable, consumers with a high monetary or emotional involvement in such products and services should have a high interest in the survival of the firm (Steinman and Jacobs, 2015). Football clubs are far from being a unique example for this. For instance, we may consider small firms selling local specialities as well as global companies like Apple. These goods are often connected to fan involvement, for which reason the perceived utility stemming from these goods is usually difficult to replace. Hence, when customers are so strongly associated with a product, a potential dropout of the producer would instantaneously lead to a total depreciation of the invested time, money and probably the social capital in the form of social networks to other fan consumers. The question is how the consumers will react and what a rational behaviour means. On the one side, they can invest in a potential bailout of the company ('loyalty'), and on the other side, they can simply leave the company ('exit') (Hirschman, 1970). The tendency to support the company should be stronger the higher the past investments and current dependencies, which leads to the assumption that highly involved consumers accept, e.g., non-risk-adjusted interest for lending capital to the firm or, in extreme cases, leave the money without further compensation.

3.2. *Emotional involvement and crowdfunding*

Crowdfunding is generally used to generate funds for a project from a large number of people, typically with the help of the Internet (Lehner, 2013). The often-cited Belleflame *et al.* (2014) define crowdfunding as "...an open call, mostly through the Internet, for the provision of financial resources either in the form of donation or in exchange for the future product or some form of reward to support initiatives for specific purposes". This quite new instrument for acquiring capital has aroused the interest of empirical researchers, especially since the supposed bypassing of classical institutional intermediaries, the opportunity to support 'hip' people and their 'cool' projects and to feel being a part of it attracted a partial new class of private investors called backers. An obvious question to ask here concerns their motives.

In the current literature, it has been already suggested that social and intrinsic determinants impact the success of crowdfunding projects and that capital providers are often not predominantly or solely motivated by monetary returns (see, e.g., Ordanini *et al.*, 2011; Belleflame *et al.*, 2014; Allison *et al.*, 2015). Most of the authors assume a limited rational behaviour of the investors (e.g., Gerber and Hui, 2013; Brem and Wassong, 2014; Lin and Viswanathan, 2015). In the field of behavioural finance, there are also various studies to explain investors' decisions to support crowdfunding projects. They deal with herd behaviour (Zhang and Liu, 2012; Agrawal *et al.*, 2015), home bias (e.g., Brem and Wassong, 2014; Lin and Viswanathan, 2015) or the feeling of solidarity (e.g., Ordanini *et al.*, 2011). According to behavioural finance's outlook, these studies suggest non-rational behaviour, and we must ask again whether this blanket assumption is appropriate. A recent study (Zhang and Chen, 2019) discusses two types of backer motivations besides the 'material' aspect which they name extrinsic motivation. The authors call the two types of motivations as self-orientation and other orientation; self-orientation denotes egoistic motivation to pursue personal satisfaction, whereas other orientation conveys altruistic motivation.

Zhang and Chen (2019) used data (concerning film projects) from the reward-based crowdfunding platform *kickstarter.com* just like the study by Trost *et al.* (2017), which analyses real projects (with a focus on technology projects). The latter's observations strongly suggest that profitability is indeed a key element of an investor's bundle of motivations, while on the other hand, backers also have a broad acceptance for negative returns. Cox *et al.* (2018) derived similar results with data from the reward-based crowdfunding platform *fundanything.com* and Bretschneider and Leimeister (2017) with data from an equity-based crowdfunding platform.

Despite the broad consensus that returns are not the sole criterion for human decision-making in crowdfunding, at the present stage, we are not able to quantify whether and to what extent emotions play a role in the bundles of backers' motives. Nevertheless, in our opinion they surely do.

3.3. *Emotional involvement and football investments*

Emotional involvement is a striking feature of football fandom, as fans usually identify strongly with their clubs (Wann and Branscombe, 1990; de Ruyter and Wetzels, 2000). If football clubs want to attract fans for financing, there are several possibilities. Fan bonds and crowdfunding are currently predominant in Germany. (Because it is not relevant for our considerations, we won't distinguish between the clubs and the capital company emitting the bonds.) Fan bonds are usually closed and unlisted, aimed at fans and other stakeholders as outside creditors (Küting and Strauß, 2011; Weimar and Fox, 2012; Fox and Weimar, 2014). However, IPOs and mezzanine capital are also used for the financial participation of fans in football clubs (Weimar and Fox, 2012; Fox, 2016). Emotions seem to play an important role in the investment decision here too (Berument and Ceyland, 2012; Weimar and Fox, 2021).

Considering fan bonds in Germany, it is interesting to note the differing degrees of success. In some cases, there was a dramatic lack of buyers (e.g., a bond was emitted in 2010 by TSV 1860 München with a sold rate of 7.5%), while in other cases, the emission's volume could be increased subsequently (e.g., the fan bond emitted in 2012 by Hamburger Sportverein had a planned volume of 12.5 Mio. EUR when the actually placed volume of 17.5 Mio. EUR was 40% higher). Some authors speculate that sentiment bias impacts the demand for such fan bonds (Weimar and Fox, 2012; Fox and Weimar, 2014). Huth *et al.* (2014) who examined real investment decisions concerning fan bonds concluded that the investment decision of fans has primarily emotional causes. However, Huth *et al.* (2014) used only a limited database and excluded non-investors from their study (Weimar and Fox, 2021).

3.4. *Emotional involvement and ESG investing*

In the recent past, a strong demand for financial investments meeting contemporary environmental, social and governance requirements emerged (Eurosif, 2018; Deutsche Bundesbank, 2019; Hale, 2021). We refer to them as ESG investments in this chapter, including the frequently used terms such as sustainable investment and sustainable finance. ESG investing is also named socially responsible investing (SRI) or ethical investing, which seems to be the oldest term. For a discussion of ethical investment in the broader field of business ethics, see Teresiene and Budriene (2021). There is a broad range of goals and constraints that may or may not be seen as ethical (Schwartz, 2003, p. 197). Therefore, it is not surprising that many definitions are quite vague and lack concrete content so as to avoid the difficulty in defining accurately. However, for our purposes, this is sufficient. We have adopted a definition by Cowton (1999, p. 60), replacing the term ethical with the ESG terms: 'ESG investing is a set of approaches which include environmental, social and governance goals or constraints as well as more conventional financial criteria in decisions over whether to acquire, hold or dispose of a particular investment'. For a more sophisticated approach, see the Darmstadt Definition of Sustainable Investments (Hoffmann *et al.*, 2004; Busch *et al.*, 2016, pp. 308–309).

First, this raises the question of why we lump together the meritorious engagement regarding 'good matters' like climate neutrality with being a football fan, presumably a quite dubious phenomenon to many outside observers. The intention is to stress the fact that we want to examine emotional involvement without any content-related judgement caused by individual ethical standards, individual tastes, or other factors. Furthermore, we want to clarify that emotional involvement in our interpretation is not a failure or mistake *per se*. In fact, appraisals like these lie in the eye of the beholder and should be avoided. It is very easy to imagine people investing money in the bond of their preferred football club instead of a sustainable investment fund and, of course, vice versa. Both investors may be emotionally involved, although in different decision situations. All aspects that we cover under the concept of emotional involvement have in common that they are relevant to some decision makers and irrelevant to others. For ESG investments, this is shown empirically by Wins and Zwergel (2014).

ESG investing, on the other hand, may certainly be a decision solely based on non-emotional considerations, regardless of whether they are financial or of some other nature. Hence, we have to look at the motives of ESG investors. According to Chatterji *et al.* (2009, p. 130), ESG investors maybe financial, deontological, consequentialist, or expressive investors (see also Busch, Bauer, and Orlitzky, 2016, pp. 312–313). Financial investors believe that ESG investments show better financial performance. Deontological investors attribute intrinsic ethical values to decision alternatives regardless of their monetary outcomes. They may also be called 'ethical investors' (for the terminology, see von Wallis and Klein, 2015, p. 63). Consequentialist investors want to influence the cost of capital for firms depending on their degree of social responsibility via generating greater capital supply for the 'good' companies. Lastly, expressive investors want to shape their social identity or image by making 'ethically correct' investments. As we see by this categorisation, it is the same as in the cases of crowdfunding or fan bond investors, respectively: Without further investigation, we cannot dismiss this behaviour as not rational, and we cannot distinguish between intuitive actions driven partially by emotions and calculated ones. We presume that emotional involvement may be seen most likely in the group of expressive investors and probably among deontological investors.

4. Financing the MSV Duisburg: An Extreme Case of Emotional Involvement

4.1. *Some facts on (German) fan bonds*

A look at the 2018/2019 season (in order to avoid the numerous effects of the coronavirus pandemic since spring 2020) shows that 28 of the 36 clubs in the 1 and 2. Bundesliga were able to achieve annual profit (DFL, 2020). On the contrary, this was not the case for most of the fan bond issuers. Due to their poor financial situation, traditional financing instruments such as bank loans were simply too expensive due to the bad credit rating of the clubs (Weimar and Fox, 2012; Fox and Weimar, 2014). All bonds except the first one were publicly placed and not to be traded at stock exchanges. In about half of the cases, the purposes were debt restructuring, liquidity improvement, or re-financing earlier fan bonds (Weimar and Fox, 2012). The short-term character of these uses without any perspective on the substantial improvement of the club's structural financial and sporting situation increases the riskiness of the investment. Ongoing lack of sporting success may cause a fatal feedback due to the frustration of the fans, thereby lowering the ticket and fan article incomes. The increased risk of fan bonds in contrast with other bonds is not reflected by the yields of the bonds (Weimar and Fox, 2012; Huth *et al.*, 2014).

Besides the consistently low minimum nominal amounts, clearly aiming at the broader football audience and the high proportion of decorative certificates issued with attached interest coupons are noticeable. In addition to sales promotion (Keller, 2008), the aim is mainly to prevent the assertion of claims for interest and redemption payments, since in this case, the jewellery loans are 'visually destroyed' (Weimar and Fox, 2012). Another reason for the different placement successes is presumably the number of potential investors. In this respect, associations with a high supra-regional popularity seem to be at an advantage and achieve higher placement rates (Weimar and Fox, 2012).

For more details on German fan bonds, we referred to the information given by Weimar and Fox (2021).

4.2. *Hypotheses development*

We will try to prove whether football fans can be viewed as a special case of EII. The basis of the following investigation is a fan bond issued by the German football club MSV Duisburg in 2013. The tendency to support a football club financially will presumably be greater the higher the emotional connection to the club is:

H1: The proportion of investors is greater among fans than among non-fans.

For the same reason, one could expect that fans will show a greater willingness to lend money without financial compensation.

H2: Among the investing fans, a larger proportion would have invested even at zero interests than among the investing non-fans.

Furthermore, we will deal with the previously discussed phenomenon that can be explained by behavioural finance: the willingness to waive interest and/or even redemption payments. A person wanting to support a club via donation should do so. There is no need to invest in a bond first and then change it to a donation. Moreover, we will investigate whether a reasonable number of investors are still willing to do so. This would be evidence for the existence of endowment effect and status quo effect because the position of the investor has shifted by time from 'I have the money in my pocket and have to decide whether I should give it away' to 'I have to decide whether I should claim to get money additional to my present wealth'. We hypothesise that the following behaviour is a significant characteristic of fans:

H3: Among the investing fans with decorative certificates, a larger proportion waives interest payments than among the investing non-fans with decorative certificates.

H4: Among the investing fans with decorative certificates, a larger proportion waives the redemption payments than among the investing non-fans with decorative certificates.

4.3. *Empirical study*

Using the data set employed by Weimar and Fox (2021), collected through the interviews of the investors and non-investors of the fan bond issued by MSV Duisburg in 2013, we will test the aforementioned hypotheses and show how the behaviour of these investors is decisively driven by their emotional attachment to the investment object.

4.3.1. *Sample and research design*

We have kept the description here as brief as possible and refer the readers to Weimar and Fox (2021) for more details, where they will find the following explanations, in addition to descriptive statistics and a thorough regression-based analysis.[1]

When MSV Duisburg issued the bond, former relegations from the first division down to the third division and remaining fix costs (e.g., stadium, youth academies, etc.) had brought the club into financial turmoil. The signing period was from 4 September 2013 to 30 April 2014 with maturity on 14 September 2018. The interest rate amounted to 5% and would have raised to 6% in case of a relegation to the second division (MSV Duisburg, 2013). A large part was sold in traditional decorative certifications. The bond was issued by the underlying club and not the capital company holding the rights of the professional football team (MSV Duisburg GmbH & Co. KGaA). This decision was due to the worse financial situation of the capital company. As depicted by the official bond prospectus, the club reported a loss of €3.9 million in 2012/2013, and the total balance total was only €6.8 million. Not surprisingly, the emission failed the maximum value of €5,000,000, but at least it collected over €650,000.

Fundamentally desirable would be a comparison of the behaviour of EII, in this case fans of MSV Duisburg, with the behaviour of 'normal' investors who are not emotionally involved with the MSV Duisburg. However, the fact is that it is difficult to generate reliable data on the part of non-EIIs due to both the rather low issue volume and the low general awareness of the issuer. As a result, we decided

[1]We thank Daniel Weimar, formerly University of Duisburg-Essen, for the permission to use his data set; see Weimar and Fox (2021).

that the population should consist of persons who have proven to know the MSV Duisburg and presumably have a basically benevolent interest in the club. For this purpose, all persons who subscribed to the MSV bond or who followed the MSV Duisburg on Facebook were contact. In the following section, we refer to this compound population as sympathisers.

The questionnaire was sent to all subscribers (approximately 1,100) of the bond at the beginning of May 2014 and a link was posted on the Facebook page of MSV Duisburg at the same time (approximately 35,000 followers). A total of 1,649 sympathisers completed the questionnaire, from which, remained 1,266 after removing data records with missing values, inconsistent answers, and minor respondents. With 556 data records approximately, 44% of all bond investors were elements of this sample, with 525 of them ordering a decorative certificate. The remaining 710 had not invested in the bond. Due to the primarily local significance of the club, both investing and non-investing sympathisers were locally centralised within a radius of 50 km around Duisburg.

4.3.2. *Variables*

For our analysis, we only need a part of the data set. First, we are interested in the variables INVESTOR (indicating whether the person has invested in the bond), INVEST IF ZERO INTEREST (denoting whether the investor would have invested if the interest rate had been zero), WAIVER INTEREST (indicating whether the person considered waiving the right to claim interest payment) and WAIVER REPAY (representing whether the person planned to waive the right to claim redemption). Furthermore, crucial for our purpose is a measure of the property 'fan of MSV Duisburg'. This variable, also used by Weimar and Fox (2021), is defined using another variable named FAN INVOLVEMENT. This is a standardised conglomerate of four variables as proxies, measuring whether the person holds a season ticket, counting the home games attended, counting the years of club membership and calculating the fan expenses per year. The last two had to be measured in relation to age and personal income. The dichotomous variable FAN takes the value one in the case of FAN INVOLVEMENT $>=$ 0 and zero otherwise. FAN separates high involvement from low involvement in a simple and robust manner.

4.3.3. *Testing for dependencies*

All of our four hypotheses concern dependencies between the first four variables and the variable FAN. To prove the hypotheses, contingency tables were calculated and examined for the significance of dependencies by the chi-square test (so-called fourfold test due to the 2×2-dimension of the tables). Table 1 shows the distribution of fans and investors among the 1,266 sympathisers.

The chi-square statistic had the value 12.68, and the dependency was therefore significant to more than the 1%-level ($p = 0.0004$).

From a total of 556 investors, 516 answered the question as to whether they would have invested even if the offered interest would have been zero (Table 2).

The chi-square statistic had the value 3.92 and the dependency was significant to the 5%-level ($p = 0.0476$).

For a group of 502 investors (those with decorative certificates), we have information about the willingness to waive interest payments (Table 3) or even redemption payments (Table 4). Note that these data do not refer to real actions because of the early date of the questionnaire, the more so as all claims may be made within 5 years after maturity.

Table 1. Joint distribution of investment and fan property.

Investor	No fan	Fan	Total
No	401	309	710
Yes	258	298	556
Total	659	607	1,266

Table 2. Joint distribution of fan property and investment without interest (hypothetical).

Without interest	No fan	Fan	Total
No	168	184	352
Yes	63	101	164
Total	231	285	516

Table 3. Joint distribution of fan property and (presumable) waiver of interest payments.

Waiver of interest (decorative certificate)	No fan	Fan	Total
No	46	35	81
Yes	176	245	421
Total	222	280	502

Table 4. Joint distribution of fan property and (presumable) waiver of redemption payment.

Waiver of redemption (decorative certificate)	No fan	Fan	Total
No	68	50	118
Yes	154	230	384
Total	222	280	502

The chi-square statistic had a value of 6.18 and the dependency was significant to slightly less than the 1%-level ($p = 0.0129$).

The chi-square statistic had the value 11.24 and the dependency was significant to more than the 1%-level ($p = 0.0008$).

4.3.4. *Discussion*

Each of the four tests shows strong dependencies between the two respective dichotomous variables, thereby confirming the hypotheses H1 to H4. Because FAN is one of the variables in every test, these results show that being a fan is an important determinant driving the willingness to lend money to the club as well as to waive compensation as contracted or, moreover, redemption. The higher significance of the fourth test in comparison with the third test shows that fan involvement is more important for waiving the redemption than for only waiving the interest payments. Since our population consists of sympathisers without any neutral persons, we may conclude that the two groups FAN and NO FAN represent two different grades of emotional involvement, significantly influencing the investment decision.

The significant relationship between fan involvement and investor decisions is not surprising. Fans have stronger incentives to bail out a club since they are intense consumers of the product, which means that they would experience a high loss in utility due to the club's insolvency. Club members and high consuming fans are more passionate about the club and, hence, more willing for investment.

These findings are consistent with the assumption that the emotional loyalty to a club is, besides wealth, at least a second influencing variable to the investors' decisions. Here, it is irrelevant whether we argue with (multi-attributive) utility theory or not. However, it would certainly be too short-sighted to call this behaviour generally irrational or bounded rational according to behavioural finance. Nevertheless, as we have argued previously, hypotheses H3 and H4 further reveal bounded-rational behaviour in the form of a sort of status quo effect. However, admittedly, the argumentation may have a weak point: Besides the time effect, donating the money in the beginning or waiving it at a later point of time has different outcomes: In the latter case, the investor possesses the decorative certificate, whereas in the first case the investor won't. Our counterargument is that assuming a consistent, i.e., totally rational, behaviour over time would mean that all investors who ordered decorative certificates and later declared their willingness to waive their payments right from the start wanted to buy the decorative certificate not as a contract but as a physical decoration of their home. We cannot prove it by now, but we don't believe that this would be a plausible assumption.

5. Conclusions

The aim of this chapter was twofold. First, we wanted to explicate the influence of emotions (as described in Section 3.1) on investment decisions. Second, we took this emotional involvement as an example to discuss the meaningfulness of some criticism to classical financial and decision theoretic models in conjunction with the seeming requirements for 'good' model building. No one believes that simple theories like the EUT and CAPM describe human behaviour correctly. There is no point in repeatedly discussing this fact. More interesting are discussions on what the consequences of this fact should be.

- Our examples showed that we should take emotional involvement into account. But how? In the case of fan bonds, we were successful in defining a variable called fan or fan involvement, respectively, serving as operationalisation. In the consequence, we could assume a preference functional depending on two variables, namely monetary outcome and fan involvement. It is very questionable whether this functional could be handled in a fruitful manner. And if so, would we be as successful when dealing with crowdfunding or ESG investing? How many additional causes of emotional involvement should we consider? Obviously, even if we ignore the induced 'hunger of data' every attempt to do so results in typical model overfitting: With respect to certain data sets, we may explain the past well, while the derived model is absolutely useless in dealing with the future.
- Descriptive research doubtlessly is crucial for broadening our knowledge about human decision-making. It is the main objective of psychologists and sociologists as well as behavioural economists. Their research brings important and interesting facts to light, which we should have in mind when making investment or other economic decisions. However, these findings cannot become part of formal models that are plain and simple, because they are too complicated.
- Then, what is the role of formal models like CAPM? They can be seen as sort of heuristic when we need quantitative information where the reality is too complex to look for total models (which is, in fact, almost always). It is the same argument justifying in the investment appraisal the use of the present value instead of the in-principle better complete financial plan (e.g., Kruschwitz and Lorenz, 2019, pp. 38–52). For example, when using discounted cash flow to calculate a company's value, we need an approximation for equity costs. Usually, this is done using the CAPM. What would be an alternative, aside from free-handed, i.e., discretionary estimation? Therefore, the professional standards for company evaluation prescribe the use of CAPM, for example, the standard IDW S1 (for the current version of this standard see IDW (2019)) in Germany. Another example for the use of CAPM is for benchmarking and performance evaluation in fund management.
- The example of emotional investment teaches another lesson: The term 'rational' is problematic. After all, despite all criticisms in

economic theory, it is usually associated with the homo economicus. Every deviation from the assumed behaviour of this construct is labelled as not rational. We have argued in all our three examples that this is not very helpful in understanding human decision-making. Behavioural finance argues using bounded rationality and calls every deviation from the homo economicus' decisions an 'anomaly'. We assume these wordings as not useful at all since it creates the impression that economists misjudge every deviation from maximising monetary outcome as not rational.

To sum up, the emotionally involved investor shows us again that most of the real human decision-making cannot be described by simple formal models, that in many cases emotion-driven decisions cannot be rejected in general as not rational and that formal models like the CAPM nowadays play a small yet important role in economic thinking, especially when the user prosaically needs a concrete number. Emotional aspects are much too complex to be incorporated into a mathematical calculus — no matter how sophisticated it may be.

References

Agrawal, A., Catalini, C., and Goldfarb, A. (2015). Crowdfunding: Geography, social networks, and the timing of investment decisions, *Journal of Economics & Management Strategy* **24**(2), 253–274.

Allison, T., Davis, B., Short, J., and Webb, J. (2015). Crowdfunding in a prosocial microlending environment: examining the role of intrinsic versus extrinsic cues, *Entrepreneurship, Theory and Practice* **39**(1), 53–73.

Andrade, E.B., and Ariely, D. (2009). The enduring impact of transient emotions on decision making, *Organizational Behavior and Human Decision Processes* **109**(1), 1–8.

Aren, S. and Hamamci, H.N. (2020). Emotional finance: determinants of phantasy, *Kybernetes* **50**(5), 1250–1276.

Bamberg, G. (1986). The hybrid model and related approaches to capital market equilibria. In: Bamberg, G. and Spremann, K. (eds.), *Capital Market Equilibria*. Berlin: Springer, pp. 7–54.

Bechara, A. and Damasio, A. (2005). The somatic marker hypothesis: a neural theory of economic decision, *Games and Economic Behavior* **52**(2), 336–372.

Belleflame, P., Lambert, T., and Schwienbacher, A. (2014). Crowdfunding: tapping the right crowd, *Journal of Business Venturing* **29**(5), 585–609.

Berument, M.H. and Ceylan, N.B. (2012). Effects of soccer on stock markets: the return-volatility relationship, *Social Science Journal* **49**(3), 368–374.

Brem, A. and Wassong, N. (2014). Wer investiert warum? Eine Analyse von Investmententscheidungen bei crowdfunding-Projekten, *Zeitschrift für KMU und Entrepreneurship* **62**(1), 31–55.

Bretschneider, U. and Leimeister, J.M. (2017). Not just an ego trip: exploring backers' motivation for funding in incentive-based crowdfunding, *Journal of Strategic Information Systems* **26**(4), 246–260.

Busch, T., Bauer, R., and Orlitzky, M. (2016). Sustainable development and financial markets: old paths and new avenues, *Business & Society* **55**(3), 303–329.

Camerer, C.F. and Loewenstein, G. (2004). Behavioral economics: past, present, future. In Camerer, C., Loewenstein, G., and Rabin, G. (eds.), *Advances in Behavioral Economics.* Princeton, Oxford: Princeton University Press, pp. 3–51.

Camerer, C.F., Loewenstein, G., and Prelec, D. (2004). Neuroeconomics: why economics needs brains, *Scandinavian Journal of Economics* **106**(3), 555–579.

Chatterji, A.K., Levine, D.I., and Toffel, M.W. (2009). How well do social ratings actually measure corporate social responsibility? *Journal of Economics & Management Strategy* **18**(1), 125–169.

Coffman, D. (2020). The trouble with minding markets: emotional finance in context, In Ahangar, R.G. and Salman, A. (eds.), *Investment Strategies in Emerging New Trends in Finance.* London: IntechOpen, pp. 115–131. Available from: https://www.intechopen.com/books/investment-strategies-in-emerging-new-trends-in-finance/the-trouble-with-minding-markets-emotional-finance-in-context.

Cowton, C.J. (1999). Playing by the rules: ethical criteria at an ethical investment fund, *Business Ethics: A European Review* **8**(1), 60–69.

Cox, J., Nguyen, T., and Kang, S.M. (2018). The Kindness of strangers? An investigation into the interaction of funder motivations in online crowdfunding campaigns, *KYKLOS* **71**(2), 187–212.

Daxhammer, R.J. and Facsar, M. (2018). *Behavioral finance: Verhaltenswissenschaftliche Finanzmarktforschung im Lichte begrenzt rationaler Marktteilnehmer* (2. Aufl.) Konstanz München: UVK.

De Bondt, W., Muradoglu, G., Shefrin, H., and Staikouras, S. (2008). Behavioral finance: quo vadis? *Journal of Applied Finance* **18**(2), 1–15.

de Ruyter, W.F.M. and Wetzels, M. (2000). With a little help from my fans: extending models of pro-social behaviour to explain supporter's intentions to buy soccer club shares, *Journal of Economic Psychology* **21**(4), 387–409.

Deutsche Bundesbank (2019). The sustainable finance market: a stocktake. Available from: https://www.bundesbank.de/en/publications/search/the-sustainable-finance-market-a-stocktake-811962. Accessed July 5, 2021.

DFL (2020). *DFL Wirtschaftsreport 2019: Die ökonomische Situation im deutsche Lizenzfußball.* Available from: https://media.dfl.de/sites/2/2020/02/DE_DFL_Wirtschaftsreport_2020_M.pdf. Accessed July 5, 2021.

Eurosif (2018). *European SRI study 2018.* Available from: https://www.eurosif.org/wp-content/uploads/2021/10/European-SRI-2018-Study.pdf. Accessed July 5, 2021.

Fox, A, (2016). Crowdfunding: Eine Alternative für professionelle Fußballclubs? *Corporate Finance* **7**(11), 403–408.

Fox, A. and Weimar, D. (2014). Fan-Anleihen als Finanzierungsmöglichkeit von Sportorganisationen außerhalb des Fußballs, *Corporate Finance* **5**(5), 242–252.

Fox, A. and Heim, S. (2015). Das Investorenverhalten bei Fan-Anleihen. *Schriften zur Finanzwirtschaft, Heft 14.* TU Ilmenau, FG Finanzwirtschaft/Investition: Ilmenau.

Gerber, E. and Hui, J. (2013). Crowdfunding: motivations and deterrents for participation, *ACM Transactions on Computer-Human Interaction* **20**(6), 1–32.

Hale, J. (2021). A broken record: flows for U.S. sustainable funds again reach new heights. Available from: https://www.morningstar.com/articles/1019195/a-broken-record-flows-for-us-sustainable-funds-aga in-reach-new-heights. Accessed July 5, 2021.

Hirschman, A.O. (1970). *Exit, Voice, and Loyalty: Responses to Decline in Firms, Organizations and States.* Cambridge: Harvard University Press.

Hoffmann, J., Scherhorn, G., and Busch, T. (eds.) (2004). *Darmstadt Definition of Sustainable Investments.* Wuppertal: Wuppertal Institut für Klima, Umwelt, Energie.

Huth, C., Gros, M., and Kühr, C. (2014). Fananleihen deutscher Fußballunternehmen: eine empirische Untersuchung des Anlageverhaltens der Zeichner. *Corporate Finance* **5**(1), 7–16.

IDW (2019). *Verlautbarungen zur Unternehmensbewertung.* IDW Sonderdruck, Düsseldorf: IDW Verlag.

Jensen, M.C. and Meckling, W.H. (1976). Theory of the firm: managerial behavior, agency costs and ownership structure, *Journal of Financial Economics* **3**(4), 305–360.

Kahneman, D. (2011). *Thinking Fast and Slow.* New York: Macmillan.

Kahneman, D. and Tversky, A. (1979). Prospect theory: an analysis of decisions under risk, *Econometrica* **47**(2), 263–291.

Kahneman, D. and Tversky, A. (1986). The framing of decisions and the evaluation of prospects. In Marcus, B., Dorn, G. J. W., and Weingartner, P. (eds.), *Logic, Methodology and Philosophy of Science VII*, 503–520.

Keeney, R.L. and Raiffa, H. (1976). *Decisions with Multiple Objectives: Preferences and Value Tradeoffs.* New York: Wiley.

Keller, C. (2008). *Steuerung von Fußballunternehmen: finanziellen und sportlichen Erfolg langfristig gestalten.* Berlin: Erich Schmidt Verlag.

Klug, T., Locarek-Junge, H., and Mihm, M. (2009). Rationale Marktübertreibungen im Zusammenhang der aktuellen Finanzmarktkrise, *Vierteljahreshefte zur Wirtschaftsforschung* **78**(1), 25–39.

Konovalov, A. and Krajbich, I. (2019). Over a decade of Neuroeconomics: what have we learned? *Organizational Research Methods* **22**(1), 148–173.

Kruschwitz, L. and Lorenz, D. (2019). *Investitionsrechnung* (15. Aufl.). Berlin: de Gruyter.

Küting, K. and Strauß, M. (2011). Finanzielle und bilanzielle Krisenstrategien im Profifußball, *Der Betrieb* **64**(47), 2613–2621.

Lehner, O. M. (2013). Crowdfunding social ventures: A model and research agenda, *Venture Capital* **15**(4), 289–311.

Lin, M. and Viswanathan, S. (2015). Home bias in online investments: an empirical study of an online crowdfunding market, *Management Science* **62**(5), 1393–1414.

Lintner, J. (1965). The valuation of risk assets and the selection of risky investments in stock portfolios and capital budgets, *Review of Economics and Statistics* **47**(1), 13–37.

Lintner, J. (1969). The aggregation of investor's diverse judgments and preferences in purely competitive securities markets, *Journal of Financial and Quantitative Analysis* **4**(4), 347–400.

Lintner, J. (1970). The market price of risk, size of market and investor's risk aversion, *Review of Economics and Statistics* **52**(1), 87–99.

Loewenstein, G. (2000). Emotions in economic theory and economic behavior. *American Economic Review* **90**(2), 426–432.

Loomes, G. and Sugden, R. (1982). Regret theory: an alternative theory of rational choice under uncertainty. *Economic Journal* 92 (December), 805–824.

Lucey, B.M. and Dowling, M. (2005). The role of feelings in investor decision-making, *Journal of Economic Surveys* **19**(2), 211–237.

Markowitz, H.M. (1952). Portfolio selection, *Journal of Finance* **7**(1), 77–91.

Merriam-Webster (2021). Definition of 'emotion'. Available from: https://www.merriam-webster.com/dictionary/emotion. Accessed July 5, 2021.

Miendlarzewska, E.A., Kometer, M., and Preuschoff, K. (2019). Neurofinance, *Organizational Research Methods* **22**(1), 196–222.

Mossin, J. (1966). Equilibrium in a capital asset market, *Econometrica* **34**(4), 768–783.

Neumann, J. von and Morgenstern, O. (1944). *Theory of Games and Economic behaviour*, Princeton: Princeton University Press.

Ordanini, A., Miceli, L., Pizzetti, M., and Parasuraman, A. (2011). Crowdfunding: transforming customers into investors through innovative service platforms, *Journal of Service Management* **22**(4), 443–470.

Persky, J. (1995). The ethology of homo economicus, *Journal of Economic Perspectives* **9**(2), 221–231.

Peterson, R.L. (2010). Neuroeconomics aund neurofinance, in Baker, H. K. and Nofsinger, J.R. (eds.), *Behavioral Finance: Investors, Corporations, and Markets*. Hoboken: Wiley, pp. 73–92.

Rick, C. and Loewenstein, G. (2008). The role of emotion in economic behaviour. in Lewis, M., Haviland-Jones, J.M. and Feldman Barrett, L. (eds.), *Handbook of Emotions* (3rd ed.) New York: Guildford, pp. 138–156.

Ross, S.A. (1973). The economic theory of agency: the principal's problem, *American Economic Review* **63**(2), 134–139.

Ross, S.A. (1976). The arbitrage theory of capital asset pricing, *Journal of Economic Theory* **13**(3), 341–360.

Samuelson, W. and Zeckhauser, R. (1988). Status quo bias in decision making, *Journal of Risk and Uncertainty* **1**(1), 7–59.

Savage, L.J. (1954). *The Foundations of Statistics*. New York: Wiley.

Schwartz, M.S. (2003). The 'ethics' of ethical investing, *Journal of Business Ethics* **43**(3), 195–213.

Sharpe, W.F. (1964). Capital asset prices: a theory of market equilibrium under conditions of risk, *Journal of Finance* **19**(3), 425–442.

Simon, H.A. (1957). *Models of Man, Social and Rational: Mathematical Essays on Rational Human Behavior in a Social Setting*. New York: Wiley.

Steinman, R.B. and Jacobs, E., (2015). Sunk costs effects on consumer choice. *Business Management Dynamics* **4**(11), 25–30.

Taffler, R. (2018). Emotional finance: investment and the unconscious. *European Journal of Finance* **24**, 7–8, 630–653.

Taffler, R.J. and Tuckett, D. (2010). Emotional finance: the role of the unconscious in financial decisions. In Baker, H.K. and Nofsinger, J.R. (eds.), *Behavioral Finance: Investors, Corporations, and Markets* Hoboken: Wiley, pp. 95–112.

Teresiene, D. and Budriene, D. (2021). Business ethics and ethical investing: from historical, ethical approach to real investments, *Technium Social Sciences Journal 17(March)*, 212–221.

Thaler, R.H. (1980). Toward a positive theory of consumer choice, *Journal of Economic Behaviour and Organization* **1**(1), 39–60.

Trost, R. (1991). *Entscheidungen unter Risiko: Bernoulliprinzip und duale Theorie.* Frankfurt/M.: Peter Lang.

Trost, R., Fox, A., and Heim, S. (2017). Geldwerte Gegenleistungen im reward-based Crowdfunding — suchen die Geldgeber doch Rendite? *Betriebswirtschaftliche Forschung und Praxis* **69**(2), 131–155.

Virlics, A. (2013). Emotions in economic decision making: a multidisciplinary approach. *Procedia Social and Behavioral Sciences* **92**, 1011–1015.

Wallis, M. von and Klein, C. (2015). Ethical requirement and financial interest: a literature review on socially responsible investing, *Business Research* **8**, 61–98.

Wann, D.L. and Branscombe, N.R. (1990). Die-hard and fair-weather fans: Effects of identification on BIRGing and CORFing Tendencies. *Journal of Sport and Social Issues* **14**(2), 103–117.

Weimar, D. and Fox, A. (2012). Fananleihen als Finanzierungsmöglichkeit von Sportclubs? Eine Bestandsaufnahme am Beispiel der Fußballbundesliga, *Corporate Finance Biz* **3**(4), 181–187.

Weimar, D. and Fox, A. (2021). Fan involvement and unusual investor behaviour: evidence from a football fan bond, *International Journal of Sport Finance* **16**(1), 16–32.

Wins, A. and Zwergel, B. (2016). Comparing those who do, might and will not invest in sustainable funds: a survey among German retail fund investors, *Business Research* **9**, 51–99.

Zhang, H. and Chen, W. (2019). Backer motivation in crowdfunding new product ideas: is it about you or is it about me? *Journal of Product Innovation* **36**(2), 241–262.

Zhang, J. and Liu, P. (2012). Rational herding in microloan markets. *Management Science* **58**(5), 892–912.

https://doi.org/10.1142/9781800611917_0004

Chapter 4

How Did Risk-Reduced Investment Strategies Perform During the Corona Crash? Lessons Learned from the Crisis for the Asset Management Industry

Friedrich Thießen* and Jörg Müller

Chemnitz University of Technology, Faculty of Economics and Business Administration, Germany

**finance@wirtschaft.tu-chemnitz.de*

Based on the Corona crash of February 2020, this chapter examines three risk-reduced investment strategies focusing on equities concerning their suitability for limiting investment risks (long-short approaches, multi-asset approaches, value-protection approaches). The sample is about 100 funds. The results show that the strategies limit the risks on average for all funds — mainly through liquidity reserves and broad allocations. The funds show heterogeneous outcomes within strategies and homogeneous across strategies. This is surprising. It is due to the freedom of fund management. Information in the sales documents is vague and undefined. Fund managers do not disclose procedures. Fund categories are used as marketing instruments. They do not reflect definitive intention. Consequently, the fact that a fund belongs to a strategy group offers little indication of the results to be expected in the event of a crisis. Investors must provide themselves beyond the sales documents with additional information about the fund management's real intentions. Only funds that very decisively restrict the management's actions show the expected results.

1. Introduction

Between mid-February and mid-March 2020, the stock markets suffered a conspicuous fall in prices due to the pandemic. Within one month, stock indices worldwide lost a good third of their value (cf. among others Büttner, 2020, p. 29). In principle, price slumps on stock markets are not uncommon. There have been three major price slumps in the first two decades of the 21st century (2000–2003, 2008, 2011) (concerning the backgrounds cf. FCIC, 2011). The price slump in the Corona crash was not limited to the stock market. It caused corporate bond prices to fall as well; it also led to tight market liquidity (cf. Englert, 2020a, p. 36). Such developments were also relevant in 2008, for example, in the scenario of the financial crisis. To protect themselves from price slumps, investors propose risk-reduced investment strategies. The usefulness of such strategies is the subject of the following chapter.

The Corona crash offers a unique environment for the analysis of risk-reduced investment strategies. It is an entirely unexpected, globally occurring phenomenon for which fund managers could not precisely adjust and prepare themselves. In the literature, the Corona crash has been described as a 'black swan event', i.e., an event with an extremely low probability (cf. Gleißner, 2020, p. 121). The pandemic study of the German Bundestag of 2013 does not name any probabilities of occurrence. Still, it does illuminate a phenomenon with a virus pandemic that could no longer be completely ruled out after the previous virus outbreaks (cf. Deutscher Bundestag, 2013). In any case, the performance of investments in a crash reflects the actual, unvarnished performance of risk-reduced strategies in unexpected or implausible situations. There is a trend in wealth management to no longer manage risks in terms of regular small fluctuations, i.e., volatility, but to focus on the large deviations from the mean, the value at risk. With its low probability of occurrence and at the same time great intensity, the Corona crash offers an excellent opportunity to test risk-reduced strategies for their characteristics concerning extraordinary risks.

1.1. *Research design*

The study focuses on three different risk-reduced investment strategies used internationally, with a focus on international equities. Their performance is compared with a broad general stock index, the MSCI All Country World Index All Cap.

We consider the following three strategy types, for which a sufficient number of investment objects are available in a standardised, comparable form, to be risk-mitigating investment strategies:

- Long-short-strategies;
- Multi-asset systems with strong diversification;
- Investments with explicit promises to secure value.

Long-short strategies aim to decouple from beta risk and attempt to achieve a return above the money market rate without systematic risk. They are also offered as 'absolute return' or 'market neutral' strategies because they reduce or even eliminate systematic market risk.[1]

With multi-asset investments, an attempt is made to achieve a favourable risk structure through vast diversification, which allows the inclusion of riskier individual assets to achieve an additional return while at the same time maintaining a low risk level due to diversification.[2] In contrast to long-short strategies, no complete decoupling from beta risk is sought. The aim is often to bring more 'calm' into the portfolio through vast diversification to create scope for the formation of small, promising investment focuses.

Value–protection concepts attempt to combine protection against loss of value with participation in opportunities for value growth (cf. Faber, 2008, p. 5; cf. Marshall, 1987, p. 115). Typically, investors define lower value limits, which must not be undercut.

The strategies considered here are widely used in asset management and have repeatedly been the subject of academic research in the past. Examples include Petukhina and Sprünken (2021) or Glas and Poddig (2018) with a focus on multi-asset investment strategies, and Chaperon (2010) with a long-short investment focus (considering the financial crisis at the time). A scientific study of investment

[1]The term 'long-short' results from the fact that assets that appear to the fund manager to be undervalued are bought, and assets that appear to be overvalued are sold short. See in the case of shares (Kaiser, 2004, p. 131).

[2]The range of multi-asset strategies extends from simple mixed funds to complex structures of various asset classes such as shares, high-yield bonds, commodities and real estate, see Englert (2020b, p. 6).

strategies in the context of the current Corona crisis is not yet to be found in the literature. The present study is intended to help fill this gap.

Our objects of investigation are public investment funds. The advantage of public investment funds for this investigation is that many information about the investment strategies and the assets' composition is regularly available. Often, the price history is also available. We obtain the data from the website Fondsweb.com/en. The site contains a large number of such funds, which are of interest in this article. In addition, the data are available in a uniformly prepared, structured, and systematised form. Furthermore, Fondsweb offers access to documents such as sales prospectuses, KIDs, and/or annual reports.

We form a sample of around 100 funds that invest globally, mainly in equity markets, and are listed in euros. We exclude those funds that cannot easily be assigned to one of the three strategies mentioned above. The allocation of funds to specific strategies has not proved to be easy. In some cases, funds do not disclose their strategies in full detail in sales prospectuses and KIDs, despite the obligation to inform customers. In some cases, there are additional secondary strategy elements and the main strategy, which are highlighted in the documents to make these funds appear particularly attractive. There is obviously a great need for funds to stand out from others to not be assigned to a particular category, which would make them easier to compare.

It is also problematic that the funds often do not commit themselves exactly. Some funds focus on a specific strategy in KIDs. The same is then found in the sales prospectuses. However, other courses of action are often mentioned there, making it difficult to see what the fund really intends to do. Often, very little is excluded. Funds strive for an enormous scope of action, enabling them to act flexibly and be legally unassailable. If an investor reads 'exactly', he or she cannot be sure what he or she is getting. We will see in the following that the return development of the funds in and after the Corona crash reflects this ambiguity.

For these reasons, the grouping of funds into groups of specific strategies is impossible without a certain degree of fuzziness. Therefore, we have decided not to group the funds ourselves but to use that of a major fund marketer, namely Fondsweb. It results a two-stage classification system.

On the upper level, a distinction is made between the three main strategies mentioned above, namely 'long-short', 'multi-asset', and 'value-protection'. On a second level, seven sub-strategies are considered, which Fondsweb uses and which are described in what follows. The sub-strategies are as follows:

(a) For the long-short strategies, the subgroups 'flexible', 'long bias', and 'market neutral' are managed.
(b) There are two subgroups for multi-asset strategies according to the automation of decisions: 'Macro-dynamic' contains funds with more discretionary interventions. At the same time, 'systematic-dynamic' is more likely to be funds that proceed algorithmically (On the discretionary character of macro-strategies, see Kaiser (2009, pp. 103–106). On the characteristics of discretionary and systematic approaches, see Hilpold/Kaiser (2010, p. 25) and Joh Berenberg, Gossler & Co. KG (2020).
(c) According to the promised level of protection, there are two subgroups of value protection strategies: 'at least 90% of the initial value' and 'below 90% of the initial value'.

The sample map in Fig. 1 provides an overview of the funds included in the study and the size of the individual categories.

The analysis period is the following: We consider three periods. The calculation of returns starts on February 17, 2020, which coincides with the coronary crash's first day. The downward phase lasted from February 17 to March 17. The adjacent phase is characterised by great uncertainty regarding further development. The losses were stopped. There was a minimal recovery in prices until mid-April. But, overall, this phase was marked by an uncertain stagnation after the crisis. Once this phase is over, the development moves into a more convinced recovery phase. On May 6. our observation period ends. All phases are about a month long. We talk about the crash phase and the 'first' and 'second' recovery phases. We examine how risk-reduced concepts behave in the immediate crisis phase and somewhat longer term through the phasing (for general theory, see Jehmlich, 2019; Rudolph, 2007; Fama, 1991, 1979, 1976). As a benchmark, we

Fig. 1. Sample map.

choose the MSCI All Country World Index All Cap ('MSCI ACWI AC'), which is listed in Euro (cf. MSCI Inc., 2020). We use the period yield as a measure of earnings. As a measure of risk, we use the standard deviation of the daily returns measured over the period under consideration (cf. Hartmann-Wendels *et al.*, 2019).

1.2. *Initial hypotheses*

The central research question is: How do risk-reduced investment strategies behave after a change in data that has a global impact and comes as a complete surprise to most asset managers? Do they perform what investors typically or textbook-wise can expect from the strategies in question, or are there entirely different developments? What factors explain any divergent outcomes?

As initial hypotheses, the following expected results are formulated:

1. Long-short approaches should, on average, be unaffected by the Corona crash and should have yielded a stable return close to the safe interest rate. That is what they are designed for. For individual funds, depending on how strictly the beta risk's neutralisation was carried out, deviations from the average result can occur.
2. Multi-asset approaches should have a specific positive correlation with the index. Still, they should take a defensive approach to value by recording less severe price losses and less volatility than the index because of their broad diversification.
3. Value–protection concepts should show a stable value development after conceptually unavoidable slight price drops, from which the strictest funds (due to depleted risk budgets) will not recover. Other funds with more flexibility (and still available risk budgets) could regain value in the post-crash phases.

2. Quantitative Data Analysis

2.1. *Comparison of returns*

In the following, we present the results of the performance (based on published fund prices) in three steps.

(1) First, risk-mitigated investment strategies are compared with the benchmark performance (see Sections 2.1.1 and 2.1.2).
(2) Then the seven sub-strategies are compared with the benchmark and the previous findings (see Section 2.1.3).
(3) Finally, the results are presented at the individual fund level (see Section 2.1.4).

2.1.1. *Strategy returns on average*

Figure 2 visualises the average returns of the three strategies and the benchmark over the entire period from February 17 to May 6.

In summary, Fig. 2 proves that on average, the risk-reduced investments were able to limit the losses relative to the benchmark.

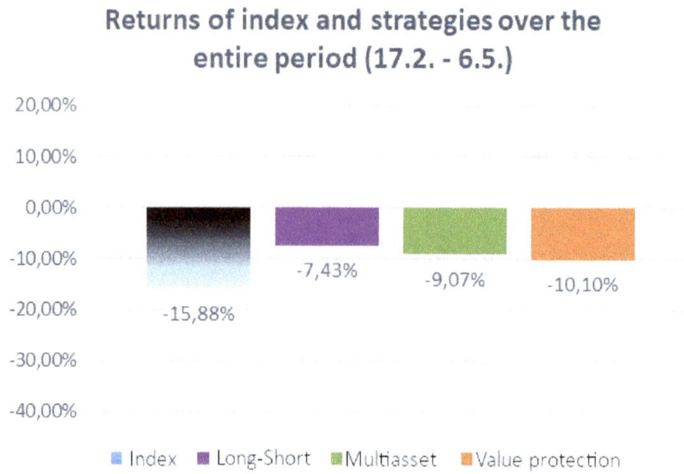

Fig. 2. Strategy returns versus index returns in the total period.

2.1.2. *Strategy comparison in partial periods*

Figure 3 allows a comparison of the strategies in the sub-periods, i.e., in the crash and in the recovery phases. It can be seen that the returns of the very different strategies (long-short, multi-asset, value–protection) lie within a narrow band. This was not to be expected (Fig. 3). Although it is possible to identify a performance that is fundamentally in line with the hypotheses formulated above — e.g., long-short strategies and value–protection strategies have lower declines than multi-asset strategies — the differences in returns are very small. One could have expected much more different results.

Besides, the results of the multi-asset strategy are not intuitively plausible. Multi-asset funds lost 41% of the index result in the crash phase. Still, they only recovered 19% of the index result in the second recovery phase. This means that they show a comparatively high correlation to the crash benchmark but a relatively low recovery correlation.

2.1.3. *Comparison of the sub-strategies*

In the following, we turn to the seven sub-strategies (Fig. 4). The left group of columns shows the performance in the crash phase. On the

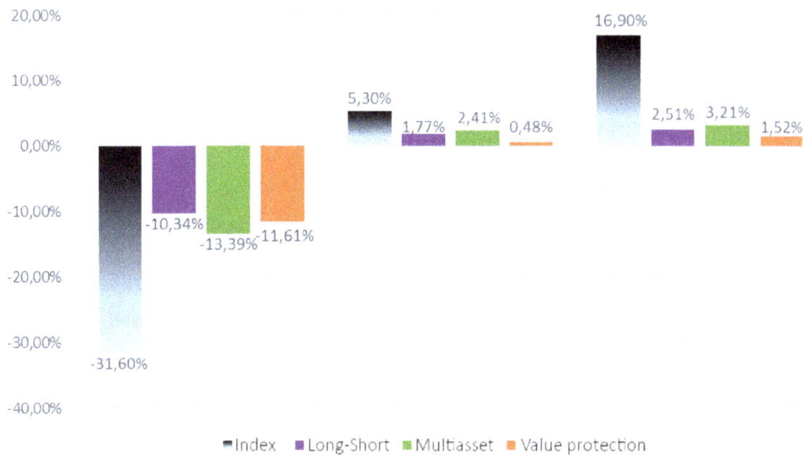

Fig. 3. Returns of the individual strategies in sub-periods.

right, the performance in the subsequent two recovery phases follows. On the far right is the loss in value over all periods.

Figure 4 shows that at the level of sub-strategies, one finds an astonishingly widespread of returns. This contrasts with the small spread of returns at the level of the three main strategies (see Fig. 2). It can also be seen that the spread of the returns of the sub-strategies runs across the main group boundaries. This means that one group can have both particularly good and bad sub-strategies. In each main group, one strategy is among the best and one that is among the worst strategies overall.

Among the four strategies with relatively low losses, two groups can be distinguished: one group are funds that already lost little in the crash, but then did not catch up. This includes strict value–protection with security levels of 'at least 90%' as well as market-neutral funds. Besides, some strategies lost more in the crash but later caught up again. These include the multi-asset strategy group 'systematic-dynamic', which provides for more rule-based, algorithm-controlled funds, and the variant of the long-short funds 'LS-Flexible', which includes funds that hedge risks through short positions but do not aim for a market neutral position.

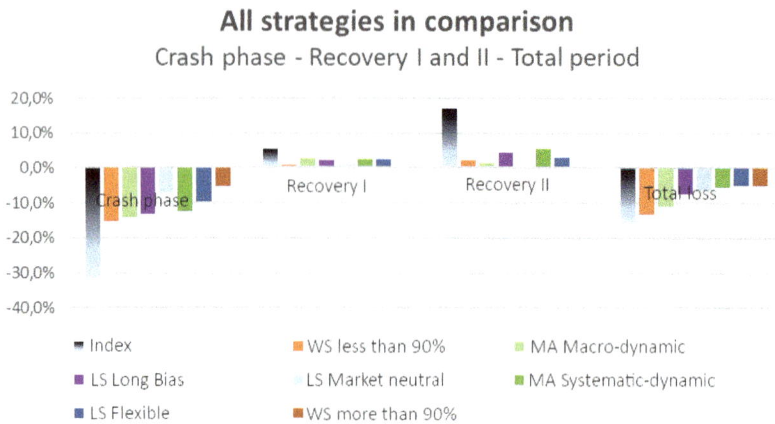

Fig. 4. The return of sub-strategies in crash and recovery phases.

All in all, the initial findings are as follows:

- Risk-reduced investment strategies lost less than the benchmark, both in the crash phase as in the whole period. Thus, they have fulfilled expectations in terms of the sign (sign test).
- The returns of the three main strategies are surprisingly close within a narrow return range. This does not meet expectations. It was not to be expected that very different strategies would show almost identical results (Fig. 2).
- All main strategies show a clearly positive correlation to the benchmark movement in the crash phase. However, strategies like 'Long–Short' or 'Value–Protection' should not have had this.
- All main strategies show strongly weakened correlations to the benchmark in the second recovery phase. This is a particularly surprising result for the 'multi-asset' strategy. Why should strategies be more strongly correlated with the index in the crash phase and less strongly in the recovery phases?

The result is that risk-reduced (equity) investment strategies, on the one hand, actually performed better in the Corona crash than the major equity indices. But one also finds that investors have practically no reliance on a strategy. In every investment strategy, one finds sub-strategies that show comparatively good results and less good results (Fig. 4). The affiliation of a fund to a particular main or sub-strategy does not seem to be a guarantee that the result will be the one most likely to be associated with that particular strategy. In the following, these findings will be examined more closely at the level of individual funds.

2.1.4. *Comparison at individual fund level*

What return development can be found at the level of the individual funds? Figure 5 shows the development of the funds in the individual categories based on the multiplicatively linked daily returns. At first glance, there are definitely clear differences between the individual funds in the individual categories. For example, the 'soft' version of value–protection does not help against losses any better than most other strategies. Long-Short strategies deliver similar results to macro-dynamic multi-asset. Only the two strictly formulated strategies 'market neutral' and 'value-protection at least 90%' show stable and expected results among the funds.

The differences and similarities will be discussed in more detail in the following section.

Figure 6 shows the development of returns of all individual funds in more detail under consideration during the crash phase (black columns) as well as the first (white columns) and second recovery phase (grey columns). The funds are grouped by sub-strategies and ranked by returns in the crash phase.

The typical return patterns look like this: In each sub-strategy, the funds record a wide range of returns in the crash phase. In all strategies and sub-strategies, returns achieved range from 0% (or even slightly positive) to values close to the benchmark. All strategies agree on this pattern. This means that no matter which strategy or sub-strategy an investor has chosen, he or she is confronted with a very heterogeneous bundle of funds with a high range of returns. This range is almost the same for all strategies.

There are only two exceptions, namely, the two strategies 'market neutral' and 'strict value-protection' with protection levels of at least 90%. These record comparatively low losses in the crash and in the overall period with a narrow bandwidth of returns within the strategies. But they do not completely escape the general pattern.

Further results are as follows:

- Of the 29 funds in the long-short group, exactly four funds have a return trend that one would associate with long-short strategies.

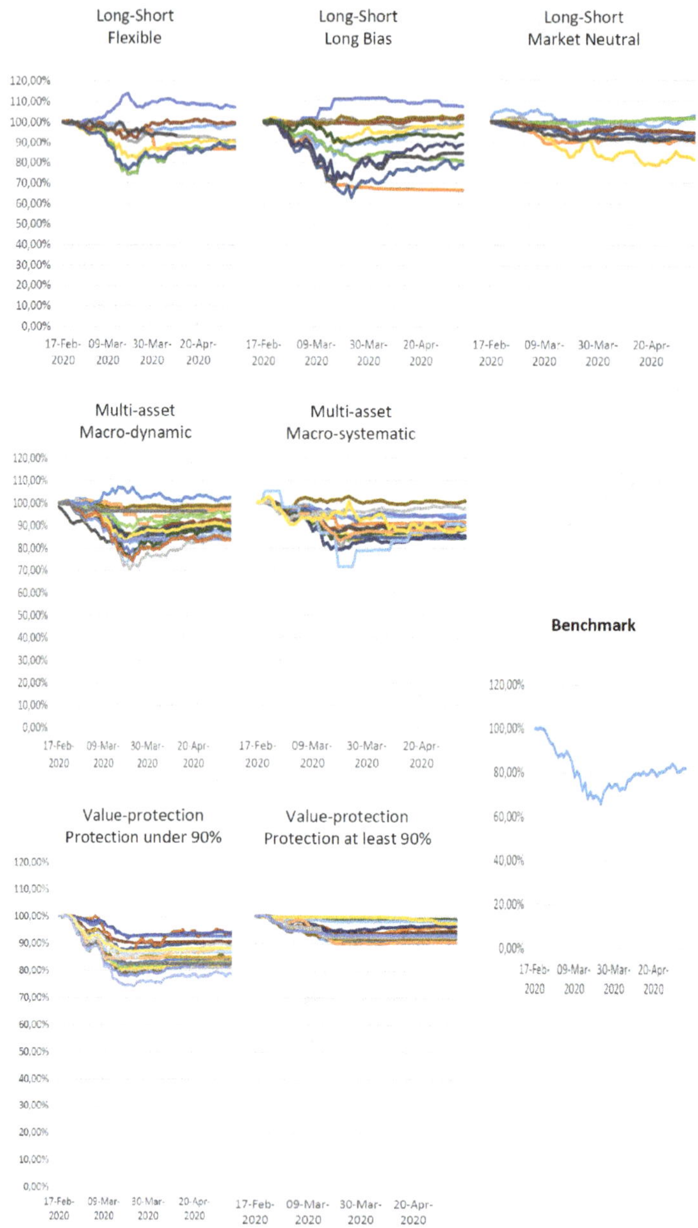

Fig. 5. Fund categories vs. benchmark: Asset performance (starting from 100%) based on multiplicatively linked daily returns.

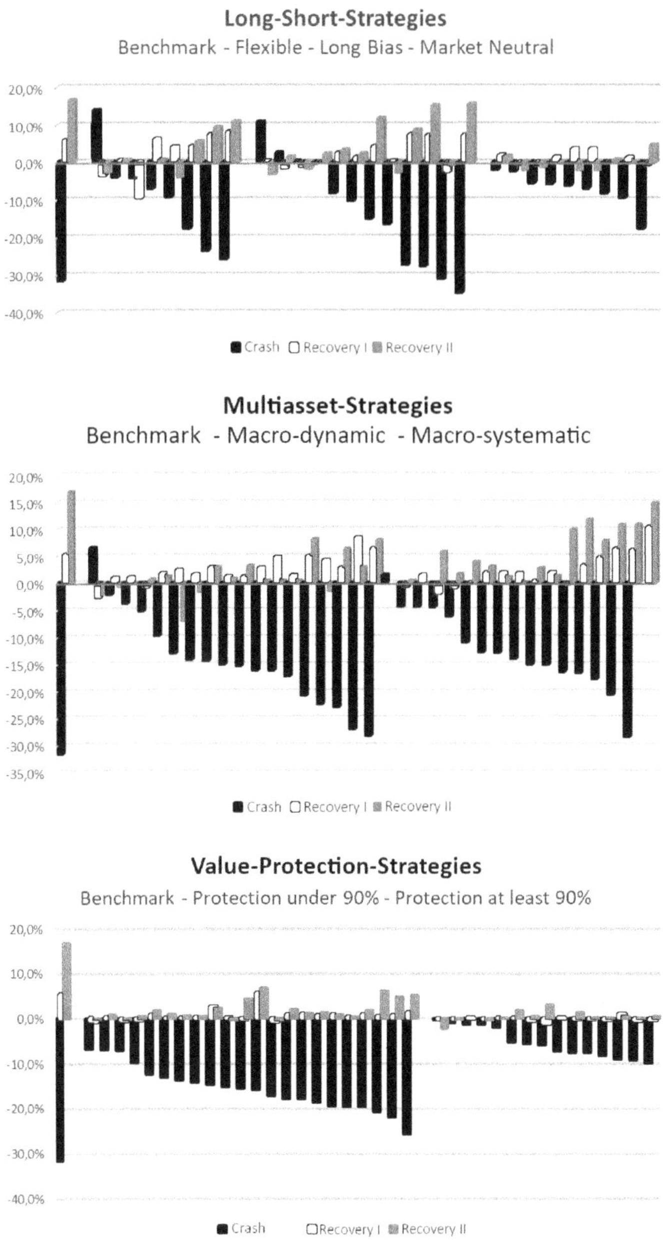

Fig. 6. Strategic returns at the individual fund level.

On the other hand, 9 of 29 funds, i.e., a good third, follow more or less the development of the index, break down significantly in the crash phase and end the entire period with a return just like the index (here an average of −17%).

- In the long bias and long flexible categories, most of the funds have yield curves that are aligned with the benchmark. This would not have been easy to expect in the long-short category.
- In the group of multi-asset funds, there are no systematics at all. There are funds with a rather defensive performance and those with a performance that is strongly based on the benchmark.
- Among the multi-asset funds in the sub-category 'systematic-dynamic', a group shows conspicuously positive returns in the second recovery phase. This is a group of funds that pursue strongly rule-based strategies.
- The value–protection strategies fall into two groups. The funds with soft lower value limits have more widely spread yield developments than the funds with at least 90% of hedging levels. The funds with soft lower limits are the worst of all fund groups discussed here: They lose a lot in a crash and do not catch up after the crash. This is the worst of all worlds.
- Meanwhile, we find that the funds with high protection levels do not catch up much after the crash, but lose much less in the crash. This therefore makes this group the safest of all strategies discussed here.

2.2. *Correlation comparison*

Figure 7 illustrates the fact that there is a correlation between the amount of losses in the crash phase and the gains in the subsequent recovery phases. Those who lost a lot in the crash have also made up a lot in the recovery phases. The horizontal axis shows the return in the crash phase. In contrast, the vertical axis shows the return in the following two recovery phases. R^2 is 0.5. For comparison, the benchmark, the MSCI ACWI AC, is shown in the upper left corner as a red dot.

The close relationship between crash losses and subsequent recovery gains leads to the need to rethink the concept of risk. This is because risk is significantly lower in the long term than over shorter periods. Investors' focus on safeguarding their assets in a stressful

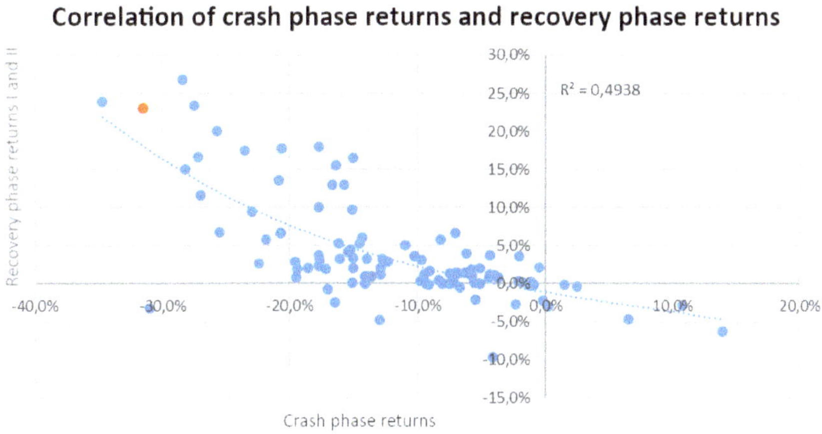

Fig. 7. Crash phase returns and recovery phase returns.

phase is too short-sighted: they cut off their chances of recovery if they invest too stress-resistant.

2.3. *Risk analysis*

Figure 8 summarises the risk structure of the strategy groups compared in this study. The first risk indicator is volatility, i.e., the standard deviation of daily returns. Extreme values are used as a further risk indicator. These are the highest negative or positive daily returns that occur in a fund of a strategy group within the overall period. The extreme values are considered because the individual funds within a strategy group show very different returns. Suppose investors are unable to determine the risk structure of the funds ex ante. In that case, it is useful information for them to know what the worst-case return could be if they were to catch the worst-case fund in a strategy group. Figure 8 shows the benchmark (left) and the three strategy groups — long-short, multi-asset and value-protection (right) — in the form of a candlestick chart. First (i) the mean of the returns, then (ii) the returns that lie one standard deviation above and below the mean, and (iii) the extreme values, i.e., the highest and lowest daily returns of the entire period, can be seen. With the yields within the candles, there is a probability of about 66%. The remaining values lie above or below the extreme values.

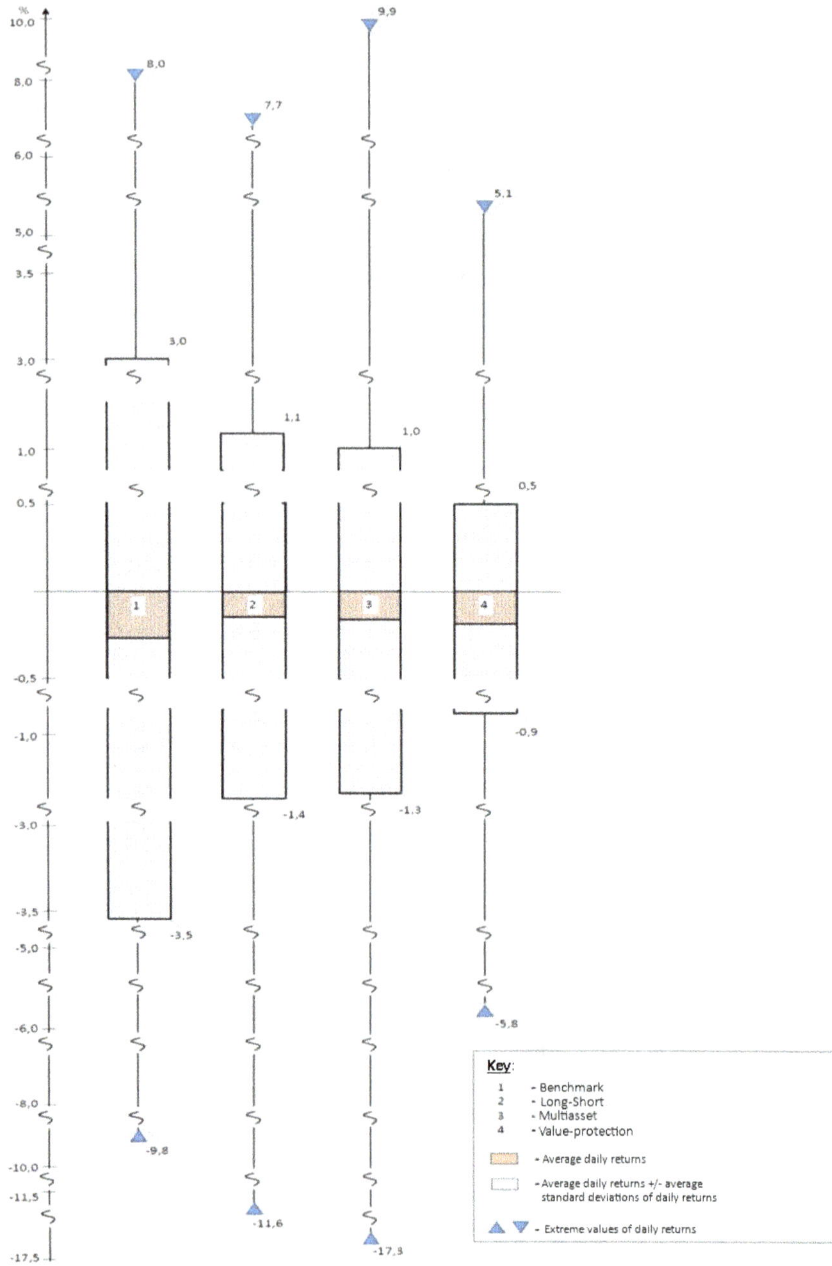

Fig. 8. Risk analysis.

One can see that the benchmark — as shown above — has the lowest average return. It also has the largest candle, i.e., the highest standard deviation of daily returns. Long-short and multi-asset strategies have a similar standard deviation. The standard deviation of the value-hedging strategies is lower. The differences in standard deviation between the benchmark and value-hedging strategies are considerable. This means that when volatility figures are considered, a risk reduction can be demonstrated by the strategies examined.

However, this does not apply when looking at the *extreme values*: the benchmark does not show the highest risk for extreme values. Here, long-short and multi-asset's strategies are in a more extensive risk range than the benchmark in terms of the downward swings. This means that an investor who randomly picks one of the funds in a strategy group and invests in it must expect to achieve significantly worse results than the benchmark.

In the following, we will take a closer look at the reasons for this poor performance of risk-reduced strategies in extreme cases.

3. Qualitative Analysis

What are the causes of the phenomena shown? In particular, why are there the very heterogeneous returns of different funds belonging to the same strategy group? And what is the reason why the funds of completely different strategies have quite similar average returns?

It seems practically impossible that the significant heterogeneity of the individual funds' returns is (exclusively) due to the strategies *per se*, i.e., long-short, multi-asset, value–protection, into which the funds were classified by Fondsweb or into which they have classified themselves. We test the hypothesis that the differences lie instead in the execution of the fund management. One cannot observe the implementation of the fund management directly from the outside. But it is possible to gain a certain insight from the sales documents. Fondsweb provides Key Investor Documents (KIDs) and sales brochures.

An analysis shows that the funds formulate their investment policies in such a way that they can act as they see fit. In many cases, the sales documents' investment policy lacks a direct link to the strategy group into which the funds are sorted. A connection with the strategy pursued is more likely to be found in the objectives and declarations of intent that precede the investment policy's descriptions. However, these are not binding (for information on practices in the early days of asset management, see Quittner, 1930, also Thießen, 2011). Vague descriptions of the investment policy supplement the non-binding targets. If you take a closer look, you will find little binding and factual information. The funds' *objectives* are usually presented in comparatively great detail — they often take up more space than the investment policy presentation. The objectives are typically formulated to connect to the respective fund category is recognisable (long-short, multi-asset, value–protection). Examples are as follows:

- It 'attempts to ensure a minimum value and simultaneously achieve the highest possible participation in price increases in the value enhancement component. The aim is to allow the investor to participate in rising markets while at the same time limiting the risk of loss in the event of falling markets'.
- '...to always achieve a positive result. At the same time, the aim is to limit the decline in value of the fund after a peak to a maximum of 5%.'
- 'The investment objective of the fund is to achieve absolute returns and reduced volatility of returns over a medium to long-term period.'

On the contrary, presentations of investment policy are often brief and characterised by many vaguenesses. It is usually no more than a sentence that characterises the policy. Everything else is non-binding filler text. The strategy categories into which the funds are divided, i.e., long-short, multi-asset, and value–protection, are often no longer found in the descriptions of the investment policy. For example, when it says

- 'The fund pursues its investment objective through exposure to the global equity and bond markets', the relation to the strategy is no longer recognisable. Similar in this case:
- The fund seeks to achieve its investment objective by investing in the EU debt securities markets and global equity markets'.

Such formulations offer little indication of what management is doing. However, in the context of the preceding goals and intentions, a picture often emerges of what management could be doing to make the two fit together.

A further characteristic of many representations of the investment policy is that the decision-making process remains in the long run open. It is the manager who decides discretionary with him known information:

- Basis of the decision is 'publicly known information' together with the 'assessment of the investment manager'.
- 'The assets to be acquired for the fund are identified discretionarily on the basis of a consistent investment process'.
- The fund hopes to benefit from advantageous 'price deviations between long/short pairs' using 'fundamental analysis'.

Several funds explain the procedure with their own systems, which are not presented in detail:

- 'The investment manager, in his own opinion, has some sources of investment income through his quantitative research process'.
- 'The fund seeks to achieve capital appreciation through a computer-based trading approach that uses mathematical models designed by the Investment Manager'.

Another conspicuous feature is where detailed information is given. In these cases, terms such as 'other', 'as a rule', 'expected', 'may exist', 'can exist', 'may consider', 'can be increased', 'in general' and many other similar statements dilute the details presented. One can also recognise framing elements here if aspects of fund management are first dealt with in detail, only to be invalidated again by the words mentioned — easily to be overlooked.

- 'Shares and equivalent securities, other securities, bank deposits, money market instruments, shares in other investment funds *and other investment instruments* may be purchased for the fund'.
- The fund draws returns from equities 'normally listed in the United States of America, the United Kingdom and the rest of the European Union, Japan, Singapore, Hong Kong, *and other global market* portfolios'.

- 'The average leverage of the Fund is expected to be in the range of 200% to 400% ... and is not expected to exceed 500% ... *although higher levels are possible*'.

In the investment principles, one fund only explains the vehicles, but not the asset classes in which it intends to invest:

- Investments are made in 'certificates, funds, hedge funds, derivatives, warrants'.

Overall, it can be seen that strategy presentations are kept rather vague and that what is actually done to achieve the previously described goals is not disclosed. Nevertheless, the overall picture seems to be often quite informative, which can be explained by the framing effect caused by the preceding presentation of objectives (cf. Oehler, 1995; Gigerenzer, 2008; Gigerenzer and Selten, 2002).

4. Summary

This chapter aims to use the Corona crash of March 2020 to test various risk-mitigated investment strategies regarding their suitability to limit investment risks. Three popular investment strategies were selected that are suitable for reducing investment risks. These are long-short approaches, which aim to eliminate beta risks. Multi-asset approaches pursue the goal of mitigating risks through markedly broad diversification. Value preservation approaches *per se* promise to preserve assets at a certain level. Approximately 100 funds have been identified, which can be assigned to one of the groups mentioned above and for which detailed information can be found in KIDs and sales prospectuses.

The investigation brought three main results:

(1) The losses in the value of risk-reduced investments are lower than those of the major stock indices.
(2) The three risk-reduced investment strategies' average returns are very similar, although the strategies are very different.
(3) One finds funds with very heterogeneous yield curves that cover a very wide range of returns within the strategies.

On average, it is possible to reduce asset losses relative to a typical benchmark by using risk-reduced strategies. But the results within each strategy-group are very heterogeneous. The reasons for the very heterogeneous results within the strategies can be seen in the very different investment policies that the funds implement. Funds show the desire to be something special. A too strict tie to one category is avoided. Presentations of the investment and strategy policy of funds are characterised by many vaguenesses and the fund management's endeavour not to limit itself. Statements of policy are formulated as non-binding declarations of intent, more as 'possibilities' than definitive plans. One finds great freedom and little in the way of concrete action. The legal safeguards may be one explanation for the wide latitude that the funds allow themselves. But that does not seem sufficient. In the sales documents, only the non-binding objectives and intentions indicate the strategy groups into which the funds are divided or which they bear in their name. In the descriptions of the investment policy, the affiliation to specific groups of investment strategies is already no longer reflected. We have not found two identical formulations of the investment policy. Each fund behaves like a unique specimen. In this respect, the descriptions of the investment policy regularly boil down to the statement that there is a great deal of freedom, which allows the fund management a great deal, in many cases even "everything". This concerns funds of very different categories.

The quintessence shows up that the investors can rely on a price development, which corresponds approximately to the type of the selected strategies, only if the investment policy is so strictly formulated that the fund management is limited effectively in its options for action. Only where rules are completely closely expressed (in the present study with 'market neutral' and strict protection of value), one finds smaller dispersion of the fund net yields. Only then, results correspond to expectations. We have identified funds that belong to this group.

The fact that the funds lost on average less than the stock index used as a benchmark during the crash is in many cases only due to the fact that the funds held a considerable amount of liquidity (fixed-interest securities, etc.). However, it was precisely these instruments that prevented the funds from following the index during the two recovery phases, so that investors were less able to regain what they had previously lost less. So, the final question that remains is whether asset protection is so important during the brief period of extreme events such as the Corona crash that it precludes a feedback loop to market developments?

Acknowledgements

The authors thank Ms. Sophia Thieme, B.Sc., for her help with the translation and the data research, and Mr. Tom Fischer, B.A., for the support in documenting the sources.

References

Büttner, T. (2020). Rallye oder Abgrund, *Portfolio Institutionell* **April 2020**, 28–31.

Chaperon, Ch. (2010). An Empirical Approach to Long/Short Equity Market Neutral Portfolio Management. Available at SSRN: https://ssrn.com/abstract=1716981 or http://dx.doi.org/10.2139/ssrn.1716981. Accessed September 13, 2021.

Deutscher Bundestag (2013). Bericht zur Risikoanalyse im Bevölkerungsschutz 2012, Drucksache 17/12051.

Englert, D. (2020a). Die Aufnahme der Schadensbilanz, *Portfolio Institutionell* **April 2020**, 36–41.

Englert, D. (2020b). Alles aus einer hand, *Portfolio Institutionell* **February 2020**, 6–9.

Faber, P. (2008). *Wertsicherung von Aktienanlagen.* Wiesbaden.

Fama, E. (1970). Efficient capital markets: a review of theory and empirical work, *The Journal of Finance* **25**(2), 383–417.

Fama, E. (1976). *Foundations of Finance — Portfolio Decisions and Securities Prices.* New York: Basic Books.

Fama, E. (1991). Efficient capital markets: II, *The Journal of Finance* **46**(5), 1575–1617.

FCIC (2011). Financial Crisis Inquiry Report. Final Report of the National Commission on the Causes of the Financial and Economic Crisis in the United States, New York.

Gigerenzer, G. (2008). *Rationality for Mortals: How people cope with uncertainty,* Oxford: Oxford University Press.

Gigerenzer, G. and Selten, R. (2002). *Bounded Rationality: The Adaptive Toolbox.* Cambridge, Massachusetts: The MIT Press.

Glas, T. and Poddig, T. (2018). Kryptowährungen in der Asset-Allokation: Eine empirische Untersuchung auf Basis eines beispielhaften deutschen multi-asset-portfolios. *Vierteljahreshefte zur Wirtschaftsforschung* **87**(3), 107–128.

Gleißner, W. (2020). Die Corona-Krise: Fakten, Prognosen und Risiken, *Corporate Finance* **11**(5), 121–130.

Hartmann-Wendels, T. *et al.* (2019). *Bankbetriebslehre* (7th edn. Berlin): Springer.

Hilpold, C. and Kaiser, D.G. (2010). Innovative Investmentstrategien. Wiesbaden.

Jehmlich, T. (2019). Effizienz und Preiskontinuität von Aktienmärkten: Notwendigkeit und Vorschläge der kontinuierlichen Effizienzsicherung im Aktienhandel. Hamburg.

Joh. Berenberg, Gossler & Co. KG (2020). Asset Management. Available at: https://www.berenberg.de/asset-management. Accessed September 13, 2021.

Kaiser, D.G. (2004). *Hedgefonds.* Wiesbaden: Gabler.

Kaiser, D.G. (2009). *Hedgefonds* (2nd edn. Wiesbaden): Gabler.

Marshall, W. J. (1987). Portfolio insurance: limiting the exposure of actively managed pension funds under statement of financial accounting Standards No. 87, in Fabozzi, F. J. and Garlicki, T. D. (eds.), *Advances in Bond Analysis & Portfolio Strategies*, Chicago: Probus Publ., pp. 115–137.

Mein Geld Medien GmbH (2017). Assetmanagement mit Makro-Strategie. Available at: https://www.mein-geld-medien.de/investmentfonds/assetmanagement-mit-makro-strategie/ Accessed September 06, 2021.

MSCI Inc. (2020), MSCI ACWI Index (EUR). Available at: https://www.msci.com/documents/10199/1ee87397-6313-4f46-87ae-6761f666558e. Accessed September 06, 2021.

Nitzsch, R. and Friedrich, C. (2000). Erkenntnisse der verhaltenswissenschaftlichen Kapitalmarktforschung — behavioral finance. *Finanz-Betrieb* (5), 311–318.

Oehler, A. (1995). Die Erklärung des Verhaltens privater Anleger, *Theoretischer Ansatz und empirische Analysen.* Stuttgart: Schäffer-Poeschel.

Petukhina, A. and Sprünken, E. (2021). Evaluation of multi-asset investment strategies with digital assets, *Digital Finance* **3**(1), 45–79.

Quittner, P. (1930). *Investment: Moderne Prinzipien der Vermögensanlage.* Berlin: Springer.

Roth, G. (2003). *Fühlen, Denken, Handeln: wie das Gehirn unser Verhalten steuert.* Frankfurt am Main: Suhrkamp.

Rudolph, B. (2007). Kapitalmarkt: Historische Entwicklung. *Knapps Enzyklopädisches Lexikon des Geld-, Bank- und Börsenwesens*, article nr. 1996, pp. 1–3.

Thießen, F. (2011). *Opportunismus und Finanzmärkte.* Wiesbaden.

https://doi.org/10.1142/9781800611917_0005

Chapter 5

The Growth of Social Banks, Investment Restrictions, and Excess Liquidity Risk

Susanne Homölle*, Nikolas Höhnke, Ulf Hübenbecker, and Philipp Winskowski

University of Rostock, Department of Banking and Finance, Germany

**susanne.homoelle@uni-rostock.de*

Social banks are expected to have excess liquidity issues, caused by the combination of massive growth of deposits and their self-restricted investment selection. In this study, we differentiated between social banks with moderate and those with strict self-restrictions. As strict social banks are expected to attract more depositors, excess liquidity issues might be a larger problem of this type of social bank. Comparing the development of deposits and excess liquidity indicators between both types based on a data set of 23 European social banks, we found that the deposits of strict social banks have indeed grown much stronger and that these banks show lower ability to transform deposits into impact assets. Moderate social banks seem to be able to easier compensate low loans-to-deposits ratios with suitable investments in shares and bonds. Liquidity surplus of (strict) social banks might decrease their efficiency, but does not seem to infringe their going concern.

1. Introduction

The deposits of social banks have grown massively over the past years (Benedikter, 2011; Höhnke and Homölle, 2018; Remer, 2014; ZEB, 2012). As deposits are social banks' primary financing tool (Paulet *et al.*, 2015), this growth of deposits enables social banks to fund more social or environmental projects, which in turn create further social or environmental value added. However, the growth of deposits might have a downside, too. Cornée *et al.* (2016) supposed that social banks face an excess liquidity issue, meaning that they hold far more deposits than financial assets, such as loans, shares, and bonds. Apart from social banks' fast growth in deposits, this imbalance might result from social banks self-restriction of investments. Some social banks *merely* invest in projects that create social or environmental value (impact investing strategy), while others exclude projects exerting a negative impact on the society and environment (exclusion strategy) and thus invest in *both* projects with a positive and those with a neutral impact (Höhnke and Homölle, 2020). As social banks with a higher extent of self-restriction of investments are even expected to attract more depositors, excess liquidity might be a larger issue for these social banks. However, so far, the relevant literature has not offered a sound analysis of social banks' growth of deposits and the potentially resulting excess liquidity issues. Therefore, the purpose of this study is to explore whether social banks have faced an excess liquidity issue in recent years and whether the degree of social banks' self-restriction of investments leads to differences in the deposit growth and extent of the liquidity surplus.

Against this background, the authors conducted a longitudinal analysis of deposits and excess liquidity indicators based on a data set of 23 European social banks. Data needed were collected from banks' annual financial statements, their websites, and a survey.

This chapter seeks to make the following contributions to the existing literature. First, as previous research on social banking has only referred to social banks' growth in the wake of the global financial crisis without detailed data analysis, we present the first comprehensive overview of the development of social banks' deposits in recent years. Second, the results of the present analysis will enable a sound assessment of social banks' risk for excess liquidity, providing important insights, particularly for customers, social banks, and conventional banks that aim to adopt the principals of social banks, such as their asset selection policy.

The remainder of this chapter is structured as follows: Section 2 forms the basis of our analysis, as the concept of social banking is briefly described. In Section 3, we explain the term 'excess liquidity' in the social banking context. Section 4 presents the methodology and data collection, before Section 5 shows our results. The findings, their implications, limitations, and resulting avenues for further research are critically discussed in Section 6. The chapter ends with a summary and conclusion in Section 7.

2. Social Banking

Social banks, also known as ethical, green, sustainable, or alternative banks (Chew *et al.*, 2016; Cornée *et al.*, 2016; Goyal and Joshi, 2011), are financial intermediaries that run a commercial banking business. The primary objective of social banks is the creation of positive social and environmental impact in addition to sufficient profits for their going concern (Höhnke and Homölle, 2018). However, social or environmental value added is not created by social banks directly, but indirectly by financing socially and environmentally impactful projects (Chew *et al.*, 2016; Lopez *et al.*, 2020; Paulet *et al.*, 2015). Most conventional banks do not offer sustainable savings deposits (Heinemann *et al.*, 2018). Social banks are thus expected to dominate this market niche by primarily collecting savings and distributing loans to social and environmental projects (Cornée *et al.*, 2016; Paulet *et al.*, 2015).

Over the past years, several newspapers and banking journals have reported that these niche-market banks have shown annual growth rates of up to 30% (Benedikter, 2011; Höhnke and Homölle, 2018, 2020; Remer, 2014; ZEB, 2012). One of the most relevant drivers of institutes total growth is the strong increase of deposits, which are social banks' primary financing tools (Paulet *et al.*, 2015). For example, the deposits of German social banks grew from €1.474 billion to €7.273 billion between 2007 and 2017, reflecting a relative growth of 493% over one decade (Höhnke and Homölle, 2020). The global financial crisis of 2007/2008 is expected to have been of vital importance for social banks' growth (Cornée and Szafarz, 2014; Köhler, 2010;

Paulet *et al.*, 2015). The annual deposit growth rate of the German GLS Bank, for instance, increased during and directly after the crisis until it reached its peak at nearly 40% in 2010. Afterwards, a continuous flattening of the relative growth was observed. However, even in 2015, the growth rate was still approximately 15%. Despite social banks' enormous growth over the past years, Krause and Battenfeld (2019) supposed that social banking has huge further potential to gain market share in commercial banking.

A comparison of social banks' growth with the development of other commercial banks, such as cooperative and savings banks, reveals that social banks have outperformed comparable conventional banks in recent years. All cooperative banks in Germany show growth rates of 'merely' 61% for loans, 58% for deposits, and 48% for total assets between 2007 and 2018 (BVR, 2020). In the same period, the cumulative total assets of German savings banks also grew by 'only' 16% (DSGV, 2008, 2019). These differences in growth rates underline the remarkable development of social banks in the aftermath of the global financial crisis. It does not seem to have been mainly driven by comparable extensive growth in the entire industry.

So far, it is expected that social banks' special placement of assets is one major reason for depositors' choice of social banks (Höhnke, 2020; Höhnke and Homölle, 2020; Krause and Battenfeld, 2019) and in turn for social banks' growth of deposits. The placement of assets, meaning the selection of investments, is an important aspect that distinguishes social from conventional banks (Paulet *et al.*, 2015; San-Jose *et al.*, 2011). Social banks do not apply speculative activities and they self-restrict their use of funds (Cornée *et al.*, 2016; Paulet *et al.*, 2015; San-Jose *et al.*, 2011). Some social banks use the so-called impact investing strategy, meaning that they merely invest in projects that create social or environmental value. We call these banks 'strict social banks'. Other social banks (henceforth referred to as 'moderate social banks') 'just' do not invest in projects that create social or environmental harm, but in all other projects providing a positive or neutral impact on the society and environment. They follow the exclusion strategy (Höhnke and Homölle, 2020). So-called investment criteria are disclosed by social banks to explain their differentiation between negative and positive projects. Fields of investments with a negative impact include, for example, nuclear energy, genetic manipulation, animal testing, pornography, drugs, and armaments (Aßländer and Schenkel, 2011; San-Jose *et al.*, 2011). Projects that are perceived to create a positive social or environmental impact include, for example, organic farming, renewable energy, social businesses, and fair trade products (Cowton, 2002; Paulet *et al.*, 2015; Pulejo *et al.*, 2015; San-Jose *et al.*, 2011).

Usually, the term 'growth' has a positive connotation in the economic context. Deposit growth enables social banks to fund more social or environmental projects. However, considering social banks' self-restriction of investments, the massive growth of deposits over the past years might have a downside, too. In this vein, Cornée *et al.* (2016) pointed out that social banks generally might have an excess liquidity issue due to their self-restriction.

3. The Excess Liquidity Issue

Social banks' concentration on granting loans and taking deposits leads to high deposits-to-assets and loans-to-assets ratios (Cornée and Szafarz, 2014). Previous studies found that social banks have significantly higher deposits-to-assets ratios than conventional banks, whereas the loans-to-assets ratios are not significantly different (Cornée *et al.*, 2016, 2020) or are even lower for social banks (Karl, 2015). Loans-to-deposits ratios that are below 100% (Karl, 2015; Scheire and De Maertelaere, 2009; Weber, 2011) mean that not all deposits are transformed into loans. Social banks convert deposits into loans to an even lesser extent than conventional banks (Cornée *et al.*, 2016) leading to an oversupply of deposits (Scheire and De Maertelaere, 2009).

The restricted reconversion capability was observed for several European social banks, e.g., Banca Etica, Triodos Bank, and GLS Bank, who "seem to be struggling with their popularity" (Scheire and De Maertelaere, 2009, p. 23). This might lead to the conclusion that social banks have severe problems fulfilling their core function (Remer, 2011). Schwedeler (2017), for instance, stated that the Triodos Bank could not expand the loan business as much as would be necessary to match the growth of the deposits. Instead, the liquidity surplus had to be invested in government bonds or deposited at the central bank.

Following Cornée *et al.* (2016), the excess liquidity issue[1] can be explained from both sides of the credit market. From the supply side, social banks' self-restriction regarding their placement of assets limits the volume of loans granted. Only borrowers that meet the relevant investment criteria will get a loan. We expect that social banks with higher degrees of self-restriction of investments attract more depositors, since German (non-church) social banks with strict self-restrictions had increased their deposits between 2007 and 2017 to a rate twice as high as social banks with moderate restrictions (Höhnke and Homölle, 2020). Therefore, we will investigate in this chapter whether the excess liquidity issue might depend on the social banks' degree of self-restriction.

Moreover, there might be a time-lag between taking deposits and granting loans due to the more extensive lending process (Scheire and De Maertelaere, 2009). Schönenbach (2012) reported on the time-consuming screening process and structural adjustments of the GLS Bank in 2001 being one reason for its low conversion rate. The implementation of regulatory requirements concerning the loan business can be another reason for the restricted loan growth (Schwedeler, 2017). Finally, social banks might prefer to hold larger liquidity buffers (Karl, 2015). However, this argument could hardly explain loans-to-deposits ratios that are significantly below 100%.

Social banks' difficulties finding enough borrowers that meet their investment criteria (Karl, 2015) may also be explained by the lack of demand in the (social) credit market. Some social enterprises might fulfill the social but not the financial criteria, for example, they cannot afford the interest rates of a loan. Other social firms do not need external finance, as rapid growth is not their primary goal. Moreover, their managers are not used to dealing with banks, even social ones, and are not willing to do so, perhaps because of restricted business skills (Cornée *et al.*, 2016).

Over-liquidity is not only an unpleasant situation but might lead to severe economic problems. Cornée *et al.* even called it the

[1]The excess liquidity issue of social banks must not be confused with the excess liquidity issue of the whole banking system. The excess liquidity in the Eurosystem is defined as "the sum of holdings of central bank reserves in excess of reserve requirements and holdings of equivalent central bank deposits" (Baldo *et al.*, 2017, p. 2).

"Achilles' heel" (Cornée *et al.*, 2016, p. 501) of the business model of social banks. As it is a challenging task to find other investments that meet the investment criteria (Feßmann, 2013), the excess liquidity is parked at very low, zero or even negative interest rates. Therefore, excess liquidity is not only a hint that social banks do not fulfill their core function, but is also inefficient and thus detrimental to their profitability. It may lead to a severe earnings risk, which we call excess liquidity risk. Thus, unprofitable excess liquidity needs to be managed (Schierenbeck *et al.*, 2014).

4. Methodology and Data

4.1. *Methodology*

This study investigates whether the degree of social banks' self-restriction of investments leads to differences (1) in the deposit growth and (2) in the extent of excess liquidity. We analysed data from two types of social banks, differing regarding their investment strategy: social banks with moderate self-restrictions of investments (exclusion strategy) and social banks with strict self-restrictions (impact investing strategy), respectively. The difference in deposit growth can be easily calculated from the data of just one balance sheet position, namely customer deposits. To measure the degree of excess liquidity, we developed three excess liquidity indicators, all of which relate to characteristics of social banks' business model and the problem itself.

The first excess liquidity indicator, ELI_1, is the 'loans-to-deposits ratio' (Karl, 2015; Scheire and De Maertelaere, 2009; Weber, 2011):

$$ELI_1 = \frac{CL}{CD},$$

where CL stands for the sum of loans to customers and CD for the sum of customer deposits. This indicator provides relevant insights into the fulfilment of social banks' core function, i.e., the transformation of customer deposits into loans. A value of ELI_1 below one gives a first indication for over-liquidity: the lower the ELI_1, the higher the excess liquidity risk.

As social banks can also use customer deposits for investments in securities that meet their investment strategy, the second excess liquidity indicator, ELI_2, is the 'impact-assets-to-deposits ratio':

$$ELI_2 = \frac{CL + S + B + OS}{CD},$$

where S stands for the sum of shares, B for the sum of bonds, and OS for the sum of other securities. The so-called impact assets (Höhnke and Homölle, 2018) comprise loans to customers, shares, bonds, and other types of securities. A comparison of ELI_1 and ELI_2 gives a hint of whether social banks are able to compensate for differences between customer deposits and loans to customers by investments in appropriate securities.

Even though social banks predominantly collect savings as their primary financing tool (Paulet *et al.*, 2015), other forms of financing, such as liabilities to banks or securitised liabilities, could also drive an excess liquidity issue. We further extend ELI_2 by other forms of borrowed capital and create the third excess liquidity indicator, ELI_3, which is called the 'impact-assets-to-liabilities ratio':

$$ELI_3 = \frac{CL + S + B + OS}{CD + LB + SL}.$$

LB stands for liabilities to banks and SL for securitised liabilities. Referring to the measurement approach of Höhnke and Homölle (2018) for social banks' growth (here in a simplified form), the numerator reflects social banks' capability to distribute loans and other investments, CAP_{Loa}, and the denominator social banks capability to take deposits and other liabilities, CAP_{Dep}. Using the example of the German GLS Bank, Höhnke and Homölle (2018) showed that the difference between CAP_{Dep} and CAP_{Loa} constantly increased between 2006 and 2015, supporting the presumption of excess liquidity issues among social banks.

4.2. *Data collection*

The analyses described so far require information about social banks' investment strategies as well as several balance sheet items. To get a sufficient number of banks, we tried to capture all European social banks. These were identified through research in other publications, e.g., San-Jose *et al.* (2011), and the websites of the relevant international associations, such as the Global Alliance for Banking on Values

(GABV), the Institute for Social Banking (ISB), and the European Federation of Ethical and Alternative Banks (FEBEA). To be considered in our study, the institutions had to be full banks and not just financial providers, such as Oikocredit, and operate an open deposit business. Contrary to Höhnke and Homölle (2020), church banks are also included in our analysis if they are considered in the social banking context (Forum Nachhaltige Geldanlage, 2020) because excess liquidity might not only be an issue in non-church social banks.

We checked the banks' websites to verify the investment selection criteria and, when the information provided was not sufficient, contacted bank employees via email. A total of 33 banks met our criteria and were thus included in the initial sample. In order to distinguish between moderate and strict social banks, we tried to identify the investment strategies of each bank. Social banks usually report on the sectors, products or business practices in which they are investing. However, they rarely provide information concerning their investment strategies. Therefore, we sent a short questionnaire to all social banks (except for those analysed by Höhnke and Homölle, 2020)[2] via email. They were asked whether they only invest in projects with positive social or environmental impact (impact investing strategy: strict) or also in neutral (exclusion strategy: moderate) or even in negative projects. Additionally, they should indicate whether they differentiate between the granting of loans and the investment in securities. Since the response rate was only mediocre after several attempts to contact them by email, contact was also tried via social media such as Facebook. For those banks that still did not answer, the authors identified the investment strategies from the information provided on the banks' websites. In total, 17 social banks took part in the survey. Furthermore, the data needed for six additional banks were found on their websites or in their annual reports. For the remaining 10 social banks, no information regarding their investment strategy were found. Therefore, these banks have not been included in this study.

To calculate the excess liquidity indicators, we used several of the sample banks' balance sheet items. Since social banks' strong growth

[2]The social banks in the study of Höhnke and Homölle (2020) have already been asked about their investment strategy.

presumably finds its origin in the global financial crisis, we observed the development of deposits and over-liquidity between 2007 and 2019. Therefore, the annual financial statements of this time period were collected. Again, we used the banks' websites as sources of information. Some social banks publish all relevant statements there, whereas other websites reveal significant gaps. In cases of incompleteness, we used the Federal Gazette ('Elektronischer Bundesanzeiger') for the German banks. The other European social banks were asked for their assistance via email. Due to the repeatedly low response rate, contact was again additionally established via social media. In the end, the data of 23 social banks were collected (for more information on the unbalanced panel, see Table 1).

5. Results

Following our approach, our final sample can be divided into two groups, moderate and strict social banks. For both groups, we calculated the aggregate volume of customer deposits of the banks for which we have complete data over the entire observation period. The largest moderate social bank was excluded because it comprised more than half of all deposits in the group, which would lead to biased results. Thus, Figure 1 shows rapid but uneven deposit growth for four banks with strict self-restrictions and 11 banks with moderate self-restrictions. The deposits of the moderate social banks have grown by 89% over the entire period, whereas the strict social banks have shown a 331% deposit growth.

In the following, we use exclusively the unbalanced panel with six banks with strict self-restrictions and 17 banks with moderate self-restrictions. For each group of social banks, we calculated the (unweighted) average excess liquidity indicators. Figure 2 shows that the first excess liquidity indicator, ELI_1, i.e., the loans-to-deposits ratio, is on average higher for strict social banks than for moderate banks. These results challenge our initial assumption. However, if we exclude one (strict) bank from our data set because of the rather limited information on its investment strategy[3] and its

[3]The allocation of this bank to the group of strict social banks was based on the authors' interpretation of website information.

Table 1. Sample of European social banks.

No.	Bank	Country	Final sample	Data source
1	Alternative Bank Schweiz	Switzerland	2007–2019	Survey
2	APS Bank	Malta	2007–2019	Website/Annual Report
3	Banca Populare Etica	Italy	2007–2019	Survey
4	ASN Bank	Netherlands	No	None
5	Bank für Kirche und Diakonie eG	Germany	2007–2019	Survey
6	Bank für Orden und Mission	Germany	2007–2019	Website/Annual Report
7	Bankhaus Schelhammer & Schattera	Germany	2015–2018	Website/Annual Report
8	Bank im Bistum Essen eG	Germany	2007–2019	Survey
9	Cassa Padana	Italy	2007–2019	Website/Annual Report
10	Cassa Rurale di Bolzano Soc. Cooperativa	Italy	2008–2011, 2013–2019	Survey
11	Charity Bank	United Kingdom	No	None
12	Caisse Solidaire	France	No	None
13	Caixa Pollenca	Spain	2011–2019	Website/Annual Report
14	Cooperative Bank	United Kingdom	2007–2019	Website/Annual Report
15	Cooperative Bank of Karditsa Coop.L.L.	Greece	No	None
16	Crédit Coopératif	France	No	None
17	Cultura Sparebank	Norway	No	None
18	Ecology Building Society	United Kingdom	No	None
19	Ekobanken	Sweden	No	None
20	Ethikbank	Germany	2007–2019	Survey

(*Continued*)

Table 1. (*Continued*)

No.	Bank	Country	Final sample	Data source
21	Evangelische Bank eG	Germany	2007–2019	Survey
22	Evenord-Bank	Germany	2007–2019	Survey
23	Freie Gemeinschaftsbank	Germany	2012–2019	Survey
24	GLS Bank	Germany	2007–2019	Survey
25	MagNet Hungarian Community Bank	Hungary	2008–2016	Survey
26	Merkur, den almennyttige andelskasse	Denmark	No	None
27	Pax-Bank eG	Germany	2007–2019	Survey
28	ProCredit	Germany	2012–2017	Survey
29	Raiffeisenbank Holzkirchen-Otterfing eG	Germany	2007–2019	Survey
30	Société financière de la NEF	France	No	None
31	Steyler Bank GmbH	Germany	2007–2019	Survey
32	Triodos Bank	Netherlands	2007–2019	Survey
33	Umweltbank	Germany	2007–2019	Survey

Notes: "No" in column "Final sample" means that no data regarding the investment strategy of the bank was available, so the bank had to be excluded from the analysis.

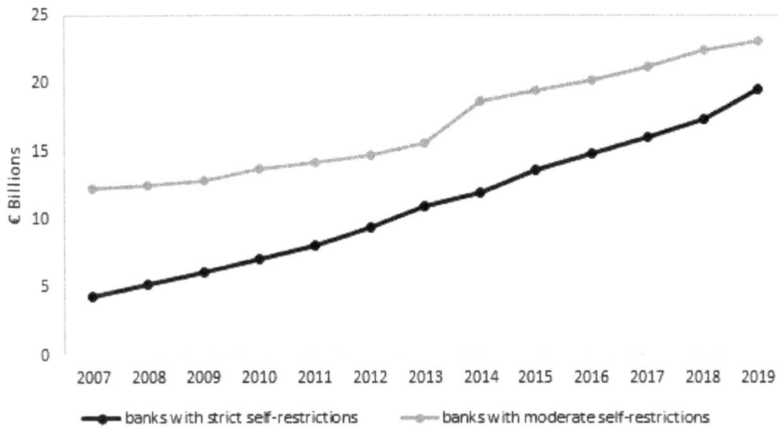

Fig. 1. Development of deposits of social banks (2007–2019).

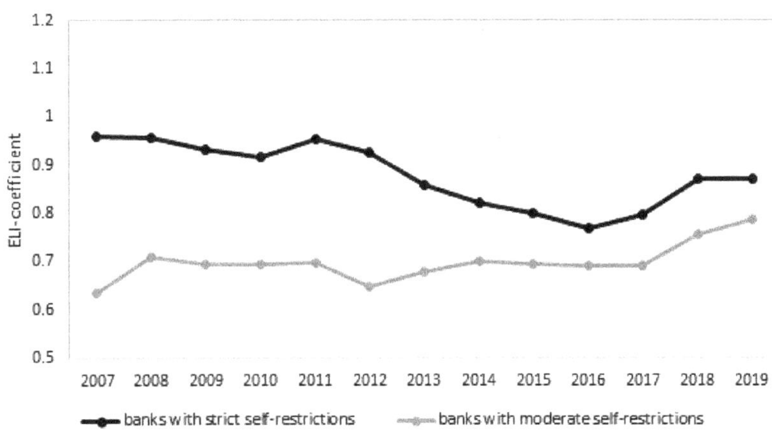

Fig. 2. Development of average ELI_1 of social banks (2007–2019) I.

strong outlier values[4], the diagram will be put into perspective (see Figure 3).[5] At least in the years 2008 to 2010, we observe the expected results. For the other years, the deviation between both groups is

[4]Figure 6 in the Appendix shows the strong outlier in scatter plots and the resulting incongruity of the excluded bank. Figures 7 and 8 show the distribution of ELI_1 of the remaining strict and the moderate social banks, respectively.

[5]This bank is also excluded from the data in Figures 4 and 5.

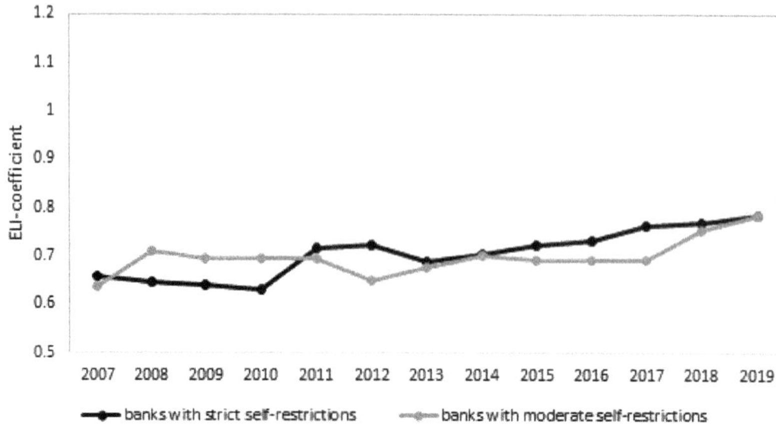

Fig. 3. Development of average ELI_1 of social banks (2007–2019) II.

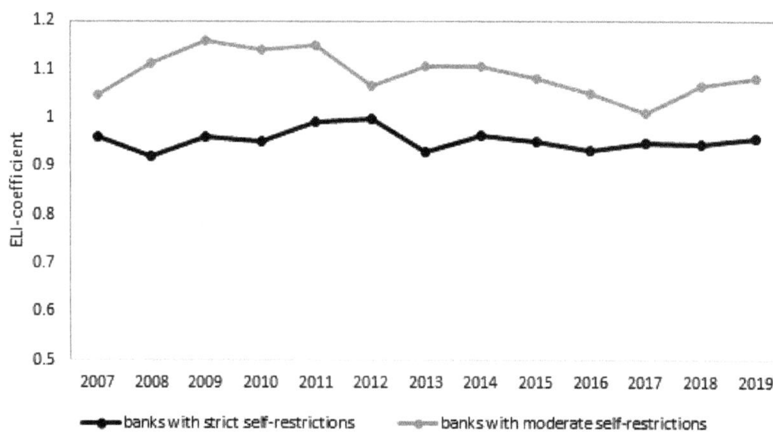

Fig. 4. Development of average ELI_2 of social banks (2007–2019).

rather small. Moreover, the loans-to-deposits ratio of both groups is always significantly below 100%.

The diagram of our second excess liquidity indicator, ELI_2, is clearer (see Figure 4). The average indicator values of strict social banks are now always below those of moderate banks. The values remain relatively stable over time for strict social banks, beginning with 0.96 in 2007 and ending at 0.95 in 2019. For moderate social banks, the fluctuations of the average impact-assets-to-deposits ratio

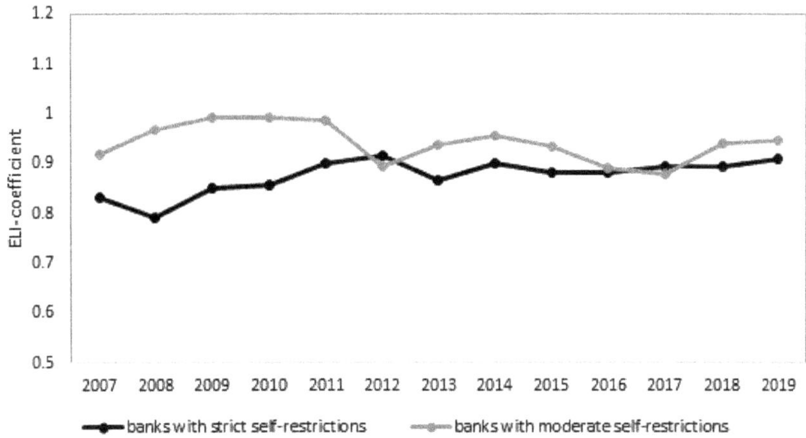

Fig. 5. Development of average ELI_3 of social banks (2007–2019).

are somewhat larger and, more importantly, the average ELI_2 is always higher than 100%.

Including additional liabilities shifts the graphs downwards, as can be seen in Figure 5. In 2012 and 2017, the average values of ELI_3 of moderate social banks are below those of strict banks. For 2012, the change can be explained by the lack of balance sheet data for a moderate social bank with otherwise comparatively high impact-assets-to-liabilities ratios, as well as the inclusion of a bank that was founded in 2012 and had very low indicator values.

6. Discussion

Our results indicate that the deposits of European social banks in general have grown massively in the wake of the global financial crisis. The 331% growth of deposits of strict social banks between 2007 and 2019 outperformed the (still impressive) 89% growth of moderate social banks by far. This finding supports the assumption of Höhnke and Homölle (2020) that strict social banks attract more depositors than moderate ones, potentially because they are attractive to a wider spectrum of customer groups, such as those who try to avoid negative investments *as well as* those who try to invest in positive projects only. However, the growth rates of both types of social banks have outperformed those of other comparable conventional commercial banks (in Germany) over the past decades.

As argued in Sections 2 and 3, fast growth could be a threat for social banks, leading to a severe earnings risk. Since strict banks have grown much faster than moderate ones and restrict their placement of assets more strongly, they might have a higher excess liquidity risk. Our findings indicate that both types of social banks show average loans-to-deposits ratios, ELI_1, significantly below 100% over the entire time of observation, indicating that social banks in general are not able to transform all their customer deposits to loans (to social projects). Furthermore, our findings reveal that strict social banks had, on average, lower loans-to-deposits ratios than moderate banks in the years directly after the global financial crisis only (until 2010). Afterwards, strict banks had equal or even higher ratios. At first glance, these findings indicate that, contrary to our expectation, strict social banks do not seem to face a higher risk for excess liquidity than moderate social banks.

The development of the average impact-assets-to-deposits ratio, ELI_2, however, implies that moderate social banks have more options to invest remaining deposits in adequate securities. Their average ratios are clearly above 100%, whereas the average ELI_2 of strict social banks is still below 100%. These findings show that strict social banks might indeed be more limited in their selection of assets, which mainly stems from their stricter self-limitation of investments in securities. Moderate social banks are able to allocate all their deposits to projects that create at least a neutral social or environmental value added, whereas strict banks struggle to direct all their deposits to projects creating a positive social and environmental benefit.

An average ELI_2 slightly below 100% does not justify labelling strict social banks in general as high-risk candidates for an excess liquidity issue. A comparison of all borrowed capital with all impact assets (see ELI_3) does not change this evaluation, as on average both types of social banks seemed to be able to transform approximately 90% of their borrowed capital into assets in recent years. Even though ratios below 100% may indicate inefficiency, we cannot conclude that there exists a general existential threat for European social banks.

These findings contribute to the relevant literature by questioning social banks' expected higher risk for excess liquidity issues. While several scholars suppose that excess liquidity issues might be a major threat for social banks, particularly during the very strong growth of deposits in the aftermath of the global financial crisis, our findings indicate inefficiency rather than an existential threat. We contribute empirical evidence to the field of literature on the characteristics of social banks, where most studies rather use pure literature approaches or case studies of few social banks.

Our findings have several implications for subsequent research and practitioners. We showed that strict social banks have grown much faster than moderate banks have done, particularly in the aftermath of the global financial crisis. As the reason for this difference is still not fully clear, we encourage further research to investigate depositors' choice between different (types of) social banks in quantitative settings. Our findings furthermore imply that strict and moderate social banks do not greatly differ in their ability to transform deposits into loans but into securities. Therefore, subsequent research attempts could try to identify the obstacles of strict social banks (or social banks in general) regarding the selection of suitable securities. In recent years, some former conventional banks have started to adopt social banking principles (e.g., investment criteria), such as Raiffeisenbank Holzkirchen-Otterfing eG in 2014 and Evenord-Bank in 2015. As sustainability has developed into an important topic even in the banking industry, further banks might think about following these early movers. However, the idea of a general heavy threat for social banks, such as an excess liquidity problem, might be a barrier for interested banks. Our results thus clear the way for followers by challenging this prevailing assumption.

Our study is not free of limitations. Sometimes, it was difficult to identify independent social banks — or whether they are subsidiaries or only branches of conventional banks — and whether separate balance sheet data were available. This limitation also affected the identification of investment strategies. Some social banks that are branches and subsidiaries, respectively, indicated that they only invest in positive projects, whereas the main bank also invests in neutral ones. If no separate financial data for these social banks were available, we have taken the investment strategy of the parent company into account as well.

A further limitation with regard to investment strategies results from the lack of cooperation of some banks. As not all banks in our initial sample answered our questions regarding investment strategies, even after repeated enquiries via various communication channels, we had to make assumptions about these strategies. These assumptions were partly based on very few or sometimes vague statements made by the banks on their websites, and therefore may not always reflect reality. Nevertheless, these data are appropriate to analyse the growth of social banks' deposits insofar as the same public information is available for their depositors. We labelled and analysed these self-identified strategies separately and double-checked our results.

The distribution of the loans-to-deposits ratio, ELI_1, among moderate social banks might be another relevant limitation of our study. As can be seen in Figure 8, the ELI_1 of moderate social banks is widely scattered. The majority of moderate social banks have a loans-to-deposits ratio below 1, some even lower than those of strict social banks (see Figure 7). In contrast, a few moderate social banks show a very high ELI_1 of up to approximately 1.5, raising the group's average significantly. However, a comparison of the ELI_1 and ELI_2 among moderate social banks with a very low ELI_1 shows that these social banks just seem to have an investment focus on securities because their ELI_2 is right around 100%. Our main result — that excess liquidity does not seem to be an existential risk for (moderate) social banks — thus remains the same, as social banks with low ELI_1 generally seem to be able to invest in securities sufficiently.

7. Summary and Conclusion

In this study, we investigated the development of customer deposits and three excess liquidity indicators among 23 European social banks to find out whether the level of restriction of investments may lead to higher growth of deposits and higher excess liquidity risk. For this reason, we differentiated between two types of social bank: first, social banks that only invest in projects creating a positive social and environmental impact (strict social banks) and second, social banks that invest in projects creating a positive or neutral social and environmental impact (moderate social banks).

According to our data, the deposits of strict social banks have indeed grown much stronger since the financial crisis. On average, social banks could not fully transform customer deposits into loans. Moderate social banks seem to be able to easier compensate low loans-to-deposits ratios with suitable investments in shares and bonds. In conclusion, the results indeed indicate excess liquidity risks in social banks with strict self-restrictions. However, as on average both groups of social banks seemed to be able to transform approximately 90% of their borrowed capital into impact assets, liquidity surplus might decrease the efficiency, especially of strict social banks, but does not seem to infringe their going concern.

Appendix

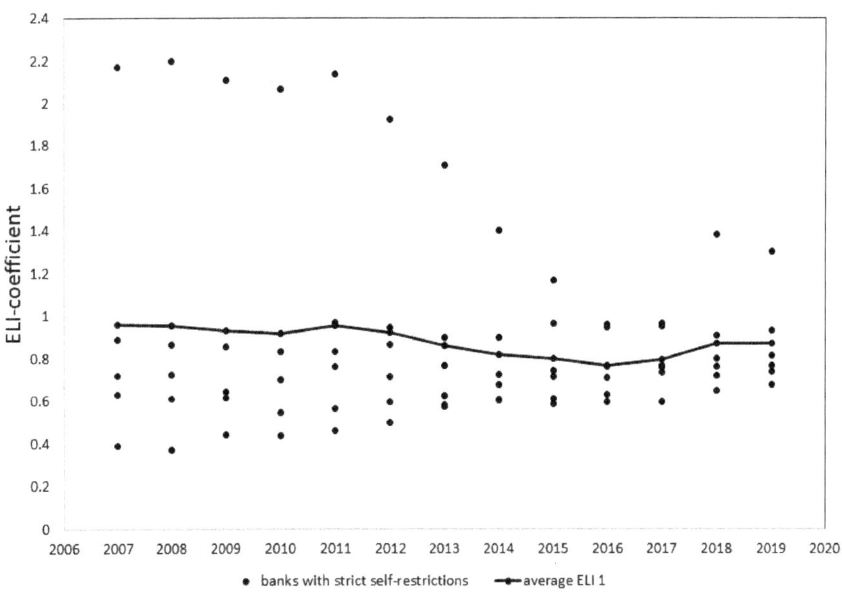

Fig. 6. Distribution of ELI_1 of strict social banks (2007–2019) I.

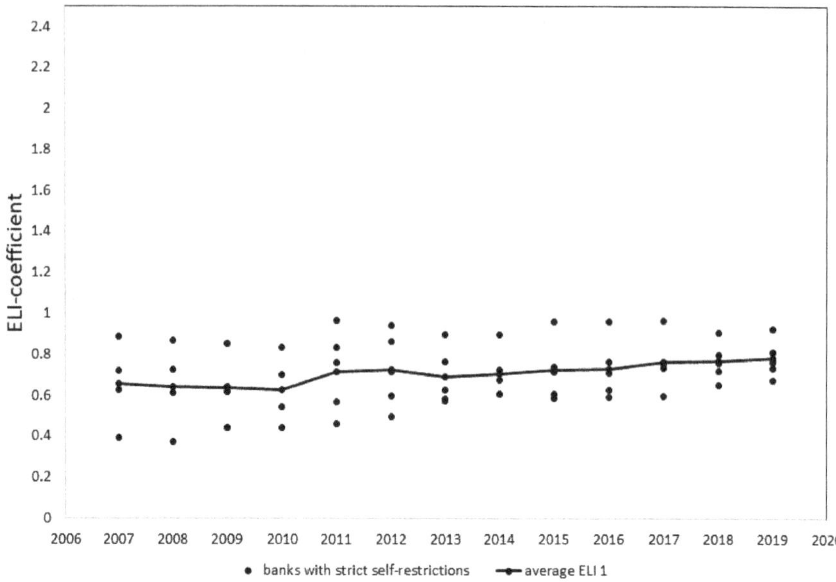

Fig. 7. Distribution of ELI_1 of strict social banks (2007–2019) II (without outliers).

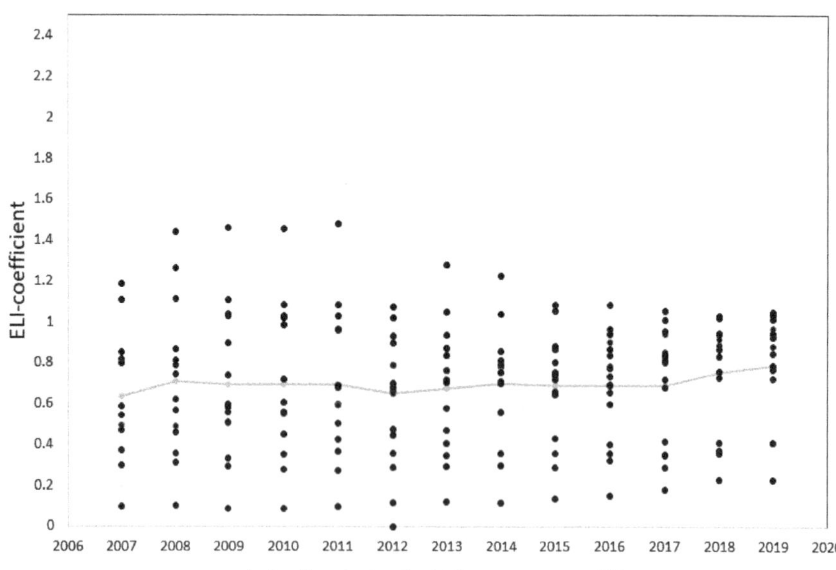

Fig. 8. Distribution of ELI_1 of moderate social banks (2007–2019).

References

Aßländer, M. and Schenkel, M. (2011). Responsible investment and exclusion criteria: A case study from a Catholic private bank. In: Vandekerckhove, W., Leys, J., Alm, K., Scholtens, B., Signori, S. and Schäfer, H. (eds.), *Responsible Investment in Times of Turmoil*, Dordrecht: Springer Science, pp. 135–150.

Baldo, L., Hallinger, B., Helmus, C., Herrala, N., Martins, D., Mohing, F., Petroulakis, F., Resinek, M., Vergote, O., Usciati, B., and Wang, Y. (2017). The distribution of excess liquidity in the euro area. Online, https://www.ecb.europa.eu/pub/pdf/scpops/ecb.op200.en.pdf. Accessed January 19, 2021.

Benedikter, R. (2011). *Social Banking and Social Finance: Answers to the Economic Crisis*. New York: Springer.

BVR (2020). Entwicklung der Genossenschaftsbanken ab 1970. Online, https://www.bvr.de/p.nsf/0/F0F8A6D1636D3A1CC1257D0A00540564/$file/Entwicklung%20der%20Banken%20seit%201970_SB.pdf. Accessed January 19, 2021.

Chew, B.C., Tan, L.H. and Hamid, S.R. (2016). Ethical banking in practice: a closer look at the co-operative bank UK PLC, *Qualitative Research in Financial Markets* **8**(1), 70–91.

Cornée, S., Kalmi, P. and Szafarz, A. (2016). Selectivity and transparency in social banking: Evidence from Europe, *Journal of Economic Issues* **50**(2), 494–502.

Cornée, S., Kalmi, P. and Szafarz, A. (2020). The business model of social banks, *Kyklos* **75**(2), 196–226.

Cornée, S. and Szafarz, A. (2014). Vive la différence: Social banks and reciprocity in the credit market, *Journal of Business Ethics* **125**(3), 361–380.

Cowton, C. (2002). Integrity, responsibility and affinity: Three aspects of ethics in banking, *Business Ethics: A European Review* **11**(4), 393–400.

DSGV (2008). Statistisches Beiheft zum Finanzbericht 2007. Online, https://www.dsgv.de/sparkassen-finanzgruppe/publikationen/finanzbericht.html. Accessed January 19, 2021.

DSGV (2019). Statistisches Beiheft zum Finanzbericht 2018. Online, https://www.dsgv.de/sparkassen-finanzgruppe/publikationen/finanzbericht.html. Accessed January 19, 2021.

Feßmann, M. (2013). Ethisch-ökologisches Banking vor dem Hintergrund der jüngsten Finanzkrise. *Vierteljahrshefte zur Wirtschaftsforschung* **82**(4), 89–106.

Forum Nachhaltige Geldanlage (2020). Marktbericht Nachhaltige Geldanlagen: Deutschland, Österreich & die Schweiz. Online, https://fng-marktbericht.org/fileadmin/Marktbericht/archiv/FNG-Marktbericht-2020.pdf. Accessed January 19, 2021.

Goyal, K. A. and Joshi, V. (2011). A study of social and ethical issues in banking industry, *International Journal of Environmental Research* **2**(5), 49–57.

Heinemann, K., Zwergel, B., Gold, S., Seuring, S., and Klein, C. (2018). Exploring the supply-demand-discrepancy of sustainable financial products in germany from a financial advisor's point of view, *Sustainability* **10**(4), 944.

Höhnke, N. (2020). Doing good or avoiding evil? An explorative study of depositors' reasons for choosing social banks in the pre and post crisis eras, *Sustainability* **12**(23), 10082.

Höhnke, N. and Homölle, S. (2018). The growth of social banks — A new measurement approach. In: Lindgreen, A., Vallaster, C., Yousafzai, S. and Hirsch, B. (eds.), *Measuring and Controlling Sustainability*, London and New York: Routledge, pp. 206–222.

Höhnke, N. and Homölle, S. (2020). Impact investments, evil investments, and something in between: comparing social banks' investment criteria and strategies with depositors' investment preferences, *Business Ethics: A European Review* **30**(3), 287–310.

Karl, M. (2015). Are ethical and social banks less risky? Evidence from a New Dataset, Online, https://www.diw.de/documents/publikationen/73/diw_01.c.508003.de/dp1484.pdf. Accessed January 19, 2021.

Köhler, M. (2010). Sonderfrage: Social Banking, *ZEW Finanzmarktreport* **18**, 3.

Krause, K. and Battenfeld, D. (2019). Coming out of the niche? Social banking in Germany: An empirical analysis of consumer characteristics and market size, *Journal of Business Ethics* **155**(3), 889–911.

Lopez, B., Torres, A., Ruozzi, A. and Vicente, J.A. (2020). Main factors for understanding high impacts on CSR dimensions in the finance industry, *Sustainability* **12**(6), 2365.

Paulet, E., Parnaudeau, M., and Relano, F. (2015). Banking with ethics: Strategic moves and structural changes of the banking industry in the aftermath of the subprime mortgage crisis, *Journal of Business Ethics* **131**(1), 199–207.

Pulejo, L., Marisca, C., and Rappazzo, N. (2015). Social reporting in European ethical banks: A comparative study, *International Journal of Managerial Studies and Research* **3**(6), 196–202.

Remer, S. (2011). Social banking and the future of social finance. In: Weber, O. and Remer, S., (eds.), *Social Banks and the Future of Sustainable Finance*, Abingdon and New York: Routledge, pp. 136–195.

Remer, S. (2014). The social banking landscape in Europe, *Global Social Policy* **14**(2), 267–269.

San-Jose, L., Retolaza, J.L., and Gutierrez-Goiria, J. (2011). Are ethical banks different? A comparative analysis using the radical affinity index, *Journal of Business Ethics* **100**(1), 151–173.

Scheire, C. and De Maertelaere, S. (2009). Banking to make a difference: A preliminary research paper on the business models of the founding member banks of the global alliance for banking on values. Online, https://www.financite.be/sites/default/files/references/files/519.pdf. Accessed January 19, 2021.

Schierenbeck, H., Lister, M., and Kirmße, S. (2014). *Ertragsorientiertes Bankmanagement: Band 1: Grundlagen, Marktzinsmethode und Rentabilitäts-Controlling.* Wiesbaden: Gabler Verlag and Springer.

Schönenbach, R. (2012). Success factors of ethic banks in Germany: Implications for Islamic banking. Online, https://www.academia.edu/23821254. Accessed January 19, 2021.

Schwedeler, A. (2017). Die Triodos Bank und ihr nachhaltiges Geschäftsmodell. In: Krämer, G., (ed.), *Finanzwirtschaft in ethischer Verantwortung*, Wiesbaden: Springer Gabler, pp. 83–93.

Weber, O. (2011). Mission and profitability of social banks. Online, https://ssrn.com/abstract=1957637. Accessed January 19, 2021.

ZEB (2012). Social banking study 2012: Management summary. Online. https://bankinghub.de/wp-content/uploads/2013/11/zeb-Social-Banking-Study-2012.pdf. Accessed January 19, 2021.

https://doi.org/10.1142/9781800611917_0006

Chapter 6

Comparative Analysis of Determining the Risk-Adequate Cost of Capital for Regulated Network Operators in Network Industries

Ulrike Stopka

Technische Universität Dresden, Chair of Information and Communication Business Management & Economics, Germany

ulrike.stopka@tu-dresden.de

Even years after liberalisation, network industries such as electricity, telecommunications and railways are characterised by the existence of essential facilities that cannot be easily duplicated by new market entrants. Regulation must therefore ensure non-discriminatory, fair-priced access for all competitors to these facilities. The article considers the approaches to tariff regulation applied by the Bundesnetzagentur in the three sectors. The focus is on the comparison of the methodological framework for determining the eligible cost of capital. The estimation of the input parameters for CAPM and the results for the eligible rate of return on equity are discussed. There are considerable particularities in the electricity sector. Then, the determination of the eligible total costs of capital is addressed. In the telecommunications and railway sectors, this is done via the WACC method while in the electricity sector different approaches are used.

1. Introduction

Infrastructure networks — e.g., road, railway, electricity, gas pipelines, water, or data transmission — have a key function in the economy. While network industries were traditionally perceived as natural monopolies in which competition is inefficient, today's view is much more differentiated. Since the mid-1980s, technical and economic developments and the resulting re-evaluation of networks in economic theory have triggered the liberalisation of several network industries traditionally run as (state) monopolies with market-dominant network operators.

In this context, the term "essential facility" was defined for resources indispensable for the emergence of competition. These facilities are needed to enter the market for newcomers and to compete with the market leaders. They cannot be reasonably duplicated by new market entrants due to their high irreversibility of costs. The Essential Facility Theory is anchored both in Article 102 of the Treaty on the Functioning of the European Union (TFEU) and in Section 19 IV of the Act against Restraints of Competition (GWB).

The key issue in the telecommunication, railway and electricity sectors is to ensure non-discriminatory access to the essential facilities at fair prices through regulation. In railways, this particularly concerns railroads and passenger stations of the railway infrastructure companies; in telecommunications, the wholesale products of market-dominant companies, such as the unbundled subscriber line at the main or cable distribution frame of the Deutsche Telekom or the bitstream access for competitors; and in electricity, e.g., the extra-high voltage networks for the power transmission over long distances. Meanwhile, it must be ensured that network operators have sufficient financial resources to operate their networks. Especially for investments, they need a long-term planning horizon and reliable economic framework conditions. In the interest of the wholesale and private customers, the charges for the use of network infrastructure elements must be calculated transparently and reasonably. This is where the wholesale regulation with its two essential components "charge regulation" and "access regulation" comes into play. Figure 1 provides an overview about the sector-specific legal bases (BNetzA, 2017a, p. 7; Knieps, 2008, p. 1).

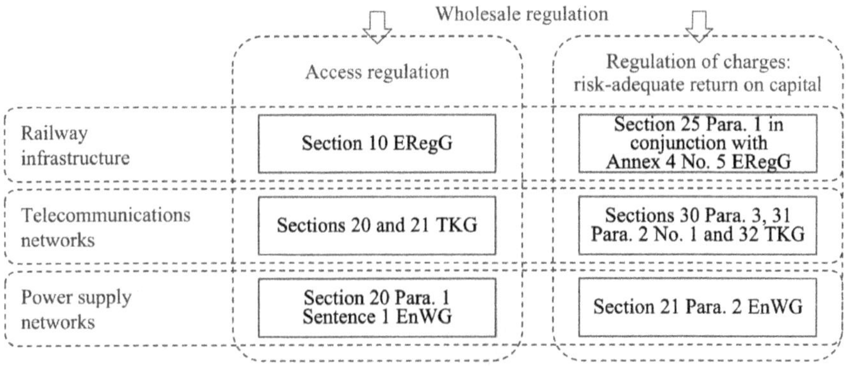

Fig. 1. Sector-specific legislative requirements for access and charge regulation.

2. The Regulation of Charges for the Use of Infrastructure and Associated Services in the Three Sectors

In the context of the regulation, the infrastructure operators in network sectors can be given by the authority cost, price and revenue caps for any single charge, service baskets or total revenues of the company (Coenen and Haucap, 2012, p. 13). If the infrastructure operator is given upper limits to the total revenue, this is referred to as Revenue Caps. Revenue Cap regulation allows the operator to change its prices within baskets of services if the change in revenue does not exceed the Revenue Cap Index. This index usually reflects the general rate of inflation in the economy, the inflation of the input prices of the operator compared to an average company in the economy, and the ability of the operator to achieve efficiency gains. Price Cap regulation follows the same approach but for prices rather than revenues. Here, too, the inflation trend in the form of the Retail Price Index, the general productivity growth rate of the economy as well as company-specific efficiency improvement targets are used to determine the eligible price cap. The efficiency of a network operator is determined by suitable benchmarking methods. In this way, a development path for prices or revenues is determined by the regulatory authority for a regulatory period (usually 2–5 years).

In all three sectors, investments in network infrastructure require considerable financial resources that must be provided by the network owners. This in turn raises the question, what is the reasonable return on investment or what costs of capital are appropriately reflected in the prices and charges to be approved by the regulatory authority. These prices must ultimately be paid by the competitors who need access to the infrastructure and, especially in the electricity market, directly by the consumers.

As can be inferred from the above, the methodological framework for determining the eligible cost of capital is very diverse. It ranges from the balance sheet method, the capital asset pricing model (CAPM) in conjunction with the weighted average cost of capital (WACC) approach or the Regulated Asset Base approach, to the determination of Cost or Revenue Caps. The methods used in the three network sectors, telecommunications, railway, and electricity, differ to a certain extent. The CAPM is used to ascertain the return on equity in all three sectors in a similar way. The imputed return on total costs of capital in the telecommunications sector is calculated by the Bundesnetzagentur (BNetzA) based on the WACC-formula as part of the determination of the long run incremental costs of efficient service provision. In the regulation of railway infrastructure companies, there is nearly the same procedure. In contrast, in the electricity sector, the relevant determination of the imputed eligible return on capital as a component of the network charges is based on the determination of a Revenue Cap in accordance with the Ordinance on the Incentive Regulation of Energy Supply Networks 2007. In what follows, this will be discussed in greater detail for each of the three network sectors.

3. The Capital Asset Pricing Model and Weighted Average Cost of Capital for Determining the Eligible Cost of Capital

The CAPM is a theoretical capital market model that opens up a statistical-econometric approach to how the non-diversifiable risk of a company can be derived from the development of the stock prices of selected companies compared to the market index or portfolio (*Frontier Economics*, 2019). Accordingly, the expected return on a security is a linear function of the risk premium of the market portfolio, i.e., the totality of all risky securities in circulation (Breuer and

Breuer, 2018). The CAPM is used in the context of charge regulation for market-dominant network operators to determine the eligible cost of equity or the expected returns for the risks of investing in essential facilities. The CAPM summarises the intuitive idea that higher risks must be rewarded with higher returns in a model and in a formula (cf. F1). In Stehle (2010, p. 57), the most important rules of the CAPM are mentioned:

- According to Modigliani and Miller (1958), a differentiation must be made at the company level between the risk associated with the real economic activities of a company and the capital structure risk.
- According to Sharpe (1963), a distinction must be made at investor level between diversifiable and non-diversifiable risks.[1] Only the latter influences the cost of equity and thus the total cost of capital of a company. The non-diversifiable risk is measured with the standardised parameter beta.

The CAPM model exists in many variations and alternative approaches, which are discussed in more detail in Stehle (2010, p. 63 ff.) for the telecommunications sector and in *Frontier Economics* (2009, pp. 39–43) for the railway sector. The basic model used for regulatory purposes by the BNetzA is as follows:

$$C_E = E(R_i) = R_f + \beta_i[E(R_m) - R_f], \tag{1}$$

where C_E is the expected return on equity, $E(R_i)$ is the expected return on the share i, or cost of equity of the company i, with the given capital structure, R_f is the "risk-free" interest rate (the interest rate for risk-free capital transfers), β_i is the (standardised) measure of non-diversifiable risk, in short, the beta of the share i(more precisely: the equity beta), $[E(R_m) - R_f]$ is the market risk premium, the difference between the expected return on the market portfolio of all available shares and the risk-free interest rate.

[1]Risks that an investor can eliminate by exploiting different investment opportunities are called diversifiable. Non-diversifiable risks are correlated with the economy, more precisely with the overall market risk, which is usually represented by a share index. They cannot be eliminated by different investment strategies.

The cost of equity in this model can also be regarded as the return on a security i (e.g., a share). From Eq. (F1), it can be seen that the cost of equity depends on several components: the beta factor, the risk-free interest rate, and the market risk premium. According to (1), the return on equity is the sum of the risk-free interest rate and a risk surcharge. The latter is calculated as the product of the beta factor and the market risk premium. The beta (β_i) provides information on the non-diversifiable risk of the share i compared to the overall market (return of the market portfolio). It is expressed by the degree of correlation between the performance of the company and the market (cf. (2)), where R_i represents the expected return of a particular share i and R_m is the return of the overall market. The covariance of these two variables is set in relation to the variance of the total market return.

$$\beta_i = \frac{\text{Cov}(R_i, R_m)}{\text{Var}\, R_m}. \tag{2}$$

This means that the beta factor indicates how sensitively the security reacts to a change in the market, i.e., how much riskier it is to invest in the share i instead of investing in a portfolio of shares. The beta value thus expresses the company-specific risk in relation to the systematic, i.e., not further diversifiable risk of the overall market. The risk of the company is higher than that of the overall market risk if $\beta_i > 1$ and lower if $\beta_i < 1$. If $\beta_i = 1$, the company risk is equal to that of the entire market portfolio. The equity beta is empirically estimated by linear regression (OLS (Ordinary Least Squares) regression) (Stehle, 2010, p. 59). The estimation of the systematic risk beta depends on a variety of assumptions regarding future technological, demand-side, and competitive developments in the markets under consideration.

The interest rate for government securities (e.g., 10-year federal bonds) is often used as the risk-free interest rate because it is theoretically assumed that these securities carry no default risk (cf. Section 5.1.1). Subtracting this risk-free interest rate from the return on the market portfolio of all shares available in the market results in the market risk premium. The market risk premium is therefore not a calculable value but is estimated in a forward-looking manner based on the averages of past return series.

Since companies need debt capital to a greater or lower extent in addition to equity capital to finance the assets necessary for operations, the total cost of capital must be determined. In addition to the risk-adequate imputed equity interest rate, it also includes the interest on debt capital as well as the target capital structure ratios of the companies. Regulatory authorities use the WACC for this purpose, which is a reference value for the minimum return on the operating capital of the company. Based on the capital structure, the equity interest rate is weighted with the equity ratio and the debt interest rate correspondingly with the debt ratio. The cost of debt capital is reduced by the tax shield. As a result of the interest subsidy, the market value of the company increases and at the same time the WACC decreases. The WACC as the return on total capital can be determined before and after taxes. Pursuant to Stehle (2010, p. 53), the WACC after taxes is calculated as follows, based on the "textbook formula" according to Copeland *et al.* (2005, p. 569):

$$\text{WACC}_{\text{after taxes}} = C_E \frac{E}{E+D} + (1-t)C_D \frac{D}{E+D}, \tag{3}$$

where C_E is the cost of equity after corporate tax or the expected return on equity, E is the market value of equity capital (number of outstanding shares multiplied by the share price), t is the relevant corporate tax rate, C_D is the cost of debt capital (in the case of risk-free debt capital, the effective interest rate), D is the market value of the debt, $E/(E+D)$ is the equity ratio, $D/(E+D)$ is the debt ratio (leverage).

The WACC before tax can be calculated by dividing the WACC after tax by $(1-t)$ (Stehle, 2010, p. 55). The WACC calculation shows that the underlying capital structure has a considerable influence on the eligible total return on capital investments for the regulated infrastructure companies. The question here is whether the capital ratios are determined based on the market value of the equity and debt capital as to be seen from formula (3) or based on the balance sheet values for the equity and debt capital (cf. Section 4).

4. The Basis for the Return on Capital and the Capital Structure

Here, the question is to be answered to which assets or facilities the interest on the capital employed relates. There are specific aspects in all three infrastructure sectors.

4.1. *Electricity sector*

In the electricity sector, the current procedure for determining the cost of capital within the framework of defining the Revenue Caps for power transmission network operators requires an individual evaluation of the capital base and structure. That means, the equity capital and debt capital of each single network operator, in particular the current assets required for operations and the capital to be deducted, have to be considered on the basis of balance sheet as well as imputed values. This leads to a high checking effort by the regulatory authority and restricts the companies' scope for the optimisation of their capital structure under regulatory aspects.

In accordance with the requirements of the Ordinance on the Incentive Regulation of Energy Supply Networks (ARegV), Revenue Caps are set for energy network operators for one regulatory period (5 years). Before the start of such a period, the regulatory authority determines the initial level for the calculation of the Revenue Cap through an individual cost audit of the network operator in the so-called base year. This is in each case 3 years before the start of a regulatory period. When fixing the initial cost level and the eligible return on equity, there is a strong focus on company-specific conditions, taking into account

- the company-specific imputed asset base,
- the company-specific capital structure,
- the current assets recognised as necessary for operations,
- the interest-bearing debt capital, and
- capital to be deducted (various liability items, provisions or building cost subsidies) (*Frontier Economics*/KPMG, 2018, p. 11).

The interest basis is the equity required for operations. Various items are included in the calculation, some of them are taken from the balance sheet and some are imputed (cf. Table 1). Depending on the capitalisation date (before or after January 1, 2006), tangible fixed assets are valued as old assets or new assets on the basis of imputed residual book values, at current values or historical acquisition and production costs. With the exception of direct pension obligations, financial assets are generally not considered as necessary for operations in regulatory practice. Required current assets are determined by the balance sheet values. The capital to be deducted as well as the interest-bearing debt capital is then subtracted from the total of the

Table 1. Determination of the equity required for operations to calculate the imputed return on equity in the electricity sector according to Section 7 Paras. 1 and 2 of the Ordinance on Charges to Access to Power Supply Networks (StromNEV) (Romer, 2016, p. 104).

	Imputed residual book values of old assets required for operations at acquisition and production costs multiplied by debt ratio ($\geq$60%)
+	Imputed residual book values of old assets required for operations at current values multiplied by equity ratio ($\leq$40%)
+	Imputed residual book values of new assets required for operations at acquisition and production costs
=	Imputed residual values of tangible fixed assets
+	Financial assets required for operations
+	Current assets required for operations
=	Assets required for operations
−	Tax portion for special reserves
−	Capital to be deducted
−	Interest-bearing capital
=	Equity required for operations

asset items. The latter is justified by the fact that the reimbursement of debt capital costs does not take place via imputed interests but, in accordance with Section 5 Para. 2 StromNEV, they are accepted as costs equal to the real expenditures. This approach entails considerable efforts in collecting the company-specific data. In addition, the high degree of complexity is accompanied by a certain degree of non-transparency and the danger of economically inappropriate incentives (*Frontier Economics*/KPMG, 2018, p. 15).

In accordance with Section 7 Para. 1 StromNEV, only 40% of the equity required for operations earns interests at the equity I interest rate. The share of the equity that exceeds 40% of the operating assets is remunerated with the lower equity II interest rate, which corresponds to the nominal interest rate on debt capital. The equity I interest rate includes a risk premium customary in the market, while the equity II interest rate is a mixed interest rate from public bonds and corporate bonds pursuant Section 7 Para. 7 StromNEV (cf. Section 5.2). What is the reason for this specific approach?

Without the above-mentioned limitations, the total costs of capital would be significantly higher, since the equity ratio in the electricity sector is relatively high and the interest rate on equity is significantly higher than the interest rate on debt. Equity ratios of up to 90% exist here. Therefore, as described in Section 6 Para. 2

StromNEV, the equity ratio is limited to a maximum of 40%. This is intended to prevent the network operators from setting an equity ratio above the usual market level arbitrarily driving up the network charges. According to the BNetzA, the 40% equity ratio represents the optimal financing structure, which can also be found in competitive markets (Romer, 2016, p. 103).

4.2. *Railway and telecommunications sectors*

The determination of the capital base in the railway sector also focuses on the capital required for operations. The starting point is the balance sheet total for the so-called minimum access package according to Annex 2 No. 1 Railway Regulation Act (ERegG), which includes the operation of the railroads, the associated control and safety systems, the associated equipment for the track-related supply of traction current, etc. Particularly in the case of allied companies, such as Deutsche Bahn (DB) AG, it is necessary to differentiate the capital base of the entire company group with regard to the intended purpose. In addition, equity, interest-bearing debt capital and other capital must be distinguished from each other. Interest-free loans, public grants and building cost subsidies (insofar as they have been capitalised) are not to be included in the capital base. This also applies to provisions (excluding pension provisions) and other interest-free capital. Here, the procedure is analogous to that in the electricity sector (capital to be deducted). This is matched by the assets required for operations on the assets side of the balance sheet. In the railway sector, as in the electricity sector, the evaluation of fixed assets is based on real capital preservation, which means at historical acquisition costs. This allows the railway companies to earn back their capital invested through depreciation and the interests on the capital still tied up in the assets.

With regard to the capital ratios accepted by the regulator, it should be noted that also in the railway and telecommunications sectors, the equity share is limited to a level customary in the market, as is done, e.g., in the context of beta adjustment in the CAPM calculation (cf. Section 5.1.2) (*Frontier Economics*, 2009, p. 95).

In the case of state-owned railway infrastructure companies, there is another special feature. According to Article 87e Para. 3 of the German Basic Law, the federal government must always hold the majority of shares in these companies. On the one hand, this raises the question of an appropriate risk-adequate return on equity: should it deviate from the usual return of non-state owned railway infrastructure companies or not? To this end, the following options are discussed (*Ibid.*, p. 16 f.):

- Setting the beta value and risk premium at the lower limit of the ranges determined in the CAPM analysis by *Frontier Economics*.
- Splitting the equity base: investments from public capital (tax money) are only remunerated with tax-adjusted debt capital costs, investments financed from DB AG's own funds with the risk premium according to CAPM.

On the other hand, federal companies have an exceptionally good ranking at the financial institutions, regardless of their debt ratio. This reduces their debt capital costs. The debt ratios of comparable companies, such as freight railways, passenger railways, ports, airports, road operators, energy networks and utilities, are used to determine a standardised debt ratio for the German railway infrastructure companies. Furthermore, the assumptions of other international regulators are used as a plausibility check. It shows that the debt ratios are most often between 50% and 60%. This approach is supported in several studies.[2] For the regulatory period 2019 to 2023, the BNetzA has determined a debt capital ratio of 64% for the regulated railway infrastructure companies[3] (BNetzA, 2017b, p. 60).

5. Determining the Eligible Costs of Capital — Similarities and Differences in the Three Sectors

In addition to the similarities and differences already mentioned in Section 4, the determination of the eligible costs of capital in the electricity, railway and telecommunications sectors indicates differences and similarities in estimating the permitted return on equity

[2] *Frontier Economics* (2009, p. 96 ff.), *Frontier Economics*/IGES (2013, p. 3) and *Frontier Economics*/IGES (2016, p. 29 f.).

[3] Includes interest-bearing and non-interest-bearing debt capital for determining the industry equity beta (levered beta).

via CAPM and return on total capital via WACC as well as the specification of their various input parameters. The first point to note is that the CAPM is used in all three sectors to determine the cost of equity. In telecommunications and railways, the equity interest rate estimated via CAPM is then used for the calculation of the total cost of capital via a classic WACC approach. In the electricity sector, special features exist that are mainly due to the determination of the cost of debt capital.

5.1. *Estimating the input parameters for CAPM*

5.1.1. *Risk-free interest rate*

The risk-free interest rate is the yield an investor would receive on the capital market for a theoretical security without risk. In the *railway sector*, fixed interest-bearing government bonds are considered as a suitable reference for this because medium to long-term bonds reflect the actual financing structure and asset lifespan of infrastructure companies best. As a result of the financial crisis as well as the European Central Bank's long-standing low interest policy, the average yields of German Government securities are continually falling, which has corresponding implications on the risk-free interest rate. While this was still stated at 4.1% in 2009 (*Frontier Economics*, 2009, p. 49), it was in a range of −0.3% to 3.0% in 2016 (*Frontier Economics*/IGES, 2016, p. 8). Finally, the BNetzA calculated the risk-free interest rate at 2.6% for the CAPM calculation in the railway sector in 2017. This was done using the current yields for federal bonds with a remaining term of ten years, starting on 31 December 2015 into the past and averaging over a period of ten years (BNetzA, 2017b, p. 61). As can be seen from Figure 2, the parameter "risk-free interest rate" is also used to determine the debt capital costs.

In the other sectors, too, there has been a continuous decline in the risk-free interest rate. To determine the risk-free interest rate in the regulatory practice of telecommunications, the daily or monthly current yields of domestic bearer bonds and public sector bonds over the last ten years are used. The risk-free interest rate is the simple mean value of the above mentioned time series (BNetzA, 2019, p. 112). This was calculated at 4.07% in 2010 (Stehle, 2010, p. 189), at

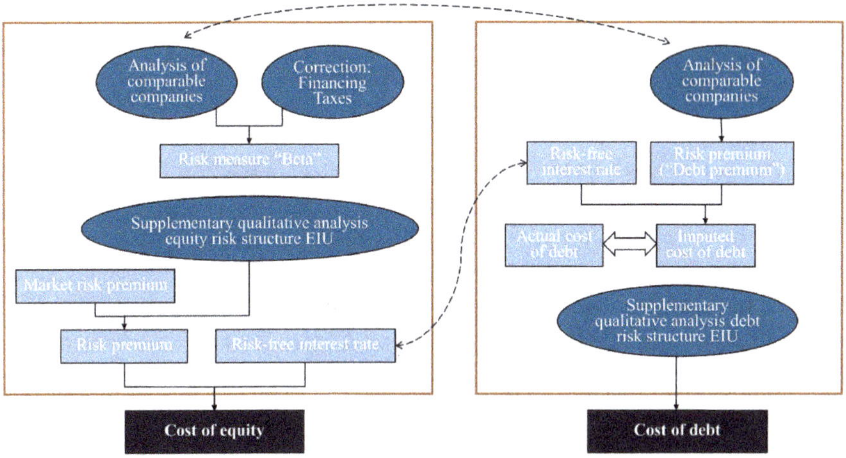

Fig. 2. Procedure for determining the eligible rate of return on equity and debt in the railway sector (*Frontier Economics*/IGES, 2020, p. 9).

2.71% in 2015 (BNetzA, 2015, p. 112) and at 1.30% in 2019 (BNetzA, 2019, p. 113).

The risk-free base rate used for CAPM in the energy sector is derived from a 10-year average of the current yields of fixed-interest securities from domestic issuers published by the Deutsche Bundesbank. These include bank bonds (mortgage bonds, public mortgage bonds, bonds of special credit institutions), corporate bonds and public-sector bonds.[4] The risk-free interest rate is 2.49% in the base year of the regulatory period 2019 to 2023 (BNetzA, 2016b, p. 4).

It is obvious that the risk-free interest rates determined in the three infrastructure sectors vary due to the inclusion of different types of securities with different maturities and the way in which the average is calculated (simple or weighted, arithmetic or geometric). This is remarkable in so far as, according to the basic understanding of the CAPM capital market model, the risk-free interest rate should be determined by the regulatory authority precisely in an industry-unspecific manner.

---

[4]In this context, Ruling Chamber 4 of the BNetzA bases its decision on the series published by the Bundesbank in the Supplements to the Capital Market Statistics.

5.1.2. *Beta factor*

The beta factor is a specific measure of risk that reflects the systematic,[5] i.e., non-diversifiable risk of a company. It depends on the risk of the company's real economic activities and on its level of debt-equity ratio. The expected returns associated with the different risks of corporate decisions are summarised by the beta factor in a single parameter. The risk factor beta represents the central element to specify the return on equity via CAPM (*Frontier Economics*, 2009, p. 4). This usually does not indicate the beta of a single company but the industry beta or levered beta, which is calculated for a peer group of companies. This is done in several steps. First, for each company in the peer group, the equity beta is empirically estimated based on stock returns and index changes. It measures the non-diversifiable risk associated with owning the share. In the second step, the asset beta or unlevered beta that a company would have if it were purely equity-financed is calculated for each company. In the third step, the average asset beta of an entire economic sector is determined. In the fourth step, the industry beta or levered beta is calculated from the average asset (unlevered) beta on the basis of the industry average capital structure (Stehle, 2010, p. 102 f.).

5.1.2.1. Railway sector

In practice, beta factors are estimated using historical capital market data of the company compared to the market index. Ideally, representative railway infrastructure companies from Germany or Europe would be considered to determine the beta values. However, such comparable companies do not exist, as pure railway infrastructure companies are not listed on the stock exchange. In the absence of a suitable comparable company, it is necessary to resort to similar companies (peer groups). In the report by *Frontier Economics*/IGES (2016), a quantitative analysis of a "long list" of 1,329 companies from the areas of railways, transport infrastructure, transport companies and infrastructure companies is used to create a "short list"

---

[5]Systematic risks are those risks that are correlated with the economy, more precisely with the so-called market portfolio, which is typically represented by a share index or similar issue. Unsystematic risks can be diversified away by investors through skilful portfolio design (*Frontier Economics*, 2009, p. 4 f.).

of 179 companies according to the filter criteria core business area, liquidity, data availability and economic environment. In the subsequent qualitative analysis, the demand risk, cost risk and regulatory risk are reflected for the short list peer groups (passenger railways, ports, freight railways, energy networks and utilities). For each of these peer groups, the unlevered beta values of the related companies are determined (*Ibid.*, p. 33 ff.). By combining the partial risks, the overall systematic risk could be determined for each group of the short list peer companies. Thus, the range of unlevered betas for railway infrastructure companies in passenger transport is between 0.29 and 0.57 and in freight transport between 0.29 and 1.07 (*Ibid.*, p. 87).

This means that rail freight transport has a higher risk than passenger transport, which is due to the greater fluctuations in demand and the greater dependence on economic cycles in the rail freight market. Based on a share of freight transport in the total turnover of federally owned railway infrastructure companies of 15.80% (average of the base years 2014–2016), the BNetzA calculated for the first regulatory period an unlevered beta of 0.47 and a levered (industry) beta of 1.07 taking into account the average debt capital ratio and tax aspects[6] (BNetzA, 2017b, p. 60).

5.1.2.2. Telecommunications sector

For the determination of the beta factor, the daily data of the share index for telecommunications companies "STOXX® Europe Total Market Index (TMI) Telecommunications" and the share index for Europe "STOXX® Europe TMI" are considered via a 5-year regression of the relevant reporting date (June 30, 2019). By using the above-mentioned share indices of the telecommunications industry, the precision of the estimates made by Stehle (2010, p. 99 ff. and Appendix 4) could be increased. The industry beta set by the BNetzA for 2019 is 0.99 (BNetzA, 2019, p. 107).

[6]Following an analogous approach, the updated *Frontier Economics*/IGES 2020 report determines the range of unlevered betas for railway infrastructure companies to be between 0.15 and 0.62 for passenger transport and between 0.15 and 1.04 for freight transport (*Frontier Economics*/IGES, 2020, p. 24).

5.1.2.3. Electricity sector

The ascertainment of the beta factor for electricity network operators is largely analogous to the procedure in the railway sector. It is based on the empirical analysis of a worldwide sample of 14 listed companies from Europe, Australia, New Zealand, and USA (peer group) with an identical risk to that of the electricity network operators in Germany. The selection criteria for the peer group companies comprise a similar regulatory environment, sufficient trading liquidity of the shares and a pure network operator status, i.e., offering mostly regulated network activities. The risks examined in the qualitative analysis include the assessment of the utilisation, substitution, market entry, price and regulatory risk (BNetzA, 2016b, p. 15 ff.).

The daily values of the sub-indices of the "Financial Times Stock Exchange (FTSE) All-World Index" are used to derive the risk factors for the companies in the peer group. In doing so, the index with the broadest possible diversification of investment alternatives is set in order to meet the risk aspects comprehensively (BNetzA, 2016b, p. 21). The betas (raw risk factors) of the involved companies are adjusted for statistical uncertainties[7] as well as capital structure effects for the calculation of the company-specific asset betas for a 5-, 3- and 1-year period (*Frontier Economics*, 2016, p. 29). From the arithmetic averages of these three periods, an average industry asset beta is calculated. Taking into account the capital structure of 60% debt capital and 40% equity (debt-equity ratio 1.5) customary in the industry as well as an average corporate tax rate in Germany, this results in an industry beta of 0.83[8] (BNetzA, 2016b, p. 27).

5.1.3. *Market risk premium*

While the beta factor measures the risk of a company's economic activities in a specific industry, the market risk premium stands for the risk on the overall market. It is calculated as the difference

---

[7] With the help of the Vasicek adjustment, the betas of the peer group companies are weighted towards a known reference value. The fuzzier the quality of the underlying regression, the greater the standard deviation of the estimated beta (*Frontier Economics*, 2016, p. 28).

[8] Industry Beta (0.83) = Industry Asset Beta (0.4025) * [1+(60/40) * Tax Shield (1 – 0.2972)] (BNetzA, 2016b, p. 27).

between the expected return on the market portfolio of theoretically all shares (total market return) and the risk-free interest rate. It corresponds to the term in the square bracket in the CAPM formula (F1). The market risk premium refers to the additional return above the risk-free interest rate that investors expect for the investment in a fully diversified portfolio (*Frontier Economics*, 2016, p. 9).

5.1.3.1. Telecommunications sector

For the estimation of the market risk premium, the following four historical return time series of shares were used with equal weighting to achieve the best possible statistical validity:

- US shares 1871 up to December 31 of the previous year;
- US shares 1926 up to December 31 of the previous year;
- UK shares 1900 up to December 31 of the previous year;
- German shares (REX/DAX Performance Index) 1955 up to December 31 of the previous year.

These series have a sufficiently high reliability because they do not contain breaks in the form of missing trading periods. The index formation is based on uniform benchmarks so that the data are comparable. The 2019 market risk premium of 4.61% is calculated from the average of the arithmetic and geometric mean of these 4 historical stock return time series (10-year average of the effective yield). This corresponds to the usual procedure for determining a market risk premium (BNetzA, 2019, p. 108).

5.1.3.2. Railway and electricity sectors

In both sectors, the analysis of long-term time series of historical financial market data is also used to determine the market risk premium. The basis for this in both industries is the study “Credit Suisse Global Investment Returns Sourcebook 2016” (Dimson *et al.*, 2016), which contains a database of 23 countries over the period 1900 to 2015 and covers more than 90% of the global stock market (BNetzA, 2016b, p. 9; BNetzA, 2017b, p. 66). Based on this very long observation period and the global portfolio (total market return), the market risk premium is calculated in comparison to medium and long-term government bonds, which practically embody the risk-free interest rate (*Frontier Economics*, 2016, p. 8). For each year included in the estimation, the difference between the nominal stock return and the nominal bond return, the so-called surplus return, is taken, and both, arithmetic mean and a geometric mean[9] are calculated from it. Since the arithmetic mean would generally lead to an overestimation and the geometric mean to an underestimation of the market risk premium, the market risk premium is calculated by the regulator as an average of the upper and lower limits (BNetzA, 2017b, p. 63; Stehle, 2016). It was calculated at 3.80% for the current regulatory period 2019–2023 in both sectors (BNetzA, 2016b, p. 9; BNetzA, 2017b, p. 63). In this context, it is worth discussing whether the market risk premium should be calculated as the difference between the historical total market return and the average of the historical risk-free interest rate or on the basis of the current risk-free interest rate. Regulated companies argue in favour of the latter since the risk-free interest rate has fallen steadily since the financial market crisis of 2008 and thus a higher market risk premium would be the result. On the one hand, however, this would result in a methodological break. On the other hand, this argument implies that the total market return is stable in the long term, which is not the case due to the expansive monetary policy, higher capital availability and investments (cf. BNetzA, 2017b, p. 64). Several expert reports[10] point out that a clearly positive or negative correlation between the market risk premium and the risk-free interest rate cannot be proven on the basis of long-term time series analyses.

5.2. *Results of the imputed return on equity via CAPM*

The return on equity is the sum of the risk-free interest rate plus the product of the industry beta and the market risk premium (cf. (1)).

[9]The arithmetic mean corresponds to the return on a hypothetical portfolio that the investor would receive for precisely 1 year. In contrast, the geometric mean represents the return achieved over the portfolio's entire investment period of several years. (BNetzA, 2017b, p. 64).

[10]Stehle (2016, Chapter V.2, pp. 43–45); *Frontier Economics* (2016, p. 14 ff. and 43 ff).

Thus, it is a purely arithmetical result of the previously discussed parameters and is determined in the *telecommunications* and *railway sectors* according to Table 2 (position cost of equity before tax 8.55%) and Table 3 (line H — equity interest rate 9.5%).

This is much more differentiated in the *electricity sector*. Here, equity I and equity II interest rates are determined via CAPM. Equity I interest rates are granted on a maximum of 40% of the imputed operating assets (cf. Section 4.1). A further differentiation is made between the equity I interest rate for new assets and old assets (capitalised before January 1, 2006). The share of equity that exceeds 40% of the assets required for operation is remunerated with the equity II interest rate.

The equity I interest rate for new investments takes into account the above-mentioned risk-free basic interest rate of 2.49% (cf. Section 5.1.1) added to the calculated risk premium to cover network operation-specific entrepreneurial risks of 3.15% (market risk premium 3.8 × beta factor 0.83 (cf. Sections 5.1.3.2 and 5.1.2.3). Thus, the equity I interest rate for new investments is 5.64% after tax (cf. Figure 3) and 6.91% before tax (BNetzA, 2016b, p. 32). The 10-year average of the price changing according to the consumer price index of the Federal Statistical Office of 1.46% is subtracted from this for old assets in accordance with Section 7 Para. 4 Sentence 2 StromNEV. This results in an equity I interest rate for old investments of 4.18% after tax and 5.12% before tax ((5.64%–1.46%) * 1.225) (*Ibid.*, p. 33).

The equity II interest rate is determined according to Section 7 Para. 7 StromNEV as the mean value of the 10-year average current yields of public bonds, corporate bonds, and mortgage bonds. It is actually 2.75% (*Frontier Economics*/KPMG, 2018, p. 12).

In order to fix the pre-tax return on equity, it is necessary to define the income tax rate. It is needed for the calculation of the industry beta (cf. footnote 8) as well as the conversion of the equity interest rate into after-tax/pre-tax. The income tax rate is set at 29.72%[11] and is included in the calculations in the telecommunications and

[11]Corporate tax 15% (Section 23 Para. 1 Income Tax Act (KStG)); Solidarity tax contribution 5.5% (Section 4 Solidarity Surcharge Act (SolzG)); Total 15.825%; Trade tax: tax rate 3.5% (Section 11 Trade Tax Act (GewStG)) * municipal rate 397% (Federal Statistical Office, 2015, p. 8); Total 13.895%; Income tax rate 29.72% (BNetzA, 2017b, p. 70).

electricity sectors via the tax increase factors. In 2019, this is 1.46 in the telecommunications sector (cf. Table 2) and 1.225 in the electricity sector (cf. Figure 3). The difference is explained by the fact that the tax factor in the electricity sector only takes corporate tax into account. The trade tax is included as an imputed cost item in accordance with Section 7, StromNEV.

6. Determination of the Interest Rate on Debt Capital as an Input Variable for the Total Return on Capital

The total return on capital (WACC) is calculated according to (3) from the return on equity and the interest rate on debt weighted by the equity ratio and the debt ratio, respectively. Therefore, the interests on debt capital based on the return requirements of the lenders must be ascertained. Depending on the credit rating of the company, the lenders demand a "risk premium" on the risk-free interest rate in order to price in a potential risk of default. To take into account the tax deductibility of interest expenses, the cost of debt capital is reduced by the so-called tax shield $(1 - t)$ (Böttger and Balks, 2017, p. 4).

6.1. *Determination of the interest rate on debt capital for railway infrastructure companies*

In the railway sector, the cost of debt capital is set by the risk-free interest rate and a risk premium, i.e., debt spread. The risk premium results from the yield spread of corporate bonds of the peer group companies belonging to the short list used in the beta analysis (cf. Section 5.1.2.1) and risk-free government bonds with an equivalent remaining term of around ten years. In deviation from the 10-year average for determining the risk-free interest rate, a 5-year average is calculated for setting the debt capital premium. In addition, the peer group data are extended by bonds of purely state-owned railway companies that could not be included in the beta peer group due to the lack of stock exchange listing, such as Österreichische Bundesbahnen (ÖBB), Société nationale des chemins de fer francais (SNCF), Network Rail and DB AG (*Frontier Economics*/IGES, 2020, p. 25 ff.). Due to significant differences in the credit rating between state-owned and private railway companies, the *Frontier Economics*/IGES 2020 report distinguishes between federally owned and non-federally owned railway infrastructure companies when calculating the risk premium. For the former, the range of the risk premium is between 0.27% and 1.12% and for the latter between 0.97% and 2.14% (*Ibid.*, p. 33).

To ascertain the initial level of the total costs for the first regulatory period 2019 to 2023, the BNetzA determined the debt risk premium for the infrastructure companies of DB AG by analysing empirical values of the parent company and other state-owned railway companies at 0.6% (this is within the range mentioned above). Added to the risk-free interest rate of 2.6% (cf. Section 5.1.1), it results in an interest rate on debt capital of 3.2% (BNetzA, 2017b, p. 71).

6.2. *Determination of the interest rate on debt capital in the telecommunications sector*

The risk premium for debt capital for regulated telecommunications companies is calculated analogous to the railway sector. It is derived from the difference (yield spread) between the yield of a corporate bond and a comparable federal bond (reference date of June 30) for each of the ten largest European telecommunications companies in the peer group[12] mentioned in Section 5.1.2.2. These bond pairs have an average remaining term of approximately ten years and are denominated in a nominal amount above 500 million euros (BNetzA, 2019, p. 117). The debt capital risk premium is finally calculated from the size-weighted average of the yield spread of the companies in the peer group. The market value of the companies serves as the weighting factor. The weighted risk premium for 2019 amounts to 1.37% (*Ibid.*, p. 118) and is added to the risk-free interest rate of 1.30% (cf. Section 5.1.1). The cost of debt capital in total (2.67%) is multiplied by the tax increase factor 1.04 (cf. Table 2).

[12]Vodafone Group, Deutsche Telekom, Telefonica, France Telecom/Orange, Telecom Italia, British Telecom, Telia Sonera, KPN, Telenor, and Telekom Austria.

6.3. *Determination of the interest rate on debt capital in the electricity sector*

When determining the cost of debt capital in the energy sector, in contrast to the telecommunications and railway sectors, two different objectives must be distinguished: on the one hand, capital remuneration in the context of determining the base level for the Revenue Cap and, on the other hand, the calculation for the nationwide efficiency comparison pursuant to Section 14 Para. 2 ARegV. The former is relevant for determining the eligible total cost of capital (cf. Figure 3). Here, the actual interest expenses for both interest-bearing debt capital and capital to be deducted (cf. Section 4.1) are taken from the profit and loss account of the different companies and set into relation to this debt capital. The interests on debt capital are recognised as equal to expenditures and eligible insofar as they do not exceed the interest rates customary on the capital market for comparable borrowings (cf. Section 5, StromNEV). That means that company-specific parameters are used instead of averaged or standardised industry values.

7. Setting the Total Cost of Capital in All Three Sectors

According to the WACC approach, the total cost of capital results from the determined return on equity and debt capital weighted with the equity and interest-bearing debt capital ratio (cf. Section 4). Table 2 shows the data in the *telecommunications sector* calculated for fixed network and mobile network operators as of June 30, 2019. These are essentially the capital costs for network infrastructures, which do not include investments in fibre-optic networks.

In contrast to the railway and electricity sectors, the total cost of capital in the telecommunications sector is calculated annually by the BNetzA. Based on a long time series analysis, which goes back to 1999, stronger fluctuations in some values are mitigated by exponential smoothing. For this purpose, the WACC before tax of the current year is multiplied by the smoothing factor $\alpha = 0.3$, and the smoothed WACC of the previous period is multiplied by $1 - \alpha = 0.7$. Then, both values are added. In this way, the high-interest rates of the

Table 2. Determination of the total cost of capital (WACC) for fixed and mobile network operators (June 30, 2019) (BNetzA, 2019, p. 103).

	Equity capital	
	Beta	0.99
*	Market risk premium	4.61%
=	**Equity risk premium Market (equity) risk premium**	**4.57%**
+	Risk free interest rate	1.30%
=	**Cost of equity after tax**	**5.87%**
X	Tax increase factor	1.46
=	Cost of equity before tax	8.55%
X	Equity ratio	37.55%
=	**Weighted cost of equity**	**3.21%**
	Debt capital	
	Risk-free interest rate	1.30%
+	Risk premium	1.37%
=	**Cost of debt after tax**	**2.67%**
X	Tax increase factor	1.04
=	**Cost of debt before tax**	**2.77%**
X	Debt ratio, interest-bearing	57.89%
=	**Weighted cost of debt capital**	**1.61%**
	Total capital	
=	**Weighted total cost of capital before tax (nominal)**	**4.82%**
–	Inflation rate	1.56%
=	**Weighted total cost of capital (WACC) before tax (real)**	**3.26%**
	Weighted total cost of capital before tax **after smoothing** (0.3 * 3.26 + 0.7 * 4.87 (smoothed WACC 2018)	4.39%

former years are still reflected in the smoothed WACC today, albeit in a decreasing manner, so that it considerably exceeds the actual total cost of capital. As shown in Table 2, the difference between the smoothed and non-smoothed WACC is 1.13 percentage points in 2019. If the smoothing of the total cost of capital were cancelled in 2019 for the first time, this would result in a significant decay of the interest rates of 33.06% compared to the reference point in 2009

(BNetzA, 2019, p. 123). To ensure stable economic conditions for competition in telecommunication markets according to Section 32 Para. 3 No. 4 Telecommunications Act (TKG), the BNetzA, therefore, adheres to the exponential smoothing till today. Nevertheless, the European Commission (EU COM) has requested the BNetzA to review and re-evaluate this procedure within the process of the 2019 fee authorisation. On the part of the regulated network operators, however, it is emphasised that the cancelling of the smoothing methodology and the determination of the cost of capital by following the European Commission's WACC notification from 6 November, 2019 would lead to a disproportionately low total cost of capital and a lower inflow of funds, which would slow down the investments in fibre-based Gigabit networks (EU COM, 2019).

The specific limiting rules for the determination of the WACC in the *railway sector* are that

- the return on equity for railway infrastructure companies has to take into account the share of freight transport on the total revenue of the operator, and
- the interest rates are applied to the capital required for the minimum access package by following Annex 2 No. 1 ERegG in connection with Section 25 Para. 1 ERegG.

Table 3 shows the corresponding parameters for setting the WACC for the regulatory period 2019–2023 based on the average values of these parameters from 2014 to 2016.

Significantly divergent from the determination of the eligible total return on capital in the telecommunications and railway sectors, two different systems of fixing capital returns are used for power supply operators in the *electricity sector* based on the ARegV and the StromNEV: (a) capital return in the context of determining Revenue Caps and (b) capital return in the frame of nationwide efficiency comparisons. For the purpose mentioned under (a), the determination of the eligible equity return is based on the CAPM approach, as in the other two sectors, Still, three different equity interest rates are applied (cf. Section 5.2 and Figure 3). These interest rates are set by the BNetzA at the same level for all power supply network operators for the duration of a regulatory period. However, the WACC method is not used to ascertain the total return on capital. There is no standardised level for the debt interest rate and the debt capital

Table 3. Determination of the total cost of capital (WACC) for federally owned railway infrastructure operators (BNetzA, 2017b, pp. 58 and 60).

Line	Position	Ø 2014 to 2016
A	Share of turnover rail freight (%)	15.8%
B	Beta unlevered (number) Unlevered Beta/Asset Beta	0.47
C	Debt capital ratio for levered beta (%)	64%
D = B*(1+(1-E)*(C/1-C))	Beta indebted (number) Levered Beta/Industry Beta	1.07
E	Tax rate (%)	29.7%
F	Market risk premium (%)	3.8%
G	Risk-free interest rate (%)	2.6%
H = (G+D*F)/(1-E)	Equity interest rate (%)	9.5%
I	Interest rate on debt capital (%)	3.2%
J	Equity (m €)	6,516
K	Interest-bearing debt capital (m €)	8,702
L = (H*J+I*K)/(J+K)	**Total cost of capital (%)**	**5.9%**

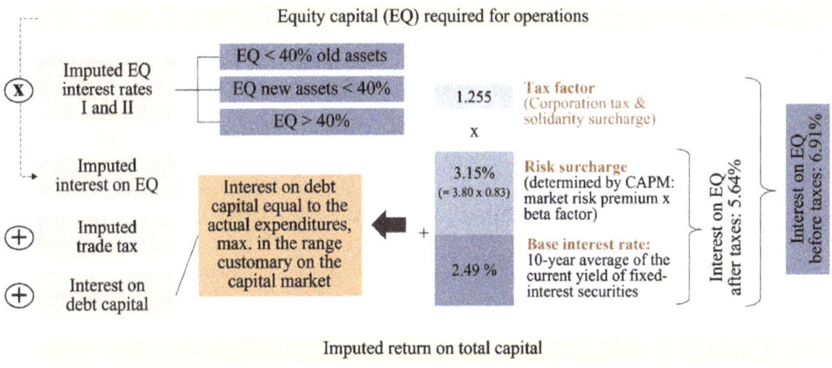

Fig. 3. Imputed total return on capital in the electricity sector (according to *Frontier Economics*/KPMG, 2018, p. 14 and BNetzA, 2017c).

ratio for all operators needed for the WACC calculation. Instead, the company's specific values are recognised (cf. Figure 3).

For the efficiency comparison mentioned under (b), the BNetzA carries out a comparability calculation of the total costs of capital.

The capital return rate is determined as the weighted average of the costs of equity and debt capital with a generalised capital structure (40% equity capital, 35% interest-bearing and 25% non-interest-bearing debt capital). The interest rate on debt capital is set as a generalised value of the current return on fixed-interest securities of domestic issuers (*Frontier Economics*/KPMG, 2018, p. 12 ff.). So, a wide variety of approaches is currently used in parallel in the electricity sector, which requires great effort for standardisation due to their complexity. This concerns in particular the application of the internationally established WACC approach, which is applied in the telecommunications and railway sectors. If this approach were implemented in the electricity sector, it would no longer be necessary to determine the equity required for operations (cf. Table 1), the actual debt capital costs, and the individual capital ratio for each single network operator. Instead, the imputed equity returns determined via CAPM (cf. Section 5.2) and an imputed interest rate on debt capital could find their way into the WACC via a standardised capital structure (e.g., of 40% equity and 60% debt capital). The use of the classic WACC approach would be associated with various improvements compared to the status quo. These relate, e.g., to the incentives for network operators to optimise the capital costs through an efficient capital structure, increased transparency, and security for investors through the application of an internationally known standard, as well as a significantly lower audit burden for the BNetzA through the reduction of company-specific parameters (*Ibid.*, p. 31 f.).

8. Summary and Comparative Assessment

The comparative compilation of the results for determining the eligible total return on capital for regulated network operators in the telecommunications, railway, and electricity sectors for 2019 is shown in Table 4.

The comparison of the beta factors illustrates the different systematic risks of the business fields in the three infrastructure sectors. However, it should be emphasised that the exact level of risk for specific companies and industries cannot be derived theoretically but must be defined empirically. This approach implies the existence of listed companies, which is not the case for the market-dominant railway infrastructure operator, DB AG.

Table 4. Results and selected influencing parameters on the eligible total return on capital in the telecommunications, railway and electricity sectors for 2019.

	Parameters		WACC/ Total return on capital (before tax)	Capital structure	
Sector	Levered beta (industry beta)	Return on equity (before tax)		Equity share	Dept share
Telecommunications	**0.99**[3, p. 107]	**8.55%**[3, p. 103]	Not smoothed: **3.26%**[3, p. 103] Smoothed: **4.39%**[3, p. 103]	**37.55%**[3, p. 114]	**57.89%**[a] [3, p. 114] **4.56%**[b] [3, p. 114]
Railway	**1.07**[2, p. 60]	**9.50%**[2, p. 58]	**5.90%**[2, p. 58]	**42.82%**[2, p. 55]	**57.18%**[2, p. 55]
Electricity	**0.83**[1, p. 27]	**Equity I interest rate** — New assets: **6.91%**[1, p. 32] Old assets: **5.12%**[1, p. 33] **Equity II interest rate:** **2.75%**[4, p. 12]	Company-specific because the costs for debt capital and the capital ratio are not determined as standardised values	Company-specific, but max. **40%/60%** for network charges; Standard threshold for efficiency comparisons: **40%** / **35%**[a]/**25%**[b] [4, p. 13]	

Notes: [a]Interest-bearing debt capital; [b]Non-interest-bearing debt capital.
Sources: [1] BNetzA (2016b), [2] BNetzA (2017b), [3] BNetzA (2019), [4] *Frontier Economics*/KPMG (2018).

The beta factor is the lowest in the electricity sector, as the demand for energy and the price development in the electricity market shows a continuous upward trend.

The company-specific risk for the fixed and mobile network operators in telecommunications is almost the same as for the overall market (beta 0.99). For investments in optical fibre-based Gigabit access networks (i.e., Fibre to the Home (FTTH) or Fibre to the Building (FTTB)), the risk is currently significantly higher due to the competitive situation with cable television and the still quite low demand for Gigabit connections and subscribers in Germany.[13]

In the railway sector, the beta factor is above 1, which the higher risks can explain in the freight transportation market in comparison to telecommunications and energy. Overall, it is debatable to what extent the infrastructure companies of the DB AG (DB Netz and DB Stationen), whose only equity provider is the German government, should obtain a return on equity via CAPM that is customary on the capital market, as is the case for infrastructure companies in the telecommunications and energy sectors. Ultimately, an implicit state guarantee comes into play here, which significantly reduces the usual market risks. The determination of the beta factor via primarily listed companies of the peer group is based on a significantly higher risk profile of these companies and is therefore not fully applicable to DB AG. Therefore, various expert opinions and statements consider that only a debt-like interest rate should be applied to the total capital employed, i.e., equating the WACC with the cost of debt capital, taking into account tax effects (Balks and Böttger, 2017, pp. 6 and 9; IGES Institute, 2016, p. 12 f.).

A problem for all network operators in the three infrastructure sectors is the low-interest policy that persists on the capital market for years. This policy has led to a steady decline in the eligible total return on capital (WACC), mainly because of the declining risk-free interest rate and the falling interest rates on debt capital. For example, the WACC in real terms before taxes in the telecommunications sector, which is fixed annually by the regulatory authority

[13]Stehle (2010, p. 120) indicates an estimated beta for investments in fibre-based networks of 1.3, which should be lowered by 0.03 per year.

as of June 30,[14] has fallen in the period 2010–2020 from 7.11% to 3.64% for fixed networks and from 7.88% to 4.42% for mobile networks (BNetzA, 2021c). The falling eligible total return on capital ultimately leads to lower cash inflows from wholesale charges paid by the competitors to use the network operators' essential facilities. This development, in turn, reduces the ability to higher investments for the market players.

A comparative look at the capital structures (equity/debt capital ratios) shows differences between the three sectors. The equity ratio is highest for the federally owned railway network operators, which causes state-owned companies' particular situation. The regulatory authority determines the capital structure in the railway sector based on the required assets or capital values for the minimum access package, i.e., the mandatory services (cf. Section 4.2). For telecommunications network operators, the capital ratios are calculated based on the market value of the equity and the book values of the debt capital of a peer group (cf. Section 4.2). On the other hand, to determine the capital structure in the electricity sector, both company-specific parameters and a standardised threshold (efficiency comparison) are used. However, the equity ratio is limited to a maximum of 40% for calculating the network charges. The reason for this is the relatively high actual equity ratio of the power supply companies. As the equity interest rate is significantly higher than the debt interest rate, the aim is to prevent the network operators from fixing an equity ratio higher than usual in the market and thus arbitrarily increasing the network charges. In the electricity sector, for historical reasons, is a strong mixture of balance sheet and imputed values in the regulatory procedure dated back from the early phases before the introduction of regulated network access in the electricity market. This gives considerable scope for an increased transition to imputed values and standardised capital structures.

[14]In contrast, in the railway sector, the eligible capital cost rates are set based on the determination of a starting level for a regulatory period of 5 years in each case. Since the third regulatory period in the energy sector, a changed determination also occurs during a 5-year regulatory period.

References

Balks, M. and Böttger, C. (2017). *Gutachten zu dem Ansatz der Kapitalkosten durch die DB Netz AG im Entgeltgenehmigungsverfahren BK10-17-0001_E.* Berlin: NEE e.V., GDL, and VPI e.V.

BNetzA (2015). *Beschluss BK2-15-002 auf Antrag der Telekom Deutschland GmbH auf Genehmigung der Entgelte für Carrier-Festverbindungen (CFV)-Ethernet ab 01.07.2015,* Bonn: BNetzA.

BNetzA (2016a). *Information für Betreiber von Schienenwegen über Vorschriften und Handhabung der Entgeltgenehmigung nach dem Eisenbahnregulierungsgesetz (ERegG),* Bonn: BNetzA.

BNetzA (2016b). *Beschluss BK 4-16-160 zur Festlegung von Eigenkapitalansätzen Für Alt- und Neuanlagen für Betreiber von Elektrizitätsversorgungsnetzen für die dritte Regulierungsperiode in der Anreizregulierung,* Bonn: BNetzA.

BNetzA (2017a). *Konsultationsdokument — Fragen der Entgeltregulierung bei FttH/B-basierten Vorleistungsprodukten mit Blick auf den Ausbau hochleistngsfähiger Glasfaserinfrastrukturen,* Bonn: BNetzA.

BNetzA (2017b). *BK10-17-0001_E/Bestimmung des Ausgangsniveaus der Gesamtkosten und Festlegung der Obergrenze der Gesamtkosten für die Netzfahrplanperiode 2018/2019,* Bonn: BNetzA.

BNetzA (2017c). *Ermittlung der Netzkosten.* [Online] Available at: https://www.bundesnetzagentur.de/DE/Fachthemen/ElektrizitaetundGas/Netzentgelte/Anreizregulierung/WesentlicheElemente/Netzkosten/Netzkostenermittlung_node.html. Accessed March 24, 2021.

BNetzA (2018). *Einsatz von Kostenmodellen in der Bundesnetzagentur.* [Online] Available at: https://www.bundesnetzagentur.de/DE/Sachgebiete/Telekommunikation/Unternehmen_Institutionen/Marktregulierung/massstaebe_methoden/kostenmodelle/kostenmodelle-node.html. Accessed March 14, 2021.

BNetzA (2019). *Beschluss BK2a-19/033 in dem Verwaltungsverfahren aufgrund des Antrags der Telekom Deutschland GmbH wegen Genehmigung von Entgelten für Carrier-Festverbindungen (CFV Ethernet 2.0),* Bonn: BNetzA.

BNetzA (2020). *Beschlussentwurf BNetzA BK 3c-20/013,* Bonn: BNetzA.

BNetzA (2021a). *Wesentliche Elemente der Anreizregulierung.* [Online] Available at: https://www.bundesnetzagentur.de/DE/Sachgebiete/ElektrizitaetundGas/Unternehmen_Institutionen/Netzentgelte/Anreizregulierung/WesentlicheElemente/elemente_anreizreg-node.html. Accessed April 13, 2021.

BNetzA (2021b). *Die Entgeltregulierung im Eisenbahnsektor.* [Online] Available at: https://www.bundesnetzagentur.de/DE/Fachthemen/Eisenbahnen/Entgelte/start.html. Accessed April 13, 2021.

BNetzA (2021c). *Kapitalkostensatz im Telekommunikationsbereich.* [Online] Available at: https://www.bundesnetzagentur.de/DE/Sachgebiete/Telekommunikation/Unternehmen_Institutionen/Marktregulierung/massstaebe_methoden/Kapitalkostensatz/kapitalkostensatz-node.htm. Accessed April 24, 2021.

Böttger, C. and Balks, M. (2017). *Gutachten zu dem Ansatz der Kapitalkosten durch die DB Netz AG im Entgeltgenehmigungsverfahren BK10-17-0001_E,* Berlin: s.n.

Breuer, W. and Breuer, C. (2018). *Capital Asset Pricing Model (CAPM).* [Online] Available at: https://wirtschaftslexikon.gabler.de/definition/capital-asset-pricing-model-capm-28840/version-252464. Accessed April 4, 2021.

Bundeskartellamt (1997). *Zugang zu Netzen und anderen wesentlichen Einrichtungen als Bestandteil der kartellrechtlichen Mißbrauchsaufsicht, Arbeitsgrundlage für die Sitzung des Arbeitskreises Kartellrecht am 9. und 10. Oktober 1997,* Berlin: s.n.

Coenen, M. and Haucap, J. (2012). *Ökonomische Grundlagen der Anreizregulierung.* Düsseldorf: Düsseldorf Institute for competition Economics (DICE).

Copeland, T.E., Weston, J.F., and Shastri, K. (2005). *Financial Theory and Corporate Policy, 4. Aufl., Pearson Education, Inc., S. 569*, 4th edn. Los Angeles: Pearson Education.

Dimson, E., Marsh, P. and Staunton, M. (2016). *Credit Suisse Global Investment Returns Yearbook,* Zurich: Credit Suisse.

EU COM (2019). *Commission Notice on the calculation of the cost of capital for legacy infrastructure in the context of the Commission's review of national notifications in the EU electronic communications sector, 2019/C 375/01,* Brussels: EU COM.

Federal Statistical Office (2015). *Fachserie 14, Reihe 10.1,* Wiesbaden: Federal Statistical Office.

Frontier Economics/IGES (Institut für Gesundheits- und Sozialforschung) (2013). *Gutachten zur Bestimmung der Kapitalkosten von Eisenbahninfrastrukturunternehmen unter den besonderen Bedingungen des deutschen Eisenbahnsektors — Aktualisierung 2013,* London: Frontier Economics Ltd.

Frontier Economics/IGES (Institut für Gesundheits- und Sozialforschung) (2016). *Gutachten zur Bestimmung der Kapitalkosten für Eisenbahninfrastrukturunternehmen unter den besonderen Bedingungen des deutschen Eisenbahnsektors — zweite Aktualisierung 2016,* London: Frontier Economics Ltd.

Frontier Economics/IGES (Institut für Gesundheits- und Sozialforschung) (2020). *Aktualisierung von Betawert und Fremdkapitalzuschlag für*

Eisenbahninfrastrukturunternehmen — Gutachten im Auftrag der Bundesnetzagentur. London: Frontier Economics Ltd.

Frontier Economics/KPMG (2018). *Weiterentwicklung der Kapitalkostenvergütung für Betreiber von Strom- und Gasversorgungsnetzen — Gutachten im Auftrag der Bundesnetzagentur,* London: Frontier Economics Ltd.

Frontier Economics (2009). *Bestimmung der Kapitalkosten im Eisenbahninfrastrukturbereich unter den besonderen Bedingungen des deutschen Eisenbahnsektors — Gutachten für die Bundesnetzagentur,* London: Frontier Economics Ltd.

Frontier Economics (2016). *Wissenschaftliches Gutachten zur Ermittlung der Zuschläge zur Abdeckung netzbetriebsspezifischer unternehmerischer Wagnisse für Strom- und Gasnetzbetreiber,* London: Frontier Economics Ltd.

Frontier Economics (2019). *Aktualisierung von Betawert und Fremdkapitalzuschlag für Eisenbahninfrastrukturunternehmen — Bericht für die Bundesnetzagentur,* London: Frontier Economics Ltd.

IGES Institute (Institut für Gesundheits- und Sozialforschung) (2016). *Auswirkung der rechtlichen Stellung der Eisenbahninfrastrukturunternehmen des Bundes auf die Verzinsung des Eigenkapitals.* Berlin: IGES Institute GmbH.

Knieps, G. (2008). *Verkehrsinfrastrukturen zwischen Wettbewerb und Regulierung, Diskussionsbeitrag N2. 121,* Freiburg i. Br.: Albert-Ludwigs-Universität Freiburg, Institut für Verkehrswissenschaft und Regionalpolitik.

Modigliani, F. and Miller, M.H. (1958). The Cost of Capital, Corporation Finance and the Theory of Investment. *The American Economic Review* **48**(3), pp. 261–297.

Romer, A. (2016). *Kapitalkosten in der Regulierung: Identifizierung und Begrenzung von Freiräumen bei der Bestimmung durch Netzbetreiber und Regulierungsbehörde,* Hohenheim: Universität Hohenheim.

Schiffer, H.-W. (2019). *Energiemarkt Deutschland — Daten und Fakten zu konventionellen und erneuerbaren Energien.* Berlin: Springer.

Sharpe, W.F. (1963). A simplified model for portfolio analysis, *Management Science*, 01, 277–293.

Stehle, R. (2010). *Wissenschaftliches Gutachten zur Ermittlung des kalkulatorischen Zinssatzes, der den spezifischen Risiken des Breitbandausbaus Rechnung trägt,* Berlin: Institut für Bank-, Börsen- und Versicherungswesen, Humboldt-Universität zu Berlin.

Stehle, R. (2016). *Wissenschaftliches Gutachten zur Schätzung der Marktrisikoprämie (Equity risk premium) im Rahmen der Entgeltregulierung,* Berlin: Wirtschaftswissenschaftliche Fakultät, Humboldt Universität Berlin.

Stehle, R. and Betzer, A. (2018). *Kurzgutachten zur wissenschaftlichen Fundierung der Festlegung der angemessenen Verzinsung im Telekommunikationsbereich durch die Bundesnetzagentur,* s.l.: s.n.

https://doi.org/10.1142/9781800611917_0007

Chapter 7

Private Equity Investments and Value Creation in Small and Medium-Sized Enterprises

Benjamin Hammer[*,‡], **Nils Härtel**[†,§], **Suleiman Naiem**[†,¶], **and Bernhard Schwetzler**[†,||]

[*]*Lancaster University, United Kingdom*

[†]*HHL Leipzig Graduate School of Management, Germany*

[‡]*b.hammer@lancaster.ac.uk*

[§]*nils.haertel@hhl.de*

[¶]*suleiman.naiem@hhl.de*

[||]*bernhard.schwetzler@hhl.de*

This chapter examines the enterprise value growth of private equity (PE)-backed buyouts in small and medium-sized enterprises (SMEs). Using a comprehensive sample of PE buyouts from 1997 to 2016 in 59 countries, we find that enterprise value growth rates are significantly higher if the portfolio firm is a small or medium-sized enterprise prior to the buyout. These results also hold for subsequent buyout rounds, i.e., the enterprise value growth of both the primary and secondary buyout is higher if the portfolio firm is a SME prior to the initial buyout. Moreover, we show that good access to finance, management buyouts, and SME investments by large funds have a negative effect on SMEs' enterprise value growth, whereas a PE firm's venture capital focus reinforces the positive enterprise value growth of SME portfolio firms. Our results are robust to different tests designed to mitigate selection concerns.

1. Introduction

It is a stylised fact that private equity (PE) firms employ various value creation measures in their acquired portfolio firms in order to achieve outstanding returns on their investments (Jensen, 1989). To generate these returns, value creation mechanisms usually include a combination of corporate governance improvements, the use of high levels of leverage in portfolio companies, and multiple expansion (Kaplan and Strömberg, 2009). However, it can be argued that these traditional value creation strategies have become somewhat commoditised and due to increasing competition for deals and higher valuations, the persistence of outstanding returns has declined (Braun *et al.*, 2017). According to the Bain Global Private Equity Report 2020, dry powder of buyout funds alone hit a record high of US$890 billion in 2019 and PE firms are faced with the task of putting all that unspent capital to work in an increasingly challenging and mature industry.

Many PE firms have started with a focus on smaller targets at the time of their foundation and shifted towards larger buyouts with increasing experience (e.g., Metrick and Yasuda, 2010; Wright *et al.*, 2006). PE firms tend to prefer larger deals and more established companies as buyout targets since the time required for conducting due diligence, closing a deal, and managing a portfolio company can take as much time for smaller buyouts as for larger buyouts. PE firms wish to undertake sizeable investments with high absolute returns instead of focusing on smaller transactions, which might increase overall fund return only marginally even though the percentage return is potentially high (Nikoskelainen and Wright, 2007). However, fierce competition for assets with stretched valuations seems to have sparked a renewed interest in smaller buyout targets and PE firms increasingly comb through the small and medium-sized enterprises (SMEs) segment in their quest for returns.[1] PE investors like SMEs due to

[1]Triton raised its first smaller mid-cap fund in 2017 with typical equity investments in the range of EUR 20 to EUR 50 million; IK Investment Partners closed its second small cap fund in 2018, which is double the size of its first small cap fund; Carlyle, which is particularly known for larger buyouts, seemingly chose an indirect route into the SME segment by acquiring a majority stake in KAP

their (still) reasonable valuations, because they are easier to grow and they can often be bought away from an auction process.[2]

In this study, we first focus on deal level returns of PE investments in the SME segment and are interested in whether the apparent enthusiasm among PE firms is justified. While previous research has examined PE returns on the fund or deal level in general (e.g., Acharya *et al.*, 2013; Achleitner *et al.*, 2011; Arcot *et al.*, 2015; Kaplan and Schoar, 2005) and some studies have taken into account some size effect (e.g., Lopez-de-Silanes *et al.*, 2015; Humphery-Jenner, 2012; Nikoskelainen and Wright, 2007), little to no attention has been paid to PE returns specifically in the SME segment. We fill this gap by investigating whether PE firms can generate higher deal level returns as measured by the enterprise value growth rate when investing in SMEs. Furthermore, we contribute to the currently scarce and almost non-existent literature positioned at the intersection between PE and SME research (Engel and Stiebale, 2014; Paglia and Harjoto, 2014). By doing so, we contribute to the following two main literature strands: (i) research on PE returns and (ii) literature at the intersection between PE research and research on SMEs.

2. Theoretical Background and Hypotheses

2.1. *General overview of the SME segment and relevance for the private equity industry*

The SME sector is often argued to be the backbone of an economy. In the European Union for example, SMEs represented 99.8% of all non-financial businesses in 2016, accounted for 67% of total employment, and generated 57% of value added (European Commission, 2017). Despite their importance as the engine of economic development, SMEs are likely to have less access to external financing and are

Beteiligungs-AG in 2016. KAP is a strategic financial holding company, which invests in and provides services to middle market businesses.

[2]Davies, Anjuli. "Big not always beautiful for European private equity". Reuters, March 15, 2013, https://www.reuters.com/article/us-private-equity-small-funds/big-not-always-beautiful-for-european-private-equity-idUSBRE92E0V920130315. Accessed July 24, 2019.

likely to be more constrained regarding growth and operations than larger firms (Carpenter and Petersen, 2002).

The general notion is that smaller firms have different optimal capital structures and rely on various sources of financing throughout the different stages of their organisational lives. Due to the reliance on private markets, SMEs are limited in terms of access to finance (Berger and Udell, 1998). In addition, Beck *et al.* (2005) show that impediments regarding legal systems are not as important as financing constraints, which in turn translate into an important growth constraint for smaller firms. Nevertheless, SMEs have long been the focus of policies aimed at improving their financing environment and within this changing environment, PE finance has also gained increasing importance over the past decades (Engel and Stiebale, 2014; Wright *et al.*, 2006). Conversely, the SME sector is also gaining importance for PE sponsors as they increasingly raise funds specifically dedicated to the SME segment as an apparent consequence of the structural changes over the past decades in the PE industry.

2.2. *Private equity deal returns and SMEs*

PE firms employ various value creation measures in their acquired portfolio firms in order to achieve outstanding returns on their investments (Jensen, 1989). According to Jensen (1989), leveraged buyouts result in corporate governance structures which reduce agency problems and create value via the following mechanisms: The use of high levels of debt in leveraged buyouts and the resulting increased interest payments discipline a company's management not to waste free cash flow and create incentives to reduce sub-optimal investments. Furthermore, managers typically receive a relatively large equity stake in the buyout which leads to additional alignment of interests between investors and managers. Finally, PE firms typically have significant board representation and are able to further reduce information asymmetries through continuous monitoring of a portfolio company's performance. The theoretical advantages of a leveraged buyout's governance structure have been confirmed by empirical studies, which show that firm performance increases after a buyout (Cumming *et al.*, 2007; Harris *et al.*, 2005; Kaplan, 1989).

As already mentioned, PE sponsors aim to maximise the returns of their investments (Jensen, 1989) since the ability to generate sufficient returns is a determining factor for a buyout fund's reputation and positively related to its ability to raise future funds (Chung *et al.*, 2012). The most prominent theoretical value creation drivers in PE deals, as suggested by Kaplan and Strömberg (2009), are changes in operating performance and changes in enterprise value/EBITDA valuation multiples and leverage. Although, to this day, general data availability of PE returns on the deal level is still insufficient, several studies have investigated the relationship between these value creation mechanisms and returns. The importance of operational improvements as a value driver has been confirmed, for example, by Acharya *et al.* (2013), Alperovych *et al.* (2013) and Achleitner *et al.* (2011). An improvement in enterprise value/EBITDA valuation multiples between entry and exit is another mechanism to increase returns. Even if EBITDA of the portfolio company stay constant between entry and exit, an increase in the EBITDA multiple leads to a higher enterprise value and, assuming constant net debt, finally to higher equity returns as well. Acharya *et al.* (2013) find that the improvement in valuation multiples between entry and exit is higher for PE owned companies than for benchmark companies not backed by financial sponsors. This is also confirmed by Achleitner *et al.* (2011), who show that EBITDA multiple expansion is another essential element to generate higher returns. Finally, the reduction of corporate taxes through the use of debt and the optimisation of the capital structure of the portfolio company is a generally acknowledged mechanism to boost PE returns and its positive impact has been empirically supported by Achleitner *et al.* (2011). To summarise, PE firms are active investors who implement the aforementioned governance structure within their portfolio companies and employ various value creation mechanisms, which in turn are to some extent simultaneously features of the buyout governance structure (such as high leverage), to achieve outstanding returns.

When discussing value creation in buyouts, it is necessary to distinguish between return on enterprise value and equity value, i.e., between value increase and equity return (Nikoskelainen and Wright, 2007). Financial sponsors aim to maximise the return on their investment, which does not necessarily indicate an increase in enterprise value. For example, assuming a constant enterprise value, the equity value can be increased solely through the accelerated repayment of debt during the holding period, which in turn might be possible due to operational improvements. In fact, Nikoskelainen and Wright (2007) find that the correlation between the internal rate of return on enterprise value and equity value is 0.62, which implies a positive but less than perfect relationship between these two return measures. Nevertheless, the growth rate of enterprise values, i.e., the value increase of the buyout target, serves as a proxy for equity IRRs and enables to measure the value creation in PE deals in case of limited data availability (e.g., Arcot *et al.*, 2015; Bonini, 2015).

Using a sample of 321 buyouts in the UK, Nikoskelainen and Wright (2007) find that larger buyouts, i.e., buyouts with an entry enterprise value above GBP 100 million, earn higher returns than medium-sized or smaller buyouts. They argue that the higher bankruptcy risk of smaller buyouts is likely one of the main reasons for this finding. However, as already outlined before, PE firms equip their target companies with tools to improve various critical elements for business success. Among other things, portfolio companies benefit from improvements in corporate governance and in operational areas such as financial accounting. Additionally, PE firms can potentially provide access to new markets and technologies via their expertise from earlier investments (Baker and Wruck, 1989). Since SMEs usually have more room for improvements than larger companies, we would assume that they benefit more from the guidance of PE firms and from the implemented mechanisms. Additionally, the operational improvements should usually increase EBITDA or free cash flow which in turn should translate into a higher enterprise value.

H1: We expect that the enterprise value growth rate is higher for small and medium-sized enterprises than for larger companies in private equity-backed buyouts.

2.3. *Additional factors potentially influencing the enterprise value growth rate*

The returns on the enterprise value of PE investments can be moderated by several factors which characterise the overall financing environment in which the portfolio firm operates (as measured by access to finance (e.g., Beck *et al.*, 2006, 2008)), the PE firm (in the form of fund size and investment focus (e.g., Lopez-de-Silanes *et al.*, 2015; Humphery-Jenner, 2012; Cumming *et al.*, 2009; Cressy *et al.*, 2007)), and the deal characteristics (such as a management buyout (e.g., Wright *et al.*, 2006; Hite and Vetsuypens, 1989)). Hence, we also investigate these potential moderating factors with regard to PE investments in the SME segment.

2.3.1. *Access to finance*

Information asymmetries occur in any lending situation since the borrowers are better informed about themselves than outsiders such as shareholders, banks, and suppliers (Jensen and Meckling, 1976). These kinds of information asymmetries are especially severe for smaller firms and due to their limited track record and restricted ability to provide collateral, SMEs are more limited in accessing external finance than larger firms. Consequently, they are often forced to pass up on growth opportunities if internal financial resources do not suffice (Carpenter and Petersen, 2002).

Several studies investigate the link between a better developed financial sector and firm performance. The general consent is that countries with better developed financial markets promote firm growth. For example, Demirgüc-Kunt and Maksimovic (1998) show that an active stock market and a large banking sector are linked to externally financed firm growth. Beck *et al.* (2006) find that firms are larger in countries with better financial intermediaries and more efficient legal systems and better property rights protection. Additionally, Beck *et al.* (2008) show that smaller companies are disproportionately positively impacted by better financial development.

PE firms provide SMEs not only with advice and support, but also an alternative source of financing which equips them with the means to pursue new investment opportunities and overcome potential growth constraints. According to the aforementioned studies, growth constraints of SMEs are aggravated by relatively underdeveloped financial markets. This potentially untapped growth potential combined with the typical PE value creation measures could translate into even higher growth for PE-backed SMEs in countries with relatively poor financial market development.

H2: We expect that PE investments in SME portfolio firms in countries with higher developed financial markets achieve lower enterprise value growth than PE investments in SME portfolio firms in countries with less developed financial markets.

2.3.2. *Investment stage focus*

Advising and mentoring is another known lever for value creation employed by PE firms. Through constructive interaction, representatives of the buyout firm nurture portfolio firms and provide them with knowledge on markets and strategy (Baker and Wruck, 1989). In addition, PE firms are also known to restore entrepreneurial spirit within the buyout target and to encourage innovation (Wright *et al.*, 2000). Portfolio managers of the PE firm are usually not involved in day-to-day operations of the buyout target. However, they are still much closer to management and operations than the board of directors in large corporations (Anders, 1992; Hite and Vetsuypens, 1989).

Companies differ in the degree of required nurturing and management expertise (Cumming *et al.*, 2005) and early stage investments require a different kind of expertise than investments in mature and established companies (Kaplan and Strömberg, 2009). PE firms differ considerably in terms of entrepreneurial stage focus with regard to their buyout targets and several studies have paid attention to this stage specialisation. Cressy *et al.* (2007) find that while investment stage specialisation does not impact profitability for PE-backed buyouts, it may provide a growth spurt. Cumming *et al.* (2009) find some evidence for a positive link between style drifting in terms of stage focus and investment performance. Regarding active involvement with portfolio companies, Bottazi *et al.* (2004) find that venture capital firms have a more active investment style when focusing solely on venture capital.

We are interested in whether PE firms' focus on early stage investments might lead to increased value generation in SMEs which in turn could be a consequence of more active involvement with the portfolio firm or a better match of PE firm expertise and target size. However, since venture capital firms frequently drift into later-stage investments, which would usually be classified as PE investments, and, conversely, PE firms also often style-drift into earlier stage investments (Cumming *et al.*, 2009), we do not focus explicitly on a 'stage focus'. We rather hypothesise that higher deal returns can be generated with SME investments, when PE firms also have early stage investments among their preferred investment ranges and thus the relevant expertise with regard to smaller firms.

H3: We expect that investments in SME portfolio firms achieve higher enterprise value growth in case the private equity firm also states venture capital as one of the preferred investment ranges.

2.3.3. *Large PE funds*

Compared to smaller PE funds, large PE funds usually have access to better financing conditions due to better connections with other financial institutions (Demiroglu and James, 2010). Additionally, larger PE firms should be more likely to expand internationally (Cumming and Dai, 2010) and since the investment environment will vary from country to country, larger funds should be able to more easily choose a favourable environment. Nevertheless, Lopez-de-Silanes *et al.* (2015) show that large PE funds perform worse than smaller PE funds. This is confirmed by Humphery-Jenner (2012), who also goes on to show that large funds generate especially low returns when they invest in small companies.

Humphery-Jenner (2012) points out that smaller companies might be better investments for smaller funds for the following reasons. Due to capital and location constraints, the number of potential investment opportunities is limited for smaller funds and since evaluating investments is time consuming, smaller funds might be better than larger funds at finding smaller companies with greater value creation potential. Additionally, larger PE funds usually have fewer investment professionals per investment which translates into less attention that each portfolio company receives from each professional (Lopez-de-Silanes *et al.*, 2015). Especially for smaller companies, which rely more on nurturing and management expertise than larger companies (Cumming *et al.*, 2005), this could be problematic in terms of value generation. While Humphery-Jenner (2012) examines the returns of large PE firms and their investments in smaller companies without a specific cut-off criterion for what constitutes smaller companies, we are interested in how larger PE firms perform in terms of enterprise value growth when they invest specifically in the SME segment.

H4: Based on the aforementioned arguments, we expect that the returns on enterprise value are lower when larger PE firms invest in SMEs.

2.3.4. *Management buyouts*

Management buyouts (MBOs) are known as transactions in which the leveraged buyout is led by the incumbent management which then typically becomes the majority shareholder, whereas outside management teams take over a firm in so-called management buy-ins (MBIs). Transactions in which PE firms lead the buyout and end up as the majority owner are referred to as institutional buyouts (IBOs) and the PE firms leading the IBO may bring in a new management team or retain some or all of the incumbent management. In any case, while managers do not end up as majority owners of the target company in buyouts led by PE firms, they typically receive relatively large equity stakes to mitigate the classical agency theory problems and to assure incentive alignment between them and the PE investors (Kaplan and Strömberg, 2009; Jensen, 1989).

Incumbent managers as "firm insiders" typically have superior company and industry specific information compared to outsiders since they have been operating the company for many years prior to the buyout. Robbie *et al.* (1992) find that MBIs perform worse than MBOs in terms of operating performance and are also more likely to end up in receivership. Additionally, Wright *et al.* (1996) found that MBOs from the UK in the 1980s had significantly lower failure rates than MBIs from the same period, thereby also implying higher information asymmetries in buyouts driven by outsiders.

However, PE firms are well known for raising performance standards for the management team and do not hesitate to replace managers in case performance benchmarks are not met (Anders, 1992; Baker and Wruck, 1989). Sound management skills are especially important for SMEs since a lack thereof hinders business growth or might even contribute to business failure. Fuller-Love (2006) points out that improving managerial capabilities within smaller firms will likely have a positive impact on their growth and competitiveness and there is a clear need to stimulate such management development. PE firms provide their portfolio companies with access to additional management and industry expertise from previous transactions, which represents a valuable source of additional managerial talent that might otherwise not have been readily available (Hite and Vetsuypens, 1989).

In case existing management acquires the majority of the company in a buyout, it will have an incentive to reduce managerial inefficiencies and to maximise value creation since it also owns the company. Additionally, existing management will have superior insider information which should further facilitate value creation after the buyout. However, as already mentioned, managerial capabilities in SMEs could well be underdeveloped, especially in comparison to the new managerial talent the PE sponsor might bring in. Moreover, PE firms are also well known for their thorough due diligence processes before acquiring any target company, which should somewhat mitigate the disadvantage of not having insider information. Following these arguments, we hypothesise that especially in SME buyouts, PE firms may be better suited to effectively 'run' the target company and that they create more value compared to the case in which the existing management becomes the new owner and steers the company.

H5: We expect that management buyouts of SME portfolio firms achieve lower enterprise value growth than leveraged buyouts of SME portfolio firms in which the incumbent management does not acquire a controlling equity stake.

3. Data

3.1. *Sample construction and data sources*

Our main data source is Bureau van Dijk's (BvD) Zephyr deal database, which has been used in various previous studies (e.g., Hammer *et al.*, 2017; Rigamonti *et al.*, 2016; Tykvová and Borell, 2012). We obtain transaction data from the Zephyr deal database by selecting institutional buyouts (IBOs), PE sponsor-backed management buyouts (MBOs), management buy-ins (MBIs), and buy-in management buyouts (BIMBOs) for which the financing is stated as "private equity" or "leveraged buyout" and which have been completed between 1 January 1997 and 31 December 2016. We do not include venture capital buyouts and private investments in public equity (PIPE). This leaves us with 19,012 worldwide PE transactions.

After refining the dataset and removing all observations for which we do not have EVs at entry and exit of the buyout, i.e., observations for which we cannot compute enterprise value growth rates we have a final sample of 2,305 deals entered between 1997 and 2016 and covering 59 countries.

Further details regarding the distribution of both the full sample are depicted in Table 1. Table 1 Panel A depicts the distribution of deals across countries. The United Kingdom accounts for the largest number of deals for both the full sample and the buyout chain sample, followed by US deals. Table 1 Panel B depicts the distribution of deals by entry year. As can be seen, the deals are widespread across entry years, with no year accounting for more than 11% of the deals. Finally, Table 1 Panel C shows the distribution of deals by industry, based on the Fama–French 10 (FF10) industry classification scheme. Most deals (18.9% and 21.0% respectively) are in Manufacturing for both the full sample and the buyout chain sample, followed by Business Equipment (15.7%) and Shops (14.7%) in the full sample and Shops (13.4%) and Consumer Non-durables (11.8%) in the buyout chain sample.

3.2. *Variables and summary statistics*

3.2.1. *Dependent variables and main explanatory variable*

In order to measure the profitability of a deal, we use the enterprise value (TEV) growth rate as our main dependent variable. As outlined above, this variable has already been used in previous studies (e.g., Arcot *et al.*, 2015; Bonini, 2015).

We calculate enterprise value changes between entry and exit, i.e., the enterprise value (TEV) growth rate as follows:

$$\text{TEV growth} = \sqrt[n]{\frac{\text{Exit EV}}{\text{Entry EV}}} - 1, \qquad (1)$$

where n is the numbers of years between entry and exit, i.e., the holding period, Exit EV is the enterprise value paid at exit, i.e., when the portfolio firm is sold, and Entry EV is the enterprise value paid at entry, i.e., when the portfolio firm is bought. As depicted in Table 3, the mean (median) enterprise value growth rate is 21.4% (13.8%).

Table 1. Sample distribution.

Panel A: Distribution of deals by target country

Country	n	in %	Country	n	in %
Australia	60	2.6	Japan	39	1.7
Belgium	21	0.9	Korea, Republic of	20	0.9
Brazil	7	0.3	Luxembourg	7	0.3
Canada	38	1.6	Netherlands	49	2.1
Cayman Islands	7	0.3	New Zealand	12	0.5
Czech Republic	9	0.4	Norway	20	0.9
Denmark	24	1.0	Poland	13	0.6
Finland	21	0.9	Spain	49	2.1
France	184	8.0	Sweden	56	2.4
Germany	112	4.9	Switzerland	20	0.9
India	13	0.6	United Kingdom	754	32.7
Ireland	16	0.7	United States	598	25.9
Israel	13	0.6	Other	75	3.3
Italy	68	3.0	Total	2,305	100.0

Panel B: Distribution of deals by entry year

Entry year	n	in %	Entry year	n	in %
1997	43	1.9	2008	107	4.6
1998	79	3.4	2008	107	4.6
1999	126	5.5	2009	56	2.4
2000	150	6.5	2010	70	3.0
2001	127	5.5	2011	81	3.5

(*Continued*)

Table 1. (*Continued*)

Panel B: Distribution of deals by entry year

Entry year	n	in %	Entry year	n	in %
2002	125	5.4	2012	85	3.7
2003	214	9.3	2013	65	2.8
2004	205	8.9	2014	45	2.0
2005	258	11.2	2015	15	0.7
2006	218	9.5	2016	7	0.3
2007	229	9.9	Total	2,305	100.0

Panel C: Distribution of deals by target industry

Industry	n	in %	Industry	n	in %
Cons. non-durables (FF1)	219	9.5	Shops (FF7)	339	14.7
Cons. durables (FF2)	86	3.7	Healthcare (FF8)	115	5.0
Manufacturing (FF3)	435	18.9	Utilities (FF9)	28	1.2
Energy (FF4)	31	1.3	Other (FF10)	598	25.9
Bus. equipment (FF5)	362	15.7	Total	2,305	100.0
Telecomm. (FF6)	92	4.0			

Notes: This table presents the sample distribution along various dimensions. Panel A shows the sample distribution by home country of the portfolio company. Panel B shows the sample distribution across buyout entry years. Panel C shows the sample distribution by industry of the company that is acquired by a PE fund, classified according to FF10 (Fama–French 10 industry classification scheme). Distributions are shown for the full sample as well as the buyout chain sample, i.e., the sample in which a portfolio firm is consecutively observed from the entry of the primary buyout until the exit of the secondary buyout. Data are from Bureau van Dijk's Zephyr database.

The main explanatory variable used in this chapter is a small and medium-sized enterprises' (SMEs) indicator. We construct this variable based on the entry enterprise value of the buyout. A portfolio firm is defined as a SME if the enterprise value is below US$100 million. Since our sample is dominated by deals in which the target portfolio company is located in Europe (over 60% of the deals in the sample are 'European' deals), we derive our SME definition by leaning on the definition criteria used by the European Commission, which requires a company to have fewer than 250 employees and less than EUR 50 million turnover.[3] Since we do not have data on staff or sales for our deals, we approximate this definition by using enterprise values and EV/Sales multiples. EV/Sales multiples are usually in the range of 1× to 3× and, according to data provided by Aswath Damodaran, the cumulated EV/Sales multiple for Europe is roughly 2×,[4] which in turn translates into an EV of roughly US$100 million[5] when using EUR 50 million sales as a cut-off criterion for defining SMEs. While there is no universally applicable definition of SMEs, we are confident that we correctly capture the enterprise value growth effects of portfolio firms in the SME segment, since our definition is also in line with Nikoskelainen and Wright (2007). They categorise small and medium-sized deals as deals with an enterprise value of less than GBP 100 million[6] by following practitioners' notions.

Table 3 depicts summary statistics for the dependent and independent variables used in this chapter (see Table 2 for detailed definitions of all variables). 39.2% of the portfolio firms in our sample can be classified as SMEs.

3.2.2. *Additional control variables*

For the analyses of the enterprise value growth effects of SME portfolio firms compared to non-SME portfolio firms, we include several

---

[3]Or alternatively, fewer than 250 employees and less than EUR 43 million balance sheet total.

[4]The cumulated multiple is obtained by adding up all company EVs and dividing them by cumulated sales across all sectors; as of January 2018; https://people.stern.nyu.edu/adamodar/New_Home_Page/datacurrent.html.

[5]We disregard minor differences which arise since EVs in different currencies are used for the comparison or are used for the approximation.

[6]*Ibid.*

Table 2. Variable definitions.

	Description
Panel A: Dependent variables full sample	
TEV growth	Annualised growth rate of the portfolio firm's enterprise value from date of entry to date of exit. This measure serves as an approximation of the deal's internal rate of return (IRR) (Arcot *et al.*, 2015). *Source*: BvD Zephyr; Preqin.
Deal rank (5-year)	Percentile rank (normalised between zero and one) with regard to TEV growth rate of a deal, computed across all deals within the same 5-year period (1997–2001, 2002–2006, 2007–2011, and 2012–2016) and geography (Asia, Africa & Middle East, Central Europe, Eastern Europe, Latin America, North America excl. US, Australia and New Zealand, UK, and US). A rank of one indicates the fund with the highest rank (Arcot *et al.*, 2015). *Sources*: BvD Zephyr; Preqin; Own analyses.
Panel B: Independent and control variables	
SME	Indicator variable equal to one if the portfolio firm is a SME, and zero otherwise. To be considered as a small or medium-sized enterprise, the enterprise value (EV) has to be below US$100 million, which is equivalent to a EV/Sales multiple of 2 (assuming Sales of US$50 million as the SME threshold). *Sources*: BvD Zephyr; Preqin.
Buy and build	Indicator variable equal to one if the portfolio firm has engaged in add-on activities after the buyout, and zero otherwise. Source: BvD Zephyr.
HEC ranking	Indicator variable equal to one if at least one of the involved PE firms is included in the HEC-DJ PE performance ranking, and zero otherwise. *Source*: HEC-Dow Jones Private Equity Performance Ranking.

Table 2. (*Continued*)

PEI50 ranking	Indicator variable equal to one if at least one involved PE firm is included in the PEI50 ranking, and zero otherwise. *Source*: Private Equity International.
Public-to-private	Indicator variable equal to one if the portfolio firm's vendor at entry is a publicly listed entity, and zero otherwise. *Source*: BvD Zephyr.
Private-to-private	Indicator variable equal to one if the portfolio has been an independent private firm before the buyout event, and zero otherwise. *Source*: BvD Zephyr.
Divisional	Indicator variable equal to one if the portfolio firm has been a corporate division or subsidiary before the buyout event, and zero otherwise. *Source*: BvD Zephyr.
Financial	Indicator variable equal to one if the portfolio firm's vendor at entry is another PE firm, and zero otherwise. *Source*: BvD Zephyr.
Privatisation	Indicator variable equal to one if the portfolio firm has been a government owned firm before the buyout event, and zero otherwise. *Source*: BvD Zephyr.
Management participation	Indicator variable equal to one if the buyout is labelled as 'management buyout', 'management buy-in' or 'buy-in management buyout' in BvD Zephyr, and zero otherwise. *Note*: Deals with management participation are only included if a PE investor is involved, i.e., pure management buyouts without any PE involvement are excluded. *Source*: BvD Zephyr.
Syndicate	Indicator variable equal to one if more than one PE sponsor backs the deal, and zero otherwise. *Source*: BvD Zephyr.
PF # of prior acq	Variable indicates the total number of acquisitions which the portfolio company has made before the buyout event. *Source*: BvD Zephyr.

(*Continued*)

Table 2. (*Continued*)

Exit channel	Categorical variable indicating whether the buyout was exited via a trade sale, initial public offering (IPO), a management buyout or another subsequent financial buyout. *Sources*: BvD Zephyr; Own analyses.
MBO	Indicator variable equal to one if the buyout is labelled as 'management buyout', in BvD Zephyr, and zero otherwise. *Note*: Deals with management participation are only included if a PE investor is involved, i.e., pure management buyouts without any PE involvement are excluded. *Source*: BvD Zephyr.
VC focus	Indicator variable equal to one if any of the involved PE sponsors in the respective buyout states 'venture capital' among the preferred investment stages, and zero otherwise. *Source*: BvD Zephyr.
Financial market development	Indicator variable equal to one if the country of the buyout target is globally above the 50th percentile based on the 10-year average (2008–2017) of the 'Financial Market Development' index provided by the World Economic Forum (WEF), and zero otherwise. The 'Financial Market Development' index is a subindex of the WEF's 'Global Competitive Index' and captures the availability of credit, equity, debt, insurance, and other financial products, and the stability of a country's financial system. *Source*: World Economic Forum.
ESAF	Indicator variable equal to one if the country of the buyout target is above the 50th percentile based on the 5-year average (2013–2017) country rank of the SME Access to Finance Index (ESAF) provided by the European Investment Fund, and zero otherwise. The ESAF index, is a composite indicator used to monitor SME external financing markets in the 28 EU countries. *Source*: European Investment Fund.

Note: This table presents the definitions and sources of the dependent and independent variables used in this article.

Table 3. Summary statistics of dependent and independent variables.

	N	Mean	S.D.	Q1	Median	Q3
Dependent variables						
TEV growth	2,305	0.214	0.515	−0.028	0.138	0.358
Deal rank (5-year)	2,305	0.502	0.288	0.250	0.502	0.750
Independent and control variables						
SME	2,305	0.392	0.488	0.000	0.000	1.000
Buy and build	2,305	0.352	0.478	0.000	0.000	1.000
HEC ranking	2,305	0.109	0.312	0.000	0.000	0.000
PEI50 ranking	2,305	0.377	0.485	0.000	0.000	1.000
Public-to-private	2,305	0.145	0.353	0.000	0.000	0.000
Private-to-private	2,305	0.210	0.408	0.000	0.000	0.000
Divisional	2,305	0.342	0.475	0.000	0.000	1.000
Financial	2,305	0.260	0.439	0.000	0.000	1.000
Privatisation	2,305	0.005	0.072	0.000	0.000	0.000
Management participation	2,305	0.160	0.366	0.000	0.000	0.000
MBO	2,305	0.143	0.350	0.000	0.000	0.000
Syndicate	2,305	0.207	0.405	0.000	0.000	0.000
PF # of prior acq	2,305	1.179	3.957	0.000	0.000	1.000
Financial market development	2,283	0.965	0.183	1.000	1.000	1.000
ESAF	1,409	0.922	0.268	1.000	1.000	1.000
VC focus	2,305	0.260	0.439	0.000	0.000	1.000

control variables in our multivariate ordinary least squares (OLS) regression model as well as the nearest-neighbor and propensity score matching analyses. These control variables can be clustered into three groups: PE firm characteristics, portfolio firm strategy, and buyout characteristics.

- *PE firm characteristics*: We control for a PE firm's reputation by including the ranking of the PE firm in the PEI50 Ranking. This ranking by Private Equity International (PEI) ranks the top 50 PE firms according to their capital under management. It has been used in several previous studies as a proxy for fund size and reputation (e.g., Boone and Mulherin, 2011; Officer *et al.*, 2010). In addition, we control for a PE firm's past performance by including a PE firm's ranking in the HEC-Dow Jones Ranking. The HEC-Dow Jones (HEC-DJ) Private Equity Performance Ranking ranks

PE firms based on their aggregated internal rate of return of all funds raised. Both the PEI50 variable and the HEC-DJ variable serve as proxies for a PE firm's reputation. Following the argument by Demiroglu and James (2010), these two reputation variables can therefore be seen as an indicator of how good the general partner (GP) is at selecting, monitoring, and restructuring portfolio companies.

- *Portfolio firm characteristics and strategy*: As outlined by Hammer *et al.* (2017), deal enterprise value growth tends to be significantly higher for deals with add-on acquisitions. Hence, we control for a portfolio firm's add-on activities by including an add-on indicator variable, called buy and build. As a company is usually more successful in implementing a buy and build strategy if it already has acquisition experience, we also control for the number of previous acquisitions made by the portfolio company prior to the buyout.
- *Buyout characteristics*: In spirit of Axelson *et al.* (2013), we control for different deal type characteristics, in particular the entry type as well as the exit type of the buyout. These could include privatisation, public-to-private and private-to-private transactions as well as divisional and financial buyouts for the entry of the buyout and trade sales, initial public offering, management buyouts or subsequent financial buyouts for the exit. In addition, we control for the possibility that a deal is carried out by more than one PE firm, i.e., in a syndicate, and the possibility that the incumbent management is involved in the deal (management participation).

4. Empirical Results

4.1. *Enterprise value growth for PE investments in small and medium-sized enterprises*

Based on the theoretical discussion, we are at first interested in potential differences in enterprise value growth rates between SME and non-SME portfolio firms. First, we address this question in a univariate setting. In a second step, we employ a multivariate ordinary least squares (OLS) regression approach followed by a nearest-neighbor and propensity score matching analysis. We discuss these aspects and results in Sections 4.1.1–4.1.3, respectively.

Table 4. Univariate analyses.

	Not SME ($N = 1,402$)	SME ($N = 903$)	Difference
Mean TEV growth	0.105	0.383	0.278***

Notes: This table presents mean differences for the mean enterprise value (TEV) growth with regard to the portfolio firm being a large firm or a SME prior to the initial buyout. Variables are explained in detail in Table 2. Statistical significance is represented at the 1% (***) level.

4.1.1. *Univariate results*

Table 4 shows univariate results for the average enterprise value growth comparing portfolio firms which are among the small and medium-sized enterprises and those which are non-SME. As depicted in Table 4, the enterprise value growth rate is around 38% for SME portfolio firms. This is around 28 percentage points (pp) higher for SME portfolio firms compared to non-SME portfolio firms. This difference is statistically significant at the 1% level and still persists when using the natural logarithm of the enterprise value growth rate instead of absolute enterprise value growth rates (not displayed).

4.1.2. *Multivariate analyses*

In order to further investigate potential differences in the enterprise value growth rate, we employ a multivariate OLS regression approach, controlling for a plethora of PE firm, portfolio firm and deal characteristics as outlined in Section 3.2.2. It is important to control for these factors as a portfolio firm's or PE firm's overall ability can impact the enterprise value growth rate. In addition, we include industry, time, and country fixed effects as well as various combinations of fixed effects (FE) in our model specifications, following Acharya *et al.* (2018) and Goetz *et al.* (2013). This allows us to address spurious results. Such results could for example occur because of time-varying shocks to an industry or a country. We therefore sequentially add country × industry fixed effects, country × entry year FE, industry × entry year FE, and country × industry × entry year FE to our baseline OLS model.

Table 5. Multivariate analyses.

Dependent variable: TEV growth					
	(1)	(2)	(3)	(4)	(5)
SME	0.211*** (0.026)	0.217*** (0.029)	0.204*** (0.032)	0.210*** (0.034)	0.195*** (0.042)
Industry FE	YES	YES	YES	YES	YES
Entry year FE	YES	YES	YES	YES	YES
Country FE	YES	YES	YES	YES	YES
Country × Industry FE	NO	YES	YES	YES	YES
Country × Entry year FE	NO	NO	YES	YES	YES
Industry × Entry year FE	NO	NO	NO	YES	YES
Country × Industry × entry year FE	NO	NO	NO	NO	YES
Constant	YES	YES	YES	YES	YES
Other controls	YES	YES	YES	YES	YES
N	2,305	2,305	2,305	2,305	2,305
R^2	0.23	0.31	0.42	0.48	0.55

Notes: This table presents results of multivariate OLS regression models with industry, time, and country fixed effects. The dependent variable is the enterprise value (TEV) growth for the full sample. SME is an indicator variable equal to one if the portfolio firm is a small or medium-sized enterprise at the initial buyout. Control variables include the involved PE firms' ranking in the HEC-Dow Jones and PEI50 Ranking, the entry type (public-to-private, private-to-private, divisional, financial, and privatisation), deal characteristics (management participation and syndicate), the number of acquisitions made by the portfolio firm prior to the buyout, an indicator variable for add-ons by the portfolio firm after each buyout as well as the exit type of the buyout. Dependent and independent variables are described in Table 2. Robust standard errors are shown in parentheses. ***denotes statistical significance at the 1% level.

Table 5 presents the results for the baseline multivariate OLS regressions with TEV growth as the dependent variable. As can be seen from Table 5 the TEV growth rate increases by up to 21.7 pp if the portfolio firm is a small or medium-sized enterprise. Despite losing many degrees of freedom through the combination of fixed effects, the results are statistically significant at the 1% level for all specifications and thus lend further support to our hypothesis that enterprise value growth rates for SMEs are higher than for non-SMEs and that this difference is also economically significant.

4.1.3. *Nearest neighbour matching and propensity score matching*

One additional concern that needs to be controlled for is that the assignment to treatment and control groups is itself not random (Faccio and Hsu, 2017). This would be the case if SME and non-SME targets differ already on various dimensions such as the buyout year, industry and country of the portfolio firm and the entry type of the buyout prior to the buyout. In order to control for these factors we employ nearest neighbour matching (NNM) and propensity score matching (PSM) analyses. We include the buyout year as well as the portfolio firm's industry and home country as matching criteria to control for potential differences in local market conditions which could lead to differences in returns between SME and non-SME portfolio firms. This approach is in line with Faccio and Hsu (2017), who compare target firms of politically connected and non-connected PE firms. In addition, we control for the entry type of the buyout, e.g., public-to-private, private-to-private, divisional, financial buyout and privatisation, participation of the incumbent management and syndication, i.e., whether more than one PE firm is involved in the deal, in order to reflect potential differences with regard to deal preferences of the involved PE firms. Finally, we control for a portfolio firm's number of previous acquisitions, i.e., acquisitions the portfolio firm made prior to the respective deal, as well as for a PE firm's HEC-DJ ranking and PEI50 ranking in order to reflect a PE firm's previous performance with regard to returns and fundraising.

We start our analyses by employing NNM on the basis of the Mahalanobis distance. This is used to identify non-SME control firms, which are virtually indistinguishable from SME firms with regard to observable attributes. After this matching, we expect these two groups to exhibit the same or at least very similar enterprise value growth characteristics. Next to the NNM, we also carry out a propensity score matching analysis. This procedure was first introduced by Rosenbaum and Rubin (1983). We model treatment assignment (here: being a small or medium-sized enterprise) using a logit regression. Similar to the NNM analysis, the PSM analysis provides us with a non-SME control group of portfolio firms, which exhibit very similar observable characteristics compared to the SME portfolio firms. It is important to note that propensity scores are estimated and not known. In order to account for this, we use the standard errors derived by Abadie and Imbens (2016). We present results for the average treatment effect on the treated (ATET) estimation using 1, 5, and 10 nearest neighbours, in order to account for the trade-off between accuracy (few nearest neighbours) and efficiency (many nearest neighbours).

Table 6 Panel A displays the results of the PSM estimation. As can be seen from the matching diagnostics, our treatment assignment model performs well in explaining cross-sectional variation in SME and non-SME target firms before matching, as the variables *public-to-private, divisional, financial, privatisation, management participation, syndicate, number of previous acquisitions by the portfolio firm, HEC ranking*, and *PEI50 Ranking* significantly discriminate between the two levels of the SME indicator. As can be seen from Table 6 Panel A, none of the coefficients — except for *PEI50 ranking* at the 5% level — is statistically significant after matching, which indicates that the covariates are sufficiently balanced after the matching.

The results for the ATET estimation for the NNM and PSM analyses are depicted in Table 6 Panel B. The dependent variable is the enterprise value growth rate.

As can be seen from Table 6 Panel B, the results of the matching estimators are in line with the univariate and multivariate regression results. There is a strong positive effect on the average enterprise value growth rate for SME portfolio firms between 13.6 pp and 19.4 pp compared to non-SME portfolio firms. These differences are statistically significant. Overall, our results indicate that PE investments in SME portfolio firms lead to higher enterprise value growth rates than investments in non-SME firms. This is in line with our first hypothesis.

4.2. *Identification of additional channels and factors*

After having analysed how the enterprise value growth rates for SME and non-SME portfolio firms differ, we are also interested in potential channels that drive these differences. As outlined in Section 2.3, we focus on four channels which are linked to the specific aspects of

Table 6. Matching estimators for enterprise value growth of SME and non-SME portfolio firms.

Panel A: Matching diagnostics

	Dependent variable: SME	
	Before matching	After matching
Public-to-private	−0.909***	0.116
	(0.330)	(0.333)
Private-to-private	−0.326	−0.029
	(0.298)	(0.317)
Divisional	−1.161***	−0.126
	(0.288)	(0.303)
Financial	−1.670***	−0.077
	(0.296)	(0.302)
Privatisation	−3.351*	−1.398
	(1.729)	(1.381)
Management participation	1.410***	−0.088
	(0.169)	(0.195)
Syndicate	−0.445***	−0.010
	(0.151)	(0.167)
PF # of prior acq	−0.366***	−0.042
	(0.075)	(0.026)
HEC ranking	−0.839***	−0.355
	(0.218)	(0.249)
PEI50 ranking	−1.378***	−0.368**
	(0.128)	(0.145)
Entry year FE	Yes	Yes
Country FE	Yes	Yes
Industry FE	Yes	Yes
N	2,305	2,305

Panel B: Treatment effects

(1) *Nearest neighbour matching (NNM)*

	Dependent variable: TEV growth
ATET with $NN = 1$	0.136**
	(0.068)
ATET with $NN = 5$	0.164***
	(0.050)
ATET with $NN = 10$	0.188***
	(0.036)

(*Continued*)

Table 6. (*Continued*)

(2) *Propensity score matching (PSM)*	
	Dependent variable: TEV growth
ATET with $NN = 1$	0.194***
	(0.041)
ATET with $NN = 5$	0.178***
	(0.042)
ATET with $NN = 10$	0.188***
	(0.032)

Notes: This table presents logit regressions on the unmatched and matched sample in Panel A, as well as the average treatment effect on the treated (ATET) for NNM and PSM estimators in Panel B with varying numbers of nearest neighbours (NNs). In Panel A, the dependent variable is the SME indicator. Omitted category is receivership for the entry channels. The constant is included. Robust standard errors are shown in parentheses. In Panel B, the dependent variable is TEV growth. Robust Abadie-Imbens standard errors are reported in parentheses. ***, **, and * denote statistical significance at the 1%, 5%, and 10% levels, respectively.

investments in SMEs: (i) access to finance in the portfolio firm's home country, (ii) a PE firm's focus on venture capital as investment stage, (iii) fund size, and (iv) management buyouts.

4.2.1. *Access to finance*

Table 7 shows the results of multivariate regressions which include interaction terms of SMEs and the described channels which might drive differences in TEV growth rates between SME and non-SME portfolio firms. We use two separate variables in order to capture access to finance for firms in a particular country. As outlined above, PE firms can fulfil the lender role and thus can potentially alleviate the growth constraint due to worse access to finance which is often experienced by SMEs. Hence, we expect both a high financial market development indicator and a high European Investment Fund SME Access to Finance (ESAF) index to have a negative effect on the TEV growth rates of PE-backed SME investments, as good access to finance potentially removes the need for PE investments. Table 7

Table 7. Interaction terms.

Dependent variable: TEV growth					
	(1)	(2)	(3)	(4)	(5)
SME	0.379***	0.305***	0.191***	0.220***	0.225***
	(0.016)	(0.037)	(0.023)	(0.013)	(0.005)
SME × Financial Market Development	−0.178***				
	(0.007)				
SME × ESAF		−0.111***			
		(0.009)			
SME × VC focus			0.080***		
			(0.003)		
SME × PEI50				−0.039	
				(0.038)	
SME × MBO					−0.124***
					(0.008)
Industry FE	YES	YES	YES	YES	YES
Time FE	YES	YES	YES	YES	YES
Country FE	YES	YES	YES	YES	YES
Constant	YES	YES	YES	YES	YES
Interacted variable stand-alone	YES	YES	YES	YES	YES
Other controls	YES	YES	YES	YES	YES
N	2,283	1,409	2,305	2,305	2,305
R^2	0.22	0.19	0.23	0.23	0.23

Notes: This table presents results of multivariate OLS regression models with industry, time, and country fixed effects. The dependent variable is the mean enterprise value (TEV) growth for the full sample. Control variables include the involved PE firms' ranking in the HEC-Dow Jones ranking, the entry type (public-to-private, private-to-private, divisional, financial, and privatisation), deal characteristics (management participation and syndicate), the number of acquisitions made by the portfolio firm prior to the buyout, an indicator variable for add-ons by the portfolio firm after each buyout as well as the exit type of the buyout. Dependent and independent variables are described in Table 2. Standard errors (clustered by deal type) are shown in parentheses. *** denotes statistical significance at 1% level.

(1) and (2) show that this is indeed the case. Both interaction terms, SME × Financial Market Development and SME × ESAF, have a negative effect on portfolio firms' TEV growth rates. This effect is between 11.1 pp and 17.8 pp and statistically significant at the 1% level.[7] This supports our hypothesis that PE investments in SME portfolio firms located in countries which are characterised by good financing opportunities, lead to lower enterprise value growth than investments in SME portfolio firms which operate in a worse financing environment.

4.2.2. *Private equity firms with venture capital as a preferred investment stage*

Next, we investigate the interaction effect between investments in SME portfolio firms and venture capital as a preferred investment stage for the involved PE firms. As outlined above, a venture capital focus indicates that the PE firm has the necessary expertise to invest in SMEs. A PE firm's venture capital focus has a positive effect of 8 pp on the enterprise value growth rate, as depicted in Table 7 (3), i.e., in case this investment stage is among the preferred investment stages, which often implies frequent investing in smaller firms, positively influences the enterprise value growth of these portfolio firms. Again, this effect is statistically significant at the 1% level and thus lends support to our hypothesis that a PE firm's venture capital focus reinforces the positive enterprise value growth effects of PE investments in SME portfolio firms.

4.2.3. *Fund size*

As outlined above, fund size can also have an effect on the PE investment returns. In order to investigate whether large funds achieve lower enterprise value growth when investing in SMEs, we interact the SME indicator variable with the PEI50 indicator variable in our multivariate regression approach. If a PE firm is ranked in the PEI50,

[7] As financial market development data were not available for 22 deals, the number of observations is reduced to 2,283 for this analysis. As the ESAF indicator is only available for European deals, we carry out this analysis with a sample size of 1,409 observations.

it is among the 50 PE firms with the most capital under management, i.e., a large and prominent fund (e.g., Officer *et al.*, 2010).

As depicted in Table 7 (4), if one of the involved PE firms is ranked in the PEI50, this has a negative effect of 3.9 pp on the enterprise value growth, i.e., if a large fund invests in a small or medium-sized enterprise, the enterprise value growth tends to be lower, albeit with the effect not being statistically significant. This finding weakly supports our hypothesis that SME target companies might simply be too small for large funds. The large funds are not capable of adequately making use of their value creation measures and thus have a negative effect on the enterprise value growth for SME investments. This is in line with Humphery-Jenner (2012), who documents that large funds' returns are lower if they invest in small companies.

4.2.4. *Management buyouts*

Finally, we are interested in the effects of MBO in SME portfolio firms on the enterprise value growth rate of these portfolio firms.

As shown in Table 7 (5), the interaction term SME × MBO has a negative effect of 12.4 pp on the enterprise value growth. This effect is statistically significant at the 1% level. Hence, MBOs underperform other types of buyouts of SMEs, i.e., when the incumbent management acquires a stake in the buyout which is larger than 50% and thereby ultimately has control over decision making, less value is generated than in institutional buyouts. This finding supports our hypothesis that PE firms are better suited to reduce potential managerial inefficiencies in SMEs when they have control over the buyout.

With regard to SME as a stand-alone variable, the coefficient is positive and statistically significant in all five specifications and thus further corroborates our previous finding that enterprise value growth is higher for SME than non-SME portfolio firms.

5. Conclusion

This chapter analyses the enterprise value growth of PE investments in SMEs. Our analyses are based on a sample of 2,305 buyouts, for which enterprise values at entry and exit are available. Our sample spans 20 years and covers 59 countries.

Our results are as follows. We first examine the enterprise value growth of PE buyouts in the SME segment by employing a cross-sectional multivariate regression including a plethora of control variables as well as carrying out a NNM and PSM analysis in order to address potential endogeneity concerns. We find a strong positive effect on the enterprise value growth rate in absolute terms if the portfolio firm is a small or medium-sized enterprise prior to the buyout. Our results are robust to different tests designed to mitigate selection concerns.

Second, we analyse different channels which drive these differences. We document that good access to finance and MBOs have a negative effect on the enterprise value growth of SME portfolio firms, whereas a PE firm's focus on the venture capital investment stage, i.e., expertise in investments in smaller firms, has a positive effect on a SME's enterprise value growth. We also show that large funds have a negative effect on the enterprise value growth of SME portfolio firms and that this effect is more pronounced if we apply a stricter SME definition.

Our study makes various contributions to the existing literature. By documenting that higher enterprise value growth rates can be achieved in both the primary and secondary buyout if the target firm is originally a small or medium-sized enterprise, we add to two main strands of literature: (i) literature on PE returns and (ii) research at the intersection between PE research and research on SMEs.

The findings of our study are interesting for both practitioners and future research. The apparent recent enthusiasm among PE firms regarding the SME segment seems justified as higher enterprise value growth rates can be achieved compared to larger buyouts. Therefore, PE firms may want to pay even more attention to the SME segment in their quest for returns. However, various moderating channels might affect the enterprise value growth of these potential SME portfolio companies and they should also be taken into account when considering SME investments. Future research might take additional factors into account that could potentially drive the enterprise value. This could include prior experience by the lead partners of each deal, i.e., SME expertise on a personal level, as well as a potential size threshold at which portfolio firms become a reasonable investment option for large funds.

References

Abadie, A., and Imbens, G.W. (2016). Matching on the estimated propensity score, *Econometrica* **84**(2), 781–807.

Acharya, V.V., Eisert, T., Eufinger, C., and Hirsch, C. (2018). Real effects of the sovereign debt crisis in Europe: Evidence from syndicated loans, *The Review of Financial Studies* **31**(8), 2855–2896.

Acharya, V.V., Gottschalg, O.F., Hahn, M., and Kehoe, C. (2013). Corporate governance and value creation: Evidence from private equity, *The Review of Financial Studies* **26**(2), 368–402.

Achleitner, A.K., Braun, R., and Engel, N. (2011). Value creation and pricing in buyouts: Empirical evidence from Europe and North America, *Review of Financial Economics* **20**(4), 146–161.

Alperovych, Y., Amess, K., and Wright, M. (2013). Private equity firm experience and buyout vendor source: What is their impact on efficiency?, *European Journal of Operational Research* **228**(3), 601–611.

Anders, G. (1992). The Barbarians in the Boardroom, *Harvard Business Review* **70**(4), 79–87.

Arcot, S., Fluck, Z., Gaspar, J.-M., and Hege, U. (2015). Fund managers under pressure: rationale and determinants of secondary buyouts, *Journal of Financial Economics* **115**(1), 102–135.

Axelson, U., Jenkinson, T., Strömberg, P., and Weisbach, M.S. (2013). Borrow cheap, buy high? The determinants of leverage and pricing in buyouts, *The Journal of Finance* **68**(6), 2223–2267.

Baker, G.P., and Wruck, K.H. (1989). Organizational changes and value creation in leveraged buyouts: The case of the O.M. Scott and Sons Company, *Journal of Financial Economics* **25**(2), 163–190.

Beck, T., Demirgüç-Kunt, A., and Maksimovic, V. (2006). The influence of financial and legal institutions on firm size, *Journal of Banking and Finance* **30**(11), 2995–3015.

Beck, T., Demirgüç-Kunt, A., Laeven, L., and Levine, R. (2008). Finance, firm size, and growth, *Journal of Money, Credit and Banking* **40**(7), 1379–1405.

Berger, A.N., and Udell, G.F. (1998). The economics of small business finance: The roles of private equity and debt markets in the financial growth cycle, *Journal of Banking and Finance* **22**(6–8), 613–673.

Bonini, S. (2015). Secondary buyouts: Operating performance and investment determinants, *Financial Management* **44**(2), 431–470.

Boone, A.L. and Mulherin, J.H. (2011). Do private equity consortiums facilitate collusion in takeover bidding?, *Journal of Corporate Finance* **17**(5), 1475–1495.

Bottazzi, L., Da Rin, M., and Hellmann, T. (2004). Active financial intermediation: Evidence of the role of organizational specialization and human capital, *ECGI Finance Working Paper* Vol. 49.

Braun, R., Jenkinson, T., and Stoff, I. (2017). How persistent is private equity performance? Evidence from deal-level data, *Journal of Financial Economics* **123**(2), 273–291.

Carpenter, R.E., and Petersen, B.C. (2002). Is the growth of small firms constrained by internal finance?, *Review of Economics and Statistics* **84**(2), 298–309.

Chung, J.-W., Sensoy, B.A., Stern, L.H., and Weisbach, M.S. (2012). Pay for performance from future fund flows: The case of private equity, *The Review of Financial Studies* **25**(11), 3259–3304.

Cressy, R., Munari, F., and Malipiero, A. (2007). Playing to their strengths? Evidence that specialization in the private equity industry confers competitive advantage, *Journal of Corporate Finance* **13**(4), 647–669.

Cumming, D., and Dai, N. (2010). Local bias in venture capital investments, *Journal of Empirical Finance* **17**(3), 362–380.

Cumming, D., Fleming, G., and Schwienbacher, A. (2009). Style drift in private equity, *Journal of Business Finance & Accounting* **36**(5–6), 645–678.

Cumming, D., Fleming, G., and Suchard, J.A. (2005). Venture capitalist value-added activities, fundraising and drawdowns, *Journal of Banking & Finance* **29**(2), 295–331.

Cumming, D., Siegel, D.S., and Wright, M. (2007). Private equity, leveraged buyouts and governance, *Journal of Corporate Finance* **13**(4), 439–460.

Demirgüç-Kunt, A., and Maksimovic, V. (1998). Law, finance, and firm growth, *Journal of Finance* **53**(6), 2107–2137.

Demiroglu, C., and James, C.M. (2010). The role of private equity group reputation in LBO financing, *Journal of Financial Economics* **96**(2), 306–330.

Engel, D., and Stiebale, J. (2014). Private equity, investment and financial constraints: firm-level evidence for France and the United Kingdom, *Small Business Economics* **43**(1), 197–212.

European Commission. (2017). Annual Report on European SMEs 2016/2017.

Faccio, M. and Hsu, H.C. (2017). Politically connected private equity and employment, *The Journal of Finance* **72**(2), 539–574.

Fuller-Love, N. (2006). Management development in small firms, *International Journal of Management Reviews* **8**(3), 175–190.

Goetz, M.R., Laeven, L., and Levine, R. (2013). Identifying the valuation effects and agency costs of corporate diversification: Evidence from the geographic diversification of US banks, *The Review of Financial Studies* **26**(7), 1787–1823.

Hammer, B., Knauer, A., Pflücke, M., and Schwetzler, B. (2017). Inorganic growth strategies and the evolution of the private equity business model, *Journal of Corporate Finance*, **45**(1), 31–63.

Harris, R., Siegel, D.S., and Wright, M. (2005). Assessing the impact of management buyouts on economic efficiency: Plant-level evidence from the United Kingdom, *Review of Economics and Statistics* **87**(1), 148–153.

Hite, G.L. and Vetsuypens, M. (1989). Management buyouts of divisions and shareholder wealth, *The Journal of Finance* **44**(4), 953–970.

Humphery-Jenner, M. (2012). Private equity fund size, investment size, and value creation, *Review of Finance* **16**(3), 799–835.

Jensen, M.C. (1989). Eclipse of the public corporation, *Harvard Business Review* **67**(5), 61–74.

Jensen, M.C. and Meckling, W.H. (1976). Theory of the firm: Managerial behavior, agency costs and ownership structure, *Journal of Financial Economics* **3**(4), 305–360.

Kaplan, S. (1989). The effects of management buyouts on operating performance and value, *Journal of Financial Economics* **24**(2), 217–254.

Kaplan, S.N., and Strömberg, P. (2009). Leveraged buyouts and private equity, *Journal of Economic Perspectives* **23**(1), 121–146.

Lopez-de-Silanes, F., Phalippou, L., and Gottschalg, O. (2015). Giants at the gate: Investment returns and diseconomies of scale in private equity, *Journal of Financial and Quantitative Analysis* **50**(3), 377–411.

Nikoskelainen, E. and Wright, M. (2007). The impact of corporate governance mechanisms on value increase in leveraged buyouts, *Journal of Corporate Finance* **13**(4), 511–537.

Officer, M.S., Ozbas, O., and Sensoy, B.A. (2010). Club deals in leveraged buyouts, *Journal of Financial Economics* **98**(2), 214–240.

Paglia, J.K. and Harjoto, M.A. (2014). The effects of private equity and venture capital on sales and employment growth in small and medium-sized businesses, *Journal of Banking & Finance* **47**, 177–197.

Rigamonti, D., Cefis, E., Meoli, M., and Vismara, S. (2016). The effects of the specialization of private equity firms on their exit strategy, *Journal of Business Finance & Accounting* **43**(9–10), 1420–1443.

Robbie, K., Wright, M., and Thompson, S. (1992). Management buy-ins in the UK, *Omega* **20**(4), 445–456.

Rosenbaum, P.R. and Rubin, D.B. (1983). The central role of the propensity score in observational studies for causal effects, *Biometrika* **70**(1), 41–55.

Tykvová, T. and Borell, M. (2012). Do private equity owners increase risk of financial distress and bankruptcy?, *Journal of Corporate Finance* **18**(1), 138–150.

Wright, M., Hoskisson, R.E., Busenitz, L.W., and Dial, J. (2000). Entrepreneurial growth through privatization: The upside of management buyouts, *Academy of Management Review* **25**(3), 591–601.

Wright, M., Renneboog, L., Simons, T., and Scholes, L. (2006). Leveraged buyouts in the UK and Continental Europe: Retrospect and prospect, *Journal of Applied Corporate Finance* **18**(3), 38–55.

Wright, M., Thompson, S., and Robbie, K. (1996). Buy-ins, buy-outs, active investors and corporate governance, *Corporate Governance* **4**(4), 222–234.

PART II
Aspects of Modern Risk Management

https://doi.org/10.1142/9781800611917_0008

Chapter 8

The Risk of the Unseen

Steffi Höse[*,‡] **and Stefan Huschens**[†,§]
[*]*Zittau/Görlitz University of Applied Sciences, Faculty of Business Administration and Economics, Germany*
[†]*Technische Universität Dresden, Faculty of Business and Economics, Germany*
[‡]*s.hoese@hszg.de*
[§]*stefan.huschens@tu-dresden.de*

What statements can be made from a statistical point of view about the probability of the existence of a black swan, if so far only white swans have been observed? We answer this question in the framework of a statistical model of repeated Bernoulli trials. Sixteen point estimates and ten interval estimates for the Bernoulli parameter are given based on different approaches to statistical inference, whereby the variety of methods ranges from the maximum likelihood method to Bayesian methods and ad hoc approaches.

1. Introduction

Events whose occurrence is regarded as a loss by an individual or organisation and whose possible occurrence is therefore perceived as a risk are referred to as risky events. Examples of such risky events are the total failure of a machine, the fatal course of an illness, a fatal accident while climbing a mountain, a plane crash, the default of a borrower, the insolvency of a company, etc. If no occurrence of the risky event has been observed so far, the question arises what can be concluded about the probability of the risky event. In other words: How likely is the occurrence of non-white swans if only white swans have been observed so far? Possible answers to this question from a statistical point of view will be given within the framework of repeated independent Bernoulli trials.

Let $X_1, \ldots, X_n$ be independent and identically Bernoulli distributed random variables with Bernoulli parameter $0 \leq \theta \leq 1$. Then

$$\mathrm{P}(X_i = 1) = 1 - \mathrm{P}(X_i = 0) = \theta \quad \text{for } i = 1, \ldots, n,$$

where the event $\{X_i = 1\}$ indicates a so-called success (occurrence of a risky event) in the ith trial and the parameter θ is the so-called probability of success.

We call the case, where in n trials no success is observed, i.e., $x_1 = 0, \ldots, x_n = 0$, the case of *zero observation*. This case is known in literature as "zero-failure data" (Bailey, 1997; Jiang *et al.*, 2015), "zero occurrence" (Basu *et al.*, 1996; Razzaghi, 2002), "no recorded failures" (Bryant, 2007), "adverse events that have not yet occurred" (Eypasch *et al.*, 1995), "zero numerators" or "no events" (Hanley and Lippman-Hand, 1983), "no defaults observed" (Pluto and Tasche, 2005) and "zero failure data" (Quigley and Revie, 2002). But how relevant is the case of zero observation or how probable or improbable is the occurrence of the event $\{X_1 = 0, \ldots, X_n = 0\}$? Since

$$\mathrm{P}(X_1 = 0, \ldots, X_n = 0) = \prod_{i=1}^{n} \mathrm{P}(X_i = 0) = (1 - \theta)^n,$$

the answer depends on the number of trials n and on the probability of success θ and is given in Table 1 for different possible constellations of n and θ. The probabilities in Table 1 show for many combinations of n and θ a — perhaps surprisingly — high probability of the case of zero observation.

In the following, we assume that the number n of observations is fixed and known, whereas the Bernoulli parameter θ is unknown. At first glance, in this situation, there is no hope to carry out any statistical inferences about θ. This raises the question: What kind of statistical inference on the Bernoulli parameter θ is possible, if the event $\{X_1 = 0, \ldots, X_n = 0\}$ has been realised and therefore $x_1 = 0, \ldots, x_n = 0$ has been observed? We approach this question within the framework of a statistical model for a finite or infinite sequence of independent homogeneous Bernoulli trials or experiments.

Table 1. Probability of the event $\{X_1 = 0, \dots, X_n = 0\}$ for different constellations of n and θ.

Number of trials, n	Probability of success θ						
	0.001	0.01	0.02	0.05	0.1	0.15	0.2
1	0.999	0.99	0.98	0.95	0.9	0.85	0.8
5	0.995	0.951	0.904	0.774	0.590	0.444	0.328
10	0.990	0.904	0.817	0.599	0.349	0.197	0.107
20	0.980	0.818	0.668	0.358	0.122	0.039	0.012
40	0.961	0.669	0.446	0.129	0.015	0.002	10^{-4}
100	0.905	0.366	0.133	0.006	$3 \cdot 10^{-5}$	$9 \cdot 10^{-8}$	$2 \cdot 10^{-10}$

1.1. *Statistical model*

Let X_i for $i = 1, 2, \dots$ be independent and identically Bernoulli distributed random variables with Bernoulli parameter $0 \leq \theta \leq 1$. This means $\text{Law}[X_i] = \text{Ber}(\theta)$ for $i = 1, 2, \dots,$ where θ is the probability of success.

1.2. *Multivariate Bernoulli distribution*

In this statistical model, the probability distribution of random vector $(X_1, \dots, X_n)$ is a multivariate Bernoulli distribution with

$$\begin{aligned} \mathrm{P}(X_1 = x_1, \dots, X_n = x_n) &= \theta^k (1-\theta)^{n-k} \\ &\text{for } (x_1, \dots, x_n) \in \{0,1\}^n, \end{aligned} \tag{1}$$

where $k \stackrel{\text{def}}{=} \sum_{i=1}^n x_i$ and $0^0 \stackrel{\text{def}}{=} 1$. In this context, n is the number of trials and k the number of observed successes. It should be noted that the observed values $x_1, \dots, x_n$ enter the probabilities in (1) only via k. Any statistical inference on θ that is based on the probabilities in (1) can therefore be performed with the sufficient statistic $K \stackrel{\text{def}}{=} \sum_{i=1}^n X_i$ describing the random number of successes. Since

$$k = 0 \iff x_1 = \cdots = x_n = 0,$$

the case of zero observation $x_1 = 0, \dots, x_n = 0$ is given more compactly by the specification $k = 0$.

1.3. *Binomial distribution*

The random number K of successes in n Bernoulli trials follows a binomial distribution with parameters n and θ, $\mathrm{Law}[K] = \mathrm{Bin}(n, \theta)$, and probabilities

$$\mathrm{P}(K = k) = \binom{n}{k} \theta^k (1-\theta)^{n-k} \quad \text{for } k \in \{0, 1, \dots, n\}. \tag{2}$$

Thus, the Bernoulli parameter of interest θ becomes a parameter of the binomial distribution. For $0 < \theta < 1$, all probabilities in (2) are positive. For $\theta = 0$ and $\theta = 1$, the corresponding binomial distributions of K are degenerated with $\mathrm{P}(K = 0) = 1$ if $\theta = 0$ and $\mathrm{P}(K = n) = 1$ if $\theta = 1$. The random number of failures, i.e., trials without success, is $n - K$ and also follows a binomial distribution, $\mathrm{Law}[n - K] = \mathrm{Bin}(n, 1 - \theta)$.

1.4. *Negative binomial distribution*

Let Y denote the number of failures (zeros) before the first success (one) occurs in a sequence of Bernoulli trials $X_1, X_2, \dots$. Then for $0 < \theta \leq 1$, the random variable Y follows a negative binomial distribution with parameters $r = 1$ and θ, $\mathrm{Law}[Y] = \mathrm{negBin}(1, \theta)$, and probabilities

$$\mathrm{P}(Y = y) = \theta(1-\theta)^y \quad \text{for } y \in \{0, 1, \dots\}. \tag{3}$$

For $\theta = 0$, it holds that $\mathrm{P}(X_1 = X_2 = \cdots = 0) = 1$ and therefore with probability one, no success will be observed.

2. Point Estimation in Case of Zero Observation

In the following, point estimates for parameter θ in case of zero observation $k = 0$ in n independent Bernoulli trials are given: The first estimate is the maximum likelihood estimate. Six further estimates are based on Bayesian estimation with uniform prior distribution or on Jeffrey's non-informative prior distribution, whereby mean, median or mode of the posterior distribution are used as point estimates, respectively. Three other estimates are motivated by a principle of prudence and are based on upper confidence limits. Two further estimates are minimax estimates, which are based on the principle of risk aversion. Whereas these twelve estimates are derived from general estimation principles, four further estimates are based on ad hoc approaches for the case of zero observation without obvious or stringent generalisation to cases with $k > 0$.

2.1. *Maximum likelihood estimate*

For a given realisation $k \in \{0, 1, \ldots, n\}$ of the random variable K with distribution $\mathrm{Bin}(n, \theta)$, the likelihood function $L_k : [0, 1] \to [0, 1]$ is defined as

$$L_k(\theta) = \binom{n}{k} \theta^k (1-\theta)^{n-k}, \quad 0 \le \theta \le 1.$$

These are the probabilities from (2) interpreted as function of θ for fixed k. For the zero observation $k = 0$, the likelihood function is

$$L_0(\theta) = (1-\theta)^n, \quad 0 \le \theta \le 1,$$

which is maximised by the likelihood estimate

$$t_1^\circ = \arg \max_{0 \le \theta \le 1} (1-\theta)^n = 0. \tag{4}$$

It should be noted that estimate $t_1^\circ = 0$ is not a regular likelihood estimate, since the likelihood function $L_0(\theta)$ has no horizontal tangent at $\theta = 0$.

2.2. *Bayesian estimates with uniform prior and with non-informative prior*

In the Bayesian approach to statistical inference, the parameter θ is seen as a realisation of a random variable $\tilde{\theta}$. In this approach, a two-dimensional probability distribution for the random vector $(\tilde{\theta}, K)$ defines the statistical model. Thereby, the marginal distribution of $\tilde{\theta}$ is the so-called prior distribution, which concentrates the probability mass on the interval $[0, 1]$, i.e., $\mathrm{P}(\tilde{\theta} \in [0, 1]) = 1$. For the conditional distributions of K given $\tilde{\theta} = \theta$, it holds that

$$\mathrm{Law}[K | \tilde{\theta} = \theta] = \mathrm{Bin}(n, \theta), \quad 0 \le \theta \le 1.$$

The conditional distribution of $\tilde{\theta}$ given a realisation k of random variable K, $\mathrm{Law}[\tilde{\theta} | K = k]$, is the so-called posterior distribution of $\tilde{\theta}$

after k is observed. The posterior distribution given k can be derived from the prior distribution and the likelihood function $L_k(\theta)$ via the Bayesian theorem. The Bayesian inference can be summarised by the transformation

$$\text{(prior distribution, observation)} \mapsto \text{posterior distribution.} \qquad (5)$$

The textbook case of Bayesian estimation in the binomial model uses beta distributions as prior distributions. If the prior distribution of $\tilde{\theta}$ is a beta distribution $\text{Beta}(c, d)$ with parameters $c > 0$ and $d > 0$, i.e.,

$$\text{Law}[\tilde{\theta}] = \text{Beta}(c, d),$$

then the posterior distribution of $\tilde{\theta}$ is also a beta distribution but with altered parameters, i.e.,

$$\text{Law}[\tilde{\theta}|K = k] = \text{Beta}(k + c, n - k + d).$$

This means that beta distributions build a so-called conjugated family of distributions for this application of Bayesian estimation. In this case, the transformation (5) specialises in

$$(\text{Beta}(c, d), k) \mapsto \text{Beta}(k + c, n - k + d). \qquad (6)$$

The case of zero observation $k = 0$ leads together with prior distribution $\text{Beta}(c, d)$ via Bayesian transformation rule (6) to posterior distribution $\text{Beta}(c, n+d)$. As one can see, the zero observation alters only the value of the second parameter.

2.2.1. *Uniform prior distribution*

For $c = d = 1$, the prior beta distribution $\text{Beta}(1, 1)$ is the uniform distribution on $[0, 1]$. The uniform distribution is often used when there is no prior information about whether certain parameter ranges have a greater a priori probability than others.

In case of zero observation $k = 0$, the posterior distribution

$$\text{Law}[\tilde{\theta}|K = 0] = \text{Beta}(1, n + 1) \qquad (7)$$

results. In general, three possible estimates for θ are the mean, the median and the mode of the posterior distribution. For the posterior distribution in (7), the *mean* is

$$t_2^\circ = \mathbb{E}[\tilde{\theta}|K = 0] = \frac{1}{n+2}, \tag{8}$$

the *median* is

$$t_3^\circ = \mathrm{Med}[\tilde{\theta}|K = 0] = 1 - (1/2)^{\frac{1}{n+1}}, \tag{9}$$

and the *mode* is

$$t_4^\circ = \mathrm{Mode}[\tilde{\theta}|K = 0] = 0. \tag{10}$$

Equations (8)–(10) follow from (A.1), (A.3) and (A.4) obeying that the parameters of the posterior distribution are 1 and $n+1$. The estimate t_4° coincides with the maximum likelihood estimate $t_1^\circ = 0$ from (4).

2.2.2. *Jeffrey's prior*

The beta distribution with $c = d = 1/2$ is known as Jeffrey's prior or non-informative prior for the estimation of the binomial parameter θ (Jeffrey, 1945). In case of zero observation $k = 0$, the posterior distribution

$$\mathrm{Law}[\tilde{\theta}|K = 0] = \mathrm{Beta}(1/2, n + 1/2) \tag{11}$$

results. Three possible estimates for θ based on zero observation are the *mean*

$$t_5^\circ = \mathbb{E}[\tilde{\theta}|K = 0] = \frac{1}{2(n+1)}, \tag{12}$$

the *median*

$$t_6^\circ = \mathrm{Med}[\tilde{\theta}|K = 0] = B_{1/2,n+1/2,1/2}, \tag{13}$$

and the *mode*

$$t_7^\circ = \mathrm{Mode}[\tilde{\theta}|K = 0] = 0 \tag{14}$$

of the posterior distribution in (11). In (13), $B_{c,d,p}$ denotes the p-quantile of $\mathrm{Beta}(c, d)$. Equations (12) and (14) follow from (A.1) and (A.5) obeying that the parameters of the posterior distribution are $1/2$ and $n + 1/2$. The estimate t_5° is used in the context of rare cancer observations (Basu *et al.*, 1996). Unlike in t_3°, the median t_6° has no explicit algebraic representation, but can numerically evaluated, compare (A.2). The estimate t_7° coincides with the maximum likelihood estimate $t_1^\circ = 0$ from (4).

The choice between mean, median and mode in (8)–(10) and in (12)–(14) of the posterior distribution is not arbitrary, but should depend on the loss function of the decision maker. The error loss function

$$\ell(\theta, t) = (t - \theta)^2$$

leads to the mean, the error loss function

$$\ell(\theta, t) = |t - \theta|$$

leads to a median and the error loss function

$$\ell(\theta, t) = \begin{cases} 0 & \text{if } |t - \theta| \leq c \\ 1 & \text{if } |t - \theta| > c \end{cases}$$

with $c > 0$ leads for $c \to 0$ to a mode of the posterior distribution (Lehmann and Casella, 1998, Corollary 1.2, p. 228).

2.3. *Upper confidence bounds as estimates*

Motivated by a principle of prudence, an upper confidence bound U for Bernoulli parameter θ with given high confidence level $1 - \alpha$ can be interpreted as conservative point estimate for θ, since $U \geq \theta$ holds at least with probability $1 - \alpha$. In the following, three upper confidence bounds based on the exact binomial distribution of K and its approximating Poisson and normal distribution, each with confidence level 95%, are used as conservative point estimates for θ.

2.3.1. *"Most prudent" estimate*

In the context of credit risk, Pluto and Tasche (2005) suggest for a given confidence level $1 - \alpha$ the upper confidence bound $1 - \alpha^{1/n}$, cp. (24), as the "most prudent" estimate for θ in case of zero observation. Usually, $\alpha = 5\%$ is used corresponding to the confidence level 95% and leads to the estimate

$$t_8^\circ = 1 - 0.05^{\frac{1}{n}}$$

for parameter θ in case of zero observation. This estimate for θ is also known in technical and biometrical applications (Eypasch *et al.*, 1995; Hanley and Lippman-Hand, 1983; Razzaghi, 2002).

2.3.2. *"Rule of three" estimate*

A binomial distribution $\mathrm{Bin}(n, \theta)$ can be approximated by a Poisson distribution with parameter $\lambda = n\theta$. In case of zero observation, an upper confidence bound with confidence level $1 - \alpha$ for the intensity parameter λ of a Poisson distribution is $-\ln(\alpha)$. For $\alpha = 0.05$ the value is $-\ln(0.05) \approx 2.9957$. When rounded off to two decimal places, the upper confidence bound 3 with confidence level 95% results for Poisson parameter λ. This bound is also known as "Höchstens-drei-Regel" (no more than three rule) (Hedderich and Sachs, 2020, p. 374) or Hanley's estimate (Hanley and Lippman-Hand, 1983; Quigley and Revie, 2002). The upper confidence bound 3 for Poisson parameter λ leads to the approximate upper confidence bound $3/n$ for parameter θ. This motivates the "rule of three" estimate $3/n$ (Eypasch *et al.*, 1995; Hanley and Lippman-Hand, 1983). For $n < 3$, this estimate has to be improved, resulting in the new estimate

$$t_9^\circ = \min\left\{1, \frac{3}{n}\right\}$$

for parameter θ in case of zero observation.

2.3.3. *Normal approximation estimate*

A binomial distribution $\mathrm{Bin}(n, \theta)$ can be approximated by a normal distribution with the same mean $n\theta$ and variance $n\theta(1-\theta)$. From the assumption $\mathrm{Law}[K] = \mathrm{N}(n\theta, n\theta(1-\theta))$ the upper confidence bound

$$U = \frac{2K + z_{1-\alpha}^2 + z_{1-\alpha}\sqrt{z_{1-\alpha}^2 + 4K(1 - K/n)}}{2(n + z_{1-\alpha}^2)}$$

for θ with confidence level $1 - \alpha$ can be derived, where z_p denotes the p-quantile of the standard normal distribution. U is obtained by taking the upper limit of the confidence interval with symmetrical allocation of α given in literature, e.g., Blyth and Still (1983, Eq. (2.1)), and by replacing $\alpha/2$ with α.

For the observed value $k = 0$, the value

$$u = \frac{z_{1-\alpha}^2}{n + z_{1-\alpha}^2}$$

of the upper confidence bound U results, which gives for $\alpha = 0.05$ and $z_{0.95}^2 \approx 2.7055$ the estimate

$$t_{10}^{\circ} = \frac{z_{0.95}^2}{n + z_{0.95}^2} \approx \frac{2.7055}{n + 2.7055}$$

for parameter θ in case of zero observation (Bailey, 1997, p. 376).

2.4. *Minimax estimates*

Risk adverse estimates result from the concept of minimax estimation. Using the *squared error loss function* $(t-\theta)^2$, the random variable

$$T_{11} = \frac{2K + \sqrt{n}}{2(n + \sqrt{n})}$$

is the unique minimax estimator for parameter θ of the binomial distribution (Lehmann and Casella, 1998, p. 312), which is also admissible (Lehmann and Casella, 1998, p. 336). In case of zero observation $k = 0$, this minimax estimator leads to the estimate

$$t_{11}^{\circ} = \frac{1}{2(1 + \sqrt{n})}$$

for parameter θ (Razzaghi, 2002, p. 329).

If the *weighted squared error loss function* $(t-\theta)^2/(\theta(1-\theta))$ is used instead, the minimax estimator

$$T_{12} = \frac{K}{n}$$

is obtained for parameter θ. For the observed value $k = 0$, this results in the estimate

$$t_{12}^{\circ} = 0$$

for parameter θ (Lehmann and Casella, 1998, p. 312). A comparison of estimates t_{11}° and t_{12}° shows that the minimax property depends strongly on the selected error loss function.

2.5. *Ad hoc estimates with zero observation*

We call the next estimates ad hoc estimates, since they are based on ad hoc approaches for the case of zero observation $k = 0$ without any obvious or stringent generalisations to cases with $k > 0$. Therefore, these estimates cannot be interpreted as realisations of corresponding estimators.

2.5.1. *"Upper bound" estimate*

The "one-failure case", in which the maximum likelihood estimate of θ is $1/n$, can be seen as an "reasonable upper bound" for the "zero-failure case" (Bailey, 1997, p. 376). This motivates the "upper bound" estimate

$$t_{13}^{\circ} = \frac{1}{n} \tag{15}$$

for parameter θ in case of zero observation.

2.5.2. *"One-third" estimate*

"One estimator for λ in the case where zero failures have been observed in time period Δt is given by $\hat{\lambda} = \frac{1/3}{\Delta t}$" (Bailey, 1997, p. 376), where λ is the intensity parameter of a Poisson distribution. This argument, which is not understandable per se, is supported by a reference (Welker and Lipow, 1974) that is not accessible to us. Equating $\Delta t = 1$ and $\lambda = n\theta$, which is motivated by the approximation of a binomial distribution by a Poisson distribution, yields the "one-third" estimate

$$t_{14}^{\circ} = \frac{1}{3n}$$

for parameter θ in case of zero observation (Bailey, 1997, p. 376).

2.5.3. *Probability 1/2 estimate*

The idea of this estimate is to determine the parameter value θ which, for given n and given zero observation $k = 0$, satisfies

$\mathrm{P}(K=0)=1/2$ with $\mathrm{Law}[K]=\mathrm{Bin}(n,\theta)$. This procedure leads to the estimate

$$t_{15}^{\circ}=1-(1/2)^{\frac{1}{n}}$$

for parameter θ in case of zero observation. This approach seems to be "currently limited to the risk analyses of energetic initiation in the explosives testing field" (Bailey, 1997, p. 375). Formally, estimate t_{15}° can be seen as a special case of the upper confidence bound $1-\alpha^{1/n}$ in (24) for $\alpha=1/2$.

2.5.4. *Pessimistic estimate*

The pessimistic estimate for θ is motivated by negative binomial sampling, where a sequence of Bernoulli trials is observed as long as the first success occurs. Let Y denote the number of failures (zeros) before the first success (one) occurs. If the given sample information is $x_1=0,\ \ldots,\ x_n=0$ and no additional information about $X_{n+1},X_{n+2},\ldots$ is available, then this means that the event $\{Y\geq n\}$ has occurred. This event has probability

$$\mathrm{P}(Y\geq n)=\mathrm{P}(X_1=0,\ldots,X_n=0)=(1-\theta)^n.$$

Maximising this probability with respect to θ in the sense of likelihood estimation leads to

$$\sup_{0<\theta\leq 1}(1-\theta)^n=1=\lim_{\theta\downarrow 0}(1-\theta)^n,$$

but $\theta=0$ makes no sense in the context of negative binomial sampling.

Therefore, if one assumes any hypothetical observed value $y\geq n$, then the corresponding maximum likelihood estimate of θ is, compare (3),

$$\arg\max_{0<\theta\leq 1}\theta(1-\theta)^y=\frac{1}{y+1}.$$

The resulting set of maximum likelihood estimates for possible values $y\geq n$ is

$$\left\{\frac{1}{n+1},\frac{1}{n+2},\ldots\right\}.$$

A conservative approach takes the largest estimate in this set and leads to

$$t_{16}^{\circ} = \frac{1}{n+1}$$

as estimate for parameter θ in case of zero observation. For large n, this pessimistic estimate is close to $t_{13}^{\circ} = 1/n$ from (15). However, for small n, t_{16}° seems to be more plausible than t_{13}°, since (15) leads to estimate $t_{13}^{\circ} = 1$ for parameter θ in case of $n = 1$ and observed value $x_1 = 0$. But $\theta = 1$ implies $\mathrm{P}(X_1 = 0) = 0$, which gives the event $\{X_1 = 0\}$ the probability zero.

Clearly, the idea behind t_{16}° corresponds to the very pessimistic view that after n observed zeros the next trial leads to a one. A more optimistic view may expect further n observed zeros followed by a one in the $(2n+1)$th trial. Then the maximum likelihood estimate $1/(2n+1)$ results, which is close to estimate $t_5^{\circ} = 1/(2n+2)$ in (12) based on Jeffrey's non-informative prior.

2.6. *Comparison of point estimates*

In the previous subsections, 16 different point estimates t_1° to t_{16}° for the parameter θ in case of zero observation in n independent Bernoulli trials are presented. Whereas $t_1^{\circ} = t_4^{\circ} = t_7^{\circ} = t_{12}^{\circ} = 0$ for all $n \in \mathbb{N}$, all other estimates are positive for all $n \in \mathbb{N}$ but strictly decreasing in n with

$$\lim_{n\to\infty} t_i^{\circ} = 0 \quad \text{for } i \in \{2, 3, 5, 6, 8, \ldots, 11, 13, \ldots, 16\}.$$

In Table 2, the estimates t_1° to t_{16}° are contrasted for different numbers $n \in \{1, 5, 10, 50, 100, 1000\}$ of observed zeros. The first group contains the four estimates which are always zero and therefore do not depend on the number n of observed zeros. These are the maximum likelihood estimate, the two Bayesian estimates using the mode of the respective posterior distribution and the minimax estimate with weighted squared error loss function. The second group is made up of Bayesian estimates using mean and median of the posterior distribution. The third group contains estimates derived from upper confidence bounds. The fourth group consists of the minimax estimate with squared error loss function and the last group contains the ad hoc estimates.

Table 2. Point estimates of θ with zero observation depending on the observed number of zeros.

	Number n of observed zeros					
Point estimate of θ	1	5	10	50	100	1000
$t_1^\circ = t_4^\circ = t_7^\circ = t_{12}^\circ = 0$	0	0	0	0	0	0
$t_2^\circ = \frac{1}{n+2}$	0.3333	0.1429	0.0833	0.0192	0.0098	0.0010
$t_3^\circ = 1 - (1/2)^{\frac{1}{n+1}}$	0.2929	0.1091	0.0611	0.0135	0.0068	0.0007
$t_5^\circ = \frac{1}{2(n+1)}$	0.2500	0.0833	0.0455	0.0098	0.0050	0.0005
$t_6^\circ = B_{1/2,n+1/2,1/2}$ [a]	0.1632	0.0423	0.0219	0.0045	0.0023	0.0002
$t_8^\circ = 1 - 0.05^{\frac{1}{n}}$	0.9500	0.4507	0.2589	0.0582	0.0295	0.0030
$t_9^\circ = \min\{1, \frac{3}{n}\}$	1.0000	0.6000	0.3000	0.0600	0.0300	0.0030
$t_{10}^\circ = \frac{z_{0.95}^2}{n+z_{0.95}^2} \approx \frac{2.7055}{n+2.7055}$ [b]	0.7301	0.3511	0.2129	0.0513	0.0263	0.0027
$t_{11}^\circ = \frac{1}{2(1+\sqrt{n})}$	0.2500	0.1545	0.1201	0.0619	0.0455	0.0153
$t_{13}^\circ = \frac{1}{n}$	1.0000	0.2000	0.1000	0.0200	0.0100	0.0010
$t_{14}^\circ = \frac{1}{3n}$	0.3333	0.0667	0.0333	0.0067	0.0033	0.0003
$t_{15}^\circ = 1 - (1/2)^{\frac{1}{n}}$	0.5000	0.1294	0.0670	0.0138	0.0069	0.0007
$t_{16}^\circ = \frac{1}{n+1}$	0.5000	0.1667	0.0909	0.0196	0.0099	0.0010

[a] $B_{c,d,p}$ denotes the p-quantile of beta distribution Beta(c, d).
[b] z_p denotes the p-quantile of the standard normal distribution.

In case $n = 1$, all positive estimates take their maximum value and these values range from 16.32% for the Bayesian estimate t_6° with non-informative prior to 100% for the "rule of three" estimate t_9° and the "upper bound" estimate t_{13}°. Among the positive estimates, t_6° is the uniformly smallest estimate for all specified n. For $n \in \{1, 5, 10\}$ the "rule of three" estimate t_9° is the largest and for $n \in \{50, 100, 1000\}$ the risk-adverse estimate t_{11}° based on the concept of minimax estimation with squared error loss function is the largest. For $n \geq 1000$, all estimates are less than or equal to 1.53%, but the smallest positive estimate t_6° and the largest estimate t_{11}° differ by a factor of 76.5. It is also noteworthy that the estimates t_3° and t_6° differ by a factor of 3.5 for $n = 1000$. Both are medians of posterior distributions, derived with the uniform prior and Jeffrey's prior, respectively. In contrast to the uniform prior, Jeffrey's prior gives more weight to the ends of the parameter range, which favours parameter values close to zero or one more than the uniform prior. The estimate t_{16}° suggested here for the first time corrects the not very plausible behaviour of the "upper bound" estimate t_{13}° for small n and integrates well into the numerical range of the other estimates. Nevertheless, point estimates are only a first step of statistical inference and should be supplemented by interval estimates to quantify the accuracy of the estimation.

3. Interval Estimation in Case of Zero Observation

Three types of interval estimates are considered: firstly, likelihood intervals for the unknown parameter θ based on the likelihood function, secondly, credible intervals as probability intervals for θ based on the posterior distribution of the Bayesian inference approach and thirdly, confidence intervals for θ based on estimators that provide stochastic lower and upper bounds for the unknown parameter.

3.1. *Likelihood intervals*

In case of zero observation $k = 0$ in n independent Bernoulli trials, the likelihood function

$$L_0(\theta) = (1-\theta)^n$$

has maximum value

$$L_{\max} = \max_{0\leq\theta\leq 1}(1-\theta)^n = 1,$$

which is reached for $\theta = 0$. A $(1-\alpha)$-likelihood set consists of all parameter values θ for which the likelihood $L_0(\theta)$ is greater than or equal to $\alpha L_{\max}$. In this context, the $(1-\alpha)$-likelihood set is

$$\begin{aligned} &\{\theta \in [0,1] \mid L_0(\theta) \geq \alpha L_{\max}\} \\ &\quad = \{\theta \in [0,1] \mid (1-\theta)^n \geq \alpha\} = [0, 1-\alpha^{1/n}]. \end{aligned}$$

Therefore,

$$I_1^{\circ} = [0, 1-\alpha^{1/n}] \tag{16}$$

is a $(1-\alpha)$-likelihood interval (Pawitan, 2013, p. 38) which contains the most plausible parameter values and excludes parameter values with small likelihood $L_0(\theta) < \alpha L_{\max}$.

3.2. *Credible intervals*

In the Bayesian approach to statistical inference, credible intervals are probability intervals for the unknown parameter based on the posterior distribution so that the random parameter $\tilde{\theta}$ takes values in these intervals with posterior probability $1-\alpha$.

3.2.1. *Uniform prior*

Using a uniform prior, the posterior distribution $\text{Beta}(1, n+1)$ results in case of zero observation $k = 0$ in n independent Bernoulli trials. With the p-quantiles $B_{1,n+1,p}$ of this special beta distribution, which are explicitly given by (A.3), a lower credible interval with credibility $1-\alpha$ can be derived as

$$I_2^{\circ} = [B_{1,n+1,\alpha}, 1] = [1-(1-\alpha)^{1/(n+1)}, 1], \tag{17}$$

and an upper credible interval with credibility $1-\alpha$ can be derived as

$$I_3^{\circ} = [0, B_{1,n+1,1-\alpha}] = [0, 1-\alpha^{1/(n+1)}] \tag{18}$$

(Pires and Amado, 2008, Table 1, Method II). A two-sided central interval with credibility $1-\alpha$ and symmetrical allocation of α is

$$\begin{aligned} I_4^{\circ} &= \left[B_{1,n+1,\alpha/2}, B_{1,n+1,1-\alpha/2}\right] \\ &= [1-(1-\alpha/2)^{1/(n+1)}, 1-\alpha/2^{1/(n+1)}]. \end{aligned} \tag{19}$$

The corresponding posterior probabilities are

$$\text{P}(\tilde{\theta} \in I_2^{\circ}|K=0) = \text{P}(\tilde{\theta} \in I_3^{\circ}|K=0) = \text{P}(\tilde{\theta} \in I_4^{\circ}|K=0) = 1-\alpha.$$

3.2.2. *Jeffrey's prior*

Using Jeffrey's prior, also known as non-informative prior, the posterior distribution $\text{Beta}(1/2, n+1/2)$ results in case of zero observation $k = 0$ in n independent Bernoulli trials. Then a lower credible interval with credibility $1-\alpha$ is

$$I_5^{\circ} = \left[B_{1/2,n+1/2,\alpha}, 1\right] \tag{20}$$

and an upper credible interval with credibility $1-\alpha$ is

$$I_6^\circ = \left[0, B_{1/2,n+1/2,1-\alpha}\right]. \tag{21}$$

A two-sided central interval with credibility $1-\alpha$ and symmetrical allocation of α is

$$I_7^\circ = \left[B_{1/2,n+1/2,\alpha/2}, B_{1/2,n+1/2,1-\alpha/2}\right] \tag{22}$$

(Brown *et al.*, 2002, Eq. (3.3)). The corresponding posterior probabilities are

$$\mathrm{P}(\tilde{\theta} \in I_5^\circ | K=0) = \mathrm{P}(\tilde{\theta} \in I_6^\circ | K=0) = \mathrm{P}(\tilde{\theta} \in I_7^\circ | K=0) = 1-\alpha.$$

3.3. *Confidence intervals*

In an application-driven perspective, the goal may be to use either a two-sided confidence interval $[L, U]$ or a one-sided confidence interval $[L, 1]$ with lower confidence bound L or $[0, U]$ with upper confidence bound U. The choice of interval depends on the particular issue in substance science.

In an alternative method-driven perspective, a confidence set may be requested as a supplement to the point estimate in order to give additional information about the accuracy of the point estimation. Then, the shape of the confidence set depends on the distribution of the random observations or of a sufficient statistic and may be a one- or two-sided interval or a more complex set.

3.3.1. *Lower one-sided confidence interval*

A lower confidence bound L for Bernoulli parameter θ with given confidence level $1-\alpha$ is a random variable depending on K with

$$\mathrm{P}(0 \le L \le \theta) \ge 1-\alpha \quad \text{for all } 0 \le \theta \le 1.$$

Since $\mathrm{P}(K=0)=1$ for $\theta=0$, the value l of an lower confidence bound L for θ based on zero observation $k=0$ is $l=0$. Therefore, the value of a lower one-sided confidence interval for θ based on zero observation is

$$I_8^\circ = [l, 1] = [0, 1]. \tag{23}$$

3.3.2. *Upper one-sided confidence interval*

An upper confidence bound U for Bernoulli parameter θ with given confidence level $1-\alpha$ is a random variable depending on K with

$$\mathrm{P}(\theta \leq U \leq 1) \geq 1-\alpha \quad \text{for all } 0 \leq \theta \leq 1.$$

The value u of an upper confidence bound U for θ based on zero observation $k=0$ is

$$u = 1-\alpha^{1/n}. \tag{24}$$

Therefore, the value of an upper one-sided confidence interval for θ based on zero observation is

$$I_9^\circ = [0, u] = [0, 1-\alpha^{1/n}]. \tag{25}$$

The interval estimates I_9° and I_1° are identical.

3.3.3. *Two-sided confidence interval*

If lower and upper confidence bounds L and U with symmetrical allocation of probability α and with

$$\mathrm{P}(L > \theta) \leq \alpha/2, \quad \mathrm{P}(\theta > U) \leq \alpha/2 \quad \text{and} \quad \mathrm{P}(L \leq \theta \leq U) \geq 1-\alpha$$

are used, then the value

$$I_{10}^\circ = [0, 1-(\alpha/2)^{1/n}] \tag{26}$$

of a two-sided confidence interval for θ based on zero observation results (Pires and Amado, 2008, Eq. (2.3)).

3.4. *Comparison of interval estimates*

In the previous subsections, 10 different interval estimates I_1° to I_{10}° for the parameter θ in case of zero observation in n independent Bernoulli trials are presented. These estimates are contrasted in Table 3 for the frequently used value $1-\alpha = 95\%$ and different numbers $n \in \{1, 10, 100, 1000\}$ of observed zeros. The table contains three groups of intervals: four two-sided intervals build the first group, three lower intervals build the second group and three upper intervals build the third group. Since the lower intervals are formed on the basis of lower bounds for θ, the upper limit for these intervals is always one resulting from the general restriction $\theta \leq 1$. The upper

Table 3. Interval estimates of θ with zero observation for $1-\alpha = 95\%$ depending on the observed number of zeros.

Interval estimate of θ	Number n of observed zeros			
	1	10	100	1000
I_1°, cp. (16)	[0.0000,0.9500]	[0.0000,0.2589]	[0.0000,0.0295]	[0.0000,0.0030]
I_4°, cp. (19)	[0.0126,0.8419]	[0.0023,0.2849]	[0.0003,0.0359]	[0.0000,0.0037]
I_7°, cp. (22)	[0.0004,0.8533]	[0.0000,0.2172]	[0.0000,0.0247]	[0.0000,0.0025]
I_{10}°, cp. (26)	[0.0000,0.9750]	[0.0000,0.3085]	[0.0000,0.0362]	[0.0000,0.0037]
I_2°, cp. (17)	[0.0253,1.0000]	[0.0047,1.0000]	[0.0005,1.0000]	[0.0001,1.0000]
I_5°, cp. (20)	[0.0015,1.0000]	[0.0002,1.0000]	[0.0000,1.0000]	[0.0000,1.0000]
I_8°, cp. (23)	[0.0000,1.0000]	[0.0000,1.0000]	[0.0000,1.0000]	[0.0000,1.0000]
I_3°, cp. (18)	[0.0000,0.7764]	[0.0000,0.2384]	[0.0000,0.0292]	[0.0000,0.0030]
I_6°, cp. (21)	[0.0000,0.7715]	[0.0000,0.1708]	[0.0000,0.0190]	[0.0000,0.0019]
I_9°, cp. (25)	[0.0000,0.9500]	[0.0000,0.2589]	[0.0000,0.0295]	[0.0000,0.0030]

intervals of the third group are derived from upper bounds for θ. Therefore, the lower limit for these intervals is always zero resulting from the general restriction $\theta \geq 0$.

Although the differences between the intervals of a particular group do not appear to be very serious for many applications, especially for large n, the interpretation of the intervals is quite different. The likelihood interval I_1° contains parameters with at least 5% of the maximum likelihood and is solely based on the likelihood function for the given observed $k = 0$. The credible intervals I_2° to I_7° are probability intervals based on posterior distributions so that the random parameter $\tilde{\theta}$ takes values in these intervals with posterior probability 95%. The intervals I_8° to I_{10}° are values of confidence intervals in the spirit of classical inference. They are realisations of stochastic intervals, which cover the non-stochastic unknown parameter value θ with a probability of at least 95%. Only the lower confidence interval I_8° does not depend on n and covers the hole parameter space of θ.

4. Concluding Remarks

The above explanations show that many competing statistical methods are available, even for the very special case of zero observation. Our selection of the procedures tries to consider the most important ones but is far from a complete coverage of all available procedures.

For a modified minimax approach to the point estimation of the Bernoulli parameter, see Quigley and Revie (2002). There are further approaches for the point estimation of a Poisson parameter with zero observation in the area of intensity and failure models, which can be transferred to the estimation of a Bernoulli parameter (Bryant, 2007; Jiang *et al.*, 2015). There are many other variants of confidence intervals for the Bernoulli parameter (Brown *et al.*, 2002; Newcombe, 2011; Pires and Amado, 2008).

Conceptually or computationally simple solutions are often chosen for applications. But the choice of a method should be driven by stronger reasons, especially since the claim of computational simplicity will become irrelevant. In order to select an appropriate statistical method, the following questions should be asked and answered: What is the research question and which are the implications for the choice of the statistical method? What information is available in addition to the data? What are the consequences of a decision for an estimate?

4.1. *Research question*

Statistical questions and adequate statistical methods should be derived from the respective research question. In contrast, a data-driven choice of statistical methods is problematic. If the research question leads to the necessity of not underestimating the Bernoulli parameter with a high degree of statistical certainty, then the specification of a lower credible or confidence interval is an adequate statistical method. In such a case, it is problematic to change the method once the data are available and, for example, to calculate in the case of a zero observation an upper credible or confidence interval while a lower interval is induced by the research question. In contrast, there is the proposal to use in a ritualised way either an upper credible interval if $k = 0$ is observed or a two-sided credible interval for $0 < k < n$ or a lower credible interval if $k = n$ is observed (Pires and Amado, 2008, p. 170).

4.2. *Available information*

The choice of a statistical method should also be determined by the prior information available and how this information can be taken into account. Bayesian modelling allows to consider prior information very flexibly through the choice of the prior distribution. In contrast, the classical approach to modelling prior information is rather limited to the choice of restricted parameter ranges, e.g., in maximising the likelihood function.

4.3. *Consequences*

The context of the research question determines the consequences resulting from the decision for a certain estimate of the Bernoulli parameter. While the classical likelihood approach is driven entirely by the statistical model and the effort to hit the unknown parameter, the decision-theoretical approach allows the consideration of possible consequences of a statistical decision by specifying an error loss function.

Appendix A. Properties of Beta Functions and Distributions

A.1. *Beta function*

The function

$$\mathrm{B}(c,d) = \int_0^1 x^{c-1}(1-x)^{d-1}\mathrm{d}x \quad \text{for } c > 0,\ d > 0$$

is called the *beta function*;

$$\mathrm{B}(x;c,d) = \int_0^x u^{c-1}(1-u)^{d-1}\mathrm{d}u \quad \text{for } 0 \le x \le 1$$

is the *incomplete beta function* and

$$\mathrm{I}_x(c,d) = \frac{\mathrm{B}(x;c,d)}{\mathrm{B}(c,d)} \quad \text{for } 0 \le x \le 1$$

is the *regularised incomplete beta function.*

A.2. *Beta distribution*

A *beta distribution* $\mathrm{Beta}(c,d)$ with parameters $c > 0$ and $d > 0$ has probability density function

$$f(x) = \begin{cases} \dfrac{x^{c-1}(1-x)^{d-1}}{\mathrm{B}(c,d)} & \text{for } 0 < x < 1 \\ 0 & \text{otherwise,} \end{cases}$$

where B denotes the beta function. For $c \geq 1$ and $d \geq 1$, the density can be defined for $0 \leq x \leq 1$ using $0^0 \overset{\text{def}}{=} 1$. The distribution function is

$$F(x) = \begin{cases} 0 & \text{for } x < 0 \\ \mathrm{I}_x(c,d) & \text{for } 0 \leq x < 1 \\ 1 & \text{for } 1 \leq x, \end{cases}$$

where I is the regularised incomplete beta function.

A.3. *Mean of beta distribution*

The mean of $\mathrm{Beta}(c,d)$ is

$$\int_0^1 x f(x) \mathrm{d}x = \frac{c}{c+d}. \tag{A.1}$$

A.4. *Quantiles and median of beta distribution*

Let $B_{c,d,p}$ denote the p-quantile of $\mathrm{Beta}(c,d)$ for $0 < p < 1$. In general, the p-quantile $B_{c,d,p}$ has no explicit algebraic representation, but can be formulated with the inverse of the regularised beta function as

$$B_{c,d,p} = \mathrm{I}_p^{-1}(c,d) \tag{A.2}$$

and can be numerically evaluated, for example, by using
— MATHEMATICA function `InverseBetaRegularized`,
— GAUSS function `cdfBetaInv` or
— R function `Rbeta.inv` (package `zipfR`).
For $p = 1/2$ results the median of $\mathrm{Beta}(c,d)$ as the quantile $B_{c,d,1/2} = \mathrm{I}_{1/2}^{-1}(c,d)$. In the special case $(c,d) = (1, n+1)$ with $n \in \mathbb{N}$, the p-quantile can be elementary formulated as

$$B_{1,n+1,p} = 1 - (1-p)^{\frac{1}{n+1}}. \tag{A.3}$$

A.5. *Mode of beta distribution*

For $c \geq 1$, $d \geq 1$ and $c + d > 2$, the mode of $\mathrm{Beta}(c,d)$ is

$$\arg \max_{0 \leq x \leq 1} x^{c-1}(1-x)^{d-1} = \frac{c-1}{c+d-2}. \tag{A.4}$$

For $0 < c < 1$ and $d \geq 1$, the mode of Beta(c, d) is 0, since

$$\begin{aligned} &0 < f(x) < \infty \quad \text{for } 0 < x < 1, \\ &\lim_{x \uparrow 1} f(x) < \infty, \quad \lim_{x \downarrow 0} f(x) = \infty. \end{aligned} \tag{A.5}$$

For $c \geq 1$ and $0 < d < 1$, the mode of Beta(c, d) is 1, since

$$0 < f(x) < \infty \quad \text{for } 0 < x < 1, \quad \lim_{x \downarrow 0} f(x) < \infty, \quad \lim_{x \uparrow 1} f(x) = \infty.$$

A.6. *Derivation of (A.3)*

The density function of Beta$(1, n+1)$ is

$$f(t) = \begin{cases} \dfrac{(1-t)^n}{\mathrm{B}(1, n+1)} = (n+1)(1-t)^n & \text{for } 0 \leq t \leq 1 \\ 0 & \text{otherwise,} \end{cases}$$

since $\mathrm{B}(1, n+1) = \int_0^1 (1-x)^n \mathrm{d}x = 1/(n+1)$. The distribution function of Beta$(1, n+1)$ is

$$F(t) = \begin{cases} 0 & \text{for } t < 0 \\ \displaystyle\int_0^t f(s)\mathrm{d}s = 1 - (1-t)^{n+1} & \text{for } 0 \leq t < 1 \\ 1 & \text{for } 1 \leq t, \end{cases}$$

since $\int_0^t f(s)\mathrm{d}s = \int_0^t (n+1)(1-s)^n \mathrm{d}s = 1 - (1-t)^{n+1}$. For $0 < p < 1$, the inverse of the distribution function of $\mathrm{B}(1, n+1)$ is

$$F^{-1}(p) = 1 - (1-p)^{\frac{1}{n+1}}, \quad 0 < p < 1.$$

References

Bailey, R.T. (1997). Estimation from zero-failure data, *Risk Analysis* **17**(3), pp. 375–380.

Basu, A.P., Gaylor, D.W., and Chen, J.J. (1996). Estimating the probability of occurrence of tumor for a rare cancer with zero occurrence in a sample, *Regulatory Toxicology and Pharmacology* **23**, 139–144.

Blyth, C.R. and Still, H.A. (1983). Binomial confidence intervals, *Journal of the American Statistical Association* **78**(381), 108–116.

Brown, L.D., Cai, T.T. and DasGupta, A. (2002). Confidence intervals for binomial proportion and asymptotic expansions, *Annals of Statistics* **30**(1), 160–201.

Bryant, R. (2007). Estimation of component failure rates for use in probabilistic safety. Assessment in cases of no or few recorded failures, *Safety and Reliability* **27**(1), 8–21.

Eypasch, E., Lefering, R., Kum, C.K. and Troidl, H. (1995). Probability of adverse events that have not yet occurred: A statistical reminder, *BMJ (British Medical Journal)* **311**, 619.

Hanley, J.A. and Lippman-Hand, A. (1983). If nothing goes wrong, is everything all right? Interpreting zero numerators, *Journal of the American Medical Association* **249**(13), 1743–1745.

Hedderich, J. and Sachs, L. (2020). *Angewandte Statistik: Methodensammlung mit R*, 17th edn. Berlin: Springer Spektrum.

Jeffrey, H. (1945). An invariant form for the prior probability in estimation problems, *Proceedings of the Royal Society A* **186**, 453–461.

Jiang, P., Xing, Y., Jia, X. and Guo, B. (2015). Weibull failure probability estimation based on zero-failure data, *Mathematical Problems in Engineering* Article ID 681232, 1–8.

Lehmann, E.L. and Casella, G. (1998). *Theory of Point Estimation*, 2nd edn. New York: Springer.

Newcombe, R.G. (2011). Measures of location for confidence intervals for proportions, *Communications in Statistics — Theory and Methods* **40**(10), 1743–1767.

Pawitan, Y. (2013). *In All Likelihood: Statistical Modelling and Inference Using Likelihood*, Oxford: Clarendon Press.

Pires, A.M. and Amado, C. (2008). Interval estimators for a binomial proportion: comparison of twenty methods, *REVSTAT — Statistical Journal* **6**(2), 165–197.

Pluto, K. and Tasche, D. (2005). Thinking positively, *Risk* **18**(8), 72–78.

Quigley, J. and Revie, M. (2011). Estimating the probability of rare events: Addressing zero failure data, *Risk Analysis* **31**(7), 1120–1132.

Razzaghi, M. (2002). On the estimation of binomial success probability with zero occurrence in sample, *Journal of Modern Applied Statistical Methods* **1**(2), 326–332.

Welker, E.L. and Lipow, M. (1974). Estimating the exponential failure rate from data with no failure events, In *Proceedings of the Annual Reliability and Maintainability Symposium*, Vol. 7, issue 2, Los Angeles, CA, pp. 420–427.

https://doi.org/10.1142/9781800611917_0009

Chapter 9

Tail Nonlinearly Transformed Risk Measure as a Capital Constraint — A Better Choice for Bank Regulation Than Conditional Value-at-Risk?

Kerstin Bergk[*,‡], **Mario Brandtner**[†,§], **and Wolfgang Kürsten**[*,¶]

[*]*Friedrich Schiller University Jena, Faculty of Economics and Business Administration, Germany*

[†]*Jena University of Applied Sciences, Department of Business Administration, Germany*

[‡]*kerstin.bergk@uni-jena.de*

[§]*mario.brandtner@eah-jena.de*

[¶]*wolfgang.kuersten@uni-jena.de*

The purpose of this chapter is to compare regulatory capital constraints based on tail nonlinearly transformed risk measure (TNT) and conditional value-at-risk (CVaR). TNT extends CVaR by additionally transforming financial positions' outcomes by means of a concave transformation function and, as such, it results that the TNT constraint is stricter than the corresponding CVaR constraint for any given confidence level. In a setting with n risky assets and one risk-free asset, we analyse the implications from imposing a TNT constraint on a bank's (μ, σ)-portfolio selection problem and compare them with those arising from imposing a CVaR constraint. We find two major outcomes: First, due to its strictness, the (convex) TNT constraint is more effective than the (linear) CVaR constraint to induce slightly risk-averse banks to select a portfolio with smaller standard deviation. Second, the benefits of using a TNT constraint may come at a price, causing highly risk-averse banks to select a portfolio with larger standard deviation. We further derive the intersections of the (μ, σ)-efficient frontier and the TNT constraint analytically.

1. Introduction

During the last financial crisis of 2007–2008, some banks had to declare bankruptcy and government bailouts were announced to stabilise the financial system. This made the relevance of efficacious banking regulation and supervision aware to the public. Despite the wide variety of regulatory tools, setting capital requirements continues to be a central pillar in attempting to reduce the fragility of banks. A key feature that is needed to link a bank's risk with an adequate regulatory capital is the choice of a suitable risk measure to quantify the bank's aggregate portfolio risk. Value-at-risk (VaR) and conditional value-at-risk (CVaR) (see, e.g., Acerbi and Tasche, 2002; Rockafellar and Uryasev, 2000) evolved as the two standard risk measures, which are nowadays used as capital constraints. Adopted from insurers' maximum probable yearly loss (MPY) risk measure (see Cummins and Freifelder, 1978; Dionne, 2013), VaR emerged as an industry standard risk measure in the banking regulation schemes Basel II/III. Given a banks uncertain portfolio value at a future point in time, VaR indicates the portfolio's loss that is only exceeded by a (small) probability α. VaR found wide-spread application and attention by scholars (e.g., Basak and Shapiro, 2001; Locarek-Junge *et al.*, 2002, 2000; Wang *et al.*, 2005). However, VaR performs poorly in supporting regulatory goals due to its inability to capture tail risk and to promote diversification (see Szegö, 2002).

Therefore, in 2016, the Basel Committee revised its standards of capital requirements by recommending to replace VaR with CVaR. Defined as the average loss in the $\alpha \cdot 100\%$ worst cases, CVaR overcomes the major drawbacks of VaR. Moreover, CVaR belongs to the class of coherent risk measures which Artzner *et al.* (1999) proposed as an axiomatic approach to define and construct risk measures that may build a sound theoretical basis for capital requirements. In fact, Artzner *et al.* (1999) formalised four properties (or axioms) that any reasonable risk measure should fulfil: monotonicity, translation invariance, positive homogeneity, and sub-additivity. However, the concept of coherent risk measures such as CVaR contains some considerable drawbacks as well. Koch-Medina and Munari (2016) argued that CVaR allows regulatory arbitrage opportunities. Brandtner (2013) showed that, due to the axioms of translation invariance and positive homogeneity, CVaR tends to corner solutions in portfolio selection problems. Kürsten and Brandtner (2009) have criticised CVaR because of its inherent, narrow understanding of risk and Brandtner (2018) found that, in a portfolio selection problem with background risk, caused by the axiom of sub-additivity, CVaR and the entire class of coherent risk measures are incompatible with risk vulnerability. Alexander and Baptista (2003, 2004, 2006) showed that, in a traditional (μ, σ)-model, relatively highly risk-averse banks may be forced to select portfolios with larger standard deviation when a CVaR constraint is imposed. These shortcomings have led some scholars to propose alternative classes of risk measures that do not rely on the relevant properties. As part of this trend, Chen *et al.* (2012) developed the tail nonlinearly transformed risk measure (TNT), which generalises CVaR by introducing a nonlinear transformation function that penalises tail-outcomes. As TNT fulfils the axioms of monotonicity and convexity only, this risk measure belongs to the new class of generalised convex risk measures.

Recently, Bergk *et al.* (2021) documented that TNT performs superior in a mean-risk portfolio selection problem when compared to CVaR. In this paper, we apply TNT as a "new" risk measure in the context of bank regulation. In particular, we continue the studies of Alexander and Baptista (2003, 2006) and Bergk *et al.* (2021) by imposing a TNT constraint in a (μ, σ)-model where returns are normally distributed and a risk-free asset is available, and the transformation function is exponential as proposed by Chen *et al.* (2012).

In line with the relevant literature, we assume that banks are (μ, σ)-decision makers (e.g., Alexander and Baptista, 2006; Hart and Jaffee, 1974; Koehn and Santomero, 1980; Rochet, 1992). We investigate the set of (μ, σ)-efficient portfolios satisfying the TNT constraint, analytically derive the intersections of the (μ, σ)-efficient frontier and the TNT constraint, and compare it with the "traditional" regulation scheme based on a CVaR constraint. We show that for slightly risk-averse banks that would select portfolios with a relatively large standard deviation, the TNT constraint is a more effective regulation tool than the CVaR constraint, as TNT-regulation yields a greater reduction in the portfolio's standard deviation.[1] At the same time, however, the TNT constraint forces highly risk-averse banks to select portfolios with a larger standard deviation than they would choose without any regulation. Compared to the CVaR constraint, this negative effect is even more pronounced under a TNT constraint.

The paper is structured as follows: Section 2 introduces CVaR and TNT and compares general theoretical properties. Section 3 derives the CVaR- and TNT-constrained (μ, σ)-efficient frontiers, examines the implications for the banks' portfolio choice and compare those with each other. Section 4 concludes and discusses the possible superiority of a TNT constraint. All proofs are given in the Online Appendix.

2. Risk Measures as Capital Constraints: Preliminaries

In this section, we provide some preliminaries on our choice of axiomatic risk measures, CVaR and TNT, and introduce the capital constraints based on these two risk measures. Throughout this paper, we consider a probability space $(\Omega, \mathcal{F}, P)$, where Ω is the set of all events, $\mathcal{F}$ is a σ-algebra on Ω, and P is a probability measure on $\mathcal{F}$. $\mathcal{X}$ is the set of all measurable, real valued random variables X; in the remainder of the paper, we will identify the random variables with (uncertain) financial positions, and portfolio returns in particular. The cumulative distribution function and the quantile function of a random variable X are given by $F_X(x) = F(x) = P(X \leq x)$ and $F_X^{-1}(p) = F^{-1}(p) = \sup\{x \in \mathbb{R} | F(x) < p\}$, $p \in (0, 1]$, and $F^{-1}(0) = \operatorname{ess\,inf}\{X\}$. In order to quantify financial risk, axiomatic risk measures ρ are introduced that map the random variable X from $\mathcal{X}$ to the real line $\mathbb{R}$.

[1]For brevity, note that hereafter we omit the qualifier "relatively".

2.1. *Coherent risk measures and CVaR*

Perceived as the cornerstone of axiomatic risk measures, Artzner *et al.* (1999) proposed the class of coherent risk measures defined as follows:

Definition 1 (Coherent risk measures). A risk measure ρ is called coherent if and only if it satisfies the four axioms of

(M) Monotonicity: $X \leq Y \Rightarrow \rho(X) \geq \rho(Y)$, $\forall X, Y \in \mathcal{X}$,
(TI) Translation invariance: $\rho(X+m) = \rho(X) - m$, $m \in \mathbb{R}$, $\forall X \in \mathcal{X}$,
(PH) Positive homogeneity: $\rho(\delta \cdot X) = \delta \cdot \rho(X)$, $\delta \geq 0$, $\forall X \in \mathcal{X}$,
(S) Subadditivity: $\rho(X+Y) \leq \rho(X) + \rho(Y)$, $\forall X, Y \in \mathcal{X}$.

Coherent risk measures were proposed as a sound theoretical basis to regulate a bank's risk by means of capital requirements. As such, a bank with a financial position X is deemed to be well capitalised with respect to the (translation invariant and positively homogeneous) risk measure ρ if it satisfies the capital constraint

$$\rho(X+K) \leq \rho(0) = 0 \Leftrightarrow \rho(X) \leq K, \tag{1}$$

with $K \in \mathbb{R}$ as the equity of the bank. The intuition is straightforward. Formalised by the properties of (TI) and (PH), the risk of the financial position $\rho(X)$ as expressed in monetary terms must not exceed bank's equity K.

By replacing traditional and ad hoc VaR in the measurement of market risk in the Basel III regulation accord, CVaR constitutes the most prominent example within the class of coherent risk measures that, in the meanwhile, exhibits a crucial role in banking regulation. First proposed by Artzner *et al.* (1999) and examined by numerous scholars thereafter (Acerbi and Tasche, 2002; Rockafellar and Uryasev, 2000, to name a few), CVaR at the confidence level $\alpha \in (0, 1]$ measures the downside risk of a financial position X by indicating the mean of its worst $\alpha \cdot 100\%$ outcomes, formally

$$\text{CVaR}_\alpha(X) = -\frac{1}{\alpha} \cdot \int_0^\alpha F_X^{-1}(p)dp. \tag{2}$$

As CVaR considers the average of the worst $\alpha \cdot 100\%$ outcomes only, it distorts the physical probabilities by assigning a constant weight of $\frac{1}{\alpha}$ to the $\alpha \cdot 100\%$ worst cases and zero weight else, so CVaR is nonlinear in the probabilities but linear in the outcomes of the financial position. Assuming normally distributed returns, $X \sim N(\mu_X, \sigma_X^2)$, we can rewrite CVaR by means of the properties of (TI) and (PH) as a linear combination of the position's mean and standard deviation,

$$\mathrm{CVaR}_\alpha(X) = \mathrm{CVaR}_\alpha\left(\mu_X + \sigma_X \cdot X_0\right) = -\mu_X + \sigma_X \cdot k(\alpha), \tag{3}$$

where X_0 is a standard normal random variable and $k(\alpha) = \mathrm{CVaR}_\alpha(X_0) = \frac{n(N^{-1}(\alpha))}{\alpha}$ (see, e.g., Alexander and Baptista, 2004, Section 2).

Suppose a bank is restricted to select a financial position $X \sim N(\mu_X, \sigma_X)$ such that $\mathrm{CVaR}_\alpha(X) \leq K$. From Eqs. (1) and (3), it follows that the CVaR constraint, in the (σ, μ)-plane, can be depicted as

$$\mu_X \geq k(\alpha) \cdot \sigma_X - K, \tag{4}$$

and appears as a straight line with intercept $-K$ and slope $k(\alpha)$, which immediately follows from the linearity axioms (TI) and (PH) of CVaR as a coherent risk measure. Admissible portfolios have to lie on or above this straight line. While the intercept of the CVaR constraint $-K$, the negative of the bank's equity, is determined by the respective bank only, the slope $k(\alpha)$ is under the control of the regulator and can be used, by means of fixing the confidence level α, to reach the required strictness of regulation. For example, to implement a stricter regulation, the slope $k(\alpha)$ has to be increased which can be accomplished by setting a lower confidence level α (*and vice versa*).

2.2. *Generalised convex risk measures and TNT*

Notwithstanding CVaR's unbroken popularity in the present banking regulation, its linearity properties (TI) and (PH) come with surprising and adverse anomalies (e.g., Brandtner, 2013, 2018; Brandtner and Kürsten, 2015; Koch-Medina and Munari, 2016; Kürsten and Brandtner, 2009). In the context of portfolio selection, for example, CVaR-minimising portfolios exhibit a tendency towards non-diversification, corner solutions, and counter-intuitive comparative statics. Similarly, in the original context of banking regulation, Alexander and Baptista (2006) have shown that a CVaR constraint can lead to an increase instead of a decrease in a bank portfolio's standard deviation. Hence, some scholars have proposed broader classes of axiomatic risk measures which come without the critical properties (TI) and (PH), respectively. To this end, the class of generalised convex risk measures introduced by Li Yang *et al.* (2016) is defined as follows:

Definition 2 (Generalised convex risk measures). A risk measure ρ is called generalised convex if and only if it satisfies the two axioms of

(M) Monotonicity: $X \leq Y \Rightarrow \rho(X) \geq \rho(Y), \forall X, Y \in \mathcal{X}$,
(C) Convexity: $\rho(\delta \cdot X + (1-\delta) \cdot Y) \leq \delta \cdot \rho(X) + (1-\delta) \cdot \rho(Y)$, $\delta \in [0,1], \forall X, Y \in \mathcal{X}$.

Note that by fulfilling (PH) and (S), the class of coherent risk measures immediately satisfies (C), i.e., is a subset of the class of generalised convex risk measures.

A first representative is the weighted expected shortfall (WES) proposed by Chen and Li Yang (2011) which penalises tail-outcomes by means of a nonlinear transformation function. Similarly, the Disutility-Based Risk Measure (DCVaR) proposed by Fulga (2016) incorporates an increasing concave disutility function in order to capture loss aversion. As a third representative, we focus on the TNT introduced by Chen *et al.* (2012) which, similar to the WES, incorporates a transformation function u that penalises larger losses more than smaller ones. Formally, TNT is defined as

$$\mathrm{TNT}_\alpha(X) = -\frac{1}{\alpha} \cdot \int_0^\alpha u(F_X^{-1}(p))dp, \tag{5}$$

with confidence level $\alpha \in (0,1]$ and u as a negative and continuous, monotonically increasing, concave transformation function. Due to the (negative) concavity of u, large losses obtain higher weights, so TNT represents risk aversion. In order to specify TNT, we follow the suggestion of Chen *et al.* (2012) and apply the exponential transformation function $u(x) = -\exp(-\lambda \cdot x)$, where $\lambda > 0$ is some investor-specific risk parameter (Chen *et al.*, 2012, p. 820) controlling both the concavity of the transformation function and the degree of the investor's risk aversion. Again assuming normally distributed returns, $X \sim N(\mu_X, \sigma_X^2)$, we can rewrite TNT as the mean of a truncated log-normally distributed random variable with parameters

$(-\lambda\mu_X, \lambda^2\sigma_X^2)$ (see Bergk *et al.*, 2021):

$$\mathrm{TNT}_{\alpha,\lambda}(X) = \exp\left(-\lambda\mu_X + \frac{1}{2}\lambda^2\sigma_X^2\right) \cdot \frac{N\left(\lambda\sigma_X + N^{-1}(\alpha)\right)}{\alpha}. \tag{6}$$

So far, TNT has only been introduced as a risk measure in portfolio selection problems, yet not as a capital constraint. In order to implement TNT as a capital constraint, we have to insert the given equity K of a bank in the TNT as, due to the lack of (TI) and (PH), equivalence property (1) cannot be applied. As a result, a bank regulated with a TNT constraint is restricted to select a position X such that

$$\mathrm{TNT}_{\alpha,\lambda}(X + K) \leq \mathrm{TNT}_{\alpha,\lambda}(0) = 1 \Leftrightarrow \mathrm{TNT}_{\alpha,\lambda}(X) \leq \exp(\lambda \cdot K). \tag{7}$$

Assuming $X \sim N(\mu_X, \sigma_X^2)$, we insert (7) in Eq. (6) and solve for μ_X, which yields the TNT constraint as

$$\mu_X \geq \frac{\lambda}{2} \cdot \sigma_X^2 + \frac{1}{\lambda} \cdot \ln(N(\lambda\sigma_X + N^{-1}(\alpha))) - \frac{1}{\lambda}\ln(\alpha) - K. \tag{8}$$

For the derivation of the TNT constraint, see also Bergk *et al.* (2021). In contrast to the linear CVaR constraint (4), the TNT constraint appears as a convex curve in the (σ, μ)-plane with intercept $-K$ and slope

$$s_{\alpha,\lambda}(\sigma_X) := \lambda \cdot \sigma_X + \frac{n(\lambda\sigma_X + N^{-1}(\alpha))}{N(\lambda\sigma_X + N^{-1}(\alpha))}, \tag{9}$$

which is obtained by differentiating (8) with respect to the standard deviation σ_X. Any admissible portfolio has to lie on or above the curve in order to satisfy the TNT constraint. By adding the TNT constraint as a regulatory constraint to the bank's objective function, a regulator now can fix two parameters, the confidence level α and, additionally, the risk parameter λ. Both serve as adjustment tools with respect to the intended strictness of regulation. The lower the confidence level or/and the higher the risk parameter, the higher the slope of the curve and the stricter the regulation is.

Put together and illustrated in Figure 1, the CVaR and the TNT constraint for the same confidence level α possess the same intercept

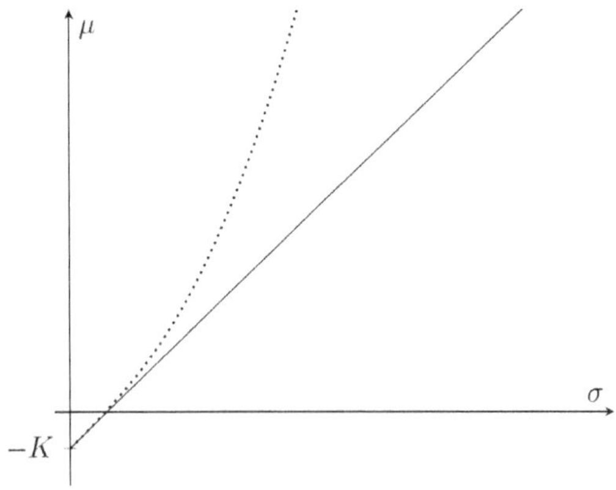

Fig. 1. Representation of a CVaR constraint (straight line) and a TNT constraint (dotted convex curve) in the (σ, μ)-space.

with the y-axis. But, due to $s_{\alpha,\lambda}(\sigma_X) \geq k(\alpha)$, the TNT constraint lies on or above the CVaR constraint in the (σ, μ)-plane (for the proof, see Bergk *et al.*, 2021, Appendix C). Therefore, the TNT constraint comes to a stricter bank regulation than the corresponding CVaR constraint does.

3. $(\mu, \sigma)_\rho$-Efficient Frontiers: The Case of n Risky Assets and a Risk-Free Asset

3.1. *Preliminaries*

In this section, our intention is to compare the implications arising from a CVaR and TNT constraint, respectively, on a bank's optimal portfolio choice. First, we establish some preliminaries. Second, we recall the portfolio analysis under a CVaR constraint (see Alexander and Baptista, 2003, 2006) and, third, extend the portfolio analysis of Bergk *et al.* (2021) under a TNT constraint by adding a risk-free asset as an additional investment opportunity with return μ_0. The risky rates of return $r = (r_1, \ldots, r_n)^T$ follow a multivariate normal distribution, where $\mu \in \mathbb{R}^n$ is the vector of the means and Σ is the $n \times n$ positive definite variance–covariance matrix. $\mathbb{1} \in \mathbb{R}^n$ denotes the n-dimensional unit vector $(1, \ldots, 1)$. We denote the set of possible portfolios including the risk-free asset by $\Theta_{n+1} = \{\theta \in \mathbb{R}^{n+1} | \sum_{j=0}^{n} \theta_j = 1\}$, where $\theta_{j=1,\ldots,n}$ indicates the share invested in risky asset j, and θ_0 indicates the share invested in the risk-free asset. For any $\theta \in \Theta_{n+1}$, $\mu(\theta)$ and risk(θ) denote the mean and the risk of the rate of return of portfolio θ. For the sake of clarity, we add the subscript L for CVaR and the subscript T for TNT, respectively. Further, we use the constants $A \equiv \mathbb{1}^T \sum^{-1} \mu$, $B \equiv \mu^T \sum^{-1} \mu$ and $C \equiv \mathbb{1}^T \sum^{-1} \mathbb{1}$.

In our analysis, we allow that there is a risk-free asset. In line with the relevant literature, we assume that the return of the risk-free asset is smaller than the return of the risky minimum variance portfolio, $\mu_0 < A/C$, in order to ensure that the risk-free asset does not dominate the risky investment opportunities. We assume a bank with a (μ, σ)-objective function that seeks to optimally split its wealth between the risk-free asset and the n risky assets. The bank finds its optimal portfolio by fixing a certain level of expected return, $\bar{\mu}$, and choosing the corresponding portfolio that minimises the variance over the set of alternatives Θ_{n+1}:

$$\begin{aligned} &\min_{\theta \in \Theta_{n+1}} \sigma^2(\theta) \\ &\text{s.t. } \theta^T \mu = \bar{\mu}. \end{aligned} \tag{10}$$

The main results are summarised in the following.

Proposition 1 (Tangency portfolio). *The portfolio $\theta^*(\bar{\mu})$ that solves $\min_{\theta \in \Theta_{n+1}} \sigma^2(\theta)$, s.t. $\mu(\theta) = \bar{\mu}$, is given by*

$$\theta^*(\bar{\mu}) = (1 - \lambda(\bar{\mu})) \cdot \begin{pmatrix} \mathbb{0} \\ 1 \end{pmatrix} + \lambda(\bar{\mu}) \cdot \begin{pmatrix} \theta_{\text{tang}} \\ 0 \end{pmatrix}, \tag{11}$$

where $\mathbb{0} = (0, \ldots, 0)^T$, $\lambda(\bar{\mu}) = (A - \mu_0 \cdot C)\frac{\bar{\mu} - \mu_0}{D(\mu_0)}$, and $\theta_{\text{tang}} \in \mathbb{R}^n$ denotes the so-called tangency portfolio which is characterised by

$$\theta_{\text{tang}} = \frac{1}{A - \mu_0 \cdot C} \Sigma^{-1} (\mu - \mu_0), \tag{12}$$

$$\text{with} \quad \mu(\theta_{\text{tang}}) = \frac{B - \mu_0 \cdot A}{A - \mu_0 \cdot C} \quad \text{and} \quad \sigma(\theta_{\text{tang}}) = \frac{\frac{B - \mu_0 \cdot A}{A - \mu_0 \cdot C} - \mu_0}{\sqrt{D(\mu_0)}}, \tag{13}$$

where $D(\mu_0) = B - 2 \cdot A \cdot \mu_0 + C \cdot \mu_0^2$. Consequently, the (μ, σ)-boundary is given by

$$\mu(\theta) = \sqrt{D(\mu_0)} \cdot \sigma(\theta) \pm \mu_0, \tag{14}$$

and the (μ, σ)-efficient frontier is characterised by

$$\mu(\theta) = \sqrt{D(\mu_0)} \cdot \sigma(\theta) + \mu_0. \tag{15}$$

For the proof, see, e.g., de Giorgi (2002, Section 5.1). As is well known, the (μ, σ)-efficient frontier (15) appears as a straight line through the risk-free asset and the portfolio θ_{tang} that touches the risky (μ, σ)-boundary at only one point, and therefore is called tangency portfolio (Tobin, 1958).

Now, let us assume that the bank is regulated with an additional restriction on the portfolio risk, ρ. Initially, we define the corresponding $(\mu, \sigma)_\rho$-boundary and $(\mu, \sigma)_\rho$-efficient frontier, where the subscript ρ indicates the capital constraint with respect to the imposed risk measure ρ, which we later specify by L for CVaR and T for TNT. The corresponding constrained optimisation problem can be summarised as follows:

$$\min_{\theta \in \Theta_{n+1}} \sigma^2(\theta) \tag{16}$$

$$s.t. \quad \theta^T \mu = \bar{\mu}$$

$$\rho(\theta) \leq \begin{cases} K & \text{if } \rho(\theta) \cong \text{CVaR}_\alpha(\theta) \\ \exp(\lambda \cdot K) & \text{if } \rho(\theta) \cong \text{TNT}_{\alpha,\lambda}(\theta). \end{cases} \tag{17}$$

This yields the $(\mu, \sigma)_\rho$-boundary.

Definition 3 ($(\mu, \sigma)_\rho$-boundary). A portfolio $\theta \in \Theta_{n+1}$ belongs to the $(\mu, \sigma)_\rho$-boundary if and only if it belongs to the (μ, σ)-boundary given by Eq. (14) and satisfies the risk measure constraint (17).

A bank with (μ, σ)-preferences only selects portfolios which are located on the upper branch on the (μ, σ)-boundary and, additionally, satisfy the regulatory capital constraint. Those portfolios lie on the $(\mu, \sigma)_\rho$-efficient frontier.

Definition 4 ($(\mu,\sigma)_\rho$-efficient frontier). A portfolio $\theta \in \Theta_{n+1}$ belongs to the $(\mu, \sigma)_\rho$-efficient frontier if and only if it belongs to the (μ, σ)-efficient frontier given by Eq. (15) and satisfies the risk measure constraint (17).

3.2. The CVaR constraint

Next, we specify the general risk measure constraint through the CVaR constraint (see Alexander and Baptista, 2003, 2006). If it exists, let θ_L indicate the portfolio which is located at the intersection of the CVaR constraint and the (μ, σ)-efficient frontier. The following result characterises the $(\mu, \sigma)_L$-efficient frontier.

Proposition 2 ($(\mu,\sigma)_L$-efficient frontier). *(i) If $k(\alpha) < \sqrt{D(\mu_0)}$ and $K < -\mu_0$, then a portfolio $\theta \in \Theta_{n+1}$ belongs to the $(\mu, \sigma)_L$-efficient frontier if and only if it belongs to the (μ, σ)-efficient frontier and $\mu(\theta) \geq \mu(\theta_L)$. (ii) If $k(\alpha) \leq \sqrt{D(\mu_0)}$ and $K \geq -\mu_0$, then the $(\mu, \sigma)_L$-efficient frontier and the (μ, σ)-efficient frontier coincide. (iii) If $k(\alpha) > \sqrt{D(\mu_0)}$ and $K = -\mu_0$, then the $(\mu, \sigma)_L$-efficient frontier only consists of the risk-free asset. (iv) If $k(\alpha) > \sqrt{D(\mu_0)}$ and $K > -\mu_0$, then a portfolio $\theta \in \Theta_{n+1}$ belongs to the $(\mu, \sigma)_L$-efficient frontier if and only if it belongs to the (μ, σ)-efficient frontier and $\mu(\theta) \leq \mu(\theta_L)$. (v) Otherwise, there is no portfolio on the $(\mu, \sigma)_L$-efficient frontier.*

For the proof, see Online Appendix A. An illustration of the cases (i)–(v) in Proposition 2 is shown in Figure 2. We further analyse cases (i)–(iv) of Proposition 2 only, as otherwise the $(\mu, \sigma)_L$-efficient frontier would be empty. The remaining cases can be subdivided with respect to the relation of the slopes and the amount of equity available to the bank. If the slope of the CVaR constraint is larger than the slope of the (μ, σ)-efficient frontier, $k(\alpha) > \sqrt{D(\mu_0)}$, we call the regulation "strict". Conversely, if $k(\alpha) \leq \sqrt{D(\mu_0)}$, we call

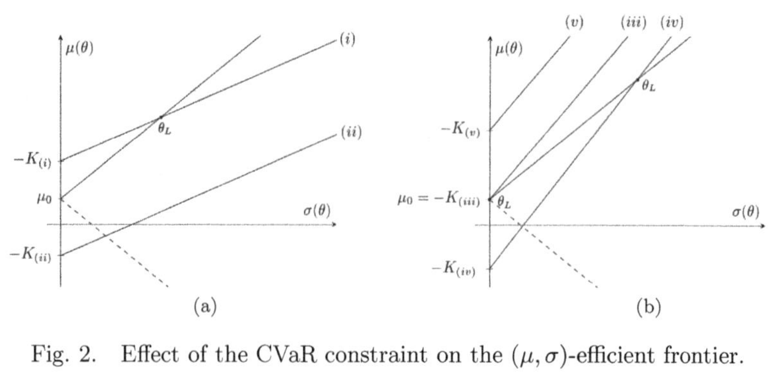

Fig. 2. Effect of the CVaR constraint on the (μ, σ)-efficient frontier.

the regulation "loose". Similarly, if for the equity holds $K < -\mu_0$, we call the equity "small" and otherwise we call the equity "large".

First, we assume a loose regulation as given in cases (i) and (ii) in Proposition 2 and Figure 2(a). Depending on the equity of a bank, there is either one intersection with the (μ, σ)-efficient frontier or there is none. As a consequence, either only portfolios with small standard deviation are precluded or a CVaR constraint does not have any regulatory effect. Particularly, in the first case, the CVaR constraint counteracts its regulatory goal, as it requires highly risk-averse banks to increase the standard deviation of their portfolio such that $\mu(\theta) \geq \mu(\theta_L)$. In summary, a loose regulation may increase the fragility of highly risk-averse banks.

Second, suppose the regulation is strict corresponding to (iv) and its special case (iii) in Proposition 2 and Figure 2(b). Within these two cases, a bank has to select a portfolio with a mean lower or equal to the one of the intersection portfolio: $\mu(\theta) \leq \mu(\theta_L)$. Here, and in line with the regulatory goal, any slightly risk-averse bank is forced to choose a portfolio with smaller standard deviation leading to a reduction in financial fragility. Table 1 summarises these observations.

Table 1. Impact of a CVaR constraint within (μ, σ)-model on portfolio efficiency and selection.

	Equity K	
Regulation	Small	Large
(a) *Efficient portfolios that are precluded by the CVaR constraint*		
Loose	Efficient portfolios with small standard deviations	None
Strict	All efficient portfolios	Efficient portfolios with large standard deviations
(b) *Impact of the CVaR constraint on a bank's optimal portfolio*		
Loose	Highly risk-averse banks will select efficient portfolios with larger standard deviations	None
Strict	There are no admissible efficient portfolios for a bank to choose	Slightly risk-averse banks will select efficient portfolios with smaller standard deviations

3.3. *The TNT constraint*

We proceed by analysing the generalised convex risk measure, TNT, as a capital constraint. If they exist, let $\underline{\theta}_T$ and $\overline{\theta}_T$ indicate the portfolios which are located at the lower and upper intersections of the convex TNT constraint and the linear (μ, σ)-efficient frontier, respectively. Further, let $\bar{K}$ be the bank's critical level of equity defined by

$$\bar{K} := \frac{\lambda}{2} \cdot \bar{\sigma}^2 + \frac{1}{\lambda} \ln(N(\lambda\bar{\sigma} + N^{-1}(\alpha))) \\ -\frac{1}{\lambda} \cdot \ln(\alpha) - (\mu_0 + \sqrt{D(\mu_0)} \cdot \bar{\sigma}), \tag{18}$$

where $\bar{\sigma}$ is implicitly given by $s_{\alpha,\lambda}(\bar{\sigma}) = \sqrt{D(\mu_0)}$. Then the following result characterises the $(\mu, \sigma)_T$-efficient frontier.

Proposition 3 ($(\mu,\sigma)_T$-efficient frontier). *(i) If $K = \bar{K} \leq -\mu_0$, then the $(\mu, \sigma)_T$-efficient frontier only consists of the portfolio $\theta_T = \underline{\theta}_T = \overline{\theta}_T$. (ii) If $\bar{K} < K \leq -\mu_0$, then a portfolio $\theta \in \Theta_{n+1}$ belongs to the $(\mu, \sigma)_T$-efficient frontier if and only if it belongs to the (μ, σ)-efficient frontier and $\mu(\underline{\theta}_T) \leq \mu(\theta) \leq \mu(\overline{\theta}_T)$. (iii) If $K > -\mu_0$, then a portfolio $\theta \in \Theta_{n+1}$ belongs to the $(\mu, \sigma)_T$-efficient frontier if and only if it belongs (μ, σ)-efficient frontier and $\mu(\theta) \leq \mu(\overline{\theta}_T)$. (iv) Otherwise, there is no portfolio on the $(\mu, \sigma)_T$-efficient frontier.*

For the proof see Online Appendix B. Figure 3 illustrates the cases proposed in Proposition 3. In case (i), the single intersection of

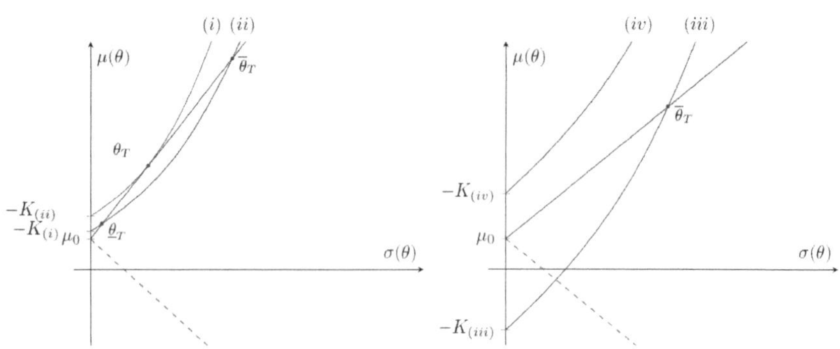

Fig. 3. Effect of the TNT constraint on the (μ, σ)-efficient frontier.

the (μ, σ)-efficient frontier and the TNT constraint, $\theta_T = \overline{\theta}_T = \underline{\theta}_T$, provides the portfolio that minimises TNT with respect to the investment opportunity set that consists of the risk free asset and the tangency portfolio, i.e., $\theta_T := \arg\min_{\theta \in \Theta_{n+1}} \mathrm{TNT}_{\alpha,\lambda}(\theta_0 \cdot r_0 + (1 - \theta_0) \cdot r(\theta_{\mathrm{tang}}))$. This portfolio's TNT amounts to $\bar{K}$, i.e., $\mathrm{TNT}_{\alpha,\lambda}(\theta_T) = \bar{K}$, and its composition has been derived by Bergk *et al.* (2021), Section 5. We further assume that the $(\mu, \sigma)_T$-efficient frontier is not empty, i.e., we address the cases (i)–(iii) only. As with the CVaR constraint, we subdivide the cases (i)–(iii) with respect to the equity of a bank. If $K < -\mu_0$, we say the equity of a bank is "small", and, otherwise "large".

Within the cases (i)–(iii), independent of the equity of a bank, portfolios with large standard deviations are precluded. In line with the goal of the regulator, slightly risk-averse banks have to choose a portfolio with lower standard deviation and, thus, decrease their fragility. However, for banks with small equity as displayed in cases (i) and (ii), the TNT constraint also precludes portfolios with a small standard deviation. Hence, among highly risk-averse banks with small equity, the standard deviation of their portfolio is higher in the presence of the constraint than in its absence resulting in an increase in their fragility. Table 2 summarises these observations.

Table 2. Impact of a TNT constraint within (μ, σ)-model on portfolio efficiency and selection.

Equity K	
Small	Large
(a) *Efficient portfolios that are precluded by the TNT constraint*	
Efficient portfolios with small and large standard deviations	Efficient portfolios with large standard deviations
(b) *Impact of the TNT constraint on a bank's optimal portfolio*	
Highly risk-averse banks will select efficient portfolios with larger standard deviations; Slightly risk-averse banks will select efficient portfolios with smaller standard deviations	Slightly risk-averse banks will select efficient portfolios with smaller standard deviations

3.4. *Comparison between CVaR-constrained and TNT-constrained optimal portfolios*

We now provide a detailed comparison of the two risk measures, CVaR and TNT, in terms of their economic implications if they are used as regulatory capital constraints. Propositions 4 and 5 give some preliminaries.

Proposition 4 (Intersection: CVaR constraint). *For a given equity K and confidence level $\alpha \in (0,1]$, and either $k(\alpha) < \sqrt{D(\mu_0)}$ and $K < -\mu_0$ or $k(\alpha) > \sqrt{D(\mu_0)}$ and $K > -\mu_0$, the intersection of the CVaR constraint and the (μ,σ)-efficient frontier is given by*

$$\sigma(\theta_L) = \frac{\mu_0 + K}{k(\alpha) - \sqrt{D(\mu_0)}}. \tag{19}$$

For the proof, see Alexander and Baptista (2004).

The intersections of the TNT constraint and the (μ,σ)-efficient frontier can be derived in a similar way when using the tangent to the TNT constraint at the intersections points. In general, the tangent to the TNT constraint is given by $\mu(\theta) = s_{\alpha,\lambda}(\theta)\cdot\sigma(\theta) + m_{\alpha,\lambda}(\theta)$, where $s_{\alpha,\lambda}(\theta) = \lambda\sigma(\theta) + N(\lambda\sigma + N^{-1}(\alpha))/n(\lambda\sigma + N^{-1}(\alpha))$ and $m_{\alpha,\lambda}(\theta) = s_{\alpha,\lambda}(\theta)\cdot\sigma(\theta) - \big(\lambda/2\cdot\sigma^2(\theta) + 1/\lambda\cdot\ln\big(N(\lambda\sigma(\theta) + N^{-1}(\alpha))/\alpha\big) - K\big)$. Then it holds the following.

Proposition 5 (Intersections: TNT constraint). *For a given equity $\bar{K} < K \leq -\mu_0$, confidence level $\alpha \in (0,1]$ and risk parameter $\lambda > 0$, the lower intersection of the TNT constraint and the (μ,σ)-efficient frontier is (implicitly) given by*

$$\sigma(\underline{\theta}_T) = \frac{\mu_0 + m_{\alpha,\lambda}(\underline{\theta}_T)}{s_{\alpha,\lambda}(\underline{\theta}_T) - \sqrt{D(\mu_0)}}. \tag{20}$$

For a given equity $\bar{K} \leq K$, confidence level $\alpha \in (0,1]$ and risk parameter $\lambda > 0$, the upper intersection of the TNT constraint and the (μ,σ)-efficient frontier is (implicitly) given by

$$\sigma(\overline{\theta}_T) = \frac{\mu_0 + m_{\alpha,\lambda}(\overline{\theta}_T)}{s_{\alpha,\lambda}(\overline{\theta}_T) - \sqrt{D(\mu_0)}}. \tag{21}$$

Proofs are given in the Online Appendix C.

In order to discuss the regulatory implications, we first address a loose regulation $k(\alpha) \leq \sqrt{D(\mu_0)}$, which can only occur under a CVaR constraint. This is because CVaR incorporates a linear mean-standard deviation-trade-off. When moving upward the (μ, σ)-efficient frontier, the mean increases yielding (c.p.) a linear reduction in CVaR, while the standard deviation increases, which (c.p.) results in a linear increase of CVaR. However, in a loose regulation, the mean outweighs the standard deviation in this linear trade-off such that CVaR can be reduced ad infinitum. This "critical" case of loose regulation does not emerge under the TNT constraint, which is caused by its strict convexity as opposed to CVaRs linearity induced by the axioms (TI) and (PH). Two regulatory consequences arise. First, for slightly risk-averse banks with small equity $K < -\mu_0$, the CVaR constraint proves to be useless, as it does not limit the standard deviation of their portfolio. In contrast, due to TNTs strict convexity, which relies on the axiom (C), the upper intersection $\sigma(\overline{\theta}_T)$ always exists. Thus, TNT always limits the standard deviation for these slightly risk-averse banks. Second, for highly risk-averse banks and small equity $K < -\mu_0$, the CVaR constraint may be even harmful. This is because it precludes portfolios with small standard deviation and, thus, forces these banks to increase their portfolio's standard deviation. For TNT, the benefits of the strict convexity of the constraint for slightly risk-averse banks come at a price for highly risk-averse banks. In formal terms, we obtain the following.

Proposition 6 (Comparison: lower intersections). *Let $k(\alpha) < \sqrt{D(\mu_0)}$ and $K < -\mu_0$. Given a bank's equity K, a confidence level $\alpha \in (0, 1]$ and risk parameter $\lambda > 0$, for the lower intersection of the (μ, σ)-efficient frontier and the TNT and CVaR constraint, respectively, it holds that*

$$\sigma(\underline{\theta}_T) > \sigma(\theta_L). \tag{22}$$

For highly risk-averse banks, the TNT constraint is even more harmful than the CVaR constraint in precluding more portfolios with small standard deviation. Consequently, highly risk-averse banks suffer a stronger increase in the standard deviation of their portfolio under the TNT constraint than under the CVaR constraint.

Second, assume a strict regulation, $k(\alpha) > \sqrt{D(\mu_0)}$, is induced by the CVaR constraint. As examined earlier, the TNT and CVaR constraint force slightly risk-averse banks to choose a portfolio with lower standard deviation. Comparing the strictness of regulation, we obtain the following result:

Proposition 7 (Comparison: upper intersections). *Let $k(\alpha) > \sqrt{D(\mu_0)}$ and $K > -\mu_0$. Given a bank's equity K, a confidence level $\alpha \in (0, 1]$ and risk parameter $\lambda > 0$, for the upper intersection of the (μ, σ)-efficient frontier and the TNT and CVaR constraint, respectively, it holds that*

$$\sigma(\overline{\theta}_T) < \sigma(\theta_L). \tag{23}$$

Like with loose regulation, the TNT constraint is also more effective in controlling slightly risk-averse banks than the CVaR constraint under strict regulation.

To summarise, the benefits of switching from a CVaR constraint to a TNT constraint need to be qualified. Given the above results, the possible superiority of the TNT constraint when compared to the CVaR constraint depends on the trade-off between the positive and the negative outcome of the TNT constraint's strict convexity: While the fragility of slightly risk-averse banks is reduced, that of highly risk-averse banks will be affected negatively.

4. Concluding Remarks

Imposing a (convex) TNT constraint on a banks (μ, σ)-portfolio selection problem opens a promising alternative when compared to the traditional (linear) CVaR constraint. This is because the constraint's shape moves from linear to convex, and further TNT provides regulation authorities with an additional parameter of control by means of the risk parameter λ. The concrete recommendation, which risk measure to use, however, depends on the specific situation at hand with respect to, e.g., the amount of equity and the bank's degree of risk aversion.

In the run up of the recent financial crisis 2007–2009, banks proved to be engaged in aggressive risk-taking which led international and national regulators to propose several regulatory changes in order to control banks' risk and protect the financial system. For instance, the Basel Committee on Banking Supervision suggested the replacement of VaR by CVaR for setting capital constraints. To provide a better control of bank's risk taking, our results suggest that the TNT constraint may be used instead, as it is more effective in controlling slightly risk-averse banks. Due to the convexity of the TNT constraint, the problem of implementing a critical "loose" regulation vanishes. Note that a loose regulation induces adverse implications for bank regulation and may be seen as a source of financial crises.

Furthermore, the additional risk parameter λ allows a more flexible adjustment of the capital constraint. One idea could be to assign different risk parameters to different banks or group of banks; especially, too-big-to-fail (TBTF) banks may receive higher risk parameters in order to induce a more prudent behaviour. Dam and Koetter (2012) and Balasubramnian and Cyree (2011) argue that any enforced *ex ante* beliefs in rescuing banks by bailout procedures leaves them with aggressive risk-taking and diminished market discipline. Boyd *et al.* (2009) show that the World's 20 largest banking firms took excessive risks in the 2000s and suffered excessive losses in the beginning of the crisis. The necessity to control these slightly risk-averse banks and their appetite of risk-taking encourage to replace the CVaR constraint by the TNT constraint with a high risk parameter. Other banks can be controlled by means of a TNT constraint with a low risk parameter or with a CVaR constraint depending on their respective size. Note that the empirical evidence on the relationship between bank size and risk taking is mixed. However, if we assume that small and medium-sized banks do not engage in aggressive risk taking, TNT can be harmful when controlling these banks. By forcing higher portfolio risk, the TNT constraint may exacerbate the too-many-to-fail problem, the risk that many banks fail together.

Overall, it is difficult to classify banks in terms of their risk aversion itself only. Depending on the current regulation, resolution mechanism, interest rate policy, creditor rights, CEO compensation, etc., banks can behave more or less risk-averse, so the concrete recommendation with respect to either TNT-based or CVaR-based regulation depends on the specific situation at hand. To summarise, there is no "one size fits all"-approach to risk measurement. Instead, our findings suggest that the use of a CVaR and TNT constraint is intertwined.

Appendix

The online supplementary material can be accessed here: https://www.worldscientific.com/worldscibooks/10.1142/q0351#t=suppl.

References

Acerbi, C. and Tasche, D. (2002). On the coherence of expected shortfall, *Journal of Banking & Finance* **26**(7), 1487–1503.

Alexander, G.J. and Baptista, A.M. (2003). CVaR as a measure of risk: Implications for portfolio selection, *EFA 2003 Annual Conference Paper*, 235.

Alexander, G.J. and Baptista, A.M. (2004). A comparison of var and CVaR constraints on portfolio selection with the mean-variance model, *Management Science* **50**(9), 1261–1273.

Alexander, G.J. and Baptista, A.M. (2006). Does the basle capital accord reduce bank fragility? An assessment of the value-at-risk approach, *Journal of Monetary Economics* **53**(7), 1631–1660.

Artzner, P., Delbaen, F., Eber, J.-M. and Heath, D. (1999). Coherent measures of risk, *Mathematical Finance* **9**(3), 203–228.

Balasubramnian, B. and Cyree, K.B. (2011). Market discipline of banks: Why are yield spreads on bank-issued subordinated notes and debentures not sensitive to bank risks? *Journal of Banking & Finance* **35**(1), 21–35.

Basak, S. and Shapiro, A. (2001). Value-at-risk-based risk management: Optimal policies and asset prices, *Review of Financial Studies* **14**(2), 371–405.

Bergk, K., Brandtner, M. and Kürsten, W. (2021). Regulating banks with the tail nonlinearly transformed risk measure — a better choice than the conditional value-at-risk? Working Paper.

Bergk, K., Brandtner, M. and Kürsten, W. (2021). Portfolio selection with the tail nonlinearly transformed risk measure — a comparison with mean-CVaR analysis. *Quantitative Finance* **21**(6), 1011–1025.

Boyd, J.H., Jagannathan, R. and Kwak, S. (2009). What caused the current what caused the current financial mess and what can we do about it? Working Paper.

Brandtner, M. (2013). Conditional value-at-risk, spectral risk measures and (non-)diversification in portfolio selection problems — a comparison with mean–variance analysis, *Journal of Banking & Finance* **37**(1)2, 5526–5537.

Brandtner, M. (2018). Expected shortfall, spectral risk measures, and the aggravating effect of background risk, or: Risk vulnerability and the problem of subadditivity, *Journal of Banking & Finance* **89**, 138–149.

Brandtner, M. and Kürsten, W. (2015). Decision making with expected shortfall and spectral risk measures: The problem of comparative risk aversion, *Journal of Banking & Finance* **58**, 268–280.

Chen, Z. and Li Yang (2011). Nonlinearly weighted convex risk measure and its application, *Journal of Banking & Finance* **35**(7), 1777–1793.

Chen, Z., Li Yang, Xu, D. and Hu, Q. (2012). Tail nonlinearly transformed risk measure and its application, *OR Spectrum* **34**(4), 817–860.

Cummins, J.D. and Freifelder, L.R. (1978). A comparative analysis of alternative maximum probable yearly aggregate loss estimators, *The Journal of Risk and Insurance* **45**(1), 27–52.

Dam, L. and Koetter, M. (2012). Bank bailouts and moral hazard: Evidence from germany, *Review of Financial Studies* **25**(8), 2343–2380.

de Giorgi, E. (2002). A note on portfolio selections under various risk measures: Working Paper.

Dionne, G. (2013). Risk management: History, definition, and critique, *Risk Management and Insurance Review* **16**(2), 147–166.

Fulga, C. (2016). Portfolio optimization with disutility-based risk measure, *European Journal of Operational Research* **251**(2), 541–553.

Hart, O.D. and Jaffee, D.M. (1974). On the application of portfolio theory to depository financial intermediaries, *The Review of Economic Studies* **41**(1), 129–147.

Koch-Medina, P. and Munari, C. (2016). Unexpected shortfalls of expected shortfall: Extreme default profiles and regulatory arbitrage, *Journal of Banking & Finance* **62**, 141–151.

Koehn, M. and Santomero, A.M. (1980). Regulation of bank capital and portfolio risk, *The Journal of Finance* **35**(5), 1235–1244.

Kürsten, W. and Brandtner, M. (2009). Kohärente risikomessung versus individuelle akzeptanzmengen — anmerkungen zum impliziten risikoverständnis des "conditional value-at-risk", *Schmalenbachs Zeitschrift für betriebswirtschaftliche Forschung* **61**(4), 358–381.

Li Yang, Chen, Z.P. and Zhang, F. (2016). Time consistency and time consistent generalized convex multistage risk measures, *IMA Journal of Management Mathematics* **27**(3), 419–437.

Locarek-Junge, H., Prinzler, R. and Straßberger, M. (2002). The estimation of market risk in portfolios of stocks and stock options, *Schmalenbach Business Review, Special Issue* **54**(1-02), 171–189.

Locarek-Junge, H., Straßberger, M. and Vollbehr, H. (2000). Die ermittlung von value-at-risk-handelslimiten zur kontrolle und steuerung von marktrisiken bei kontinuierlicher überprüfung. In Inderfurth, K., Schwödiauer, G., Domschke, W., Juhnke, F., Kleinschmidt, P. and Wäscher, G. (eds.), *Operations Research Proceedings 1999*, Springer Berlin Heidelberg, pp. 317–322.

Rochet, J.-C. (1992). Capital requirements and the behaviour of commercial banks, *European Economic Review* **36**(5), 1137–1170.

Rockafellar, R.T. and Uryasev, S. (2000). Optimization of conditional value-at-risk, *Journal of risk* **2**(3), 21–42.

Szegö, G.P. (2002). No more var (this is not a typo), *Journal of Banking & Finance* **26**(7), 1247–1251.

Tobin, J. (1958). Liquidity preference towards risk, *Review of Economic Studies* **67**(2), 65–86.

Wang, C.P., Shyu, D. and Huang, H.H. (2005). Optimal insurance design under a value-at-risk framework, *The Geneva Risk and Insurance Review* **30**(2), 161–179.

https://doi.org/10.1142/9781800611917_0010

Chapter 10

Objectification of Subjective Risk Assessments

Lars Hengmith* **and Sophia Licht**†
50Hertz Transmission GmbH, Berlin, Germany
**lars.hengmith@50hertz.com*
†sophia.licht@50hertz.com

Risk quantification in enterprises often is based on a large degree of subjectivity. While subjectivity is necessary to get all the relevant information and to assess the complex risk situation, it might lead to problems when risks are compared, aggregated and control measures are derived based on the risk assessment. We developed a methodology to reduce subjectivity by systematically combining opinions of several experts.

1. Introduction

> "If someone asked me how I would describe my experience of 40 years at sea, I could answer this question with 'unspectacular'. I have never seen a wreck, nor have I been in distress myself or otherwise found myself in a predicament that threatened to turn into a disaster." (Edward John Smith, 1907)

According to the legend, this was the statement of John Edward Smith, the captain of the RMS Titanic. Five years later, on 14 April 1912, the passenger ship sank and over 1,500 people lost their lives (Koldau, 2012, p. 7). One of them was the captain. He himself assessed the risk of danger in the Titanic's voyage as too low and that only because he referred to his experience. This is an example of how blind trust in one's own experience without taking into account new possible risks can become a danger. This makes it clear that the problem of subjective self-assessment was already an issue back then. Today, too, one encounters similar problems in everyday life. Perceived risks often do not coincide with risks based on empirical data. An example of this is that a car journey is 10 times more deadly than a plane journey. However, people consider the latter to be far riskier (Drommert, 2008). This was also made very clear by the aftermath of September 11. Fearing that they might suffer the same fate as the people in said plane, people began to choose the car as an alternative means of transport in the months following the disaster. This decision to avoid the risks of flying then resulted in an above-average increase in the number of deaths from car accidents. Thus, more people died as a result of the attack than during the attack itself (Gigerenzer, 2014, p. 22).

Another point is that people have a natural aversion to risks, which is why they are often consciously or unconsciously ignored. They are frequently associated with management mistakes and thus deliberately not analysed (Gleißner, 2018, p. 27).

However, there is usually not enough data available for a sufficient risk assessment in companies. In addition, the causes and potential effects are so diverse and complex that the subjective assessment of experts, often also their gut feeling, is an important source for the evaluation of risks.

Even at 50 Hertz Transmission GmbH and (hereafter 50 Hertz), the risk assessment is mostly based on the subjective opinion and experience of employees. This creates discrepancies in the approach to risk assessment within the different areas and between those involved. In order to obtain comparable results and also a more precise determination of the probability of occurrence and the impact of risks, a procedure that is more independent of subjective factors is needed.

The aim of this chapter is to give an overview of the methods for risk identification and assessment. The assessment methods used in the company will be examined and compared with regard to accuracy and decision support. In particular, the advantages and disadvantages of objective and subjective methods will be examined.

Subsequently, a method will be developed to help objectify the results of subjective methods in order to mitigate the disadvantages of subjective risk assessment.

2. Definition of Terms

2.1. *Risk/opportunity*

In a company, planned or forecast values are set as relevant goals. A forecast or forecast value is a target value that is to be achieved at a certain point in the future. These can be monetary values, such as the planned budget of a project or the expected net profit, or non-monetary target values, such as the maximum accident rate. However, since the future is unknown, it is almost certain that deviations from the planned values will occur. The possibility of a negative deviation is called a risk. If it is a positive deviation, it is called an opportunity. Risk management thus encompasses all activities in the company where possible opportunities and risks can arise (Gleißner, 2017a, p. 25). If a risk is considered before the mitigation measures are implemented, it is called a gross risk. After the measures have been taken into account, it is a net risk (Diederichs, 2018, p. 139).

2.2. *Objectivity/subjectivity*

The terms objectivity and subjectivity originate in philosophy and refer to the assessment or description of a fact or event. Numerous definitions exist for the two terms in the literature. In the following, objectivity is defined as 'value-free judgement' (Ritsert, 1999, p. 52). Here, a matter is classified on the basis of the neutrality with which something is evaluated. The more neutral the point of view, the more objective the assessment, and the more independent the estimation is of the person carrying out the assessment. In this context, the possibility of absolute objectivity seems impossible (Perler, 2006, p. 158). The contrast to this is subjectivity. Here, feelings and own opinions are included in the assessment. Subjectivity is defined as a 'form of everyday knowledge that leads to convictions through the repetition of subjective experience via associations' (Achterberg, 2015, p. 2; Popper, 2002, p. 21). The result of a subjective assessment is thus highly dependent on the experiences, expectations, beliefs, etc. of the person making the assessment.

3. Methods for Risk Identification and Risk Assessment

3.1. *Risk identification*

For all subsequent steps of the risk management process, risk identification is the first that becomes necessary. This forms the basis of risk management and has a strong influence on its quality and efficiency. The essential goals of identification are to record all sources of hazards, damage and disruptions and to recognise potential links between the individual causes. The information required for risk identification can be collected by different methods and separated according to the type of risk (Vanini, 2017, p. 69).

The identification of risks is strongly linked to the assessment. There are three basic methods for this, on which all procedures used are based. These are the loss data collection (Kaiser and Köhne, 2004, p. 75), which has an objective view of identification and assessment, expert estimates (Kaiser and Köhne, 2004, p. 88 ff.), which are characterised by subjectivity, and risk indicators (Kaiser and Köhne, 2004, p. 105 ff.).

The first way to identify a risk is to collect loss data and then assess the new risks against data that have already been identified. Loss data include information about negative events that have occurred (Kaiser and Köhne, 2004, p. 75). It is not only possible to identify potential risks, but also to determine proposals for evaluation and to check the effectiveness of control measures. In order to be able to evaluate the loss data accordingly, extensive documentation is necessary. Attention must be paid to completeness, accuracy, consistency and clear allocability (Röckle, 2002, p. 68 ff.). Once the possible risks have been identified, the collected data can be used to make an assessment. The derived probability of occurrence and the expected amount of loss play a key role in the assessment (Faisst and Kovacs, 2003, p. 342 ff.). In order to not generate too much data, an interval limit must be set in which the loss levels must be located. Also, the incurred loss values cannot be taken over one-to-one if the negative event lies several years in the past. In this case, the values must be compounded to adjust for inflation. In order to determine the effectiveness of measures, the values prior to the introduction of mitigation measures should be used for the evaluation, in order to compare them later with the losses after the implementation of the measures (Hengmith, 2008, p. 28 ff.) (see Table 1).

The contrast to the objective loss data collection is the more subjective expert estimates. The corresponding risk situation is assessed by suitable experts. However, before the expert looks at the risk, four statements must be made about the respective risk. First, it is determined whether the risk is a net or gross risk. Furthermore, the business sector in which the particular risk falls must be defined. In addition, it must be specified how the determined risk is to be stated. This can be done in monetary units or by using a qualitative scale, such as indicating the time impact in the categories high/medium/low. Finally, it must be decided who will make the assessment. This can be done by an internal staff member or an external expert (Kaiser and Köhne, 2004, p. 88 ff.). The risks are then quantified similarly to the loss data collection by the determined values of the probability of occurrence and the expected loss amount (Faisst and Kovacs, 2003, p. 342 ff.) (see Table 2).

The last method of identifying risks to be considered here is the use of risk indicators. These are key figures that combine objective data already collected with a possible assessment for the future. Thus, this method builds on the loss data collection and expert estimates. The relationship between the characteristic of the indicator and the respective risk is considered. A suitable risk indicator for this method is a key figure that can generally represent risks (Hengmith, 2008, p. 33). These can be financial values such as cash flow or organisational aspects such as employee satisfaction. In this approach, as a first step the indicators are to be identified. This can be done through expert assessments. Subsequently, three ranges are defined for each indicator, which usually include a green range, which is considered uncritical; a warning range, in which a risk should be constantly monitored; and an alarm range, which requires immediate action. Once these indicators have been established, they must be regularly monitored and re-measured (Kaiser and Köhne, 2004, p. 105 ff.). By comparing the methods, various advantages and disadvantages of the individual approaches emerge (see Table 3).

Table 1. Advantages and disadvantages of loss data collection.

	Loss data collection
Advantages	+ Method enables objective assessment of risks. + Data are relatively easy to quantify (Hengmith, 2008, p. 34). + Allows validation of data by relying on values that have already occurred. + Large losses can be derived from smaller losses that have already occurred (Muermann and Oktem, 2002).
Disadvantages	– In practice, there is often not enough data available for certain types of risk to make an appropriate assessment. – Not all recorded losses are equally relevant, which entails an elaborate verification process. – The damage of a risk occurrence can sometimes only be indicated after a longer period of time has elapsed. – Incentive problems, because risks are often caused by people who report or record the losses (Hengmith, 2008, p. 28 ff.). – Only the past is considered, so that a changed risk situation is only taken into account after a longer period of time (Hengmith, 2008, p. 34).

Table 2. Advantages and disadvantages of the expert estimates.

	Expert estimates
Advantages	+ New risks that have not yet occurred can be identified (Hengmith, 2008, p. 34). <u>Risk assessment by internal staff:</u> + Internal staff know the area of risk well and can accordingly assess the extent (Kaiser and Köhne, 2004, p. 99). + The method creates internal risk awareness (Minz, 2004, p. 78).
Disadvantages	– Purely subjective assessment of risks. – Problematic quantifiability of the data (Hengmith, 2008, p. 34). <u>Risk assessment by internal staff:</u> – Incentive problems because staff may feel that risk assessment is an evaluation of the quality of their own work. – Fewer staff have experience with systematic risk identification and assessment (Kaiser and Köhne, 2004, p. 100).

Table 3. Advantages and disadvantages of risk indicators.

	Risk indicators
Advantages	+ Consider present and future. + One-time definition of indicators with subsequent reuse. + Use objective data from the past (Hengmith, 2008, p. 34).
Disadvantages	– Require concrete connection between indicator and risk (Hengmith, 2008, p. 34). – Regular monitoring is necessary. – Subjective determination of indicators by experts.

3.2. *Methods for risk quantification*

3.2.1. *Overview*

Building on the methods for risk identification, quantification methods are formed such as interviewing techniques (e.g., expert interviews), indicator approaches (key figures or systems of key figures), stochastic methods (statistical distribution functions) and causal methods (e.g., Bayesian networks) (Faisst and Kovacs, 2003).

For assessment by experts, either interviews with external experts are conducted or it can be a self-assessment, i.e., a survey of internal employees. An example of a possible approach to an expert interview is the Delphi method. The Delphi method is an applied technique for the identification and simultaneous assessment of risks by experts. In this process, experts are systematically interviewed. The results of this survey are then returned to the respondents in the next step to review and reassess (Häder and Häder, 1994, p. 14 ff.). This multi-stage survey secures the established results and is a simultaneous review and expansion of what has already been established. In this way, the quality of the expert estimates can also be checked. The core aspect here is the anonymity of the respondents, so that no influence can be exerted on each other. Dominant character traits of certain persons also play no role in this regard (Hansmann, 1979; Häder and Häder, 2000, p. 22 ff.). In comparison, this cannot be avoided in group discussions with several experts. On the other hand, the execution of the complete Delphi method can be time-consuming and costly and offers little room for development due to the fixed specification of questions in the second execution (Hansmann, 1979; Geschka, 1977).

Building on the defined risk indicators for identifying risks, extended indicator approaches can be developed. These can be branched indicator systems such as scorecards. This involves linking and aggregating the risk indicators that have been defined individually for certain risks in order to present the overall situation of the company (Haubenstock and Hause, 2006, p. 23; Schawel and Billing, 2012, p. 28). The measured level of the individual risks, including the quality of the regularly performed control measurements, is then presented. The scorecard summarises all risks, provides an overview of the overall situation and additionally shows the effectiveness of the repeated measurements (Blunden, 2003, p. 236; Anders and Sandstedt, 2003, p. 48).

3.2.2. *Quantification by means of statistical distribution function*

Quantification is executed with the help of statistical distribution functions. By describing a risk by means of a distribution function, a risk measure or key figure can then be derived that makes the risks comparable. Risk management in practice usually uses one of the following three distribution functions (Albrecht and Maurer, 2016, p. 107 ff.).

Triangular distribution: The triangular distribution enables an assessment of the risks without much prior knowledge of statistics. For the distribution, three different values are needed, which have to be given for the risky variable. The first is the minimum value. This reflects the smallest numerical value of the corresponding variable. In contrast to this is the maximum value. It shows the highest case of loss, should the risk occur in full. The third and middle point of the distribution is the most probable value. This is an indication of which value is most likely to occur or which amount of damage is most likely. The key figure derived from the triangular distribution is the expected value, which can be calculated with the following formula:

$$\mu = \frac{a+b+c}{3}. \tag{1}$$

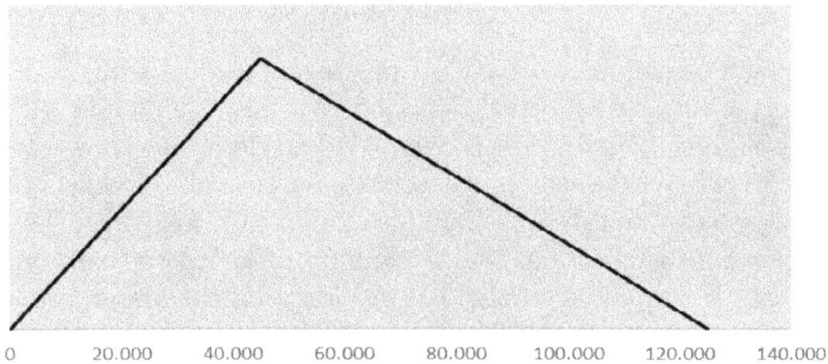

Fig. 1. Triangular distribution for loss of key personnel (Gleißner, 2017b, p. 93; 2011b, p. 188).

In addition, the standard deviation of the triangular distribution is calculated with the formula:

$$\sigma = \sqrt{\frac{a^2 + b^2 + c^2 - ab - ac - bc}{18}}. \tag{2}$$

This is an indication of the dispersion around the mean of the distribution. Figure 1 shows an example of a triangular distribution for the loss of key personnel in a company (Gleißner, 2017b, p. 92 ff.; 2011b, p. 187 ff). The damage amounts to zero in the minimum case, 50,000 in the most probable case and 125,000 in the maximum case.

Normal distribution: The normal distribution is based on the limit theorem. This states that deviations from the planned values are normally distributed if the risky variable consists of many smaller variables that are independent of each other. The normal distribution can also be described with the help of an expected value and a standard deviation (Gleißner, 2017b, p. 93 ff.; Gleißner, 2011b, p. 187).

Binomial distribution: The binomial distribution is based on the Bernoulli experiment, in which there are two events (A and B) that occur with a probability of p or $1-p$. These do not change with experimental repetitions and the individual experiments are not linked to each other. The Bernoulli experiment can be repeated any number of times (n times). The distribution then gives the probability that and one of the events (A) occurs k times (Gleißner, 2017b, p. 94 ff.; 2011b, p. 186).

3.2.3. *Combination of distribution functions*

In the case of a complex situation where using one distribution is not sufficient, several distribution functions can also be combined. The first probability distribution is then used to determine how often a loss occurs while the second represents the uncertain amount of loss. A court case can be taken as a simple example of this. With the help of a Bernoulli distribution, the probability of losing the case can be calculated. The amount of the loss can then be calculated with the help of the minimum, most likely and maximum values. The expected value of the two distributions can then be offset against each other, resulting in a combined expected value of the risks (Gleißner, 2017b, p. 95 ff.; 2011b, p. 188 ff.).

If an expert is unable to provide a suitable estimate needed for the corresponding distribution, the statement can be made that the required estimate itself is subject to risk and should also be described by a distribution. If one is not able to give a definite value for the distribution and thus another distribution is needed, one speaks of a so-called 'meta-risk'. In the case of a triangular distribution, it can be a meta-risk if the minimum value and the maximum value are estimated by the expert, but the most probable value is itself represented by a triangular distribution. If meta risks are not included in the assessment, this can lead to an underestimation of the respective risk. Meta risks can also be differentiated (Gleißner, 2011a, p. 215 ff.):

1. **Type one:** The probability distribution type of the risk can be determined with certainty, but the parameters needed for the distribution are seen as random variables.
2. **Type two:** The parameters of the distributions are known and fixed with certainty. But several probability distributions come into question for the description of the risk. The probability of which probability distribution type is present is also unknown. Therefore, a probability distribution must be created that indicates the probability of the probability distributions being present.
3. The third type combines the first two. First of all, it is therefore unclear which probability distribution is involved, which is why a probability distribution is required to determine it. Furthermore, the individual parameters of the probability distributions are not

clearly defined, which is why probability distributions are also necessary for them.

3.3. *Intermediate conclusion*

The most reliable evaluation, which simplifies comparisons between different risks and without the subjective fluctuations mentioned, is achieved by using the objective methods. However, these are usually based on a large amount of data. If the subjective methods are considered, it can be seen that they form an important core of risk identification and assessment, but are very strongly coupled to the opinion and assessment of the person performing the task. This fact opens a source for misjudgements and prevents an objective evaluation and comparison. For this reason, a method is developed in the following, which tries to objectify the subjective assessments to a certain extent.

4. Combination of Expert Assessments

4.1. *General procedure*

In risk management, the risk identification is followed by the evaluation and assessment of the risks by the respective expert. For the development of the methodology, the assessment of the risk takes place by means of a probability distribution. The risk is represented with the help of a triangular distribution. The triangular distribution is chosen, because it is easy to understand, even for project staff who are not familiar with statistics and risk topics, since no probabilities have to be given. Since these staff members are the best choice to assess the risk, and their input is therefore crucial for a high-quality risk assessment, the ease of understanding of the assessment method is of high importance.

Moreover, in many cases, it depicts the density function sufficiently with a minimum amount of parameters. The triangular distribution assumes a probability of occurrence of 100%, which is why only the impact of the risk is required from the expert. The impact is characterised by the minimum, most probable and maximum amount of damage. Here, the net risks, i.e., after mitigation through measures, are taken into account in order to show the real relevance for the company. In order to mitigate the aforementioned disadvantages of subjectivity, at least three experts are interviewed about the respective risk. The corresponding values are then weighted using different criteria, which are presented in what follows.

4.2. *Expert experience*

The first factor included in the weighting is the experience of the respective expert (referred to as e thereafter). To make this easier to evaluate, the weighting can be divided into five different classes. Class one includes, among others, a person who has no professional experience at all, while class five refers to an expert who has been working in the professional field for more than 10 years.

Table 4 shows the subdivision into the different classes.

The year specifications of the classes are only suggestions in order to clarify a distinction. The values can be changed on a case-by-case basis. In addition, not all conditions have to be fulfilled for an assessment of the classes, but only one or more have to apply.

Table 4. Classification of expert experience.

Class	Example/description
1	No work experience (0–1 year), new to the company/industry (0–1 year), only theoretical knowledge, no overlapping of training and subject area.
2	First work experience (1–3 years), first experience gained in the company/industry (1–3 years), theoretical and first practical knowledge, little overlapping of training and subject area.
3	Little work experience (3–5 years), little experience in the company/industry (3–5 years), theoretical and first practical knowledge, basic overlapping of training and subject area.
4	Basic professional experience (5–10 years), basix experience gained in the company/industry (5–10 years), basic theoretical and practical knowledge, pronounced overlapping of training and subject area.
5	Many years of professional experience (>10 years), many years of work in the company/industry (>10 years), extensive theoretical and practical knowledge, complete overlapping of training and subject area.

4.3. *Precision*

The second factor that plays a role in the weighting is the precision (referred to as p thereafter). This involves checking the consistency of the respective expert's assessment with the reality in the past. This is a factor that turns out to be difficult to track or evaluate in practice, since for many experts there is no documentation on the consistency between the assessment and reality. For this reason, a medium value is generally determined for this factor, i.e., a classification into class three. In individual cases, a decision has to be made, whether there is an upward or downward deviation from this value, if the necessary information is available. Table 5 shows the classification of the precision in the respective class.

4.4. *Gut feeling*

A third factor that is relevant for an expert's assessment and often plays a role in everyday life is the gut feeling of the risk manager (referred to as m thereafter), who interviews the experts and then carries out the weighting. Since the gut feeling is to be seen as a rather subjective aspect, it cannot be classified into the respective classes on the basis of strict parameters. Instead, the classification is made on the basis of a separate evaluation according to soft factors. These include the subjective assessment of the competence and thus the expertise of the experts with regard to the respective topic. The interest of the respective expert is also assessed and how much commitment he or she shows to the topic. In addition, the demeanour of a person is often an important criterion that is decisive for the gut

Table 5. Classification of precision.

Class	Example/description
1	Regular deviation from assessment and reality over a long period of time.
2	Occasional deviation from assessment and reality.
3	Average correlation between assessment and reality.
4	Recurring correlation between assessment and reality.
5	Regular correlation between assessment and reality over a long period of time.

feeling. In this case, the self-confidence, but also the fact how much someone stands behind his/her own opinion, is verified. Finally, the subjective evaluation of the expert's argumentation is also taken into account. This is the risk manager's opinion on the extent to which the reasoning for the expert's respective assessment sounds plausible. Based on these factors, the risk manager then assigns a rating from one to five according to his own assessment. One factor (e.g., interest) can be particularly high, but another (e.g., subjective evaluation of the argumentation) can be particularly low, which in this example would lead to a rating of three.

4.5. *Self-assessment*

The last factor that plays a role in the weighting of the expert opinion is the respective self-assessment of the expert (referred to as s thereafter). This is often defined in literature as the reciprocal of the variance of the corresponding distribution. Just as the standard deviation (see formula (2)), the variance is a measure of dispersion around the centre of gravity of a probability distribution. The variance itself is the standard deviation squared. After the variance has been calculated, the reciprocal value of the variance is determined with (Ocker, 2010, p. 170 ff.)

$$s = \frac{1}{\sigma^2}. \tag{3}$$

This is then seen as the expert's self-assessment and is thus based on the hypothesis that an expert who specifies a lower range of variation in the results believes he can make more reliable predictions than an expert who specifies a higher range of variation.

4.6. *Weighting factors*

These four individual factors must still be weighted individually after the evaluation, in order to determine the general weight of the expert estimate. For this purpose, the assessments of all experts must be considered. The determined value of an individual expert (e, p, m or s) is divided by the sum of all values of all experts determined in this category. This results in the following formula (where n is the number of experts interviewed):

$$ge_i = \frac{e_i}{\sum_{i=1}^{n} e_i}, \quad gp_i = \frac{p_i}{\sum_{i=1}^{n} p_i}, \quad gm_i = \frac{m_i}{\sum_{i=1}^{n} m_i}$$
$$\text{and} \quad gs_i = \frac{s_i}{\sum_{i=1}^{n} s_i}. \tag{4}$$

These individual values determined are then weighted again with the following formula in order to clarify their relevance in the actual weighting:

$$g_i = 0,4 \cdot ge_i + 0,1 \cdot gp_i + 0,3 \cdot gm_i + 0,2 \cdot gs_i. \tag{5}$$

The weighting factors used are fixed, but can be changed by the responsible risk manager under certain circumstances. However, this reduces the standardisation of the final results. After the weighting for the respective expert has been determined, the assessed value is then multiplied by the new weighting. This has to be executed for the minimum, the most probable and the maximum value with the corresponding formulas:

$$W_{a,i} = a_i \cdot g_i, \quad W_{b,i} = b_i \cdot g_i \quad \text{and} \quad W_{c,i} = c_i \cdot g_i. \tag{6}$$

In order to link the weighted values of the experts with each other, the sum of the individual estimates for the three required data is calculated:

$$E_a = \sum_{i=1}^{n} W_{a,i}, \quad E_b = \sum_{i=1}^{n} W_{b,i} \quad \text{and} \quad E_c = \sum_{i=1}^{n} W_{c,i}. \tag{7}$$

The three assessments needed to create the triangular distribution were determined. Not only the assessments of several experts were considered, but the individual experts were also implemented differently in the decision based on their 'quality'.

5. Application at 50 Hertz

5.1. *Company profile 50 Hertz*

50 Hertz operates the electricity transmission system in the north and east of Germany, which it expands as needed for the energy

transition. Its extra high voltage grid has an electrical circuit length of about 10,490 km, or the distance between Berlin and Rio de Janeiro. The 50 Hertz control area covers the Lander of Brandenburg, Mecklenburg-Western Pomerania, Saxony, Saxony-Anhalt and Thuringia, as well as the city states of Berlin and Hamburg. Within these regions, 50 Hertz and its 1,300 employees ensure that 18 million people are supplied with electricity around the clock. 50 Hertz is a forerunner in the field of secure integration: in its grid area, more than 60% of the electricity consumed is already generated from renewable sources. The objective is until 2032 to integrate 100% of renewable energy securely (50 Hertz Company Website, 2020).

5.2. *Risk management at 50 Hertz*

The risk management at 50 Hertz can roughly be split in two areas: The first area covers only the top risks and is managed by the enterprise risk management process (ERM process), whereas the second area covers also smaller risks that need to be managed on department-level or on project-level. Only large risks are relevant for the ERM process, and risks can not only result from projects but from different areas and processes. To connect the risk management on department-level with the ERM process the top project risks are reported. In certain cases such a top risk is an aggregated risk which comprises several minor risks, e.g., there might be a risk of delays that has several different potential causes.

It is often challenging to communicate the added value of the ERM process and the risk aggregation to the people responsible for project risk management, because this is not directly needed for project management. Additionally, the concrete meaning of the points of the triangular distribution are not always clear to the people involved in the projects. That's why it is necessary to make clear if it is a conditional triangular distribution, that is only to apply if the risk occurs (means: If the risk occurs, what would be the lowest, the expected and the maximum damage?), or if it is an unconditional triangular distribution (here the lowest damage could be zero in case the risk doesn't occur, or even an upside might be realised). And it should be clear what the target values are, that would be missed in case the risk occurs. For example, if there is a delay for bad weather included in the schedule, only additional delays can be seen as 'damage' in the sense of the triangular distribution, and the possibility that the delay is shorter than the scheduled one presents an upside.

Risk management at 50Hertz is dominated by subjectivity. Reason for this are the types of relevant risks that only seldom show a history that can be used for assessment because of the many changes in connection with the energy transition, regulatory changes and new technologies.

The views on what is seen as a risk differ from department to department, mostly depending on their daily business. Also, the different personalities and experiences of the employees foster a heterogeneous understanding of the risk situation. And the feeling, what the identified risk might show about the quality or quantity of the work of the assessing person can play a role in the risk assessment. For example, there might be the feeling that a reported risk indicates an error in the process and as such might show that the processes for which the person is responsible are not sufficiently under control. This can have the result that some risks are 'kept secret', or that the assessing person is unconsciously biased towards seeing these risks as not relevant. On the other hand, if a certain objective shall be reached, or a signal shall be sent, risks might be reported that objectively are not relevant. Also, overconfidence can lead to underestimation of the risks because the assessing expert could be of the opinion that he or she can solve the problem before the risk occurs.

These are the reasons why there have been many efforts in the past years to develop a better understanding for the requirements and added value of the ERM-process to reach a more homogeneous risk assessment. For instance, checklists are used to better detect recurring risks (especially typical project risks) and consistently capture them. Risk workshops are held at least on a yearly basis by the risk manager and the respective departments to make sure the requirements of the ERM-process are understood throughout the enterprise. One of the main problems here is that the risk assessment according to the requirements of the ERM-process is not part of the daily work of the experts because it often differs from the risk management that is needed for the project management.

Because of all these reasons, subjectivity heavily affects the risk assessment at 50Hertz. This assessment is a central part of the risk management, mainly because the decisions on control measures are based on the assessment, so an objectification of the risk assessments would create a better overview over the companies' risk situation and enable better decisions.

5.3. *Test of the methodology*

To test the applicability of the methodology from Section 4, three expert interviews have been carried out. Because of the COVID-19 situation they took place by phone instead of personally. The interview guide was sent to the experts upfront so that they had time to think about the questions and the respective risk.

For the test of the methodology, the project South-East-Link was chosen. Here two different risks were assessed. The first one is a market price risk that might occur because of a limited number of suppliers on the market and resulting supply bottlenecks, which in turn would result in higher prices for material and personnel, as well as project delays. Here only the higher prices will be regarded.

The second risk is also a market price risk that can result in higher prices for material and personnel. Here the price deviations are derived from mid-price calculations of pre-studies with inquired budget calculations.

Three experts were questioned who are involved in the project. The first part of the interview consisted of general questions regarding the professional background and the experiences in risk management of the experts. Experiences in this professional area and in risk management reached from 8 to 15 years. Two of the experts additionally dealt privately with risk topics. The educational background was nearly identical, mainly focusing on technical aspects.

In the second part of the interview, the experts were asked to assess the above mentioned two risks. For the first risk in two of three cases, the value from the risk register was determined as the most probable value in the triangular distribution. There might have been larger deviations had this risk been assessed for the first time (since the risks were already captured in the risk register).

Table 6 shows the results from the interviews and calculations for the first risk (numbers have been changed by a factor for reasons of corporate secrecy). As depicted in following Table 6, the estimates

Table 6. Application of methodology: Risk 1.

Risk 1	Expert 1	Expert 2	Expert 3	Weight	Result
Experience (e)	5	5	4	0,4	
Precision (p)	3	3	3	0,1	
Gut feeling (m)	3	5	4	0,3	
Self-assessment (s)	6,521E-09	5,683E-09	2,667E-08	0,2	
Minimum (a)	10.000€	10.000€	15.000€		
Most probable (b)	21.114€	21.114€	22.500€		
Maximum (c)	40.000€	42.000€	30.000€		
ge	0,357	0,357	0,286		
gp	0,333	0,333	0,333		
gm	0,250	0,417	0,333		
gs	0,168	0.146	0,686		
g	0,285	0,330	0,385		
Wa	2.847€	3.304€	5.772€		
Wb	6.012€	6.977€	8.659€		
Wc	11.390€	13.878€	11.545€		
μ	23.705€	24.371€	22.500€		
σ^2	153.355.777	175.971.777	37.500.000		
Ea					11.924€
Eb					21.647€
Ec					36.813€
μ					23.461€
σ					5.121€

of the experts 1 and 2 are pretty similar, whereas expert 3 had a different view. Since experts 1 and 2 have more experience, their estimates were weighted more than the estimates of expert 3.

The result of the calculations shows that the maximum value significantly differs from the 'single' estimations of the experts, because here the estimations were spread rather far. For the other values, there was no significant spread and therefore the results from the calculation are close to the estimates. This can either mean that we can be pretty sure that the risk distribution is correct or that we see the disadvantages of an already captured risk, where experts tend to stick near the values they already know.

The differences in the expert assessments are visible in Figure 2. It shows the three separate triangular distributions that are based on the expert assessments, and the resulting distribution from the

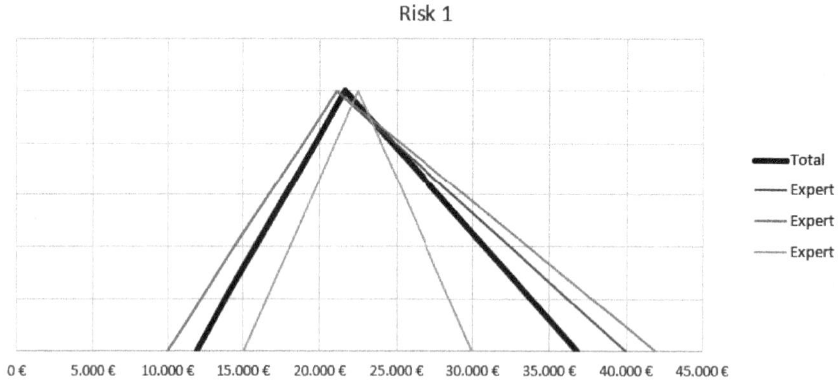

Fig. 2. Triangular distributions of the expert assessments and combined distribution for risk 1.

application of the methodology. The values of the single distributions are spread rather broadly, whereas the combined distribution has a more narrow range, which points to a higher confidence in the aggregated assessment. The expected value is 23.5 T€ and the standard deviation is 5.1 T€.

The results from the assessment of the second risk show an even broader spread (here also numbers have been changed by a factor). While the most probable value was nearly the same for all of the experts, there were significant differences for the maximum and minimum values. Experts 1 and 3 estimated the minimum value between 13 and 15 T€. In contrast expert 2 even saw an upside here, giving a negative value. This means that payments will be repaid or budget will not be used. Also, the maximum values show a significant spread. The range was from 27 to 40 T€. The combined distribution has a minimum value of 3.2 T€, which is pretty far from all of the experts' assessments (lower in case of experts 1 and 3, higher in case of expert 2).

An overview over the results can be seen in Table 7, the corresponding triangular distributions are shown in Figure 3 (here the numbers also have been changed for reasons of corporate secrecy). The large spread in the assessment of expert 2 stands out — this leads to a low weighting coefficient for the self-assessment. The combined distribution has an expected value of 18.8 T€ and a standard deviation of 5.8 T€.

Table 7. Application of methodology: Risk 2.

Risk 1	Expert 1	Expert 2	Expert 3	Weight	Result
Experience (e)	5	5	4	0,4	
Precision (p)	3	3	3	0,1	
Gut feeling (m)	3	5	4	0,3	
Self-assessment (s)	2,571E-08	1,636E-09	3,174E-08	0,2	
Minimum (a)	15.000€	−19.500€	13.750€		
Most probable (b)	20.000€	20.000€	20.650€		
Maximum (c)	30.000€	40.000€	27.500€		
ge	0,357	0,357	0,286		
gp	0,333	0,333	0,333		
gm	0,250	0,417	0,333		
gs	0,435	0,028	0,537		
g	0,338	0,307	0,355		
Wa	5.073€	−5.981€	4.882€		
Wb	6.765€	6.135€	7.332€		
Wc	10.147€	12.269€	9.764€		
μ	21.667€	13.500€	20.633€		
σ^2	38.888.889	611.166.667	31.510.556		
Ea					3.974€
Eb					20.231€
Ec					32.180€
μ					18.795€
σ					5.780€

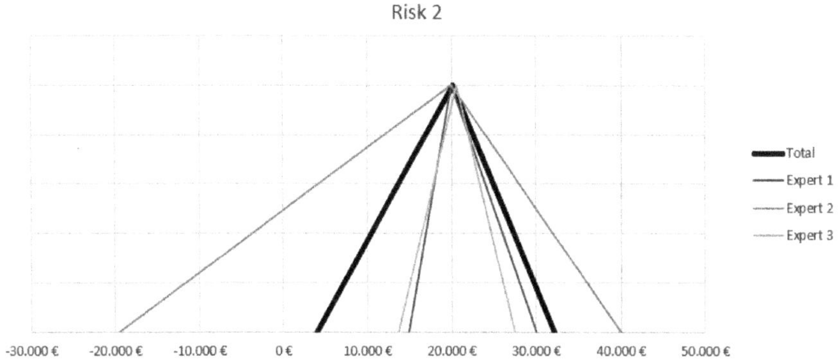

Fig. 3. Triangular distributions of the expert assessments and combined distribution for risk 2.

5.4. *Summary*

Compared with the current assessment of the risks in the project risk register, the described methodology leads to different values. The mean values slightly changed by this assessment. But in this case study the main improvement is assumed in the assessment of the minimum- and maximum-values. Expert knowledge was systematically combined and so subjectivity could be reduced in the risk assessment.

Nevertheless, some potential problems need to be considered. The knowledge that the experts themselves are being assessed via the weighting coefficients might bias their contributions. On the other hand, this knowledge might motivate them to a better assessment. Additionally, the methodology brings better results if new risks are being assessed, where no risk values are known yet. Otherwise, it is likely that the experts tend towards the already known values, as probably happened in the case of the two risks in Section 5.3, and thus produce biased results. Another aspect to be considered is that the interviews, the assessment of their experience, competence, etc. requires a high expenditure of time that is not feasible in smaller projects. And for every risk a number of experts must be found that are able to assess the risk in question, which for some risks might be difficult.

However, for important risks, where a number of experts are able to contribute, the methodology seems suitable to reduce subjectivity by means of 'swarm intelligence'.

6. Conclusion

The objective of this chapter was to examine the different methods for risk assessment, to compare them and to derive a methodology to objectify subjective risk assessments. The methodology was developed and tested with expert interviews at 50Hertz.

It could be shown that subjectivity is necessary in risk assessments in enterprises, and objectification is only possible to some extent, because subjectivity cannot be eliminated completely. Expert knowledge of some complex issues is crucial in risk assessment, and often this knowledge can only be expressed by means of the experts gut feeling. Data analysis would not be sufficient to assess complex risks in changing environments, in projects with new technologies or other situations, where the future risk situation cannot (or only to some limited extent) be assessed by data from the past.

The application of the methodology at 50Hertz shows only minor differences in the expected values that were estimated by the experts. The reason might be that the risk was already captured and assessed in the projects risk register, and the risk value from the register had the effect of an anchor value. In addition, a number of three experts might be rather low to reduce subjectivity. The methodology needs at least two experts that can contribute to the risk assessment, but there is no limit as to how many experts can be interviewed, or the limit is rather set by practical issues such as how much effort and how many resources can be put into the risk assessment and the consideration that the marginal utility of every additional expert declines.

The resulting 'objectivity' is based on the concept of swarm intelligence. Swarm intelligence means that "... a group of actors that form a swarm [...] is able to show 'intelligent behavior' in its entirety that the single actors would not be capable of" (Schmickl, 2009, p. 143 ff.). This concept shows that a large number of individuals can assess certain issues better than a single individual can.

It should be noted that the methodology itself is based on subjective assessments (in the determination of some of the weighting coefficients). If the risk manager is biased or makes some erroneous assessments this might lead to a lower quality of the results. Additionally, if the experts have already formed a common opinion on the risk in question, e.g., because the project leader often talked about it and all the other experts more or less 'acquired' his opinion, the quality of the results could be affected as well.

With the implementation and repeated application of the methodology new data can be gathered that can be used for future applications regarding the weighting coefficients. Once the methodology is in place application takes less effort and can also be used for smaller projects. Results should be documented and, after the project has finished, compared with the risks that have occurred. This backtesting can help to improve the methodology and to realise potential weak points. The longer the methodology is in place, the more added value it will bring for risk management and the better it will support decisions.

References

Achterberg, M. (2015). *The Possibility of Objectivity in Science in Karl R. Popper and Jürgen Habermas.* Munich: GRIN Publishing House.

Albrecht, P. and Maurer, R. (2016). *Investment and Risk Management: Models, Methods, Applications.* 4th edition, Stuttgart: Schäffer-Poeschel Publishing House.

Alexander, C. (2003). Managing operational risks with Bayesian Networks. In: Alexander, C. (ed.), *Operational Risk: Regulation, Analysis and Management.* London: Prentince Hill Financial Times, pp. 285–295.

Anders, U. and Sandstedt, M. (2003). An operational risk scorecard approach. In: *Risk*, No. 01/2003. London: Infopro Digital, pp. 48–51.

Ansoff, H.I. (1975). Managing strategic surprise by response to weak signals, *California Management Review* **18**(2), Berkley: BerkleyHaas, pp. 21–33.

Blunden, T. (2003). Scorecard approaches. In: Alexander, C. (ed.), *Operational Risk: Regulation, Analysis and Management.* London: Pretence Hall Financial Times, pp. 229–240.

Bol, G., Nakhaeizadeh, G., and Vollmer, K.-H. (2000). *Datamining und Computational Finance.* Heidelberg: Physica-Publishing House Heidelberg.

Cruz, M.G. (2002). *Modeling, Measuring and Hedging Operational Risk.* Chichester: John Wiley & Sons Ltd.

Diederichs, M. (2018). *Risk Management and Risk Controlling*, 4th edn. Munich: Vahlen Publishing House.

Döring, N. and Bortz, J. (2016). Science-theoretical foundations of empirical social research. In: Döring, N. and Bortz, J. (eds.), *Research Methods and Evaluation in the Social and Human Sciences.* Berlin, Heidelberg: Springer-Publishing House, pp. 31–79.

Drommert, J. (2008). The scaredy cats. Consumers mostly evaluate dangers according to feelings. But the perceived risk often does not coincide with the statistically calculable risk. In: *THE TIME*, No. 14/2008, 27.03.2008, O. S., [online] https://www.zeit.de/2008/14/GS-Risiko (17.02.2020).

Faisst, U. and Kovacs, M. (2003). Quantifying operational risks — a comparison of methods. In: *The Bank*, Issue 5, pp. 342–349.

Geschka, H. (1977). Delphi. In: Bruckmann, G. (ed.), *Long-term Forecasts. Possibilities and Methods of Long-term Prognostics of Complex Systems.* Würzburg: Physica Publishing House, pp. 27–44.

Gigerenzer, G. (2014). *Risk: How to make the Right Decisions.* 3rd edn., Munich: btb Publishing House.

Gleißner, W. and Romeike, F. (2005). *Risk Management. Implementation, Tools, Risk Assessment*, 1st edn., Munich: Haufe Group.

Gleißner, W. (2011a). Risk management: Data problems and uncertain probability distributions. In: Klein, A. (ed.), *Risk management and Risk Controlling*, 1st edn. Munich: Haufe Group, pp. 205–222.

Gleißner, W. (2011b). Quantitative methods in risk management: Risk aggregation, risk measures and performance measures. In: Klein, A. (ed.), Risk management and risk controlling. 1st edn. Munich: Haufe Group, pp. 179–204.

Gleißner, W. (2017a). Risk management: Overview of objectives and subtasks. In: Gleißner, W. and Klein, A. (eds.), *Risk Management and Controlling*, 2nd edn. Munich: Haufe Group, pp. 23–38.

Gleißner, W. (2017b). Quantification and Aggregation of Risks. In: Gleißner, W. and Klein, A. (eds.), *Risk Management and Controlling*. 2nd edn. Munich: Haufe Group, pp. 85–110.

Gleißner, W. (2018). Controlling and risk management in the joint fight against risk blindness. In: Risk Management Association E. V./ Internationaler Controller Verein E. V. (eds.), *Networking Risk Management and Controlling*. Berlin: Erich Schmidt Publishing House, pp. 21–33.

Grüning, M. and Winkler, A. (2018). Document analysis and rating conferences as instruments to capture different teaching cultures of teacher education institutions. In: Rothland, M. and Biederbeck, I. (eds.), *Practice Phases in Teacher Education in the Focus of Educational Research. Contributions to Teacher Education and Educational Research* Volume 4, Münster, New York: Waxmann Publishing House, p. 209.

Häder, M. and Häder, S. (1994). *The Basics of the Delphi Method: A Literature Review. ZUMA-Arbeitsberichte*, No. 02/1994, Mannheim: Center for Surveys, Methods and Analyses.

Häder, M. and Häder, S. (2000). The Delphi method as an object of methodological research. In: Häder, M. and Häder, S. (eds.), *The Delphi Technique in the Social Sciences*. Wiesbaden: West German Publishing House.

Hansmann, K.-W. (1979). Heuristic forecasting methods. In: *WISU No. 5/79*, Düsseldorf: Lange Publishing House, pp. 229–233.

Haubenstock, M. and Hause, J. (2006). Practical decisions to successfully model operational risk capital. In: Davis, E. (ed.), *The Advanced Measurement Approach to Operational Risk*. London: Risk Books, pp. 15–34.

Hengmith, L. (2005). Business process modeling and simulation as a tool for operational risk management. In: *Banking and Information Technology*, Issue 2, pp. 17–29.

Hengmith, L. (2008). *Management of Operational Risks. Financing, Capital Markets and Banks Volume 60*, Cologne: Eul-Publishing House.

Kaiser, T. and Köhne, M.F. (2004). *Operational Risks in Financial Institutions — Ways to Implement Basel II and CAD 3.* Wiesbaden: Gabler-Publishing House.

Koldau, L.M. (2012). *Titanic: The Ship, the Sinking, the Legends.* Munich: C.H. Beck Publishing House.

Kühnel, S. and Dingelstedt, A. (2019). Causality. In: Baur, N. and Blasius, J. (eds.), Handbook of Methods of Empirical Social Research. 2nd edn. Wiesbaden: Springer VS, pp. 1401–1413.

Mangold, U. and Kunert, A. (2007). Qualitative observation methods. In: Naderer, G. and Balzer, E. (eds.), *Qualitative Market Research in Theory and Practice: Principles, Methods and Applications.* Wiesbaden: Gabler Publishing House, pp. 309–319.

Marotzki, W. (2006). Research methods and methodology of educational biographical research. In Krüger, H.-H. and Marotzki, W. (eds.), *Handbook of Educational Biographical Research.* 2nd edn. Wiesbaden: VS Publishing House for Social Sciences, pp. 111–135.

Mayring, P. (2015). Qualitative Content Analysis: Basics and Techniques, 12th edn. Weinheim: Beltz Publishing House.

Meuser, M. and Nagel, U. (1991). Expert interviews — much tried, little thought: a contribution to the qualitative method discussion. In: Garz, D. and Kraimer, K. (eds.), *Qualitative-empirical Social Research: Concepts, Methods, Analyses.* Opladen: Westdt. Ltd, pp. 441–471.

Minz, K.-A. (2004). *Operational Risks in Credit Institutions.* 1st edn. Competence Center Finance and Bank Management Vol. 2, Frankfurt am Main: Bankakad-Publishing House.

Muermann, A. and Oktem, U. (2002). The Near-Miss Management of Operational Risk, In: Emerald Publishing (ed.), *Journal of Risk Finance* Vol. 4, No. 1, Bingley: Emerald Group Publishing, pp. 25–36.

Ocker, D. (2010). *Fuzzy Risk Analysis of Strategic Event Risks.* Papers on corporate planning Vol. 83, Frankfurt am Main: Peter Lang GmbH.

Perler, D. (2006). *Doubt and Certainty: Skeptical Debates in the Middle Ages.* Philosophical essays Volume 92, Frankfurt am Main: Klostermann Publishing House.

Popper, K. (2002). *Logic of Research.* Tübingen: Mohr Siebeck Publishing House.

Prüfer, P. and Stiegler, A. (2002). *Conducting Standardized Interviews: A Guide.* ZUMA How-to series Volume 11, Mannheim: Center for Surveys, Methods and Analysis.

Ritsert, J. (1999). Dimensions of scientific objectivity. In: Glatzer, Wolfgang (ed.), *Views of Society: Frankfurt Contributions from Sociology and Political Science.* Contemporary Studies — Special Issue Volume 11,

Wiesbaden: VS Publishing House for Social Sciences / Springer Specialist Media, pp. 51–58.

Röckle, S.A. (2002). *Loss Databases as a Tool for Quantifying Operational Risk in Credit Institutions.* Study Series of the Credit Industry Foundation at the University of Hohenheim Volume 35, Sternfels: Science and Practice Publishing House.

Schawel, C. and Billing, F. (2012). Balanced Scorecard (BSC): Key figures and concepts of corporate management. In: Schawel, C. and Billing, F. (eds.), *Top 100 Management Tools.* 4th edn. Wiesbaden: Gabler Publishing House, pp. 28–31.

Schmickl, T. (2009). Swarm intelligence using the example of ant trails. In: Province of Upper Austria/Upper Austrian State Museum/Biology Center/OÖ LANDES-KULTUR GMBH / Weidinger, A. (ed.), *Treasured, Cursed, Ubiquitous: Ants in Biology and Popular Culture.* Denisia vol. 25, pp. 141–155, https://www.zobodat.at/pdf/DENISIA_0025_0141-0155.pdf (06.11.2020).

Schmidt, F. (2018a). Interview procedures. An overview. In: Boelmann, J.M. (ed.), *Survey and Evaluation Procedures.* Empirical Research in German Didactics Volume 2, Baltmannsweiler: Schneider Publishing House Hohengehren GmbH, pp. 23–34.

Schmidt, F. (2018b). Guided interviews. In: Boelmann, J.M. (ed.), *Survey and Evaluation Methods.* Empirical Research in German Didactics Volume 2, Baltmannsweiler: Schneider Publishing House Hohengehren GmbH, pp. 51–66.

Sombé, L. (1992). Causal models. In: Sombé, Léa (ed.), *Reasoning with Uncertain Knowledge in Artificial Intelligence: Comparing Formalisms by Example.* Wiesbaden: Vieweg+Teubner Publishing House, pp. 105–112.

Vanini, U. (2017). Tools for a systematic identification of risks. In: Gleißner, W. and Klein, A. (eds.), *Risk Management and Controlling,* 2nd edn. Munich: Haufe Group, pp. 67–84.

Vesely, W.E., Goldberg, F.F., Roberts, N.H., and Haasl, D.F. (1981). *Fault Tree Handbook.* Washington, D.C.: U.S. Nuclear Regulatory Comission.

Wittkowski, J. (2013). *The Interview in Psychology: Interview Technique and Coding of Interview Material.* Berlin, Heidelberg: Springer-Publishing House. C. Jarlskog, CP Violation. World Scientific, Singapore (1988).

https://doi.org/10.1142/9781800611917_0011

Chapter 11

Model Risk as Multiplicative Risk Factor

Stefan Huschens[*,‡] **and Gerhard Stahl**[†,§]

[*]*Technische Universität Dresden, Faculty of Business and Economics, Germany*

[†]*HDI AG, Hannover, Germany*

[‡]*stefan.huschens@tu-dresden.de*

[§]*gerhard.stahl@hdi.de*

The aggregation of risks is usually discussed in the context of an additive model, which is adequate for many kinds of risk. In contrast, we prefer to capture model risk through a multiplicative risk factor.

1. Introduction

The focus of our chapter is on the aggregation of two variables X and Y which are different by their very nature, where X captures the financial risk of a portfolio and Y stands for the model risk. Typically, aggregation of risk variables is closely related to diversification. This relationship is extensively discussed in the literature of coherent risk measures within a framework based on additive aggregation. The additive approach treats X and Y in a symmetrical manner. While the portfolio risk is based on observable variables and risk factors, the model risk is induced by unobservable variables and latent risk factors. Model risk depends on the basic portfolio risk. This justifies to call it a second order or meta risk. To capture these stylised facts, an approach based on mixture distributions is more appropriate.

We assume a loss variable X as genuine random variable from a complex stochastic model for financial risks, e.g., in the banking and insurance industry. Usually, the random variable X is an additive aggregate $X = X_1 + \cdots + X_m$ of several variables which represent the risk contributions of different divisions, business lines or departments. On the way to the specification of the distribution function F_X, several assumptions are necessary for the independence of component variables, risk factors must be identified, plausible distributions must be specified and parameters must be estimated with statistical methods or determined by expert judgment. The distribution of random variable X resulting from this process is therefore subject to model risk in various ways.

For a given loss variable X, a second non-negative variable Y reflects the model risk inherent in the determination of the distribution of X. The choice of an appropriate distribution function F_Y in a pre-specified parametric family $\mathbb{F}_Y$ of distribution functions depends highly on the respective distribution function F_X of random variable X. This dependency reflects the second order character of the model risk.

While in the following models, the random variables Y and X are assumed to be stochastically independent, this independence is only conditional on the chosen pair

$$(F_X, F_Y) \in \mathbb{F} \times \mathbb{F}_Y,$$

where $\mathbb{F}$ denotes the set of all distribution functions. If we symbolise with Θ the process of the choice of (F_X, F_Y), then X and Y are stochastically independent conditional on Θ. We do not necessarily assume that a three-dimensional probability distribution for (X, Y, Θ) exists, but assume conditional independence in the wider sense of Dawid (1979).

We consider three approaches to combine the stochastically independent variables X and Y with the aim of aggregating the two risks which are associated with the variables X and Y.

(1) In the additive model, the sum variable

$$Z = X + Y \tag{1}$$

represents a modified loss variable including the model risk. This is the standard approach to risk aggregation. The risk factor Y plays the role of a stochastic additive safety margin.

(2) In the multiplicative model, the product variable

$$Z = XY \tag{2}$$

represents the modified loss variable including the model risk. The nonnegative risk factor Y plays the role of a stochastic multiplicative safety margin.

(3) A third approach to reflect model risk is

$$Z = \mathbb{E}[X] + (X - \mathbb{E}[X])Y \tag{3}$$

for random variables X and Y with finite means. In this approach, the deviations of X from the expected value $\mathbb{E}[X]$ are reduced by values of Y less than one and are stretched by values of Y greater than one, whereas the mean is unaffected.

In the following, we call these three alternative ways to implement the model risk by an additional random variable Y the *location model*, the *scale model* and the *location-scale model* since there is a strong connection to location, scale and location-scale families of distributions.

Let random variable V have distribution function F. Then for the linearly transformed random variable $a + bV$ with $a \in \mathbb{R}$ and $b > 0$, it holds that

$$\mathrm{P}(a + bV \le t) = \mathrm{P}(V \le (t - a)/b) = F((t - a)/b) \quad \text{for all } t \in \mathbb{R},$$

so that the random variable $a + bV$ has the distribution function

$$F(t; a, b) = F((t - a)/b), \quad t \in \mathbb{R}.$$

For any fixed distribution function F, the set of distribution functions

$$\{F(\cdot; a) \mid F(\cdot; a) = F(\cdot - a),\ a \in \mathbb{R}\}$$

defines a *location family* of distributions with *location parameter* a, the set of distribution functions

$$\{F(\cdot; b) \mid F(\cdot; b) = F(\cdot/b),\ b > 0\}$$

defines a *scale family* of distributions with *scale parameter* b and the set

$$\{F(\cdot; a, b) \mid F(\cdot; a, b) = F((\cdot - a)/b),\ a \in \mathbb{R},\ b > 0\}$$

defines a *location-scale family* of distributions with *location parameter* a and *scale parameter* b (Lehmann and Casella, 1979, p. 17). We show in the following sections that in the three models in (1)–(3) the resulting distribution of Z, which integrates the model risk, can be interpreted as mixtures of location, scale and location-scale families of distributions, respectively.

In Sections 2–4 the methodological aspects of these approaches are discussed. Section 5 discusses an application in the insurance industry. All technical derivations are deferred to the last section.

2. Location Model to Integrate Model Risk

In this section, we assume that X and Y are stochastically independent random variables with distribution functions F_X and F_Y and we focus on the sum $Z = X + Y$. The factor Y has the function of a stochastic additive safety margin. Therefore, we assume that Y is a non-negative continuous random variable with density function f_Y.

2.1. *Convolution*

The distribution function F_Z of random variable Z can be gained from F_X and F_Y by the well-known formula

$$F_Z(z) = \int_{-\infty}^{\infty} F_X(z-y)\mathrm{d}F_Y(y), \quad z \in \mathbb{R}.$$

This formula is known as convolution of the two distribution functions and denoted as $F_Z = F_X * F_Y$. Since Y is assumed to be a non-negative continuous random variable with density function f_Y, the formula for F_Z simplifies into

$$F_Z(z) = \int_{0}^{\infty} F_X(z-y)f_Y(y)\mathrm{d}y, \quad z \in \mathbb{R}. \tag{4}$$

If X is a continuous random variables with density function f_X, then Z is a continuous random variable with density function

$$f_Z(z) = \int_{-\infty}^{\infty} f_X(z-y)f_Y(y)\mathrm{d}y, \quad z \in \mathbb{R}.$$

2.2. *Mixture distribution*

The convolution formula (4) can be interpreted as mixture of the family $\{F_X(\cdot - y) \mid y \in \mathbb{R}\}$ of distribution functions with mixing distribution defined by F_Y. This family of distributions functions defines a location family of distributions with location parameter y. For the mixture interpretation of the convolution, the alternative formulation

$$F_Z(z) = \mathbb{E}[F_X(z - Y)], \quad z \in \mathbb{R}$$

of the convolution in (4) illustrates that F_Z is a mean of distribution functions and Y can be interpreted as a random parameter in the distribution of F_X.

Example 1. Let $X \sim \mathrm{N}(0, 1)$ and $Y \sim \mathrm{Exp}(1)$ with density function $f_Y(y) = \mathrm{e}^{-y}$ for $y \geq 0$ and $f_Y(y) = 0$ otherwise. Let Φ denote the distribution function of $\mathrm{N}(0, 1)$. Then

$$F_Z(z) = \int_0^\infty \Phi(z - y)\mathrm{e}^{-y}\mathrm{d}y, \quad z \in \mathbb{R}.$$

Since $\Phi(\cdot - y)$ is the distribution function of $\mathrm{N}(y, 1)$, the distribution of Z can be seen as a mixture of normal distributions with different means $y \in [0, \infty)$ and the same variance 1.

This example shows that even in simple cases, no closed form representation for the distribution function F_Z can exist, so that numerical approximations or simulations are indispensable.

2.3. *Aggregation of quantiles and risk measures*

A quantile z_p or the deviation $z_p - \mathbb{E}[Z]$ of a quantile from the expected value is a frequently used risk measure. In general, there is no simple formula which links the p-quantiles x_p, y_p and z_p of the random variables X, Y and Z. Normal distributions build an important exception, since Z is normal distributed if X and Y are normal distributed and since a p-quantile is a relatively simple function of p and the distribution parameters. For $X \sim \mathrm{N}(\mu_X, \sigma_X^2)$ the p-quantile of X is $x_p = \mu_X + \Phi^{-1}(p)\sigma_X$.

Example 2. Let $X \sim \mathrm{N}(0, \sigma_X^2)$ and $Y \sim \mathrm{N}(0, \sigma_Y^2)$. Then

$$z_p = \sqrt{x_p^2 + y_p^2} \quad \text{for } 1/2 \leq p < 1. \tag{5}$$

Example 3. Let $X \sim \mathrm{N}(\mu_X, \sigma_X^2)$ and $Y \sim \mathrm{N}(\mu_Y, \sigma_Y^2)$. Let $\dot{x}_p = x_p - \mathbb{E}[X]$, $\dot{y}_p = y_p - \mathbb{E}[Y]$ and $\dot{z}_p = z_p - \mathbb{E}[Z]$ denote the difference between p-quantile and expected value of the respective variable, then

$$\dot{z}_p = \sqrt{\dot{x}_p^2 + \dot{y}_p^2}, \quad 1/2 \leq p < 1. \tag{6}$$

Formulas (5) or (6) are sometimes used as an aggregation rule for quantiles or risk measures even in cases where the random variables X and Y are not normally distributed, where (5) is sometimes applied even when the means are different from zero. But then the approximation errors can be large, as the following example shows.

Example 4. Let $X \sim \mathrm{uni}(0, 1)$ and $Y \sim \mathrm{uni}(0, 1)$. Then $x_p = y_p = p$ for $0 < p < 1$ and

$$z_p = 2 - \sqrt{2(1-p)} \quad \text{for } 1/2 \leq p < 1. \tag{7}$$

An approximate calculation of z_p with aggregation formula (5) leads to

$$z_p \approx z'_p = \sqrt{x_p^2 + y_p^2} = \sqrt{2}p, \quad 0 < p < 1.$$

A second approximation using aggregation formula (6) and taking $\mathbb{E}[X] = \mathbb{E}[Y] = 1/2$ and $\mathbb{E}[Z] = 1$ into account leads to

$$z_p \approx z''_p = \mathbb{E}[Z] + \sqrt{\dot{x}_p^2 + \dot{y}_p^2} = 1 + \sqrt{2}(p - 1/2), \quad 1/2 < p < 1.$$

Table 1 contrasts z_p with the approximations z'_p and z''_p for several values of p. While z'_p considerably underestimates the p-quantile for all considered values of p, z''_p and z_p agree for $p = 0.5$; for $p \in \{0.75, 0.9\}$ the p-quantile is overestimated by z''_p and for larger values of p the p-quantile is considerably underestimated by z''_p.

Table 1. Quantile z_p from Example 4 and approximations z'_p and z''_p for different values of p.

p	0.5	0.75	0.9	0.95	0.975	0.99	0.995	0.999
z_p	1.000	1.293	1.553	1.684	1.776	1.859	1.900	1.955
z'_p	0.707	1.061	1.273	1.344	1.379	1.400	1.407	1.413
z''_p	1.000	1.354	1.566	1.636	1.672	1.693	1.700	1.706

3. Scale Model to Integrate Model Risk

In this section, we assume that X and Y are stochastically independent random variables with distribution functions F_X and F_Y and focus on the product variable $Z = XY$. The factor Y has the function of a stochastic multiplicative safety margin. Therefore, we assume that Y is a non-negative continuous random variable with density function f_Y.

3.1. *Product distribution*

The distribution function F_Z of the random variable Z is given by

$$F_Z(z) = \int_0^\infty F_X(z/y) f_Y(y)\mathrm{d}y, \quad z \in \mathbb{R}. \tag{8}$$

If additionally X is a continuous random variable with density function f_X, then

$$f_Z(z) = \int_0^\infty \frac{1}{y} f_X(z/y) f_Y(y)\mathrm{d}y, \quad z \in \mathbb{R} \tag{9}$$

is the density function of Z, cp. Shorack (2000, p. 188).

3.2. *Mixture distributions*

This formula can be interpreted as a mixture with respect to a scale parameter, since the set $\{F_X(\cdot/y) \mid y > 0\}$ of distribution functions defines a scale family of distributions with scale parameter y. Also, (9) defines a mixture distribution, since $\frac{1}{y} f_X(\cdot/y)$ is the density function which belongs to the distribution function $F_X(\cdot/y)$. The set $\{(1/y)f_X(\cdot/y) \mid y > 0\}$ of density functions characterises the same scale family of distributions with scale parameter y.

4. Location-Scale Model to Integrate Model Risk

In this section, we assume that X and Y are stochastically independent random variables. Let X have expected value $\mu_X = \mathbb{E}[X]$ and standard deviation $\sigma_X = \sqrt{\mathbb{V}[X]}$ which is assumed to be finite and positive. We assume that Y is a non-negative random variable with finite variance and density function f_Y. The aggregated variable Z is linked with X and the non-negative random variable Y through

$$Z = \mathbb{E}[X] + (X - \mathbb{E}[X])Y. \tag{10}$$

This approach has two basic properties:

- Since $\mathbb{E}[(X - \mathbb{E}[X])Y] = 0$, it follows that
$$\mathbb{E}[Z] = \mathbb{E}[X]$$
for each distribution of Y, so that the expected value of Z is unaffected by Y.
- From $Z - \mathbb{E}[Z] = (X - \mathbb{E}[X])Y$ it can be seen that deviations of X from the expected value $\mathbb{E}[X]$ are shrunk by values of Y less than one and stretched by values of Y greater than one.

The approach of leaving the mean unchanged is motivated by applications in the insurance industry, where expected losses are typically covered by premia. Therefore, model risk related to the mean is minor.

4.1. *Mixture distributions framing model risk*

For the distribution function F_Z of random variable Z, which is defined by (10), the representation

$$F_Z(z) = \int_0^\infty F_X\left(\frac{z - \mu_X}{y} + \mu_X\right) f_Y(y)\mathrm{d}y, \quad z \in \mathbb{R} \tag{11}$$

as a mixture distribution holds. The derivation of (11) is deferred to the last section. The distribution function F_Z is a mixture of distribution functions in the set

$$\mathbb{F}_X = \left\{F \in \mathbb{F} \;\middle|\; F(\cdot) = F_X\left(\frac{\cdot - \mu_X}{b} + \mu_X\right),\ b > 0\right\} \tag{12}$$

of distribution functions, which is a parametric subset of the set $\mathbb{F}$ of all distribution functions. $\mathbb{F}_X$ builds a location-scale family of distributions with scale parameter b and fixed location parameter μ_X. All distributions in $\mathbb{F}_X$ have the same mean μ_X and standard deviations $b\sigma_X$, cp. (15) and (16). For $b = 1$, the distribution function F_X results as an element of $\mathbb{F}_X$.

Example 5. Let $X \sim \mathrm{N}(\mu_X, \sigma_X^2)$ and $Y \sim \mathrm{Exp}(1)$ with density function $f_Y(y) = \mathrm{e}^{-y}$ for $y \geq 0$ and $f_Y(y) = 0$ otherwise. Then the distribution function of Z is

$$F_Z(z) = \int_0^\infty \Phi\left(\frac{z - \mu_X}{y\sigma_X}\right) \mathrm{e}^{-y} \mathrm{d}y, \quad z \in \mathbb{R}. \tag{13}$$

Since $\Phi((\cdot - \mu)/\sigma)$ is the distribution function of $\mathrm{N}(\mu, \sigma^2)$, the distribution of Z is a mixture of normal distributions with common mean μ_X but different standard deviations in the set $\{y\sigma_X \mid y \geq 0\} = [0, \infty)$.

4.2. *Risk measure and location-scale model*

The family of distribution functions $\mathbb{F}_X$ in (12) has an interesting property in connection with the risk measure

$$\varrho_p(F) \stackrel{\text{def}}{=} Q_p(F) - \mu(F), \tag{14}$$

where

$$Q_p(F) = \inf\{x \in \mathbb{R} \mid F(x) \geq p\}$$

denotes the p-quantile of the probability distribution that is defined by distribution function F and where

$$\mu(F) = \int_{\mathbb{R}} x \mathrm{d}F(x)$$

denotes the mean of this probability distribution. This risk measure ϱ_p with a high probability level, e.g., $p = 99.5\%$, is used for example in the insurance industry. This is reasonable because premia should cover those risks related to the expectation.

Theorem 1. *Let for a given distribution function F_X with finite mean μ_X the family $\mathbb{F}_X$ be defined by* (12)*. Let further for a given probability $0 < p < 1$ the risk measure ϱ_p defined by* (14)*. Then for all $F \in \mathbb{F}_X$ it holds that*

$$\mu(F) = \mu(F_X), \tag{15}$$

$$\sigma(F) = b\sigma(F_X), \tag{16}$$

and

$$\varrho_p(F) = b\varrho_p(F_X).$$

The proof of this theorem may be found in the last section.

4.3. *Modeling with standardised random variables*

Let F^* denote the distribution function of the standardised random variable

$$X^* = \frac{X - \mu_X}{\sigma_X}.$$

Then the representation

$$F_Z(z) = \int_0^\infty F^\star\left(\frac{z - \mu_X}{\sigma_X y}\right) f_Y(y)\mathrm{d}y, \quad z \in \mathbb{R} \tag{17}$$

of the distribution function of Z can be gained. The derivation of (17) is deferred to the last section. This formula can be interpreted as mixture with respect to the scale parameter of the distributions in the location-scale family defined by the set

$$\{F(\cdot; a, b) \mid F(\cdot; a, b) = F^\star((\cdot - a)/b) \mid a \in \mathbb{R}, b > 0\}$$

with fixed location parameter $a = \mu$ and scale parameter b. For $a = \mu$ and $b = \sigma$ the distribution function of X is contained in this family as $F_X(\cdot) = F(\cdot; \mu, \sigma)$.

5. Processing the Quantification of Model Risk

A short look back on the history of quantitative risk management since the mid-90s provides the context of practical aspects for the management of model risk. This evolutionary sketch will help to bridge the gap between the already outlined multiplicative setting and practical challenges that have to be tackled in order to satisfy simultaneously the expectations of multiple stakeholders (management board, supervisors and rating agencies).

This section is organised as follows:

- the introductory subsection headlined by *From past to now* shows that model risk motivated regulatory setting from the time of deregulation until the aftermath of the financial crisis;
- the second subsection, *Managing model risk*, highlights different levels of managing model risk, depending on the gathered experience;
- the next two subsections, *Model risk in practice — Parts I and II*, show how these different levels may be implemented in practice, where Part I uses an additive approach and Part II uses an multiplicative approach;
- the last subsection, *Practical implementation*, outlines the practical set-up. Last but not the least, follow some empirical results and conclusions.

5.1. *From past to now*

For financial institutions, the ongoing story of the application of stochastic models for firm specific and regulatory purposes started in the mid-1990s with the famous RiskMetrics framework (Morgan, 1995). Though deregulation was highly prioritised at those times of Reaganomics, see e.g., Padoa-Schioppa (2004), the treatment of model risk was already on the top of the regulatory agenda, see Stahl (1997), who introduced a regulatory capital buffer for market risk, which was motivated by model uncertainties.

At that time, model risk was seen as an idiosyncratic type of risk, which is related to a specific modelling approach chosen by a financial institution (Office of the Comptroller of the Currency, 2011; Sibbertsen *et al.*, 2008). More recently, in a second step, pioneered by the financial crisis, another perspective, known as systemic risk, has been incorporated into risk modelling (Cont and Schaanning, 2017; Kemp, 2017). These strategies are motivated in order to control global spill-overs. As a consequence out of the lessons from the financial crisis, financial institutions have to evidence by means of a substantiated analysis that their capitalisation allows to buffer also those risks which are beyond those already quantified by $\varrho(X)$ (either by an internal model or a standard formula-based approach).

Under Solvency II, the so-called Own Risk and Solvency Assessment (ORSA), see Scherer and Stahl (2020) for a short summary, is regulatory compulsory in order to convince the board of management and the regulatory bodies as well (supervisory authorities and rating agencies) that the present capital buffer is sufficient. The outcome of this process is an estimate of the so-called *own solvency needs.*

5.2. *Managing model risk*

The level of management of model risk evolves with the experience gathered over time by running an internal model. At the very beginning, the meaning and materiality of model risk and the practical implications are far from evident. Hence, along with the first implementation of an internal model, it seems difficult to manage model risk actively.

Therefore, a conservative, however passive approach by putting a certain amount of capital aside, makes sense. Let C_Y denote the amount of capital put aside in order to buffer model risk Y. Then a first simple approach is to determine

$$C_Y = \nu \times \varrho[X] \tag{18}$$

as a percentage $\nu \in (0, 1)$ of $\varrho[X]$, the capital to buffer risks from X. For an insurance company, $\varrho[X]$ is the calculated solvency capital requirement (SCR). In this section, $\varrho[X]$ can interpreted as the risk measure $\varrho(F_X)$ defined in (14), where F_X denotes the distribution function of X.

From the available capital C, the buffer C_Y is subtracted. Then the residual capital

$$C_r = C - C_Y \tag{19}$$

is the input in the capital allocation process. This approach in so far seems conservative as possible diversification effects between X and Y are not taken into account.

After applying an internal model over a time span of say 5 to 10 years, additional insights are gathered and further tools in order to tackle model risk are developed that allow a more matured approach to manage to model risk. We spot light some sources related to that progress:

- A deepened understanding of operational risk as a consequence of an approved internal model approach for that risk category. In that respect, undertakings may have access to additional external data sources like ORX (Operational Riskdata eXchange Association and KPMG, 2016). The ORX consortium institutionalises exchanges among peers. Furthermore, benchmark studies, e.g., by European Insurance and Occupational Pensions Authority (EIOPA) give further insights in the variability of internal models.
- The lessons learned by the application and usage of the internal model allow to move from a pure risk based approach to a risk-informed one, see, for example, the NASA Handbook of risk management (National Aeronautics and Space Administration, 2011), where the role of experts relatively to model output in so far is strengthened as the disciplined incorporation of their knowledge in the decision process and risk assessment as well is fostered.
- Last but not least, statistical tools have been developed for a better control numerical uncertainties, e.g., the Monte-Carlo sampling error.

In order to take into account the progress related to an active risk management of model risk, the augmentation of C_r is at hand. This may be achieved by a diversified aggregation of X and Y. Instead of the simple approach in (18), the capital buffer C_Y may be computed as $\varrho[Y]$ from a distribution for Y and the aggregation may be based on the additive approach $X+Y$, where the random variables X and Y are assumed to be stochastically independent. Experience has shown that model risk is of a substantial amount, hence an additive approach of aggregating X and Y as independent random variables is not feasible, because the resulting required capital buffer would be too low. Furthermore, to base the aggregation of X and Y on correlations is also not convincing due to the consecutive, i.e., asymmetric nature of model risk (first the model is chosen, then the model risk is determined).

5.3. *Model risk in practice — Part I*

In practice, the determination of own solvency needs may, for example, split into the following possible risk categories: model risk or model uncertainty, emerging risks and strategic risks.

Table 2. Risk components of model risk as percentages of solvency capital requirement.

Risk component	%
Numeric uncertainty	3
Stochastic uncertainty	10
Epistemic uncertainty (approximations)	4
Netted aggregated model risk	~12

In the following, the focus is on the determination of model risk, which splits up, for example in numerical, stochastic and epistemic risks ($Y_i, i = 1, 2, 3$), see Stahl (2016). Table 2 highlights for an insurance company the corresponding risk measures $\varrho[Y_i]$ as percentages

$$\pi_i = \frac{\varrho[Y_i]}{\varrho[X]} \tag{20}$$

of solvency capital requirement $\varrho[X]$.

The percentages (20) in Table 2 are outcomes of the validation process, e.g., in the sense of ORSA, where empirical analysis goes hand in hand with expert judgments in order to judge the level of capital adequacy in the light of the validation of the model. Furthermore, the quantification of model risk by aggregating the components of model risk mirrors an advanced understanding of the validation process, see Stahl (2019). With respect to Table 2, the following remarks are important:

- The large contribution of stochastic uncertainty to overall model risk mirrors the fact that the underlying sample sizes (typically 100–200 observations) are relatively small compared to the required level of significance (e.g., $\alpha = 99.5\%$) and the number of risk factors (often more then 1000), see Stahl (2016).
- The percentages in the table are the output of an elicitation as part of the validation process (O'Hagan *et al.*, 2006). This elicitation process can be set-up in such a way that the regulatory requirements for the so-called expert judgements are fulfilled. The latter, by and large, minimise expert bias in the sense of Tversky and Kahnemann (1974).

- The numbers in first three rows are prone to various double counting, the so-called boundary risks, see Operational Riskdata eXchange Association and KPMG (2016). For example, $\varrho[X]$ comprises already operational risk or other components (emerging and strategic risk) of the own solvency needs. These double counting effects can be netted after their aggregation.
- Typically, the netted figure, ν, for model risk might be in a range $\nu \in (15\%, 20\%)$ from the calculated solvency capital requirement $\varrho[X]$.

5.4. *Model risk in practice — Part II*

Like modelling, validation is a process that combines empirical techniques (backtesting, sensitivity analysis, etc.) with expert judgments. If the targeted outcome of the validation process is defined as a binary result (acceptance, non-acceptance of the model) the expert judgment comes mainly into play in the final judgment which qualifies a model, and hence the calculated capital, as adequate or inadequate.

In the light of the progress achieved by active management of model risk and the related matured processes with respect to the treatment of model risk, a continuous approach for tackling validation might be preferable. Such an approach would increase the efficiency of the exhaustion of the available information about the quality of the applied model. To that end, an elicitation process $\mathcal{E}$, seen as a business process (Schmelzer and Sesselmann, 2008), may be implemented. The participants of this process comprise risk managers, modellers and representatives of senior management among others. All participants are involved either in the modelling, validation or application of the risk management system at hand.

The outcome of elicitation process $\mathcal{E}$ is a distribution function

$$F_Y(y \mid \mathcal{E}), \quad y \in \mathbb{R} \tag{21}$$

for variable Y that represents model risk. A facilitator provides the J participants $e_1, \ldots, e_J$ of the elicitation workshop with the necessary information (registered losses, near misses, validation reports, etc.) to express their expert knowledge by means of a distribution of Y. Each member is asked to determine a distribution function

$$F_Y(\cdot \mid e_j), \quad j = 1, \ldots, J.$$

The aggregation of the J distribution functions may be achieved either by a consensus or by a formal aggregation procedure, for example, by averaging the J expert judgments, so that

$$F_Y(y \mid \mathcal{E}) = \frac{1}{J}\sum_{j=1}^{J} F_Y(y \mid e_j), \quad y \in \mathbb{R}$$

results. By means of a scoring process, the outcome (21) of the elicitation process $\mathcal{E}$ is validated. Compared to a binary approach to validation, the scoring of the elicitation process yields an additional valuable feedback to $\mathcal{E}$. Evidently, each expert e_j elaborates $F_Y(\cdot \mid e_j)$ *conditioned* on the chosen model for X, the quality of the modellers, the performance of the model, etc.

A practical approach is to determine F_Y using a gamma distribution derived by a consensus approach. In a final step, the distributions of X and Y are aggregated by (3), where the distribution of Z is approximated by a Monte-Carlo simulation.

5.5. *Practical implementation*

In practice, very often, only a Monte-Carlo approximation for the distribution function of X is at hand, for example, an empirical distribution function

$$F_n(t) = \frac{1}{n}\sum_{i=1}^{n} \mathbf{1}_{(-\infty,t]}(x_i), \quad t \in \mathbb{R}, \tag{22}$$

where $x_1, \ldots, x_n$ denote given data points in $\mathbb{R}$. In order to apply an approach that aggregates X and Y by mixing distributions, a parametric setup has to be defined in a first step. To that end, a location-scale model based on (22) induced by a standardisation $F_n^\star(t)$ of $F_n(t)$

$$F_n^\star(t) \stackrel{\text{def}}{=} F_n\left(\mu_n + t\sigma_n\right), \quad t \in \mathbb{R}$$

is introduced. The resulting family of distribution functions

$$\{F(\cdot; a, b) \mid F(\cdot; a, b) = F_n^\star\left((\cdot - a)/b\right), \ a \in \mathbb{R}, b > 0\}$$

has location parameter a, scale parameter b and contains the empirical distribution function F_n for the parameter $a = \mu_n$ and

$b = \sigma_n$, i.e.,

$$F_n(t) = F(t; \mu_n, \sigma_n) = F_n^\star\left(\frac{t-\mu_n}{\sigma_n}\right), \quad t \in \mathbb{R}.$$

The representation $F_n^\star((\cdot - \mu_n)/\sigma_n)$ of the empirical distribution function F_n makes it possible to modify F_n by mixing the distribution functions with respect to the additive parameter s:

$$F_Z(z) = \int_0^\infty F_n^\star\left(\frac{z-\mu_n}{\sigma_n + s}\right) f_S(s)\mathrm{d}s, \quad z \in \mathbb{R}. \tag{23}$$

In practice, a two-parameter gamma distribution is determined by $\mathcal{E}$.

This approach is formally equivalent to the multiplicative setting

$$F_Z(z) = \int_0^\infty F_n^\star\left(\frac{z-\mu_n}{\sigma_n y}\right) f_Y(y)\mathrm{d}y, \quad z \in \mathbb{R}, \tag{24}$$

cf. the representation (17), if for fixed σ_n, the variables S and Y are related by $\sigma_n + S = \sigma_n Y$. Although s in (23) is additive to the standard deviation, the variable S in the final effect acts as a multiplicative risk factor by changing the standard deviation and thus the scale factor. Therefore, it is only a matter of practicability whether the approach (23) or (24) is used to implement the location-scale-model (10).

Results. For a concrete situation of an insurance company, the outcome of the elicitation workshop specified the parameters of a gamma distribution $\Gamma(\alpha, \beta)$ as $\alpha = 0.18$ and $\beta = 0.95$. The application of (23) gives

$$F_Z(z) = \int_0^\infty F_n^\star\left(\frac{z-\mu_n}{\sigma_n + s}\right) g(s; 0.18, 0.95)\mathrm{d}s, \quad z \in \mathbb{R},$$

where $g(s; \alpha, \beta)$ denotes the density function of a gamma distribution with parameters α and β. Using the risk measure $\varrho[Z] = \varrho_p(F_Z)$ defined in (14), the enhanced solvency capital

$$\varrho[Z] = 105\% \varrho[X] \tag{25}$$

results, which includes a buffer for model risk.

- Sensitivity analysis, not included in this chapter, has shown that (25) is robust with respect to moderate changes of parameters α and β.

- The chosen approach captures the conditional dependency relation between the model and the model risk.
- In the chosen approach (3), the variables X and Y are assumed to be independent, but the induced additive impact of Y is not independent of X. Model (3) is equivalent to the additive formulation

$$Z = X + Y' \quad \text{with} \quad Y' \stackrel{\text{def}}{=} (X - \mathbb{E}[X])(Y - 1).$$

The variables X and Y' are not stochastically independent since

$$\mathbb{C}\text{ov}[X, Y'] = \mathbb{V}[X](\mathbb{E}[Y] - 1). \tag{26}$$

They are positive correlated, if $\mathbb{E}[Y] > 1$.
- Hence, model (3) with mixture representation (11) implicitly defines a dependence structure and a copula for the pair of random variables X and Y'. Whereas the chosen approach by elicitation is fully transparent for the experts, on the other hand, it is well known that it is difficult to extract copula functions directly from experts.

6. Derivations and Proof

Derivation of (5). The p-quantiles are $x_p = \Phi^{-1}(p)\sigma_X$ and $y_p = \Phi^{-1}(p)\sigma_Y$ for $0 < p < 1$. Further, $Z \sim \mathrm{N}(0, \sigma_X^2 + \sigma_Y^2)$ and

$$z_p = \Phi^{-1}(p)\sqrt{\sigma_X^2 + \sigma_Y^2} = \text{sign}(\Phi^{-1}(p))\sqrt{x_p^2 + y_p^2},$$

so that (5) follows. It should be noted that

$$z_p = -\sqrt{x_p^2 + y_p^2} \quad \text{for } 0 < p < 1/2.$$

Derivation of (6). The p-quantiles are $x_p = \mu_X + \Phi^{-1}(p)\sigma_X$ and $y_p = \mu_Y + \Phi^{-1}(p)\sigma_Y$ for $0 < p < 1$. Further, $Z \sim \mathrm{N}(\mu_X + \mu_Y, \sigma_X^2 + \sigma_Y^2)$, so that

$$z_p = \mu_X + \mu_Y + \Phi^{-1}(p)\sqrt{\sigma_X^2 + \sigma_Y^2}.$$

From this equation for the differences $\dot{x}_p$, $\dot{y}_p$ and $\dot{z}_p$ between p-quantile and the expected value of the respective variable follows (6).

Derivation of (7). $Z = X + Y$ has density function

$$f_Z(z) = \begin{cases} 0 & \text{for } z < 0 \text{ and } z \geq 2 \\ z & \text{for } 0 \leq z < 1 \\ 2 - z & \text{for } 1 \leq z < 2, \end{cases}$$

and distribution function

$$F_Z(z) = \begin{cases} 0 & \text{for } z < 0 \\ z^2/2 & \text{for } 0 \leq z < 1 \\ -1 + 2z - z^2/2 & \text{for } 1 \leq z < 2 \\ 1 & \text{for } z \geq 2. \end{cases}$$

Therefore, the p-quantiles of Z are given by

$$z_p = F_Z^{-1}(p) = \begin{cases} \sqrt{2p} & \text{for } 0 < p < 1/2 \\ 2 - \sqrt{2(1-p)} & \text{for } 1/2 \leq p < 1. \end{cases}$$

Derivation of (11). For the centred random variables $\dot{X} = X - \mu_X$ and $\dot{Z} = Z - \mathbb{E}[Z] = Z - \mu_X$, the multiplicative model $\dot{Z} = \dot{X}Y$ holds. From (8), it follows that

$$F_{\dot{Z}}(t) = \int_0^\infty F_{\dot{X}}(t/y) f_Y(y) \mathrm{d}y, \quad t \in \mathbb{R}.$$

With $F_Z(z) = \mathrm{P}(Z \leq z) = \mathrm{P}(\dot{Z} \leq z - \mu_X) = F_{\dot{Z}}(z - \mu_X)$ and with the substitution $t = z - \mu_X$, it follows that

$$F_Z(z) = \int_0^\infty F_{\dot{X}}\left(\frac{z - \mu_X}{y}\right) f_Y(y) \mathrm{d}y, \quad z \in \mathbb{R}. \tag{27}$$

Then (11) follows from $F_{\dot{X}}(t) = \mathrm{P}(X - \mu_X \leq t) = \mathrm{P}(X \leq t + \mu_X) = F_X(t + \mu_X)$.

Derivation of (13). The distribution function of X is

$$F_X(x) = \Phi\left(\frac{x - \mu_X}{\sigma_X}\right).$$

Then

$$F_X\left(\frac{z-\mu_X}{y}+\mu_X\right)=\Phi\left(\frac{\frac{z-\mu_X}{y}+\mu_X-\mu_X}{\sigma_X}\right)=\Phi\left(\frac{z-\mu_X}{y\sigma_X}\right),$$

so that (13) follows from (11).

Derivation of (17). With

$$F_{\dot{X}}(t)=\mathrm{P}(X-\mu_X\le t)=\mathrm{P}\left(\frac{X-\mu_X}{\sigma_X}\le\frac{t}{\sigma_X}\right)=F^*(t/\sigma_X),$$

it follows that

$$F_{\dot{X}}\left(\frac{z-\mu_X}{y}\right)=F^*\left(\frac{z-\mu_X}{\sigma_X y}\right).$$

With this, (17) follows immediately from (27).

Proof of Theorem 1. For each distribution function

$$F(\cdot)=F_X((\cdot-\mu_X)/b+\mu_X)\in\mathbb{F}_X$$

it holds that

$$\begin{aligned}
\mu(F)&=\mu(F_X((\cdot-\mu_X)/b+\mu_X))=\mu\left(F_X\left(\frac{\cdot-(1-b)\mu_X)}{b}\right)\right)\\
&=\mathbb{E}[bX+(1-b)\mu_X]=b\,\mathbb{E}[X]+\mu_X-b\mu_X=\mu_X=\mu(F_X),\\
\sigma(F)&=\sigma(F_X((\cdot-\mu_X)/b+\mu_X))=\sigma\left(F_X\left(\frac{\cdot-(1-b)\mu_X)}{b}\right)\right)\\
&=\sigma[bX+(1-b)\mu_X]=b\sigma[X]=b\sigma(F_X),\\
Q_p(F)&=Q_p(F_X((\cdot-\mu_X)/b+\mu_X))=Q_p\left(F_X\left(\frac{\cdot-(1-b)\mu_X)}{b}\right)\right)\\
&=bQ_p(F_X)+(1-b)\mu_X=b(Q_p(F_X)-\mu_X)+\mu_X\\
&=b\varrho_p(F_X)+\mu_X,
\end{aligned}$$

and

$$\varrho_p(F)=Q_p(F)-\mu(F)=b\varrho_p(F_X)+\mu_X-\mu_X=b\varrho_p(F_X).$$

Derivation of (26). It holds that $\mathbb{E}[Y']=0(\mathbb{E}[Y]-1)=0$ and

$$\begin{aligned}
\mathbb{C}\mathrm{ov}[X,Y']&=\mathbb{E}[(X-\mathbb{E}[X])Y']=\mathbb{E}[(X-\mathbb{E}[X])^2(Y-1)]\\
&=\mathbb{V}[X](\mathbb{E}[Y]-1).
\end{aligned}$$

References

Cont, R. and Schaanning, E. (2017). *Fire Sales, Indirect Contagion and Systemic Stress Testing.* Technical Report, Norges Bank.

Dawid, A.P. (1979). Conditional independence in statistical theory, *Journal of the Royal Statistical Society Ser. B (Meth.)* **41**(1), pp. 1–31.

Kemp, M. (2017). *Systemic Risk.* New York: Palgrave Macmillan.

Lehmann, E.L. and Casella, G. (1979). *Theory of Point Estimation*, 2nd edn. New York: Springer.

Morgan, J.P. (1995). *RiskMetrics Technical Manual.* New York.

National Aeronautics and Space Administration (2011). *NASA Risk Management Handbook.* Hanover.

Office of the Comptroller of the Currency (2011). *Sound Practices for Model Risk Management: Supervisory Guidance on Model Risk Management*, OCC Bulletin 2011–12 [replaces Bulletin OCC 2000–16, *Model Validation*].

O'Hagan, A., Buck, C.E., Daneshkhah, A., Eiser, J.R., Garthwaite, P.H., Jenkinson, D.J., Oakley, J.E., and Rakow, T. (2006). *Uncertain Judgements: Eliciting Experts' Probabilities.* New York: Wiley.

Operational Riskdata eXchange Association (ORX) and KPMG (2016). Geneva. *Defining the Boundary — An Industry-Wide Appraisal of the Operational Risk-Insurance Risk Boundary.*

Padoa-Schioppa, T. (2004). *Regulating Finance — Balancing Freedom and Risk.* Oxford: Oxford University Press.

Scherer, M. and Stahl, G. (2020). The standard formula of Solvency II: A critical discussion. *European Actuarial Journal*, https://doi.org/10.1007/s13385-020-00252-z.

Schmelzer, H.J. and Sesselmann, W. (2008). *Geschäftsprozessmanagement in der Praxis*, 6th edn. München: Hanser.

Shorack, G.R. (2000). *Probability for Statisticians.* New York: Springer.

Sibbertsen, P., Stahl, G., and Luedtke, C. (2008). Measuring model risk, *The Journal of Risk Model Validation* **2**(4), 65–81.

Stahl, G. (1997). Three cheers, *Risk* **10**(October), 67–69.

Stahl, G. (2016). Model uncertainty in a holistic perspective, In Kallsen, J. and Papapantoleon, A. (eds.), *Advanced Modelling in Mathematical Finance.* New York: Springer, pp. 189–215.

Stahl, G. (2019). Kommentar zu den §§ 96–121. In Kaulbach, D., Bähr, G., and Pohlmann, P. (eds.), *Versicherungsaufsichtsgesetz — Kommentar*, 6th edn. München: Beck, pp. 740–800.

Tversky, A. and Kahnemann, D. (1974). Judgement under uncertainty: heuristics and biases, *Science* **185**(4157), 1124–1131.

https://doi.org/10.1142/9781800611917_0012

Chapter 12

Model Risk in Option Pricing — Estimation Risk of Volatility Parameter

Krzysztof Jajuga

Wroclaw University of Economics and Business, Poland

krzysztof.jajuga@ue.wroc.pl

The advancement of financial theory designed for option pricing based on quantitative methods has been observed in the last 40 years. The main problem of the application of these methods is that these methods may not be well suited to the real world in some cases. This chapter discusses the main background to analyse model risk in option pricing. The chapter concentrates on model risk resulted from uncertainty as to the parameters of the model, which in option pricing is the volatility of the underlying price. The proposal is to measure model risk by sensitivity measures, particularly for the Black–Scholes–Merton model.

One of the sources of model risk resulted from the uncertainty of the volatility estimate may result from using the volatility index as this estimate. The empirical example compares expected volatility provided by VIX with realised volatility.

1. Option Pricing — Introduction

Option pricing is one of the mainstream areas in financial market theory and practice. It took a considerable amount of time to derive a model which has been accepted by researchers as well as practitioners, for classical types of options (the so-called vanilla options).

As it is well known, the earliest attempt to derive an option pricing model was made by Bachelier (1900), who applied arithmetic Brownian motion as the underlying process for option pricing. It is probably less known that a few years later, a model, which can be considered as an option pricing model was proposed by Bronzin (1908).

Later, the other proposals were given by Sprenkle (1964), Boness (1964), and Samuelson (1965). They, however, did not meet theoretical requirements, for example, the assumption of a realistic underlying process.

The seminal paper, where the model was proposed, is of course the one by Black and Scholes (1973), extended at the same time by Merton (1973), therefore today it is known as the Black–Scholes–Merton model. In 1997, Myron Scholes and Robert Merton were awarded The Sveriges Riksbank Prize in Economic Sciences in Memory of Alfred Nobel (simply called Nobel Prize in Economic Sciences) for a new method to determine the value of derivatives.

Despite its wide acceptance, the Black–Scholes–Merton model is derived only for limited types of options, namely:

- European options on stocks, stock market indices, currencies, also options on futures on these underlying instruments.
- American call options on these underlying instruments given that underlying does not pay cash flows before the expiration of the option.

The second most widely used option pricing model is the Cox–Ross–Rubinstein model (Cox *et al.*, 1979), suggested by Sharpe in 1978. The main feature of this model is the discrete time process of the underlying index. This model is widely used in cases when the Black–Scholes–Merton variant is not available or not recommended. This refers to most American options as well as some interest rate options.

It can be proved for binomial model (sometimes called binomial tree model), that in the limit, when the number of periods goes to infinity, the length of each period becomes infinitesimal, the binomial model converges to the Black–Scholes–Merton.

Since 1973 many other option pricing models were elaborated. Several areas can be mentioned:

- American options, usually by approximate formulas (e.g., Barone-Adesi and Whaley, 1987; Bjerksund and Stensland, 1993).

- Exotic options, for example, barrier options (e.g., Rubinstein and Reiner, 1991; Ritchken, 1995) and compound options (e.g., Geske, 1979).
- Interest rate options (e.g., Hull and White, 1990; Heath *et al.*, 1992, Brace *et al.*, 1997).

The extended treatment of option pricing is given by Hull (2018) and Haug (2007).

With the advancement of technology, it is now common to use Monte-Carlo simulation to price options for which there is no analytical closed form available.

It is worth mentioning that option pricing models founded a new thinking in finance, called Contingent Claims Analysis. This term refers to the situation when there is a claim on some assets, which is contingent on the outcome of future events and this claim should be valued. This fits exactly the problem of option pricing.

Contingent Claim Analysis can be applied to the valuation of corporate debt and corporate equity, considering all stakeholders to hold contingent claims on the assets of the corporation. This proposal was developed in the paper by Merton (1974), in which

- equity is considered as long position in a call option on company assets;
- debt is considered as long position on risk-free asset plus short position on company assets.

The first paper which proposed the application of option pricing in corporate finance was written by Myers (1974). The general description of Contingent Claim Analysis in financial theory is summarised by Neave and Fabozzi (2012) and in corporate finance by Damodaran (2012).

The paper by Myers is now considered as the first one where the famous concept of real options (not using this name) was proposed. A comprehensive overview of this area with the particular emphasis on option pricing is given by Copeland and Antikarov (2001), Dixit and Pindyck (1994), Smit and Trigeorgis (2004) and Trigeorgis (1996).

In this chapter, I look at the problem of model risk in option pricing. The price-setting parameters in the Black–Scholes–Merton and the binomial model (they are also main price-setting parameters in the other models) are underlying price, strike price, risk-free rate, time to maturity, underlying price volatility as well foreign risk-free rate, dividend yield. All of them except the underlying price volatility are observable (either given in the contract or observed in the market). The volatility parameter creates some risk. Therefore, the main emphasis in this chapter is on the volatility parameter, which must be estimated.

The chapter gives some straightforward proposals on how to assess model risk related to the estimation of volatility parameter. Section 2 contains an introduction to the problem of model risk as well general approaches to its assessment. In Section 3, some methodology to measure model risk is given. Section 4 contains the specific application of this methodology in option pricing. Section 5 presents the specific use of these methods in the assessment of model risk in binary option pricing. Section 6 provides empirical studies on how the volatility index performs in applying market expectations of volatility compared to future realised volatility. Finally, Section 7 gives some conclusions.

2. Model Risk — Introduction

Models in finance (particularly the ones applied in the financial market) are approximations to the financial world, which is driven not by models but by people using these models. This statement is a counterargument to many models used in natural sciences (for example, in physics), which often describe deterministic natural phenomena.

Therefore, the application of the financial model raises the issue of an incorrect description of the real world (for example, the description of the financial market), which can lead to wrong decisions made by the participants in the financial world.

The notion 'model risk' can be defined in a general and simplified way:

Model risk is a risk resulting from the erratic model used in the real world.

One of the very first papers in which this notion was coined was the report by Derman (1996). He simply described model risk through the following quote: "The most fundamental of risks is that modelling is just not applicable."

A very good common sense explanation of model risk is given by Robert Merton. He stated that:

> "At times we can lose sight of the ultimate purpose of the models when their mathematics becomes too interesting. The mathematics of financial models can be applied precisely, but the models are not all precise in their application to the complex real world. Their accuracy as a useful approximation to that world varies significantly across time and place. The models should be applied in practice only tentatively, with careful assessment of their limitations in each application (Merton, 1994)."

In his statement, Robert Merton did not use the term 'model risk', but in fact, he referred to this problem. He indicated that the main source of model risk is the attempt to use precise (possibly sometimes complex) mathematical tools. It is one of the causes of model risk.

There are three main sources of model risk (Kato and Yoshiba, 2000; Jajuga, 2010), also called uncertainty, resulting in this risk:

(1) Uncertainty as to the structure of the model.

This refers, for example, to the situation in which some important factors (variables) are omitted; there is a wrong functional form of relationship between the variables in the model, there is no adjustment of the model for illiquidity in the market, etc.

A good example is the bond pricing model stated as a linear function, which does not fit into reality, because of the convex relationship between price and yield.

(2) Uncertainty as to the parameters of the model.

Even if the structure of the model is correct, some parameters of the model usually need to be estimated. Model risk occurs since there are different estimation methods, possibilities of using different data sets, etc. This source of model risk is also called 'estimation risk'.

A good example is the determination of estimation of beta coefficient based on historical data containing may outliers when regression is estimated by least squares method, which is not robust to outliers.

(3) Uncertainty as to the application of the model.

This refers to the situation when the model that was correctly constructed and estimated is not a good description of the real case, for example, it was derived for the developed market, but it is used in the emerging market, also when there are structural changes in the market.

A good example is the use of the dividend discount model for stock pricing in the emerging market, in which participants are mostly short-term investors and do not care about dividends but only about short-term changes of stock prices.

This chapter concentrates on the second type — uncertainty as to the parameters of the model. The main reason lies in the fact, that this type of uncertainty can (comparing to the other types of uncertainty) be analysed under the unified structure. One possible way is given in this chapter.

Using financial models without a clear understanding of uncertainty lying behind these models may lead to consequences in the financial market, including severe losses.

The first significant case of losses resulted from model risk occurred during the collapse of the hedge fund Long-Term Capital Management in 1998. One of the main reasons was that their models were not properly adjusted for the case of extreme shocks which happened during the East Asian crisis in 1997 and the Russian crisis in 1998.

The second well-known case of model risk happened during the great financial crisis in 2007–2009. It refers to the pricing of collateralised debt obligations (CDO) and the other mortgage backed securities (MBS), as well as credit default swaps (CDS). The prevailing model of pricing assumed that the dependence in multivariate distributions of the portfolio credit risk can be well captured by normal (Gaussian) copula (Li, 2000), which is based on the unrealistic assumption of the tail independence property of normal copula.

Model risk — in my opinion — should be evaluated. The methods to assess model risk can be either qualitative or quantitative.

Among qualitative methods I mention the following:

(1) Analysis of the justifiability of assumptions lying upon models. This allows to reduce uncertainty as to the structure of the model and/or uncertainty as to the application of the model.

(2) Analysis of the market for which pricing model is to be used. This allows reducing uncertainty as to the application of the model.

Among quantitative methods I mention the following:

(1) **Backtesting**: This refers to the verification of the model using past data — if the model does not perform well on the past data, this might be an indication of higher risk as to the application of this model in the future.
(2) **Stress testing**: This is the verification of the model using data generated subject to extreme shocks — this shows how the model performs in the case of such shocks; usually occurrence of instability of the model is not a good recommendation for future application.
(3) **Scenario analysis**: This is the verification of the model using data generated by assuming different scenarios created by the user of the model — this shows the possible future outcomes of the model.
(4) **Monte-Carlo simulation**: This refer to the verification of the model using many (possibly millions) generated possible values according to some stochastic model. This shows the distribution of model outcomes.
(5) **Sensitivity analysis**: This refer to the verification of how the model is sensitive to the changes of the input values. Of course, large sensitivity means high model risk.
(6) **Analysis of estimation errors**: this verification is possible when one is interested in how large errors can be made in the estimation of the parameters of the model. This verification can be conducted when one relies on statistical estimation and the formula for estimation errors is available. In the Black–Scholes–Merton option pricing model, this can be done by looking at estimation error for standard deviation (volatility parameter).

All the mentioned quantitative methods practically allow to reduce all types of uncertainty, but mainly uncertainty as to the parameters of the model.

In this chapter, we concentrate on the fifth group: sensitivity analysis, because it is the most common approach used in financial risk analysis by practitioners.

The best source for the use of quantitative methods in option pricing is the book by Hull (2018).

3. Model Risk Measurement — General Remarks

In this section, I give some proposals as model risk measurement is concerned. These proposals refer to the uncertainty as to the parameters of the model, which is estimation risk.

The starting point for this proposal is the classification of market risk measures given by Jajuga (2016):

1. Sensitivity measures;
2. Distribution-based measures.

3.1. *Sensitivity measures*

These measures are derived from the function linking the risk variable to risk factors. The most used description of the sensitivity measure for ith risk factor is given as

$$\mathrm{sm} = \frac{\partial g(X_1, X_2, \ldots, X_m)}{\partial X_i}, \tag{1}$$

where sm is the sensitivity measure, X_i is the ith risk factor and g is the risk function.

Equation (1) shows that a sensitivity measure is defined about each risk factor as the partial derivative of the risk function for a particular risk factor. This is a 'what if' type of measure since it results in the change of the risk variable given that the risk factor changes by some small unit while the other factors remain unchanged.

In the literature, very many sensitivity measures have been proposed, for example, duration (Macaulay, 1938) or beta (Sharpe, 1963).

3.2. *Distribution-based measures*

Here, one analyses the distribution of the estimate of the parameter. The larger the dispersion of this distribution, the higher is the model risk resulting from the estimation of this parameter.

Here, the risk is being captured by the statistical distribution of the risk variable. In the case of the option pricing model, this risk variable is assumed to be the market price of an option at a future moment. Three basic types of measures can be distinguished:

1. Volatility measures;
2. Quantiles of distribution;
3. Values of the distribution function.

Volatility measures are dispersion measures for this distribution, e.g., standard deviation, mean deviation, interquartile range. Here, the risk is understood as a two-sided risk. These measures show how much typically option price given by the model differs (up or down) from the market price.

The difficulty with measuring model risk using volatility measures lies in the fact that one must know the distribution of risk variable. In the case of the option pricing model, it can be derived by looking at empirical distribution using historical data. However, if significant changes are taking place, this may lead to errors.

The other two types of measures are based on the concept of downside (one-sided) risk. However, in the model risk for option pricing, we do not distinguish between positive and negative deviations from the referred value, therefore these two types of measures are not recommended here.

One should consider that the distribution of the estimator of the parameter depends on the distribution of the risk variable, which should be known. Therefore, our recommendation is to use a nonparametric approach, like sensitivity analysis, which is explored in this chapter.

4. Model Risk Measurement in Black–Scholes–Merton Option Pricing

Now, I turn to the problem of model risk measurement in Black–Scholes–Merton (BSM) option pricing and concentrate on estimation risk, resulting from the uncertainty as to the parameters. In the BSM framework, the main parameter to be considered in the analysis of model risk is volatility, measured as the standard deviation of returns of the underlying instrument. The other parameters are either known, because they are given in the contract (strike price, time to expiration), or they are given through market information (underlying price, domestic risk-free rate, foreign risk-free rate, dividend yield).

4.1. *Sensitivity measure applied to model risk analysis*

One possible (and straightforward) measure of model risk is the sensitivity measure of the model output for a parameter. In the case of the option pricing model, this is a partial derivative of the option value for volatility, which is *vega* (also called *kappa*). This measure is usually applied in hedging with options, but here, I propose to use it as natural sensitivity measure of model risk.

In Black–Scholes–Merton option pricing model, *vega* for call and put option is given as

$$\text{vega} = Se^{(b-r)T} n(d_1)\sqrt{T}, \tag{2}$$

$$d_1 = \frac{\ln\left(\frac{S}{X}\right) + (b + 0.5\sigma^2)T}{\sigma\sqrt{T}}, \tag{3}$$

where S is the value of underlying index, X is strike price, T is time to expiration (in years), r is risk-free interest rate, b is cost-of-carry rate, σ is volatility (standard deviation of underlying returns) and $n(x)$ is the value of the density of standard normal distribution at x, which is derivative of the distribution function.

The cost-of-carry rate is used here to capture several variants of the BSM model in one formula, namely (Haug, 2007):

- $b = r$ — results in stock option pricing model if the stock does not pay a dividend (Black and Scholes, 1973);
- $b = r - q$ — results in the stock option pricing model, where q is dividend yield (Merton, 1973);
- $b = 0$ — results in futures option pricing model (Black, 1976);
- $b = r - rf$ — results in currency option pricing model, where rf is the foreign risk-free rate (Garman and Kohlhagen, 1983).

In the case of the classical Black–Scholes model (value of the option on stock not paying dividend), the cost-of-carry rate is equal to risk-free interest rate and we have

$$\text{vega} = Sn(d_1)\sqrt{T}, \tag{4}$$

$$d_1 = \frac{\ln\left(\frac{S}{X}\right) + (r + 0.5\sigma^2)T}{\sigma\sqrt{T}}, \tag{5}$$

where $n(x)$ is the value of the density of standard normal distribution at x, which is derivative of the distribution function.

It should be mentioned that this simple approach can be used when there is the assumption of constant volatility, which is the case of the BSM model. When we refer to the case of stochastic volatility, the proposals by Hull and White (1987) are given for the case when there is the correlation of volatility with the price of an underlying asset.

The main intention to use the *vega* coefficient as a measure of model risk lies in the fact that when a wrong estimate of volatility is used, one obtains the option price which differs from the 'true' price — given that market follows the model (like BSM). The higher the coefficient, the higher is the model risk related to the volatility estimate. If we have an at-the-money option and the volatility is not correctly estimated, there is the risk that in fact, we may end with an option that is in-the-money or out-of-the-money. This will lead to a decision based on inappropriate analysis of the characteristics of an option. On the other hand, when an option is out-of-the-money (or in-the-money), the wrong estimate of volatility will not change the classifying of this option from out-of-the-money into another class (because of low *vega* coefficient).

Here, I present simple illustrative examples to use this approach for the classical Black–Scholes model.

Tables 1 and 2 in these examples show the values of *vega* for different strike prices and time to expiration.

Examples.
In the first example, $S = 100$, $r = 5\%$, $\sigma = 10\%$. In the second example, $S = 100$, $r = 5\%$, $\sigma = 20\%$.

The main conclusions from these examples are as follows:

- when the time to expiration of an option is relatively short (up to one month), the model risk occurs only for at-the-money options;

Table 1. Results for the first example.

	Time				
Strike price	1 day	1 month	3 months	6 months	1 year
50	<0.01	<0.01	<0.01	<0.01	<0.01
60	<0.01	<0.01	<0.01	<0.01	<0.01
70	<0.01	<0.01	<0.01	<0.01	<0.01
80	<0.01	<0.01	<0.01	0.05	0.83
90	<0.01	<0.01	1.17	4.83	11.03
100	2.52	11.37	19.21	26.15	34.29
110	<0.01	0.08	5.27	17.81	36.78
120	<0.01	<0.01	0.07	0.11	17.74
130	<0.01	<0.01	<0.01	<0.01	4.65
140	<0.01	<0.01	<0.01	<0.01	0.80
150	<0.01	<0.01	<0.01	<0.01	0.08

Table 2. Results for the second example.

	Time				
Strike price	1 day	1 month	3 months	6 months	1 year
50	<0.01	<0.01	<0.01	<0.01	0.03
60	<0.01	<0.01	<0.01	0.02	0.59
70	<0.01	<0.01	0.02	0.61	4.10
80	<0.01	<0.01	1.10	5.33	13.63
90	<0.01	1.80	9.38	17.24	27.16
100	2.52	11.46	19.64	27.36	37.52
110	<0.01	3.46	14.73	25.76	39.58
120	<0.01	0.11	5.13	16.40	34.07
130	<0.01	<0.01	0.99	7.75	25.12
140	<0.01	<0.01	0.12	2.91	16.42
150	<0.01	<0.01	0.01	0.91	9.77

- for options with longer time to the expiration, the model risk is significant for at-the-money options, as well as for these in-the-money options and out-of-the-money options, for which strike prices differ by at most 10% from at-the-money options;
- the longer time to expiration, the higher model risk;
- the higher the volatility, the higher the model risk.

The presented approach can be used to directly assess the model risk of option pricing. It is, however, well known that option prices are used (indirectly) in hedging. A very popular hedging strategy is the so-called delta-gamma-vega hedging, in which a portfolio is constructed with the use of options and underlying instrument in such a way that all three Greek coefficients of this portfolio are equal to zero. This means robustness of the value of this portfolio to the changes of the price of underlying, to the changes of the delta, and the changes of volatility.

Then the question arises of model risk of this strategy. Similarly, as in the option pricing model, here also volatility parameter is the only one that should be considered while assessing the model risk of this strategy.

We propose to use the same concept as already presented, being sensitivity measures.

These are partial derivatives of the respective Greek coefficients for volatility (see e.g., Haug, 2007):

- Vanna — sensitivity of delta to the changes of volatility;
- Zomma — sensitivity of gamma to the changes of volatility;
- Vomma — sensitivity of vega to the changes of volatility.

5. Model Risk Measurement in Binary Option Pricing

In the previous section, I discussed model risk for Black–Scholes–Merton option pricing, which is the model elaborated for the simplest type of options (these options belong to the so-called 'plain-vanilla' options). I mentioned previously the other large class — exotic options, which are mostly OTC options. Now I consider the simplest class of exotic options, namely binary options.

The basic types of binary options are *cash-or-nothing* options. Here,

- A binary *call* option gives the constant payoff equal to Q if the value of an underlying instrument is higher than the strike price;
- The binary *put* option gives the constant payoff equal to Q if the value of an underlying instrument is lower than the strike price.

Option pricing model for binary *call* and *put* is given through the following formulas:

$$c = Qe^{-rT}N(d_2), \tag{6}$$

$$p = Qe^{-rT}N(-d_2), \tag{7}$$

$$d_2 = \frac{\ln\left(\frac{S}{X}\right) + (b - 0.5\sigma^2)T}{\sigma\sqrt{T}}. \tag{8}$$

I use the same idea of sensitivity measure as for the BSM model. It is defined as a partial derivative of the option value for volatility. For option on the instrument which does not pay cash flows (before the expiration of option), it is given in the following formulas (separate ones for *call* and *put*):

$$\text{vega}(call) = -\frac{e^{-rT}}{\sigma}d_1 n(d_2), \tag{9}$$

$$\text{vega}(put) = \frac{e^{-rT}}{\sigma}d_1 n(d_2), \tag{10}$$

where $n(x)$ is the value of the density of standard normal distribution at x, which is on derivative of the distribution function.

6. Impact of Volatility Indices on Model Risk — A Simple Example

Volatility parameter is usually the main challenge in option pricing — for classical (plain-vanilla) options. As it is well known, either historical volatility or implied volatility (resulting from the model used by participants) could be used. In the developed market, characterised by high liquidity and the large variety of options (for example, Chicago Board of Options Exchange), implied volatility is preferred. Some reservations can be made, because there are different methods of volatility estimation, including the necessity to analyse volatility surface.

The idea of the creation of different volatility indices, which are treated as the estimate (given through market expectations) of the volatility of underlying is to partially overcome this issue. As a rule, they are determined for the most popular underlying instruments.

The first and the most well-known volatility index is VIX, established in 1993, by the Chicago Board of Options Exchange. This index is the estimate of one month expected volatility of the Standard and Poor's 500 index. Options on S&P 500 are probably the most popular options on the stock market index traded in the United States. There are several dozens of volatility indices reported on CBOE, they measure implied volatility of numerous underlying instruments.

The participants on the option market use VIX as the estimate of volatility in option pricing. Therefore, model risk in option pricing may depend on the performance of VIX in the estimation of volatility. In other words, the question arises, how VIX as the measure of market volatility expectations predicts realised volatility. To check it, empirical verification was conducted.

In this verification, I compared VIX with realised volatility in the monthly period for which VIX was stated. In this exercise, the monthly periods from January 2005 to April 2021 were considered. Value of VIX on the last day of the preceding month was taken. The realised volatility for the month was calculated as the standard deviation of daily logarithmic returns on the S&P 500 during this month.

This exercise intends to show that in the case when realised volatility is different from estimated volatility by VIX, the option prices obtained using VIX may be different from option prices determined by actual (realised) volatility — which is the realisation of model risk related to volatility.

In addition, this exercise shows the standard problem of many financial studies, how *ex-ante* estimated characteristic may lead to the wrong financial decision when it turns out that *ex-post* realisation of this characteristic is significantly different.

The results are visualised in the Figure 1. The main conclusions from this exercise are as follows.

The average absolute value of differences is 6.44%, the median is 5.19%, which suggests slight skewness to the right.

There are much more positive differences (158) than negative differences (38), this shows that VIX generally overestimates volatility.

However, there are exceptions, there are several very large negative differences, below −20%, they refer to the following events:

- The large financial crisis (September 2008 and October 2008);
- Eurozone crisis (August 2011);
- Pandemic (March 2020) — this is the largest absolute difference.

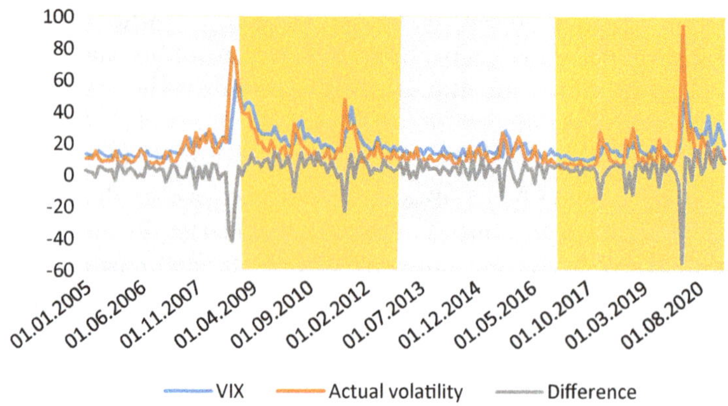

Fig. 1. The comparison of VIX and actual volatility.

This shows negative surprise due to extreme events. In this case, VIX underestimated volatility. It proves that market expectations do not capture possible extreme events. However, once they happen, the market updates the expectations.

There is also one positive difference above 20% in November 2020, it looks like it refers to US elections showing positive surprise due to the victory of Joe Biden.

This leads to a general conclusion, that implied volatility estimation using VIX may increase the model risk for option pricing.

7. Conclusions

This chapter discussed the main background to analyse model risk in option pricing. The considerations were concentrated on model risk resulted from uncertainty as to the parameters of the model, which in option pricing is the volatility of the underlying price. The proposal was to measure model risk by *vega* coefficient, particularly for the Black–Scholes–Merton model. Individual solutions were given.

One of the sources of model risk resulted from the uncertainty of the volatility estimate, may result from using the volatility index as this estimate. In this chapter, the empirical example compared the expected volatility provided by VIX with the realised volatility. The conclusions are that VIX generally overestimates volatility. But there are cases of negative surprise due to extreme events. In these cases, VIX underestimated volatility. This refers to the large financial crisis (September 2008 and October 2008), Eurozone crisis (August 2011), and Pandemic (March 2020). There is also one positive surprise (November 2020), it can be explained by US elections showing positive surprise due to the victory of Joe Biden.

References

Bachelier, L. (1900). *Theory of Speculation in The Random Character of Stock Market Prices.* Cootner, P. (ed.), Cambridge: MIT Press.

Barone-Adesi, G. and Whaley, R.E. (1987). Efficient analytic approximation of American option values, *Journal of Finance* **42**, 301–320.

Bjerksund, P., and Stensland, G. (1993). Closed-form approximation of American options, *Scandinavian Journal of Management*, **9**, 87–99.

Black, F. (1976). The pricing of commodity contracts, *Journal of Financial Economics* **3**, 167–179.

Black, F. and Scholes, M. (1973). The pricing of options and corporate liabilities, *Journal of Political Economy* **81**, 637–654.

Boness, A. (1964). Elements of a theory of stock-option value, *Journal of Political Economy* **72**, 163–175.

Brace, A., Gątarek, D., and Musiela, M. (1997). The market model of interest rate dynamics, *Mathematical Finance* **7**(2), 127–155.

Bronzin, V. (1908). Theorie der Prämiengeschäfte, Franz Deuticke. Described in: Zimmermann H. and Hafner W. (2005). *Vincenz Bronzin's option pricing theory: Contents, contribution, and background*, WWZ Forschungsbericht, No. 04/05, Universität Basel, Wirtschaftswissenschaftliches Zentrum (WWZ), Basel.

Copeland, T.E. and Antikarov, V. (2001). *Real Options: A Practitioner's Guide.* Texere: New York.

Cox, J.C., Ross, S.A., and Rubinstein, M. (1979). Option pricing: A simplified approach, *Journal of Financial Economics* **7**, 229–263.

Damodaran, A. (2012). *Investment Valuation: Tools and Techniques for Determining the Value of any Asset.* New York: Wiley.

Derman, E. (1996). *Model Risk*, Quantitative Strategies Research Notes. New York: Goldman Sachs.

Dixit, A. and Pindyck, R. (1994). *Investment Under Uncertainty.* Princeton: Princeton University Press.

Garman, M. and Kohlhagen, S.W. (1983). Foreign currency option values, *Journal of International Money and Finance* **2**, 231–237.

Geske, R. (1979). The valuation of compound options, *Journal of Financial Economics* **7**, 63–81.

Haug, E.G. (2007). *The Complete Guide to Option Pricing Formulas.* 2nd edn. New York: McGraw-Hill.

Heath, D., Jarrow, J.A., and Morton A. (1992). Bond pricing and the term structure of interest rates: A new methodology, *Econometrica*, **60**(1), 77–105.

Hull, J. (2018). *Options, Futures and Other Derivatives.* 10th edn. New York: Pearson.

Hull, J. and White, A. (1987). Pricing of options with stochastic volatilities, *Journal of Finance* **42**, 281–300.

Hull, J. and White, A. (1990). Pricing interest rate derivative securities, *Review of Financial Studies* **3**, 573–592.

Jajuga, K. (2010). Assessment of model risk in financial markets, *Optimum Studia Ekonomiczne* **48**, 35–43.

Jajuga, K. (2016). From duration analysis to GARCH models — An approach to systematization of quantitative methods in risk measurement, *Economics and Business Reviews* **16**, 7–19, Poznań.

Kato, T. and Yoshiba, T. (2000). Model risk and its control, *Monetary and Economic Studies*, **18**(2), 129–156.

Li, D.X. (2000). On default correlation: A copula approach, *Journal of Fixed Income* **13**, 43–54.

Macaulay, F. (1938). *Some Theoretical Problems Suggested by the Movements of Interest Rates, Bond Yields and Stock Prices in the US Since 1856.* NBER, New York: Columbia University Press.

Merton, R.C. (1973). Theory of rational option pricing, *Bell Journal of Economics and Management Science* **4**, 141–183.

Merton, R.C. (1974). On the pricing of corporate debt: The risk structure of interest rates, *Journal of Finance* **29**, 449–70.

Merton, R.C. (1994). Influence of mathematical models in finance on practice: Past, present and future, *Philosophical Transactions* **1684**, 451–463.

Myers, S.C. (1974). Interactions of corporate financing and investment decisions: Implications for capital budgeting, *Journal of Finance* **29**, 11–25.

Neave, E.H. and Fabozzi, F.J. (2012). *Introduction to contingent claims analysis.* In *Encyclopedia of Financial Models.* New York: Wiley.

Ritchken, P. (1995). On pricing barrier options, *Journal of Derivatives* **3**(2), 19–28.

Rubinstein, M. and Reiner, E. (1991). Breaking down the barriers, *Risk* **9**, 28–35.

Samuelson, P. (1965). Rational theory of warrant pricing, *Industrial Management Review* **6**, 13–31.

Sharpe, W.F. (1963). A simplified model for portfolio analysis, *Management Science* **19**, 277–293.

Smit, T.J. and Trigeorgis, L. (2004). *Strategic Investment: Real Options and Games.* Princeton: Princeton University Press.

Sprenkle, C. (1964). Warrant prices as indicators of expectations and preferences. In Coolner, P. (ed.), *The Random Character of Stock Market Prices*, Cambridge: MIT Press.

Trigeorgis, L. (1996). *Real Options: Managerial Flexibility and Strategy in Resource Allocation.* Cambridge: MIT Press.

https://doi.org/10.1142/9781800611917_0013

Chapter 13

Reference Framework for Success Factors of Resilient Supply Chains and Practical Application on a Supply Chain Disruption

Rainer Lasch[*,†] **and Karl Dietrich**[*,‡]
[*]*Technische Universität Dresden, Faculty of Business and Economics, Germany*
[†]*rainer.lasch@tu-dresden.de*
[‡]*karljohannes.dietrich@outlook.com*

The purpose of this chapter is to develop and apply a reference framework which illustrates the success factors of resilient supply chains. The basis of this reference framework is an extensive literature review focussing on identified success factors. After developing the reference framework, it was applied in the form of a case study analysing the reaction of two supply chains to a disruption. This chapter extends the research stream of reference frameworks for supply chain resilience by classifying existing success factors into three layers: fundamental, mediating, and directly influencing success factors. Furthermore, hypotheses regarding the impact of new digital technologies on supply chain resilience were developed. Managers can use this reference framework to analyse the reaction of their company to past supply chain disruptions (SCDs) and consider optimisation needs.

1. Introduction

In this chapter, we focus on supply chain disruptions (SCDs). Due to their low probability of occurrence and significant impact, as well as the lack of availability of sufficient historical data with which to make predictions, the application of traditional supply chain risk management (SCRM) is difficult (Simchi-Levi *et al.*, 2014). The SCDs resulting from the Coronavirus are current examples for the relevance of this topic (O'Leary, 2020). One solution for coping with the increasing vulnerability to SCD is the design of resilient supply chains. By creating supply chain resilience (SCR), it is no longer necessary to evaluate every possible cause of disruptions (Lasch, 2018, p. 295). SCR refers to the ability of a supply chain to make preparations in order to reduce the probability of the occurrence or the negative impact of foreseeable and unforeseeable SCD, as well as to react as quickly as possible in order to adapt to the situation and to derive appropriate measures (Barroso *et al.*, 2008, p. 1872; Craighead *et al.*, 2007, p. 146; Dolgui *et al.*, 2018, pp. 421–422; Hohenstein *et al.*, 2015). Furthermore, resilient supply chains can recover faster from SCDs than the competition and attain an improved competitive situation (Sheffi and Rice, 2005, p. 44). In this chapter, the focus is on reference frameworks that outline the success factors of resilient supply chains. Prior researchers have already established such reference frameworks. Biedermann (2018) has developed the most comprehensive one to date. This chapter extends his framework by additionally illustrating the impact of modern digital technologies on SCR and presenting an advanced understanding of the concept of SCR. Since the existing reference frameworks lacked practicality, several specific measures have been assigned for each essential success factor. The rest of this chapter is structured as follows: First, a general understanding of SCR is provided. Afterwards, based on the analysis of existing reference frameworks for SCR, a new reference framework is developed. In order to validate the gained insights, the reference framework is tested in a case study covering a past SCD. Finally, conclusions are drawn and further need for research is pointed out.

2. Understanding the Concept of Supply Chain Resilience

SCDs have played a unique role in corporate risk management, directly influencing the operational processes and stability of the supply chain. They can be both predictable and unpredictable (Barroso *et al.*, 2008, p. 1872). A low probability of occurrence characterises predictable SCD. However, there is usually a lack of historical events to adequately identify and assess them in the context of traditional SCRM. Unpredictable SCDs are not considered at all in conventional SCRM due to their lack of probability of occurrence (Lasch, 2018, pp. 294–295; Zegordi and Davarzani, 2012, p. 210).

The concept of SCR arose from a research gap in the field of traditional SCRM regarding SCDs. Resilient supply chains can effectively deal with the problems which are associated with SCDs. In contrast to the approach of a conventional SCRM, it is not necessary to assess each possible cause of an SCD individually, as it is assumed that not all risk events can be prevented (Jüttner and Maklan, 2011, p. 1; Lasch, 2018, pp. 295–296). Instead, companies in resilient supply chains develop capabilities that enable them to prepare for, respond to, and recover from SCDs. By effectively managing SCDs, resilient supply chains can subsequently assume an improved state (Hohenstein *et al.*, 2015, p. 96; Ponomarov and Holcomb, 2009, p. 131).

Those capacities mentioned above describe the understanding of SCR in this chapter. In line with Biedermann (2018, p. 61), this chapter focusses on the success factors of SCR which are necessary characteristics of supply chains and contribute to an effective reaction to SCD. The identified success factors will be presented in the next chapter in the form of a reference framework.

Concerning coping with SCD in resilient supply chains, four different phases can be distinguished: readiness, reaction, recovery, and growth (Hohenstein *et al.*, 2015, p. 96; Ponomarov and Holcomb, 2009, p. 135). The readiness phase is the basis of SCR, as in this phase measures are taken that can reduce the probability of SCD occurring or can mitigate possible negative influences on the supply chain (Hohenstein *et al.*, 2015, p. 107). As soon as the event has occurred, the reaction phase begins. The goal of the reaction phase is to bring the situation under control and to avoid collateral damage (Sheffi and Rice, 2005, p. 42). The quicker the supply chain reacts to the SCD during the reaction phase and adapts to the situation, the faster it can recover (Craighead *et al.*, 2007, p. 146; Hohenstein *et al.*, 2015, p. 107). Preparatory activities for this already begin in the readiness and reaction phase (Sheffi and Rice, 2005, p. 43). These activities are defined in the form of emergency plans and build

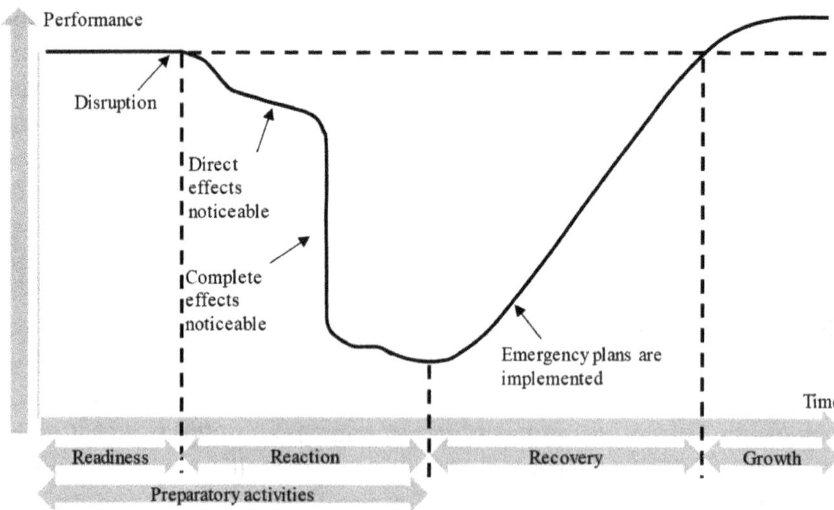

Fig. 1. Phases of coping with SCD.
Source: Adapted from Sheffi and Rice (2005, p. 42) and Biedermann (2018, p. 55).

upon the redundant resources already created (Dolgui *et al.*, 2018, pp. 421–422). The recovery phase begins with the implementation of these emergency plans (Biedermann, 2018, p. 55; Dolgui *et al.*, 2018, pp. 421–422). In addition, Hohenstein *et al.* (2015, p. 96) have identified a fourth phase, the growth phase. It goes beyond the recovery phase, as it aims not only to return to the initial state, but also to attain an improved position (Hohenstein *et al.*, 2015, p. 96). If supply chains react quickly enough to SCD, they can secure new market shares from slower supply chains (Sheffi and Rice, 2005, p. 44). Figure 1 illustrates the discussed phases.

3. Developing the Reference Framework

3.1. *Research methodology*

The reference framework is based on a comprehensive literature review of the current state of the art in the research area of supply chain resilience. Table 1 lists the core terms, as well as related terms and synonyms, which were used to find relevant papers. Boolean operators connected the terms in every search query. Phrase search

Table 1. Executed search queries.

Search query	Key term 1	Key term 2
1	**Resilienz*** OR Widerstandsfähigkeit* OR Widerstandskraft* OR Strapazierfähikeit*	AND '**Supply Chain***' OR Lieferkette* OR 'logistische Kette*' OR Versorgungskette* OR
2	**Resilient*** OR Widerstandsfähig* OR Zäh* OR resistent*	Liefernetz* OR Unternehmensnetzwerk* OR 'Supply Chain' Management'
3	**Resilience** OR robustness OR resistance	AND '**Supply Chain***' OR 'chain of supply' OR
4	**Resilient** OR robust OR resistant	'logistics network*' OR 'supply network*' OR 'value added network*' OR 'corporate network*' OR 'Supply Chain Management'

was used to narrow down the search results and truncation was used to expand them. The following databases were used for the literature research: Academic Search Complete, Business Source Complete, EconLit, and Emerald Insight. Based on the title search in the four databases mentioned above, a total of 1013 papers were found. After eliminating duplicate articles, 510 publications remained from the original population. Papers were considered which rated at least C on a scale from A to D, according to the rating of VHB-JOURQUAL3 (VHB, 2019). Based on this condition, the number of suitable publications was reduced to 262. In the subsequent phase, the titles and abstracts of the publications were checked for thematic relevance. The goal was to identify success factors in the papers researched. The basis for the understanding of the success factors of SCR was the publication of Hohenstein *et al.* (2015, p. 105). Their compilation was modified and extended through an extensive literature review. Publications were considered which describe new success factors of SCR or further analyse established success factors. Based on these criteria, only 82 papers remained eligible. Eventually, the full text of the remaining publications was evaluated. This analysis laid the basis for the final listing of success factors and specific measures.

Table 2. Frequency of the addressed success factors in papers.

Success factor	Addressed in number of papers
Flexibility	25
Agility	21
Human resources management	16
Redundancy	15
Collaboration	15
Robustness	13
Digital technologies	6
Lean processes	2

Table 2 shows how often the success factors were addressed within the analysed papers. This shows that flexibility and agility were the most significant success factors in past research. Human Resources Management, redundancy, collaboration, and robustness were commonly addressed, whereas digital technologies and lean processes have played a subordinate role so far.

In the next step, existing reference frameworks for SCR are analysed in order to outline the need for further research. Finally, a new reference framework is developed, with the approach of Rößl (1990, pp. 100–109) serving as an orientation. Rößl first defined rough categories, labelled in this publication as success factors. He then assigned dimensions to the categories, which operationalise the reference framework. In this chapter, these are referred to as specific measures. Following Rößl's approach, hypotheses regarding the relationships between the dimensions, i.e., specific measures, are further developed.

3.2. *Analysing current reference frameworks for supply chain resilience*

Frameworks for SCR were developed by Christopher and Peck (2004), Blackhurst *et al.* (2011), Purvis *et al.* (2016), Ali *et al.* (2017), Chowdhury and Quaddus (2017), Jain *et al.* (2017), Biedermann (2018), and Adobor (2019). All of those papers have in common the fact that SCR is the central object of investigation, specific success factors and relationships between the success factors are reported, and that their goal was to provide a complete, context independent list of all success factors for SCR. Biedermann (2018) has developed, up to this point, the most profound and extensive reference framework yet. He provided a comprehensive summary of success factors and numerous specific measures while thoroughly outlining the relationships between them. However, his framework lacks coverage regarding the impact of new digital technologies on SCR. Furthermore, there was no differentiation between various levels of success factors and their respective influence on SCR. Finally, there was no clear distinction between more general success factors and specific practical measures that contribute to SCR on a more operational level.

After the current status regarding reference frameworks for SCR has been derived, the following requirements are imposed on the development of a new reference framework:

- It must cover the state of the art concerning success factors for SCR and their relationships to each other.
- To be easily applicable for practitioners, there must be a clear distinction between general success factors and specific measures that enhance SCR.

4. Introducing Success Factors for Supply Chain Resilience

The identified success factors can be divided into three levels: fundamental (lower level), mediating (medium level), and directly (top level) influencing success factors.

4.1. *Fundamental success factors*

Fundamental success factors on the lower level lay the basis for SCR. They influence the two upper levels heavily. When seeking to improve SCR, companies should begin with the strengthening of fundamental success factors.

4.1.1. *Digital technologies*

The use of big data analytics (BDA) increases forecast accuracy and improves transparency in the supply chain (Ivanov *et al.*,

2019, p. 836). Cyber physical systems (CPS) enable production data to be available at any time. This increases transparency in production and, thus, in the entire supply chain (Theorin *et al.*, 2017). Additive manufacturing enables more flexible production, reducing the impact of SCD caused by changes on the end customer side (Ivanov *et al.*, 2019, p. 836). With the help of Advanced Tracking and Tracing Technology (ATTT), potential SCDs can be anticipated more quickly (Ivanov *et al.*, 2019, p. 836).

4.1.2. *Lean processes*

A lean process is characterised by little or no surplus or waste regarding effort, resources, and time. Therefore, lean processes are very efficient (Purvis *et al.*, 2016, p. 581).

4.1.3. *Redundancy*

By creating redundancy, sudden fluctuations in supply (procurement view) or increased variability in demand (sales view) can be dealt with (Purvis *et al.*, 2016, p. 582). Thus, in the reaction phase, the immediate effects of SCD can be reduced (Dolgui *et al.*, 2018, p. 421). Redundancy in the supply chain can be achieved by maintaining reserve capacities in production and transport (Christopher and Peck, 2004, p. 8). Fattahi *et al.* (2017) show the importance of redundant storage and production sites. Another measure is the use of multiple sourcing (Tomlin, 2006). A measure complementary to multiple sourcing is the reservation of products with substitute suppliers (Namdar *et al.*, 2018, p. 2345). Finally, another important measure is establishing risk mitigation inventory (RMI) (Lucker and Seifert, 2017, p. 6).

4.1.4. *Human resources management*

Emphasis should be placed on an appropriate risk management culture. For example, employees should be encouraged to make autonomous decisions in the event of an SCD in order to realise a shorter reaction time (Treiblmaier, 2018, p. 447). Christopher and Peck (2004, p. 11) emphasise that leadership support is essential to make the shift to a more risk management oriented company. Gölgeci and Ponomarov (2015, pp. 276–277) have demonstrated the relevance of companies' innovative ability regarding the resilience of supply chains. The reason for this is that innovative problem solving skills help companies to reinvent themselves (Nonaka and Yamanouchi, 1989, p. 299). Furthermore, appropriate education and training are necessary for employees to equip them with the relevant skills for coping with SCD (Blackhurst *et al.*, 2007, p. 380). Companies that learn from past SCDs are better prepared for future SCD (Blackhurst *et al.*, 2007, p. 380). For this reason, companies should implement learning mechanisms within their routines (Scholten, 2019).

4.2. *Mediating success factors*

Mediating success factors form the second level of the reference framework. Success factors on the lower level influence them. Furthermore, they have a direct effect on the success factors of the top level and thus have an indirect influence on SCR. The better the implementation of the mediating success factors, the bigger the immediate impact on SCR through the directly influencing success factors.

4.2.1. *Flexibility*

Flexibility can be described as the ability of supply chains "to quickly assess identified needs and provide appropriate measures for adaptation" (Lasch, 2018, p. 296). The resources created by building redundancy lay the basis for this in the readiness phase. In this way, flexible measures can be implemented in the form of contingency plans. These plans depend on the resource activated (Dolgui *et al.*, 2018, pp. 421–422). For example, redundant production sites can be used to design and implement a flexible contingency plan to redirect resources in case of an SCD (Blackhurst *et al.*, 2011, p. 383). Other examples are the flexible usage of capacities (production, transport), flexible inventory management (RMI), and flexible supplier management (multiple sourcing, reserving materials).

4.2.2. *Collaboration*

The more the partners in a supply chain collaborate, the better the mitigation of the impact of SCD (Christopher and Peck, 2004, p. 9). One important measure is to strengthen the exchange of information and knowledge between supply chain partners, as this can reduce uncertainties (Christopher and Peck, 2004, p. 9). Building cooperative relationships increases the sense of responsibility in supply chains, as companies help each other anticipate potential risks (Wieland and Wallenburg, 2013, p. 306). Furthermore, the strengthening of trust between supply chain partners is essential when seeking to achieve cooperative relations (Vlachos and Bourlakis, 2006, p. 78).

4.3. *Directly influencing success factors*

Directly influencing success factors form the top level of the reference framework. As they have a direct impact on SCR, great emphasis should be put on their implementation. They are influenced by success factors of the preceding levels. For this reason, when applying the concrete measures of those success factors, companies should be aware of the dependencies.

4.3.1. *Agility*

Christopher and Peck (2004, p. 10) define agility in supply chains as "the ability to react quickly to unforeseeable changes on the supply or demand side". Lasch (2018, p. 296) presents two measures for creating agility in the supply chain: strengthening the situational awareness and increasing the supply chain velocity. Another critical measure is the increase in visibility in supply chains. All processes and elements in the supply chain should always be transparent to every supply chain partner (Christopher and Peck, 2004, p. 10). An agile supply chain is also able to reorganise itself quickly and flexibly after an SCD (Blackhurst *et al.*, 2011, p. 38).

4.3.2. *Robustness*

In line with Wieland and Wallenburg (2012, p. 890), robustness is defined as the ability of a supply chain to withstand SCD without changing its initial configuration. According to Ali *et al.* (2017, p. 26), the robustness of a supply chain is mainly determined by its structure. It is recommended that, instead of one global supply chain, several regional supply chains consisting of local customers and suppliers are built up in order to react faster to changes (Chopra and Manmohan, 2014, pp. 76–77; Treiblmaier, 2018, p. 448). High supply chain complexity, i.e., the number of organisational units and the degree of interaction between them, reinforces the effects of SCDs (Craighead *et al.*, 2007, p. 141; Giannoccaro *et al.*, 2018, p. 627). For this reason, the complexity in supply chains should be kept as low as possible. A further measure is the fortification of sites to reduce the impact of SCDs (Ivanov and Dolgui, 2019, pp. 5122–5123).

4.4. *Relationships between the measures of the success factors*

Here, the relationships between the specific measures which are assigned to the general success factors are described. In this way, it is possible to clarify the detailed dependencies within this reference framework. For each success factor, associated measures are listed what follows and their respective influence on other measures. We focus only on relationships in which one measure positively influences another measure.

4.4.1. *Digital technologies*

BDA increases visibility in the supply chain by transforming unstructured data into usable knowledge (Jodlbauer, 2018; Ivanov *et al.*, 2019, pp. 837–838). CPS guarantee access to production data at any time (Theorin *et al.*, 2017). It is assumed that this increases transparency in the production of companies and, thus, across the entire supply chain. Since additive manufacturing can be used to integrate several functions in one component, the number of different components to be procured is reduced. This reduces complexity in procurement, production, and logistics (Jodlbauer, 2018, p. 113). It is therefore assumed that the supply chain complexity can be reduced using additive manufacturing. Furthermore, additive manufacturing enables shorter lead times (Ivanov *et al.*, 2019, p. 836). According to the understanding of Christopher and Peck (2004, p. 10), it can be deducted that the use of additive manufacturing increases the velocity of the entire supply chain in the case of an SCD. ATTT used between the supply chain partners enables end-to-end tracking of the material flow in the supply chain. It can be argued that the application of this technology thus increases supply chain visibility (Ivanov *et al.*, 2019, pp. 836–838).

4.4.2. *Lean processes*

Purvis *et al.* (2016, pp. 581–582) suggest that efficient processes with minimal waste improve agility in the supply chain by enhancing the velocity in case of an SCD (Christopher and Peck, 2004, p. 10).

4.4.3. *Redundancy*

Lasch (2018, p. 297) argues that redundancy is the basis for flexible decisions in supply chains. Therefore, it is assumed that measures to create redundancy influence flexible contingency plans.

4.4.4. *Human resources management*

According to Biedermann (2018, pp. 180–186), an open company culture enables a better exchange of information and knowledge as well as stronger cooperation. Biedermann (2018, pp. 142–186) has also shown that top management support has a direct influence on the risk management culture of the company. Furthermore, he has demonstrated that the education and training of employees influence the company culture. Top management can provide the necessary support for a corresponding risk management orientation of the company (Biedermann, 2018, pp. 181–186). Finally, Biedermann (2018, p. 181) describes the relationship between learning and training/education of employees. According to him, the knowledge gained through continuous learning from past SCDs can be passed on to employees through training. Following Gölgeci and Ponomarov (2015, p. 270), it is assumed that a high level of innovative strength has a positive influence on the ability of the supply chain to restructure itself flexibly after an SCD.

4.4.5. *Flexibility*

Lasch (2018, p. 296) explains that the flexibility of the companies in a supply chain determines the agility of the entire supply chain. The better the flexible measures (in the form of contingency plans) are adapted to the SCDs, the state of the supply chain, and the available resources, the more agile the response of the supply chain to the SCDs and any subsequent redesign of the supply chain itself.

4.4.6. *Collaboration*

According to Christopher and Peck (2004, p. 10), collaboration is essential for a high level of visibility in supply chains and is a prerequisite for an active exchange of information. According to Brandon-Jones *et al.* (2014, p. 60) and Dubey *et al.* (2017, pp. 3–4), the successful exchange of information between supply chain partners leads to higher transparency in the supply chain. Morgan and Hunt (1994, p. 26) and Dubey *et al.* (2017, p. 3) have shown that trust building in a supply chain has a positive effect on the collaborative behaviour between supply chain partners.

4.4.7. *Agility*

Purvis *et al.* (2016, pp. 581–582) and Biedermann (2018, p. 186) have shown that agility directly influences SCR. Accordingly, it is assumed that the corresponding specific measures have a direct effect on SCR.

4.4.8. *Robustness*

The view of Purvis *et al.* (2016, p. 581) that robustness is a directly influencing success factor on SCR is shared in this chapter. Following them, the assumption is made that the associated measures directly contribute to SCR.

4.5. *Discussing the framework*

The reference framework in Figure 2 has a theoretical character, as it serves to summarise the findings on success factors of SCR. However, the listing of specific measures enhances its practical applicability, which is an improvement compared to the framework developed by Biedermann (2018). Furthermore, four hypotheses regarding dependencies of new digital technologies on SCR have been derived based on the current state of the art found in the literature. Additionally, in comparison to Biedermann's approach, the segmentation of the success factors into three levels provided in this framework is a new systematic illustration of the principle of SCR. For example, the quality of a contingency plan based on flexible capacities (mediating level) is dependent on the extent to which the creation of redundancy

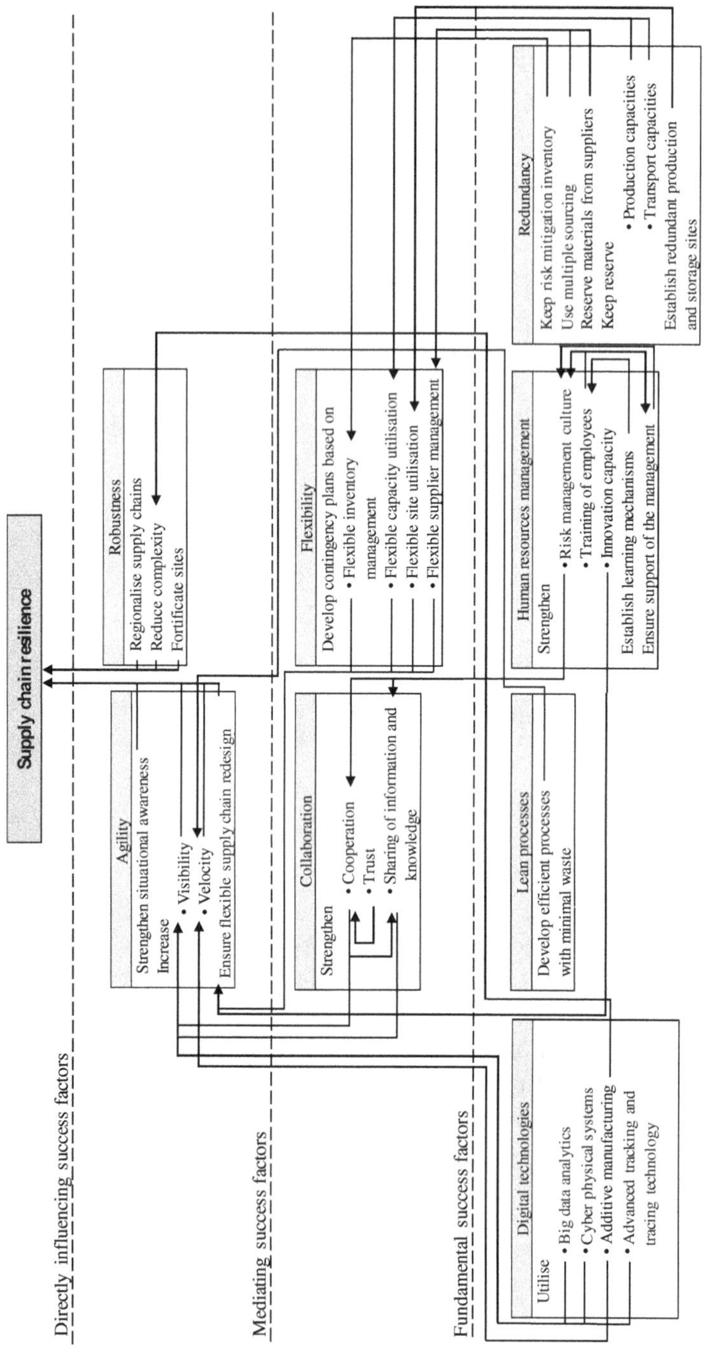

Fig. 2. Reference framework for success factors of resilient supply chains.

has been included in capacity planning (fundamental level). The correct implementation of these contingency plans is, in turn, crucial for an agile redesign of the supply chain (directly influencing level). This chain of effects shows that SCR is a holistic concept that is made up of a multitude of interacting factors. Supply chain managers must consider the relationships between these individual measures.

5. Case Study

5.1. *Research methodology and context of the case study*

A case study will be carried out to demonstrate the applicability of the developed reference framework. Using the reference framework, two supply chains are analysed concerning their mitigation strategy regarding a past SCD in order to outline the success factors involved. Afterwards, the SCR of each supply chain is measured using our own method based on the findings of Hohenstein *et al.* (2015, p. 107).

In this case study, two mobile phone supply chains are analysed with the focus on the production companies and the supplier. In both supply chains, Philips acted as a supplier of chips that were later built into the mobile phones produced by Ericsson and Nokia (Latour, 2001; Mukherjee, 2008). The SCD both supply chains dealt with was caused by a natural disaster. On 17 March, 2000, due to a lightning strike, a fire broke out in a chip factory operated by Philips. Both wafers and stored chips used in Nokia's and Ericsson's mobile phones were destroyed (Mukherjee, 2008).

5.2. *Analysing Nokia's reaction to the supply chain disruption*

5.2.1. *The initial reaction of Nokia to the SCD*

An employee from Nokia noticed an anomaly in the routine input of Philips a few days after the SCD. He forwarded this incident immediately to his supervisor. After Nokia had already detected this anomaly, a Philips employee called Nokia's senior purchasing manager on 20 March, 2000, informing him about the SCD, stating that it would last about a week. The manager again forwarded this information to his supervisor (Murkherjee, 2008). In response to this line of communication, the status of components manufactured at the Philips factory was checked daily instead of the usual weekly cycles (Murkherjee, 2008). The basis for Nokia's successful response to the SCD was the company's strong situational awareness. The predefined processes (checking routine input and monitoring critical components) for detecting early warning signs laid the basis for this. Besides, the open communication culture regarding the forwarding of problem cases can be emphasised positively. Nokia's risk management culture strengthened the collaboration within the company. The strong cooperation and extensive exchange of information, in turn, increased the visibility within Nokia. On this information base, agile decisions were made.

Philips again approached Nokia on 31 March, 2000. This time, they spoke of several weeks needed to restore the operability of the production facility in Albuquerque. Furthermore, it was communicated that stocks of microchips produced within several months were damaged (Latour, 2001, p. 4). Nokia then took three main steps to mitigate the effects of the SCD (Mukherjee, 2008) as follows:

- *Redistribution of the production of ASIC chips in cooperation with Philips*: Two types of chips manufactured by Philips in Albuquerque were essential to Nokia's production: the (Application Specific Integrated Circuit ASIC) chip and the Amplifier chip. The ASIC chip at that time was manufactured exclusively by Philips and its direct suppliers. In several meetings between senior executives of Philips and Nokia, Nokia made it clear that the company would not tolerate a long-term SCD. Nokia requested information from Philips about the capacity situation in other Philips factories. As part of a close cooperation between Philips and Nokia, capacities in Philips' factories in Eindhoven and Shanghai were restructured so that ASIC chips could be produced there (Latour, 2001, pp. 4–5). The basis for this approach was the redundancy created by Philips in the form of production sites where ASIC chips could also be manufactured. Thus, a flexible contingency plan was implemented for the reallocation of the production to Eindhoven and Shanghai. This, in turn, made the supply chain more agile, as a redesign of the supply chain was possible. That was also an example of good cooperation between Nokia and Philips. Cooperative negotiations between the two supply chain partners and an intense exchange of information and knowledge about Philips' capacity situation ensured visibility and thus agility.

- *Redesign of the chips and increase of the production output*: Nokia's management assembled an interdisciplinary team of supply chain managers, chip developers, and executives. The group was assigned the task of developing solutions which would mitigate the SCD while also keeping lines of communication with Philips constantly open. The impetus for this action was the result of a learning process from a previous SCD (Latour, 2001, p. 4). The team created a new design for the required chips so that they could be manufactured at other Philips production sites or by other suppliers (Mukherjee, 2008). Also, an existing project to increase production output was given high priority. Once Philips' Albuquerque factory was operable again, a compensation of the loss of more than 2 million microchips was possible (Latour, 2001, p. 5). This approach was based on Nokia's human resources management; based on the recommendation from top management, an interdisciplinary team was put together. This recommendation was most likely the result of lessons learned from a past incident, leading the company to be better prepared for future SCD. These measures strengthened the company's risk management culture. The work within the team strengthened the cooperation between employees at Nokia's different sites and between Nokia and Philips and improved the exchange of information. This close collaboration increased visibility in the supply chain. The innovative approaches of the team members (chip redesign and increased production output) ensured that the supply chain could be flexibly redesigned and adapted to the SCD.
- *Procurement of the amplifier chip through multiple sourcing*: Nokia was able to use suppliers that had already been approved for this chip. Two suppliers agreed to produce several million amplifier microchips (Latour, 2001, pp. 4–5). The basis for this solution was the existing redundancy created using multiple sourcing. This made it possible to develop and implement a contingency plan to compensate for the damaged amplifier chips. Through this course of action, a flexible redesign of the supply chain was possible.

5.3. *Analysing Ericsson's reaction to the supply chain disruption*

Just like Nokia, Ericsson received a call from Philips on 20 March, 2000, in which the company communicated an initial assessment of the SCDs. The significant difference between Ericsson and Nokia was that Ericsson itself had not noticed any discrepancies in the supply of the microchips until then (Mukherjee, 2008). Furthermore, the incident was not directly reported to top management (Latour, 2001, pp. 4–5). As a result of this, no follow-up action was taken by Ericsson (Latour, 2001; Mukherjee, 2008). After Philips had briefed Ericsson on the actual impact of the SCD, it also took time for the information to be passed on from middle management to top management. This delay prevented Philips from responding to Ericsson's request to provide the required demand for chips, as Philips' capacities had already been exhausted by that time (Latour, 2001, pp. 4–5). No success factors of SCR concerning Ericsson's reaction to the SCD could be identified.

5.4. *Measuring the supply chain resilience*

Following Reed *et al.* (2009, p. 175), SCR is measured within a specific time interval. This fixed interval allows the comparison of the two production companies, Nokia and Ericsson. The performance of both companies is assumed to be representative of the performance of the associated supply chains. The first fixed point in the time axis is January 2000, which was chosen because it represents the initial situation of Nokia and Ericsson before the SCDs. The second fixed point is set in January 2001, after the SCD (Latour, 2001). Following the proposed metrics of Hohenstein *et al.* (2015, p. 107) for measuring SCR, the goal was to compare the shift in market share between Nokia and Ericsson.

If the market share of the company at fixed point 2 is as high or higher than at fixed point 1, the company has recovered from the SCD within the given period or has been able to move into an improved competitive position. Consequently, the SCR is high. However, if the market share at fixed point 2 is lower than the performance at fixed point 1, the company has not fully recovered from the SCD in the given period. Accordingly, this is referred to as a low SCR. Figure 3 shows the estimated curve of the market share

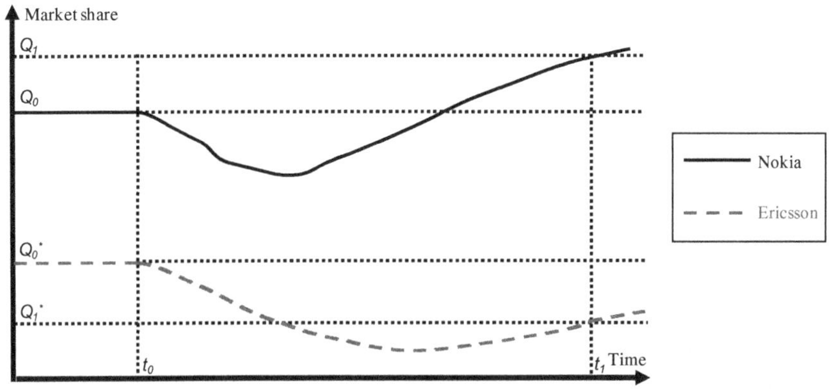

Fig. 3. Comparison of the estimated market share curve between Nokia and Ericsson.

of Nokia and Ericsson. In January 2000 at time t_0, Nokia had an initial global market share in the mobile phone sector Q_0 of 27%, which increased to a value $\underline{Q}_1$ of 30% at time t_1 in January 2001. Ericsson's initial global market share Q_0* at time t_0 was 12%, which had fallen to a market share Q_1* of 9% at time t_1 (Latour, 2001, p. 2). The course of the market share of both companies shows the different levels of success in their responses to the SCD. Since Nokia was able to increase their market share after the SCD, its SCR is considered as high, whereas Ericsson's significant market share drop is an indication for its low SCR.

5.5. *Discussing the case study*

This case study demonstrated the practical applicability of the reference framework. By pointing out the success factors incorporated by Nokia, and Ericsson's lack of them, it has been illustrated why Nokia was able to mitigate the SCD better than Ericsson. Therefore, its SCR was higher. Through the analysis of Nokia's measures following the relationships between the three levels of success factors, the concept of SCR is demonstrated. Furthermore, it is argued that the shift of the market share of the two companies is a result of their different reactions to the SCD. Nokia was able to respond better to and recover faster from the SCDs than Ericsson by applying specific measures that enhanced its SCR. Concretely, Nokia was able to procure the necessary chips for its production earlier than Ericsson.

Nokia was then able to use them for their mobile phones, generating sales revenue that Ericsson missed out on. The result of this rapid recovery was a global market share gain in Nokia's mobile phone sector. It can be assumed that Nokia's 3% market share gain was primarily made possible by Ericsson's 3% market share loss (Latour, 2001, p. 2).

6. Conclusions and Future Work

This chapter focusses on reference frameworks displaying success factors for SCR. By analysing existing papers regarding this research stream, a new state-of-the-art reference framework was developed. It extended previous research in several ways. Firstly, the latest findings regarding the impact of modern digital technologies on supply chain management were incorporated and hypotheses about the effects on SCR were formulated. Secondly, a more in-depth understanding of the concept of SCR was provided by classifying the success factors for SCR in three levels and illustrating the relationships between them. Lastly, the reference framework focusses on high practicality by linking specific measures to every essential success factor. Managers may use this reference framework to assess past dealings with SCD and conclude what needs to be improved to mitigate future SCDs more effectively. They can also use it proactively to compare their measures to increase SCR to the measures listed in the reference framework.

Since this reference framework is based exclusively on an extensive literature review, it needs to be validated through interviews and surveys. Furthermore, the case study conducted in this chapter was limited to the secondary data available online. Primary data, for example, gathered through industry cooperation, could provide a more in-depth insight into the mitigation of SCD. Future research could also use the success factors and measures as a basis to develop a model weighing the impact of each measure on SCR depending on the characteristics of both the supply chain and the SCDs.

References

Adobor, H. (2019). Supply chain resilience: A multi-level framework, *International Journal of Logistics Research and Applications* **22**(6), 533–556.

Ali, A., Mahfouz, A., and Arisha, A. (2017). Analysing supply chain resilience: integrating the constructs in a concept mapping framework via a systematic literature review, *Supply Chain Management: An International Journal* **22**(1), 16–39.

Barroso, A.P., Machado, V.H., and Machado, V.C. (eds.) (2008). A supply chain disturbances classification. *IEEE International Conference on Industrial Engineering and Engineering Management*. Singapore.

Biedermann, L. (2018). *Supply Chain Resilienz Konzeptioneller Bezugsrahmen und: Identifikation zukünftiger Erfolgsfaktoren* (Doctoral dissertation). Bremen, Germany. Available at: https://link.springer.com/content/pdf/10.1007%2F978-3-658-23516-1.pdf.

Blackhurst, J., Dunn, K., and Craighead, C. (2011). An empirically derived framework of global supply resiliency, *Journal of Business Logistics* **32**(4), 374–391.

Brandon-Jones, E., Squire, B., Autry, C.W., and Petersen, K.J. (2014). A contingent resource-based perspective of supply chain resilience and robustness, *Journal of Supply Chain Management* **50**(3), 55–73.

Chopra, S. and Manmohan, S. (2014). Reducing the risk of supply chain disruptions, *MIT Sloan Management Review* **55**(3), 73–81.

Chowdhury, M. and Quaddus, M. (2017). Supply chain resilience: Conceptualization and scale development using dynamic capability theory, *International Journal of Production Economics* **188**(1), 185–204.

Christopher, M. and Peck, H. (2004). Building the resilient supply chain, *International Journal of Logistics Management* **15**(2), 1–14.

Christopher, M., Mena, C., Khan, O., and Yurt, O. (2011). Approaches to managing global sourcing risk, *Supply Chain Management* **16**(2), 67–81.

Craighead, C.W., Blackhurst, J., Rungtusanatham, M.J., and Handfield, R.B. (2007). The severity of supply chain disruptions: Design characteristics and mitigation capabilities, *Decision Sciences* **38**(1), 131–156.

Dolgui, A., Ivanov, D., and Sokolov, B. (2018). Ripple effect in the supply chain: an analysis and recent literature, *International Journal of Production Research* **56**(1–2), 414–430.

Dubey, R., Gunasekaran, A., Childe, S.J., Papadopoulos, T., Blome, C., and Luo, Z. (2017). Antecedents of resilient supply chains: An empirical study, *IEEE Transactions on Engineering Management* **66**(1), 8–19.

Fattahi, M., Govindan, K., and Keyvanshokooh, E. (2017). Responsive and resilient supply chain network design under operational and disruption risks with delivery lead-time sensitive customers, *Transportation Research Part E* **101**(1), 176–200.

Gölgeci, I. and Ponomarov, S.Y. (2015). How does firm innovativeness enable supply chain resilience? The moderating role of supply uncertainty and interdependence, *Technology Analysis & Strategic Management* **27**(3), 267–282.

Hendricks, K.B. and Singhal, V.R. (2011). Supply chain disruptions and corporate performance. In Gurnani, H., Mehrotra, A. and Ray, S. (eds.), *Supply Chain Disruptions: Theory and Practice of Managing Risk*. London: Springer-Verlag, pp. 1–19.

Hohenstein, N., Feisel, E., and Hartmann, E. (2015). Research on the phenomenon of supply chain resilience A systematic review and paths for further investigation, *International Journal of Physical Distribution & Logistics* **45**(1–2), 90–117.

Ivanov, D. and Dolgui, A. (2019). Low-certainty-need (LCN) supply chains: A new perspective in managing disruption risks and resilience, *International Journal of Production Research* **57**(15–16), 5119–5136.

Ivanov, D., Dolgui, A., and Sokolow, B. (2019). The impact of digital technology and Industry 4.0 on the ripple effect and supply chain risk analytics, *International Journal of Production Research* **57**(3), 829–846.

Jain, V., Kumar, S., Soni, U., and Chandra, C. (2017). Supply chain resilience: Model development and empirical analysis, *International Journal of Production Research* **55**(22), 6779–6800.

Jodlbauer, H. (2018). *Digitale Transformation der Wertschöpfung*. Stuttgart: W. Kohlhammer Verlag.

Jüttner, U. and Maklan, S. (2011). Supply chain resilience in the global financial crisis: an empirical study, *Supply Chain Management: An International Journal* **16**(4), 246–259.

Lasch, R. (2018). *Strategisches und operatives Logistikmanagement: Prozesse*. 2nd edn. Wiesbaden: Springer Gabler.

Latour, A. (2001). *Trial by Fire: A Blaze in Albuquerque Sets Off Major Crisis For Cell-Phone Giants*. Retrieved from https://stuff.mit.edu/afs/athena/course/15/15.795/WSJ_Nokia%20Handles SupplyChainShock.pdf.

Lucker, F. and Seifert, R.W. (2017). Building up resilience in a pharmaceutical supply chain through inventory. dual sourcing and agility capacity, *Omega* **73**(1), 114–124.

Morgan, R. and Hunt, S. (1994). The commitment-trust theory of relationship marketing, *The Journal of Marketing* **58**(3), 20–38.

Mukherjee, A.S. (2008). *The Fire That Changed an Industry: A Case Study on Thriving in a Networked World*. Available at: https://www.informit.com/articles/article.aspx?p=1244469.

Namdar, J., Li, X., Sawhney, R., and Pradhan, N. (2018). Supply chain resilience for single and multiple sourcing in the presence of disruption risks, *International Journal of Production Research* **56**(6), 2339–2360.

Nonaka, I. and Yamanouchi, T. (1989). Managing innovation as a self-renewing process, *Journal of Business Venturing* **4**(5), 299–315.

O'Leary, L. (2020). *The Modern Supply Chain Is Snapping. The Coronavirus Exposes the Fragility of an Economy Built on Outsourcing and Just-in-Time Inventory.* Available at: https://www.theatlantic.com/ideas/archive/2020/03/supply-chains-and-coronavirus/608329/.

Ponomarov, S. and Holcomb, M. (2009). Understanding the concept of supply chain resilience, *The International Journal of Logistics Management* **20**(1), 124–143.

Purvis, L., Spall, S., Naim, M., and Spiegler, V. (2016). Developing a resilient supply chain strategy during "boom" and "bust", *Production Planning & Control* **27**(7–8), 579–590.

Rößl, D. (1990). Die Entwicklung eines Bezugsrahmens und seine Stellung im Forschungsprozess, *Journal für Betriebswirtschaft* **40**(1), 99–110.

Scholten, K., Stevenson, M., and Van Donk, D.P. (2020). Dealing with the unpredictable: Supply chain resilience, *International Journal of Operations & Production Management* **40**(1), 1–10.

Sheffi, Y. and Rice, J.B. (2005). A supply chain view of the resilient enterprise, *MIT Sloan Management Review* **47**(1), 41–48.

Simchi-Levi, D., Schmidt, W., and Wei, Y. (2014). *From superstorms to factory fires: Managing unpredictable supply-chain disruptions.* Available at: https://hbr.org/2014/01/from-superstorms-to-factory-fires-managing-unpredictable-supply-chain-disruptions.

Theorin, A., Bengtsson, K., Provost, J., Lieder, M., Johnsson, C., Lundholm, T., and Lennartson, B. (2017). An event-driven manufacturing information system architecture for Industry 4.0, *International Journal of Production Research* **55**(5), 1297–1311.

Tomlin, B. (2006). On the value of mitigation and contingency strategies for managing supply chain disruption risks, *Management Science* **52**(5), 639–657.

Treiblmaier, H. (2018). Optimal levels of (de) centralisation for resilient supply chains, *The International Journal of Logistics Management* **29**(1), 435–455.

VHB (2019). *Alphabetische Gesamtliste der Fachzeitschriften in VHB-JOURQUAL3.* Available at https://vhbonline.org/vhb4you/vhb-jourqual/vhb-jourqual-3/gesamtliste.

Vlachos, I.P. and Bourlakis, M. (2006). Supply chain collaboration between retailers and manufacturers: Do they trust each other? *Supply Chain Forum: An International Journal* **7**(1), 70–80.

Wieland, A. and Wallenburg, C.M. (2012). Dealing with supply chain risks: Linking risk management practices and strategies to performance, *International Journal of Physical Distribution & Logistics Management* **42**(10), 887–905.

Wieland, A. and Wallenburg, C. (2013). The influence of relational competencies on supply chain resilience: a relational view, *International Journal of Physical Distribution & Logistics Management* **43**(4), 300–320.

Zegordi, S. and Davarzani, H. (2012). Developing a supply chain disruption analysis model: Application of colored Petri-nets, *Expert System with Applications* **39**(1), 2102–2111.

https://doi.org/10.1142/9781800611917_0014

Chapter 14

Assessment of the Systemic Risk in the German Banking Industry

Katarzyna Kuziak* **and Krzysztof Piontek**†

Wroclaw University of Economics and Business, Poland

**katarzyna.kuziak@ue.wroc.pl*

†*krzysztof.piontek@ue.wroc.pl*

In this chapter, systemic risk refers in a very narrow sense to a risk of breakdown or major dysfunction in a banking system. Some researchers use the term to include the potential insolvency of a major entity in the financial system or its component. In this work, financial indicators and the approach of Conditional Value-at-Risk (CoVaR) is used to empirically analyse the systemic risk for the German financial system. Results indicate that the differences in the systemic risk assessment by using composite measure and delta CoVaR may occur as the result of the composite measure being determined by selected financial ratios, the adopted normalisation and ordering method, and the group of banks. The relationship between a bank's financial condition and systemic risk is not obvious for complex financial systems, and both approaches use data of different frequency, which affects quality of the assessment.

1. Introduction

The global financial crisis 2007–2009 has highlighted the importance of prudent monitoring and assessment of systemic risk and has increased the concern about systemic risk among academics, regulators, and central banks. Systemic risk refers to the risk of a breakdown of an entire financial system rather than simply the failure of an individual financial institution. Compared with individual risk, systemic risk has five basic characteristics: complexity, suddenness, rapid contagion, wide spread, and great harm (Zhang, 2010). Therefore, it has many dimensions and it seems to be a complex phenomenon, thus, is not easy to measure.

Hansen (2013) considered three possible notions of systemic risk. Firstly, there is bank run, which is triggered by liquidity concerns. Secondly, financial network vulnerability, in which adverse consequences of internal shocks spread and magnify within the network itself. Finally, the potential insolvency related to a major institution and/or a component of the financial system.

Due to the complexity of the systemic risk phenomenon, there is no golden standard measurement, yet. Bisias *et al.* (2012), Hattori *et al.* (2014), and Benoit *et al.* (2015) provided overviews of a large number of studies about measurement methods.

There are many approaches to measure the systemic risk (Hansen 2013, Benoit *et al.*, 2015), but the major distinction includes financial soundness indicators and advanced systemic risk models. Since international financial markets are susceptible to turbulence, the IMF began an initiative to identify a list of internationally comparable indicators that can be used for financial sector surveillance. In the second group of measures — advanced models of systemic risk — advanced statistical and econometric tools have been applied. They are based on the statistical multivariate distributions or on the stochastic processes (Benoit *et al.*, 2015).

The goal of this work is to combine delta CoVaR (Conditional Value-at-Risk) and measures of financial condition in the systemic risk assessment. Delta CoVaR (measured with DCC and quantile regression approach) proposed by Adrian and Brunnermeier (2016) is used to measure the systemic risk. The composite indicator — a classical measure of development proposed by Hellwig (1968) — is used as a measure of financial condition.

The second section provides directions in measurement approaches. The third section is devoted to CoVaR estimation methods. In the fourth section, the composite measure is described. The fifth section scrutinises information about the

German banking sector. The last two sections present the results from the empirical study and conclude this work.

2. Systemic Risk Measurement

Jajuga (2015) proposes two main approaches in the systemic risk measurement:

1. focused on "input" to financial instability (systemic risk) — indicators of financial stability — which can be treated as warning signals of a systemic event;
2. focused on "output" of financial instability (systemic risk) — more advanced models of systemic risk — which can be treated as a result of a systemic event.

In the second group, many systemic risk measures have been proposed but two have gained particular attraction: CoVaR and MES (Marginal Expected Shortfall). The CoVaR proposed by Adrian and Brunnermeier (2016) is derived from the VaR measure. This measure was extended by taking more dimensions into account. The Multi-Conditional-VaR (MCoVaR) was then proposed by Cao (2013). The MES is derived from the Expected Shortfall proposed by Acharya *et al.* (2010) and Brownlees and Engle (2012). Dičpinigaitienė and Novickytė (2018) found that the application of various methods based on the network methodology in the systemic risk analysis has particularly increased. Among the other important systemic risk measures the following are to be considered:

- the Shapley Value approach (Tarashev *et al.*, 2010);
- the Component Expected Shortfall (Banulescu and Dumitrescu, 2012);
- the Systemic RISK measure (SRISK) (Acharya *et al.*, 2012; Brownlees and Engle, 2016);
- Distress Insurance Premium (Huang *et al.*, 2009, 2010, 2011);
- Joint Probability of Distress (Segoviano and Goodhart, 2009);
- the Expected Financing Requirements (Popescu and Turcu, 2017);
- the Impact Susceptibility Index (Silva *et al.*, 2017).

Dičpinigaitienė and Novickytė (2018) concluded that the appropriate method for measuring the systemic risk has not yet been found, and that there can be no single method or model for measuring the overall systemic risk. Some authors emphasise the weaknesses or advantages of certain methods, looking for ways to improve them. Others introduce new methods or new approaches.

This study is based on the CoVaR methodology initially proposed by Adrian and Brunnermeier (2016) and then modified by Girardi and Ergün (2013), and entails the financial indicators composite measure.

3. Conditional Value at Risk Estimation

The general idea behind CoVaR is to use the conditional distribution of a random variable X^j representing a particular financial institution (or the entire financial system) given that another institution, represented by a random variable X^i, is under stress.

There are two alternative definitions of CoVaR in the current literature. The original definition by Adrian and Brunnermeier (2016) is derived from the conditional distribution of X^j given that $X^i = \mathrm{VaR}_q^i$. The second one uses conditioning on $X^i \leq \mathrm{VaR}_q^i$. This modification was proposed by Girardi and Ergün (2013) to improve the comparability of CoVaR with nonparametric estimation methods.

The measure of risk used by financial institutions, the Value at Risk (VaR) focuses on the risk of an individual institution. Similarly to VaR, the CoVaR is defined as (Adrian and Brunnermeier, 2016):

$$P\big(X^j \leq \mathrm{CoVaR}_q^{j|i} \,|\, X^i = \mathrm{VaR}_q^i\big) = q, \tag{1}$$

where q is a quantile of the distribution of X^j taking into account the financial system.

The CoVaR measures the VaR of the financial system conditioning on a financial institution that is in financial distress. The delta CoVaR is the difference between the CoVaR conditional on the distress of an institution and the CoVaR conditional on the normal state of the institution. It captures the contribution of a particular institution, in a non-causal sense, to the overall systemic risk (Adrian and Brunnermeier, 2016).

The delta CoVaR is directional. It ensures the answer which institutions attribute most to the financial system when a financial crisis occurs. Reverting the conditioning allows to answer which institutions are most at risk in the event of a financial crisis.

There are a few methods of CoVaR and delta CoVaR estimation: quantile regression, multivariate GARCH, copula function, Extreme Value Theory, and bootstrap approach. In this work, quantile regression and GARCH will be applied.

3.1. *Quantile regression*

The quantile regression approach is based on Koenker and Basset's (1978) quantile regression proposition. According to Adrian and Brunnermeier (2016), it is an efficient way to estimate CoVaR.

The quantile regression models the relation between a predictor variable (or a set of predictor variables) and specific quantiles of the response variable. While estimating CoVaR, the focus is on a specific low quantile of a distribution and, therefore, it is convenient to use quantile regression here:

$$X_q|x = F_y^{-1}(q|x) = \alpha_q + \beta_q x. \tag{2}$$

The predicted value is an estimate of the quantile q of y as a linear function of x, where $F^{-1}(q|x)$ is the inverse CDF conditional on x.

In the quantile regression with financial system j versus institution i:

$$X_t^j = \alpha_q^i + \beta_q^i X_t^i + \epsilon_t^i; \tag{3}$$

after estimation:

$$\hat{X}_t^j = \hat{\alpha}_q^i + \hat{\beta}_q^i X_t^i. \tag{4}$$

CoVaR can be obtained in the following way:

$$\text{CoVaR}_{q,t}^{j|X_i=\text{VaR}_q^i} = \hat{\alpha}_q^{j|i} + \hat{\beta}_q^{j|i}\text{VaR}_{q,t}^i, \tag{5}$$

$$\text{CoVaR}_{0.5,t}^{j|X_i=\text{VaR}_{0.5}^i} = \hat{\alpha}_q^{j|i} + \hat{\beta}_q^{j|i}\text{VaR}_{0.5,t}^i, \tag{6}$$

then, finally, delta CoVaR is equal to

$$\Delta\,\text{CoVaR}_{q,t}^{j|i} = \hat{\beta}_q^{j|i}(\text{VaR}_{q,t}^i - \text{VaR}_{0.5,t}^i). \tag{7}$$

3.2. *GARCH approach*

Using GARCH approach is popular not only in case of the systemic risk measurement (Walther *et al.*, 2017).

The GARCH approach follows a two-step procedure:

(1) the volatility part of the joint normal distribution is estimated. For this purpose, the respective underlying GJR-GARCH(1,1) model is fitted to each bank's return series.
(2) the correlation part is estimated with the estimates from step one, which serve as the input. Thus, given the estimates from the Dynamic Conditional Correlation (DCC) approach, the conditional covariance matrix Σ_t can be specified entirely.

The VaR of each institution i is obtained by estimating a univariate GJR-GARCH(1,1) as follows:

$$r_t = \mu + \epsilon_t = \mu + \sqrt{h_t} z_t, \quad z_t \sim N(0,1), \tag{8}$$

where conditional variance is

$$h_t = \omega + (\alpha + \alpha^- I_{(\epsilon_{t-1}<0)})\epsilon_{t-1}^2 + \beta h_{t-1}, \tag{9}$$

and then VaR:

$$\mathrm{VaR}_{q,t}^i = \sqrt{h_t} \cdot quantile(\hat{z}_t^i, q). \tag{10}$$

The DCC specification for the institution i and the financial system is the following:

$$\begin{gathered} X_t = \mu + \epsilon_t, \quad \epsilon_t | F_{t-1} \sim N(0, D_t R_t D_t) \qquad (11) \\ D_t^2 = diag\{H_t\} \\ H_{i,t} = \omega_i + \alpha_i + \epsilon_{i,t-1}^2 + \beta_i H_{i,t-1} \\ z_t = D_t^{-1} \epsilon_t. \end{gathered}$$

Following Engle (2002), the specification of the conditional correlation matrix is

$$R_t = diag\{Q_t\}^{-1/2} Q_t diag\{Q_t\}^{-1/2}, \tag{12}$$

where $\text{diag}\{Q_t\}$ is the (2×2) matrix with Q_t on the diagonal and zeros off-diagonal, as follows:

$$Q_t = \Omega + \alpha z_{t-1} z'_{t-1} + \beta Q_{t-1}, \quad \Omega = \bar{R}(1 - \alpha - \beta) \tag{13}$$

$$\hat{\gamma}_{ji,t} = \hat{\rho}_{ij,t} \frac{\sqrt{\hat{h}_{j,t}}}{\sqrt{\hat{h}_{i,t}}},$$

where $\gamma_{ji,t}$ is the linear projection coefficient of the system return j, on the financial institution return i, $\rho_{ij,t}$ is the correlation between the system and the financial institution at time t. Finally, the delta CoVaR is defined as

$$\Delta\, \text{CoVaR}_{q,t}^{j|i} = \gamma_{ji,t}(\text{VaR}_{q,t}^{i} - \text{VaR}_{0.5,t}^{i}). \tag{14}$$

It is noted that in both approaches of the measurement, the delta CoVaR is defined in the same way as a difference between VaR for a financial institution is calculated on the q and 0.5 level multiplied by different coefficient: β and γ.

4. Composite Indicator of Financial Ratios

Systemically Important Financial Institutions (SIFIs) or Global Systemically Important Banks (G-SIBs) remain an important issue in the systemic risk analysis. SIFIs or G-SIBs are financial institutions whose failure might trigger a financial crisis (they are "too big to fail"). The Basel Committee has identified five factors for assessing whether a financial institution is systemically important: its size, its complexity, its interconnectedness, the lack of readily available substitutes for the financial infrastructure it provides, and its global activity. The Financial Stability Board publishes a list of Global Systemically Important Financial Institutions (G-SIFI) in November each year. Two German banks, Deutsche Bank and Commerzbank, analysed in the following sections in this chapter are considered as SIFI/G-SIB.

It seems that evaluating the financial condition of such institutions at an appropriate frequency, using financial ratios, could provide a warning signal indicating financial difficulties and be part of the assessment of the systemic risk. Therefore, it has been proposed

Table 1. Selected financial indicators.

	Ratio	Type	Variable
X1	Impaired Loans/Gross Loans %	Quality of loans	Destimulant
X2	Impaired Loans/Equity %	Quality of loans	Destimulant
X3	Equity/Total Assets %	Leverage	Stimulant
X4	Net Interest Margin %	Profitability	Stimulant
X5	Net Interest Revenue/Avg Assets %	Profitability	Stimulant
X6	Return on Avg Assets (ROAA) %	Profitability	Stimulant
X7	Return on Avg Equity (ROAE) %	Profitability	Stimulant
X8	Cost to Income Ratio %	Efficiency	Destimulant
X9	Recurring Earning Power %	Efficiency	Stimulant
X10	Net Loans/Total Assets %	Liquidity	Destimulant
X11	Net Loans/Total Deposits & Short Term funding %	Liquidity	Destimulant
X12	Liquid Assets/Total Deposits & Borrowing %	Liquidity	Destimulant

by the authors to use financial ratios in the systemic risk assessment. In such an assessment, the given banks have been ordered according to their financial condition (Kuziak and Piontek, 2018).

The IMF's Executive Board prepared the list of Financial Soundness Indicators (IMF, 2006, 2013). Based on these indicators, financial ratios have been selected by the authors and presented in Table 1. They will be scrutinised in the empirical study.

Linear ordering by the measure of development (also called composite indicator) has been applied. The concept of the pattern of development and the measure of development in English was presented by Professor Zdzisław Hellwig at the UNESCO conference in Warsaw in 1967 (see details e.g., Hellwig (1968), Walesiak (2016)). Linear ordering requires initial identification of variables as stimulants z_j^S, destimulants z_j^D and nominants (indicated in Table 1). Before calculations are made, all nominants should be converted to the stimulants.

Then the pattern of development and finally calculation of the measure of development (distance from the pattern of development) will be conducted. In the first step, standardisation was made. Elements z_{0j} of the pattern of development are as follows:

$$O_0 = [z_{oj}], \tag{15}$$

where

$$z_{oj} = \begin{cases} \max_i\{z_{ij}\} & \text{for } z_j^S \\ \max_i\{z_{ij}\} & \text{for } z_j^D. \end{cases} \tag{16}$$

In the next step, the linear ordering of a set of objects is carried out, based on the Manhattan distance from the pattern (perfect) object (elements z_{0j}), as follows:

$$\mathrm{d}_{i0} = \sum_{j=1}^{m} |z_{ij} - z_{0j}|. \tag{17}$$

The measure of development (composite indicator) is constructed based on distances as follows:

$$s_i = 1 - \frac{d_{i0}}{d_0}, \tag{18}$$

where d_0 is defined as

$$d_0 = \bar{d_0} + 2S(d_0) \tag{19}$$

and

$$\bar{d_0} = \frac{1}{n}\sum_{i=1}^{n} d_{i0},$$

$$S(d_0) = \left[\frac{1}{n}\sum_{i=1}^{n}(d_{i0} - \bar{d_0})^2\right]^{0.5}. \tag{20}$$

The higher the value of the measure of development (composite indicator, s_i), the better the financial condition of a bank (see comparable study for the Polish market Kuziak and Piontek (2019)).

5. German Banking Sector Until 2015

The German banking system consists of three groups of banks: private banks (including the "big banks"), banks with government involvement, and cooperative banks (including large Landesbanken and the smaller savings banks).

In 2014, the value of total assets of German banks was almost EUR 6.8 trillion. That corresponds to roughly 250% of Germany's GDP and 28% of the total assets in the monetary union. In Germany, there is also a comparatively large number of banks. The German banking sector is relatively large and heterogeneous. Small and medium-sized banks, which include savings banks, account for around 35% of the total balance sheet of the German banking sector (ECB, 2015).

The financial crisis of 2007–2009 affected the German banking system including large banks from the private sector. Hypo Real Estate, Industrie-Kreditbank, Deutsche Bank, and Commerzbank experienced large losses due to risky investments. Three of them were rescued by the government, only Deutsche Bank survived the crisis without government help (Behr and Schmidt, 2016).

Domestically, the largest German banks and insurance companies are highly interconnected. The highest degree of interconnectedness can be found between Allianz AG, Munich Re AG, Hannover Re AG, Deutsche Bank, Commerzbank, and Aareal Bank, with Allianz being the largest contributor to systemic risks among the publicly-traded German financials. Both Deutsche Bank and Commerzbank are the source of outward spillovers to most other publicly listed banks and insurers (IMF, 2016).

Among G-SIBs, Deutsche Bank appears to be the most important net contributor to systemic risks (followed by HSBC and Credit Suisse). An important bank in Germany, Commerzbank, does not appear to be a contributor to systemic risks globally. Commerzbank tends to be the recipient of inward spillover from the U.S. and European G-SIBs. The relative importance of Deutsche Bank underscores the importance of risk management, intense supervision of G-SIBs, and the close monitoring of their cross-border exposures, as well as rapidly completing capacity to implement the new resolution regime (IMF, 2016).

In this study, the focus is on the largest private banks. Because of merger processes in the years 2006–2015, the research is limited in use of financial data and stock prices only to four largest banks in Germany listed on Deutsche Börse between 2006–2015: Aareal Bank (ARL), Comdirect (COM) Bank, Commerzbank (CBK), and Deutsche Bank (DBK).

6. Empirical Study

The presented methodology was applied for the German market. Due to the small sample of analysed banks, this study should be considered as preliminary research for a large sample.

An important simplifying assumption was that the financial system was composed only of banks (it is a narrow definition of the systemic risk, in which the focus is set on the banking sector) and a banking industry index — DAXsector Banks Performance — is taken as a proxy of financial system in delta CoVaR calculations. The sample period was from 2 January 2006 to 25 December 2006 (before the crisis), from 4 January 2010 to 27 December 2010 (just after the crisis) and from 5 January 2015 to 28 December 2015 (after the crisis). Weekly logarithmic rates of return are calculated from closing prices (Reuters database). VaR was estimated by historical simulation filtered with GARCH.

For the same four banks for years 2006, 2010, and 2015, twelve financial ratios indicted in Table 1 (for each bank separately) were calculated (Scopus database). The total asset values in EUR for pointed years are also collected from Scopus database.

Figures 1(a)–4(b) present delta CoVaR values in time for both 0.01 and 0.05 significance levels and applied methods of estimation, DCC and quantile regression. For both significance levels, shape of delta CoVaR in time is the same — the only difference between results obtained for different significance levels is value — higher for 0.01 level. Mostly, results for quantile regression are higher compared to DCC; the exception remains the results for Commerzbank at 0.01 significance level. The higher values of delta CoVaR in the crisis time (around 2008) may be noticed in all given banks.

Results in Tables 2–4 present linear ordering of a set of objects (banks) based on the pattern of development (Hellwig, 1968) and on the delta CoVaR as well as on the size of a bank (measured by the value of total assets in EUR). The largest values of measure of development and assets or lowest values of delta CoVaR were indicated with bold font.

The results of delta CoVaR at level 0.05 obtained from quantile regression were higher compared to DCC. Only in the case of two banks (Comdirect Bank and Commerzbank) in 2015, the opposite result were obtained by the authors (delta CoVaR using DCC

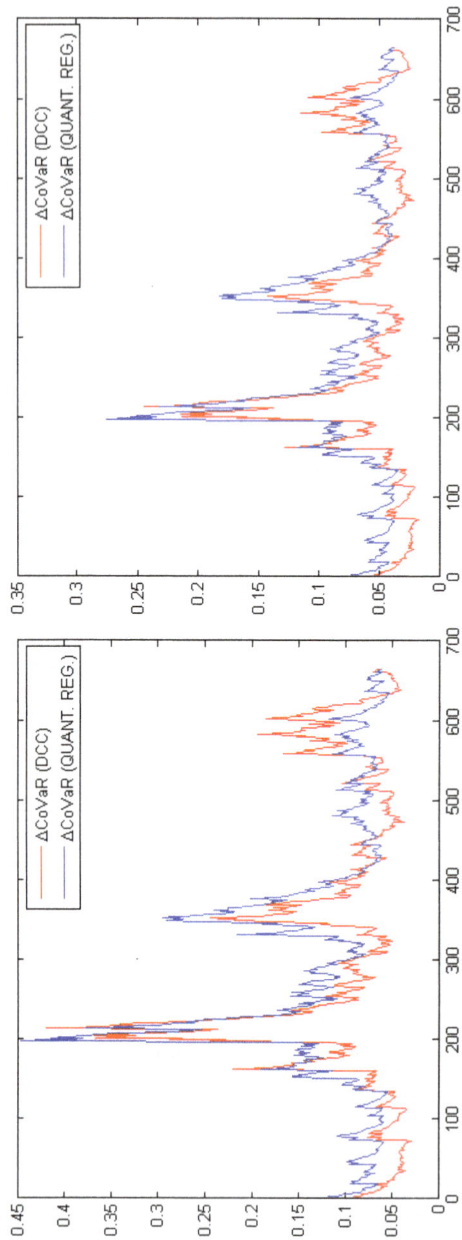

Fig. 1. (a) Delta CoVaR for ARL 0.01. (b) Delta CoVaR for ARL 0.05.

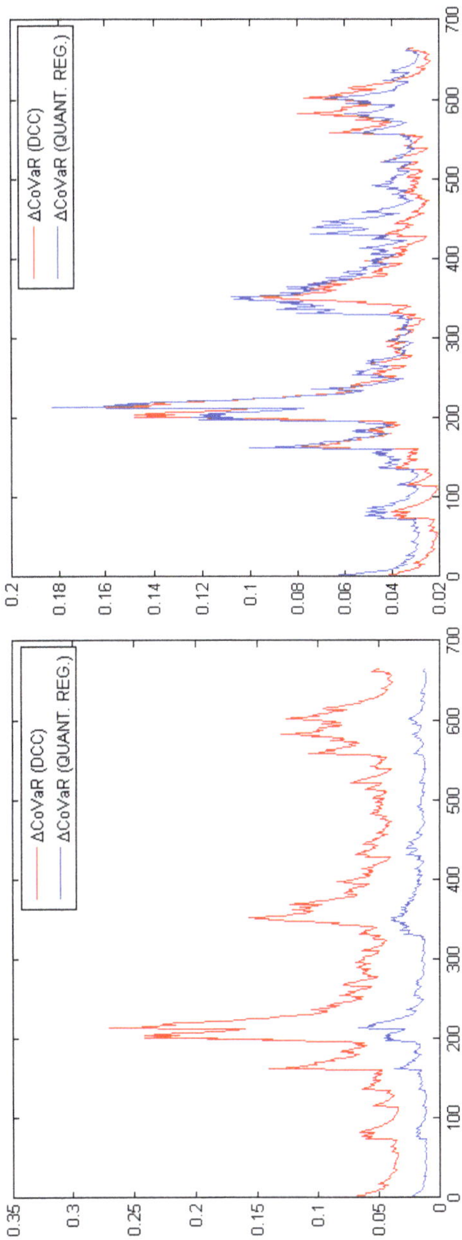

Fig. 2. (a) Delta CoVaR for CBK 0.01. (b) Delta CoVaR for CBK 0.05.

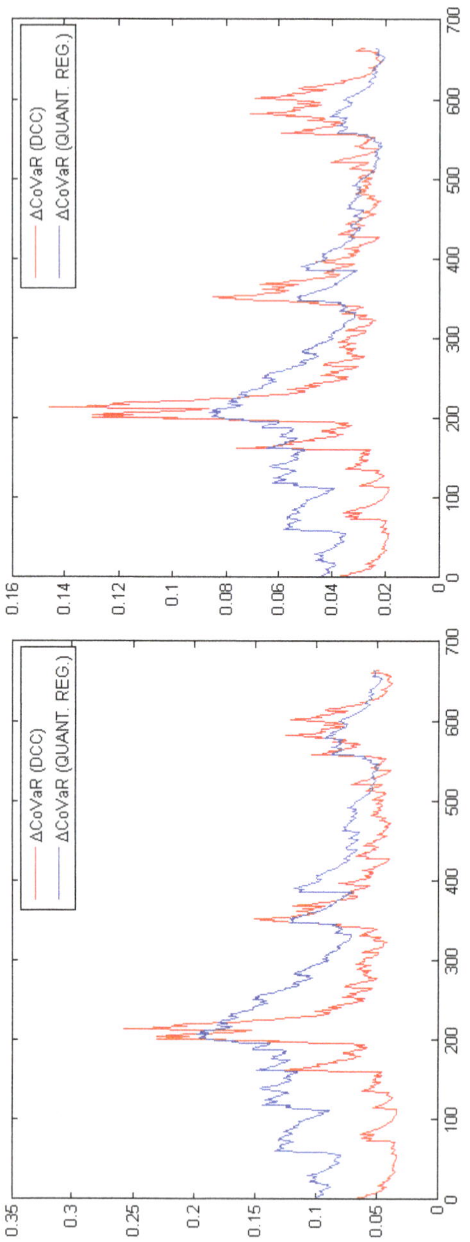

Fig. 3. (a) Delta CoVaR for COM 0.01. (b) Delta CoVaR for COM 0.05.

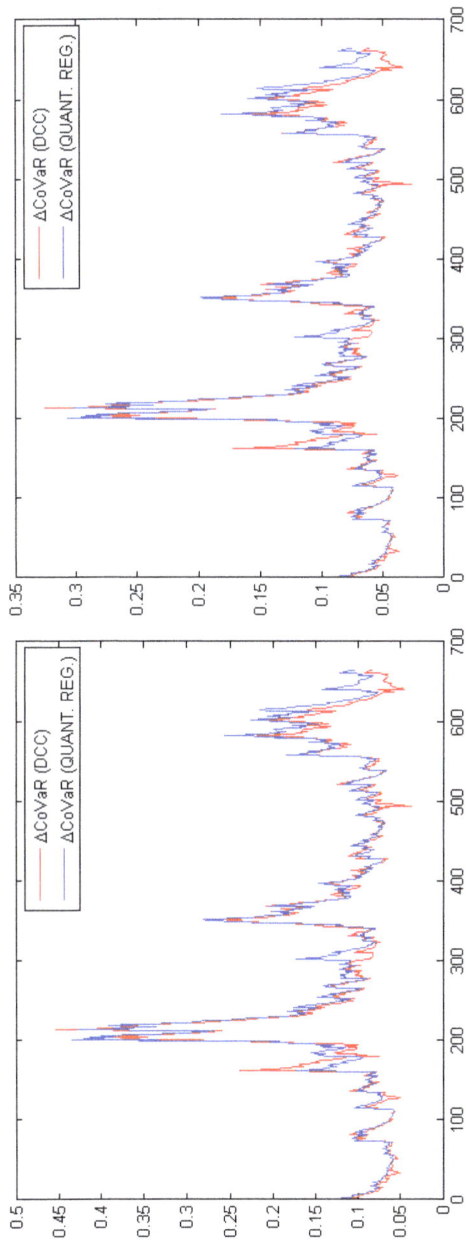

Fig. 4. (a) Delta CoVaR for DBK 0.01. (b) Delta CoVaR for DBK 0.05.

Table 2. Results for 2015.

	DCC 0.05		QR 0.05		Measure		Assets		DCC 0.01		QR 0.01	
Aareal Bank AG	0.0530	3	0.05149	3	0.60237	2	51 948 000	3	0.089548	3	0.08193	3
Comdirect Bank AG	**0.03426**	1	**0.02784**	1	**0.70371**	1	16 768 700	4	**0.060205**	1	0.06336	2
Commerz-bank AG	0.03789	2	0.03677	2	0.55091	3	532 641 000	2	0.061983	2	**0.01364**	1
Deutsche Bank AG	0.07545	4	0.07660	4	0.32258	4	**1 629 130 000**	1	0.104254	4	0.10754	4

Table 3. Results for 2010.

	DCC 0.05		QR 0.05		Measure		Assets		DCC 0.01		QR 0.01	
Aareal Bank AG	0.05104	3	0.07132	3	0.39063	3	41 217 000	3	0.08667	3	0.11412	3
Comdirect Bank AG	**0.03359**	1	0.04579	2	**0.77372**	1	11 040 200	4	**0.05933**	1	0.10477	2
Commerz-bank AG	0.03760	2	**0.03792**	1	0.28657	4	754 299 000	2	0.06151	2	**0.01406**	1
Deutsche Bank AG	0.07350	4	0.08475	4	0.49700	2	**1 905 630 000**	1	0.10165	4	0.11910	4

Table 4. Results for 2006.

	DCC 0.05		QR 0.05		Measure		Assets		DCC 0.01		QR 0.01	
Aareal Bank AG	0.02869	3	0.04532	2	0.23655	3	38 279 000	3	0.04833	3	0.07190	2
Comdirect Bank AG	**0.02424**	1	0.05072	3	**0.83039**	1	5 300 900	4	**0.04286**	1	0.11613	4
Commerz-bank AG	0.02717	2	**0.03643**	1	0.19191	4	608 339 000	2	0.04446	2	**0.01351**	1
Deutsche Bank AG	0.05348	4	0.05465	4	0.39050	2	**1 571 768 000**	1	0.07357	4	0.07639	3

approach was higher compared to QR). The same phenomenon can be noted for the delta CoVaR results calculated at significance level 0.01.

The highest value of measure of development (which means better financial standing compared to the others) is found for Comdirect Bank, the lowest for Deutsche Bank for all years which are subject to the analysis. It means that Deutsche Bank had weak financial standing compared to others.

7. Conclusions

CoVaR and ΔCoVaR extend the VaR framework to measure the systemic risk rather than the individual institution risk. ΔCoVaR is higher for the quantile regression compared to the DCC approach. The results are similar to Girardi and Ergün (2013), Benoit *et al.* (2013), and Kuziak and Piontek (2018).

Mostly, lower values of measure of financial condition (composite indicator) were not reflected in higher values of the delta CoVaR.

For measuring the delta CoVaR, the authors have approximated the system with the DAXsector Banks Performance index instead of accounting data since information coming from accounting data is lagged and the data frequency is low. In the case of financial markets, the data frequency (for prices) is high, therefore, the use of stock prices of banks and the banking index seems reasonable. The construction of delta CoVaR allows using market prices, however, applying the banking index might be problematic. The banking index is dependent on the individual stock price, therefore, the interpretation of results is biased. It is hard to attribute the result to the bad financial condition of the bank or to the size of the given bank. The obtained results indicate that index approximation, if used frequently, might not be appropriate — cf. Kuziak and Piontek (2018) studying the Polish banking sector.

This issue could be tackled by constructing a broad index (using broader definition of the system than the banking sector) or removing the bank from the index (when calculating CoVaR for a given bank).

Kuziak and Piontek (2018) reached a similar conclusion for the Polish banking sector. Additionally, they proved that the delta CoVaR is more influenced by the size of the bank than its financial condition. It is confirmed by the positive, large, and statistically significant correlation coefficients between delta CoVaR and the size, and by the smaller and mostly insignificant correlation coefficients between the delta CoVaR and the measure (composite indicator).

The differences in the systemic risk assessment by using the composite measure and delta CoVaR may arise due to the following:

1. the result is determined by selected financial ratios, the adopted normalisation and ordering method, and the group of banks,
2. the relationship between a bank's financial condition and systemic risk is not obvious for complex financial systems,
3. both approaches use data of different frequency, which affects the quality of the assessment.

References

Acharya, V., Pedersen, L., Philippon, T. and Richardson, M. (2010). Measuring Systemic Risk, *Working Paper*, New-York University, Available at SSRN: http://ssrn.com/abstract=1573171, referred on (20/05/2021).

Acharya, V.V., Engle, R. and Richardson, M.P. (2012). Capital shortfall: A new approach to ranking and regulating systemic risks, *American Economic Review* **102** (3), pp. 59–64.

Adrian, T. and Brunnermeier, M.K. (2016). CoVaR, *American Economic Review* **106** (7), pp. 1705–1741.

Banulescu, G.D. and Dumitrescu, E.I. (2012). A Component Approach to Systemic Risk. Which are the Riskiest Financial Institutions of Them All? *Proceedings of CREDIT 2012 Conference.*

Behr, P. and Schmidt, R.H. (2016). *The German Banking System In book: The Palgrave Handbook of European Banking*, available at https://www.researchgate.net/publication/312447349_The_German_Banking_System, referred on (20/05/2021).

Bisias, D., Flood, M., Lo, A.W. and Valavanis, S. (2012). A Survey of Systemic Risk Analytics, *The Office of Financial Research, US Treasury.*

Benoit, S., Colliard, J.-E., Hurlin, C. and Perignon, C. (2015). Where the risks lie: A survey on systemic risk, *HEC Paris Research Paper*, FIN-2015-1088.

Brownlees, C.T. and Engle, R.F. (2012). Volatility, Correlation and Tails for Systemic Risk Measurement. Available at https://faculty.washington.edu/ezivot/econ589/VolatilityBrownlees.pdf, referred on (20/05/2021).

Brownlees, C.T. and Engle, R.F. (2016). SRISK: A Conditional Capital Shortfall Measure of Systemic Risk. Available at http://papers.ssrn.com/sol3/papers.cfm?abstract_id=1611229, referred on (20/05/2021).

Cao, Z. (2013). Multi-CoVaR and Shapley value: A Systemic Risk Measure. Available at https://docs.google.com/viewer?a=v&pid=sites&srcid=ZGVmYXVsdGRvbWFpbnx6aGlsaWNhbzIwMnxneDo1ZmM0ZWY3YTk5NjJjYjFk, referred on (20/05/2021).

Dičpinigaitienė, V. and Novickytė, L. (2018). Application of systemic risk measurement methods: A systematic review and meta-analysis using a network approach, *Quantitative Finance and Economics* **2** (4), pp. 798–820.

ECB. (2015). Report on financial structures, October.

Engle, R.F. (2002). Dynamic conditional correlation: A simple class of multivariate generalized autoregressive conditional heteroscedasticity models, *Journal of Business and Economic Statistics* **20**, pp. 339–350.

Hansen, L.P. (2013). Challenges in Identifying and Measuring Systemic Risk. Available at SSRN: http://ssrn.com/abstract=2158946, referred on (20/05/2021).

Hattori, A., Kikuchi, K., Niwa, F. and Uchida, Y. (2014). A Survey of Systemic Risk Measures: Methodology and Application to the Japanese Market, *Discussion Paper No. 2014-E3.*

Hellwig, Z. (1968). Zastosowanie metody taksonomicznej do typologicznego podziału krajów ze względu na poziom ich rozwoju i strukturę wykwalifikowanych kadr [Procedure of evaluating high level manpower data and typology of countries by means of the taxonomic method], *Przegląd Statystyczny* **15** (4), pp. 307–327.

Huang, X., Zhou, H. and Zhu, H. (2009). A Framework for Assessing the Systemic Risk of Major Financial Institutions, *Finance and Economics Discussion Series*, Divisions of Research & Statistics and Monetary Affairs, Federal Reserve Board, Washington, D.C.

Huang, X., Zhou, H. and Zhu, H. (2010). Assessing the systemic risk of a heterogeneous portfolio of banks during the recent financial crisis, *BIS Working Papers No 296.*

Huang, X., Zhou, H. and Zhu, H. (2011). Systemic Risk Contributions. *Finance and Economics Discussion Series*, Divisions of Research & Statistics and Monetary Affairs, Federal Reserve Board, Washington, D.C.

IMF (2006). Compilation Guide on Financial Soundness Indicators.

IMF Policy Paper (2013). Modifications to the Current List of Financial Soundness Indicators (FSIs), November 13.

IMF (2016). Country Report No. 16/189, Germany Financial Sector Assessment Program. Financial System Stability Assessment.

Jajuga, K. (2015). Measuring Systemic Risk, unpublished work.

Koenker, R. and Basset, Jr. G. (1978). Regression auantiles, *Econometrica* **46** (1) pp. 33–50.

Kuziak, K. and Piontek, K. (2018). *Assessment of Systemic Risk in the Polish Banking Industry*, A chapter in Contemporary Trends and Challenges in Finance, pp. 145–158 from Springer.

Popescu, A. and Turcu, C. (2017). Sovereign debt and systemic risk in the eurozone: A macroeconomic perspective, *Economic Modelling* **67**, pp. 275–284.

Segoviano, M. and Goodhart, C. (2009). Bank Stability Measures. *IMF Working Paper*, WP/09/4.

Silva, T.C., Souza, S.R.S.D. and Tabak, B.M. (2017). Monitoring vulnerability and impact diffusion in financial networks, *Journal of Economic Dynamic Control* **76**, pp. 109–135

Tarashev, N., Borio, C. and Tsatsaronis, K. (2010). Attributing systemic risk to individual institutions. Methodology and policy applications, *BIS Working Papers No. 308.*

Walesiak, M. (2016). Visualization of linear ordering results for metric data with the application of multidimensional scaling, *Ekonometria = Econometrics* **2** (52), pp. 9–21.

Walther, T., Klein, T., Thu, H.P. and Piontek, K. (2017). True or spurious long memory in European non-EMU currencies, *Research in International Business and Finance* **40**, pp. 217–230.

Zhang, X.P. (2010). A study on systemic financial risk: Evolution, causes and supervision, *Studies of International Finance* **7**, pp. 58–67.

PART III
Aspects of Modern Commodity Finance

https://doi.org/10.1142/9781800611917_0015

Chapter 15

Oil and Stock Market Returns: Direction, Volatility or Liquidity?

Harald Kinateder* and Niklas Wagner†

University of Passau, School of Business, Economics and Information Systems, Germany

**harald.kinateder@uni-passau.de*

†*niklas.wagner@uni-passau.de*

We examine how oil market variables affect short-term stock market returns in the US and in six other major oil-importing countries. Apart from oil price direction, we also consider oil market volatility and liquidity. Analysis of daily returns during the 2007–2017 period reveals that oil price direction has a significant positive effect on returns for all markets, which can be interpreted as evidence of oil as a business climate indicator. Furthermore, for the US market, shocks to implied oil market volatility negatively affect stocks, this effect is significantly asymmetric, and declining oil market liquidity predicts declining stock prices.

1. Introduction

As oil is a major input factor in most economies, it is important to understand the relation between oil and stock markets, which is not only vital for investors but also plays a major role in climate finance (see, e.g., Batten *et al.*, 2018, 2021). However, past research in the oil-stock market nexus mostly considers the impact of oil price shocks on stock markets (see, e.g., Degiannakis *et al.*, 2018 for a detailed review). Recently, some papers have focused on implied volatility in oil markets (see, e.g., Christoffersen and Pan, 2018; Dupoyet and Shank, 2018; Luo and Qin, 2017) as well as the price volatility and volume relationship (see, e.g., Batten *et al.*, 2019a; Fousekis and Tzaferi, 2020). Apart from oil price direction and volatility, a third characteristic of oil markets, namely liquidity, may also drive stock market returns. Given these different oil market variables, it remains an open issue of how and to which extent they impact on stock market returns.

In this chapter, we contribute to the ongoing discussion on stock-oil relationship. For this purpose, the study examines the relation between oil and stock market returns in the US and six other major oil-importing economies. To do so, we employ a vector autoregressive model with exogenous explanatory variables.[1] This approach allows us to study the lead–lag relationship in international stock market returns and the effect of a set of explanatory variables including oil price direction, oil market volatility and liquidity as well as commonly used control variables. Volatility in the oil market is assessed by an implied volatility measure given by the Chicago Board Options Exchange (CBOE) implied oil volatility index (OVX), whose computation is based on the VIX method.[2] Moreover, we study potential asymmetric response of stock markets to positive and negative

[1]There are different approaches how this relation can be examined. Apart from this study, there is some research that analyses the level of integration between oil and stock markets, which is found to be strongest during periods of financial market stress (see, e.g., Batten *et al.*, 2017). In this context, Locarek-Junge and Walther (2017) point out that return series are often biased due to structural breaks. Therefore, the use of Markov-Switching models could be useful for analysing the stock oil market integration (see, e.g., Batten *et al.*, 2019b). Other papers examine the risk-return relationship in stock and oil markets (see, e.g., Belhassine and Bouzid, 2019; Dupoyet and Shank, 2018; Mollick and Assefa, 2013). In addition, Klein and Walther (2016) and Nguyen and Walther (2020) study oil price volatility forecasts. Finally, a different strand in the literature deals with the predictive value of oil prices for stock returns (see, e.g., Brigida, 2018; Kumar *et al.*, 2020).

[2]Christoffersen and Pan (2018) show that OVX and VIX do not capture the same source of volatility. For daily data, OVX provides additional information that is not included in VIX.

shocks in OVX.[3] Since our aim is to go beyond the study of return and volatility data only, we also focus on oil market liquidity. For this purpose, we use Amihud's (2002) price impact measure, Corwin and Schultz's (2012) high/low estimator, and Roll's (1984) implicit bid-ask spread to calculate oil market liquidity. As individual liquidity approaches do not capture all aspects of market liquidity and can be contaminated by individual model errors, we consider the first principal component of these measures.

Besides the US, we are focusing on other oil-importing countries to avoid biases due to differences arising from countries being net oil exporters. We study daily returns during the 10 May 2007 to 31 August 2017 period. The starting date of the sample corresponds to the beginning of the OVX calculation. Since CBOE uses options on the United States Oil Fund ETF to calculate OVX, we also construct our measures of oil price direction and liquidity based on this ETF to have a consistent set of oil price variables. The results display that oil price direction is the only oil variable that has a significant positive impact on returns of all stock markets. We interpret this as evidence for oil price direction being a short-term business climate indicator for oil-importing countries. As such, a rise (drop) in oil prices implies an improvement (deterioration) in the business climate of the respective countries. We further find that oil market volatility and liquidity matter not only in the US market, but for all markets in our sample (i.e., for Australia, France, Germany, and the United Kingdom) except the Asian markets. Moreover, an asymmetric effect of shocks in oil market volatility on US stock markets is documented. For non-US markets, the results for volatility asymmetry are mixed.

The remainder of this chapter is organised as follows. Section 2 describes the data set and conducts a preliminary analysis of the used variables. Section 3 contains results on the impacts of oil market variables on international stock market returns and discusses several other findings. Finally, Section 4 concludes.

[3]Following Park and Ratti's (2008) method for oil price shocks, Dupoyet and Shank (2018) separate OVX returns into their positive and negative parts. However, no asymmetric response to OVX returns is documented for US industry returns. Instead of focusing on industry returns, we analyse asymmetry on the market level. In contrast to the above-mentioned papers, we outline a test for asymmetry.

2. Approach and Data

2.1. *VARX model*

We use a vector autoregressive model with k endogenous and d exogenous variables (henceforth VARX(p) model):

$$Y_t = c + \sum_{i=1}^{p} \Phi_i Y_{t-i} + \Lambda X_t + \epsilon_t \quad \text{for } t = 1, \ldots, T, \tag{1}$$

where Y_t is a $(k \times 1)$ vector of dependent variables and X_t is a $(d \times 1)$ vector of exogenous explanatory variables; Φ_i is a $(k \times k)$ matrix and Λ is a $(d \times d)$ matrix. c is a $(k \times 1)$ vector of constants and ϵ_t is a $(k \times 1)$ vector of unobservable residuals with $\mathbb{E}(\epsilon_t) = 0$ and time-invariant covariance matrix $\mathbb{E}(\epsilon_t \epsilon_t') = \Sigma_\epsilon$. The optimal lag order p is determined by the Bayesian information criterion (BIC) and maximum likelihood estimation is used to estimate the parameters of the VARX model.

2.2. *Data*

Our data set contains daily data retrieved from Thomson Reuters Eikon and Federal Reserve Economic Database. The sample is from 10 May 2007 to 31 August 2017. The beginning of the sample coincides with the introduction of the OVX.

2.2.1. *Endogenous variables*

The stock indices comprise the following representative markets: S&P 500 (United States), ASX (Australia), CAC (France), DAX (Germany), FTSE (United Kingdom), SSE (China), and TOPIX (Japan). These countries are among the world's top 30 oil importers, with China and the United States being the two largest ones.[4]

[4]This statistic ranks countries based on their total amount of crude oil imported in barrels per day (bbl/day): US (7,969,000 bbl/day, 2017 est.) and China (6,710,000 bbl/day, 2015 est.) imported almost twice as much as Japan (3,208,000 bbl/day, 2017 est.), followed by Germany (1,836,000 bbl/day, 2017 est.), France (1,147,000 bbl/day, 2017 est.), United Kingdom (907,100 bbl/day, 2017 est.), and Australia (341,700 bbl/day, 2017 est.). *Source*: The World Factbook, Central Intelligence Agency, https://www.cia.gov/the-world-factbook/field/crude-oil-imports/, Available at: (accessed on 14.06.2021).

In our empirical analysis, we consider the time-t continuously compounded return of stock market index i, which is calculated as $R_{i,t} = \ln(P_{i,t}) - \ln(P_{i,t-1})$, where $P_{i,t}$ is the daily index close level in US dollars. Given that the vector of endogenous variables is $Y_t = (R_{\text{S\&P500},t}, R_{\text{ASX},t}, R_{\text{CAC},t}, R_{\text{DAX},t}, R_{\text{FTSE},t}, R_{\text{SSE},t}, R_{\text{TOPIX},t})'$.

2.2.2. *Exogenous explanatory variables*

This section contains a description of our explanatory variables including their expected relation to stock market returns.

2.2.2.1. Oil price direction

To analyse how movements in the oil market influence stock markets, we follow Dupoyet and Shank (2018) and use the return of the United States Oil Fund ETF, i.e., $R_{\text{OIL},t}$.[5] This oil ETF is used to calculate the OVX and therefore offers a consistent framework to analyse impacts of oil price direction, oil market volatility and liquidity. Falling oil prices should negatively impact the stocks of energy companies as their profits shrink. At the overall market level, the effect could also be negative. The reason is that a drop in oil prices can be regarded as a negative indicator for the performance of the global economy. Given this logic, $R_{\text{OIL},t}$ should have a positive impact on stock markets. However, evidence in previous literature is mixed. Studies that find a positive relation are, for example, Gupta (2016) and Luo and Qin (2017).

2.2.2.2. Oil market volatility

In May 2007, the CBOE introduced an implied oil volatility index (OVX), which measures the market's expectation of 30-day volatility of crude oil prices based on options on the United States Oil Fund ETF. We model oil market volatility by using changes in OVX, i.e., ΔOVX_t, where Δ denotes the first difference operator. During times

---

[5]We do not account for asymmetry in oil price shocks as unreported results document no asymmetric effect in positive and negative oil price shocks. In addition, former papers of Herrera *et al.* (2015) and Dupoyet and Shank (2018) report that there is no asymmetric effect on OECD countries industrial production and US industry sector returns, respectively. Park and Ratti (2008) also do not find asymmetric effects of oil price shocks on European stock returns.

of low volatility, stock markets are usually rising while the opposite is observed in tranquil periods. We assume that volatility in oil markets is perceived by investors in the same way as volatility in stock markets. Thus, we expect a negative relation between stock market returns and oil market volatility, which is also confirmed by the previous work of Diaz *et al.* (2016), Dupoyet and Shank (2018), and Luo and Qin (2017).

Asymmetric stock market volatility is an important characteristic of market volatility dynamics (see, e.g., Aboura and Wagner, 2016). Given that we also account for potential asymmetric effects of oil implied volatility on stock markets, therefore, OVX changes are split up into their positive and negative parts, respectively: $\Delta \text{OVX}_t^+ = \max\{0, \Delta OVX_t\}$ and $\Delta \text{OVX}_t^- = \min\{0, \Delta OVX_t\}$. We test for potential asymmetry by testing the null hypothesis H_0: "$\hat{\theta} = \hat{\beta}_{\Delta \text{OVX}^+} - \hat{\beta}_{\Delta \text{OVX}^-} = 0$" against the alternative H_1: "$\hat{\theta} = \hat{\beta}_{\Delta \text{OVX}^+} - \hat{\beta}_{\Delta \text{OVX}^-} < 0$". The respective t-statistic is

$$t_{\hat{\theta}} = \frac{\hat{\theta}}{\sigma(\hat{\theta})} = \frac{\hat{\beta}_{\Delta \text{OVX}^+} - \hat{\beta}_{\Delta \text{OVX}^-}}{\sqrt{[\sigma(\hat{\beta}_{\Delta \text{OVX}^+})]^2 + [\sigma(\hat{\beta}_{\Delta \text{OVX}^-})]^2 - 2Cov(\hat{\beta}_{\Delta \text{OVX}^+}, \hat{\beta}_{\Delta \text{OVX}^-})}}, \tag{2}$$

where $\sigma(\cdot)$ denotes the standard error and $\hat{\beta}$ is the estimated coefficient. The one-sided test statistic, $t_{\hat{\theta}}$, is Student t-distributed with $T - k$ degrees of freedom, where k is the number of estimated coefficients.

2.2.2.3. Oil market liquidity

The impact of oil market liquidity on stock markets is examined using three different liquidity measures, which are calculated on the United States Oil Fund ETF, namely Amihud's (2002) price impact measure, Corwin and Schultz's (2012) high/low estimator, and Roll's (1984) implicit bid-ask spread.[6] As individual liquidity approaches do not capture all aspects of market liquidity and can be contaminated by individual model errors, we consider the first principal component (PC_1) of these measures and employ a commonly used restriction for

[6]Apart from Amihud (2002), there are earlier volume based liquidity approaches (see, e.g., Cooper *et al.*, 1985; Martin, 1975).

liquidity: $LI_t = \max\{0, PC_{1,t}\}$.[7] The measure is built in a way that an increase in LI_t refers to a decline in oil market liquidity. To avoid collinearity with oil price direction, we use lagged changes instead of contemporaneous changes in PC_1, i.e., ΔLI_{t-1}, as our proxy for oil market liquidity. Our hypothesis suggests that the stock markets respond to an increase in oil market illiquidity in the same way as to an increase of oil market volatility, i.e., we expect a negative sign.[8]

2.2.2.4. Expected inflation

The change in expected inflation, ΔEI_t, calculated as the yield differential between 10-year US treasury bonds and 10-year inflation linked US treasury bonds, should have an immediate influence on stock markets (see, e.g., Dupoyet and Shank, 2018; Mollick and Assefa, 2013). Since an increase of expected inflation indicates future economic growth, we expect a positive effect on stock markets.

2.2.2.5. Term spread

The term spread is obtained by the yield differential between the 10-year and 2-year US treasury bonds. We use changes in the term spread, ΔTS_t, which are an indicative of prospective economic climate. Positive changes indicate future economic growth, whereas negative changes signal a decline in economic growth.

2.2.2.6. Default spread

The yield spread between Moody's Baa- and Aaa-rated US corporate bonds is often regarded as default spread. However, positive values of ΔDS_t signal not only greater credit risk but also greater funding illiquidity (see, e.g., Amihud and Noh, 2021), which should yield to a decline in stock markets.

---

[7] The usage of the first principal component is further underpinned by the fact the individual liquidity measures are not highly correlated. Therefore, it is a common practice in literature to use the first principal component if data for various liquidity proxies is available.

[8] Previous research has shown that stock market liquidity is a priced factor (see, e.g., Czauderna *et al.*, 2015). Given this finding, we expect a similar result for the oil market.

Table 1. Summary statistics.

	Mean	Maximum	Minimum	Std. Dev.	Skewness	Kurtosis	JB
Panel A: Endogenous Variables							
$R_{S\&P500}$	0.000189	0.109572	−0.094695	0.012981	−0.326800	13.35033	11643.00
R_{ASX}	−0.000051	0.132318	−0.146036	0.015992	−0.610240	11.99587	8969.523
R_{DAX}	0.000134	0.126464	−0.094678	0.016940	−0.018778	9.698910	4900.921
R_{CAC}	−0.000114	0.122383	−0.115334	0.017479	−0.038892	9.487840	4636.056
R_{FTSE}	−0.000118	0.111479	−0.116066	0.015053	−0.319346	11.68329	8237.734
R_{SSE}	−0.000009	0.090271	−0.090952	0.017425	−0.594909	7.097623	1907.856
R_{TOPIX}	0.000005	0.113460	−0.120052	0.014744	−0.252926	9.565286	4570.747
Panel B: Exogenous Explanatory Variables							
R_{OIL}	−0.000618	0.092987	−0.114260	0.022238	−0.148097	5.303507	583.8870
ΔOVX^+	0.672550	23.93000	0.000000	1.504471	5.343361	48.11413	240922.1
ΔOVX^-	−0.652480	0.000000	−24.60000	1.312251	−6.837367	86.15152	795923.2
ΔLI	−0.000038	6.651774	−6.848243	0.797541	0.127648	15.79356	18359.38
ΔEI	−0.000240	0.330000	−0.360000	0.037807	−0.269526	12.74652	10251.11
ΔTS	0.000325	0.210000	−0.280000	0.043306	−0.072728	6.097788	1034.276
ΔDS	−0.000089	0.350000	−0.150000	0.023948	2.082538	33.81730	104038.8

Notes: This table contains descriptive statistics of all endogenous variables (Panel A) and exogenous explanatory variables (Panel B). JB is the Jarque-Bera normality test. The sample period is from May 10, 2007 to August 31, 2017.

In summary, we consider three dimensions of oil markets (direction, volatility, and liquidity) and three commonly used control variables. Table 1 reports summary statistics of stock market returns and our set of explanatory variables. Among stock market indices, we document the lowest (highest) standard deviation for the S&P 500 (0.012981) and CAC (0.017479), respectively. All stock market indices display kurtosis higher than three, indicating a leptokurtic distribution of stock market returns. The skewness of stock market returns is slightly negative, which is typical for returns of stock market indices. Concerning the exogenous explanatory variables, we document substantial kurtosis for positive as well as negative OVX returns. Returns of the oil ETF show lower kurtosis than stock market returns, but its kurtosis is still leptokurtic. The outcomes of the Jarque-Bera test indicate that the daily distributions of all variables are not normal.[9] In addition, unreported results of an unit test

[9]While our analysis distinguishes between normal and non-normal returns, further investigation on knowledge discovery as proposed by Ultsch and Locarek-Junge (2010) could categorise returns into three different types: random, losses and wins.

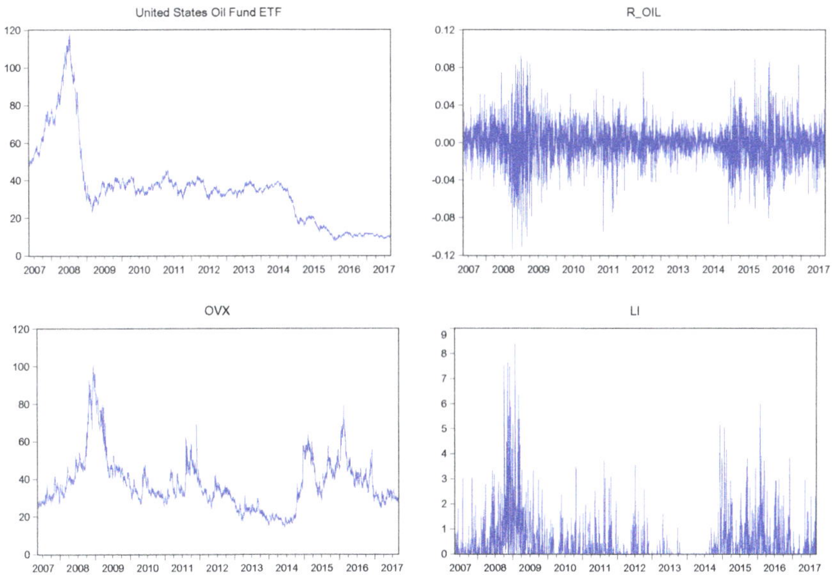

Fig. 1. This figure plots the used oil variables: Closing prices of the United States Oil Fund ETF in US dollars and corresponding returns (R_{OIL}), the level of OVX, and the level of liquidity (LI) which is calculated from the United States Oil Fund ETF. Sample period: 10 May 2007 to 31 August 2017.

reveal that all variables presented in Table 1 do not contain a unit root. A graphical representation of the used oil variables is given in Figure 1.

3. Results

We now report the main findings from our empirical analysis. Maximum likelihood estimation results for the VARX model defined in Eq. (1) are presented in Table 2. According to the BIC, the optimal lag length has been set to one. In the developed markets, the adjusted R-squared statistics range between 27.51% and 35.83% percent, but the only emerging market (SSE) has a much lower adjusted R-squared (5.94%).

Next, we discuss the lead–lag relationship of daily stock market returns and then report our findings for oil and control variables.

Table 2. VARX model estimates.

	$R_{S\&P500,t}$	$R_{ASX,t}$	$R_{DAX,t}$	$R_{CAC,t}$	$R_{FTSE,t}$	$R_{SSE,t}$	$R_{TOPIX,t}$
$R_{S\&P500,t-1}$	-0.1686^{***}	0.3769^{***}	0.2996^{***}	0.3630^{***}	0.3604^{***}	0.1579^{***}	0.4778^{***}
	[−7.11]	[13.39]	[9.68]	[11.66]	[13.92]	[4.35]	[18.59]
$R_{ASX,t-1}$	−0.0312	-0.1465^{***}	0.0377	0.0414	0.0334	−0.0270	−0.0127
	[−1.59]	[−6.28]	[1.47]	[1.60]	[1.56]	[−0.90]	[−0.60]
$R_{DAX,t-1}$	0.1387^{***}	0.0720	0.0915^{*}	0.0587	0.0638	0.0150	−0.0507
	[3.56]	[1.55]	[1.80]	[1.15]	[1.50]	[0.25]	[−1.20]
$R_{CAC,t-1}$	-0.1097^{***}	0.0094	-0.1816^{***}	-0.2044^{***}	-0.1838^{***}	0.0357	0.0985^{**}
	[−2.58]	[0.19]	[−3.27]	[−3.66]	[−3.96]	[0.55]	[2.14]
$R_{FTSE,t-1}$	0.0314	0.0969^{**}	-0.1130^{***}	-0.0943^{**}	-0.0890^{**}	0.0452	0.1441^{***}
	[0.94]	[2.44]	[−2.59]	[−2.15]	[−2.44]	[0.88]	[3.98]
$R_{SSE,t-1}$	0.0047	−0.0230	−0.0253	−0.0224	−0.0160	0.0753^{***}	−0.0178
	[0.37]	[−1.50]	[−1.50]	[−1.32]	[−1.14]	[3.81]	[−1.27]
$R_{TOPIX,t-1}$	−0.0083	−0.0243	0.0106	−0.0058	−0.0091	-0.0595^{**}	-0.1065^{***}
	[−0.47]	[−1.16]	[0.46]	[−0.25]	[−0.47]	[−2.21]	[−5.59]
c	0.0007^{**}	0.0003	0.0007^{*}	0.0003	0.0000	0.0005	0.0002
	[2.50]	[0.83]	[1.88]	[0.73]	[0.07]	[1.25]	[0.81]
$R_{OIL,t}$	0.1638^{***}	0.1740^{***}	0.2036^{****}	0.2086^{***}	0.2040^{***}	0.0594^{***}	0.0211^{*}
	[14.84]	[13.28]	[14.14]	[14.40]	[16.93]	[3.52]	[1.76]
ΔOVX_t^+	-0.0012^{***}	-0.0006^{***}	-0.0010^{***}	-0.0011^{***}	-0.0008^{***}	−0.0003	-0.0004^{**}
	[−7.58]	[−3.43]	[−4.92]	[−5.66]	[−4.90]	[−1.45]	[−2.25]
ΔOVX_t^-	-0.0007^{***}	-0.0004^{**}	-0.0004^{*}	-0.0008^{***}	-0.0008^{***}	0.0001	−0.0001
	[−4.18]	[−2.10]	[−1.88]	[−3.42]	[−4.28]	[0.48]	[−0.42]

ΔLI_{t-1}	-0.0005^{**}	-0.0010^{***}	-0.0018^{***}	-0.0020^{***}	-0.0017^{***}	0.0000	-0.0001
	[−2.06]	[−3.07]	[−5.15]	[−5.86]	[−5.84]	[0.08]	[−0.36]
ΔEI_t	0.0793^{***}	0.0799^{***}	0.0960^{***}	0.1032^{***}	0.0958^{***}	0.0317^{***}	0.0018
	[12.35]	[10.48]	[11.45]	[12.24]	[13.66]	[3.22]	[0.26]
ΔTS_t	0.0002	-0.0117^{*}	0.0283^{***}	0.0259^{***}	0.0006	-0.0021	-0.0191^{***}
	[0.03]	[−1.89]	[4.19]	[3.81]	[0.11]	[−0.26]	[−3.40]
ΔDS_t	-0.0273^{***}	-0.0533^{***}	-0.0220^{*}	-0.0302^{**}	-0.0324^{***}	-0.0315^{**}	-0.0094
	[−3.02]	[−4.97]	[−1.86]	[−2.54]	[−3.29]	[−2.28]	[−0.96]
R^2	0.2789	0.3331	0.2862	0.3205	0.3617	0.0643	0.3379
Adj. R^2	0.2751	0.3296	0.2824	0.3169	0.3583	0.0594	0.3344
SSR	0.3202	0.4517	0.5451	0.5521	0.3819	0.7514	0.3760
LogL	8336.6	7873.9	7621.0	7603.8	8099.7	7189.3	8120.4

Notes: This table reports estimated coefficients and t-statistics in parentheses of VARX(1) model for daily data. SSR and LogL denote the sum of squared residuals and log likelihood, respectively. The sample period is from 10 May, 2007 to 31 August, 2017. Significance at the 1%, 5%, and 10% level is denoted by ***, **, and *, respectively.

3.1. *Lead–lag relationship of stock markets*

Our results for the lead–lag relationship of daily stock market returns reveal important conclusions. First, the lagged US return is the only predictor that shows a pronounced forecasting power for returns of all other markets. These findings are consistent with the results of Wagner (2008) and Rapach *et al.* (2013). Interestingly, the strongest significance is documented for the TOPIX (t-value = 18.59) and the least pronounced significance reveals the SSE (t-value = 4.35). The low t-value of SSE compared with the other developed markets can be explained by the fact that lagged US returns have a lower impact on emerging markets. Second, lagged returns from ASX and SSE cannot predict returns from other markets. Third, all stock markets show significant first-order autocorrelation, but with different signs. Regardless of the direction, Bao *et al.* (2011) argue that this autocorrelation can be interpreted as an indicator of illiquidity. A possible explanation would be that stock markets react to new information in a delayed manner due to a lack of liquidity.

3.2. *Impact of oil price and controls on stock markets*

The direction of the oil price, R_{OIL}, is the only exogenous variable that has a significant positive impact on returns of all stock markets. However, we document a weaker relation for Asian stock markets. Positive shocks in oil market volatility yield to a decline in all stock markets. In contrast, negative shocks have no significant impact on the Asian markets. At first glance, it seems that positive changes in implied oil market volatility have a stronger impact on stock market returns than negative changes. We further investigate this issue by applying a test statistic that tests the null hypothesis that $\hat{\beta}_{\Delta\mathrm{OVX}^+}$ and $\hat{\beta}_{\Delta\mathrm{OVX}^-}$ are equal against the alternative "$\hat{\beta}_{\Delta\mathrm{OVX}^+} - \hat{\beta}_{\Delta\mathrm{OVX}^-} < 0$". The results are summarised in Table 3. Our findings reveal that the null can be rejected for S&P 500 and DAX at the 5% significance level and for CAC and SSE at the 10% significance level. Given that result and the fact that for the TOPIX only positive changes in OVX are significant, we conclude that there is a mild asymmetric effect of oil market volatility on stock returns, which is market-specific. Except for Asian markets,

Table 3. Asymmetric effect of OVX changes on stock market returns.

	$R_{\text{S\&P500},t}$	$R_{\text{ASX},t}$	$R_{\text{DAX},t}$	$R_{\text{CAC},t}$	$R_{\text{FTSE},t}$	$R_{\text{SSE},t}$	$R_{\text{TOPIX},t}$
$\hat{\theta}$	−0.00046**	−0.00021	−0.00057**	−0.00038*	−0.00003	−0.00046*	−0.00030
t-value	[−2.02]	[−0.76]	[−1.92]	[−1.29]	[−0.14]	[−1.33]	[−1.20]

Notes: This table presents results of a test for potential asymmetric effects of OVX changes on stock market returns. To do so, we use the estimated coefficients from Table 2 and test for equality of the difference $\hat{\theta} = \hat{\beta}_{\Delta \text{OVX}+} - \hat{\beta}_{\Delta \text{OVX}-}$ using the one-sided t-test given in Eq. (2). Significance at the 5% and 10% level is denoted by ** and *, respectively.

positive (negative) shocks in lagged oil market liquidity are followed by an increase (decrease) in stock market prices. Moreover, this effect is more pronounced in European markets compared with other non-Asian markets. The less pronounced relation between oil variables and Asian stock markets is not due to different closing times as the Australian market, which shows similar results as European and US markets, has almost identical closing times.[10]

We next discuss the results of other exogenous control variables, namely changes in expected inflation, the term spread and default spread.[11] Interestingly, changes in expected inflation are positively related to all markets, except for TOPIX. The consistent positive significance as well as the lower effect on Asian markets complies with our findings for the direction of oil prices. Changes in the default spread also yield to consistent but negative effects in all markets, however they are not significant for TOPIX. The last control variable, i.e., changes in the term spread, displays irregular results among the various markets.

3.3. *Implications for investors*

Many investors are seeking for a portfolio that performs well in different market conditions, the so-called 'all weather portfolio'. For

[10]Closing times of the stock markets are as follows: Australian Securities Exchange 5:00 GMT, Shanghai Stock Exchange 7:00 GMT, Tokyo Stock Exchange 6:00 GMT.

[11]Unreported results show that the main findings of Table 2 are unaffected if we omit the given control variables.

this purpose, it is of vital importance to diversify over various industries and asset classes as well as to understand the relation between equity markets and other asset classes such as oil, the most important industrial commodity.

A significant collapse in oil demand is often accompanied by a global economic downturn. In early 2020, there was an enormous collapse in oil prices alongside the stock markets due to the global shock from COVID-19. Our findings that underline a significant positive relation between stock market returns and oil direction confirm this observation. This point is very important for investors as they can use this information either as an indicator for stock market performance or developing hedging strategies. The latter is addressed by Batten *et al.* (2021) using a dynamic conditional correlation approach for studying the performance of stock-oil hedges. Their findings clearly show that positive jumps in the stock-oil hedge ratio are likely to occur in crisis periods. In addition, hedge portfolio returns are negatively affected by shocks in implied stock market volatility. Our results confirm this result in the same way for implied volatility of the oil market.

Despite recent developments in climate change policy, oil is still a major input factor in many economies. It is not only an important source of energy, it also plays a substantial role in the chemical industry. Even if the internal combustion engine should be abolished, oil and gas power plants will still be needed to generate enough electricity and hydrogen. Nevertheless, investors should bear in mind that there is a broad consensus to reduce carbon dioxide emissions. As a result, energy investors need to diversify this risk. Our findings provide a rich understanding between the stock-oil market relation and therefore help investors to develop appropriate strategies such as hedging or an oil market integration index (see Batten *et al.*, 2018).

4. Concluding Remark

This chapter discusses impacts of several oil price based variables on stock markets of major oil-importing countries. A novelty is the consideration not only of oil price direction and volatility but also of oil market liquidity. As oil price direction has a significant positive impact on returns of all stock markets, it can be regarded as a business climate indicator. The study further reveals that oil market volatility and liquidity are also important for the pricing of US stocks. In contrast, the results for the remainder stock markets are mixed. A fruitful topic for future research could be the analysis of our set of oil variables for oil-exporting countries.

Acknowledgements

The second author acknowledges fruitful research and teaching tasks at TU Dresden under the guidance of Professor Hermann Locarek-Junge during the years 2000 to 2002. The authors would like to thank two anonymous referees for their insightful comments and suggestions. All omissions and errors are their own.

References

Aboura, S. and Wagner, N. (2016). Extreme asymmetric volatility: Stress and aggregate asset prices, *Journal of International Financial Markets, Institutions and Money* **41**, 47–59.

Amihud, Y. (2002). Illiquidity and stock returns: cross-section and time-series effects, *Journal of Financial Markets* **5**, 31–56.

Amihud, Y. and Noh, J. (2021). The pricing of the illiquidity factor's conditional risk with time-varying premium, *Journal of Financial Markets* **56**, 100605.

Bao, J., Pan, J., and Wang, J. (2011). The illiquidity of corporate bonds, *Journal of Finance* **66**, 911–946.

Batten, J.A., Kinateder, H., Szilagyi, P., and Wagner, N. (2017). Can stock market investors hedge energy risk? Evidence from Asia, *Energy Economics* **66**, 559–570.

Batten, J.A., Kinateder, H., Szilagyi, P., and Wagner, N. (2018). Addressing COP21 using a stock and oil market integration index, *Energy Policy* **116**, 127–136.

Batten, J.A., Kinateder, H., Szilagyi, P., and Wagner, N. (2019a). Liquidity, surprise volume and return premia in the oil market, *Energy Economics* **77**, 93–104.

Batten, J.A., Kinateder, H., Szilagyi, P., and Wagner, N. (2019b). Time-varying energy and stock market integration in Asia, *Energy Economics* **80**, 777–792.

Batten, J.A., Kinateder, H., Szilagyi, P., and Wagner, N. (2021). Hedging stocks with oil, *Energy Economics* **93**, 104422.

Belhassine, O. and Bouzid, A.B. (2019). Further insights into the oil and equity market relationship, *Studies in Economics and Finance* **36**, 291–310.

Brigida, M. (2018). New results on the predictive value of crude oil for US stock returns, *Studies in Economics and Finance* **35**, 97–108.

Christoffersen, P. and Pan, X. (2018). Oil volatility risk and expected stock returns, *Journal of Banking & Finance* **95**, 5–26.

Cooper, S.K., Groth, J.C. and William, E.A. (1985). Liquidity, exchange listing, and common stock performance, *Journal of Economics and Business* **37**, 19–33.

Corwin, S.A. and Schultz, P. (2012). A simple way to estimate bid-ask spreads from daily high and low prices, *Journal of Finance* **67**, 719–760.

Czauderna, K., Riedel, C., and Wagner, N. (2015). Liquidity and conditional market returns: Evidence from German exchange traded funds, *Economic Modelling* **51**, 454–459.

Diaz, E., Molero, J., and Perez de Gracia, F. (2016). Oil price volatility and stock returns in the G7 economies, *Energy Economics* **54**, 417–430.

Degiannakis, S., Filis, G., and Arora, V. (2018). Oil prices and stock markets: A review of the theory and empirical evidence, *Energy Journal* **39**, 85–130.

Dupoyet, B.V. and Shank, C.A. (2018). Oil prices implied volatility or direction: Which matters more to financial markets?, *Financial Markets and Portfolio Management* **32**, 275–295.

Fousekis, P. and Tzaferi, D. (2020). Monotonicity, linearity and symmetry in the price volatility-volume relationship—Evidence from energy futures markets, *Studies in Economics and Finance* **37**, 110–133.

Gupta, K. (2016). Oil price shocks, competition, and oil & gas stock returns — Global evidence, *Energy Economics* **57**, 140–153.

Herrera, A.M., Lagalo, L.G., and Wada, T. (2015). Asymmetries in the response of economic activity to oil price increases and decreases?, *Journal of International Money and Finance* **50**, 108–133.

Klein, T. and Walther, T. (2016). Oil price volatility forecast with mixture memory GARCH, *Energy Economics* **58**, 46–58.

Kumar, S., Demirer, R., and Tiwari, A.K. (2020). Oil and risk premia in equity markets, *Studies in Economics and Finance* **37**, 697–723.

Locarek-Junge, H. and Walther, T. (2017). Markov-Regime-Switching-Modelle in der Finanzwirtschaft, *WiSt — Wirtschaftswissenschaftliches Studium* **46**, 4–9.

Luo, X. and Qin, S. (2017). Oil price uncertainty and Chinese stock returns: New evidence from the oil volatility index, *Finance Research Letters* **20**, 29–34.

Martin, P. (1975). Analysis of the impact of competitive rates on the liquidity of NYSE Stocks. Economic Staff Paper, 75–3, Securities and Exchange Commission.

Mollick, A. and Assefa, T. (2013). US stock returns and oil prices: The tale from daily data and the 2008–2009 financial crisis, *Energy Economics* **36**, 1–18.

Nguyen, D.K. and Walther, T. (2020). Modeling and forecasting commodity market volatility with long-term economic and financial variables, *Journal of Forecasting* **39**, 126–142.

Park, J. and Ratti, R.A. (2008). Oil price shocks and stock markets in the US and 13 European countries, *Energy Economics* **30**, 2587–2608.

Rapach, D.E., Strauss, J.K., and Zhou, G. (2013). International stock return predictability: What is the role of the United States?, *Journal of Finance* **68**, 1633–1662.

Roll, R. (1984). A simple implicit measure of the effective bid-ask spread in an efficient market, *Journal of Finance* **39**, 1127–1139.

Ultsch, A. and Locarek-Junge, H. (2010). Knowledge discovery in stock market data. In: Locarek-Junge, H., and Weihs, C. (eds.), *Classification as a Tool for Research. Studies in Classification, Data Analysis, and Knowledge Organization*, Heidelberg: Springer, Berlin, pp. 621–628.

Wagner, N. (2008). On the dynamics of market illiquidity. In: Lhabitant F.-S., and Gregoriou, G.N. (eds.), *Stock Market Liquidity: Implications for Market Microstructure and Asset Pricing*. Hoboken: Wiley; pp. 349–357.

https://doi.org/10.1142/9781800611917_0016

Chapter 16

Risk Reduction by Law: An Assessment of the German Renewable Energy Sources Act

Sven Loßagk

Berufsakademie Sachsen, University of Cooperative Education Dresden, Germany

sven.lossagk@ba-sachsen.de

Since the early beginning, the continuously amended German Renewable Energy Sources (RES) Act (Erneuerbare–Energien–Gesetz, EEG) is an important contribution to the reduction of carbon dioxide, by setting a framework for investments in RES projects, e.g., wind onshore. Besides many other aspects, the substantial change in the reference yield model from EEG 2014 to EEG 2017 should increase the incentives in realisation of projects by reducing the financial risk, resulting from future wind conditions. This study analyses the risk situations of lenders and shareholder in a project finance structure in different EEG-versions using Monte-Carlo simulation and different risk metrics on the basis of the annual debt service cover ratio (ADSCR), loan life cover ratio (LLCR) and net present value (NPV). The simulation results confirm the decrease in financial risk for both capital holders (EEG 2014 vs. EEG 2017), however, the degree of risk reduction is surprisingly high.

1. Introduction

The human-induced climate change is one of the biggest threats of our generation (IPCC, 2021). The main outcome of the Climate Change

Conferences of Paris in 2015,[1] the so-called Paris Agreement, is the commitment of the undersigned nations to "holding the increase in the global average temperature to well below 2°C above pre-industrial levels and pursuing efforts to limit the temperature increase to 1.5°C above pre-industrial levels, recognising that this would significantly reduce the risks and impacts of climate change" (UNFCCC, 2021). The emission of greenhouse gases, especially carbon dioxide (CO_2), causes the global warming and the major contribution comes from the production of energy, e.g., electricity production (Statistisches Bundesamt (Destatis), 2021; IEA, 2021). CO_2 emissions can be reduced by either increasing the efficiency of production and consumption or changing the production to CO_2 neutral technologies.[2] Although, nuclear power can be in general one of these low-carbon sources. However due to short-term danger (maximum credible accident) and very long-term impact of nuclear waste, Germany neglects it. Instead, the German government tries to support the development of technologies that produce energy from the so-called renewable sources (RES), e.g., biomass, photovoltaic energy and wind energy, since 1991 by legal regulations (RES acts[3]).

This chapter is part of a Festschrift in honour of Hermann Locarek-Junge. Next to all his achievements in the academic world as finance professor, he served as Chairman of the Supervisory Board of a German developers of biomass projects. In this function, he supported the transition to a more climate-friendly energy production in Germany.

The electricity producing infrastructure investments are typically characterised by a high proportion of capital expenditures (CAPEX) to operating expenditure (OPEX)[4] and a long but determined

---

[1]Even though the Climate Change Conferences take places every year, the last seminal agreement after the so-called Kyoto Protocol was signed by 196 nations during the conference in 2015 in Paris.

[2]Germany will end the production of electrical energy by hard coal and lignite in 2038 (KVBG, 2020).

[3]The Stromeinspeisungsgesetz in 1991 was followed by the first Erneuerbare-Energien-Gesetz (EEG) in 2000 with several amendments (2004, 2009, 2012, 2014, 2017). The current version of the EEG came into effect in 2021.

[4]The relatively low proportion of OPEX is based on the fact that the resources of the electrical energy production a generally free of charge.

project horizon (Hürlimann, 2018, p. 12). The level of risk of a RES project is fundamentally different in various project phases.[5] While the development phase, which ends by receiving the building permission, is characterised by a relatively high level of risk, the stage of operation bears a relatively low level of risk.[6] The future revenue in general depends on two aspects: (1) how many units will be sold (volume risk) and (2) what will be the price for a single unit (price risk). Over the last decade, the German RES acts tried to reduce the price risk for RES projects with different support schemes, e.g., guaranteeing a fixed price for a produced unit of electrical energy (feed-in-tariff). Within the different versions of the RES acts, the method of the support scheme varies, which leads to a different risk situation for the RES projects (cf. Section 2).

Among other aspects, most projects are partly debt financed especially due to high CAPEX (Böttcher and Blattner, 2013). The sector of German RES developers is characterised by a wide plurality of relatively small actors, which are often shareholders in the development stage, but sometimes also committed in the operating stage of the project. Therefore, while the fossil fuel power plants traditionally were financed by a corporate finance approach, RES projects nowadays use project finance structures (Steffen, 2020). The main advantage of this special financing type for the developers, in contrast to the corporate finance, is the potential of relatively high debt proportions and the absence of recourse instruments in case of financial distress of the project (Yescombe and Farquharson, 2018, p. 301).

This study investigates whether the above-mentioned regulations provide sufficient risk-return incentives for shareholders and debtholders to realise RES projects for reaching the aim of the Paris Agreement. To this end, we will analyse the risk situation of share- and debtholders within the operating phase of a RES project on the basis of various risk measurements focusing on different

---

[5]We are focusing only on the direct financial risk perspective. For an overview of different risk types in RES projects, which have also an indirect financial effect see, e.g., (Böttcher, Blattner, 2013, p. 74ff.) or (Yescombe and Farquharson, 2018, p. 146f).

[6]Only after determining the concept and understanding of risk is it possible to measure or quantify the level of risk. Section 3 will introduce the term risk for this study.

support schemes. Different RES technologies use distinct technical approaches for the production of electrical energy. Hence, different aspects are relevant for assessing the risk in the operating phase. Therefore, we are focusing on wind onshore which reflects the largest share of RES in Germany with about 88 terawatt hours in 2017 (Agentur für Erneuerbare Energien, 2021). Using a sophisticated financial cash flow model, we show that the wind onshore projects supported by the recent version of the EEG have reduced financial risk for the debtholders.

We contribute by quantitatively analysing the individual risk assumption of share- and debtholders in a project finance structure based on results of a Monte-Carlo simulation. The chapter is structured as follows: Section 2 will briefly provide information about the legal regulations in Germany, which are relevant to the topic. Section 3 discusses the features of the project finance approach and the methodology for the examination is shown. Section 4 presents and discusses the results. Finally, Section 5 concludes the chapter.

2. Legal Regulation for RES in Germany

In the following section, we are going to present the fundamental points of the EEG regarding the economic perspective of wind onshore projects in Germany. All other points, for the realisation of RES projects highly relevant technical issues, e.g., priority of energy feed-in by RES projects, will not be discussed.

From an economic point of view, the most important aspect is the price that can be achieved for the fed-in produced electricity. The reduction of the price risk over the whole operational period (in general 20 years[7]) is one crucial instrument since the beginning of RES laws. One can observe a development in the way of compensation over time. It started with a fixed price per kWh, not considering that due to geographical reasons the northern part of Germany is much more attractive for wind projects, because wind speed and wind stability (supply of wind or wind conditions) are more suitable for this technology. Furthermore, the regional characteristics

[7]The period of federal financial support differs slightly. For details in EEG 2014 and EEG 2017, cf. Sections 2.1 and 2.2.

(sparsely populated flat land) enable relatively low transportation and construction cost. As a result, the first wind farm projects were realised in Northern Germany, e.g., the first wind farm in Kaiser-Wilhelm-Koog (Schleswig-Holstein).[8]

To achieve the aim of the EEG, that 65% of the German gross electricity consumption has to be generated by RES by 2030, wind turbines must be erected also in other parts of Germany. However, the above-mentioned disadvantages of wind farms in the middle or southern parts reduce the expected return for the shareholders. The legislator reacted on these circumstances and implemented some mechanisms, e.g., in the EEG 2014, to create an economic incentive to develop and operate wind farms all over Germany. The mechanism is called 'reference yield model' (*Referenzertragsmodell*) and works in general as a price adjustment for the fed-in produced electrical energy, but differs in the method between EEG 2014 and EEG 2017.[9]

2.1. *Reference yield model of EEG 2014*

Although there are some very detailed regulations about the financial support scheme within the law (beginning from §22 EEG 2014), the following key facts will sketch the general situation.

The financial support in the form of a determined price for fed-in produced electrical energy is paid from the day of commissioning of the wind farm till the end of the first calendar year plus the following 20 calendar years. The price (*Anzulegender Wert*) depends on two aspects: (1) the year of commissioning (§29 EEG 2014), due to a quarterly reduction of at least 0.4% from beginning of 2016, depending on the net installed capacity in a relevant period (in megawatt); (2) the implemented reference yield model (§49 EEG 2014). After commissioning, the fed-in electrical energy is compensated with the so-called beginning price (*Anfangswert*), which is considerably higher than the

[8]In contrast to wind farms, a much higher number of photovoltaic energy projects were realised in Southern Germany (e.g., Bavaria), due to much longer and more intense sunlight.

[9]The mechanism of the price adjustment of EEG 2017 and EEG 2021 is nearly the same and differs only in one point (lower boundary of the site quality).

base price (*Grundwert*),[10] which was paid over the duration of the period-of-high-compensation (PHC) (*Dauer der Anfangsvergütung*) of at least 5 years after commissioning. The length of extension of this PHC depends on the amount of fed-in electrical energy within the first 5 years in relation to the reference yield of the wind farm.[11] This ratio is called site quality SQ (*Standortgüte*). In accordance with §49 (2) EEG 2014, the PHC per month can be calculated as

$$\text{PHC} = 60 + \frac{\max(1.3 - SQ; 0)}{0.0036} + \frac{\max(1 - SQ; 0)}{0.0048}. \tag{1}$$

The PHC of a wind farm with SQ of 90% (0.9) gets the high beginning price for 192 months (16 years) after the commissioning date. Afterwards, each produced and fed-in kWh is compensated at the base price until the end of the supporting period. This mechanism leads to the result that wind farms with a poorer SQ get the higher beginning price for longer. Since revenues are calculated by the product of fed-in energy (kWh) and price, the gap of overall revenues (over the whole operation period) between wind farms with different SQ should decrease in contrast to earlier yield models.

The crucial point of this regulation is that the SQ is determined only once after 5 years of operation. If the wind level, which results in produced electrical energy of the wind turbine, of the first five-year period differs from the rest of the operational period, the overall revenues can be higher or lower than what was intended by the regulatory. To illustrate this point, imagine a wind farm with a relatively low energy production in the first 5 years due to the level of wind. This leads to a low SQ and, hence, to a long PHC. If the remaining 15 years are then characterised by a high wind level of wind, the overall revenues are too high compared to the intention of the law and vice-versa.

---

[10] Considering all price reductions, e.g., the beginning price for wind farms with commissioning in January 2017 was 8.38 Ct./kWh, whereas the base price was 4.66 Ct./kWh.

[11] The wind turbine manufacturer publish for each type (depending on the nominal capacity of the generator, hub height and rotor diameter) the reference yield of a 5-year operating period. Detailed information about the reference yield and the relevant amount of fed-in electrical energy can be found in EEG 2014 Appendix 2 Subsection (7).

From the shareholders' point of view, the reference yield model increases the revenues of the wind project in contrast to an absence of this type of mechanism. The estimated revenues and therefore also the estimated returns of the projects depend on the expected wind levels on the site of the wind farm. Nevertheless, a certain volatility in the annual numbers can be expected.

2.2. *Reference yield model of EEG 2017*

The EEG 2017 brought some major changes regarding the economic aspects. Instead of presetting the price for the fed-in electrical energy by law (including the price reduction scheme described in Section 2.1) the wind onshore projects have, in general,[12] to compete against each other in a pay-as-bid auction. Each wind farm project has to bid on a certain price for a certain nominal power (installed capacity in kW). Due to a limitation of auctioned nominal power, only the wind farms with the lowest prices will get an acceptance of the bid. In contrast to other well-known pay-as-bid auctions (tender procedure of central banks), the reference yield model is included in the auction system.

Instead of bidding on the nominal price that will be paid for a kWh fed-in electrical energy (*Anzulegender Wert*), the bid price (*Gebotswert*) should be based on a hypothetically 100%-site-quality wind farm of this specific configuration. The nominal price will then be calculated by multiplying this 100%-bid-price with a so-called correction factor. The correction factor varies from 1.29 for real site-quality of 70% and below to 0.79 for real site-quality of 150% and above.[13] Therefore, a wind farm project with a SQ of 70%, that won a bid price of, e.g., 5 Ct./kWh will get 6.45 Ct./kWh for each kWh fed-in electrical energy. As in the former versions of the law this mechanism should ensure that also wind farms of the southern parts of Germany can be profitably realised.

[12]Section 22 of EEG 2017 mentions exceptions of projects that do not have to compete for the price within the auction, e.g., projects with less than 750 kW nominal power or specific wind turbines as pilot plants.

[13]The detailed values of SQ and corresponding correction factors can be found in §36h EEG 2017. The most recent version EEG 2021 expands the lower boundary to 60% with a correction factor of 1.35 so that the incentives for realisation of wind farms in 'non-windy'-areas are even bigger.

The initial SQ of a wind farm project (and therefore the relevant correction factor) has to be estimated by an accredited expert opinion in advance of the commissioning (EEG 2017 Appendix 2, no. 7.1). After 5, 10, and 15 years of operation of the wind farm, the SQ has to be re-examined, considering in general the produced electrical energy of the past 60 months.[14] If the actual SQ differs more than 2% points from the previous SQ, the sales of the previous 60 months will be compensated in the one or the other way (too high sales, based on a too high expected correction factor (too poor SQ) have to be refunded from the wind farm and vice versa). Moreover, the SQ for the future is adjusted to the most recent SQ.

In contrast to the reference yield model of EEG 2014, where the price for fed-in electrical energy changes only once over the operating period of 20 years, within the EEG 2017 supporting scheme, the price can change up to three times, depending on the wind potential over the lifetime of the project. Because the correction factors and, therefore, the price depend on the wind potential (which leads to produced electrical energy), the volatility of the wind potential over the project lifetimes determines the size of the changes. For example, if an accredited expert would estimate the SQ of a wind farm perfectly and the resulting wind energy yields (kWh) are completely stable over time, then the initial SQ and therefore the price is uniform over 20 years.

2.3. *Expected price and sales in EEG 2014 and EEG 2017*

Although the methods and forecasting models of the accredited wind expert are permanently improving, the prediction of the expected wind potential still involves uncertainty. The overall uncertainty reflects the combined uncertainty of different fields, e.g., historical wind yields, wind park model, and energy loss factors (FGW TR 6, 2021). The expert opinion reports an expected value of the annual

[14]The technical guideline no. 10 of FGW e.V. (TR 10 – Bestimmung der Standortgüte nach Inbetriebnahme) in accordance with §36h (4) EEG 2017 mentions the detailed procedure of the determination of the relevant amount of kW in respect of times, when the wind farm was not able to produce electrical energy due to technical unavailability (e.g., because of maintenance).

wind energy production (kWh/a). Furthermore, the uncertainty of this prediction is quantified as percentage deviation.[15] Even from a theoretical point of view, it is at least worthy of discussion[16] that the practitioners often use the standard distribution approach to determine other percentiles that reflect more their risk appetite. Since values below the expected value of the standard deviation have a cumulative probability of 50%, one can be interested in a value of this distribution that has a cumulative short fall of only 25% (in the wind industry this value is often called p75-value, because it is exceeded by 75% cumulative probability).

From the debt- and shareholders perspective, the expected price for the fed-in electrical energy is a crucial parameter for the *ex-ante* investment decision. Therefore, the prediction quality of the wind potential (deviation of predicted and realised production of electrical energy) has to be as good as possible. Different risk aspects exist between the two supporting schemes: In EEG 2014, the two prices (high beginning price and lower base price) are fixed, but the future point in time of switching from one to the other is uncertain. In EEG 2017, the time points of (possible) price switching are fixed but the prices are uncertain. To illustrate the situation, we will look at a wind farm project with a predicted SQ of 90%. With Eq. (1), the predicted PHC (e.g., 8.38 Ct./kWh) will be 192 months. Thereafter, the wind farm will get the base price (e.g., 4.66 Ct./kWh). Let us assume that the expert opinion underestimated the performance of the wind farm and that the certified SQ, based on the realisation of the fed-in produced electrical energy of the first 60 months is 100%. In this case, the realised PHC is only 143 months, which means an earlier drop to the lower, nearly halved, base price (see left panel of Figure 1).

The situation of the EEG 2017 is shown in the right panel of Figure 1. Based on a bid price of 5.00 Ct./kWh, the price for the

---

[15] Based on the author's experience, the overall uncertainty lies in a realistic range of 9% to 12%.

[16] The expected value is the arithmetic mean of realisation of an independent random experiment, which is repeated 'very frequently'. Since the annual basis of the wind energy production leads realistically to only 20–25 realisations of this random variable, only in a great portfolio of wind farm projects the expected value is represented by the mean of realised kWh.

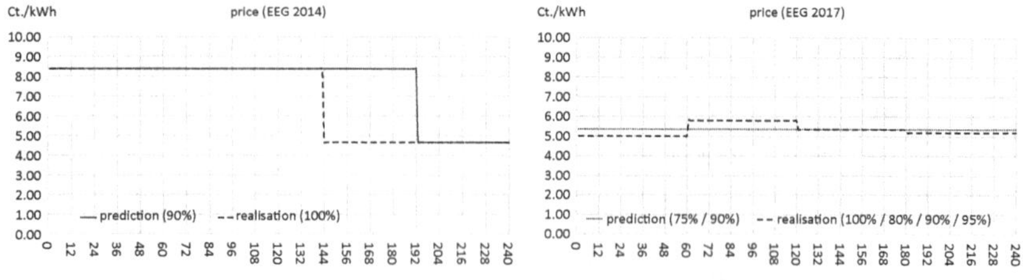

Fig. 1. Simulation of the price structure in EEG 2014 and EEG 2017.

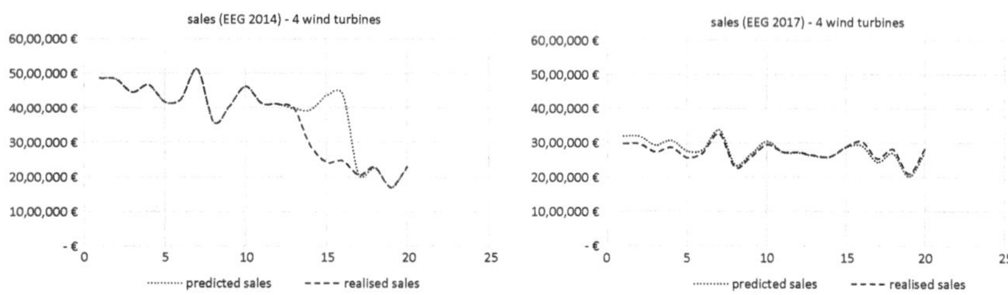

Fig. 2. Simulation of the sales in EEG 2014 and EEG 2017.

initial 60 months will be 5.35 Ct./kWh (correction factor of 1.07), assuming there is also a variation in the realised wind energy production during the operation period of 20 years. Although there are changes of 10% points, the price differences at the switching points are clearly smaller than in EEG 2014.

In Figure 2, the difference of the prediction and realisation of sales within EEG 2014 and EEG 2017 of a hypothetical wind farm project with four wind turbines (3,600 kW nominal power) are simulated. Here, the annual wind energy production is a random variable from a normal distribution with mean of 90% SQ and standard deviation of 10%. Considering the price adjustment mechanisms above, we find the type of deviation between simulated annual prediction and realisation in EEG 2014 and EEG 2017 to be different. Even though there are small deviations in some periods for EEG 2017, the big gap around year 15 in the EEG 2014 scheme could be a dramatic change in advantageousness of the investment for debt- and shareholders.

Although the perspective of sales is insufficient, the result of this preliminary consideration leads to the hypothesis that the newer supporting scheme of EEG 2017 (and EEG 2021) will reduce the risk for both capital providers in contrast to EEG 2014. For a detailed analysis, the following section will outline the characteristics of project finance structures and the relevant risk measurements of the different capital providers. Afterwards, the results of cash flow model-based Monte-Carlo-simulations will be discussed.

3. Project Finance and Methodology of the Study

3.1. *Fundamentals of project finance*

A project is characterised by its uniqueness, the determined end, which is significantly different to the nature of corporations (ongoing concern), and its specific aim (Böttcher, 2009, p. 20). When the investment volume of a project exceeds the amount which a single corporation (initiator) will raise by itself, often a special form of debt financing, called project finance, is used (Böttcher, Blattner, 2013, p. 3). In this vein, an independent legal entity (special purpose vehicle, SPV) is founded by the initiator (due to the provided equity stake, also called sponsor) and will be the holder of all project rights (e.g., building and operation permit, land lease agreements) (Steffen 2018, p. 281). In contrast to corporate finance structures, where debt is raised by a company which already exists and does have a history for the assessment of the creditworthiness by banks, project finance structures are based on a different approach (Yescombe and Farquharson, 2018, pp. 301–302). Due to considerations of risk reduction at the initiator level, the project finance is often structured as non-recourse (sometimes limited-recourse) financing (Finnerty, 2013, p. 1), where "the lender looks primarily to the revenues generated by a single project, both as the source of repayment and as security for the exposure." (Bank for International Settlements, 2017, p. 54). This means, also from the lender's perspective, that the investment decision is based on the level and the stability of the future cash flows of the project, which can be used for debt service (Steffen, 2020, p. 2).

Due to their uniqueness, all project finance structures differ with respect to number of facilities, terms, repayment schedules, collaterals, and covenants. Nevertheless, the high competition within the banking sector led to some industry 'gold standards' for wind farm projects in Germany during the last years. Since many debt financings are refinanced by promotional banks, e.g., KfW-group, the predominant portion of loans is repaid in equal instalments with a grace period up to 2 years. This grace period is typically used for funding a capital reserve account (e.g., debt service reserve account, DSRA), which increases the probability of payment of the debt service from the borrower to the lender, even if the operational cash flow of energy production is not sufficient in a certain time period.[17]

Considering the time frame of the RES support scheme in Germany, the typical period of long terms facilities is 15–18 years. The resulting time difference is called the cash flow tail and can be used for restructuring the loan (e.g., suspend repayments), if the borrower gets into temporary cash difficulties (Yescombe and Farquharson, 2018, p. 346).

3.2. *Key figures of project finance structures*

In general, the uncertainty in timing and amount of cash flow influences the profitability and probability of default for the capital holder of the project (Wang *et al.*, 2020, p. 484). The most relevant figure that determines the debt size (by given period) is called cash flow available for debt service (CFADS) and is calculated as the part of the operating cash flow of the project, which is not paid out as operating expenses, taxes, and the funding of reserve accounts in a certain period of time, e.g., 1 year (Wolf *et al.*, 2011, p. 85).[18] The CFADS can be used for interest payments and loan repayments. After the debtholders are served as agreed in the facility agreement, the remaining cash can be paid out to the shareholders as dividends. This distribution order of cash in the form of a cash-flow cascade (waterfall payment structures) is a typical regulation of a facility agreement (Yescombe and Farquharson, 2018, p. 405). Theoretically, the sum of the annual CFADS within the loan period results in the

---

[17]Based on the author's experience, other types of repayment, e.g., debt sculpting structures or cash sweeps, are uncommon, at least in the German project finance structure.

[18]Even if this definition of the CFADS seems to be relatively clear, there is a wide variety of detailed approaches of the detailed calculation scheme (Wiebusch, 2017, p. 25).

maximum amount of debt plus all interests. Due to uncertainty in the amount of the projected cash flows of the project, and consequently the CFADS, banks use a discount of the CFADS projections to fulfill their risk attitude.

One of the important ratios, based on the CFADS, is the annual debt service cover ratio (ADSCR_t). Generally, it is computed by dividing the annual CFADS_t by debt service DS_t (interests I_t and repayments R_t) of year t:

$$\mathrm{ADSCR}_t = \frac{\mathrm{CFADS}_t}{DS_t} = \frac{\mathrm{CFADS}_t}{I_t + R_t}. \tag{2}$$

As the repayments of the loan are made from after-tax-cash flow, the term R_t in the denominator can be adjusted by tax effects to $R_t/(1-\tau)$, where τ is the proportional tax rate of the SPV (Nevitt, Fabozzi, 2000, p. 53; Finnerty, 2013, p. 148f.). Since a common practice in project finance is to agree on establishing and funding a DSRA over the project lifetime for cases of temporary cash difficulties, another adjustment of (2) can be done by adding the periodic value of the DSRA to CFADS_t (Böttcher, 2009, p. 121).

The ratio should be at least one, otherwise the loan cannot be served properly. For structuring the project finance, banks can use predefined minimum ADSCR-values based on projection values of CFADS.[19] Based on the high competition in the banking industry, for wind onshore projects finance structures, a minimum ADSCR of 1.1 (for projects with good ratings) based on the p75-value is applied for wind onshore projects, resulting in a 10% buffer.[20]

Next to the short-term view of the ADSCR, the long-term perspective of CFADS can be applied for the assessment of the project finance structure in form of the so called 'present value cover ratios' (Wolf *et al.*, 2011, p. 108). From the lender's perspective, the loan life cover ratio LLCR_t depicts the potential of repayment suspensions

[19]In terms of risk mitigation from lender's perspective, the ADSCR based on historic numbers can also be used as a covenant in the facility agreement, e.g., minimum of 1.05 (Enders, 2018, p. 136).

[20]Since each bank defines its individual minimum ADSCR, the tax adjustment in the repayment can be easily omitted. Instead, a slightly higher demanded minimum ADSCR can fulfill the risk attitude without estimating the corporate tax rate τ.

until the end of the loan term T. The sum of the present values of the projected end of calculation period CFADS is divided by the outstanding debt at the beginning of the calculation period (3), where i is the (weighted) cost of debt D (Yescombe and Farquharson, 2018, p. 352; Wiebusch, 2017, p. 27):

$$\mathrm{LLCR}_t = \frac{\sum_{j=t+1}^{T} \mathrm{CFADS}_j \cdot (1+i)^{-(j-t)}}{D_t}. \tag{3}$$

The minimum of the periodic LLCR has to be above one, having in mind that the sum of present values of DS_t on each period results in outstanding debt (Kruschwitz, 2018, pp. 126–128). From the lender's point of view, a typical hurdle rate of the initial LLCR ($t = 0$) for 'standard' projects is around 1.2 (Yescombe and Farquharson 2018, p. 352). This results in enough 'restructuring potential' over the complete term of the loan without stretching into the 'tail period'.

The project life cover ratio PLCR is quite similar to the LLCR, but uses all CFADS over the complete project life time N (instead of the end of the loan term T). The PLCR_t can be computed for $t \leq T - 1$:

$$\mathrm{PLCR}_t = \frac{\sum_{j=t+1}^{N} \mathrm{CFADS}_j \cdot (1+i)^{-(j-t)}}{D_t}. \tag{4}$$

Since the sum of the discounted CFADS basically equals the project value on each calculation date (end of period t), the PLCR_t can be interpreted as the value-to-loan ratio and therefore informs the lender about the potential of expanding repayment period into the 'tail period' (Yescombe and Farquharson, 2018, p. 352; Wolf *et al.*, 2011, p. 109; Wiebusch, 2017, p. 28). To increase the probability of a successful project, the project finance structure has to establish mechanisms and incentives that debt- and shareholders act through parallel behaviour as a community-of-interest (Finnerty, 2013, p. 14; Wolf *et al.*, 2011, p. 87). Due to the residual character of dividends for the shareholder (waterfall principle), the data relating to the numbers of ADSCR_t, LLCR_t, and PLCR_t are informative for sponsors, but the internal rate of return of equity IRR, the net present value of equity NPV (Donkor and Duffey, 2013) and the variance of the

IRR are more common metrics for investors,[21] because they can be compared with other investments in different asset classes.[22]

3.3. *Methodology of the study*

As mentioned above, the aim of this study is to analyse the risk situations of share- and debtholder within the operating phase of a wind project in different EEG financial support regimes in Germany. Therefore, we will apply Monte-Carlo simulation, a method that is typically used to cope with uncertainty in project finance setting[23] (Wang *et al.*, 2020, p. 491). A sophisticated financial model in a spreadsheet environment, based on annual data, computes the projected $CFADS_t$ for the calculation of the risk assessment figures. The financial model consists of typical elements such as an investment plan for tax effects of depreciation, a profit and loss account with fixed and variable cost (payout) components,[24] which finally leads to cash flow projections. The initial price for the produced and fed-in electrical energy (first 5-years' operating period) is a basic assumption in the financial model (cf. Appendix A).

One mechanism, to fulfil the 'community-of-interest'-demand in project finance structures of wind onshore projects, involves long lasting contracts with all material contract partners (especially land lease agreements as well as maintenance, repair and insurance contracts). Next to some minor risks (e.g., counterparty risks, insignificant price risks for short-term contracts) the wind energy yield, based on the future wind conditions, is the main source of uncertainty in the operating phase of the project with respect to economic success. For this reason, the annual wind energy production yield (kWh) is the only

[21]Definitions and formulas of these figures exist in almost every standard finance textbook, e.g., Perridon *et al.*, 2017.

[22]In modern portfolio theory, the (estimated) correlation in returns of different assets is also necessary for the asset allocation, but this is not the focus of the present study.

[23]Recently, Breitenstein *et al.* (2022), used Monte-Carlo simulations to assess the value of stranded coal-fired power plants in Germany.

[24]Contrary to common understanding, variable payable costs in this context depend on the sales of the wind energy production and the fixed payable costs are independent on the sales.

stochastic variable for the Monte-Carlo Simulation. The annual wind energy production yield for each of the 20-year project lifetime is a realisation of a normal distributed random variable with mean of 95% SQ at the p50-value[25] and standard deviation of 10%. To avoid extreme values, the used realisations for the annual wind energy production yield is winsorised at the 1% and 99%-quantiles.

The capital structure of the project is assumed deterministic with two senior debt facilities and equity as the residual to the CAPEX. For structuring the project financing from the lender's perspective (banking case), we follow the principles outlined in Table 1.

For assessing the risk situation of the capital holders in the different RES federal financial support schemes (cf. Section 2) the outputs of six different scenarios are analysed.[26] For a better comparison of the investor's metrics, the specific assumptions regarding CAPEX and OPEX are in that way adjusted such that the expected equity *IRR* (based on p75-value wind energy production yield) is 5% p.a.

Table 1. Banking case principles for project finance debt structure.

Security level for cash flow projections (wind energy production yield)	p75-value
Facility I	
Duration (from starting operation phase)	16 years
Interest rate (until end of duration)	1.75% p.a.
Facility II	
Duration (from starting operation phase)	10 years
Interest rate (until end of duration)	1.45% p.a.
Type of repayment (both facilities)	Equal repayments
Grace period (both facilities)	6 months
Level for Debt Service Reserve Account (DSRA)	50% of debt service of the following year
Minimum ADSCR (without DSRA)	1.1

[25]For example, based on the EEG 2017 the 5-year reference yield for a wind turbine of type Nordex N149/4.0–4.5 with a hub height of 164 m is 86,571,658 kWh, so that the one-year 95% at the p50-value results in 16,448,615 kWh.

[26]Three different financial support schemes (EEG 2014, EEG 2017, EEG 2021) in each case with either a low or high degree of operating leverage (OL), which is the ratio of fixed to variable payable operating costs (responsiveness in respect to deviations of sales over the project lifetime).

in each scenario. This results theoretically in an equity NPV of 0. The specific numbers can be found in Appendix A.

3.4. *Hypotheses and study design*

Given all the above presented details about the different RES federal financial support schemes in Germany, especially the difference in the reference yield models and the characteristics of project finance structures, the following hypotheses should be true:

H1: The risk that **debt**holders bear decreases with changes of the EEG over time (EEG 2014>EEG 2017>EEG 2021).
H2: The risk that **share**holders bear decreases with changes of the EEG over time (EEG 2014>EEG 2017>EEG 2021).
H3: Debtholders bear lower risk in projects with low operating leverage (OL) than in projects with high OL.

For empirical testing of hypothesis H1, we use the adjusted ADSCR $adj.ADSCR_t$ (including the periodic value of the DSRA) as risk metric, since the DSRA can also be used for debt service in case of poor CFADS[27]:

$$\text{adj.ADSCR}_t = \frac{\text{CFADS}_t + \text{DSRA}_t}{\text{DS}_t} = \frac{\text{CFADS}_t + \text{DSRA}_t}{I_t + R_t}. \quad (5)$$

In addition, we use LLCR_t as presented in (3) as a second risk metric from the lender's perspective.

For each of the 1,000,000 simulation in each of the six scenarios, the minimum of the adj.ADSCR_t and the LLCR_t over the debt duration (16 years) is determined and the proportions of adj.ADSCR_t and LLCR_t less than one are calculated. As presented before, an adj.ADSCR_t below one results in an event of default (short-term perspective), because debt service cannot be fully paid in a certain period, whereas an LLCR_t below one even means no restructuring potential over the time period of the loan duration. Finally, a two-sample-Z-test is applied to compare the proportions of the scenarios.

[27]In case of usage of the DSRA in one period, the cash flow model considers the funding of the DSRA in future periods of the project until the level is reached.

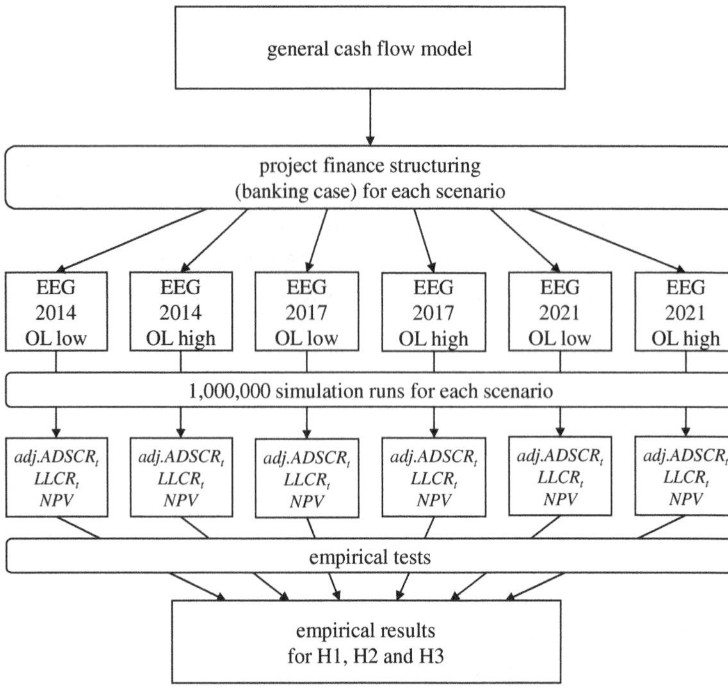

Fig. 3. General study design.

To evaluate the risk situation of the shareholder (H2), we compare the proportions of NPVs (at 5%-level) below zero in each scenario and apply also two-sample-Z-tests. Furthermore, we will use the Levene-test to check for significant differences of variance of NPV in the scenarios.

The third hypotheses (H3) validates the functioning of our complex financial model. We compare all the above-mentioned metrics in the respective low and high OL-scenarios with the two-sample-Z-test. We summarise our study design in Figure 3.

4. Empirical Results and Discussion

In Table 2 the empirical results relating to H1 are presented for the three scenarios with low OL (Panel A) and high OL (Panel B). The difference in certain risk metrics between EEG 2014 and EEG 2017

Table 2. Proposition of minimum adj.ADSCR$_t$ and minimum LLCR$_t$ less than one.

	EEG 2014		EEG 2017		EEG 2021
Panel A:			Low OL (ca. 30% fixed payable costs)		
Proportion minimum $adj.ADSCR_t < 1$	0.5315		0.2167		0.2169
Delta		0.3148***		−0.0002	
			0.3146***		
Proportion minimum $LLCR_t < 1$	0.5316		0.0954		0.0954
Delta		0.4363***		0.0000	
			0.4363***		
Panel B:			High OL (ca. 40% fixed payable costs)		
Proportion minimum $adj.ADSCR_t < 1$	0.6099		0.2375		0.2381
Delta		0.3723***		−0.0006	
			0.3718***		
Proportion minimum $LLCR_t < 1$	0.6091		0.1055		0.1057
Delta		0.5036***		−0.0002	
			0.5034***		

as well as EEG 2014 and EEG 2021 are highly statistically significant[28]. There is no different risk situation for lenders between EEG 2017 and EEG 2021, since the only difference is the adjusted border of the supported SQ from 70% to 60%. Based on the fact that the expected value of SQ for the wind project is 95%, only few realisations of the wind energy production are below this threshold.

The empirical results support hypothesis H1 only partially. There is strong evidence that the change in the RES financial support scheme (especially in the reference yield model) from EEG 2014 to EEG 2017 and EEG 2021 reduces the risk which debtholders have to bear. The figures of the ADSCR-metric are more than halved and the LLCR-metrics are reduced by approximately 80%. The change in the reference yield model of EEG 2017 to EGG 2021 does not affect the risk situation of the lenders in the considered case (base

[28]Here and in the following tables, the statistical significance level of 1% is denoted by ***.

Table 3. Proposition of NPV less than one and standard deviation of NPV.

	EEG 2014		EEG 2017		EEG 2021
Panel A:			low OL (ca. 30% fixed payable costs)		
Proportion NPV < 0	0.1605		0.0183		0.0185
Delta		0.1422***		−0.0002	
			0.1420***		
Standard deviation NPV (in €)	853,622		$282,490$		282,285
Delta (€)		571.132***		204	
			571.337***		
Panel B:			high OL (ca. 40% fixed payable costs)		
Proportion $NPV < 0$	0.1628		0.0133		0.0132
Delta		0.1495***		0.0001	
			0.1495***		
Standard deviation NPV (in €)	918,566		$297,905$		297,901
Delta (€)		620.660***		4	
			620.664***		

case of 95% SQ at p50-level), but can have an effect on wind onshore projects with 'poorer' expected SQ around 65%–70%.

The interpretation of empirical results for the risk metrics of shareholders based on the NPV is similar to the one of debtholders, but the risk reduction effect is even stronger. The absolute number of the proportion of negative NPV in the EEG 2017 (and similar in EEG 2021) in the low OL-scenario (see Table 3) is only 1.83% and therefore 85% smaller than in the EEG 2014. In the high OL-scenario, the decrease of the negative NPV proportion is higher because of the higher 'upside potential' for shareholders in years of good wind conditions (cf. footnote 26). The systematic change in the reference yield model (EEG 2014 to EEG 2017) also reduces the risk situation for shareholders. Hence, H2 cannot be rejected in this respect.

The empirical results regarding H3, presented in Table 4, lead to the clear statement that the risk situation for debtholders are always better in low OL-scenarios than in high OL-scenarios (all

Table 4. Differences in risk metrics for debt holders in both operating leverage scenarios (low minus high OL).

	EEG 2014	EEG 2017	EEG 2021
Delta of proportion $adj.ADSCR_t < 1$	-0.0783^{***}	-0.0208^{***}	-0.0212^{***}
Delta of proportion $LLCR_t < 1$	-0.0775^{***}	-0.0101^{***}	-0.0104^{***}

figures are smaller than one and the differences are highly statistically significant). As mentioned before, this result was expectable, but confirms the correct functioning of the financial model (spreadsheet).

Three limitations in the present study provide possibilities for future research. First of all, the simulations are done with only one set of assumptions on the project. Especially, a variation in the used initial SQ (e.g., around the lower boundary of the reference yield model of EEG 2017 and EEG 2021) can improve the general explanatory power of this study design. Also, other risk mitigating mechanisms besides a DSRA are not included in the financial model (e.g., cash sweeps), which would lead to a further reduction of the risk situation for lenders. Secondly, due to the central aim of the study of assessing the financial risk effects in different German RES-acts, we are focusing only on a few financial risk metrics, which are widely used in the project finance practice. Applying other risk metrics that are used in modern capital market research, e.g., value-at-risk approaches, could be further steps. The last point relates to the modelling of the future wind conditions. In line with the outcome of the accredited experts' opinion, we are modelling the annual wind energy production (kWh/a) as a normally distributed independent variable over the project life of 20 years. Even though the empirical results could change, if another distribution is used, we expect that the general message would probably remain.

5. Conclusion

Our analysis provides a strong indication that the change in the RES federal financial support scheme, especially in the applied reference yield model (EEG 2014 to EEG 2017), reduces the direct financial risk situation of lenders as well as sponsors. The stretching of the lower boundary of the correction factor to 60% SQ (EEG 2017 to EEG 2021) does not have a statistically significant effect for the present case.

Based on the used metrics, the risk situation of the debtholders lowers more than 50% at the new reference yield model of EEG 2017[29]. With an 85% reduction, the change in the risk situation of shareholders is even more pronounced. Although there is still a little number of projects which do not earn their expected rate of return within the simulation, looking on the risk-and-return trade-off, German wind onshore projects appear to be an interesting asset class for equity investors.

With EEG 2017 the German legislator wanted to increase the incentives for investing in wind onshore projects, which can be interpreted as accomplished by this study. It remains questionable whether this level of financial risk mitigation[30] was even intended.

[29]We analyse also the proportion of minimum PLCR_t less than one and find that the risk disappears completely in EEG 2017 (against ca. 39%–45% in EEG 2014). We do not report the details because of the little different understanding of PLCR_t as risk measurement (restructuring potential into the tail period of the project finance).

[30]As mentioned before, we abstract here from minor types of other risks in the operating phase, e.g., counterparty risks, insignificant price risks in short-term contracts.

Appendix A. General Assumption of the Six Scenarios

	EEG 2014		EEG 2017		EEG 2021	
	Low OL	High OL	Low OL	High OL	Low OL	High OL
Price per kWh energy:						
High beginning price	8.38 Ct./kWh	8.38 Ct./kWh				
Bid price (100%-reference quality)			5.00 Ct./kWh	5.00 Ct./kWh	5.00 Ct./kWh	5.00 Ct./kWh
OPEX (2% p.a. inflation indexation):						
Fixed (independed of energy production sales)	30%	41%	30%	41%	30%	41%
Variable (depended on energy production sales)	70%	59%	70%	59%	70%	59%
CAPEX	37,597,000€	37,559,000€	27,927,000€	27,705,000€	27,927,000€	27,705,000€
Equity	6,897,000€	6,859,000 €	5,627,000€	5,405,000€	5,627,000€	5,405,000€
Debt:						
Facility I (16 years, 1.75% p.a.)	23,900,000€	23,900,000€	22,300,000€	22,300,000€	22,300,000€	22,300,000€
Facility II (10 years, 1.45% p.a.)	6,800,000€	6,800,000€	-€	-€	-€	-€

References

Agentur für Erneuerbare Energien (2021). Available at: https://www.foederal-erneuerbar.de/uebersicht/bundeslaender.

Bank for International Settlements (2017). *Basel III: Finalising Post-Crisis Reforms.* Available at: https://www.bis.org/bcbs/publ/d424.pdf.

Böttcher, J. (2009). *Finanzierung von Erneuerbare-Energien-Vorhaben,* Oldenbourg, München.

Böttcher, J. and Blattner, P. (2013). *Projektfinanzierung: Risikomanagement und Finanzierung,* 3rd edn. München: Oldenbourg.

Breitenstein, M., Anke, C.-P., Nguyen, D.K., and Walther, T. (2022). Stranded asset risk and political uncertainty: The impact of the coal phase-out on the german coal industry, *Energy Journal* **43**(5). https://doi.org/10.5547/01956574.43.5.mbre.

Donkor, E.A. and Duffey, M. (2013). Optimal capital structure and financial risk of project finance investments: A simulation optimization model with chance constraints, *The Engineering Economist* **58**(1), pp. 19–34.

Enders, C. (2018). *Strukturierte Finanzierungen: Von ABS und Leverage Buyouts bis zur Projektfinanzierung.* Stuttgart: Kohlhammer.

FGW e.V. Fördergesellschaft Windenergie und andere Dezentrale Energien (2021). *Teil 6 (TR 6) Bestimmung von Windpotenzial und Energieerträgen — Revision 11.* Berlin.

Finnerty (2013). *Project Financing : Asset-Based Financial Engineering,* 3rd edn. Hoboken: Wiley.

Hürlimann, C. (2019). *Valuation of Renewable Energy Investments : Practices among German and Swiss Investment Professionals.* Wiesbaden: Springer Gabler.

IEA, International Energy Agency (2021). Available at: https://www.iea.org/data-and-statistics/?country=WORLD&fuel=CO2%20emissions&indicator=CO2BySector.

IPCC, Intergovernmental Panel on Climate Change (2021). *AR6 Climate Change 2021: The Physical Science Basis,* Available at: https://www.ipcc.ch/report/ar6/wg1/downloads/report/IPCC_AR6_WGI_SPM_final.pdf.

Kruschwitz, L. (2018). *Finanzmathematik : Lehrbuch der Zins-, Renten-, Tilgungs-, Kurs- und Renditerechnung,* 6th rev. edn. Berlin/Boston: De Gruyter Oldenbourg.

KVBG Kohleverstromungsbeendigungsgesetz (2020). BGBl. Teil I, Nr. 37, S. 1818.

Nevitt, P. and Fabozzi, F. (2000). *Project Financing,* 7th edn. London: Euromoney.

Perridon, L., Steiner, M., and Rathgeber, A. (2017). *Finanzwirtschaft der Unternehmung*, 17th rev. edn. München: Vahlen.

Statistisches Bundesamt (Destatis) (2021). *Nachhaltige Entwicklung in Deutschland — Indikatorenbericht 2021.*

Steffen, B. (2018). The importance of project finance for renewable energy projects, *Energy Economics* **69**, 280–294. https://doi.org/10.1016/j.eneco.2017.11.006.

Steffen, B. (2020). Estimating the cost of capital for renewable energy projects, *Energy Economics* **88**, 104783. https://doi.org/10.1016/j.eneco.2020.104783.

UNFCCC United Nations Framework Convention on Climate Change (2021). Available at: https://unfccc.int/sites/default/files/english_paris_agreement.pdf.

Wang, X., Shi, L., Wang, B., and Kan, M. (2020). A method to evaluate credit risk for banks under PPP project finance, *Engineering, Construction and Architectural Management* **27**(2), 483–501. https://doi.org/10.1108/ECAM-06-2018-0247.

Wiebusch, A. (2017). *Grundlagen einer Projektfinanzierung: Charakteristika und Risikomanagement*, In Böttcher, J. and Wiebusch, A. (eds.), *Krise und Sanierung von Projektfinanzierungen*. Berlin/Boston: De Gruyter Oldenbourg, pp. 1–30.

Wolf, B., Hill, M., and Pfaue, M. (2011). *Strukturierte Finanzierungen: Grundlagen des Corporate Finance, Technik der Projekt- und Buy-out-Finanzierung, Asset-Backed-Strukturen*, 2nd edn. Stuttgart: Schäffer-Poeschel.

Yescombe, E.R. and Farquharson, E. (2018). *Public-Private Partnerships for Infrastructure: Principles of Policy and Finance*, 2nd edn. Cambridge: Butterworth-Heinemann.

https://doi.org/10.1142/9781800611917_0017

Chapter 17

Corporate Risk Management with Power Purchase Agreements

Andreas Horsch* **and Steffen Hundt**†

Technische Universität Bergakademie Freiberg,
Faculty of Business Administration, Germany
**andreas.horsch@bwl.tu-freiberg.de*
†steffen.hundt@bwl.tu-freiberg.de

Power purchase agreements (PPAs) are a new way of purchasing (esp. green) electricity by directly linking institutional electricity consumers to the owners of renewable energy assets. Since these contracts fix electricity prices for a long-term tenor, they enable both contractual parties, buyers and sellers, to hedge against market price risk. However, PPAs may also induce new risk exposures which strongly depend on the specific price mechanism negotiated in a PPA. This chapter shows the gain and risk structure of major PPA types and evaluates the performance of the largest PPA closed in continental Europe during the COVID-19 crisis. Our results indicate that buyers should carefully match their risk appetite and price expectation with the available PPA price mechanism to negotiate the optimal solution.

1. Introduction

Our world is characterised by uncertainty, which constantly challenges entrepreneurs and the institutions run by them. As fundamental uncertainty implies a rather extensive nescience of the options a person has, of the consequences a particular action taken will generate, and which probability these outcomes have, this uncertainty is tough to handle. Economic science and economic practice alike have decided to focus on an idealised subtype of uncertainty known as risk, which is based on the assumption of 'knowing what one does not know' so that expected values, volatility measures, and further quantifications become feasible.[1] The respective 'risk management'— that at least partly is an attempt of 'uncertainty management' — task usually is depicted as a (circular) process of

- identification/analysis,
- modelling/measurement/quantification,
- management/control (i.e., application of risk management instruments), and
- monitoring,

against the backdrop of an underlying risk management strategy.[2]

By its very nature, any of these fields of addressing risk means assessing the future, so that risk management cannot escape being an educated yet fallible guess. Consequently, theory and practice of risk management are driven forward by human action destined to enhance the quality of this very educated guess while reducing uncertainty.[3] Over the years, risk measurement and risk control have emerged as the main pillars of this risk management process, as well as particular risk categories, such as market price risk or credit risk, have become the focus of attention of both researchers in the academic world and risk managers in the company world.

While belonging to the former, Hermann Locarek-Junge, whom this Festschrift celebrates, also knew about the latter's view: He became a distinguished player of the academic disciplines of research

---

[1]On the fundamental distinction between risk and certainty, see the seminal dissertation of Knight (1921).

[2]As standard textbook on risk management, see, e.g., Crouhy/Galai/Mark (2014, pp. 1–22). See also Locarek-Junge/Hengmith (2003, p. 209) and Locarek-Junge/Straßberger (2003, p. 650).

[3]On the seminal concept of human action, see the eponymous opus magnum of Ludwig von Mises (1949). Later, this market process approach — among others — inspired Dieter Schneider (1995, 1997, 2011) to lay out *Business Economics* (*Betriebswirtschaftslehre*) as the science of reducing income-related uncertainties by creating and sustaining institutional designs.

and lecturing and also a highly valued consultant of various, primarily financial firms. Before that, his academic career had started with a dissertation on knowledge-based systems of analysis (Locarek, 1988). Based hereupon, he entered the realm of (financial) risk management, where he congruously focused on risk measurement/modeling approaches during the 1990s. Among others, this decade included the (in fact re-)discovery of the concept of value at risk (VaR). After being practised by several financial institutions, selected publications combined with the regulatory adoption of VaR by banking regulators, particularly the architects of the new Basel II framework on banking regulation, made the VaR concept spread through risk management literature and concepts. Hermann Locarek-Junge contributed to this discussion by various papers which delivered both timely and critical assessments of the VaR (Locarek-Junge and Prinzler, 1998, 1999; Locarek-Junge *et al.*, 2002; later, also Locarek-Junge and Büch, 2006, particularly, pp. 121–125). Whereas his research focused on risk measurement, he also dealt with risk management instruments and techniques such as hedging or limit systems (Locarek-Junge *et al.*, 2000; Locarek-Junge, 2001; Locarek-Junge and Klein, 2016). After discussing risk measurement consequences for governmental regulation based on regimes such as Basel II and its subsequent reissues, a growing part of research at the chair of Hermann Locarek-Junge has been dedicated to (price) volatilities of other traded goods, especially of commodities (e.g., Klein and Walther, 2016; Nguyen and Walther, 2020) recently.

Already, the brief outline above illustrates that our contribution to this Festschrift can pick up only parts of the topics and achievements of the person it honours. We hope to do so appropriately by discussing a risk management — rather than risk measurement — approach, which rediscovers another traditional instrument, and does so to help market participants control the market price risk of a particular energy commodity, i.e., electricity (on (the forecasting of) volatile electricity prices, see the overview of Weron and Ziel, 2019; also Ziel and Steinert, 2018). The market price (risk) of this particular underlying has become more urgent by the year recently, as price ranges and volatilities increased, leading — amongst others — to extremely low and even negative prices (e.g., de Lagarde and Lantz, 2018; Ziel and Steinert, 2018; Aust and Horsch, 2020). Whereas these phenomena were linked to market processes of supply and demand — and respective distortions by political interference, such as the promotion of renewable energy — the COVID-19 crisis has added additional momentum since early 2020, as it strongly affected the profitability and creditworthiness of counterparties of suppliers as well as the demand for electricity — and, consequently, the price level. Both developments significantly amended the risk exposure of electricity-related undertakings.

Moreover, corporates' growing electricity price exposure led to the evolution of respective tools of risk measurement and management in general and the (re-)discovery of long-term off-take contracts in particular. To discuss the design and effects of the latter, we structure our contribution as follows: Section 2 briefly elaborates the idea of the risk management instrument of long-term fixed-price off-take contracts (LTOC) and then segues into the particular LTOC-type of power purchase agreements (PPAs). In the subsequent section, we demonstrate the hedging effects of PPAs in general. Finally, Section 4 illustrates the application of PPAs using the example of the largest PPA closed in (continental) Europe so far.

2. From Long-Term Off-Take Contracts to Power Purchase Agreements

Power purchase agreements (PPAs) are a variation of long-term, fixed-price off-take contracts. Whereas the long-term element can help mitigate information asymmetry and respective transaction cost, the fixed-price element serves the purpose of mitigating price risk by allowing 'risk-averse decision-makers to hedge against price uncertainty for components by specifying a fixed price for the duration of the contract' (Cohen and Agrawal, 1999, pp. 783–784). This risk attitude can be found both on the supplier's and the off-taker's side, who seek to either make their revenue or their cost more calculable. However, a long-term contract helps mitigate (price) risk and enhances (credit) risk, as both parties have to rely heavier on the trust-/creditworthiness, i.e., the ability and willingness to either deliver or off-take and pay, of their respective counterparty. Consequently, no long-term fixed-price off-take contract represents a risk management cure-all, but it could shift a party's risk exposure in a way it is better prepared to handle.

As long-term fixed-price off-take contracts have a long tradition, especially in energy markets with floating prices (e.g., Sund and Hausken, 2012; much earlier Hamrin, 1989), it appears rather congruous that this contractual design became used by electricity market participants, too, once electricity prices turned from regulated stability to free-market volatility. Thus, since the first long-term electricity hedges appeared in the USA after 2010, buyers and sellers of electricity mitigate the price risk of either output/sales volumes or acquired volumes by power purchase agreements. The latter can be defined as bilateral contracts between a producer/seller of electricity on the one hand and a corporate off-taker/buyer (e.g., industrial or utility company) of electricity on the other hand on the delivery of a particular amount of electricity at particular dates at a fixed price over a particular, long-term period. Table 1 illustrates the common denominator of various PPA definitions used in economics and practice (see also Shrimali *et al.*, 2019; Bonetti *et al.*, 2010; EU recast Art 2 No. 17).

Based hereupon, PPAs are classified across several criteria, such as the

1. institutional character of the off-taker,
2. way of settlement,
3. specification of the source of electricity,
4. volume mechanism, and
5. price mechanism.

2.1. *Institutional character of the off-taker*

According to the off-taker type, PPAs of the corporate type (Corporate-PPAs) are characterised by being closed between the producer/seller (e.g., owner of a wind farm) on the one hand, and one or multiple corporates on the other hand, which not only buy but also feed the acquired electricity in their respective processes of production (of, e.g., alloy). In contrast, Utility-PPAs (= Merchant PPAs) include a utility company as the off-taker, who does not intend to consume the electricity but to resell it instead (e.g., Miller and Carriveau, 2020). As the off-taker represents the credit risk as seen by the seller, different kinds of off-takers induce different levels of creditworthiness, which will be reflected in the contractual features, particularly the (risk premium included in) price of the PPA (also Hundt *et al.*, 2021).

Table 1. PPA definitions.

Authors	Definition of power purchase agreements
BakerMcKenzie	A PPA is a contract between a buyer and generator to purchase (whether physically or notionally) electricity at a pre-agreed price for a pre-agreed period of time.
Coussi/Harada	'...agreements under which a corporate customer agrees to purchase renewable electricity directly from the electricity producer...'
Energy Brainpool	A Power Purchase Agreement (PPA) is a long-term electricity supply agreement concluded directly (bilateral) between a buyer (electricity consumer) and a seller (plant operator). This agreement regulates the supply of electricity at a defined price or an equivalent financial compensation.
TaylorWessing	A PPA can be understood in principle as a long term electricity supply contract, which is concluded between the power producer and a company. Those companies are usually end consumers, but traders or energy supply companies could also be considered as contract partners of a PPA.
Dai	'...long-term power purchase agreements (PPAs) which require the purchasers to buy all of the wind energy generated at a fixed price.'
wbcsd**	A PPA is a contract between the buyer (off-taker) and the power producer (developer, Independent Power Producer, investor) to purchase electricity at a pre agreed price for a pre-agreed period of time.

Notes: Council on the promotion of the use of energy from renewable sources (recast).
**World Business Council for Sustainable Development.

2.2. *Way of settlement*

Regarding the way of settlement, a PPA can be either structured as a classic supply contract including the physical delivery (and off-taking) of electricity (Physical PPAs) or be designed as a pure financial hedge without physical delivery (Virtual PPAs). In the case of a Physical PPA, the PPA contract also includes a balancing party responsible for electricity balancing, usually a utility or energy trading company that does not off-take but intermediates, i.e., takes care of the physical transport of the delivered electricity output.

The long-term (fixed-price) tenor of Physical PPAs represents the main difference to a standard power supply contract (Tang and Zhang, 2019). In contrast, a Virtual PPA is a mere financial hedge designed to fix electricity prices based on an underlying synthetic (i.e., virtual) electricity amount. Structured as a contract for difference (CfD), the off-taker will compensate the producer for the difference between a pre-agreed strike price and a lower market price (settlement price). If market prices are higher than the strike price, in contrast, the producer has to pay the difference to the off-taker.

In contrast to Physical PPAs, Virtual PPAs thus induce the transfer of cash instead of electricity. Moreover, since they are much easier to negotiate and less transaction cost-intensive in general, Virtual PPAs have become more frequent than Physical PPAs, especially in the thriving US market (e.g., Miller and Carriveau, 2020; also Tang and Zhang, 2019). Figure 1 displays the relationship between a producer and the off-taker under a Virtual PPA with a CfD structure.

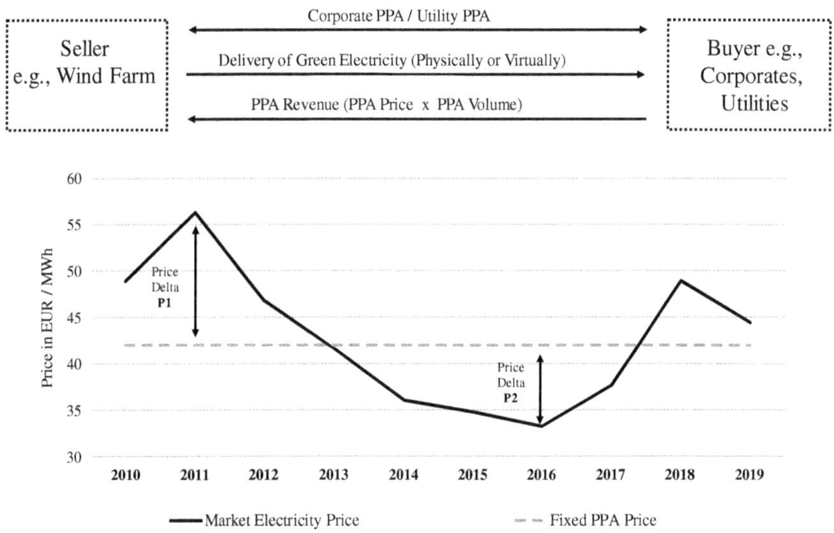

Fig. 1. PPA price mechanism and relevant stakeholders.

Notes: The graph shows the relationship between the seller and the buyer and Sweden's historical electricity wholesale prices. In the example, a fixed PPA price is assumed at 42 EUR/MWh. Thus, P1 describes a situation when power market prices exceed the fixed PPA price and vice versa related to P2. As a result, P1 has to be paid from the seller to the buyer, whereas P2 is paid from the buyer to the seller.

Under a Virtual PPA, price delta P1 is paid by the producer/seller to the off-taker since market prices are above the pre-agreed strike price. In the case of price delta P2, payments would be directed from the off-taker to the seller instead, thus compensating for the market price's downswing. As every deviation is compensated by one party and shared between seller and buyer accordingly, there 'are parallels between PPAs and interest rate swaps' (Edge, 2015, p. 1) or comparable, unconditional derivatives like futures or forwards. From a lender's perspective, the PPA turns the risk related to the seller's revenue stream from a market price risk into a credit risk related to the off-taker.

2.3. *Source of electricity*

Whereas the features mentioned above and the subsequent ones have been part of PPAs from the beginning, the source of electricity has been added in recent years and has turned into a rather distinctive feature in the wake of the ongoing climate change/renewable energy debate very quickly. In contrast to unspecified PPAs, a PPA specifying the source of electricity creates an additional obligation for the producer/seller of the negotiated electricity amount, and also an additional benefit for the off-taker, as the seller adds a qualitative guarantee to the quantities (volume, price) he has already promised. These days, this quality means the origin of the electricity sold under the PPA being renewable (renewable energy, RE), i.e., the seller is obliged to provide 'green' energy to the off-taker so that the latter in turn is entitled to declare this part of his business 'green', sustainable, or comparable. Even though the quality of green is anything but clearly defined yet (see already Wynne, 1991; in a finance context see, more recently, e.g., Horsch and Richter, 2017, with further references; also Berrou *et al.*, 2019), and even the camouflaging of un-green energy as green (greenwashing, see, e.g., de Jong *et al.*, 2020) has become a severe problem, a guarantee to receive renewable energy can help the off-taker meet sustainability goals — and respective goals of enhancing his reputation, too. Consequently, a PPA that is specified will rather be RE-linked. As other specifications are unusual, PPAs can be considered either RE-linked or unspecified.

2.4. *Volume mechanism*

Another parameter to structure the scope of PPAs is the volume mechanism, i.e., according to the question, which counterparty takes the risk of available energy output according to the specific time when the off-taker needs the electricity (extensively, see Bruck *et al.*, 2018). Insofar as RE technologies produce the electricity volume, this risk is closely related to weather risk and, therefore, to the probability of wind- and solar-related energy output. In the case of a so-called as-produced PPA, the producer delivers the electricity output produced. If this amount delivered undercuts the amount the off-taker requires, the latter has to buy the deficit amount on secondary markets at spot, i.e., unfixed, variable — and thus probably, unfortunately high — market prices. In contrast, a Fixed Volume PPA — i.e., a long-term, fixed-price, fixed-volume off-take agreement — enables the off-taker to require a pre-agreed fixed amount of electricity output from the seller. In this case, the supplier bears the risk of having to buy deficit amounts of electricity in case of underproduction on his side to meet his delivery obligations. At the same time, fixed volumes induce not only a risk reduction but also a risk increase for the off-taker: He now bears a particular accounting risk if his consumption load falls below the fixed delivery amount: In this case, the off-taker has to handle the overshooting amount, most probably by re-selling it to another off-taker. In the eyes of accounting laws, however, this turns the original off-taker into an energy trader. Especially under IFRS 9, the PPA thus has to be treated as a derivative requiring sophisticated mark to market evaluation (see Deloitte, 2016).

One of the most important categories to structure the scope of PPAs is the (way of addressing the) market price risk remaining with the off-taker (Hundt *et al.*, 2021). Therefore, the distinction of the respective subsidy schemes is elaborated in more detail in the subsequent sections.

3. Market Price Risk and Power Purchase Agreements

PPAs hedge against volatile market prices as suppliers and off-takers usually agree on a fixed strike price. This pattern evolved against the backdrop of contract designs used in previous decades, which allowed suppliers to sell their electricity output under two major subsidy schemes, i.e., feed-in tariff/FiT and feed-in premium/FiP (Wagner, 2019).

- Under the FiT scheme, the supplier sells the electricity output to off-takers — like a public utility — at a fixed price (e.g., Vietnam or Iran, see Watson Farley and Williams, 2019; IEA, 2018).
- In contrast, the supplier submits a price bid as part of a public auction under the FiP scheme. Once rewarded, the seller sells the electricity output at variable market prices to a public or private off-taker. At the same time, the seller signs a CfD with a public hedge provider. If the market price falls below the rewarded bid price, the former receives a premium from the latter covering the price difference between market price and bid price (e.g., Germany[4] or France, see CEER, 2018).

Concerning the price mechanism, a PPA structured as a CfD indicates that the supplier and the corporate off-taker negotiate a fixed PPA (strike) price (Fixed for Floating PPA). In addition, both parties mutually agree upon a settlement price commonly represented by the day ahead price of the corresponding electricity spot market. The compensation payment of the PPA is then determined by the opportunity costs or gain induced by comparing the strike price with settlement price (so-called Full Merchant). In the case of a Fixed for Floating PPA, the compensation payment of the PPA for the off-taker increases with higher power prices, as the compensation amount received from the supplier would rise accordingly. Thus, the opportunity payments for off-taker i $\mathrm{OP}_{i,t}$ at time t are calculated as follows:

$$\mathrm{OP}_{i,t} = (\mathrm{WP}_t - \mathrm{Strike}) \cdot \mathrm{PPAV}_t. \tag{1}$$

[4]The latest update of the German Law on Renewable Energies (Erneuerbare–Energien–Gesetz, EEG, 2021) however modified the underlying calculation by introducing an amendment factor which takes into account the location of the RE plant by upgrading the output volumes of under-average locations and downgrading the output volumes of above-average locations, thus causing differences between bidded value (Gebotswert) and value to be attributed (anzulegender Wert) see, e.g., Buchmüller (2020).

WP_t is the production-weighted average settlement price based on the P50 energy output[5], and PPAV_t is the agreed PPA volume that can be either fixed or variable depending on the contracted volume type. If WP_t > Strike, the off-taker i receives the full difference, and vice versa: If WP_t < Strike, he is obliged to pay the respective amount.

Alternatively to the Fixed for Floating mechanism, an off-taker can be incentivised to reduce the strike price to lower the risk of payment obligation under the PPA. However, this so-called Market Following or Floor Price structure needs to convince the supplier as well, since a lower Strike would reduce their expected cash-inflows and thus the PPA's compensation payment. Moreover, in the case of increasing WP_t, the supplier increasingly gives away the revenue upside of a Full Merchant sales scenario. Therefore, Market Following PPAs are used more frequently since this contract type reduces the payment risk for off-takers while at the same time enabling suppliers to benefit from price upsides, i.e., when settlement prices are higher than the Strike. However, the off-taker commonly requires a discount on the price upside in addition to a lower floor price. Therefore, the opportunity payments under a Market Following PPA $\mathrm{MF}_{i,t}$ for off-taker i at time t can be written as follows:

$$\mathrm{MF}_{i,t} = \begin{cases} \mathrm{WP}_t \cdot \mathrm{DIS} \cdot \mathrm{PPAV}_t, & \text{if } \mathrm{WP}_t > \mathrm{Floor} \\ (\mathrm{WP}_t - \mathrm{Floor}) \cdot \mathrm{PPAV}_t, & \text{if } \mathrm{WP}_t < \mathrm{Floor}, \end{cases} \tag{2}$$

where DIS is a discount in % of WP_t and DIS > 0%. If the settlement price is higher than the market price, the off-taker receives DIS, which reduces the costs of physical electricity consumption. This cost-saving effect increases with higher settlement prices. In contrast, the supplier receives $[\mathrm{WP}_t \cdot (1 - \mathrm{DIS})]$ and would see increasing revenues with rising settlement prices. If the settlement price falls below the Floor, off-taker i has to pay the difference to the supplier equally to a Fixed for Floating PPA. However, the Floor of a Market Following PPA is commonly lower than the Strike of a Fixed for Floating PPA because otherwise, the off-taker would face an asymmetrical

[5]The P50 energy output refers to the expected production volume of a renewable energy asset on a confidence level of 50% indicating that the real produced electricity output could be higher or lower with a probability of 50%.

Table 2. Fixed for Floating PPA vs. Market Following PPA.

	Fixed for Floating PPA	Market Following PPA	Evaluation of the compensation
Off-taker/Buyer			
WP_t > Fixed Price	Off-taker fully compensated by (WP_t – Strike)	Off-taker partly compensated by WP_t (1 – DIS)	Higher compensation with Fixed for Floating PPA
WP_t < Fixed Price	Off-taker has to pay full amount (Strike – WP_t)	Off-taker has to pay full amount (Floor – WP_t)	Higher costs with Fixed for Floating PPA
Supplier/Seller			
WP_t > Fixed Price	Supplier has to pay full amount of (WP_t – Strike)	Supplier has to pay amount of WP_t (1 – DIS)	Higher revenues with Market Following PPA
WP_t < Fixed Price	Supplier fully compensated by (Strike – WP_t)	Off-taker has to pay full amount (Floor – WP_t)	Higher compensation with Fixed for Floating PPA

higher payment risk compared to a Fixed for Floating PPA. Table 2 illustrates the risk and chances of each revenue scenario.

Altogether, the comparison shows that off-takers get more compensated under a Fixed for Floating PPA in case of rising settlement prices but face lower payment risks when settlement prices decrease. Thus, there is no superior contract structure available. The selection of the particular PPA depends more on the off-taker's degree of risk aversion and the off-taker's expectation concerning power price developments. However, both PPA types reduce the risk of being fully exposed to volatile market prices (merchant risk).

To investigate the off-taker risk of both PPA types, we have conducted a case study based on the Swedish wind farm Markbygden ETT with a total capacity of 650 MW. In 2017, the Norwegian aluminum producer Norsk Hydro closed a long-term Fixed for Floating PPA with this wind farm. The case study provides insights into the effects of COVID-19 on the risk structure of both PPA types.

4. Case Study: Swedish Corporate PPAs

Markbygden ETT represents phase I of a larger cluster of three phases and includes three wind farms (Kilberget, Gråberget,

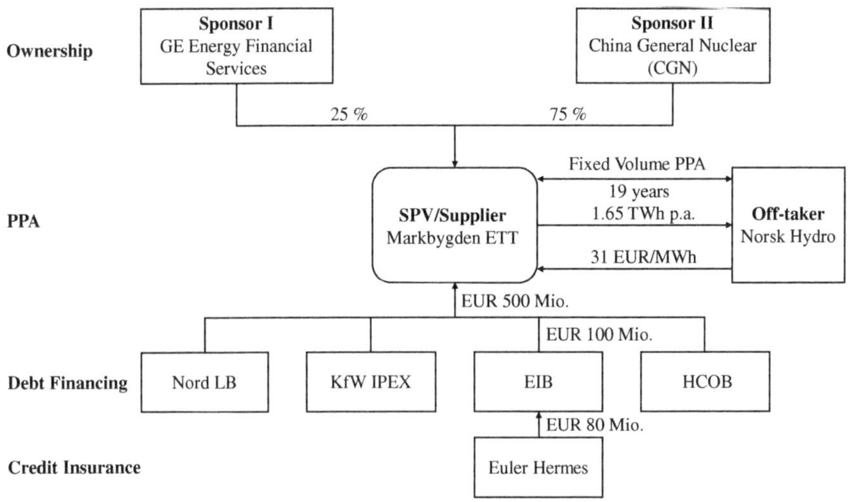

Fig. 2. Markbygden ETT transaction overview.
Source: Authors' illustration, based on Power Technology (2019). Debt volumes of Nord LB, KfW IPEX, and HCOB have not been published.

and Snöbergen) in Northern Sweden (in detail, see Ejdemo and Söderholm, 2015). The PPA closed for these RE entities became the biggest onshore wind PPA transaction in Continental Europe until early 2021. Project development started about 15 years ago, driven by the Swedish wind developer Svevind before the assets were acquired jointly by GE Energy Financial Services and Green Investment Group from Svevind in 2018 for about EUR 800 m. The wind farm has started operation at the end of 2019 (Power Technology, 2019). Figure 2 displays major parties involved in the Markbygden structure as well as their contractual relationships.

The construction of the wind farm was initially financed with sponsor's equity of EUR 300 million (estimated equity ratio 37.5%), of which 50% (EUR 150 million) as provided by Green Investment Group (GIG) and GE Energy Financial Services (GEEFS) each. However, in July 2019, GIG sold its entire stake, and GEEFS sold half of its stake (i.e., 25% of the total shares) to Chinese utility company China General Nuclear (CGN) subsidiary CGN Energy Europe (e.g., D'Angelo, 2020). The residual amount was provided by European Investment Bank (EIB), Nord LB, KfW IPEX, and Hamburg Commercial Bank (formerly known as HSH Nordbank) loan facilities, with

80% of the EIB transaction being backed by credit insurance from Euler Hermes.

Based on a confidence interval of 50% (P50), the Markbygden wind farm has an estimated annual energy production (AEP) of approximately 2.2 TWh. Based hereupon, off-taker Norsk Hydro and Markbygden ETT (i.e., the SPV running the Markbygden I project) had closed a (Physical) PPA with a tenor of 19 years and a fixed volume of $PPAV_t = 1.65\,\text{TWh}$ p.a., causing a hedge ratio of $1.65/2.2 = 75\%$. To illustrate the exact risk management effects of the PPA, (price) data is necessary, which is rather confidential than published, in particular the PPA price. Consequently, we have to base our analysis on reasonably assumed prices.

- As the Markbygden I wind farm is located in the Swedish pricing zone SE1 in Northern Sweden, we assume that SE1 is used as the settlement zone for the PPA.
- We assume a PPA price of 31 EUR/MWh based on Bloomberg data for Sweden's levelised cost of energy in 2018 and a monthly settlement period.

Figure 3 shows the compensation payment of the Fixed for Floating PPA for Norsk Hydro. As Markbygden ETT started operation at the end of 2019, 2020 was the first full PPA year, but we also considered 2019 a benchmark. As displayed in Figure 3, the day ahead price of SE1 (settlement price) dropped significantly throughout the first quarter of 2020, then moved sideways and became volatile again during H2 2020.

By spring and late autumn 2020, market prices in the SE1 region reached the lowest level according to the price tracking by Nord Pool. One of the main reasons is the overproduction of renewable energy assets in the northern price zones SE1 and SE2, which can also be tracked on Nord Pool using the Electricity Price Area Differentials (EPAD). During 2020, the overall production in SE1 increased by 19.3% up to 24.1 TWh, with an annual increase in overproduction of 37% compared to the SE1 production volume in 2019, according to Nord Pool data. Another reason is the COVID-19 effect and the corresponding decrease in product and service demand, which is

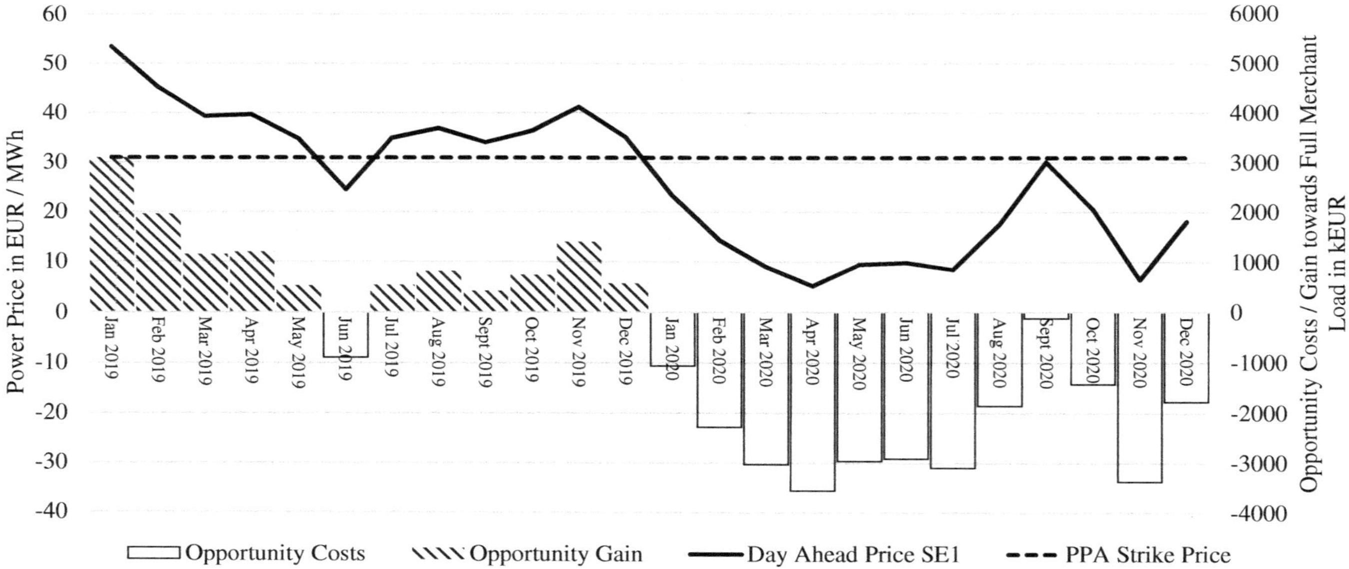

Fig. 3. Estimated performance for Norsk Hydro 2019–2020 (Fixed for Floating PPA).

Notes: This figure displays the monthly Swedish day ahead price (solid line) in the price zone SE1 where the wind farm portfolio is located. Since the PPA price was not published, we assume an average PPA price of 31 EUR/MWh based on a monthly PPA settlement provided by Nord Pool (2021).

Source: Authors' illustration.

surprising since Sweden did not officially impose a nationwide lockdown compared to the majority of other European countries (see Zhang *et al.*, 2020). As a result, the cumulated electricity consumption in the southern price zones SE3 and SE4 decreased by approximately 3% down to 87.9 TWh within the year 2020. In sum, a higher production volume in SE1 and decreasing electricity consumption in the Southern zones SE3 and SE4 significantly decreased the SE1 settlement price.

Consequently, Figure 3 shows a significant amount of opportunity costs compared to a full merchant electricity consumption. In 2020, the annual amount of cash outflows paid by Norsk Hydro under the Fixed for Floating PPA accounted for EUR 27.4 million That means Norsk Hydro would have realised a loss of EUR 27.4 million at an assumed PPA price of 31 EUR/MWh compared to consumption based purely on market prices.

In the case of a Market Following PPA structure, the opportunity costs during 2020 are expected to be lower compared to a Fixed for Floating PPA due to a lower floor. Therefore, by assuming a 22 EUR/MWh floor and a discount of 15%,[6] we have calculated a total loss of EUR 13.9 million compared to a full merchant electricity consumption. Figure 4 summarises the cash inflows and outflows, and opportunity costs according to the assumption catalogue.

The graph shows that the price downfall in 2020 does not induce negative consequences compared to a Fixed for Floating PPA. However, a possible gain for Norsk Hydro would also be smaller since the off-taker would only receive the discount instead of the full difference between strike and settlement price. Therefore, the pricing structure should match the off-taker's degree of risk aversion. Moreover, the availability of Market Following PPAs strongly depends on the supplier's preference, who exposes its revenue stream to volatile market prices when they are higher than the floor price. Finally, suppliers' access to particular project financing for building up new renewable

[6]The exact specifications of the PPA have remained confidential until now. The assumed floor/discount are assumptions based on various exchanges of the authors with PPA market participants and can be considered as an educated guess.

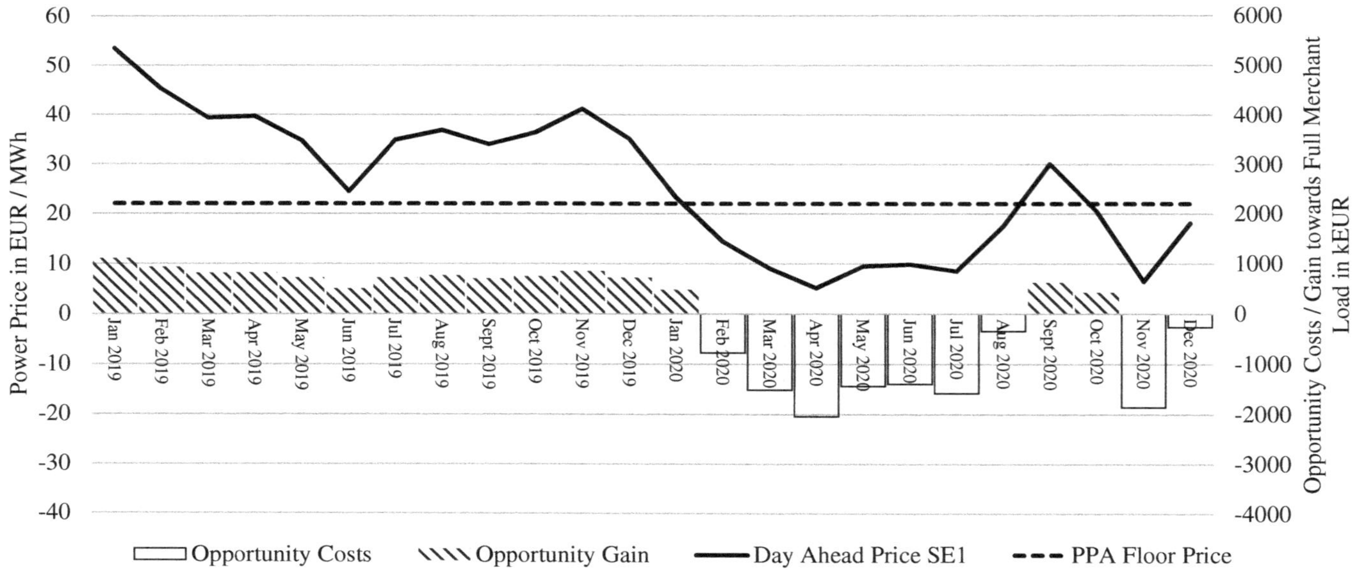

Fig. 4. Estimated performance for Norsk Hydro 2019–2020 (Market Following PPA).

Notes: This figure displays the monthly Swedish day ahead price (solid line) in the price zone SE1 where the wind farm portfolio is located. Since the PPA price was not published, we assume a 22 EUR/MWh floor price and a discount of 15% based on a monthly PPA settlement provided by Nord Pool (2021).

Source: Authors' illustration.

energy assets is limited since banks relate their debt sizing to the fixed price, which is the floor price in case of a Market Following PPA.

5. Conclusion

Power Purchase Agreements are a new kind of purchasing – especially green – electricity directly from the producer. These contracts enable off-takers like corporates or utilities to fix electricity prices and volumes and even qualities for a long-term horizon. Compared to a full merchant scenario, PPAs shift the risk of increasing power market prices to the supply side. However, due to a lack of standardisation of these forward agreements, PPAs allow for two primary price mechanisms called Fixed for Floating PPA and Market Following PPA. In the case of Fixed for Floating PPAs, off-takers can fully transfer the risk of rising settlement prices to the supplier while at the same time being forced to forward cost savings to the supplier if settlement prices fall below a pre-agreed strike. In contrast, Market Following PPAs reduce the payment risk for off-takers due to lower floor prices, but the cost-saving effect in case of increasing settlement prices is also limited since the off-taker would receive only a part of the compensation, which is represented by a discount.

In order to shed more light on the risk allocation of these two PPA types, we have conducted a case study of the biggest PPA closed in Continental Europe so far, which is under operation since the end of 2019. The analysis indicates that a Market Following PPA would be more beneficial in terms of cashflows as the contracted Fixed for Floating PPA. The value-added of this PPA type is mainly driven by a substantial downfall of electricity prices, especially in the price zone SE1 where the wind farm is located. However, this evaluation will be different if power prices start to recover or even increase again. Therefore, off-takers and suppliers should carefully select the specific market price mechanism of a PPA according to their individual risk appetite and future price expectations. In doing so, they will need comprehensive scientific research on electricity prices and PPA-based hedging, which in turn requires distinguished risk management experts — meaning that future PPA market participants would in particular benefit from future research of Hermann Locarek-Junge and the academics he educated. This is one more reason to wish them many more years of — in every respect — healthy research and valuable discoveries of yet undiscovered knowledge.

References

Aust, B. and Horsch, A. (2020). Negative market prices on power exchanges: Evidence and policy implications from Germany, *The Electricity Journal* **33**(3), art. 106716.

Berrou, R., Ciampoli, N., and Marini, V. (2019). Defining green finance: Existing standards and main challenges. In Migliorelli, M. and Dessertine, P. (eds.), *The Rise of Green Finance in Europe*, Cham: Palgrave Macmillan, pp. 31–51.

Bonetti, V., Caselli, S., and Gatti, S. (2010). Off-taking agreements and how they impact the cost of funding for project finance deals: A clinical case study of the Quezon Power Ltd Co, *Review of Financial Economics* **19**(2), 60–71.

Bruck, M., Sandborn, P., and Goudarzi, N. (2018). A leverage cost of energy (LCOE) model for wind farms that include power purchase agreements (PPAs), *Renewable Energy* **122**, 131–139.

Buchmüller, C. (2020). Gesetzliche Grundlagen — Der Katalysator für die deutsche Energiewende. In Meier, D. and Rietz, S. (eds.), *Projektmanagement in der Windenergie — Strategien und Handlungsempfehlungen für die Praxis*, Wiesbaden: Springer Gabler, pp. 27–45.

CEER — Council of European Energy Regulators (2018). *Status Review of Renewable Support Schemes in Europe for 2016 and 2017*. Ref: C18-SD-63-03, Dec 14. Available at: https://www.ceer.eu/documents/104400/-/-/80ff3127-8328-52c3-4d01-0acbdb2d3bed.

Cohen, M.A. and Agrawal, N. (1999). An analytical comparison of long and short term contracts, *IIE Transactions* **31**, 783–796.

Coussi, M. and Harada, L.-N. (2020). Power purchase agreements: An emerging tool at the centre of the European energy transition — a focus on France, *European Energy & Environmental Law Review* **29**, 195–205.

Crouhy, M., Galai, D., and Mark, R. (2014). *The Essentials of Risk Management*, 2nd ed. New York: McGraw-Hill.

D'Angelo, M. (2020). *Onshore Wind Energy: Market Analysis of Sweden, Poland, and Romania*. Master of Science Thesis, KTH School of Industrial Engineering and Management, Doc. Energy Technology TRITA-ITM-EX 2020:469, Stockholm.

Dai, T. (2017). Optimum bidding of renewable energy system owners in electricity markets. In Ozan, E. (ed.), *Optimization in Renewable Energy Systems*, Amsterdam: Elsevier, pp. 117–158.

de Jong, M.D.T., Huluba, G., and Beldad, A.D. (2020). Different shades of Greenwashing: Consumers' reactions to environmental lies, half-lies, and organizations taking credit for following legal obligations, *Journal of Business and Technical Communication* **34**(1), 38–76.

de Lagarde, C.M. and Lantz, F. (2018). How renewable production depresses electricity prices: Evidence from the German market, *Energy Policy* **117**, 263–277.

Deloitte (2016). *Power and Utilities — Accounting, Financial Reporting, and Tax Update*. Deloitte Development LLC.

Edge, P. (2015). An approximation of counterparty credit risk in long term power purchase agreements (PPAs). *2015 12th International Conference on the European Energy Market (EEM), Lisbon, Portugal, 2015*, doi: 10.1109/EEM.2015.7216645.

Ejdemo, T. and Söderholm, P. (2015). Wind power, regional development and benefit-sharing: The case of Northern Sweden, *Renewable and Sustainable Energy Reviews* **47**(C), 476–485.

Hamrin, J. (1989). Nonutility power and the reliability issue, *The Electricity Journal* **2**(5), 14–27.

Horsch, A. and Richter, S. (2017). Climate change driving financial innovation: The case of green bonds, *The Journal of Structured Finance* **23**(1), 79–90.

Hundt, S., Jahnel, J., and Horsch, A. (2021). Power purchase agreements and financing renewables — an interdependency, *The Journal of Structured Finance* **27**(1), 35–50.

IEA — International Energy Agency (2018). *Iran Feed-in Tariff*. Last modified March 1, 2018. https://www.iea.org/policies/4819-iran-feed-in-tariff.

Jorion, P. (1997). *Value at Risk*, Chicago: Irwin; 3rd ed. New York *et al.*: McGraw-Hill (2007).

Jorion, P. (2002). How informative are value-at-risk disclosures? *The Accounting Review* **77**(4), 911–931.

Klein, T. and Walther, T. (2016). Oil price volatility forecast with mixture memory GARCH, *Energy Economics* **58**, 46–58.

Knight, F.H. (1921). *Risk, Uncertainty, and Profit*. Boston: Houghton Mifflin.

Locarek, H. (1988). *Wissensbasierte Systeme zur Durchführung statistischer Analysen — Konzeption und Implementation eines Prototypen*, Frankfurt/M.: Peter Lang, also: Augsburg, Univ., PhD thes., 1987.

Locarek-Junge, H. (2001). Hedging. In Gerke, W. and Steiner, M. (eds.), *Handwörterbuch der Finanzwirtschaft*, Stuttgart: Schäffer-Poeschel, pp. 1016–1022.

Locarek-Junge, H. and Büch, C. (2006). Sind Bankenrisiken messbar? In Kürsten, W. and Nietert, B. (eds.), *Kapitalmarkt, Unternehmensfinanzierung und rationale Entscheidungen, Festschrift Wilhelm*, Berlin and Heidelberg: Springer, pp. 109–128.

Locarek-Junge, H. and Hengmith, L. (2003). Management des operationalen Risikos der Informationswirtschaft in Banken. In Geyer-Schulz, A. and Taudes, A. (eds.), *Informationswirtschaft: Ein Sektor mit Zukunft*, Bonn: Gesellschaft für Informatik, pp. 207–221.

Locarek-Junge, H. and Klein, T. (2016). Währungs-Hedging mit Derivaten, *Das Wirtschaftsstudium* **45**(3), 298–304 & 335.

Locarek-Junge, H. and Prinzler, R. (1998). Estimating value-at-risk using neural networks. In Weinhardt, C. *et al.*, (eds.), *Informationssysteme in der Finanzwirtschaft*, Wiesbaden: Gabler, pp. 385–397.

Locarek-Junge, H. and Prinzler, R. (1999). Using ANN to estimate VaR. In Gaul, W. and Locarek-Junge, H. (eds.), *Classification in the Information Age, Proceedings of the 22nd Annual GfKI Conference*, Berlin: Springer, pp. 460–466.

Locarek-Junge, H., Prinzler, R., and Straßberger, M. (2002). The estimation of market risk in portfolios of stocks and stock options, *Schmalenbach Business Review*, Special Issue, **54**(1–2), 171–189.

Locarek-Junge, H. and Straßberger, M. (2003). Standards für das Asset- und Risikomanagement, *Finanz Betrieb* **5**(10), 648–651.

Locarek-Junge, H., Straßberger, M., and Vollbehr, H. (2000). Dynamische Limitsetzung. In Rudolph, B. and Johanning, L. (eds.), *Handbuch Risikomanagement*, 2 Volumes, Vol. 2, Bad Soden: Uhlenbruch, pp. 833–849.

Miller, L. and Carriveau, R. (2020). Corporate renewable energy procurement: Comparison of the market in Canada versus the U.S. to Enable CPPAs in Canada. In Ting, D.S.-K. and Vasel-Be-Hagh, A. (eds.), *Sustaining Tomorrow*, Cham: Springer Proceedings in Energy, pp. 93–112.

Mises, L. von (1949). *Human Action — A Treatise on Economics.* New Haven: Yale University Press.

Nguyen, D.K. and Walther, T. (2020). Modeling and forecasting commodity market volatility with long-term economic and financial variables, *Journal of Forecasting* **39**(2), 126–142.

Power Technology (2019). *Projects — Markbygden ETT Windfarm*, https://www.power-technology.com/projects/markbygden-ett-windfarm/ (accessed March 10, 2021).

Schneider, D. (1995). *Betriebswirtschaftslehre*, 4 Volumes, Vol. 1. Grundlagen, 2nd ed., München and Wien: Oldenbourg.

Schneider, D. (1997). *Betriebswirtschaftslehre*, 4 Volumes, Vol. 3. Theorie der Unternehmung, München and Wien: Oldenbourg.

Schneider, D. (2011). *Betriebswirtschaftslehre als Einzelwirtschaftstheorie der Institutionen*. Wiesbaden: Springer Gabler.

Shrimali, G., Vaibhav, P.S., and Vinit, A. (2019). A payment security mechanism for off-taker risk in renewable energy projects in India, *The Journal of Structured Finance* **25**(2), 87–99.

Sund, K.A. and Hausken, K. (2012). Fixed price contract versus incentive-based contract in the oil and gas industry, *International Journal of Global Energy Issues* **35**(5), 371–410.

Tang, C. and Zhang, F. (2019). Classification, principle and pricing manner of renewable power purchase agreement. *IOP Conference Series: Earth and Environmental Science* 295 052054. doi:10.1088/1755-1315/295/5/052054.

Wagner, J. (2019). Grid investment and support schemes for renewable electricity generation, *Energy Journal*, **40**(2), 195–221.

Watson Farley and Williams (2019). *New Feed-in Tariff Mechanism for Vietnamese Solar Energy Projects*. Briefing, March 2019. Available at: https://www.wfw.com/wp-content/uploads/2019/03/WFW-Briefing-New-Feed-in-tariff-mechanism-for-Vietnamese-solar.pdf.

Weron, R. and Ziel, F. (2019). Electricity price forecasting. In Soytaş, U. and Sarı, R. (eds.), *Routledge Handbook of Energy Economics*, London and New York: Routledge, pp. 506–521.

Wynne, R.D. (1991). Defining green: Toward regulation of environmental marketing claims, *University of Michigan Journal of Law Reforms* **24**(3–4), 785–820.

Zhang, X., Pellegrino, F., Shen, J., Copertaro, B., Huang, P., Saini, P.K., and Lovati, M. (2020). A preliminary simulation study about the impact of COVID-19 crisis on energy demand of a building mix at a district in Sweden, *Applied Energy* **280**, art. 115954.

Ziel, F. and Steinert, R. (2018). Probabilistic mid- and long-term electricity price forecasting, *Renewable & Sustain. Energy Review* **94**, 251–266.

https://doi.org/10.1142/9781800611917_0018

Chapter 18

The Christenson Gold Price Model Reconsidered

Thomas Burkhardt* and Dominik Möhring
University of Koblenz-Landau, Chair of Finance, Germany
**tburkha@uni-koblenz.de*

The Christenson gold price model is an analytical model to predict the general direction of gold price movements. The model is charmingly simple, based on plausible variables, and seems to provide surprisingly good results. We analyse the model and use appropriate out-of-sample tests for our evaluation. As a result, we find that the proposed model is not useful and that the seemingly good results are a consequence of only in-sample fitting. We consider this as a case study to demonstrate that models promoted in popular investment media should be considered with care.

1. Introduction

"Gold 10 000 $?" is the title of the book by Christenson and Müller (2016), in which they present a model for the prediction of future gold prices which is at the focus of this contribution. This book is a slightly updated and adapted German version of the earlier English book by Christenson (2014).[1] We refer to this model henceforth as the Christenson model. At the time of this writing, September 2021, the gold price is around 1800$/oz., about 200$/oz. down its nominal

[1]We refer to a version of this book in epub format. Page numbers are therefore not available, and references are made to the respective chapters.

all-time high during winter 2020/2021, the first winter of the COVID crisis. The crisis, accompanied by an unseen monetary expansion, aroused special interest in gold and gold prices of the general public, as it is seen by many market participants as a potential save haven and inflation hedge.[2] In such an environment, there is a growing demand for analysis, which popular media attempt to satisfy. And for some analysts, there might be a relation between their predictions and their commercial interests. This occurs to us as a rather typical problem of investment analysis and advice in popular media and spurred our interest to find out to what extent such analysis might be reliable.

In this context, we analyse the Christenson model. It is an example of a seemingly scientific model of gold price movements, yet addressed to the retail investor.[3] We attempt to evaluate the performance of this model to gain a better understanding of the extent one might trust popular scientific work from interested practitioners. Our analysis might in this sense be regarded as a small case study.[4]

2. The Christenson Model

2.1. *Model objectives*

Christenson (2014), Chapter 1, provides a discussion of various expert opinions on the future of gold prices, concluding that "In fact,

---

[2]See, e.g., Brown (1982) for a broader discussion of hedge investments in general and in Chapter 9 on gold and silver in particular.

[3]It is not the goal of this contribution to review the extensive literature on gold and gold valuation. For a compact survey see, e.g., Shafiee and Topal (2010). We rather focus on potential problems with "practitioner" approaches, which might be influenced by commercial interests.

[4]The books providing the model address the general retail investor and give a fundamentally positive perspective on the future prices of gold. The development of a seemingly scientifically justified rational model fosters the trust of the reader in the competence of the authors, who both are involved in the promotion of precious metals and especially gold. Christenson operated an investment website www.deviantinvestor.com and is a contributor to www.goldseiten.de. Müller publishes popular investment books (Müller, 2007, 2014) and provides services to precious metal investors through his web sites www.ekg-sachwerte.de and www.goldsilber.org. Both authors emphasise their educational background in the sciences as well as their business experience.

they cannot even agree as to whether gold is likely to trade higher or lower in the next three years" — a quite common observation in any financial market. This leads him to the formulation of his modeling objectives:

> We need an objective model to project the value of gold. We need a model that bypasses the propaganda, self-serving forecasts, market manipulations, media disinformation, and the influence of high-frequency trading to "manage" the gold market.
>
> We need a simple and understandable empirical model for gold prices based on macro-economic variables that are relatively easy to measure and project several years into the future.

Chapter 5 enlarges on that:

> A gold model should function accurately and consistently during all conditions in the financial markets. In other words, it should be accurate and effective during gold bull markets and gold bear markets, during stable and unstable political conditions, and during stock and bond market crashes and rallies. ...
>
> Hence my goal was the replication of the smoothed gold price with the short term volatility removed. The model is based on a formula that works under all market conditions and is intellectually honest.

Chapter 3 discusses further guidelines and potential variables of the desired model. The following guidelines describe the objectives in more detail, which refer to a "smoothed gold price" as target variable, which we will discuss later:

- Replicate the smoothed prices for gold since President Nixon closed the "gold window" on August 15, 1971. By executive order, he announced that the United States would no longer exchange foreign owned dollars for gold. His action enabled the reduction in value and purchasing power of the dollar through massive inflation of the money supply.
- Use inputs that are easy to identify, measure, and are intuitively sensible in their causal relationship to gold prices.
- Use inputs that can be projected into the future with some degree of confidence.

- Keep it simple and easy to understand. A simple model is more credible and less susceptible to "curve-fitting" that forces agreement with the smoothed gold price.
- Calculate an equilibrium or "fair" market value for gold prices that has been smoothed to filter out the noise, short-term manipulations, high frequency trading distortions, political pressures, and temporary supply and demand changes.
- Do NOT attempt to predict weekly or monthly gold market prices.
- Do NOT use past or current gold prices to predict future gold prices.
- Do NOT expect perfection.

Such a model for sure would be very useful to the investor, especially because of its long-term focus, and its fundamental approach. A central question then is what variables to use as an input for the model. Christenson discusses a wide range of potential variables and claims that he "tested many of these macro-economic variables", but in conclusion "used variables that are logically connected with the price of gold and optimised their weighting to create a model that accurately replicates the smoothed price of gold."

2.2. *Model structure*

Christenson, after "extensive testing ... simplified the model to include only three variables":

- Official national debt;
- Price of crude oil;
- S&P 500 stock price index.

Besides these three underlying input variables, the final model uses one additional, derivative variable, which is the annual rate of change of the official national debt. Including this, the final model has four input variables.

The target variable that is to be explained by the model is the "smoothed gold price". This variable is defined in a rather tricky way (Chapter 1)[5]:

[5]Accentuations by the authors.

> Each monthly price was smoothed with a 13 month *centered* moving average. Example: the smoothed price for July 1987 gold was the simple average of all the monthly prices from January 1987 through January 1988. To create an annual smoothed gold price, the monthly smoothed prices for January–December of each year were averaged. However, to further smooth the gold price, I took the annual prices, as calculated above, and smoothed them with a three year *centered* moving average. Example: the additionally smoothed 1987 gold price was the average of the smoothed 1986, 1987 and 1988 gold prices.

This smoothing procedure is also applied to some of the inputs: Crude oil and S&P 500 index (Chapter 6).

Using centered moving averages seems problematic in a model that should predict the future: The centered average replaces the original value of the time series with an average that already includes information about future values, which are to be predicted. We will come back to this issue in our later model evaluation.

The final model is expressed by the following formula (Christenson, 2014, Chapter 5). Christenson "tried many combinations [of the variables] and the best one ... found is this."

$$\mathrm{EGP}_t = \frac{K \cdot \mathrm{ND}_{t-1}^a \cdot \mathrm{CL}_{t-1}^b \cdot \text{ND-ROC}_{t-1}^d}{\mathrm{SP}_{t-1}^c}. \tag{1}$$

We stick to his notation for easy comparison, but add appropriate time indices to the formula, which are not in the source, as the "formula calculates the equilibrium gold price using a plus one year offset. For example, the equilibrium gold price for 1998 is based on the 1997 values for national debt and its rate of change, crude oil, and the S&P 500 Index." K is a constant factor, ND is the official national debt in million dollars, ND-ROC is the annual rate of change of ND, CL is the price of crude oil in \$/Barrel/10 and SP the S&P 500 Stock Price index /100. EGP represents the estimate of the model for the smoothed gold price and is termed by Christenson "Equilibrium Gold Price". This term is misleading, as the model does not contain macroeconomic equilibrium considerations. We prefer to use the term calculated or estimated gold price instead, keeping in mind that not the gold price itself is estimated, but the smoothed gold price.

The scaling of the variables is not important, as the overall effect of such scaling is only a change of the constant K in the model.

The model has five parameters to be estimated to give useful predictions: K, a, b, c, d.

2.3. *Model fit and results*

Fitting the model to the data and subsequent testing requires at least the following steps: Defining (1) training data; (2) fitting procedure for the parameters; and (3) criteria for test evaluation. Christenson's exposition of these issues is not completely clear. In Chapter 6, a 42-year period, seemingly from 1972 to 2013, is considered. This implies that the whole available data set is used in fitting the model, so that out-of-sample tests are precluded. A formally defined fitting procedure to find the parameters was not applied. In Chapter 5 we find that Christenson "tested hundreds of combinations of those five constants" and found that the following "combination worked quite well": $K = 0.51, a = 0.41, b = 0.90, c = 0.36, d = 2.00$. In the subsequent publication, Christenson and Müller (2016) use the same procedure but data up to 2015, resulting in slightly different parameter estimates: $K = 0.55, a = 0.42, b = 0.75, c = 0.32, d = 2.00$ (p. 42).

The interpretation of the term "quite well" remains opaque. The parameters were chosen in such a way as to fit the model "quite well" to the overall data set, and criteria for the precluded out-of-sample tests became obsolete.

Christenson (2014) presents the model results in Chapter 6.[6] Provided are graphs that show the smoothed gold price together with the corresponding model estimate with the prediction horizon of one year, for the whole data set. These results appear to be appealing: The model seems to capture both direction and strength of price movements quite accurately, the correlation coefficient is 0.98, although the pointwise estimation error is mostly in the order of magnitude of 20%–30%, as we can read out from the graphs. But such estimation errors are probably not worse than those we have to face in many other valuation problems.

But serious methodological concerns remain. They cast doubt that the model really can cope with "all market conditions and is intellectually honest". We address this in the subsequent section.

[6] Christenson and Müller (2016) correspondingly with slightly updated data. We focus here on the resulting gold price estimates in Dollars, which are better than those for the Euro.

3. Model Evaluation

3.1. *Review of the methodology*

The main purpose of the model is to provide useful predictions. The model fit used by Christenson is essentially an in-sample fit, which is well known to tend to show poor out-of-sample performance. To neglect out-of-sample testing is a neglect of standard scientific procedure and a major drawback of Christenson's approach.

The second issue, as mentioned above, is the smoothing procedure. Data smoothing might in such an application be a good idea, but using *future* data in the design of a prediction model is not. The procedure used leads to a situation in which input data to the model (crude oil and S&P 500 index) contains data up to two years into the future,[7] the same as with the target variable gold price. This leads to the situation, that the model which is supposed to provide predictions one year ahead requires smoothed inputs that require data two years ahead — so the model provides essentially estimates 1 year in the past. This is a principal drawback of Christenson's approach. But for sure purely formally these predictions can be done, and this is what we do first in our subsequent evaluation to stay within Christenson's framework.[8] On the other hand, we would like to know if his approach can be useful in principle. The problem is his smoothing procedure. We solve this by shifting the data windows involved in the past so that each smoothed data point contains only information

[7]The first centered monthly average uses data six months into the future. The second average over the calendar year, resulting in a value for the middle of the year, involves the monthly estimate for December, which requires data six months ahead, altogether already 1 year ahead of the middle of the year. The third average of three such yearly data points adds another year ahead, so altogether 2 years.

[8]As discussed, for the calculation of each smoothed data point, we need two years of data in the future and the past. So, a precise application of the smoothing procedure is only possible for time points two years after the beginning up to 2 years before the end of the available data. To be able to have smoothed data points for all time points in the data set, we decided to do the smoothing at the borders of the data set by averaging only over the available data points as an approximation. Although it is not mentioned by Christenson, we conclude from his graphs that he probably used a similar procedure.

up to its point in time,[9] and redo the analysis with the modified data sets. We will refer to this approach as non-anticipative smoothing.

Although Christenson's model is formally designed for predictions one year ahead, it seems that his idea of how to apply it is a different one. Chapter 7 of Christenson (2014), and more detailed Chapter 7 of Christenson and Müller (2016) discuss predictions based on scenarios for the input variables. These discussions are not very careful with respect to modelled time lags. Rather, they develop scenarios for future values for the inputs, and, based on them, use the model to come up with predictions for the future gold price. Christenson and Müller (2016) provide a "low", "medium" and "blow off" scenario up to 2021. Such applications require quite subjective projections, and at least we do not see why it should be easier to estimate inputs like future oil or stock index prices than the gold price itself. We will not enlarge on that approach here but stick to the analysis of the one-year ahead predictions. Nevertheless, our out-of-sample tests with model parameters fixed up to 5 years in the past will allow us to develop some perspective on this issue, too.

3.2. *Out-of-sample tests*

We address these issues with out-of-sample tests: (1) We use three different settings for training and test data,[10], as detailed in the

---

[9]Each monthly price is smoothed with a 13-month moving average. For example, the smoothed gold price for July 1987 is the simple average of all the monthly prices from July 1986 through July 1987. To create an annually smoothed gold price on a monthly basis, the price of a month is replaced by the average of these smoothed prices over the past 12 months, including the month under consideration. To further smooth the gold price, each monthly value so created is replaced by its average over the last three values with yearly distance. For example, the July 1987 value is replaced by the average value of July 1987, 1986 and 1985. The resulting monthly time series is used for parameter estimation and prediction.

[10]Christenson (2014) and Christenson and Müller (2016) provide links to the data sets used in their analysis. At the time of this writing, they do not work any more. For that reason, we bought the data for the prices of gold, crude oil, and the S&P index from MacroTrends (https://macrotrends.dpdcart.com) on a monthly basis (Gold Prices monthly nominal, WTI Month-End Prices nominal, S&P 500 index monthly nominal). The data of the national debt was available for download

following subsections. (2) We need to define a reproducible fitting procedure for the parameters. We decided to use a simple least-squares regression model based on the logarithm of the model, that is,

$$\begin{aligned}\log \mathrm{EGP}_t = K' &+ a \cdot \log \mathrm{ND}_{t-1} + b \cdot \log \mathrm{CL}_{t-1} \\ &+ d \cdot \log \text{ND-ROC}_{t-1} + c' \cdot \log \mathrm{SP}_{t-1} \end{aligned} \quad (2)$$

with $K' = \log K$ and $c' = -c$. This regression is run on the training data sets providing estimates of the model parameters, and then the model is applied with these parameters out-of-sample. (3) We need to set criteria for test evaluation. As such, we use graphs to compare the target variable with its estimate and calculate absolute as well as relative prediction errors.

These prediction errors we consider for predictions out-of-sample up to 5 years, always with a prediction horizon of one year according to the model.[11] This gives a perspective as mentioned above on the use of the Christenson model in the context of scenarios. In these scenarios, the model parameters are fixed, and assumptions are made about future values of the inputs to come up with a 1-year ahead prediction of the gold price. In our approach, we keep the model parameters also fixed at the time the training data ends. But then we use actual inputs of the following up to 5 years to produce the forecasts. This corresponds to the scenario approach, but eliminates potentially erroneous assumptions about future inputs and captures solely the accuracy of the model itself.

In addition, we compare these errors with a *trivial* prediction, which is simply the last known value of the smoothed gold price.

---

at TreasuryDirect (https://www.treasurydirect.gov/govt/reports/pd/histdebt/histdebt.htm) on a yearly basis. We used the data from https://www.treasurydirect.gov/govt/reports/pd/histdebt/histdebt_histo4.htm and https://www.treasurydirect.gov/govt/reports/pd/histdebt/histdebt_histo5.htm. Monthly debt values were approximated by using a cubic spline approach. As a result, we have an overall monthly data set, which contains the yearly data set of Christenson. Our data range from August 1971 to June 2020.

[11] If we, e.g., use training data up to 2000, then we use this data to estimate the model parameters and keep these parameters fixed. With the fixed model, we first predict the future gold price for 2001 based on input data of 2000. Then we use inputs of 2001 to predict the gold price for 2002. This we continue up to the prediction of the gold price in 2005, which is then based on inputs of 2004.

3.2.1. *Applying the Christenson model up to 2020*

First, we simply apply the Christenson model with the parameter estimates as provided in Christenson and Müller (2016), and redo their analysis with our data up to 2020. The result is shown in Figure 1. This figure shows four curves: (1) the original Christenson estimate, (2) the smoothed gold price,[12] (3) the Christenson estimate based on parameters according to our regression Eqs. (2)[13] and (4), the trivial prediction, that is, the smoothed gold price of the previous year. The graph of the trivial prediction is simply that of the smoothed gold price shifted one year to the right.

Both parameter estimates are based on data up to 2016, which is the last year included in the training data. It is marked in the

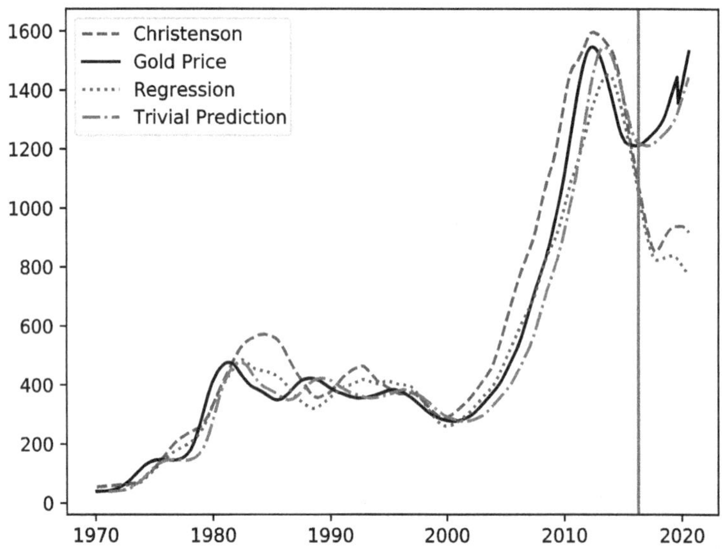

Fig. 1. Smoothed gold price in Dollar/oz. and estimates as a function of time. Estimates are based on the Christenson model with the original parameters according to Christenson and Müller (2016, p. 42) (Christenson), with parameters according to our regression approach (Regression) and based on the trivial prediction. The vertical line marks the year 2016, which is the last year included in the training data.

[12]This corresponds to the first figure in Christenson (2014, Chapter 6) and Christenson and Müller (2016, Abb. 6.1, p. 43).
[13]These are $K = 0.0017, a = 0.8756, b = 0.6737, c = 0.8314, d = -1.9984$.

graph by a vertical line. The model predictions out-of-sample are grossly wrong and substantially worse than in-sample. Furthermore, the model using the regression-based parameters seem to fit a bit better than the original ones, but nevertheless the prediction quality is poor. Most of the time even the trivial prediction is superior to the Christenson model, especially out-of-sample. This observation cast doubt on the overall usefulness of the model.

In the following subsections, we apply the Christenson model using expanding and sliding windows for the training data and investigate absolute and relative prediction errors[14] for forecasts of one up to 5 years beyond the last year in the training set.

3.2.2. *Applying the Christenson model with an expanding training set*

We create expanding windows for the training set simply by using a 20-year data set from August 1971 to August 1991 to start with,[15] and then increase the final date up to 2015. As we have data up to 2020, this leaves us always the one to five years out of sample which we need for our tests. Figure 2 shows the results. The upper two graphs show the absolute and relative prediction errors for the smoothed gold price at the respective date. The values are given for the Christenson model using regression parameters which are based on training data that end one up to 5 years before the respective date. The lower two graphs show the absolute and relative prediction error for the trivial forecast. Here, we see only one curve, as we consider the one-year prediction as in the upper graphs, but there is no need to distinguish various time lags for parameter estimations.

Again, we see that the Christenson model results in quite substantial prediction errors, which are mostly even worse than the trivial prediction. Furthermore, it becomes clear that the model will also not help in a scenario context. Even if the future inputs are correct, as is implied in our calculations, the model predictions are poor.

---

[14]The absolute error is defined by the dollar-difference of the forecast minus the actual value. The relative error is defined by the absolute error divided by the actual value.

[15]Shorter data sets give even worse results and are not included in the graph.

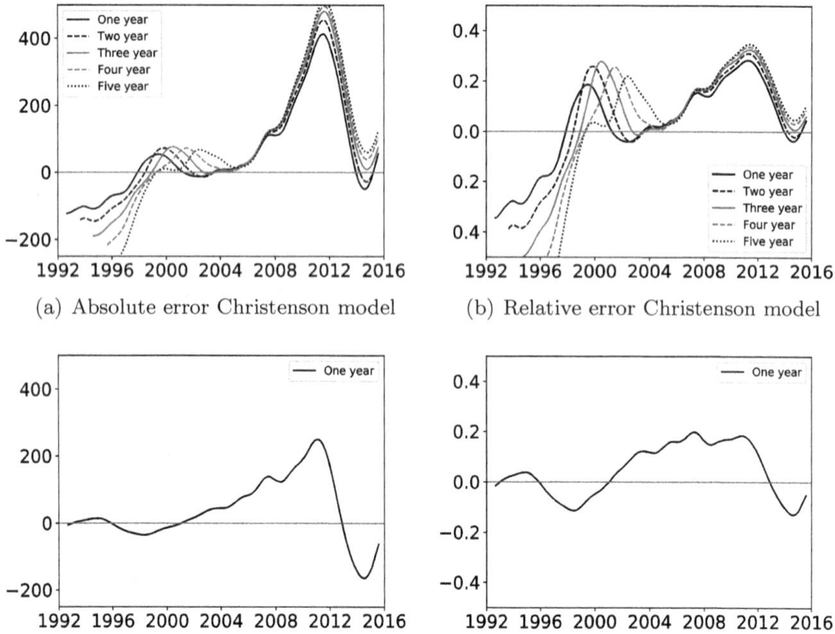

(a) Absolute error Christenson model (b) Relative error Christenson model

(c) Absolute error trivial prediction (d) Relative error trivial prediction

Fig. 2. Expanding window: Absolute and relative errors for 1-year predictions of the smoothed gold price as a function of time. The upper two graphs show results for the Christenson model if the parameters were estimated with data up to 1 to 5 years before the shown date. The lower two graphs show the results for the trivial prediction. Absolute errors are in Dollar/oz.

Furthermore, there is a tendency that the errors increase with the time passed since the last parameter update, as is to be expected.

3.2.3. *Applying the Christenson model with a sliding training set*

We create a sliding window for the training set by fixing a window of, e.g., 20 years, and then move it forward with the final date of the window. The sliding window approach should give improved results compared to the expanding windows if structural changes are in the data. If so, omitting outdated data in the parameter estimation should yield better estimates. Our calculations show very poor predictions for short windows. Figure 3 therefore shows the results only for windows of 20 and 30 years. The upper two graphs show

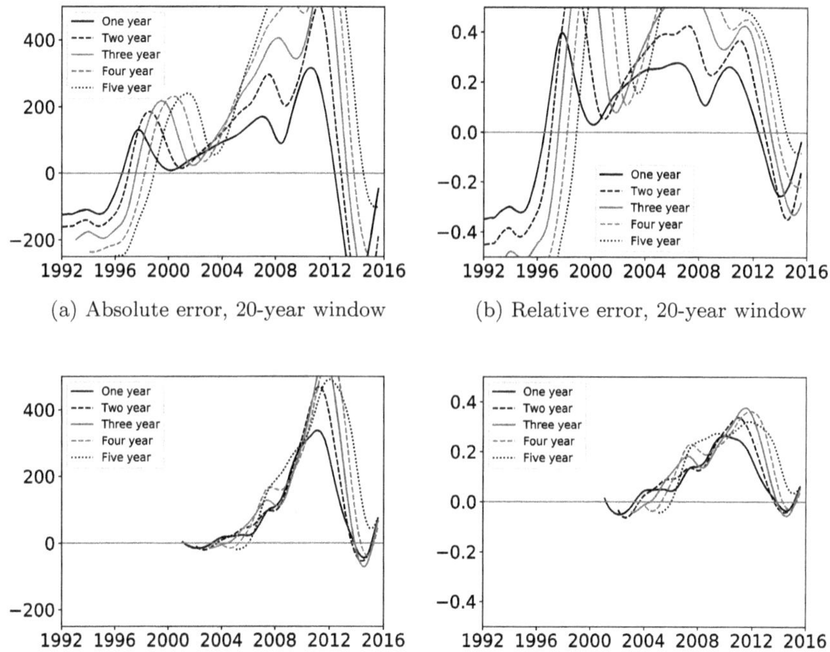

(a) Absolute error, 20-year window (b) Relative error, 20-year window

(c) Absolute error, 30-year window (d) Relative error, 30-year window

Fig. 3. Sliding window: Absolute and relative errors for 1-year predictions of the smoothed gold price as a function of time. The upper two graphs show results for the Christenson model if the parameters were estimated with data up to 1 to 5 years before the shown date for a 20-year window, the lower two graphs for a 30-year window. Absolute errors are in Dollar/oz.

the absolute and relative prediction error for the 20-year window, the lower two graphs for the 30-year window. The display format corresponds to Fig. 2 and shows the effect of the various time lags for parameter estimations. For ease of comparison, all graphs use the same scaling.[16]

It seems that the prediction quality increases with the window size. We conclude that the expanding window approach is preferable, which means that using sliding windows provides no improved performance of the model.

[16]This results in clipping very high errors. For the 20-year window, the five-year error reaches 717 Dollar or 84%. For the 30-year window, the errors are more moderate.

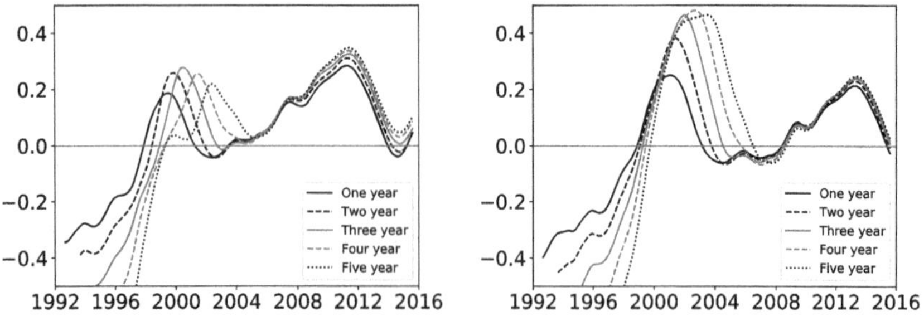

(a) Expanding Window, Christenson's smoothing

(b) Expanding Window, non-anticipative smoothing

Fig. 4. Comparing the prediction errors for Christenson's and the non-anticipative smoothing procedure. Shown are the relative prediction errors for the expanding window as a function of time.

3.3. *Using non-anticipative smoothing*

Christenson requires in his centered smoothing of the data information about the future, which is not available at the point in time when a prediction is to be made. To investigate the effect this has on the model's predictions, we did all out-of-sample tests also with the non-anticipative smoothing procedure described earlier. It should be expected that denying the model information about the future should result in larger prediction errors. Figure 4 shows the results as expected for the expanding window. This we used as it showed the best performance with the Christenson model. The display format corresponds to Fig. 2. Only relative prediction errors are shown. The left graph shows the prediction errors for Christenson's,[17] the right graph for the non-anticipative smoothing.

4. Conclusion

We discussed some methodological deficiencies of the Christenson model. These were shown to result in poor quality predictions of the gold price. Out-of-sample prediction errors are large and mostly worse than from using a trivial prediction based on the last known

[17]This is a copy of the upper right graph of Fig. 2 and put here for the ease of comparison.

gold price. The model also does not provide relevant structural information on the formation of gold prices, which might be useful in a scenario context. Even with true future input values, the model provides only forecasts which tend to be worse than the trivial predictions. We consider the Christenson model as just one case of a model promoted in the popular investment literature, where related commercial interests cannot be precluded. One more time it was found that if it looks too good to be true it usually is.[18]

References

Brown, B. (1982). *A Theory of Hedge Investments.* Macmillian Press: London and Basingstoke.

Christenson, G. (2014). *Gold Value And Gold Prices from 1971–2021: An Empirical Model.* Balboa Press: Bloomington.

Christenson, G. and Müller, J. (2016). *Gold 1000$? Was eine neue Modellrechnung über die Zukunft des Goldpreises sagt und warum Sie einen Teil Ihres Vermögens jetzt in Edelmetall anlegen sollten*, Kopp Verlag: Rottenburg.

Müller, J. (2007). *Generation Gold — Wie ihr Vermögen und ihre Altersvorsorge einen Staatsbankrott und eine Weltwirtschaftskrise unbeschadet überstehen*, 2nd edn. Kopp Verlag: Rottenburg.

Müller, J. (2014). *Drei-Speichen-Regel.* Kopp Verlag: Rottenburg.

Shafiee, S. and Topal, E. (2010). An overview of global gold market and gold price forecasting, *Resources Policy* **35**, 178–189.

[18]We communicated a preliminary German version of this paper to Dr. Jürgen Müller, coauthor of Christenson and Müller (2016). He had no objections against our analysis. He even stated that it confirms the gut feeling that the formula (Christenson model) does not work any more.

https://doi.org/10.1142/9781800611917_0019

Chapter 19

In Gold We Trust: Should German Investors Consider Gold in Stock Portfolios?

Siegfried Köstlmeier* **and Klaus Röder**†

University of Regensburg, Center of Finance, Germany

**siegfried.koestlmeier@ur.de*

†*klaus.roeder@ur.de*

Gold has similar expected returns and risk properties as stocks. The Sharpe ratio maximising allocation of gold in addition to diversified German stock portfolios varies between 42% and 75%. When tilting away from the market portfolio among firm-characteristics, hedge-based considerations suggest to increase the gold ratio when the underlying stock portfolio is riskier. As the correlation between monthly returns of both asset classes is close to zero in Germany, we find that investors can maximize the Sharpe ratio by decreasing the gold weight in more riskier portfolios and vice versa.

1. Introduction

International stock markets become increasingly integrated among few geographical regions. Investors perceive this ongoing development in an increasing correlation between international stock market returns. The sudden stock market crash in spring 2020 in consequence of the COVID-19 pandemic resulted in both a high volatility and an unexpected sharp decline in international equity returns. Accordingly, investors seek alternative investments that have a low correlation with stock returns to benefit from portfolio diversification and higher risk-adjusted returns.

It is widely believed that gold is able to provide these benefits as an alternative investment. For many decades, the market portfolio has a central role as the single risk-factor in asset pricing models. Fama and French (1993) propose additional factors related with firm size and book-to-market ratio to account for several limitations of a single market-factor. In addition, Fama and French (2015) add factors related with operating profitability and investment behavior to the well-known Fama/French five-factor model. The ongoing development of non-market factors to capture robust patterns in stock returns, not related to fluctuations in the market return, provides evidence, that investors may tilt away from holding the market portfolio. The purpose of this chapter is therefore to analyse the optimal weighting for gold not only with regards to the market portfolio, but also to determine the optimal gold ratio in diversified stock portfolios among several firm characteristics.[1] We focus on the risk-return relationship proposed by prominent asset pricing models to reveal implications of adding gold to equity portfolios. The remainder of this study is organised as followed. Section 2 provides a review of the related literature. Section 3 describes the data and variables used in this study. Section 4 presents the main results, whereas Section 5 presents concluding remarks.

2. Literature Review

Ratner and Klein (2008) compared the performance of investments in gold and US-equities for the sample period 1975–2005 and conclude that stock portfolios outperform the gold investment by an average premium of 4.6% p.a. Similar results are obtained by Conover *et al.* (2009) and Coudert and Raymond-Feingold (2011). Their overall results document that real returns on gold investments are on

[1]We use the term *German Investor* as mentioned in the title of this study for any person who exclusively invests in stocks on the German capital market and does not hold any other international assets.

average 3.2%, which is significantly left less compared to the average 8.3% p.a. on US equities. In addition, the annual volatility of gold investments is also 4.2 percentage points higher, which is an undesirable outcome for investors who aim to maximise the Sharpe ratio of their investments.

Focusing not only on the risk-return properties of pure equity or gold investments but rather on the combination of both asset classes, Jaffe (1989), Chua *et al.* (1990) and McCown and Zimmerman (2006) find a very low correlation between the according returns and a negligible exposure towards market risk. This is also documented in Baur and Lucey (2010) and Sumner *et al.* (2010) who analysed volatility spillovers between stocks and gold and find no channel of equity drawdowns in times of financial crisis to impact the return of gold. Although gold is considered an undesirable asset when held alone, adding gold to stock portfolios increases the risk-adjusted portfolio return. The main driver of enhanced risk-return measures is the reduction of the overall portfolio volatility when gold is added to stock portfolios as shown in Emmrich and McGroarty (2013). This raises the question of the optimal weighting of gold. Based on traditional optimisation asset allocation methods, Jaffe (1989) and Lucey *et al.* (2006) suggest a weight of 4%–10% for gold. Taking into account the positive skewness of gold returns, the optimal weight may be reduced to 2%–4%. Increasing the gold weighting up to 36% is recommended in Estrada (2016) if the original portfolio consists of 60% stocks and 40% bonds. Faced with the allocation of stocks, bonds and gold, Lucey *et al.* (2019) find that investors with a target Sharpe ratio of one and a fixed bond weight of 50% are indifferent in holding up to 30% gold or no gold at all. Active portfolio management decisions on the target weight of gold are seriously affected by choosing an appropriate weight, as there is no clear consensus on the optimal target weight. This ideal weight further depends on the investment horizon. Whereas gold contributes an equal amount of risk to the portfolio return for short term investing, its risk contribution significantly reduces with an increasing investment horizon. Investors who try to achieve a certain exposure to gold investments face a broad choice of related funds. Jensen *et al.* (2018) document that synthetic ETFs underperform bullion ETFs and that risk-return characteristics as well as the tracking error differs significantly among these gold-based funds.

For the German capital market, Baur and McDermott (2010) find that gold is both a hedge and a safe haven for stocks.[2] Michis (2014) shows that the risk-reduction of gold investments is prevalent in long-run investment horizons. Up to a holding period of four month, the risk contribution of gold is similar to stocks. To the best of our knowledge, academic studies on the optimal gold ratio when holding stocks and portfolios different than the market portfolio for the German capital market are non-existent. Most often, the widely suggested gold ratio between 5% and 10% is based on generalised propositions made by popular finance magazines or investment practitioners.[3] The most related study to our analysis is Belousova and Dorfleitner (2012), who also investigate both the diversification and return contribution of several commodities to equity indices. From the perspective of a euro investor, they find that precious metals have strong diversification properties while simultaneously enhancing the overall portfolio return. Further, energy and precious metals have the highest Sharpe ratio among the commodity sectors.

3. Data and Variables

We study the German equity market by collecting monthly total return data on common stocks from Thomson Reuters Datastream and firm-level accounting data from Worldscope. The sample period is from July 1990 to September 2020, but for the construction of some variables accounting data going back to 1988 is required. All data are denominated in euro. We apply the name filters proposed by Campbell *et al.* (2010) to exclude securities that are not ordinary share issues like ADRs, funds, preferred stocks or warrants. To ensure high data quality, we further conduct the recommended screens proposed by Ince and Porter (2006). More specifically, a company is required to be located in Germany and only primary quotations of stocks are considered. Any return observation above 300% that is

[2]Based on Baur and Lucey (2010), the designation hedge (safe haven) stands for the property of gold having a near-zero or negative correlation with another assets on average (in periods of extreme market turmoils).

[3]See, e.g., Platt (2019); Wolf (2020) or Hinkel (2019).

reversed within one month or a single return observation above 990% is excluded.[4]

To ensure that results are not influenced by tiny or illiquid stocks, we follow Ang *et al.* (2009) and exclude any firm-level data where the firms market capitalisation is among the smallest 5% of market equity at each portfolio formation date. To further mitigate the influence of outliers, we winsorise all firm-level variables besides market capitalisation and return data at the 1% and 99% levels. Firms are required to have a non-negative book value of equity as in Fama and French (1992).[5]

According to Fama and French (1992, 1993), we match any accounting information for the fiscal year end in the previous calendar year with stock returns from July of the current year to June of the subsequent year. Banks and financial firms having a SIC code within the range 6,000 to 6,799 are excluded from our sample. We use the Fibor rate (until the end of 1998) and the 3-month Euribor rate (from the beginning of 1999) as the riskless rate of interest (RF). The gold return in euro is based on the according spot price (PM fixing) provided by the London bullion market.

The variable SIZE denotes firm size in millions, measured as stock price multiplied by the number of shares outstanding as of June of each year. Book-to-market ratio (BM) is the ratio of book equity for the fiscal year ending in the previous year to market equity at the end of December the previous year. Operating profitability (OP) is revenues minus cost of goods sold and interest expense, all divided by book equity.[6] Investment (INV) is the annual change in total assets divided by lagged total assets. Momentum (MOM) is the cumulative prior 12-month stock return, skipping the most recent month (see Jegadeesh and Titman (1993)).

---

[4]If R_t or R_{t-1} is greater than 300% and $(1 + R_{t-1})(1 + R_t) - 1 < 50\%$, both R_{t-1} and R_t are omitted.

[5]Over the sample period, there are 724 firm-year observations with negative book-values of equity. Their median firm size is just 4.77 million euro.

[6]We do not include selling, general, and administrative expenses, as this item is not broadly available among German firms. The return predictability of operating profitability as documented in Novy-Marx (2013) or Fama and French (2015) is, however, not affected by this adjustment.

Table 1. Descriptive statistics, July 1990-September 2020.

Variable	Mean	SD	25th	Median	75th
SIZE	1,432.67	5,998.52	32.41	106.92	444.13
BM	0.70	0.61	0.32	0.55	0.88
OP	1.18	1.60	0.43	0.81	1.36
INV	0.14	0.46	−0.04	0.04	0.16
MOM	0.08	0.39	−0.15	0.03	0.24
MKT-RF	0.43	5.08	−2.37	0.79	3.55
GOLD-RF	0.36	4.48	−2.44	−0.07	2.66
RF	0.23	0.22	0.02	0.22	0.36

Table 1 reports summary statistics for our sample period. We observe a total of 14,853 firm-year observations with an average of 479 firms per year. A typical firm in the German stock market has a size of 1,432.67 million euro in terms of market capitalization, an average book-to-market ratio of 0.70 and a growth rate of 14% regarding total assets. The past 12-month return is on average 8%.

In addition to firm characteristics, Table 1 shows the excess return of a value-weighted market portfolio based on all German firms in our sample. On average, the equity risk-premium is 0.43% p.m. with a standard deviation of 5.08%. In comparison, the monthly excess return of gold is 0.36% while the volatility is less than the volatility of the market-portfolio. In effect, the annualised Sharpe ratio (see Sharpe (1966)) of gold (0.28) is similar to the Sharpe ratio of the market portfolio (0.29) over the total sample period.

4. Results

To examine the optimal gold weight for diversified portfolios which tilt away from the market portfolio, we begin our analysis by sorting stocks based on several firm-characteristics. At the end of each June, we allocate stocks into three groups based on BM, operating profitability and investment. The allocation for our momentum portfolio is updated at the end of each month. Independently, each stock is additionally grouped into three portfolios based on firm size. The breakpoints separating each subportfolio are accordingly 30% and 70% percentiles.

Table 2. Monthly subportfolio excess returns.

	Excess ret. (size)			t-stat (size)		
	Small	Medium	Big	Small	Medium	Big
Panel A: Size-B/M portfolios						
Low	0.14	0.05	0.27	0.42	0.17	0.86
Medium	0.13	0.36	0.46	0.49	1.30	1.60
High	0.23	0.44	0.74	0.72	1.30	2.20
Panel B: Size-OP portfolios						
Low	−0.04	0.03	0.06	−0.11	0.09	0.18
Medium	0.17	0.41	0.55	0.64	1.50	1.90
High	0.38	0.42	0.53	1.20	1.30	1.70
Panel C: Size-INV portfolios						
Low	0.12	0.30	0.55	0.36	0.92	1.70
Medium	0.24	0.50	0.58	0.95	1.90	1.90
High	−0.06	0.02	0.07	−0.19	0.06	0.22
Panel D: Size-MOM portfolios						
Low	−0.22	−1.10	−0.11	−0.51	−2.50	−0.26
Medium	0.22	−0.01	0.26	0.83	−0.05	0.86
High	0.40	0.87	0.64	1.40	3.20	2.10

Notes: This table reports average monthly value-weighted excess returns of portfolios sorted independently on size and selected firm-characteristics. The according t-statistics are based on Newey and West (1987) adjusted standard errors using a lag of six.

Table 2 shows average monthly value-weighted returns in excess of the riskless rate of interest for the intersection of all portfolios.[7] Across all Panels, we notice an inversion of the size-effect documented in Banz (1981) and Fama and French (1992). Different from US studies, German firms with higher market capitalisation outperform small stocks in general. This is surprising as the finding that small firms tend to outperform big firms in North America is weak for the period from 1990 to 2015 and not existent in the aggregated European market (see Fama and French (2017)).

Panel A refers to the value-effect documented in Stattman (1980) and Rosenberg *et al.* (1985). We observe an average monthly

[7]Brückner *et al.* (2015) give an extensive overview on German anomaly portfolio returns and related studies.

value-premium of 0.30% for small stocks and 1.34% for big stocks. Big firms with a high BM ratio have an average monthly excess return of 0.74% which is statistically significant at the 5% level. While the reported results are in line with similar studies (Brückner *et al.*, 2015; Hanauer *et al.*, 2013), the value premium seems to decline in recent times. In Panel B, we see portfolios sorted on operating profitability and firm size. We notice that high profitable firms outperform low profitable firms in general. Compared to the market excess return of 0.43% p.m., we find that the return difference is mainly driven by an underperformance of stocks having a low operating profitability. While Dirkx and Peter (2020) find no clear relationship between investment and average excess returns, we observe higher excess returns for low investing (conservative) firms. Within big stocks, the corresponding hedge return is 0.48% p.m. and statistically significantly distinguishable from zero. Panel D shows results for portfolios sorted on past 12 month returns (skipping the most recent month) and firm size. The return difference between high and low momentum portfolios on average is a large 1.13% p.m. and thus both economically and statistically significant. The strong dominance of the momentum anomaly in Germany is similar as reported in Schmidt *et al.* (2014).

4.1. *Gold and the market portfolio*

We begin our analysis on the optimal gold ratio with the value-weighted German market portfolio as our main investment.

Figure 1 visualises the market portfolio and gold excess returns as cumulative indices starting with an initial value of 1 euro at the end of June 1990.[8] Until September 2020, the initial investment would be worth 2.99 euro for the market portfolio and 2.61 euro for the gold investment. We clearly notice that gold tends to underperform until mid of 2005. During times of the financial and European debt crisis between 2009 and 2013, gold significantly outperformes

[8]Starting in June 1990, our sample covers the Gulf War beginning in August 1990. The market portfolio lost a total of 14.60% (16.34%) on August (September) that year. Ending in September 2020 covers the COVID-19 related market turbulence in spring 2020. Excluding these events from our sample period does not affect our main findings in this study.

Fig. 1. Cumulative returns in excess of the risk-free interest rate on an initial 1 euro investment in the German market portfolio and gold.

the market portfolio. A similar behavior can be noticed during the COVID-19 pandemic and the related market turmoils in spring 2020. While the stock market had a total return of −24.19% in the first quarter of 2020, gold increased its valuation by 8.47%. The overall correlation between gold and the market portfolio return is a negligible −0.03. This obvious contrary development of equity and gold investments enables potential diversification possibilities to improve risk-return metrics.

In Figure 2, we evaluate risk- and performance key figures for all combinations of holding the market portfolio and gold. While the monthly excess portfolio return shown in the upper left panel varies between 0.43% and 0.36%, panel SD reflects the according volatility. The global minimum variance portfolio invests 56.02% into gold and the remaining 43.98% into the market portfolio. As their correspondings correlation is near zero, the portfolio offering the highest annualised Sharpe ratio of 0.41 has a similar optimal gold ratio of 51.92%. Adding gold to the market portfolio has tremendous improvements for portfolio risk metrics. Even held alone, the gold investment has a lower value at risk (VAR 6.14%), conditional value at risk (CVaR 8.81%) and expected loss (EL 2.97%) compared to the market portfolio (VaR 8.22%, CVaR 12.13%, EL 4.01%). Minimising the value

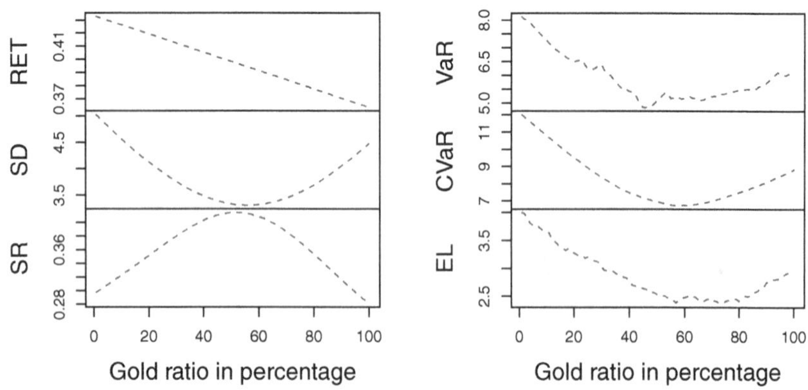

Fig. 2. Risk-return properties of market portfolio and gold investments for various gold weights. We evaluate the monthly expected excess return (RET), the monthly return volatility (SD), the annualised Sharpe Ratio (SR), the value at risk (VaR), the conditional value at risk (CVaR) and the expected loss (EL). All variables besides the Sharpe ratio are stated in percentage.

at risk (conditional value at risk), one should hold 46.47% (58.41%) gold to supplement broad equity investments.

4.2. *Gold and firm-characteristic sorted portfolios*

For our analysis on the optimal gold ratio when holding the firm-characteristic sorted portfolios presented in Table 2, we focus on maximising the Sharpe ratio of the combined gold/stock portfolio. We derive this optimisation criteria based on our results in Section 4.1, where the Sharpe ratio maximising gold ratio for the market portfolio is very similar to the ratio also optimising key risk figures. As short-selling is typically restricted or highly regulated in Germany, we constraint our optimization on long-only investment possibilities. Table 3 reports the optimal weight for gold among the intersection of sorted stock portfolios as well as the according annualised Sharpe Ratio and the average monthly excess returns.

The manifold results are easily summarised. We find an average minimum (maximum) gold ratio of 38.87% (81.09%) among all available subportfolios. This result is somewhat counterintuitive, as Jaffe (1989) and Lucey *et al.* (2006) suggest an optimal weight of 4%–10% for gold. However, long-run studies for the US-market typically include the decade of the 1980s, where gold performed relatively

Table 3. Sharpe ratio maximising gold ratio.

	Gold ratio in % (size)			Annualised Sharpe Ratio (size)			Mean excess return (size)		
	Small	Medium	Big	Small	Medium	Big	Small	Medium	Big
Panel A: Size-B/M portfolios									
Low	69.41	70.23	63.42	0.52	0.51	0.56	0.29	0.27	0.33*
Medium	54.65	45.83	54.62	0.57	0.68	0.66	0.26	0.36*	0.41**
High	54.10	48.56	53.08	0.59	0.70	0.75	0.30	0.40*	0.54***
Panel B: Size-OP portfolios									
Low	75.30	74.46	73.44	0.49	0.50	0.51	0.27	0.28	0.28
Medium	53.44	43.77	53.24	0.58	0.72	0.70	0.28	0.39**	0.45**
High	48.41	48.07	54.18	0.48	0.69	0.67	0.37*	0.39**	0.44**
Panel C: Size-INV portfolios									
Low	63.13	55.70	54.27	0.53	0.61	0.70	0.27	0.33*	0.45**
Medium	46.37	36.62	51.59	0.66	0.82	0.71	0.30*	0.45**	0.47**
High	78.83	74.64	75.44	0.48	0.50	0.50	0.27	0.28	0.29
Panel D: Size-MOM portfolios									
Low	95.85	100.00	90.51	0.46	0.46	0.47	0.34	0.36*	0.32
Medium	48.62	65.45	62.90	0.62	0.51	0.58	0.29*	0.23	0.32*
High	48.81	29.24	51.57	0.67	1.06	0.72	0.38**	0.73***	0.50***

Notes: Asterisks ***, **,* show significance at the 1,5,10% level, based on Newey and West (1987) adjusted standard errors using a lag of six. We impose short selling constraints which is not allowed in maximising the Sharpe ratio.

poorly compared to the US-stock market. As Figure 1 highlights, gold also performed poor up to the year 2005, so the risk reducing hedge property of gold proposed here may be a novel manifestation of the last decade. Besides the risk reducing aspect of adding gold to the present portfolios, we additionally notice a positive return contribution when including gold in the overall investment. Each subportfolio having the lowest return is typically suggested to be held with the maximum gold ratio. The return of small and low profitable stocks is on average −0.04%, but when held in combination with a total of 75.30% gold, the return rises to 0.27%. In contrast, subportfolios which already offer investors higher returns on their own, e.g., the portfolio consisting of big, value stocks (0.74%) or big, low-investing stocks (0.55%), exhibit lower mean excess returns when gold is added. While the lower average returns for these portfolios are clearly obvious (the return difference for big, value stocks with or without the ideal gold ratio is 0.20%), it is the optimal weight increasing the Sharpe ratio from an initial 0.43 to the maximum 0.75.

Panel D in Table 3 provides evidence for the hedge properties of gold when holding diversified portfolios. The portfolio of low momentum stocks has an average excess return of −0.48%, but holding a gold ratio between 90.51% and 100.00% yields an average excess return of 0.32% while simultaneously enhancing the average Sharpe ratio to 0.46. On the other hand, holding portfolios of high momentum stocks gains an average excess return of 0.64%, but still an average gold ratio of 43.21% is suggested to be held to maximize the Sharpe ratio. This high gold ratio for already well-performing stock portfolios is a rather surprising outcome, but the average Sharpe ratio of 0.82 of high momentum portfolios with additional gold holdings significantly outperforms the standalone market portfolio which has a Sharpe ratio of just 0.29.

4.3. *Gold and buy-and-hold portfolios*

To test the robustness of our results above, we conduct a historical simulation based on realistic and practical considerations. At the end of each month, we randomly select 30 stocks having a market capitalisation greater than the according cross-sectional 70% percentile of all stocks available in this month. As a result, we get diversified portfolios of highly liquid stocks with a minimum market capitalisation of

307.30 million euro on average. This ensures that most of all stocks will be included in the prominent indices DAX, MDAX or SDAX. We replicate the monthly random stock selection 30 times for each month and report the average mean excess returns. This procedure results in a total of 10.560 randomly compound portfolios each with 30 stocks.

As the results for the optimal gold ratio for both holding the market portfolio or firm-characteristic sorted portfolios are roughly within the range of 40%–80%, we form an equal-weighted portfolio of holding the randomly selected stocks and gold at the beginning of our investment period. The stock portfolio on its own is value-weighted in subsequent periods. We hold the combined stock/gold portfolio up to three years without readjusting the asset weights to the initially equal weighting. In addition to our total sample period from 1990/06–2020/09, we additionally examine two subperiods of equal length.

As gold investments like the highly liquid Xetra-gold are accompanied by monthly fees, we subtract the according costs of 0.025% per month from our portfolio return. We explicitly include taxes an capital gains as follows. First, at the end of the holding period, we check if the stock portfolio gained a positive total return. If so, we consider a tax rate of 26.375% on these capital gains,[9] but for practical purposes, tax-deductible loss compensations are not considered. Second, Xetra-gold is seen as an equivalent to physical gold bars which can be sold tax free after a holding period of 12 month. Thus, we do not need to consider taxes on our gold investment, as the minimum holding period is exactly one year.

To make results comparable, Table 4 separately reports our findings for the buy-and-hold portfolio with initially equal-weighting gold and 30 value-weighted randomly selected stocks (Panel B) and for the same equity portfolio without holding any gold (Panel A). We notice that for the total sample period, the combined equity/stock buy-and-hold portfolios gain an average after-tax excess return of 0.27%–0.34%. Over the total sample period, the excess-returns and

[9]Since 2009, fiscal authorities levy a final tax of 25% plus an additional 5.5% solidarity surcharge which adds up to 26.375% (neglecting potential church taxes). We consider this taxation procedure for our whole sample period.

Table 4. Buy-and-hold portfolios with initially equal-weighting gold and 30 value-weighted, randomly selected stocks.

	Mean excess return (year)			t-stat (year)			Ann. Sharpe Ratio (year)		
	1	2	3	1	2	3	1	2	3
Panel A: Stand-alone equity buy-and-hold portfolio									
1990/06-2020/09	0.20	0.27	0.33	1.08	2.00	3.33	0.32	0.31	0.32
1990/06-2004/12	0.13	0.24	0.36	0.51	1.24	2.29	0.22	0.27	0.35
2005/01-2020/09	0.26	0.29	0.30	1.03	1.63	2.62	0.43	0.35	0.28
Panel B: 50%/50% equity/gold combined buy-and-hold portfolio									
1990/06–2020/09	0.27	0.30	0.34	2.23	3.57	5.17	0.32	0.34	0.36
1990/06–2004/12	−0.01	0.10	0.20	−0.08	0.85	2.08	−0.01	0.13	0.23
2005/01-2020/09	0.55	0.51	0.50	3.57	4.99	6.88	0.65	0.56	0.51

Note: The t-statistics are based on Newey and West (1987) adjusted standard errors using a lag of six.

according Sharpe ratios are quite similar to the stand-alone equity portfolio. However, our results confirm the findings of Michis (2014), that the risk reducing property of gold investments depends on the investment horizon. While the Sharpe ratios of our portfolios with and without gold are identical for a 1-year investment horizon, their difference is 0.04 for a three-year holding period. This is an interest finding, because in Section 4.2 we document not only a risk reduction when adding gold to stock portfolios, but also a positive return contribution. This positive return contribution thus is only prevalent when holding specific style portfolios (sorted on firm-characteristics). When holding stocks without a certain investment preference, the positive return contribution vanishes while the portfolio risk reduction still remains.

The first sub-period from 1990/06 to 2004/12 implies an obvious underperformance when equally holding gold and stocks without readjusting the weights over time. As Figure 1 shows, this result is driven by the underperformance of gold until mid of 2005. Our results indicate that at least the market turmoils of the financial and European debt crisis in 2009 started a tremendous shift towards perceiving gold as a desirable investment if the euro as currency fails.[10] During the most recent subperiod beginning in January 2005, our buy-and-hold portfolio excess return is 0.55% (0.50%) for a holding period of 1 year (3 years). The finding that gold has similar risk-return properties as stocks explains the decreasing return for longer holding periods because of the lack of readjusting the initial weights. Most remarkable is the finding that the Sharpe ratios of the equity/gold portfolios significantly exceed the Sharpe ratios of the pure equity portfolios. This is also true for the overall market portfolio, which has a Sharpe ratio of 0.48 for that subperiod when being held for one year. Our buy-and-hold strategy confirms our aforementioned results, that a significantly higher gold ratio than the typically suggested 5%–10% is optimal under various conditions and investment preferences, especially for the last decade. In similar buy-and-hold analysis for the period 1976 to 2004, Hillier *et al.* (2006) also find that the optimal initial weight for gold is as high as approximately 30%.

---

[10]In May 2012, the financial and political crisis in Greece led to strong speculations of that the country would leave the eurozone shortly (Ross, 2012).

5. Conclusions

In this chapter, we analyse the optimal gold ratio when holding diversified portfolios of German stocks over the sample period from July 1990 to September 2020.

First, we notice that gold has similar risk-return properties as stocks while having a near zero return correlation with the market excess return. The Sharpe ratio maximising gold ratio for the market portfolio under short-selling constraints is 51.92%. The minimum variance portfolio invests 56.02% in gold, whereas the value at risk minimising portfolio holds 46.47% gold. These results are in strong contrast to prior US evidence, suggesting a much smaller gold ratio of 5%–10%.

Second, analysing portfolios sorted on market capitalisation and various firm-characteristics (BM ratio, operating profitability, investment and momentum), we find that the optimal gold ratio varies on average between 38.87% and 81.09%. Despite the risk-reducing hedge property of gold, we also find evidence of simultaneously positive return contributions. If the initial equity portfolio has low (high) expected returns, investors profit twofold of lower volatility and higher return when holding more (less) than the average suggested gold ratio of 59.98% for these portfolios.

Third, our buy-and-hold analysis shows that the positive risk-return effects of such high gold ratios are mainly a modern effect since the financial and European debt crisis. Starting in 2005, our buy-and-hold strategy of equally weighting gold and a portfolio of randomly selected stocks mainly listed in the most prominent indices DAX, MDAX and SDAX significantly outperforms the market portfolio even when taxes on capital gains are considered. The average after-tax excess return (Sharpe ratio) of our buy-and-hold combined gold/stock portfolio is a remarkable 0.52% p.m (0.57) and drops to 0.28% p.m. (0.35) when gold is not added to the equity portfolio.

Our analysis contradicts the widely suggested advice for asset management practitioners of allocating between 5% and 10% into gold investments. As a practical implication for investors in the German stock market, we suggest them to significantly increase gold holdings. A word of caution is warranted that investing half of the investors' wealth in gold is in contrast to a well-diversified asset allocation. We address this concern as follows. First, our firm-characteristic sorted portfolios comprise on average 409 stocks and are well diversified on their own. Exchange traded funds which replicate the aforementioned risk-factor portfolios offer a low-cost protection against idiosyncratic risks and potential defaults of single stocks. Second, diversification is no guarantee against huge losses as occurred during the market turmoils of the Dot-com crises (2000), financial crisis (2007) or COVID-19 crisis (2020). According to these extreme events, Smith and Timmermann (2021) provide evidence that they mark structural breaks in the time-series of equities and strongly affect future expected stock returns. Gold as an alternative asset class does not suffer from these structural regime shifts and even significantly outperforms equities in these times, so overall, a large gold ratio should not be a huge surprise. Third, our analysis does not account for the individual risk-preference of a certain investor or distinct groups of investors. Using the framework presented in Fama and French (2007), disagreement and tastes for different assets like stocks or gold may persuade investors to choose a gold ratio as high as 42%–75%, which our statistical analysis suggests as the optimal choice for the average investor on the German capital market.

An in-depth analysis of the optimal gold ratio when investors face other asset classes like corporate bonds or real estate is beyond the scope of this chapter but seems to be an interesting focus for future research.

References

Ang, A. Hodrick, R.J. Xing, Y. and Zhang, X. (2009). High idiosyncratic volatility and low returns: International and further U.S. evidence, *Journal of Financial Economics* **91**(1), 1–23.

Banz, R. (1981). The relationship between return and market value of common stock, *Journal of Financial Economics* **9**(1), 3–18.

Baur, D.G. and Lucey, B.M. (2010). Is gold a hedge or a safe haven? an analysis of stocks, bonds and gold, *Financial Review* **45**(2), 217–229.

Baur, D.G. and McDermott, T.K. (2010). Is gold a safe haven? international evidence, *Journal of Banking & Finance* **34**(8), 1886–1898.

Belousova, J. and Dorfleitner, G. (2012). On the diversification benefits of commodities from the perspective of euro investors, *Journal of Banking & Finance* **36**(9), 2455–2472.

Brückner, R. Lehmann, P. Schmidt, M.H. and Stehle, R. (2015). Non-u.s. multi-factor data sets should be used with caution. *Working Paper.*

Campbell, C.J. Cowan, A.R. and Salotti, V. (2010). Multi-country event-study methods, *Journal of Banking & Finance* **34**(12), 3078–3090.

Chua, J.H. Sick, G. and Woodward, R.S. (1990). Diversifying with gold stocks, *Financial Analysts Journal* **46**(4), 76–79.

Conover, C.M. Jensen, G.R. Johnson, R.V. and Mercer, J.M. (2009). Can precious metals make your portfolio shine? *The Journal of Investing* **18**(1), 75–86.

Coudert, V. and Raymond-Feingold, H. (2011). Gold and financial assets: are there any safe havens in bear markets, *Economics Bulletin* **31**(2), 1613–1622.

Dirkx, P. and Peter, F.J. (2020). The fama-french five-factor model plus momentum: Evidence for the german market, *Schmalenbach Business Review*, **72**, 661–684.

Emmrich, O. and McGroarty, F. (2013). Should gold be included in institutional investment portfolios? *Applied Financial Economics* **23**(19), 1553–1565.

Estrada, J. (2016). Alternatives: How? how much? why? *Journal of Wealth Management* **19**(3), 49–61.

Fama, E. and French, K. (1992). The cross-section of expected stock returns, *The Journal of Finance* **47**(2), 427–465.

Fama, E. and French, K. (1993). Common risk factors in the returns on stocks and bonds, *Journal of Financial Economics* **33**(1), 3–56.

Fama, E. and French, K. (2007). Disagreement, tastes, and asset prices, *Journal of Financial Economics* **83**(3), 667–689.

Fama, E. and French, K. (2015). A five-factor asset pricing model, *Journal of Financial Economics* **116**(1), 1–22.

Fama, E. and French, K. (2017). International tests of a five-factor asset pricing model, *Journal of Financial Economics* **123**(3), 441–463.

Hanauer, M., Kaserer, C. and Rapp, M.S. (2013). Risikofaktoren und multifaktormodelle für den deutschen aktienmarkt, *Betriebswirtschaftliche Forschung & Praxis* **65**(5), 469–492.

Hillier, D., Draper, P. and Faff, R. (2006). Do precious metals shine? an investment perspective, *Financial Analysts Journal* **62**(2), 98–106.

Hinkel, A. (2019). Sollten anleger ihren anleihe-anteil im depot zugunsten von gold verringern? *XETRA-Gold News*. Available at: https://www.xetra-gold.com/gold-news/news/sollten-anleger-ihren-anleihe-anteil-im-depot-zugunsten-von-gold-verringern/.

Ince, O.S. and Porter, R.B. (2006). Individual equity return data from thomson reuters datastream: Handle with care! *Journal of Financial Research* **29**(4), 463–479.

Jaffe, J.F. (1989). Gold and gold stocks as investments for institutional portfolios, *Financial Analysts Journal* **45**(2), 53–59.

Jegadeesh, T. and Titman, S. (1993). Returns to buying winners and selling losers: Implications for stock market efficiency, *The Journal of Finance* **48**(1), 65–91.

Jensen, G.R., Johnson, R.R. and Washer, K.M. (2018). All that's gold does not glitter, *Financial Analysts Journal* **74**(1), 59–76.

Lucey, B.M., Poti, V. and Tully, E. (2006). International portfolio formation, skewness and the role of gold, *Frontiers in Finance and Economics* **3**(1), 49–68.

Lucey, B.M., Peat, M., Sevic, A. and Vigne, S. (2019). What is the optimal weight for gold in a portfolio? *Annals of Operations Research.*

McCown, J.R. and Zimmerman, J.R. (2006). Is gold a zero-beta asset? analysis of the investment potential of precious metals.

Michis, A.A. (2014). Investing in gold: Individual asset risk in the long run, *Finance Research Letters* **11**(4), 369–374.

Newey, W. and West, K. (1987). A simple, positive semi-definite, heteroskedasticity and autocorrelation consistent covariance matrix, *Econometrica* **55**(3), 703–708.

Novy-Marx, R. (2013). The other side of value: The gross profitability premium, *Journal of Financial Economics* **108**(1), 1–28.

Platt, C. (2019). Gold: Warum das edelmetall jetzt ins depot gehört. Börse Online. Available at: https://www.boerse-online.de/nachrichten/rohstoffe/gold-warum-das-edelmetall-jetzt-ins-depot-gehoert-1027865259.

Ratner, M. and Klein, S. (2008). The portfolio implications of gold investment, *The Journal of Investing* **17**(1), 77–87.

Rosenberg, B., Reid, K. and Lanstein, R. (1985). Persuasive evidence of market inefficiency, *Journal of Portfolio Management* **11**(3), 9–17.

Ross, A. (2012). Grexit and the euro: an exercise in guesswork. *Financial Times.* Available at: https://www.ft.com/content/9719aced-b9dc-34a7-a85d-95b53cdbeda2.

Schmidt, P.S., Schrimpf, A., von Arx, U., Wagner, A.F. and Ziegler, A. (2014). On the construction of common size, value and momentum factors in international stock markets: A guide with applications. Swiss Finance Institute Research Paper, No. 10–58.

Sharpe, W.F. (1966). Mutual fund performance. *The Journal of Business* **39**, 119–138.

Smith, S.C. and Timmermann, A. (2021). Break risk, *The Review of Financial Studies* **34**, 2045–2100.

Stattman, D. (1980). Book values and stock returns, *The Chicago MBA: A Journal of Selected Papers.* **4**, 25–45.

Sumner, S., Johnson, R. and Soenen, L. (2010). Spillover effects among gold, stocks, and bonds, *Journal of Centrum Cathedra* **3**(2), 106–120.

Wolf, B. (2020). Flossbach setzt auf liquide sachwerte: Assetmanager erhöht goldanteil auf 20 prozent — kritik an etf. *Börsen-Zeitung.* Available at: https://m.boersen-zeitung.de/artikel/2020-05-16/2020094005/flossbach-setzt-auf-liquide-sachwerte.

https://doi.org/10.1142/9781800611917_0020

Chapter 20

Dynamic Correlation of Precious Metals and Equity Markets: A Mixed Data Sampling Approach

Tony Klein* **and Thomas Walther**†,‡

Queen's University Belfast, Queen's Management School, United Kingdom

† *Utrecht University, Utrecht School of Economics, The Netherlands*
Technische Universität Dresden, Faculty of Business and Economics, Germany

‡ *t.walther@uu.nl*

We re-examine the conditional volatility and dynamic correlation of precious metals and equity markets of developed countries by employing mixed data sampling. We find that Gold and Silver serve as short-term safe-haven with decreasing correlation towards zero during equity market recessions. A similar behaviour, albeit not as pronounced, is found for Platinum and Palladium. During normal market periods, Gold might be characterised as a hedge, while the other precious metals show features of a diversifier.

1. Introduction

Precious metals, such as Gold and Silver, are perceived as a *safe* investment with little volatility, especially in times of crises and turmoil in financial markets. For more than a century, physical Gold has been used as an investment vehicle — in different forms — to protect from inflation, market downturns, and prolonged periods of economic uncertainty. However, the recent decades have tellingly shown that this simple relationship — Gold protects against crises — can neither be simplified nor generalised and a much more particularised approach is necessary. In this vein, we review how prices and volatility of precious metals develop in comparison to financial markets in terms of correlation and connectedness. We aim to further extend the discussion of the safe-haven status of Gold and the behaviour of other precious metals and surrogate safe-haven investments.

A safe-haven investment is considered to be able to protect from portfolio losses by offsetting these losses with price increases; showing a negative correlation with general market movements. This is related to the so-called *flight-to-quality* phenomenon, in particular during highly volatile market phases as documented in Hammoudeh *et al.* (2010), where investors focus on such assets while liquidating other positions. However, this hedging capacity is only of temporary nature to further differentiate from a classical hedging allocation. In their seminal work, Baur and McDermott (2010) classify assets in view of correlation behaviour and bin assets in three distinctively different categories. The classical definition of a hedge is given "as an asset that is uncorrelated or negatively correlated with another asset or portfolio *on average*" (Baur and McDermott, 2010, p. 219). A safe-haven asset differs in a sense that only during market downturns this hedging potential is observed; that is, correlations between this asset and a market turn negative or move towards zero. A safe-haven asset could otherwise be positively correlated in *normal* market phases, which is the definition of a diversifier (Baur and McDermott, 2010). As such, we find a safe-haven asset to be a mixture of hedge and diversifier in which the hedging capacity is observed in downward markets only.

Seeking to identify flight-to-quality and possible safe-haven properties of precious metals such as Gold, Silver, Platinum, and Palladium implies that market downturns are properly identified. We follow two different approaches in identifying times of financial distress. Firstly, and in accordance to replicating existing findings (Klein, 2017), we use ℓ_1-trends to identify phases of significant financial distress separately for each of the utilised indices: the US S&P 500, the German DAX30, and the British FTSE 100. These downturn phases are then used to distinguish between a possible diversifier or a safe-haven status of any of the four precious metals. Additionally, we are using NBER recession data to identify macroeconomic downturns on a greater scale and review the relationship between the four precious metals and financial markets during these times.

We re-examine the findings of Klein (2017) on the dynamic correlation between precious metals and developed markets but extend the modelling framework. From the short- to medium-term perspective in Klein (2017), we now focus on modelling an underlying long-term component in the correlation which is used to address the categorisation of assets on a generalised level. This extends the employed models by offering a more granular and detailed view on the persistence of volatility and correlation, which plays an essential role in the correlation models employed in Klein (2017). Using recent advancements of the widely-adapted Generalised Autoregressive Conditional Heteroskedasticity (GARCH) and Dynamic Conditional Correlation (DCC) models, we disentangle short- from long-term volatility and correlation, respectively. In particular, the Mixed Data Sampling (MIDAS) technique is used to model the long-term dynamics of both, volatility and correlation. This approach builds on the recently proposed model of Colacito *et al.* (2011). Nguyen and Walther (2020) employ GARCH-MIDAS to examine the volatility long-term drivers of various commodities including Gold and Silver. Walther *et al.* (2019) also use a GARCH-MIDAS framework to identify volatility drivers for cryptocurrencies in an out-of-sample setting. Dinh *et al.* (2021) investigate the volatility and correlation of the precious metal markets using GARCH-MIDAS and DCC-MIDAS. We build on these findings and combine the proposed augmentation of the DCC by Klein (2017) with a MIDAS component as in Dinh *et al.* (2021) to include long-term drivers of volatility and correlation.

The remainder of this chapter is organised as follows. Section 2 introduces the extension of the DCC with MIDAS components and addresses the estimation procedure. Section 3 offers some insight on the utilised data sets and futures series. The results of the volatility and correlation modelling are discussed in Section 4, including a review of the categorisation of precious metals. This chapter concludes in Section 5.

2. Methodology

In this study, we employ a two-step approach to estimate the correlation: (1) we model the assets' volatility on GARCH-MIDAS and (2) we use the residuals from the first step for DCC-MIDAS to model the correlation between two assets.

We model the individual asset's volatility with GARCH-MIDAS (Engle *et al.*, 2013) which disentangles the volatility into a short-term and a long-term component. While the short-term dynamics follow a standard GARCH model, the long-term component is driven by the past realised volatility of the asset itself. In contrast to the original GARCH models, the long-term variance is not constant but time-varying.

The asset's logarithmic returns are defined as $r_{t,m} = \log P_{t,m} - \log P_{t-1,m}$, where t refers to the day in month m. The return process is given as follows:

$$r_{t,m} = \mu + \sqrt{\tau_m g_{t,m}}\varepsilon_{t,m} \qquad \forall t = 1, \ldots, N_m, \tag{1}$$

where N_m is the number of trading days in month m and $\varepsilon_{t,m}|\Phi_{t-1,m} \sim$ Student-$t(0, 1, \nu)$ with $\Phi_{t-1,m}$ being the information set up to day $(t-1)$ of month m. The factors τ_m and $g_{t,m}$ are the long- and short-run variance components, respectively. According to Engle *et al.* (2013), $g_{t,m}$ follows a standard GARCH(1,1) model with unit variance:

$$g_{t,m} = (1-\alpha-\beta) + \alpha\frac{(r_{t-1,m}-\mu)^2}{\tau_m} + \beta g_{t-1,m}, \tag{2}$$

with non-negativity and stationary conditions $\alpha, \beta \geq 0$ and $\alpha + \beta < 1$. Alternatively, we employ the GJR variant (Glosten *et al.*, 1993) similar to Opschoor *et al.* (2014):

$$g_{t,m} = (1-\alpha-\beta) + \left(\alpha + \gamma I_{(r_{t-1,m}-\mu)<0}\right)\frac{(r_{t-1,m}-\mu)^2}{\tau_m} + \beta g_{t-1,m}, \tag{3}$$

where γ is the coefficient to measure the asymmetric response of the variance to past negative returns.

The long-term component τ_m is modelled using the MIDAS technique on the realised volatility RV_t:

$$\log(\tau_m) = \omega + \theta_V \sum_{k=1}^{K} \varphi_k(\omega_{V,1}, \omega_{V,2}) RV_{m-k}, \tag{4}$$

where θ_V is the coefficient for the influence of the past K monthly realised volatility observations and ω is a constant variance level.

We define $RV_m = \sqrt{\sum_{t=1}^{N_m} r_{t,m}^2}$. Following Ghysels *et al.* (2007), we use beta lag polynomials to weigh the past realised variance:

$$\varphi_k(\omega_{V,1}, \omega_{V,2}) = \frac{(k/K)^{\omega_{V,1}-1}(1-k/K)^{\omega_{V,2}-1}}{\sum_{j=1}^{K}(j/K)^{\omega_{V,1}-1}(1-j/K)^{\omega_{V,2}-1}}. \tag{5}$$

After modelling the individual asset returns and volatility, we employ the DCC-MIDAS model (Colacito *et al.*, 2011) which disentangles the dynamic correlation into a short-term and a long-term component in a similar fashion as the GARCH-MIDAS.

We denote C_t as the conditional covariance matrix of a pair of assets:

$$C_t = D_t \Omega_t D_t, \tag{6}$$

with D_t as the diagonal matrix with the asset's conditional volatility from Eq. (1) on the diagonal and Ω_t as the conditional correlation matrix of returns at time $(t-1)$ information:

$$\begin{aligned} \Omega_t &= E_{t-1}[\eta_t \eta_t'], \\ \eta_t &= D_t^{-1}(r_t - \mu), \end{aligned} \tag{7}$$

where η_t are the standardised residuals. Hence, $r_t = \mu + C_t^{1/2}\eta_t$ with $\eta_t \overset{\text{i.i.d.}}{\sim} \mathcal{N}(0, I_n)$.

The dynamic correlation is based on the quasi-correlation matrix Q_t:

$$\Omega_t = Diag(Q_t)^{-1/2} Q_t Diag(Q_t)^{-1/2}. \tag{8}$$

The elements of Q_t follow GARCH-like dynamics:

$$q_{ij,t} = \overline{\rho}_{ij,t}(1-a-b) + a\eta_{i,t-1}\eta_{j,t-1} + bq_{ij,t-1}, \tag{9}$$

where $\overline{\rho}_{ij,t}$ is the slowly moving long-term correlation between asset i and asset j, and $q_{ij,t}$ is the short-term correlation. Following Colacito *et al.* (2011) and Conrad *et al.* (2014), the long-term correlation is modelled using a Fisher-z transformation:

$$\overline{\rho}_{ij,t} = \frac{\exp(2z_{ij,t}) - 1}{\exp(2z_{ij,t}) + 1}, \tag{10}$$

where $z_{ij,t}$ is driven by the realised correlation between asset i and j:

$$z_{ij,t} = c + \theta_C \sum_{k=1}^{K} \varphi_k(\omega_C, 1) RC_{ij,t-k}, \tag{11}$$

where

$$RC_{ij,t} = \frac{\sum_{k=t-N_m}^{t} \eta_{i,k}\eta_{j,k}}{\sqrt{\sum_{k=t-N_m}^{t} \eta_{i,k}^2}\sqrt{\sum_{k=t-N_m}^{t} \eta_{j,k}^2}}. \tag{12}$$

Thus, the coefficient θ_C represents the impact of the realised correlation on the long-term correlation.

We follow Engle *et al.* (2013), Colacito *et al.* (2011), and Conrad *et al.* (2014) and estimate the parameters of the GARCH and DCC models using quasi-maximum-likelihood-estimation. We set $K = 36$ for GARCH-MIDAS and DCC-MIDAS.

3. Data

We obtain daily prices of the nearest futures of Gold, Silver, Palladium, and Platinum from January 3, 2000 to December 31, 2020. For comparability with results of Klein (2017), we utilise the same proxies for financial markets and use daily index points of the equity indices S&P500, DAX30, and the FTSE100.[1] This data period yields between $n_{\max} = 5\,472$ and $n_{\min} = 5\,266$ observations. Data series are synchronised after calculating idiosyncratic volatilities.

While all four metals are commonly seen as precious metals, a significant share of Palladium and Platinum demand originates from industrial applications of these metals, for example in the automotive industry. It has been shown that prices of Palladium and Platinum, especially futures prices, are prone to demand shocks due to a changing or rapidly deteriorating economic situation. We address this in detail when comparing correlations during equity downturns as well as NBER recessions.

[1]All data are obtained from Bloomberg.

Table 1. Downturns (S&P500) and NBER recessions during the estimation period.

Equity downturns	NBER recessions
16-10-2007–04-03-2009	01-01-2008–01-06-2009
06-05-2011–27-09-2011	
19-05-2015–04-02-2016	
17-09-2018–24-12-2018	
07-02-2020–20-03-2020	01-03-2020–01-05-2020

Table 1 provides an exemplary overview of significant downturns of the S&P500 and NBER recessions. In the estimation window, which is shorter due to the implemented lag structure of the MIDAS framework, we identify five sharp declines in equity markets and two NBER recessions. Both the first and the last equity downturns coincide with an NBER recession: the Global Financial Crises and the COVID-19 crisis. Three shorter periods of market turmoil are detected in the S&P500 that last between three and eight months but are not associated with an economic recession.

Summary statistics and preliminary analyses of all utilised data sets prior to synchronisation are given in Table 2. All return series are empirically of non-normal shape by featuring much heavier tails and pronounced asymmetry. Gold features the lowest standard deviation across all series. We find Silver returns to show the highest kurtosis of all precious metals which also reflects on the minimum and maximum returns recorded throughout the sample period. The skewness is negative across all series, albeit of lower magnitude for the financial indices compared to the selection of precious metals. This indicates that highly negative returns occur more often than their positive equivalent, which is a typical observation for financial time series.

Results of the preliminary analyses in Table 2, in particular on autocorrelation of returns and squared returns tested for with the Ljung-Box test, reveal that GARCH-type models are a viable choice to model idiosyncratic volatility of the return series. Additionally, we find a varying degree of persistence with the GPH test statistic of Geweke and Porter-Hudak (1983). This, in turn, implies that

Table 2. Preliminary statistics and tests of daily returns of precious metals and major indices from January 3, 2000 to December 31, 2020.

	Gold	Silver	Palladium	Platinum	S&P500	DAX30	FTSE100
Obs.	5472	5468	5396	5471	5284	5329	5266
Mean (%)	0.03	0.03	0.03	0.02	0.02	0.01	−0.00
St.Dev (%)	1.08	1.88	2.08	1.44	1.26	1.49	1.20
Min. (%)	−9.51	−20.39	−22.20	−13.64	−12.77	−13.05	−11.51
50%	0.04	0.08	0.08	0.03	0.06	0.08	0.04
Max. (%)	10.25	13.18	18.81	10.09	10.96	10.80	9.38
Skew.	−0.25	−1.22	−0.52	−0.61	−0.39	−0.16	−0.33
Kurt.	9.39	14.20	10.61	9.60	13.95	8.75	10.94
JB($\times 10^3$)	9.36*	29.85*	13.23*	10.25*	26.48*	7.35*	13.90*
ADF	−75.33*	−51.54*	−35.45*	−14.20*	−13.47*	−28.22*	−14.16*
LB Q(20)	25.23	25.06	57.73*	44.83*	177.09*	35.07*	86.66*
LB Q^2(20)	921.58*	1107.88*	1133.20*	2274.74*	7499.14*	3863.92*	4870.22*
GPH	0.46	0.31	0.29	0.38	0.31	0.50	0.37

Note: *Rejection of the null-hypothesis at the 1% level.

GARCH variants that cover prolonged persistence compared to the baseline GARCH are needed. These characteristics are in line with existing literature and well-documented. Klein (2017) employs a FIGARCH (Bollerslev and Mikkelsen, 1996) and FIAPARCH (Tse, 1998) to directly model this implied long memory. We choose a differing approach by using the MIDAS framework to cover long-range memory of the variance process as outlined in the previous section. A key finding of Klein (2017) is that asymmetric long-memory models dominate all other GARCH variants for the equity indices. This finding underlines the importance of including shock persistence and the asymmetric impact of positive and negative returns on volatility, where negative returns induce a higher subsequent volatility than positive returns of the same magnitude.

4. Results and Discussion

4.1. *Idiosyncratic volatility properties*

In a first step, idiosyncratic volatilites of precious metals returns as well as returns of the equity indices are estimated. We present the Bayesian Information Criterion (BIC) for all estimations in Table 3 and the coefficients for the best-fitting models in Table 4.

Table 3. BIC of the applied univariate models on unsynchronised return data of precious metals and indices from January 3, 2000 to December 31, 2020.

	Gold	Silver	Palladium	Platinum	S&P500	DAX30	FTSE100
GARCH [1]	13040	18025	**18285**	**15311**	11544	14073	11815
GJR [2]	**13031**	18011	18292	15317	11413	13949	11676
GARCH-MIDAS [3]	13063	18021	18294	15324	11557	14086	11816
GJR-MIDAS [4]	13054	**18008**	18302	15332	**11395**	**13934**	**11653**

Note: Bold font marks the respective model choice.

The findings are in line with what is expected in view of existing results (Arouri *et al.*, 2012; Chkili, 2016; Klein, 2017). We identify asymmetric properties for Gold as the GJR-GARCH outperforms all other models in terms of in-sample performance. Silver, on the other hand, shows signs of long memory and asymmetry, which is covered by the GJR-MIDAS framework. Both metals show a negative asymmetry parameter γ indicating that negative returns are followed by lower volatility. For Palladium and Platinum, neither long memory nor asymmetry is pronounced as the baseline GARCH is found to be best fitting. For all equity indices, we confirm that modelling asymmetry and long memory yields a superior fit. The asymmetry parameters for the equity indices are positive as expected, representing the stylised fact that negative returns are followed by higher volatility. The MIDAS components for Silver and the equity indices show that a time-varying long-term trend of the volatility exists for these assets in contrast to a constant volatility level. The realised volatility influences the equity indices' volatility rather quickly within the first year, while the influence on Silver's long-term volatility is dissipating more slowly.[2]

These results underline the importance of including long memory and asymmetry when modelling dynamic correlations as features of the idiosyncratic volatility also transfer to the calculated correlations. Therefore, we use the best-fitted model for each asset in the following analysis of the dynamic correlation.

[2]The parameters $\omega_{V,1}$ and $\omega_{V,2}$ determine the slope of weights of the beta function φ. See Section 2.

Table 4. Coefficients of the conditional volatility models (unsynchronised) and the DCC-MIDAS of pairwise synchronised residuals for chosen metal/index combinations.

	Gold-S&P500		Gold-DAX30		Gold-FTSE100		Silver-S&P500		Pall.-S&P500		Plat.-S&P500	
	h_{11} [2]	h_{22} [4]	h_{11} [2]	h_{22} [4]	h_{11} [4]	h_{22} [4]	h_{11} [2]	h_{22} [4]	h_{11} [1]	h_{22} [4]	h_{11} [1]	h_{22} [4]
μ	0.054	0.055	0.054	0.061	0.054	0.023	0.077	0.055	0.100	0.055	0.038	0.055
ω	0.768	−1.251	0.768	7.438	0.768	−1.316	−0.371	−1.251	1.462	−1.251	0.642	−1.251
α	0.058	0.000	0.058	0.000	0.058	0.000	0.070	0.000	0.089	0.000	0.057	0.000
β	0.956	0.832	0.956	0.890	0.956	0.836	0.934	0.832	0.893	0.832	0.931	0.832
γ	−0.034	0.247	−0.034	0.219	−0.034	0.212	−0.038	0.247		0.247		0.247
θ_V		0.250		−0.458		0.255	0.227	0.250		0.250		0.250
$\omega_{V,1}$		2.206		1.000		2.978	1.000	2.206		2.206		2.206
$\omega_{V,2}$		15.163		23.260		22.285	1.424	15.163		15.163		15.163
ν	5.206	6.347	5.206	6.384	5.206	9.918	4.100	6.347	5.988	6.347	6.866	6.347
a	0.044		0.027		0.028		0.040		0.022		0.031	
b	0.930		0.950		0.944		0.940		0.954		0.949	
c	0.011		-0.011		0.002		0.169		0.148		0.108	
θ_C	1.032		0.939		0.796		0.434		0.612		0.665	
ω_C	1.000		2.325		1.589		12.736		7.821		5.938	

Note: Robust standard errors are available upon request. Numbers in brackets refer to the respective univariate variance model in Table 3.

4.2. *Dynamic correlation properties*

After we established the idiosyncratic volatility patterns of each asset, we turn to the bivariate dynamic conditional correlation between the four precious metals and the equity markets.

A selection of estimation results for DCC-MIDAS is also given in Table 4. All sets of a and b for the different metal-equity pairs depict a high persistence of the short-term correlation dynamics as their sum is close to unity. The long-term dynamics, however, vary for the various metals. The coefficient ω_C represents the inverse persistence. Hence, low figures for Gold-equity pairs lead to long-lasting influence of past realised correlation. In case of Gold-S&P500, we even see this persistence over the full 36 months we account for. For Silver, Palladium, and Platinum, the influence of past correlation decays much faster and is not as impactful in terms of size (θ_C) as for Gold. For Silver, e.g., $\omega_C = 12.736$ indicates that only the past 16 months affect the level of correlation.

In view of possible safe-haven properties of the precious metals under investigation, we turn to dynamic correlations with the S&P500 as calculated in Eq. (8). These correlations are visualised in Figure 1 for Gold and Silver and in Figure 2 for Palladium and Platinum. We recall the findings of Klein (2017) who identifies safe-haven properties for Gold and Silver before 2013 and only short-termed hedging capabilities thereafter as well as some safe-haven properties of Platinum in extreme market conditions.

From Figure 1, it is obvious that we replicate these findings with the DCC-MIDAS. Correlations of Gold, and to some extent of Silver, turn negative during the first NBER recession in our sample that coincides with a strong equity downturn. In the following phases of market turmoil, we find that both metals react quickly to these deteriorating market conditions and correlations are negative. However, we also find that these hedging capacities are short-lived and do not hold for a prolonged time as observed during the European Debt Crisis. Interestingly, we observe that the long-term correlation of Gold is positive in the beginning of our sample but turns negative around 2016. With regard to the definitions of Baur and McDermott (2010), this might be an indication that Gold dominates in its role as hedge rather than a safe-haven investment, at least in the long-run.

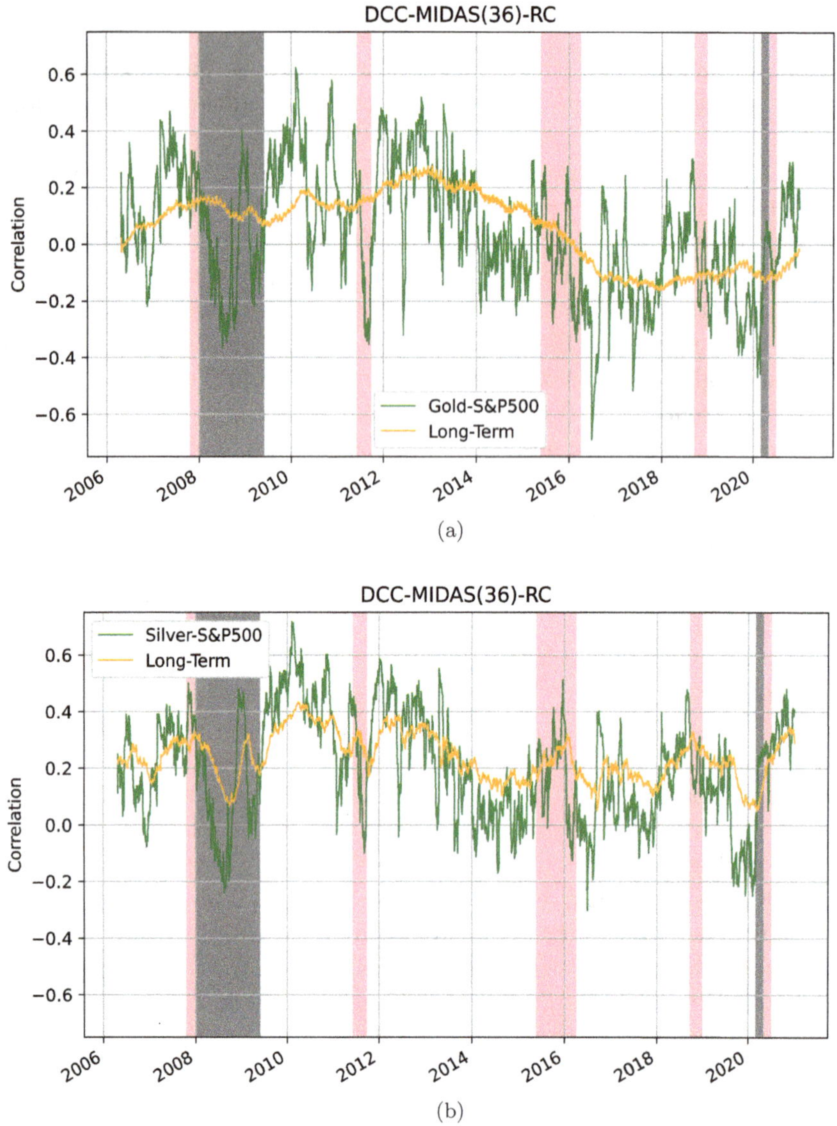

Fig. 1. Short-and long-term correlation from the (a) Gold and (b) Silver with the S&P500 with DCC-MIDAS for the period April 24, 2006 to December 31, 2020. Gray shaded areas are NBER recessions. Pink shaded areas represent equity downturns.

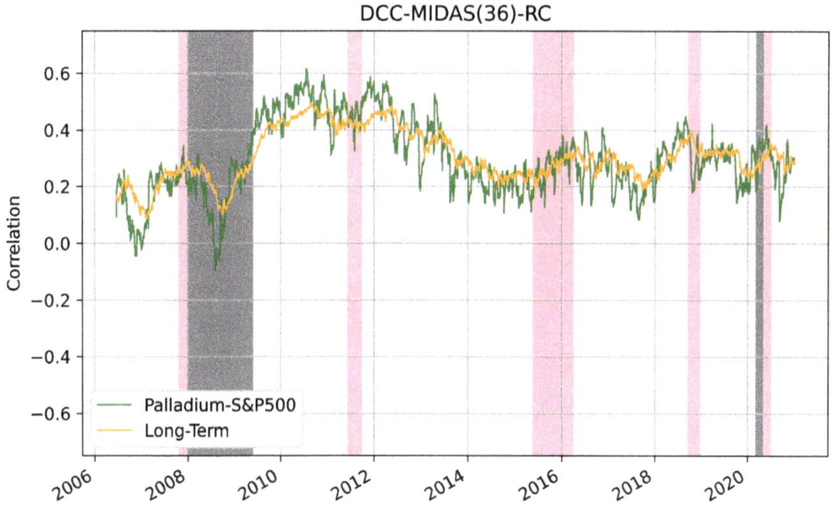

(a)

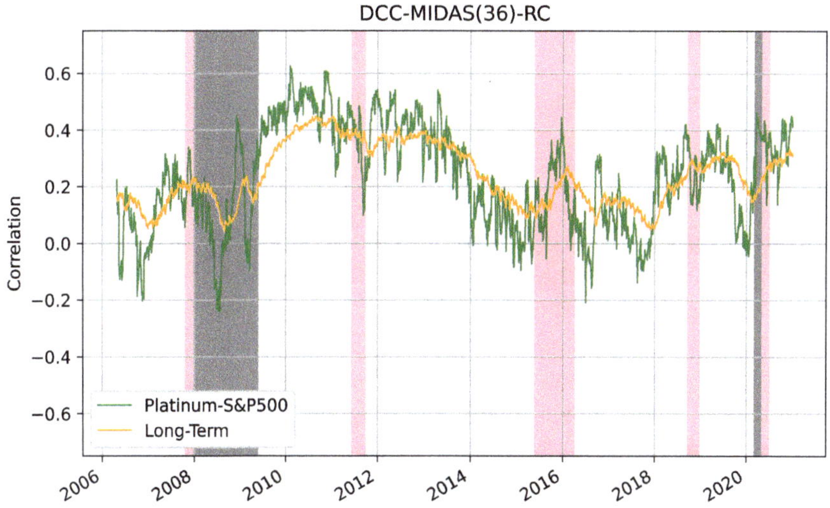

(b)

Fig. 2. Short- and long-term correlation from the (a) Palladium and (b) Platinum with the S&P500 with DCC-MIDAS for the period April 24, 2006 to December 31, 2020. Shaded areas are NBER recessions. Pink shaded areas represent equity downturns.

We observe a similar downwards long-term trend in Silver correlations albeit of strictly positive values. It is noteworthy that equity markets have been subject to a rapid growth phase since 2015 which might explain the change in the underlying long-term correlation.

For Platinum and Palladium, we observe similar findings as in Klein (2017). Correlations, both short- and long-term, are mainly positive. Platinum shows some short-term decoupling reactions to equity downturns offering limited safe-haven properties. However, for longer-lasting downturns, correlations of Platinum and equity markets are increasingly positive. Similar to Gold and Silver, we observe a relatively high long-term correlation from 2010 to 2014, which is decreasing thereafter. Given that both of these metals are mainly used for industry applications, it appears that commodity and raw material markets grew on a slower pace than equity markets.

5. Conclusions

We reassess the findings of Klein (2017) and analyse the dynamic correlation of precious metals with developed equity markets. Overall, we find that Gold and Silver serve as short-term safe-havens since correlations with financial markets react downwards quickly. However, in the case of Silver, correlations do not necessarily turn negative. A similar behaviour is found for Platinum but we note that the behaviour of Platinum and Palladium, as classical industrial metals, is different from Gold and Silver. Compared to Klein (2017), we confirm the usefulness of modelling idiosyncratic features of variance. In addition, findings with regard to the short-term reactivity of Gold and Silver correlations align. Interestingly and in some supplementing character to Klein (2017) and Nguyen and Walther (2020), we find long-term correlations of precious metals with equity markets to decline in recent years, reducing their diversifying characteristics in the long run.

Future research could analyse the drivers of the dynamic correlation replacing the realised correlation in the long-term factor with macroeconomic variables.

References

Arouri, M.E.H., Hammoudeh, S., Lahiani, A. and Nguyen, D.K. (2012). Long memory and structural breaks in modeling the return and volatility dynamics of precious metals, *The Quarterly Review of Economics and Finance.* **52**(2), 207–218. doi:10.1016/j.qref.2012.04.004.

Baur, D.G. and McDermott, T.K. (2010). Is gold a safe haven? International evidence, *Journal of Banking & Finance* **34**(8), 1886–1898. doi:10.1016/j.jbankfin.2009.12.008.

Bollerslev, T. and Mikkelsen, H.O. (1996). Modeling and pricing long memory in stock market volatility, *Journal of Econometrics* **73**(1), 151–184. doi:10.1016/0304-4076(95)01736-4.

Chkili, W. (2016). Dynamic correlations and hedging effectiveness between gold and stock markets: Evidence for BRICS countries, *Research in International Business and Finance* **38**, 22–34. doi:10.1016/j.ribaf.2016.03.005.

Colacito, R., Engle, R.F. and Ghysels, E. (2011). A component model for dynamic correlations, *Journal of Econometrics* **164**(1), 45–59. doi:10.1016/j.jeconom.2011.02.013.

Conrad, C., Loch, K. and Rittler, D. (2014). On the macroeconomic determinants of long-term volatilities and correlations in U.S. stock and crude oil markets, *Journal of Empirical Finance* **29**, 26–40. doi:10.1016/j.jempfin.2014.03.009.

Dinh, T., Goutte, S., Nguyen, D.K. and Walther, T. (2022). Economic drivers of volatility and correlation in precious metal markets, in: *Journal of Commodity Markets*, forthcoming. DOI:10.1016/j.jcomm.2021.100242.

Engle, R.F., Ghysels, E. and Sohn, B. (2013). Stock market volatility and macroeconomic fundamentals, *Review of Economics and Statistics* **95**(3), 776–797.

Geweke, J. and Porter-Hudak, S. (1983). The estimation and application of long memory time series models, *Journal of Time Series Analysis* **4**(4), 221–238. doi:10.1111/j.1467-9892.1983.tb00371.x.

Ghysels, E., Sinko, A. and Valkanov, R. (2007). MIDAS regressions: further results and new directions, *Econometric Reviews* **26**(1), 53–90. doi:10.1080/07474930600972467.

Glosten, L.R., Jagannathan, R. and Runkle, D.E. (1993). On the relation between the expected value and the volatility of the nominal excess return on stocks, *Journal of Finance* **48**(5), 1779–1801. doi:10.2307/2329067.

Hammoudeh, S.M., Yuan, Y., McAleer, M. and Thompson, M.A. (2010). Precious metals–exchange rate volatility transmissions and hedging strategies, *International Review of Economics & Finance* **19**(4), 633–647. doi:10.1016/j.iref.2010.02.003.

Klein, T. (2017). Dynamic correlation of precious metals and flight-to-quality in developed markets, *Finance Research Letters* **23**, 283–290. doi:10.1016/j.frl.2017.05.002.

Nguyen, D.K. and Walther, T. (2020). Modeling and forecasting commodity market volatility with long term economic and financial variables, *Journal of Forecasting* **39**(2), 126–142, doi:10.1002/for.2617.

Opschoor, A., van Dijk, D. and van der Wel, M. (2014). Predicting volatility and correlations with Financial Conditions Indexes, *Journal of Empirical Finance* **29**, pp. 435–447. doi:10.1016/j.jempfin.2014.10.003.

Tse, Y.K. (1998). The conditional heteroscedasticity of the yen-dollar exchange rate, *Journal of Applied Econometrics* **13**(1), 49–55. doi:10.1002/(SICI)1099-1255(199801/02)13:1⟨49::AID-JAE459⟩3.0.CO;2-O.

Walther, T., Klein, T. and Bouri, E. (2019). Exogenous drivers of Bitcoin and Cryptocurrency volatility — A mixed data sampling approach to forecasting, *Journal of International Financial Markets, Institutions and Money* **63**, 101–113. doi:10.1016/j.intfin.2019.101133.

https://doi.org/10.1142/9781800611917_0021

Chapter 21

Cryptocurrencies as an Asset Class — Holding Bitcoin in German Equities Portfolios

Mario Straßberger

Zittau/Görlitz University of Applied Sciences, Faculty of Business Administration and Economics, Germany

m.strassberger@hszg.de

We examine the diversification benefits and hedging abilities of cryptocurrencies like Bitcoin for German stock market investors. From an economic perspective, we interpret cryptocurrencies as an additional asset class and incorporate Bitcoin into portfolios of equities. Using German stock market data and Bitcoin data from January 2012 to December 2020, we yearly add Bitcoin to different long equities portfolios and apply performance and risk measures on them. Further, we use Bitcoin for hedging equities differing positive and negative stock market movements. Our results show improved performances of equities-Bitcoin portfolios over equities-only portfolios but limited properties of Bitcoin as a means to absorb market downturns, suggesting that Bitcoin can provide substantially enhanced portfolio risk-return exposures, but is constrained efficient as a hedge to the stock market.

1. Introduction

Since more than 12 years, cryptocurrencies have enormously widespread, and currently they are reaching new highs in value. Among all of them, Bitcoin is the oldest, most prominent, and most familiar so-called digital currency summarising about 60% of the market capitalisation of all cryptocurrencies at this time (Aleti and Mizrach, 2021, p. 195). The field of cryptocurrency-investors has changed in recent years. Not only some speculative private investors but also institutional agents accept to invest in cryptocurrencies especially in Bitcoin to an increasing degree. Faucette *et al.* (2018) report that more than 200 funds with more than seven billion USD in assets were actively trading in the cryptocurrencies market by end of 2018. The reasons of this growing interest are manifold. Initially, the rising acceptance of cryptocurrencies by private investors attracts the institutional ones. Moreover, the accretive regulation attempts by governments, central banks, and financial supervisors provide additional confidence (Auer and Claessens, 2018; Chimienti *et al.*, 2019). Some derivatives exchanges, first and foremost the Chicago Mercantile Exchange, quote futures contracts on Bitcoin (Aleti and Mizrach, 2021, p. 194 ff.), and in the meantime, effective payment possibilities have developed for cryptocurrencies (Stulz, 2019, p. 90). For example, PayPal currently allows customers to transfer Bitcoin. A driving force to cryptocurrencies also seems to be the macroeconomic trend to large quantities of money supply at low interest rates by central banks. The cheap money may search for new asset classes with attractive returns leading to a substantial asset price inflation (Gali, 2014; Miao *et al.*, 2019). Against the background of a growing interest on sustainable investments (Ammann *et al.*, 2019; Capelle-Blancard and Petit, 2019), even the high energy consumption of Bitcoin production (Küfeoglu and Özkuran, 2019; Schinckus *et al.*, 2020) does not negatively affect the attraction of Bitcoin to investors so far.

Thus, is this development of cryptocurrencies just an unfounded overstatement or is it part of a greater transformation in the world of finance? To be more concrete, is Bitcoin a meaningful digital asset, is it suitable to be used as a portfolio admixture, and is it perhaps effective as a hedge to other assets like equity securities?

The related literature on cryptocurrencies mainly focuses on three strands. First, technological issues are addressed by Böhme *et al.* (2015), Dwyer (2015), and Schinckus (2020) for example. A second strand deals with aspects of valuation and pricing. Among others, Schilling and Uhlig (2019) discuss general equilibrium models, Liu *et al.* (2019) study factor models. Third, the microstructure of related markets is considered by Ghysels and Nguyen (2019) analysing order books and by Aleti and Mizrach (2021) studying relations between spot and futures markets. There is not too much literature on the impacts of cryptocurrencies on portfolio composition so far. If portfolio effects are considered, most authors investigate hedging properties of cryptocurrencies deducing ambivalent results. Dyhrberg (2016), Bouri *et al.* (2017), Fang *et al.* (2018) and Bouri *et al.* (2020a) confirm hedging abilities of cryptocurrencies regarding different macroeconomic features, whereas Klein *et al.* (2018) reject hedging capabilities of Bitcoin as to different assets. Only few authors explicitly explore portfolio diversification affirming positive impacts (Guesmi *et al.*, 2019). Recently, Trimborn *et al.* (2020) explicitly model liquidity constraints and show improved risk-return profiles when including cryptocurrencies into different portfolios. Similar results depending on investor types draw Petukhina *et al.* (2021), applying diverse portfolio construction rules.

After discussing some economics of cryptocurrencies in Section 2, and describing the data in Section 3, we aim for giving answers on the aforementioned questions in Section 4. We research diversification effects and hedging abilities of Bitcoin in portfolios of German equities. Our findings are summarised in Section 5.

2. Economics of Cryptocurrencies

For an economic assessment of the phenomenon cryptocurrencies especially Bitcoin, in the first instance, it seems to be helpful to differ between a technological and an economic perspective. Bitcoin as a payment token is based on a so-called distributed ledger technology or the blockchain technology, respectively. Thus, in the technological perception, it is the aggregate of a network of about 10,000 data processing nodes around the world permanently synchronising each other. Bitcoin transactions are documented in a decentralised and redundantly recorded history of payments in a computer network — the blockchain. The technological perspective was discussed e.g., by Böhme *et al.* (2015), Dwyer (2015), Risius and Spohrer (2017) and more recently Stulz (2019) and Schinckus (2020). As a medium of exchange and a means of payment, unlike fiat money, Bitcoin does not rely on central institutions but on a decentralised technology with evenly spread power and mutual control.

Economically, Bitcoin is seen to be a new kind of commodity — a digital commodity made by computers and traded on a non-institutionally created market. As a maximum of 21 million Bitcoins there can be generated, Bitcoin is rather scarce. Therefore, Bitcoin is seen as an intangible means of value.

Other comparable entities like Ethereum offer a broad range of applications inclusive smart contracts and initial coin offerings (Adhami *et al.*, 2018). Bitcoin commonly is referred to as cryptocurrency. But, could Bitcoin be characterised as a currency or as money, respectively? According to the monetary theory, to be classified as money, some medium has to fulfil three critical functions. Money simultaneously serves as a medium of exchange and payment, as a vehicle for storing value, and as a unit of account (Hubbard and O'Brien, 2014, pp. 56–57). A unit of account includes a social convention to express prices as well as to denominate contracts in units of currency. It is essential for the effectiveness of central bank's monetary policy (Brunnermeier *et al.*, 2019).

Bitcoin is seen to be limited mainly regarding the other two functions of money. Because of its technological restrictions of scalability, it is rather convenient to be a payment instrument. Separate from comparatively high transaction cost of currently about 1.50 Euro per transaction, in practice, four to five transactions per second can be processed in Bitcoin (Böhme *et al.*, 2015). The so-called second-layer solutions netting transactions between parties may accelerate processing times. However, payment service providers and credit card companies handle up to 1,500 transactions in the same time. This fact might not necessarily slow down the acceptance of Bitcoin. Bitcoin could also reach a function as a kind of reserve currency when payment service providers just carry back with a number of Bitcoins hold by themselves instead of processing transactions on the Bitcoin blockchain.

To be a store of value, Bitcoin is less suitable because of its enormous price volatility. Between 2012 and 2020, the volatility was 63% p.a. on average with highest volatility of 101% p.a. in 2013 (Table 1). For these reasons, instead of being a stable currency or a money-like investment, Bitcoin should rather be interpreted as a risky and speculative digital commodity (Baur and Dimpfl, 2021).

What Bitcoin distinguishes from other assets is the way its value is originated. Both stocks and bonds securitise claims against the issuer.

Their value mainly results from future cashflows. Investors trust issuers to be able to fulfil the claims in the future. In case of a currency, investors have confidence in the central bank who guaranties for it. The value of Bitcoin and other cryptocurrencies is very much based just on the trust of investors in that value (Dyhrberg, 2016). In contrast to the so-called Stablecoins like Tether which is strictly bound at the US-Dollar, Bitcoin itself is not backed with any other asset. The value of Bitcoin is primarily obtained from the equivalent value in a conventional currency.

Taking all these characteristics and arguments together, Bitcoin is rather a digital commodity than a currency. In what follows, we consequently interpret Bitcoin as a new original asset class for investors.

3. Data

For our analysis, we use daily settlement prices of the German stock market index DAX and daily Euro Bitcoin prices close to 5.45 pm middle European time for a period from January 2, 2012 until December 30, 2020. As Bitcoin is traded continuously, we select a Bitcoin price near DAX closing auction settlement. DAX data are provided by the Karlsruhe Capital Market Database,[1] Bitcoin prices (BTC) are collected from "Bitcoin.de"[2] which is currently the largest regulated exchange platform for Bitcoin in Germany. Where required, we use risk free interest rates at one-year maturities provided by Deutsche Bundesbank.[3]

Daily discontinuous returns $r_{i,t}$ of DAX and Bitcoin prices are calculated according to $r_{i,t} = (p_{i,t} - p_{i,t-1})/p_{i,t-1}, i = \text{DAX}, \text{BTC}$, where $p_{i,t}$ is the DAX settlement price on day t or the Bitcoin price on day t, respectively. Conducting our analysis, we split the entire data sample into nine yearly time periods.

Table 1 presents the summary statistics for DAX and BTC returns. Over the entire sample period, DAX returns average 4.5 basis points per day, while BTC returns average 47 basis points per day.

[1]https://fmi.fbv.kit.edu/149.php.

[2]https://www.bitcoin.de/en.

[3]https://www.bundesbank.de/dynamic/action/en/statistics/time-series-databases/time-series-databases/759784/759784?listId=www_skms_it03a.

Table 1. Summary statistics.

	n	Mean (%)	Median (%)	STD (%)	SKEW	KURT	CORR
Full sample							
DAX	2,275	0.045	0.083	1.237	−0.461	9.329	
		(11.20)	(20.69)	(19.57)			
BTC	2,275	0.469	0.235	3.976	0.167	8.830	0.1046
		(117.2)	(58.85)	(62.87)			
2012							
DAX	254	0.107	0.141	1.187	−0.071	1.243	
		(26.87)	(35.32)	(18.76)			
BTC	254	0.498	0.462	3.085	0.113	7.632	0.0827
		(124.4)	(115.4)	(48.78)			
2013							
DAX	253	0.094	0.123	0.920	−0.263	1.041	
		(23.49)	(30.65)	(14.55)			
BTC	253	1.771	0.909	6.383	−0.609	6.590	0.1004
		(442.6)	(227.3)	(100.9)			
2014							
DAX	252	0.016	0.078	1.055	−0.120	0.753	
		(3.98)	(19.38)	(16.68)			
BTC	252	−0.230	−0.416	2.669	0.744	5.806	−0.0247
		(−57.5)	(−103.9)	(42.20)			
2015							
DAX	253	0.047	0.136	1.483	−0.094	0.486	
		(11.76)	(34.01)	(23.44)			
BTC	253	0.193	0.037	2.770	0.948	9.815	0.0839
		(48.35)	(9.20)	(43.79)			
2016							
DAX	255	0.035	0.139	1.312	−0.695	2.849	
		(8.67)	(34.64)	(20.75)			
BTC	255	0.354	0.235	2.210	1.425	16.279	−0.1395
		(88.41)	(58.66)	(34.94)			
2017							
DAX	252	0.049	0.050	0.669	0.547	2.544	
		(12.25)	(12.48)	(10.58)			
BTC	252	1.132	1.226	4.337	0.126	2.459	0.0699
		(282.9)	(306.6)	(68.57)			
2018							
DAX	251	−0.076	−0.059	0.978	−0.322	0.252	
		(−18.9)	(−14.78)	(15.46)			
BTC	251	−0.436	−0.036	4.200	0.036	3.241	0.1588
		(−109.1)	(−8.88)	(66.41)			

Table 1. (*Continued*)

	n	Mean (%)	Median (%)	STD (%)	SKEW	KURT	CORR
2019							
DAX	251	0.094	0.170	0.882	−0.309	1.983	
		(23.58)	(42.40)	(13.94)			
BTC	251	0.353	0.148	4.174	0.957	5.667	−0.0677
		(88.14)	(37.01)	(65.99)			
2020							
DAX	254	0.035	-0.001	2.076	−0.574	8.130	
		(8.85)	(−0.24)	(32.83)			
BTC	254	0.578	0.277	3.942	−0.157	7.214	0.3764
		(144.6)	(69.33)	(62.32)			

Notes: Sample mean and median returns, sample standard deviations (STD), skewness (SKEW), and kurtosis (KURT) for the daily DAX and BTC returns from 2012 till 2020, next to the correlation (CORR) between the two. In brackets there are given annualised parameters.

The sample standard deviation of daily BTC returns is 3.98% and thus more than three times higher than the one of the daily DAX returns. Sample median returns in comparison to sample mean returns do not specify very distinct skewed distributions. The correlation between DAX and BTC returns is 0.105, indicating a very weak positive relation. Weak correlations of Bitcoin with equities are reported by prior studies, too (e.g., Bouri *et al.*, 2020b, p. 294).

Splitting the sample into different time periods and considering the separate years, DAX returns are mostly in line with overall average. In 2012, DAX data show the highest sample mean return of about 11 basis points per day, whereas in 2018, the lowest sample mean return is at −7.6 basis points per day. The sample standard deviation of daily DAX returns does not show many specifics. Only in 2020, it is comparatively high with 2.08% per day which might be caused by the Coronavirus pandemic. More attention is attracted by BTC returns. The data show very high sample mean returns of 177 basis points per day in 2013 and 113 basis points per day in 2017. In parallel there are very high negative sample mean returns of −23 basis points per day in 2014 and even −44 basis points per day in 2018. Consequently, the sample standard deviation of BTC returns is two to three times higher than the one of DAX returns reaching a maximum of 6.4% per day in 2013. The correlation between DAX and

BTC returns in the separate years closely varies around zero ranging from −0.14 in 2016 to 0.16 in 2018. An exception only marks the comparatively high correlation of 0.38 in 2020 demonstrating a stronger positive relation than in the years before.

4. Portfolios of Equities and Bitcoin

One of the reasons why Bitcoin is in great demand might be the effort of investors to diversify and to hedge their assets. Since the 2008 financial crisis, there is in some respects a trend away from capital markets towards private equity and alternative investments. Additionally, since then investors face a persisting period of huge money supply and low interest rates. Independently from securities markets, Bitcoin as the oldest and best-known cryptocurrency offers a new asset class. In this section, we research for diversification benefits and hedging properties of Bitcoin in portfolios of German equities.

4.1. *Diversification effects*

Since investors are usually risk averse, they are interested in assets which would improve the risk-return ratio of their portfolio (Kumar, 2009). Given the findings in Table 1, we incorporate Bitcoin into portfolios of equities. To be largely independent of further specific assumptions regarding investors preferences, according to portfolio selection theory (Markowitz, 1952) we construct two types of portfolios. First, we build portfolios (P) of DAX and BTC with the same projected standard deviation of return like for the pure stock portfolio. The risk acceptance of investors then exactly corresponds to the one for a stand-alone DAX investment. So, keeping the portfolio risk constant, we maximise the portfolio's return expectation moving upward to the efficient frontier. Secondly, out of the resulting set of efficient DAX-BTC portfolios, we search for the minimum-variance-portfolio (MVP) assuming investors would simply seek to minimise portfolio risk (Elton *et al.*, 2014, p. 65 ff. hereinafter).

Starting point for determining the favoured portfolios are the following parameter estimates: the DAX and BTC sample mean returns $\bar{r}_{\text{DAX},t}$ and $\bar{r}_{\text{BTC},t}$, the sample standard deviations of DAX and BTC returns $s_{\text{DAX},t}$ and $s_{\text{BTC},t}$, and the sample coefficient of correlation between DAX and BTC returns c_t, all assessed annually at portfolio construction date $t =$ January, 1 based on the n daily return observations of the previous year. Hence, the first portfolio of both types in each case is built at date t equal to 1, January 2013 based on parameter estimates from days $t - 254$ to $t - 1$. Subsequently, the portfolios are held to 31 December of the year and rebuilt subject to the same procedure. Here, we do not account for any short sale constraints just in case investors would be able to short Bitcoin via futures or certificates, respectively.

To calculate for the portfolio weights $w_{\text{DAX,P},t}$ of the first type of DAX-BTC portfolios, at portfolio construction date t we equal the projected standard deviation of portfolio return to $s_{\text{DAX},t}$ and solve for the following equation:

$$\begin{aligned} 0 = &(s^2_{\text{DAX},t} + s^2_{\text{BTC},t} - s_{\text{DAX},t}s_{\text{BTC},t}c_t)w^2_{\text{DAX,P},t} \\ &+ (s_{\text{DAX},t}s_{\text{BTC},t}c_t - 2s^2_{\text{BTC},t})w_{\text{DAX,P},t} \\ &+ s^2_{\text{BTC},t} - s^2_{\text{DAX},t}. \end{aligned} \tag{1}$$

Table 2 presents the resulting portfolio weights of DAX and BTC over all periods considered. In addition, there are given the portfolio return expectation and the projected standard deviation of portfolio return. They are contrasted with the *ex-post* realised return and standard deviation of return for the portfolio.

The annual admixture of BTC to the portfolio strongly varies over the years considered. Always based on the parameter estimation in the previous year window, we see low shares of Bitcoin of just 2.7% for example in 2014 along with high shares of Bitcoin of 55% for example in 2017. Strictly following our portfolio composition rule, we even build portfolios with negative return expectations in 2015 and 2019. This is due to the negative BTC sample mean returns in the estimation periods which are below the DAX sample mean returns in these years. Thus, in fact, we do not move on the efficient frontier and a single DAX investment would have been a superior strategy in these years. However, in the ex-post view, DAX-BTC portfolios resulted in higher realised returns (21.9% in 2015 and 28.1% in 2019) than DAX-alone portfolios (11.8% in 2015 and 23.5% in 2019). At the same time, DAX-BTC portfolios offer lower realised standard deviations of return (21.3% in 2015 and 13.6% in 2019) than DAX (23.4% in 2015 and 13.9% in 2019). Generally, we can state that we

Table 2. DAX-BTC-portfolios with equal risk like DAX-alone-portfolios.

	$w_{\mathrm{DAX,P},t}$	$w_{\mathrm{BTC,P},t}$	$\mu_{\mathrm{P},t}$ (%)	$\sigma_{\mathrm{P},t}$ (%)	$r_{\mathrm{P},t+1}$(%)	$s_{\mathrm{P},t+1}$ (%)
2013	0.7633	0.2367	49.95	18.76	122.69	26.84
2014	0.9731	0.0269	34.77	14.55	2.33	16.26
2015	0.7236	0.2764	−13.01	16.68	21.87	21.25
2016	0.5746	0.4254	27.32	23.44	42.59	18.40
2017	0.4509	0.5491	52.45	20.75	160.88	38.11
2018	0.9637	0.0363	22.09	10.58	−22.16	15.28
2019	0.9288	0.0702	−25.21	15.46	28.11	13.61
2020	0.9022	0.0978	29.89	13.94	22.12	31.34

Notes: DAX and BTC portfolio weights ($w_{\mathrm{DAX,P},t}$, $w_{\mathrm{BTC,P},t}$), yearly *ex-ante* portfolio return expectations ($\mu_{\mathrm{P},t}$) and *ex-ante* standard deviation of return projections ($\sigma_{\mathrm{P},t}$), yearly *ex-post* realised portfolio returns ($r_{\mathrm{P},t+1}$) and *ex-post* realised standard deviations of return ($s_{\mathrm{P},t+1}$) from 2013 till 2020.

produce significantly higher returns (Figure 1) at just slightly higher risks by adding BTC to DAX portfolios. In some cases, DAX-BTC portfolios even exhibit lower risks than DAX-alone portfolios like in 2016 and 2020.

The second type of DAX-BTC portfolios with minimum variance is produced by minimising Eq. (1) and calculating for the portfolio weights $w_{\mathrm{DAX,MVP},t}$ according to

$$w_{\mathrm{DAX,MVP},t} = \frac{-(s_{\mathrm{DAX},t}s_{\mathrm{BTC},t}c_t - 2s^2_{\mathrm{BTC},t})}{2(s^2_{\mathrm{DAX},t} + s^2_{\mathrm{BTC},t} - s_{\mathrm{DAX},t}s_{\mathrm{BTC},t}c_t)}. \tag{2}$$

Table 3 presents the resulting portfolio weights of DAX and BTC. Again, there are additionally given the portfolio return expectation and the projected standard deviation of portfolio return contrasted with the *ex-post* realised return and standard deviation of return for the portfolio.

Similarly, within minimum variance portfolios the share of BTC rather fluctuates between periods. Like in type-one portfolios, we

Table 3. DAX-BTC-portfolios with minimal variance.

	$w_{\mathrm{DAX,MVP},t}$	$w_{\mathrm{BTC,MVP},t}$	$\mu_{\mathrm{MVP},t}$ (%)	$\sigma_{\mathrm{MVP},t}$ (%)	$r_{\mathrm{MVP},t+1}$(%)	$s_{\mathrm{MVP},t+1}$(%)
2013	0.8817	0.1183	38.41	17.75	73.09	17.96
2014	0.9865	0.0135	29.14	14.48	3.16	16.46
2015	0.8618	0.1382	−4.51	15.45	16.82	21.33
2016	0.7873	0.2127	19.54	21.02	25.63	17.47
2017	0.7255	0.2745	30.56	17.28	86.57	20.57
2018	0.9818	0.0182	17.17	10.50	−20.52	15.32
2019	0.9649	0.0351	−22.05	15.28	25.85	13.57
2020	0.9511	0.0489	26.74	13.54	15.48	31.94

Notes: DAX and BTC portfolio weights ($w_{\mathrm{DAX,MVP},t}$, $w_{\mathrm{BTC,MVP},t}$), yearly *ex-ante* portfolio return expectations ($\mu_{\mathrm{MVP},t}$) and *ex-ante* standard deviation of return projections ($\sigma_{\mathrm{MVP},t}$), yearly *ex-post* realised portfolio returns ($r_{\mathrm{MVP},t+1}$) and *ex-post* realised standard deviations of return ($s_{\mathrm{MVP},t+1}$) from 2013 till 2020.

identify the lowest share of Bitcoin in 2014 which is at 1.4% then, and the highest share of Bitcoin in 2017 which is at 27.5%. Anyway, the differences are not as large as before. Expectedly, the minimum variance strategy builds portfolios with higher return prospects and lower risk projections than DAX in most periods. In 2015 and 2019, for the same reasons as for type-one portfolios, the minimum variance strategy produces portfolios with negative return expectations, too. Nevertheless, *ex-post*, we reach higher returns (16.8% in 2015 and 25.9% in 2019) at lower risks (21.3% in 2015 and 13.6% in 2019) compared to the DAX-alone investment in these cases here too. In general, in the *ex-post* view, the same is true like for type-one portfolios. Typically, we realise portfolios with higher returns and slightly higher risk exhibitions. What is notable is the fact that in some cases in the *ex-ante* perspective, especially the risk parameters of minimum variance portfolios are not far away from those of DAX-alone and DAX-BTC portfolios of type one. This is due to a comparatively flat hyperbolic function representing the efficient frontier of DAX-BTC portfolios.

As a performance measure of the portfolios created, we yearly *ex-post* calculate the reward-to-variability-ratio, henceforward denoted as Sharpe-measure $SM_{i,t}$, according to (Sharpe, 1966)

$$SM_{i,t} = \frac{r^*_{i,t} - r_{f,t-1}}{s^*_{i,t}}, \quad i = \text{DAX, P, MVP}, \tag{3}$$

where $r^*_{i,t}$ is the annual realised portfolio return on year t, $r_{f,t-1}$ is the risk-free rate of interest with a one-year maturity on year $t-1$, and $s^*_{i,t}$ is the annual standard deviation of realised portfolio return on year t.

As pointed in Table 4, except in periods with negative Bitcoin returns, which is the case in 2014 and 2018, in all years the DAX-BTC portfolios generate superior performances than DAX-alone portfolios.

Table 4. Performance and risk of DAX-alone- and DAX-BTC-portfolios.

	$SM_{\text{DAX},t+1}$	$SM_{\text{P},t+1}$	$SM_{\text{MVP},t+1}$	$VaR_{\text{DAX},t}$	$VaR_{\text{P},t}$	$VaR_{\text{MVP},t}$
2013	1.6166	4.5727	4.0718	0.1685	−0.0623	0.0293
2014	0.2317	0.1359	0.1845	0.1040	−0.0088	0.0461
2015	0.5056	1.0338	0.7927	0.3488	0.5188	0.4050
2016	0.4372	2.3368	1.4899	0.4285	0.2729	0.2943
2017	1.2372	4.2428	4.2478	0.3968	−0.0410	0.0970
2018	−1.1763	−1.4046	−1.2938	0.1239	0.0256	0.0730
2019	1.7393	2.1135	1.9535	0.5489	0.6122	0.5764
2020	0.2891	0.7262	0.5049	0.0889	0.0258	0.0480

Notes: *Ex-post* Sharpe-measures of DAX-alone portfolios ($SM_{\text{DAX},t+1}$), DAX-BTC portfolios ($SM_{\text{P},t+1}$), and DAX-BTC-minimum-variance-portfolios ($SM_{\text{MVP},t+1}$); Value-at-Risk for 1 year with probability level 99% of DAX-alone portfolios ($VaR_{\text{DAX},t}$), DAX-BTC portfolios ($VaR_{\text{P},t}$), and DAX-BTC-minimum-variance-portfolios ($VaR_{\text{MVP},t}$) from 2013 till 2020.

Thereby, the Sharpe measure of a DAX-BTC portfolio can be considerable in height. It can reach more than the fivefold level compared to the measure for a DAX investment in the same period (e.g., 5.3-fold in 2016).

For further portfolio assessment, as a risk measure, we apply the one-sided Value-at-Risk instead of the two-sided standard deviation of portfolio return. We yearly *ex-ante* evaluate Value-at-Risk $VaR_{i,t}(p)$ for a 1-year time horizon with a probability level of $p = 0.99$ investing one Euro into the different portfolios. Using the delta-normal-approximation, assuming normally distributed returns and a linear loss function for the portfolios, we estimate (Locarek-Junge *et al.*, 2002; Straßberger, 2006, p. 27)

$$VaR_{i,t}(p) = \bar{r}_{i,t} - z_p \cdot s_{i,t} \quad i = \text{DAX, P, MVP}. \tag{4}$$

Thereby, z_p denotes the p-quantile of the standard normal distribution. Despite the statistics given in Table 1 not necessarily suggesting to assume normally distributed returns, we do so for convenience reasons.

Besides the performance measures, Table 4 presents the Value-at-Risk estimates of DAX-alone portfolios, DAX-BTC portfolios with equal risk projection like DAX, and DAX-BTC portfolios with minimum variance. Except for two periods, Value-at-Risk of both types of DAX-BTC portfolios is clearly lower than the one of DAX-alone. This illustrates that investors also can reach superior risk positions in terms of a quantile risk measure. Similar to the before stated results, in 2015 and 2019, Value-at-Risk of DAX-BTC portfolios turns out higher than Value-at-Risk of DAX. In these years, the BTC sample mean returns of the previous period, on which the estimate is based on, show negative values. Remarkably, Value-at-Risk even shows negative values for type-one DAX-BTC portfolios in years when DAX and BTC sample mean returns are comparatively high together with moderate sample standard deviations of return. The return distribution of these portfolios is specifying that instead of a loss, a profit is estimated at a 99% probability level.

Altogether for both types of portfolios created, we clearly see improved risk-return combinations for German stock market investors across all market cycles. Sharpe measures as well as Value-at-Risk estimates are enhanced for Bitcoin-equities-portfolios

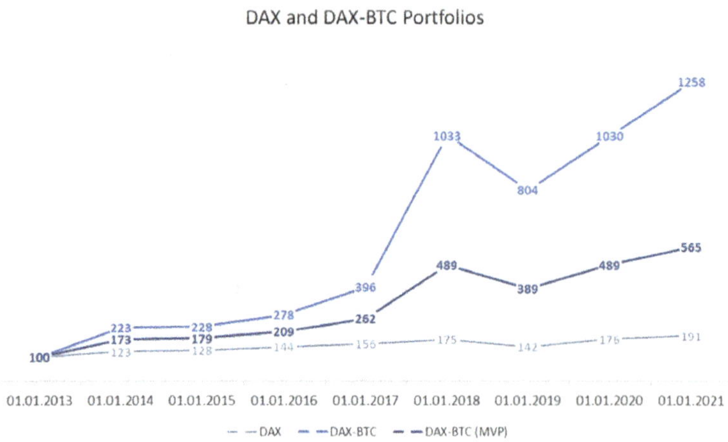

Fig. 1. Theoretical portfolios incorporating Bitcoin as an asset.

compared to equities-only ones. Based on our data used, the diversification characteristics of Bitcoin seem to be evidently distinct.

Figure 1 demonstrates the predominant performance of the two types of DAX-BTC portfolios constructed through the periods. Possibly, the improved portfolio performances could even be reached by naive diversification because of the estimation error in portfolio optimisation (DeMiguel *et al.*, 2009).

4.2. *Hedging abilities*

There exist several assets whose returns are negatively correlated with such equities on average. However, these assets cannot provide the desired hedging properties against market recessions because return correlations often become positive in phases of distress (Szado, 2009). By incorporating Bitcoin into equities portfolios, the question arises to what extent the new asset would be able to hedge equity market downturns without resigning upside. This is why — next to their risk aversion — investors typically seek to avoid negatively skewed payoffs, and wish to limit their risk exposures (Kumar, 2009). First, to understand the relationship between DAX and BTC returns, the following regression is estimated (Greene, 2018, p. 52 ff.):

$$r_{\text{BTC},t}=\alpha+\beta r_{\text{DAX},t}+\varepsilon_t, \tag{5}$$

Table 5. Relation between BTC and DAX returns.

	α	β	R^2
Full sample	0.0045	0.3362	0.0109
2012	0.0047	0.2150	0.0068
2013	0.0171	0.6963	0.0101
2014	−0.0023	−0.0626	0.0006
2015	0.0019	0.1567	0.0070
2016	0.0036	−0.2349	0.0195
2017	0.0111	0.4535	0.0049
2018	−0.0038	0.6822	0.0252
2019	0.0038	−0.3206	0.0046
2020	0.0055	0.7146	0.1417

Notes: Regression constant α, and regression coefficient β resulting from the regression of Eq. (5) for the full sample, and for single years from 2012 till 2020. R^2 denotes the coefficient of determination.

where $r_{\text{BTC},t}$ is the BTC return on day t, $r_{\text{DAX},t}$ is the DAX return on day t, α is a constant, and ε_t is the residual on day t.

Table 5 presents the estimation results. Whereas the sample intercept α ranges near zero in all periods, the sample slope β strongly varies over time taking 0.34 over the entire sample. For negative values, which are desired for hedging purposes, beta just takes in three periods with the according to amount highest value of −0.32 in 2019. The fact that beta is positive in most periods suggests short positions in Bitcoin could be more appropriate for hedging purposes. Guesmi *et al.* (2019) report similar results for different assets. Nevertheless, the coefficients of determination are extremely low over all periods specifying that DAX returns account for almost none of the variabilities of BTC returns, and suggesting that there exist very high errors of prediction. These results correspond to the weak correlations between DAX and BTC returns documented in Table 1. Over the entire sample, just 1% of variability of BTC returns is explained by DAX returns. Striking is the comparatively high coefficient of determination in 2020 when DAX returns at least explain 14% of variability of BTC returns.

Examining the hedging abilities of Bitcoin, in a next step, the entire data sample is distinguished in days in which DAX and BTC returns have positive signs and days in which they have negative signs. Within the total number of 2,275 return observations for each asset, we find 1,223 positive signed returns, and 1,052 negative signed returns for DAX as well as 1,276 positive signed returns, and 999 negative signed returns for BTC. To continue, we study the joint occurrence of equal signed returns and particularly different signed returns of DAX and BTC. Once this evaluation is done unconditionally, and once it is done under the condition of the given sign for DAX return.

The results of the assessments are presented in Table 6. As suggested by the weak correlations between DAX and BTC returns, if unconditioned outcomes are considered, the percentages of equally

Table 6. Percentage of outcomes of equally and different signed DAX and BTC returns.

		DAX+	DAX–	cond. DAX+	cond. DAX–
Full sample	BTC+	0.3081	**0.2527**	0.5732	**0.5466**
	BTC–	0.2295	0.2097	0.4268	0.4534
2012	BTC+	0.3110	**0.2756**	0.5725	**0.6034**
	BTC–	0.2323	0.1811	0.4275	0.3966
2013	BTC+	0.3715	**0.2925**	0.6667	**0.6607**
	BTC–	0.1858	0.1502	0.3333	0.3393
2014	BTC+	0.2262	**0.1706**	0.4043	**0.3874**
	BTC–	0.3333	0.2698	0.5957	0.6126
2015	BTC+	0.2964	**0.2134**	0.5435	**0.4696**
	BTC–	0.2490	0.2411	0.4565	0.5304
2016	BTC+	0.3294	**0.2784**	0.6176	**0.5966**
	BTC–	0.2039	0.1882	0.3824	0.4034
2017	BTC+	0.3571	**0.3214**	0.6667	**0.6923**
	BTC–	0.1786	0.1429	0.3333	0.3077
2018	BTC+	0.2470	**0.2470**	0.5082	**0.4806**
	BTC–	0.2390	0.2669	0.4918	0.5194
2019	BTC+	0.3108	**0.2311**	0.5379	**0.5472**
	BTC–	0.2669	0.1912	0.4621	0.4528
2020	BTC+	0.3228	**0.2441**	0.6457	**0.4882**
	BTC–	0.1772	0.2559	0.3543	0.5118

Notes: Unconditioned percentage of outcomes for positive (BTC+, DAX+) and negative (BTC–, DAX–) returns of BTC and DAX; conditioned percentage of outcomes where DAX return is given to be positive (cond. DAX+) and negative (cond. DAX–), all from 2012 till 2020; most important data for hedging purposes (DAX– in combination with BTC+) are emphasised.

and different signed asset returns are rather balanced over all four possible cases. Inside the full sample, different signed returns arise in 48.2% of all cases, but negative DAX returns in combination with positive BTC returns occur in just 25.3% of all cases. This portion is not substantially exceeded during the single years. The maximum percentage of negative DAX returns and coincident positive BTC returns is observed in 2017 with 32.1%. In some years, the percentages of equally signed BTC and DAX returns are higher than those of different signed returns indicating that a short position in Bitcoin might have more hedging effect then. Under the condition that DAX return is given to be negative, within the full sample in 54.7% of the cases, the BTC return is positive then. Again, the maximum percentage of positive BTC returns when DAX return is negative is detected in 2017 with 69.2%.

Given the differentiation in positive and negative signed asset returns, to further understand to which extent BTC returns would be able to hedge DAX returns additionally, the following multiple regression is estimated (Greene, 2018, p. 52 ff.):

$$r_{\mathrm{BTC},t} = \alpha + \beta_1 r^{+}_{\mathrm{DAX},t} + \beta_2 r^{-}_{\mathrm{DAX},t} + \varepsilon_t. \tag{6}$$

Thereby, $r^{+}_{\mathrm{DAX},t}$ and $r^{-}_{\mathrm{DAX},t}$ denote positive and negative signed DAX returns on day t now. Thus, positive and negative DAX changes are separated and included together. Baur and Lucey (2010) apply a similar approach but with step-wise quantiles of the return distribution.

Table 7 presents the estimation results which are little better than the ones of the single regression from the perspective of hedging. Again, the partial regression coefficients β_1 and β_2 strongly vary over time. In fact, β_2 indicates a stronger relation between BTC returns and negative signed DAX returns over the full sample, but this result does not hold through the single years. In five of nine periods, β_2 takes negative values, and in four periods, it takes positive values. Despite the coefficients of determination being slightly higher than the ones of the single regression, they are still extremely low. In many cases, just about 2% of variability of BTC returns are explained by positive and negative signed DAX returns. Noticeable in turn is the comparatively high coefficient of determination of 18% in 2020.

All in all, we cannot identify both an appreciable relation between BTC and DAX returns and a considerable hedging ability of Bitcoin

Table 7. Relation between BTC and different signed DAX returns.

	α	β_1	β_2	R^2
Full sample	0.0063	0.1207	0.5312	0.0131
2012	0.0008	0.6425	−0.2466	0.0198
2013	0.0234	−0.2000	1.6399	0.0178
2014	−0.0029	0.0185	−0.1390	0.0010
2015	0.0026	0.0872	0.2253	0.0076
2016	0.0022	−0.0723	−0.3670	0.0228
2017	0.0086	0.8995	−0.1529	0.0079
2018	−0.0045	0.7822	0.6086	0.0254
2019	0.0037	−0.3026	−0.3380	0.0046
2020	0.0122	0.1686	1.1596	0.1803

Notes: Regression constant α, and partial regression coefficients β_1 and β_2 resulting from the regression of Eq. (6) for the full sample, and for single years from 2012 till 2020. R^2 denotes the coefficient of determination.

for German equities across all market cycles. There is little explanatory power of DAX returns for BTC return variability, of irrespective whether we differ between positive and negative signed DAX returns or not. The often-supposed heterogeneity in cryptocurrencies and equities cannot be confirmed. Eventually, the hedging abilities of Bitcoin do not seem to be very distinct for investors to date. Klein *et al.* (2018) also find no evidence for stable hedging abilities. Some results rather hypothesise hedging effectiveness with short positions in Bitcoin.

5. Conclusion

Interpreting cryptocurrencies as an additional asset class, in this chapter, we study the diversification effects and hedging capabilities of Bitcoin from the perspective of investors in German equities. Based on German stock market data and Euro-Bitcoin data from 2012 to 2020, we incorporate Bitcoin into different equities portfolios. First, we compose Bitcoin-equities-portfolios of equal risk like equities-only portfolios and maximise expected portfolio return. Secondly, we compose minimum-variance-portfolios of Bitcoin and equities. Both types of portfolios lead investors to improved risk-return positions.

We clearly find improved portfolio performances and quantile risk measures when including Bitcoin as an additional asset next to equities investments. Researching the hedging qualities of Bitcoin, we differ in positive and negative equity market movements, examine the joint occurrences of different signed Bitcoin and equities returns, and estimate regressions on them. For the time period and market under review, we show that Bitcoin does not act as a hedge against stock market downturns. Thus, all together for investors incorporating Bitcoin in their German equities portfolios, there can be substantial diversification effects but rather no hedging possibilities. Besides, for periods other than reported, e.g., quarterly or monthly investments, there are substantially no further findings. Despite Bitcoin is not capable of reducing the downside risk for equities investments, because of its clear diversification potential, it should play the role of a valuable digital asset for equities investors.

Acknowledgement

The author thanks to Arvid Müller for help in provisioning Bitcoin data.

References

Adhami, S., Giudici, G., and Martinazzi, S. (2018). Why do businesses go crypto? An empirical analysis of initial coin offerings, *Journal of Economics and Business* **100**, 64–75.

Aleti, S. and Mizrach, B. (2021). Bitcoin spot and futures market microstructure, *Journal of Futures Markets* **41**, 194–225.

Ammann, M., Bauer, C., Fischer, S., and Müller, P. (2019). The impact of the morningstar sustainability rating on mutual fund flows, *European Financial Management* **25**(3), 520–553.

Auer, R. and Claessens, S. (2018). Regulating cryptocurrencies: assessing market reactions, *BIS Quarterly Review* **September**, 51–65.

Baur, D.G. and Dimpfl, T. (2021). The volatility of Bitcoin and its role as a medium of exchange and a store of value, *Empirical Economics* **61**, 2663–2683.

Baur, D.G. and Lucey, B.M. (2010). Is gold a hedge or a safe haven? An analysis of stocks, bonds and gold, *Financial Review* **45**(2), 217–229.

Böhme, R., Christin, N., Edelman, B., and Moore, T. (2015). Bitcoin: Economics, technology, and governance, *Journal of Economic Perspectives* **29**(2), 213–238.

Bouri, E., Gkillas, K., and Gupta, R. (2020a). Trade uncertainties and the hedging abilities of Bitcoin, *Economic Notes* **49**(3), 1–10.

Bouri, E., Molnar, P., Azzi, G., Roubaud, D., and Hagfors, L.I. (2017). On the hedge and save haven properties of Bitcoin: Is it really more than a diversifier? *Finance Research Letters* **20**, 192–198.

Bouri, E., Shahzad, S.J.H., and Roubaud, D. (2020b). Cryptocurrencies as hedges and safe-havens for US equity sectors, *Quarterly Review of Economics and Finance* **75**, 294–307.

Brunnermeier, M.K., James, H., and Landau, J.-P. (2019). *The Digitalization of Money.* Working Paper, Princeton University.

Capelle-Blancard, G. and Petit, A. (2019). Every little Helps? ESG news and stock market reaction, *Journal of Business Ethics* **157**, 543–565.

Chimienti, M.T., Kochanska, U., and Pinna, A. (2019). Understanding the crypto-asset phenomenon, its risks, and measurement issues. *ECB Economic Bulletin*, Issue 5/2019.

DeMiguel, V., Garlappi, L., and Uppal, R. (2009). Optimal versus naive diversification: how inefficient is the 1/N portfolio strategy? *Review of Financial Studies* **22**(5), 1915–1953.

Dwyer, G.P. (2015). The economics of Bitcoin and similar private digital currencies, *Journal of Financial Stability* **17**, 81–91.

Dyhrberg, A.H. (2016). Hedging capabilities of bitcoin. Is it the virtual gold? *Finance Research Letters* **16**, 139–144.

Elton, E.J., Gruber, M.J., Brown, S.J., and Goetzmann, W.N. (2014). *Modern Portfolio Theory and Investment Analysis*, 9th edn. Hoboken: Wiley.

Fang, L., Bouri, E., Gupta, R., and Roubaud, D. (2018). Does global economic uncertainty matter for the volatility and hedging effectiveness of Bitcoin? *International Review of Financial Analysis* **61**, 29–36.

Faucette, J., Graseck, B., and Shah, S. (2018). Update: Bitcoin, cryptocurrencies and blockchain. Morgan Stanley Research Report.

Gali, J. (2014). Monetary policy and rational asset price bubbles, *American Economic Review* **104**(3), 721–752.

Ghysels, E. and Nguyen, G. (2019). Price discovery of a speculative asset: Evidence from a Bitcoin exchange, *Journal of Risk and Financial Management* **12**(4), 1–26.

Greene, W.H. (2018). *Econometric Analysis*, 8th edn. Harlow: Pearson.

Guesmi, K., Saadi, S., Abid, I., and Ftiti, Z. (2019). Portfolio diversification with virtual currency: Evidence from bitcoin, *International Review of Financial Analysis* **63**, 431–437.

Hubbard, R.G. and O'Brien, A.P. (2014). *Money, Banking, and the Financial System*, 2nd edn. Harlow: Pearson.

Klein, T., PhamThu, H., and Walther, T. (2018). Bitcoin is not the new gold — A comparison of volatility, correlation, and portfolio performance, *International Review of Financial Analysis* **59**, 105–116.

Küfeoglu, S. and Özkuran, M. (2019). Bitcoin mining: A global review of energy and power demand, *Energy Research and Social Science* **58**, article 101273.

Kumar, A. (2009). Who gambles in the stock market? *Journal of Finance* **64**, 1889–1933.

Liu, Y., Tsyvinski, A., and Wu, X. (2019). Common risk factors in cryptocurrency. NYU Stern School of Business. Available at SSRN: https://ssrn.com/abstract=3379131.

Locarek-Junge, H., Prinzler, R., and Straßberger, M. (2002). The estimation of market risk in portfolios of stocks and stock options, *Schmalenbach Business Review* **54**(Special Issue 1), 171–189.

Markowitz, H. (1952). Portfolio Selection, *Journal of Finance* **7**, 77–92.

Miao, J., Shen, Z., and Wang, P. (2019). Monetary policy and rational asset price bubbles: Comment, *American Economic Review* **109**(5), 1969–1990.

Petukhina, A., Trimborn, S., Härdle, W.K., and Elendner, H. (2021). Investing with cryptocurrencies — evaluating their potential for portfolio allocation strategies, *Quantitative Finance* **21**(11), 1825–1853.

Risius, M. and Spohrer, K. (2017). A blockchain research framework. What we (don't) know, where we go from here, and how we will get There, *Business and Information Systems Engineering* **59**, 385–409.

Schilling, L. and Uhlig, H. (2019). Some simple bitcoin economics, *Journal of Monetary Economics* **106**, 16–26.

Schinckus, C. (2020). The good, the bad and the ugly: an overview of the sustainability of blockchain technology, *Energy Research and Social Science* **69**, article 101614.

Schinckus, C., Nguyen, C.P., and Ling, F.C.H. (2020). Crypto-currencies trading and energy consumption, *International Journal of Energy Economics and Policy* **10**(3), 355–364.

Sharpe, W.F. (1966). Mutual fund performance, *Journal of Business* **39**, 119–138.

Straßberger, M. (2006). Risk limit systems and capital allocation in financial institutions, *Banks and Bank Systems* **1**(4), 22–37.

Stulz, R.M. (2019). FinTech, BigTech, and the future of banks, *Journal of Applied Corporate Finance* **31**(4), 86–97.

Szado, E. (2009). VIX futures and options: A case study of portfolio diversification during the 2008 financial crisis, *Journal of Alternative Investments* **12**, 66–85.

Trimborn, S., Li, M., and Härdle, W.K. (2020). Investing with Cryptocurrencies — a liquidity constrained investment approach, *Journal of Financial Econometrics* **18**(2), 280–306.

https://doi.org/10.1142/9781800611917_bmatter

Index

E

F

CPSIA information can be obtained
at www.ICGtesting.com
Printed in the USA
JSHW050355250622
27351JS00001B/4

9 781800 611900